Historical Studies of
Rhetoric and Rhetoricians

HISTORICAL STUDIES

of

RHETORIC *and* RHETORICIANS

EDITED BY
RAYMOND F. HOWES

CORNELL UNIVERSITY PRESS
Ithaca, New York

CORNELL UNIVERSITY PRESS

First published 1961

Library of Congress Catalog Card Number: 61-16667

PRINTED IN THE UNITED STATES OF AMERICA
BY VAIL-BALLOU PRESS, INC.

TO

EVERETT LEE HUNT

a pioneer in the Cornell movement to
revive classical rhetoric and the author
of distinguished rhetorical studies, this
book is offered by his students and colleagues as a mark of personal affection
and professional respect.

The Study of Rhetoric

IT is "study"—advanced study—that will give enduring satisfactions, will convince the omnipresent sceptic that we know our business, will enable us to take rank with those who know in other fields, will mitigate the grind of drill, will enable us perhaps to illumine by a word or a reference the path of the willing and intelligent student, will add to the growing content of our field, will enable us to assimilate the labor of workers in other fields to our own, will give us some sense of the power that comes with knowledge, will give us increased dignity, will enable us to "play the academic game"—and win "recognition" where we still need and can deserve recognition. Nor can we doubt that it will enable us to offer fuller preparation and wiser training to those now entering the profession than were offered us.

—ALEXANDER M. DRUMMOND

Preface

I TAKE my text from Everett Hunt. In the introduction to *The Rhetorical Idiom* he said this:

Our friends the psychologists tell us that the study of communication is only beginning, and already the language of their treatises has become highly technical. Perhaps this is inevitable, and we shall have to learn to interpret the interpreters of the processes of communication. But a grounding in the traditions of classical rhetoric will show something of the unity of the human spirit in all of this. If we can keep as basic our conception that the humanities embrace whatever contributes to the making of free and enlightened choices, whether it be knowledge scientific, sociological, or poetic, and that in addition to adequate knowledge of all the alternatives there must be imagination to envisage all the possibilities and sympathy to make some of the options appeal to the emotions and powers of the will, we can see that rhetoric is an essential instrument for the enterprises of the human spirit. A familiarity with the history of its theory and practice cannot but have a liberalizing effect in the midst of technical specialties. The influence of the Cornell tradition in rhetoric has already extended far beyond the boundaries of any one university group, and rhetorical studies now flourish in many places. It is to be hoped that these diverse groups of students may have something of the sense of delight at the union of ancient traditions and modern practice which has been felt by the students of rhetoric at Cornell.

It is unnecessary to belabor the points he makes—the importance of rhetoric to liberal education and to effective living, the widespread interest today in rhetorical theory and practice, and the central place of the Cornell group in modern rhetorical study. It seems wise, however, to describe briefly the purpose of this book in this context.

Preface

All the contributors have belonged to the Cornell group as students, faculty members, or both. They do not constitute the entire group, however, nor do the essays here collected represent all their interests. This volume includes historical studies only; additional volumes could be compiled from noteworthy essays of Cornell authors on modern concepts of rhetoric and on the teaching of speech, not to mention the related field of drama.

The selection and arrangement of material have been influenced by my bias in favor of a volume which invites the reader to begin at the beginning and continue to the end, rather than to sample at random. The introduction sets the stage by defining and illustrating the concept of rhetoric. Then come consecutive glimpses of developments in rhetorical theory from the time of the pre-Platonic sophists to the period of William Wordsworth and his circle. In the second section of the book, devoted to rhetorical practice, a discussion of the special function of rhetorical criticism is followed by a series of critical essays. The method of presentation varies from detailed analysis of a single speech to consideration of the entire range of a writer's ideas, and the subjects include numerous forms of discourse, such as lecturing, preaching, parliamentary debate, argumentative writing, and advocacy in the courtroom. The epilogue relates the field of rhetoric to the companion realm of literature.

It is a special privilege to bring together three essays by Hoyt Hudson and two by Everett Hunt. Of the five, three have never before appeared in a book, and two are reproduced from a volume long out of print. All are classics. Both Hudson and Hunt participated in the pioneer seminar in classical rhetoric which opened at Cornell in 1920. Two other early leaders in the movement, Harry Caplan and Herbert Wichelns, are here represented by essays. It would have been asking too much in this imperfect world to find a historical study by Alexander M. Drummond, but I did discover, in one of his infrequent articles in the *Quarterly Journal of Speech*, a cogent paragraph concerning the importance of rhetorical studies and have used it in lieu of a foreword.

To all the contributors, or their representatives, who offered reprints, revised previous studies, or wrote new pieces, I express sincere gratitude. I am especially indebted to Herbert Wichelns for sage advice during every phase of the project, and have profited from the assistance of the other members of an informal advisory committee, Wilbur

Gilman, Karl Wallace, Donald Bryant, and Carroll Arnold. Encouragement and support have come from many other sources, particularly Arthur S. Adams, president of the American Council on Education, who permitted me to use the Council's resources for correspondence and miscellaneous typing, and my secretary, Mrs. Margaret Markley, who willingly and effectively did the work.

Surely all who have taken part in this venture share my hope that the collection of these essays forty years after the inauguration of studies in classical rhetoric at Cornell will give new currency to some of the major achievements of the past and consequently point the way to comparable achievements in the future.

R. F. H.

Washington, D.C.
December 31, 1960

Contents

Contents

xiv

INTRODUCTION

The Field of Rhetoric

HOYT H. HUDSON

WHEN Bishop Whately published his *Elements of Rhetoric,* he confessed in his preface that he had hesitated to use the word "rhetoric" in his title, because, he said, it is "apt to suggest to many minds an associated idea of empty declamation, or of dishonest artifice; or at best, a mere dissertation on Tropes and Figures of speech." We can appreciate the good bishop's hesitancy. For "rhetoric" is one of those words which has been so unfortunate as to lose most of its good connections and to be known by the bad company it has sometimes kept. There are five or six meanings given for "rhetoric" in the dictionary; but we are prone to think of only one, and that is "artificial elegance of language, or declamation without conviction or earnest feeling." Thus we are likely to speak of certain pieces of writing or speaking as "mere rhetoric"; or of a writer or speaker as "indulging in meaningless displays of rhetoric." It suggests an inflation of style to cover weakness of thought, or, in our American phrasing, something spread-eagle or highfaluting—and, as I have suggested, only for display.

Yet some respectable connotations have managed to cling to "rhetoric" through the centuries. Walking along a city street not long ago, I passed a building marked "School of Expression," with a sort of menu-card posted by the door showing the subjects that were taught in this school. Very lowest on the list, which included two or three kinds of dancing, elocution, dramatics, public speaking, and oratory, there was offered "rhetoric." I was reminded of Charles Lamb's answer to the saying that a pun is the lowest form of wit: it is the lowest, Lamb insists, only because it is the foundation of all. And if this school of

3

expression had included in its list courses in salesmanship and personal efficiency, as do some similar schools, it would be very much like the schools of the sophists in ancient Athens, wherein rhetoric was the foundation for a training in all the accomplishments and graces necessary to business and social success.

We are more familiar with the word "rhetoric" in the titles of textbooks on writing, of which many published within the past two or three decades have been named "Composition and Rhetoric"; though I am tempted to believe that if you asked the authors of some of these books to tell you which pages were composition and which were rhetoric, they would be at a loss. Some books named "Rhetoric" alone strikingly resemble others named "Composition and Rhetoric" or still others named "Composition" alone. Yet careful writers have maintained a distinction here, one which will throw light on what I have to say a little later about rhetoric in ancient times. Turning to one of the best secondary school texts I know of, Clippinger's *Composition and Rhetoric*, I find these sentences:

Rhetoric and composition are not always distinguished, because they are usually studied together; however the difference between them should be understood. Composition *produces* discourse; rhetoric *analyzes* discourse to determine its structure.

In other words, speaking roughly, a distinction is here being made between the pure science (rhetoric) and the applied science (composition); or, if we prefer, between the science of discourse (rhetoric) and the art of discourse (composition). A product of composition might be an essay; a product of rhetoric, in this sense, would be an outline or analysis of an essay, perhaps with a list of forms of arrangement and figures of speech employed in it. A similar distinction must have been in the minds of those who used to teach rhetoric and oratory; rhetoric was the theory, oratory was the practice. And yet there have been some, and the author of the definition in the *New International Dictionary* is among them, who have overlooked this distinction and have made rhetoric mean "the art of discourse"—the theory and the practice. It is all very confusing; and I trust you are ready to turn back, with me, to another meaning of the word "rhetoric," one which, with whatever incrustations of additional meanings it may have gathered, the word has held for some students and writers and speakers in every generation for nearly twenty-five centuries.

4

The Field of Rhetoric

Wherever we approach the subject of rhetoric, or the subject of oratory or eloquence, we do not go far without meeting finger-posts that point us to the work of Aristotle. Welldon, the translator of Aristotle, refers to his *Rhetoric* as being "perhaps the solitary instance of a book which not only begins a science, but completes it." Welldon says a little too much. A better statement is that of Hugh Blair, the Scottish preacher whose lectures on rhetoric formed the standard text-book both in England and America for fifty years. Blair wrote in 1759:

Aristotle laid the foundation for all that was afterwards written on the subject. That amazing and comprehensive genius . . . has investigated the principles of rhetoric with great penetration. Aristotle appears to have been the first who took rhetoric out of the hands of the sophists, and introduced reasoning and good sense into the art. Some of the profoundest things that have been written on the passions and manners of men, are to be found in his Treatise on Rhetoric.

Sears includes in his *History of Oratory* a chapter on "Aristotle, the Rhetorician," from which I shall quote two sentences:

He must be recognized as the father of rhetorical science, and as the man who in an age of orators compassed the whole scale of their practice. It has been observed that in the most perfect example of persuasive oratory on record —the creation of the greatest genius among the English-speaking race— Shakespeare's speech of Mark Antony—the rationale of it all had been set forth by the great Greek scientist eighteen centuries before.

In Henry Peacham's *Compleat Gentleman,* a popular work on polite accomplishments which was first published in 1622, Aristotle's *Rhetoric* is said to have been deemed by some as "being sufficient . . . to make both a Scholler and an honest man." The study of rhetoric, it is needless to say, has not always been credited with such effects.

At any rate, we do well to begin with Aristotle in building up our concept of rhetoric. With him rhetoric is a useful art, the art of persuasion, based upon a pure science. It is a useful art, because it supplements rather than imitates nature; it supplements nature, in that it helps truth and justice maintain their natural superiority. In his book Aristotle begins with the subject as a science, for he defines rhetoric not as the art of persuasion, but as "the faculty of finding, in any subject, all the available means of persuasion." That is, he makes the rhetorician a sort of diagnostician and leaves it to others to be the practitioners; the rhetorician is the strategist of persuasion, and other men execute his plans and do the fighting. In practice, however, and in any study of the subject, this distinction can hardly be maintained, since the person who determines the available means of persuasion in regard to a given subject must also be, in most cases, the one to apply those means in persuasive speech and writing. In passing I might suggest, however, that if anywhere, either in the profession of law or in advertising or in any sort of publicity work, you know a person who spends his time in analyzing subjects given him and deciding how they can best be presented, what appeals can be based upon them, yet who does not himself present the subjects or make the appeals, there you come near to having the pure rhetorician, in the narrow Aristotelian sense.

But in ancient as in modern times (as we have noted in the case of "Composition and Rhetoric") it was found impossible to divorce theory from practice. The rhetorician and the orator were one; and if not in Aristotle himself, at least in the Aristotelian school and tradition, rhetoric is the whole art of persuasion. It does not satisfy itself alone with the finding of means of persuasion; it also includes the persuasive arrangement and presentation of the speaker's material. A product of rhetoric, in this sense, then, is neither an analysis of some speech already made, with a list of figures and tropes, nor an analysis of a subject upon which a speech is to be made, showing what means of persuasion can be employed. Rather it is a speech, or some piece of persuasive discourse, persuasively presented.

I know of no statement of this meaning more simple than the earliest one to be found in any English publication: it is taken from Caxton's translation of *The Mirrour of the World,* published by himself in 1481. Caxton worded it thus: "Rhethoryke is a scyence to cause another man by speche or by wrytynge to beleue or to do that thynge whyche thou woldest haue hym for to do." This identification of rhetoric with persuasion is frequently met with in English literature throughout the sixteenth and seventeenth centuries. Thus Samuel Daniel has a line,

Sweet, silent rhetoric of persuading eyes.

Nowadays we have a proverb, "Money talks," meaning usually, "Money is the most powerful means of persuasion." A seventeenth century writer of epigrams wrote a couplet embodying the same idea; he called his epigram, "New Rhetorique," and it runs,

6

The Field of Rhetoric

Good arguments without coyn, will not stick;
To pay and not to say's best Rhetorick.

Obviously, such an epigram would be understandable only among readers who were accustomed to think of rhetoric as persuasion. In this sense, plainly, the man who speaks most persuasively uses the most, or certainly the best, rhetoric; and the man whom we censure for inflation of style and strained effects is suffering not from too much rhetoric, but from a lack of it.

Let us proceed with this meaning in mind. We recognize that in ancient times persuasion was carried on almost entirely by the spoken word. We know the great place held by public speaking in Greece and Rome, at least in their democratic phases. We know also of the place of preaching in the early church: "How shall they believe in him of whom they have not heard?" asks St. Paul. "And how shall they hear without a preacher?" After the invention of the printing-press we find persuasion carried on more and more by writing, through the pamphlet and the journal, until in our own day if we run over the principal manifestations of the persuasive art we find as many of them in type as in the spoken word. Editorial writing, pamphleteering, the immense business of advertising and the still more immense business of propaganda,—these are occupations which modern rhetoricians may follow. Yet there are also open to them the occupations calling for public speech, those of preaching, of law, of politics, the lecture and chautauqua platform, business and culture clubs. In commerce, corresponding to advertising, there is the great field of salesmanship, carried on for the most part by speaking. We expect of our publicist that he shall both write and speak.

Yet in spite of our habit of thinking of writing and speaking as separate processes, the practice of persuasion is essentially one, in that the same principles apply everywhere in the field. A writer on public speaking at the present time would hesitate to call his work "Rhetoric," because the word is now usually applied to written discourse. But less than a hundred years ago the case was exactly reversed. Bishop Whately, in the preface already cited, gives as another reason against the use of the title, "Rhetoric," that "it is rather the more commonly employed with reference to public speaking alone." E. L. Godkin, the great American editor, wrote ninety years ago: "The art of rhetoric differs from some others in having arrived long ago at perfection. The rules are the same today as they were in the

7

days of Quintilian and Demosthenes. The art, however, has now two distinct branches, writing and oratory." A writer in "The Nation," reviewing Donelly's *The Art of Interesting,* has said: The author "is a sound classical scholar. He has done us the service of showing conclusively that the underlying principles of classical rhetoric are fundamentally valid today—that Aristotle, Cicero, and Quintilian knew not only how to make speeches, but how to preach sermons, write editorials, and sell groceries."

Then, too, in spite of the great bulk of printed material in the modern world, public speaking and eloquence have by no means lost their potency; and to consider the subject of persuasion apart from speech would be indeed to play Hamlet with the prince left out. The printed word can be passed by or laid aside; the persuasive speaker wins willing and continuous attention. "What is read is accepted inertly, or, if questioned for authenticity, affords no easy measures for resolving doubt. When man listens to speaking, however, he has a definite guide for his reaction: he can look the speaker in the eye, study his face, watch his actions and bearing, analyze his voice, penetrate into the man himself, and then know whether or not he finds him worthy of credence. This is the reason why, when men really care, when an issue is deeply at stake, when the crisis impends, they resort not so much to the writer as to the speaker." [1] We may say further that speaking is still the *norm* of writing; the writer tests his article by reading it aloud "to see how it sounds," and the would-be persuasive writer can do no better than to write as a good speaker would speak.

We might now glance over the field historically, with a view to estimating the body of tradition which has grown up in the study of rhetoric. Greek rhetoric is a large field in itself, too large to be plotted here. Besides Aristotle the other great master of rhetorical theory in Greece was Isocrates, a successful teacher, who gave to his work a more immediately practical turn than Aristotle; the pupils of Isocrates were the great orators, generals, and statesmen of their time. It seems that Isocrates not only taught the form and means of persuasion, but also offered a certain content or body of doctrine which was to provide the subject-matter of his pupils' persuasive efforts. I suppose that when, at the present time, we combine work in Americanization or studies in patriotism with Public Speaking, preparing students to speak on principles of Americanism, we are doing somewhat as Isocrates did in his time. In Rome, Cicero and Quintilian are the great names, though by no means the only ones.[2] St. Augustine was a teacher of rhetoric, and it was as a connoisseur going to hear a great artist that Augustine went to listen to the preaching of St. Ambrose, whose persuasion led to his conversion. Rhetoric was one of the seven liberal arts of the mediaeval curriculum—and in that statement we are summing up many centuries of rhetorical pedagogy and practice, with some changes which we shall note later. Among the Humanists we find Melanchthon writing a treatise on rhetoric, while Erasmus wrote widely in rhetorical subjects; the *De Copia Verborum* of Erasmus was used as a school text in rhetoric for many years. Coxe and Wilson, two of the English Humanists, wrote the first works on rhetoric in our language.

It is interesting to find how many men who became eminent for other reasons made, at some time in their lives, researches in the field of rhetoric. Sir Francis Bacon tried to recall scholars in his day to the classical view of the subject, and also found time, in the midst of his other pursuits, to become a great speaker,—in the opinion of Ben Jonson the best speaker of his generation. One of the works of Thomas Hobbes is an abridgement of the *Rhetoric* of Aristotle, with an appended treatise of his own on the same subject. Isaac Barrow, Vice-Chancellor of Cambridge University and Head of Trinity College, who was famous both as a preacher and as a mathematician second only to Newton in Newton's time, was in his early days a teacher of rhetoric and gave a year's lectures on the *Rhetoric* of Aristotle. Adam Smith, author of *The Wealth of Nations,* lectured on rhetoric for several years. John Quincy Adams was the first to hold the Boylston Chair of Rhetoric and Oratory at Harvard, and his lectures form one of the principal American contributions to the tradition of the subject. Bishop Whately, great as a logician, and Alexander Bain, great as a psychologist, were the principal British writers on rhetoric in the nineteenth century.

But in addition to writers on the theory of rhetoric, the student of the subject must take into his account the practitioners,—the men who have gone to the rostrum or the senate-house, to the pulpit or the hustings, and have attempted to influence men by persuasive speech. The names of the great orators comprise too long a list to be enumerated here. It should be noted, however, that the student of rhetoric investigates eloquence, not for its graces and ornaments, and not with regard to its effect upon him as he reads it; our admiration may be excited by a splendid figure in Burke or Canning; we may gain considerable pleasure from perceiving the skill with which words have been joined euphoniously and rhythmically,—but such admiration and pleasure are incidental and are shared by the student of literature or the general reader. The student of rhetoric looks upon each oration as an effort in persuasion; he must learn what he can of the audience to which it was addressed; he takes note of the appeals that are made, with reference to the motives that are touched, the emotions that are aroused. He must know the character and reputation of the speaker at the time when the speech was made; for a speech otherwise persuasive may fail of effect because the speaker lacks a persuasive *ethos;* whereas at times one sentence from a man of great ethical weight is sufficient to perform a difficult task of persuasion. It is true that we must also take into account matters of style and ornament and delivery; but these, too, are to be estimated with reference to their persuasive effect. Figures and tropes, neat turns of speech and well-drawn pictures, are used to feather the arrow of argument and appeal; but they can also impede its flight.

It is true that there are passages in oratory where the orator seems to throw off the bonds of rhetoric as a useful art and to enter the realm of the fine arts. The end of persuasion is for the moment forgotten in sheer delight at beauty of conception and expression. It is as if a stone-cutter, carving out a figure for some public building, should be touched by inspiration and become a sculptor, making of his figure a statue worthy of standing alone, and more important as art than the whole of the building. Mr. Logan Pearsall Smith, whose work as an anthologist of beautiful passages of prose is well known, says in the introduction to his volume of *Selected Passages from Donne's Sermons:*

It is in the sermon, therefore, that we find some of the highest achievements of English prose—in the sermon, or in prophetic or didactic or even political eloquence written with the same high impulse and inspiration. For great prose needs a great subject-matter, needs great themes and a high spectacular point of vision, and solemn and clear and steadfast conception of life and its meaning.

Such passages we can share with the student of literature, asking him, however, to acknowledge the credit due to the rhetorical discipline and practice which brought the orator to such a measure of perfection, and also taking into account the persuasive task which provided the occasion.

For the most part the student of rhetoric is dealing with broader effects. Goldwin Smith speaks of John Pym as the "first great wielder of public opinion in England." It is the *wielder of public opinion* that the student of rhetoric is interested in. What are the secrets of his power? The rhetorical element in statesmanship is a whole field of study in itself. How many a good policy has been beaten or postponed for want of proper presentation! How many a just and able man has suffered because of an unpersuasive announcement of his purposes! The defeat of Blaine in 1884 is laid, as we know, at the door of his campaigner who untactfully launched against the Democrats the charge of "Rum, Romanism, and Rebellion" phrased with such perverse effectiveness. I shall not enlarge upon the wielding of public opinion which was carried on by Theodore Roosevelt and Woodrow Wilson in later times, by means of their powers of presentation. Enough if I have suggested that in political life a man must be something other than a pure statesman on the one hand or a literary artist on the other; he must know and use rhetoric as a technique of power.

In recent times also we have seen a unique example of the wielding of power through propaganda in the case of the Russian revolution. I recall from John Reed's *Ten Days that Shook the World* a story of how in the first days of the Bolshevik revolution, when the forces of Kerensky were within a few miles of Petrograd and threatening to retake the city, a courier from the battleline came in haste to the city for aid. "Do you want more soldiers?" he was asked. "No, we want orators!" he said. And a truckload of orators was mobilized and hurried to the scene of conflict. Many have wondered how the Bolsheviki, representing the opinion of only a small fraction of the Russian people, have been able to hold power, conduct military operations, and even extend their sovereignty over new territory. Their use of rhetoric as a technique of power helps answer the question. General C. Birdwood-Thompson of the English Army, writing in the *Manchester Guardian*, relates a conversation held with Trotsky, in which General Thompson asked about the "new form of war" carried on by Russia, in which the territory to be conquered was "leavened by political agents" and then easily occupied by a small military force. He goes on:

Trotsky's reply was curious. He said: "War by propaganda is not the invention of a Russian, but rather of an Englishman." And then by way of explanation he added: "Do you remember the story of Oliver Cromwell, who refused to punish one of his subordinates 'because,' he said, 'this man is a good preacher'?"

Historical Studies of Rhetoric

Some question is sure to arise concerning the relation of rhetoric, in our sense, to other fields of study. It is undeniable that rhetoric draws on other fields with considerable disregard for the airtight partitions sometimes put up between college departments. A student of architecture, whose aim is to learn to design buildings, cannot study that subject alone. Without becoming an engineer, he must draw on the special field of engineering for a knowledge of materials and construction. Without becoming a painter or sculptor he must know freehand drawing, color, and relief. He does well to learn something of surveying and landscape gardening. If he expects not only to design buildings but also to superintend their construction, there are a great many other subjects he must know; yet at the end of it all, he is an architect. The case with the rhetorician is analogous. He must learn much from the psychologist, especially with regard to the subjects of attention and emotion. From the social psychologist he draws what knowledge he can of the crowd-mind and the formation of public opinion. There are certain fundamental problems of society which a publicist is continually going to deal with, usually in relation to political questions. Aristotle, in discussing deliberative rhetoric, says that the subjects embraced are finance, war and peace, defence of the country, imports and exports, and legislation. Yet the rhetorician does not necessarily become an expert in those fields. He attempts to learn the authorities and sources of information in each, and to develop a method which he can apply to specific problems as they arise. He learns, in any given situation, what questions to ask—and to answer. The peculiar contribution of the rhetorician is the discovery and use, to the common good, of those things which move men to action—intangible, obscure, mystic, even, as these things may be; yet you and I and our communities find them intertwined with every problem of life.

The question of the relation of rhetoric to the work of the department of English is too involved for me to attempt an answer. From what we have already seen of the field of rhetoric, however, I think one or two suggestions might be drawn. The work of departments of English is already very broad, ranging from courses in Old English and Middle English to those in short-story writing, dramatic structure, biographical studies of authors, and historical studies of literary tendencies. If the department of English absorbs, in addition, the work in rhetoric, at least it should do so with complete knowledge of the breadth and importance of it, and aware of the distinction between rhetoric and other forms of literature. So far as English is the study of language, philology, it is not very closely related to rhetoric; so far as it is a study of literature it deals with a fine art; whereas we have seen that rhetoric is to be classed with the useful arts. Aristotle intended his *Poetics* to treat of discourse designed to delight; he wrote his *Rhetoric* to treat of discourse designed to persuade. We can cite John Milton as a man great in both fields. The student of literature will be especially interested in Milton's poetry. To the student of rhetoric, however, the most important part of Milton's life is the twenty years when, after having written "Lycidas" and "Comus" and other poems, he turned to writing controversial prose for the influencing of public opinion.

The writer in pure literature has his eye on his subject; his subject has filled his mind and engaged his interest, and he must tell about it; his task is expression; his form and style are organic with his subject. The writer of rhetorical discourse has his eye upon the audience and occasion; his task is persuasion; his form and style are organic with the occasion. As for showing this distinction in our curricula, might it not be possible to put all study of exposition and argumentation into a course or group of courses together with other work in rhetoric and public speaking; while the teaching of narration and description, or of such literary forms as the short-story, the familiar essay, and the play, might be kept in closer relation to the courses in literature and in distinction from the forms of writing and speaking as a useful art. There is surely a closer kinship between writing a piece of argumentation and the delivery of an argumentative speech than between the writing of the same piece of argumentation and the reading of Tennyson's poems. Surely it is not asking too much to have this fact somehow recognized.

We may wonder, if the forgoing is a true description of the field of rhetoric, how it has come about that rhetoric usually includes, in present-day usage, only matters of style and ornament. A modern discussion of rhetoric will often consist of chapters on diction, figures of speech, and forms of arrangement, such as antithesis, periodicity, and balance. The identification of rhetoric with persuasion seems to have vanished. This has come about through a process of substituting a part for the whole or of losing sight of the end in the means. For example, in the Middle Ages, there were centuries when there was not a great deal of public speaking, and what was done was in a formal way upon certain conventional themes. At such times, the chief care of the speaker was in the phrasing of his material. His subject-matter was always old —probably dictated down to minute details by the conventions of the occasion; his skill was to be shown in his diction and embellishment. So rhetoric came to be the study of embellishment, and is so defined in some mediaeval and Renaissance rhetorics. At such times, the identification of rhetoric with display is quite warranted; and we can see the ground for the prevalent meaning we noted at the beginning of the paper.

This degradation of rhetoric can be traced quite clearly. The Roman rhetoricians divided the subject into five parts; to quote Cicero's statement, the orator "ought first to find what he should say (*inventio*), next to dispose and arrange his matter, not only in a certain order, but with a sort of power and judgment (*dispositio*), then to clothe and deck his thought with language (*elocutio*); then to secure them in his memory (*memoria*); and lastly to deliver them with dignity and grace (*pronuntiatio*)." Aristotle devotes practically all of his first two books to the subject of invention; in the third he treats of disposition, elocution or style, and very briefly of delivery, omitting the subject of memorizing. But it is plain that in any period when subject-matter was conventionalized, the consideration of invention would be neglected. Disposition would require only the slightest attention, whereas stylistic embellishment, memorizing, and delivery would constitute the orator's task. Some teachers of rhetoric, indeed, by the plan of having students use only the works of others, reduce the study entirely to that of the last two of the five parts—memorizing and delivery.

As we are aware, not in the Middle Ages alone has rhetoric thus been narrowed. In any and all times the tendency is present—the tendency to depend upon tradition or convention for material and devote oneself wholly to style in writing and delivery in speaking; so that rhetoric becomes a study of how to vary a phrase, how to turn a compliment, write certain kinds of letters and formal addresses, how to declaim great orations, or how to deliver a set speech suitable to a certain occasion. Order of words, with regard to emphasis and balance, beauty of figures, dignity and sonorousness become the matters of highest concern. Rhetoric is then an affair of the court and the chamber —or the parlor; and is brought back to its true self only when some divisive issue, a revolution or a great national danger, calls men to sterner tasks of discussion and persuasion. In these times of stress, oratorical power grows out of the subject-matter, eloquence is organic and not an embellishment or flourish added from without. Such eloquence, imbued with great earnestness of persuasive effort, has a simplicity of diction and style which, like poetry in its great periods, lies very close to the common speech of men, and yet at the same time exercises an exalting and purifying influence upon the language. Might it not be possible that in matters of purity and strength of speech the orators, the speaking men—such as Bunyan, Jeremy Taylor, Pitt, Fox, Burke, and Lincoln—have exerted as great an influence upon the language as the poets and essayists? Yet the speakers are too often overlooked when investigations are made upon these points.

But it occurs to me, as I glance back, that my subject is too large to cover even in a paper of such inordinate length as this one is about to assume. I shall attempt no formal summary, hoping that as we have travelled about this field, some of its contours have become clearer and its boundary-lines more definite. I have tried to show that in the field of persuasive discourse, which traditionally and still to a great extent practically is to be identified with oratory and public address, we have a rather definite body of theory and practice, with an honorable history and an excellent academic pedigree. I have mentioned some distinctions that set off rhetorical discourses from all other forms, whether oral or written; notably, that in rhetoric a study of the audience is fundamental; and the essence of it is adaptation to the end of influencing hearers. Rhetoric does not include all the work done by our present departments of public speaking: it does not include the oral interpretation of literature, nor dramatics, nor studies designed to improve the pronunciation and diction of ordinary conversation. But estimated historically and by its influence upon the affairs of the world, rhetorical discourse seems the most important subject with which we have to do. In addition to all we inherit from the past, with modern researches in psychology to draw upon, with modern wielders of publicity to observe, and with the increasing use of a method for sending human speech broadcast, so that a speaker may address thousands where he once addressed scores, the significance of persuasive discourse is continually being enhanced. Surely it would be a mistake to overlook this significance, and in proportioning our emphasis I do not see how we can give any but a central position to rhetorical study.

RHETORICAL THEORY

Plato and Aristotle on Rhetoric and Rhetoricians

EVERETT LEE HUNT

I

THE art of rhetoric offered to the Athenian of the fifth century B.C. a method of higher education and, beyond that, a way of life. Plato attacked both. He gave rhetoric a conspicuous place in his dialogues because it represented in Athenian life that which he most disliked. His pictures of the rhetoricians are so broadly satirical that at times they become caricatures; but his literary power and philosophical originality have so impressed themselves upon succeeding ages that the sophists and rhetoricians of Athens have become symbolical of false pretense of knowledge, overweening conceit, fallacious argument, cultivation of style for its own sake, demagoguery, corruption of youth through a scepticism which professed complete indifference to truth, and, in general, a ready substitution of appearance for reality.

We have the more readily accepted Plato's account because these faults have never been absent from civilization. If the sophists and rhetoricians of Plato's dialogues had not existed, it would have been necessary to invent them. The qualities they typify are so universal that certain collective names for them have become a necessity for thought. Even Grote, the great defender of the historical sophists, when he desires to point out the fallacies of the Platonic Socrates, finds it convenient to accuse Plato of "sophistry." [1] These qualities are not only objectively ever present, but we attribute them readily to any persons or arguments when for any reason our approval has not been won. An argument which we do not accept is sophistical, and the person who presents it a sophist. An appeal to the feelings of men which does not happen to warm our own hearts is rhetorical, and its author a rhetorician. It was so in Plato's time, and it was no more safe then than now to take the words "sophistry" and "rhetoric" at their face value.

When we ask, who were the sophists, what did they teach, and what is the connection between sophistry and rhetoric, we have asked questions involving great historical and philosophical dispute. Generations of historians of philosophy, accepting Plato's account, have made the sophists the scapegoats for all intellectual—and, at times, moral—delinquencies. It is to Hegel that the sophists owe their rehabilitation in modern times.[2] G. H. Lewes, five years before Grote published his famous defense of the sophists, characterized them as professors of rhetoric,[3] and pointed out the bias which had caused their unfair treatment at the hands of Plato. Grote's classic treatment of the sophists in his *History of Greece*[4] was termed by Henry Sidgwick "a historical discovery of the highest order." "Before it was written," says Professor Sidgwick, "the facts were all there, but the learned world could not draw the right inference." In two vigorous essays he defends Grote and makes some significant contributions to the controversy.[5] John Stuart Mill, in an extended review of Grote's *Plato*, defends his interpretation in almost all points, and furnishes many additional arguments in defense of the sophists.[6] E. M. Cope, in his essays on the sophistic rhetoric, rejects many of Grote's conclusions.[7] Zeller is not inclined to look upon the sophists with favor.[8] Chaignet, in his history of rhetoric, accepts the conventional contrast between Plato and the sophists.[9] Jowett, Plato's translator, accepts many of Grote's conclusions, but rejects others.[10] Gomperz, in his *Greek Thinkers*, written fifty years after Grote's history was published, says of his own contemporaries among historians of philosophy:

They still begin by handsomely acknowledging the ambiguity of the word "sophist," and the injustice done to the bearers of that name in the fifth century B.C. by the ugly sense in which the term came to be used, and they admit that restitution is due. But the debt is forgotten before it is paid; the debtor reverts to the old familiar usage, and speaks of the sophists once more as if they were really mere intellectual acrobats, unscrupulous tormentors of language, or the authors of pernicious teachings. The spirit may be willing, but the reason is helpless against the force of inveterate habits of thought. Verily the sophists were born under an evil star. Their one short hour of triumphant success was paid for by centuries of obloquy. Two invincible foes were banded against them—the caprice of language, and the genius of a great writer, if not the greatest writer of all times.[11]

The itinerant sophists founded no schools, and most of their works have been lost. The evidence in the case is therefore of the kind which makes endless argument possible. A few conclusions may, however, be stated as generally agreed upon. The term sophist originally had no unfavorable connotation, and was applied to any man who was thought to be learned. Thus the seven sages of Greece, universally honored, were at times called sophists.[12] In the time of Plato the word carried with it something of reproach, but it was not a definitely understood term. Rival teachers employed it against each other. Thus Isocrates regarded speculative thinkers (Plato among them) as sophists, because he thought their speculations fruitless. He also attacked as sophists other teachers of rhetoric whose instruction he regarded as unintelligent, and whose promises to their pupils he thought impossible of fulfilment.[13] The general public used the term with almost no discrimination, and Aristophanes seized upon Socrates as the sophist who could be most effectively lampooned.

As to what they taught, it has been established that such terms as a sophistic mind, a sophistic morality, a sophistic scepticism, and others implying a common basis of doctrine are quite without justification. Their common characteristics were that they were professional teachers, that they accepted fees, and that rhetoric was a large element in the teaching of virtually all of them. The general emphasis upon rhetoric does not mean that, as scholars, all the sophists found their intellectual interests centered in rhetoric. But rhetoric was the one subject with which they could be sure to make a living. The conditions which made rhetorical training a universal necessity in Athens have been frequently set forth. The sophist who was a master of rhetoric had a number of possibilities before him. He could win power and repute by the delivery of eulogistic orations at public funerals, or deliberative addresses at times of political crises. He could appear at games, or upon occasions of his own making, with what we sometimes call occasional, or literary, addresses, expounding Homer or other works of Greek literature. He could write speeches for clients who were to appear in court. He was not allowed to appear in person as an advocate unless he could show that he had a direct connection with the case, but the profession of logographer was profitable. Finally, he was more certain of pupils in rhetoric than in any other subject.[14] It is not strange, then, that with a wide range of individual interests, the sophists, with varying emphasis, should unite upon rhetoric as the indispensable part of their stock in trade.

The claim to impart virtue has at times been held to be the distinguishing mark of the sophist, and the attempt has been made to divide the sophists from the rhetoricians upon this basis. This cannot be done, for the two activities of making men virtuous and making them eloquent were inextricably intermingled. Hegel has pointed out what he regards as an essential difference between the sophists and modern professors.[15] The professor makes no pretension to making men good or wise; he only presents to students his organized knowledge, realizing that knowledge comes but wisdom lingers. The sophists, on the other hand, laid claim to some actual effect from their teachings; they made men wise. This was at least in part due to the dominance of rhetoric. Aristotle might lecture upon the theoretical aspects of rhetoric—a procedure which seems to have been productive of little eloquence—but the prime purpose of the teaching of rhetoric was practical. Certain sophists made the payment of their fees dependent upon some proof that they had actually given to a pupil the ability to persuade an audience. With such a background, it is natural that the teaching of ethics as abstract knowledge would seem about as futile as the teaching of an abstract rhetoric. A man who taught ethics taught it practically, with injunctions and exhortations, and he expected practical consequences to follow. But one of the consequences always looked for was that the pupil should become such a person as to be persuasive when speaking in a public assembly. Ethics thus was often absorbed in rhetoric. The failures of many pupils to become either good or persuasive gave rise, then as now, to cynical reflections upon the futility of education, and there were many arguments as to whether virtue or rhetoric could be taught. In these arguments there were two extreme positions. Some inclined to believe that if you teach a man to be virtuous he will naturally be eloquent, and rhetorical instruction is unnecessary. Other sophists believed it quite impossible to teach virtue, but by constant attention to becoming a persuasive speaker virtue would be unconsciously acquired. The controversy over the relation of virtue to eloquence runs through the history of rhetoric, and may be viewed as a technical question in that field. The attitude of sophists toward the teaching of virtue, then, cannot distinguish the sophists from the rhetoricians, and for the purposes of our study the two terms may be used almost synonymously—the word sophist, perhaps, being somewhat more inclusive.

II

The way in which the sophists combined their own intellectual interests with the teaching of rhetoric may best be made clear by a brief study of the four principal figures: Prodicus, Hippias, Protagoras, and Gorgias. Since these are the men most often referred to by Plato, it is also desirable to have some historical knowledge of them with which to correct the impressions given by the Platonic pictures.

Protagoras and Gorgias were older than Prodicus and Hippias, but they lived longer and matured later. They were therefore more affected by the movement away from the natural sciences, and as humanists devoted a larger portion of their energies to definitely rhetorical instruction.

Prodicus of Ceos has been called the earliest of the pessimists.[16] He was frail of body, but with a powerful voice he moved his audiences by descriptions of the different ages of man from birth to second childhood and death. He would depict death as "a stony-hearted creditor, wringing pledges one by one from his tardy debtor, first his hearing, then his sight, and next the free movement of his limbs." [17] His pessimism had none of the usual consequences—passive resignation, retreat from the world, or a great desire to seek pleasures while they might be found. To face death courageously was a virtue, and he taught his disciples that while we are, death is not; when death is, we are not. Life, while it lasted, was to be lived vigorously. His most famous lecture, *The Choice of Hercules*, has been preserved by Xenophon,[18] who tells us that Socrates quoted it with approval; through many centuries it has had a great effect in exalting the ideals of labor, hardihood, and simplicity. It was not in popular religion that Prodicus found his sustaining faith, for his speculations upon the origin of religion have the point of view of the modern critical historian. He accounted for the divinities of the various nations by pointing out that peoples deified the objects most useful to them—sun, moon, rivers, fruits of the field, and heroic men.

The more technical instruction of Prodicus was devoted to a study of language. He sought to collect and compare words of similar meaning. He desired to reduce the ambiguities in the arguments of the Greeks, and to aid in the development of literary style. He attempted to clarify ideas by insisting upon accuracy in the use of words, believing, with Hobbes, that "the light of human minds is perspicuous words."

The lectures of Prodicus were well known in all the cities of Greece, and commanded large sums in all places except Sparta, where foreign teachers were discouraged by a law against the payment of fees. Nevertheless he was welcomed there. He served his native island frequently as ambassador, and in the discharge of his civic duties displayed the qualities which in his lectures he urged upon youth.

Prodicus, then, was the rhetor rather than the teacher of rhetoric; and his chief contributions to the thought of his time were made as philosopher and grammarian.

Hippias of Elis, whom Plato especially disliked, is chiefly remembered for his versatility.[19] As an orator he was known throughout Greece. He recited certain well-known compositions of his in which figures of the Iliad are compared upon the basis of their virtues, or old men give advice to aspiring youths. He was rewarded by being made a freeman of many cities, and it is especially significant that his lectures on history and ethics were also acceptable to the conservative Spartans. He never gave himself to the routine of perfecting his students in rhetoric, but was occupied with innumerable pursuits. He was a mathematician of considerable note; he wrote on theories of sculpture and painting, on phonetics, rhythm, and music; he developed a system that enabled him to perform surprising feats of memory in his old age; he was an ambassador for his native city, Elis; he attempted most of the prevailing forms of literature; and he prided himself upon his facility in mastering all the arts and crafts.

The antithesis between nature and convention seems to have originated with Hippias. He observed the variety and changeability of the laws of the Greek democracies, and felt that only laws possessing the universality and permanence of the laws of nature should be really sacred and binding. To give validity to the laws of men, the laws of all states should be compared, and the universal elements in them selected as the "natural" laws for the governing of nations. In believing that all men were by nature equal, Hippias was perhaps the originator of the doctrine of natural rights. When the distinction between nature and convention has been clearly made, one may, of course, espouse either. Hippias was one of the first preachers of a return to nature. This suggests a reason for his efforts to achieve so wide a versatility. The return to nature is only possible when each person is relatively self-sufficient, and self-sufficiency was a favorite doctrine with Hippias. He doubtless believed, as have men of other ages, that the development of personality gained by the consciousness of being equal to any situation more than offsets the dissipation of energy and efficiency incurred by the performance of all sorts of tasks; but one motive was clearly that of independence, and the development of the sort of ingenuity that enables a Robinson Crusoe to exist. Such a man would live by his work as well as by his wits. Rhetoric would not be the chief means of obtaining what he desired, and it is not surprising that rhetoric should be relatively less important to those who would be governed by nature than to those who saw in convention the power that offers the best government.

Hippias was more than a popular orator preaching to the cities of Greece. In his thought we have the beginnings of the cosmopolitanism of the later Cynics, the self-sufficiency of the Stoics, the belief in natural rights, and the ideal of versatility as a means of developing the whole man.

Protagoras of Abdera accepted the distinction of Hippias between nature and convention; but he had no sympathy for the return to nature.[20] In the variety and changeability of the laws of men lay the great hope of progress. He therefore turned away from the natural sciences and devoted himself to the "humanities." He, too, was a man of great versatility; he invented a porter's pad; as a friend of Pericles, he was given the task of framing the laws for the colony at Thurium. As a teacher, his instruction was chiefly intended to offer a training for public life. He included within his curriculum oratory and its auxiliary arts, educational theory, jurisprudence, politics, and ethics. In his teaching of public speaking he insisted upon the value of practical exercises. He declared that there were two sides to every proposition, and that a speaker should be able to set forth the arguments on either side. His practice of having his students argue upon both sides of certain general themes may have been responsible for the charge against him, recorded by Aristotle, that he made the worse appear the better reason. But as this was a standing reproach against philosophers as well as rhetoricians, and as we have no evidence which impeaches his moral

25

character, we may believe that this charge applied no more to his teaching than to all instruction in the art of reasoning.

In addition to the training in debate, Protagoras practised his pupils in the development of what were called commonplaces. Speeches were made which praised or blamed certain human qualities, such as patriotism, friendship, courage, cupidity. These speeches had no reference to a concrete situation, but they equipped the pupils with a stock of thoughts and phrases for use when a real occasion demanded ready utterance. The debates developed keenness and dexterity; the commonplaces gave the speakers a certain copiousness and elegance.

Grammar was also given attention, and Protagoras is recognized as the first to introduce the subject into his curriculum. It has been remarked that the level attained by Greek literature before Protagoras wrote his book *On Correct Speech* seems to indicate that a mastery of language may be acquired quite independently of conscious rules. But the desire of Protagoras to introduce order and consistency in the tenses of the verb, moods of predication, and genders of substantives, was in harmony with the intellectual tendencies of the times, and shows him to have been by no means totally absorbed in the practical business of advising youth how to get on in the world.

The ethical theory of Protagoras was set forth in the lost work, *On the Incorrect Actions of Mankind.* In his seventieth year he read publicly, at the house of Euripides, his work, *On the Gods.* Only the first sentence has been preserved.

In respect to the gods, I am unable to know either that they are or that they are not, for there are many obstacles to such knowledge, above all the obscurity of the matter, and the life of man, in that it is so short.[21]

Whether Protagoras meant to assail the belief in the gods, or whether he meant merely to point out that in the nature of the case we could not have *knowledge* of them, we do not know. At any rate, his scepticism so alarmed certain of his contemporaries that his book was publicly burned, and he was exiled.

The philosophical doctrine for which Protagoras is chiefly known, and for which he was vigorously assailed by Plato, is summarized in the dictum that man is the measure of all things. Since we have only the first sentence of the work in which this doctrine was developed, it is not strange that scholars are far apart in their interpretation of the meaning of Protagoras; but they are generally agreed that the Platonic interpretation of it in the *Theætetus* is quite unfair. Few in-

terpreters now consider it to involve the degree of relativity and sub-
jectivism with which Protagoras and the sophists generally have been
burdened. Gomperz points out that a man who preached that anything
was true which anyone believed to be so, would not be the man to
suffer for a denial of the possibility of knowledge of the gods. Professor F. C. S. Schiller, in his *Studies in Humanism*, devotes two dialogues to Protagoras; one explaining his humanism, and the other
defending his scepticism. In his introduction to the volume Professor
Schiller says:

Our only hope of understanding knowledge, our only chance of keeping
philosophy alive by nourishing it with the realities of life, lies in going back
from Plato to Protagoras, and ceasing to misunderstand the great teacher who
discovered the measure of man's universe.[22]

But this is not the place to discuss the philosophical aspects of the
teachings of Protagoras; it is only desired to make it clear that there
are grounds for regarding him as did Hegel:

[He was] not merely a teacher of culture, but likewise a deep and solid
thinker, a philosopher who reflected on fundamental questions of an altogether universal kind.[23]

Gorgias of Leontini,[24] who first appeared in Athens as the head of
an embassy petitioning for aid against the aggressions of Syracuse upon
Sicilian cities, is known as the founder of the art of prose. Chiefly
interested in oratory of the epideictic type, he employed what is termed
the "grand" style. The resources of the poets, whose works were so
successful in holding the attention of Greek audiences, were turned
to the purposes of the orator. Gorgias was interested in style for style's
sake; his foreign accent and distinguished air delighted the Athenians;
and throughout his career he sought to persuade by pleasing. The
extravagances and artificialities of his style have often been pointed
to as the source of the euphuism of the seventeenth century, and of
the stylistic eccentricities of other periods of decadence.

It cannot be said, however, that the oratory of Gorgias was devoid
of ideas. In common with other itinerant teachers, he preached Pan-
Hellenism in all the cities of Greece. In his Olympian oration he urged
the Greeks to cease their internal rivalries, and to turn their spears
against the barbarians. In the Athenian funeral oration he warned his
hearers that victories over their fellow Greeks called for dirges of

lament. As a teacher of oratory, Gorgias was condemned by Aristotle for placing too much emphasis upon memorization and declamation.[25] Little is known concerning his pedagogical method, but there is no reason to suppose that it differed markedly from the custom of having the pupils declaim speeches written by themselves and by the master, drill in topics of amplification and depreciation, and practise upon commonplaces and disputations. Although an epideictic speaker would be constantly praising virtue and censuring vice, and in so doing could hardly avoid entertaining certain ethical theories, Gorgias never announced himself as a teacher of virtue. He agreed with Isocrates that one who tried to become persuasive in discoursing about justice and virtue and expediency would probably become as virtuous as mere knowledge could make him.

As a philosopher, Gorgias engaged in controversy with the Eleatic school. All we know of his book *On Nature or Not-Being* is its threefold thesis that "Being does not exist; if it did exist it would not be cognizable; and if it were cognizable, the cognition would not be communicable." [26] We cannot here enter upon metaphysical questions; but the conventional construction put upon this thesis is that it goes beyond Protagoras, and is the ultimate of sophistical scepticism, that it is a nihilism which makes all knowledge impossible, that it makes immediate plausibility the sole standard of the critical judgment, and that rhetoric was the chief of all subjects for Gorgias because the one certainty of life was that the man who could persuade others to do his will was, temporarily at least, the possessor of great power. This interpretation is not justified either by an examination of the philosophical disputes of the time or by a study of the life of Gorgias himself. The Eleatic school following Parmenides and Melissus, was quite willing to doubt all evidence of the senses, and yet to trust implicitly in *a priori* reasoning about Absolute Being. The protest of Gorgias against this was quite in harmony with the growing modesty of the scientific endeavor of the times, which was beginning to see the necessity of increasing knowledge bit by bit, and to question the claim of the philosophers to a higher knowledge. Had Gorgias, in denying the tenets of the Eleatics, meant that he believed scientific truth to be unattainable, it is not likely that he would have written upon physics, nor that a statue would have appeared upon the tomb of Isocrates representing Gorgias as directing the attention of his pupil to a globe. The attack of Gorgias upon the

28

contradictions of his predecessors in philosophy does not show that he abandoned all search for truth. Socrates attacked his philosophical predecessors in a similar manner, he abandoned all inquiry in natural science, and he had as little confidence in the attributes of being as Gorgias; yet he is not accused of denying the validity of established scientific truth, or of abandoning all belief in the possibility of knowledge. The account of Gorgias offered by many historians of philosophy is a *reductio ad absurdum* rather than an interpretation.

Although we think of Gorgias chiefly as an orator and a teacher of oratory, and as a creator of a style which is now looked upon unfavorably, he was too active a participant in the philosophical controversies of his time for us to dismiss him as intellectually insignificant. Since we have lost his philosophical works, we cannot prove that he made a constructive contribution to the thought of his time, but his attack upon an absolutistic philosophy was something, and the evidence certainly does not warrant the supposition that he was guilty of meaningless absurdities, or that his teaching was necessarily immoral in its implications.

Numerous other rhetoricians might be mentioned—Polus and Thrasymachus especially—but our information concerning them is scanty, and the four we have dealt with are the most significant when we consider their prominence as rhetoricians, their contribution to the thought of the time, and the attention they received from Plato.

III

One is inevitably led to ask why such men as these have suffered so greatly in the estimation of posterity. Why has Plato's opinion been accepted uncritically and its perversions further distorted by later commentators? In addition to what has already been suggested—that we need the terminology of the attack upon the Athenian sophists to describe an ever present sophistry—there is the fact that Athenian hostility to the sophists has often been taken as a confirmation of Plato's account. This is to forget that Athenian public opinion distrusted the sophists for reasons similar to those which led it to execute Socrates, and that the disagreement between Plato and the Athenian public was profound. The activities which gave these teachers their influence with the Athenians were just the ones which led Plato to condemn them; while many aspects of their thought which led to popular disfavor were the ones which Plato would have regarded with approval. We may learn much about the sophists by contrasting the typical Athenian criticism of them with that of Plato.

In accounting for the disfavor with which the Athenians looked upon the sophists it must not be forgotten that a complementary picture of their power and influence could quite as easily be drawn, and that both are necessary to a true estimate of their position in Athenian life. The sophists exerted a much greater influence upon their times than Plato, and the element of jealousy should not be entirely overlooked in considering his attitude toward them.[27] But the conservative elements of the city, of whom Aristophanes was a prominent representative, charged the sophists with corrupting the youth. Plato dissented from this charge in the case of Socrates, and defended the sophists generally from it, asserting that the real corrupter of youth in Athens was public opinion, which the sophists only reflected.[28] John Stuart Mill, who had reasons for analyzing the motives of those who are overzealous in protecting the young, has stated the case most clearly:

When the charge of corrupting youth comes to be particularized, it always resolves itself into making them think themselves wiser than the laws, and fail in proper respect to their fathers and seniors. And this is a true charge; only it ought to fall, not on the Sophists, but on intellectual culture generally. Whatever encourages young men to think for themselves, does lead them to criticize the laws of their country—does shake their faith in the infallibility of their fathers and elders, and make them think their own speculations preferable. It is beyond doubt that the teaching of Socrates, and of Plato after him, produced these effects in an extraordinary degree. Accordingly, we learn from Xenophon that the youths of rich families who frequented Socrates, did so, for the most part, against the severe disapprobation of their relatives. In every age and state of society, fathers and elder citizens have been suspicious and jealous of all freedom of thought and all intellectual cultivation (not strictly professional) in their sons and juniors, unless they can get it controlled by some civil or ecclesiastical authority in which they have confidence. But it had not occurred to Athenian legislators to have an established Sophistical Church, or State Universities. The teaching of the Sophists was all on the voluntary principle; and the dislike of it was of the same nature with the outcry against "godless colleges," or the objection of most of our higher and middle classes to any schools but denominational ones. They disapproved of any teaching unless they could be certain that all their own opinions would be taught. It mattered not that the instructors taught no heresy; the mere fact that they accustomed the mind to ask questions, and require other reasons than use and wont, sufficed at Athens, as it does in other places, to make the teaching dangerous in the eyes of self-satisfied respectability. Accordingly, respectability, as Plato himself tells us, looked with at least as evil an eye on Philosophers as on Sophists.[29]

This explanation of Mill's is more applicable to the ethical and philosophical, than to the rhetorical, aspects of the sophists' teaching. To be sure, the rhetoricians professed to be able to speak upon either side of any case, and to impart this ability to their pupils; this was the cause of a certain distrust analogous to that with which lawyers are sometimes viewed today. But when lawyers turn public orators, they are the most vigorous and platitudinous upholders of the *status quo*. So the sophists, as public orators, illustrated and re-enforced the received dogmas of Athenian society. Their speeches were acceptable to the most conservative. Even their teaching of the art of speaking upon either side of any case did not rest so much upon a willingness to attack prevalent morality and customs as it did upon the cultivation of an ability to make either side of the case *appear* to be consistent with common standards of right and justice. Rhetoric as the art of persuasion must always appeal to the people upon the basis of whatever beliefs they may happen to have. It is not likely, then, that it was the rhetoric of the sophists which led to the charge that they broke down religion and corrupted youth. It was rather that they concerned themselves enough with philosophy to incur something of the distrust with which speculative thought has always been viewed. In all the disputes between the earlier schools of philosophy there was one point upon which they were agreed; namely, that the popular beliefs and explanations of phenomena were entirely wrong. For them, as for modern philosophers, the incarnation of ignorance was "the man in the street." Their arrogance and their contempt for the public naturally roused resentment. Their lofty pretensions were contrasted with their apparent practical helplessness, and the story of Thales falling into a well while gazing at the stars is typical of the popular attitude toward philosophers. The popular distrust of the sophists was not so much that, as rhetoricians, they were different from Socrates and Plato, but that, as philosophers, they were so much like them.

There was a certain aspect of the rhetorical teaching which caused a portion of the public to dislike the popular teachers. After the downfall of the Thirty in Athens, it was evident that democracy was the order of the day. Members of the aristocracy could retain their power in the state only by developing their ability to persuade an audience. Teachers of rhetoric, in such a situation, were indispensable. But the fees charged by the sophists placed their instruction beyond the reach of many, who naturally resented what seemed an unfair advantage possessed by those more adequately trained for public life.

The fees of the sophists seem to have been a cause of universal reproach, but the feeling was too complex to be explained simply. There was, of course, the aristocratic bias of Athenian life. Physicians were the only wage-earners who suffered no loss of social standing. Sculptors were artisans rather than artists because their work was a method of gaining a livelihood. Plato, the man of wealth and family, was for once in agreement with the popular prejudice, and he attacked the sophists both for the insignificance of their petty fees and for the large fortunes that they made.[30] The acceptance of fees marked a certain institutionalizing and mechanizing of higher education, which was disliked. The philosopher whose chief occupation was the pursuit of truth might impart his wisdom to such persons and at such times as suited him, without seriously interrupting his own thinking. He probably found a certain number of disciples a stimulus. But the introduction of fees and the acceptance of responsibility for practical training in public speaking made the teacher seem to be a servant of the pupil. He became a professional educator, and as such insisted disagreeably upon the importance of education. As philosophers, the sophists could probably have retained the measure of freedom and leisure that Plato demanded, even while accepting pay for their work. But as teachers of rhetoric they tended to become submerged in the routine of schoolmastering.

As philosophers, the sophists incurred a different sort of penalty for their fee-taking. Then, as now, certain activities of what may perhaps be termed men's higher natures were especially removed from thoughts of gain. We do not like to think that popular preachers are making money; we deplore the commercialized theatre, and the novel written only to sell. These activities, we believe, should be ends in themselves. It is not difficult to understand why the spectacle of foreign teachers coming to Athens to teach virtue for a price should have roused a resentment somewhat distinct from that of those who disliked the teaching of rhetoric.

Plato and Aristotle

IV

Turning to Plato, we have already noted that he shared the general dislike of fee-taking; but we should consider also those aspects of his thought which led him to dislike any persons who accepted Athenian life and institutions and participated actively in public affairs. Mill has pointed out:

> Plato, if he returned to life, would be to the full as contemptuous of our statesmen, lawyers, clergy, authors, and all others who lay claim to mental superiority as he ever was of the corresponding classes at Athens.[31]

This would be true because Plato would find that our life bears a much closer resemblance to the Athens he knew, than to his *Republic*. We may cite the *Republic* and the *Laws* as sufficient evidence of Plato's discontent with the sorry scheme of things entire. He was not a reformer who could be contented with a gradual evolution in the direction of his ideals; nor did it disturb him that his Republic was not an earthly city; he was satisfied to believe that its pattern was laid up in the heavens. Scholars are becoming increasingly conscious, however, that his gaze was not exclusively heavenward as he wrote the *Republic*. He knew what he disliked in Athens, and his utopia owes at least as much to his dislikes as to his desires. Had the sophists and rhetoricians been the only objects of his scorn he might not have been driven to writing the *Republic*. But the politics, poetry, art, education, and religion of Athens were all wrong—so wrong that it was easier to paint a utopia than seriously to attempt the reformation of Athens. We may say in the beginning, then, that Plato's condemnation of rhetoric and rhetoricians is merely a small part of his condemnation of all contemporary civilization. We may note in passing, that rhetoric has its uses even for those who attack it; and that Plato's contrast between the rhetorician's world of appearance and the philosopher's world of reality was drawn with consummate rhetorical skill.

The supreme remedy for the ills of civilization, Plato believed, lay in the government of philosopher-kings. But until philosophers were kings, and could govern autocratically by their wisdom, without the necessity for persuading the multitude, they were to remain aloof from public affairs.

> The lords of philosophy have never, from their youth upwards, known their way to the Agora, or the dicastery, or the council, or any other political

assembly; they neither see nor hear the laws or votes of the State written or spoken; the eagerness of political societies in the attainment of offices,—clubs, banquets, and revels, and singing maidens, do not even enter into their dreams.[32]

In Plato's ideal realm, there was no place for rhetoric as a political agency. Large questions of policy were to be settled by the philosophers. Administration of routine affairs was to be in the hands of experts. There would be no litigation, for there would be no laws. Laws were as absurd and useless for philosopher-kings as decrees of the public assembly would be for pilots and physicians, whose actions were governed by their own arts. Later in life Plato despaired of finding philosophers, even in utopia, who could be trusted to govern without laws, or of inducing people to have confidence in them, even if they could be found, and his *Laws* is a concession to that feeling. But even in his later utopia there was no freedom of utterance, without which, of course, the development of rhetoric would be an impossibility. With the dogmatism of age upon him, he laid down laws which were to be permanent. The games of children,[33] the restrictions upon foreign travel,[34] the denial of freedom of speech, and the enforcement of ethical and theological dogmas,[35] were all designed to protect the city against changes of any sort. The use of rhetoric in administering and interpreting the laws was also carefully guarded against.[36]

Although rhetoric had no place in the courts or political assemblies of Plato's ideal realms, its scope in another field was to be greatly increased. All the literature and art of the Greeks was to be examined with a single eye to its effect upon the morals of the citizens. Truth and beauty were subordinated to goodness—to goodness as Plato conceived it. Whenever the attempt is made to govern the ideals of a people by censoring art in the interests of a dogmatic morality, all art tends to become rhetorical. To say that rhetoric was banished from the Republic, then, is not quite true. It was driven out the door only to fly in at the window. The unsympathetic interpreter of Plato would say that literature became part of the educator's rhetoric, with Plato as chief educator and chief rhetorician; a better Platonist, however, would hold that literature and education became philosophy, with Plato as chief philosopher.

One source of rhetoric and rhetoricians in any democracy is the continual and restless striving of the people to better their individual conditions. They perpetually seek to become what they are not, and in doing this they strive to bend the wills of others to their own ends. This state of affairs Plato avoided, in his *Republic*, by having a fixed and settled order of society, an order of experts, in which every man did his own work, and no man attempted the work of another. In this way ambitious, self-seeking demagoguery was to be eliminated.

There is no indication in the *Republic*, that even under philosopher-kings, with a scheme of education devised by Plato himself, and with art and literature revised in the interest of morals, the mass of the people were expected to rise to greater heights than a certain efficiency in minding their own routines. It is not particularly strange, then, that Plato had a great contempt for the people of Athens, who lived under a government so little influenced by Platonism. Plato adhered to the philosophic tradition in regarding public opinion as always wrong both because it was public and because it was merely opinion. Plato despised mere opinion almost as much as he did the public. He was never tired of contrasting the knowledge of the philosopher, who had attained real knowledge by dialectical investigation, and by contemplation of Ideas, with that shadow knowledge called opinion.[37] Sometimes, of course, opinion would turn out to be right. And right opinion had a certain value as a guide to action in practical affairs; but even right opinion fell far short of philosophic knowledge. Plato never believed that probability was the guide of life. Education, for him, was a process of keeping the mass of people at their tasks with as few opinions as might be, and of enabling the few whose intelligence would permit, to attain philosophic knowledge. Those who knew were to abandon the pleasures of knowing, at stated intervals, and govern those who did not know. Thus opinion was largely to be eliminated from the State. The education given by the sophists and rhetoricians, on the other hand, was for the purpose of enabling a man to get on in a world of conjecture. Isocrates (whom we have not discussed, because, though he receives passing mention, he is hardly a figure in the Platonic pictures of contemporary rhetoricians) stated as his philosophy of education:

It is impossible to attain absolute knowledge of what we ought or ought not to do; but the wise man is he who can make a successful guess as a general rule, and philosophers are those who study to attain this practical wisdom.[38]

Akin to this is the educational aim of Protagoras—given us by Plato, but probably quite acceptable to Protagoras:

If a young man comes to me he will learn prudence in affairs private as well as public, he will learn to order his own house in the best manner, and he will be best able to speak and act in affairs of state.[39]

The education given by the sophists varied with individual teachers, but in general it aimed to enable the pupils to become leaders of men in a democracy. It was practical in the sense in which all training for public affairs is practical; and it sought to enable the individual to use existing institutions rather than to overthrow them. The perversions of such education—half-knowledge, propaganda, demagoguery, philistinism, worship of the appearance of success—are probably even more prevalent now than then. Whether they are worse than the perversions of Platonism is too large a question to be argued here. But whether for good or ill, the conception of the aims and purposes of the American liberal college, as set forth by the most distinguished modern educators, is much closer to Isocrates and Protagoras than to Plato.

It is evident, from Plato's literary activities as an idealistic reformer and creator of utopias, from his conception of the philosopher as the true governor of mankind, and from his social, political, and educational philosophy, that he would have differed profoundly from the sophists and rhetoricians, even had all of them possessed the highest character and wisdom.

V

It will be convenient to discuss Plato's treatment of rhetoric and rhetoricians under four heads: the pictures he has given us of the individual rhetoricians, his general indictment of rhetoric in Athens, his suggestions for the creation of a nobler and better rhetoric, and his later attack upon the eristical rhetoricians who imitated the argumentative methods of Socrates.

The Platonic pictures of the sophists are scattered throughout the dialogues; but the most extended and vivid characterizations of them are in the *Protagoras,* the *Hippias Major* and *Hippias Minor,* the *Gorgias,* and the *Euthydemus.* Plato constantly contrasts them with the ironical Socrates. Socrates affects a great humility, the sophists are conceited and self-confident; Socrates is skilled in closely reasoned argument, the sophists are helpless in his hands; Socrates defines his terms, but the sophists, accustomed to haranguing uncritical audiences, use their terms with all the looseness and inaccuracy of common conversation.

Protagoras is pictured at the head of a group of admiring listeners, pleased at an opportunity to lecture in the presence of rival sophists.[40] Although the reader feels that in the discussion with Socrates common sense is with Protagoras, he cannot but be amused at the spectacle of the eloquent, deep-voiced orator unable to defend even a sound argument against the dialectical attack of Socrates. Protagoras, with his popular lectures and his conventional morality, was too powerful a figure to please Plato, who was somewhat neglected in the Academy.

Hippias seems to have incurred the most vigorous enmity of Plato.[41] In the *Hippias Minor* Socrates exposes the fallacies in the popular lecture on Homer that Hippias was accustomed to give before approving audiences. In the picture of Hippias at the Olympic games in garments, rings, and accoutrements of his own make, there is no suggestion that he was attempting to re-enforce his favorite doctrine of self-sufficiency; the Platonic view is that Hippias was insufferably conceited over his versatility.

The references to Prodicus are scattered and incidental. He is described as a "taker to pieces of words," [42] as "drawing useless distinctions about names," [43] and as beginning his instruction with "initiation into the correct use of terms." [44] In the *Cratylus* there is a satirical reference to the relationship between the fees of Prodicus and the amount of knowledge imparted.[45]

Gorgias is portrayed in the dialogue bearing his name [46] as professing to be able to answer any questions which may be asked him, and as being so familiar with all possible subjects of discussion that for many years he has heard no new question. He indulges in oratorical praise of the art of rhetoric, and is shown to be quite incapable of dialectical argument.

Polus,[47] a young pupil of Gorgias, Callicles,[48] a practical politician rather than a professional rhetorician, and Thrasymachus,[49] the spokesman for doctrines that Plato wished to discredit, are described as being much like the better-known sophists.

Euthydemus and Dionysodorus, who belong to a later group of sophists, are caricatured in the *Euthydemus* with a dramatic vivacity and comic force which almost equals the *Clouds* of Aristophanes. They are characterized as "a new importation of sophists," who "will give lessons in speaking and pleading, and in writing speeches." [50] This occupation is new to them, for they were previously teachers of the art of fighting in armor. They also profess to be teachers of virtue.

Although there are no formal charges made against any individual sophists in any of the dialogues, Plato has used all his literary resources to add to the effectiveness of his philosophical attack upon them.

VI

There is in the *Gorgias* a deeper purpose than an exhibition of the deficiencies of the predominant rhetorical technique. Plato here gives us a contrast between the true and the false life. The philosophic import of the dialogue has led some commentators to believe that the treatment of rhetoric is only incidental, or that rhetoric is used merely as introductory to the higher themes of philosophy. But Plato, for all his idealism, took as the point of departure for his reforms the weaknesses which he thought he saw in Athens, and rhetoric is, after all, a chief subject of the dialogue. Rhetoric, as philosophy, was a way of life. Rhetoric dealt not only with form and style; it also treated the matter and policy of public speaking. It offered something of a philosophy to the orator. It was almost indistinguishable from political science, and to the general public the orator was the statesman.

If there was anything which could pretend to dispute with philosophy the position of a master knowledge, or put forward a rival claim for the guidance of life and affairs, it was this art of rhetoric, which professed to train men for politics, and to make them able to act as well as speak efficiently. The teacher of philosophy had thus to be vindicated against the teacher of rhetoric; the philosophical statesman had also to be vindicated against the orator-statesman of actual Athenian politics.[51]

In contrasting the philosopher and the rhetorician, Plato at times gives the impression of being on the defensive. This is not merely because rhetoric is more popular, but also because he had felt the reproaches of his friends for his inactivity in Athenian affairs. He was keenly conscious of the criticism of the philosopher which he put into the mouth of Callicles:

He [the philosopher] creeps into the corner for the rest of his life, and talks in a whisper with three or four admiring youths, but never speaks out like a freeman in a satisfactory manner.[52]

One way to establish the supremacy of philosophy was to show that the claims of rhetoric as "the art of becoming great in the city," [53] were not to be taken seriously. There must be an appeal to higher values. The belief that might makes right, the trust in things that are seen, must be replaced with a desire for the goods of the soul. The ignorance, prejudice, and selfishness of the rhetorician must be exposed; the most popular of arts must be shown to be no art at all when subjected to the scrutiny of a philosophical mind. The *Gorgias,* then, undertakes to refute the claims made for rhetoric by Gorgias, Polus, and Callicles. Socrates defeats each one in turn, so that we really have three dialogues in one, each antagonist advancing a somewhat different claim for rhetoric.

Gorgias, in the beginning, praises rhetoric for the power and influence it confers. He also defends it from the oft-repeated charge that it is frequently used wrongfully and works mischief in the state. But the definition of rhetoric is what Socrates seeks, and Gorgias appears to be as devoid of abstract ideas with which to frame a definition as the other rhetoricians. The art of formal logic did not yet exist, and Socrates presses Gorgias with various analogies and ambiguities which both appear to mistake for valid arguments. Logic and rhetoric have not yet been clearly conceived as universal arts or sciences which admit of application to any subject matter; and it is not strange that Gorgias was unable to furnish the clear conception that Socrates sought. Socrates, then, had no great difficulty in establishing his own definition, that *rhetoric is the art of persuading an ignorant multitude about the justice or injustice of a matter, without imparting any real instruction.* Rhetoric is most powerful with the ignorant many, because the rhetorician, as rhetorician, does not really know what he is talking about; he only appears to know, and the appearance is persuasive only with the ignorant. Plato here limits rhetoric to the discussion of matters concerning justice. He probably chose to discuss the forensic rather than the deliberative or epideictic rhetoric because the contemporary rhetoricians devoted most of their attention to it.

Socrates also compels Gorgias to admit that *rhetoricians do not really know their business,* for they do not teach their pupils about justice and injustice (an essential part of rhetoric, by the definition previously established). The actions of the pupils show that they have never learned to know justice—any rhetorician must admit that his pupils often act unjustly. Two things are to be noted about this argument. Gorgias and Socrates have different ideas of what it means to know justice. Gorgias means by it a sufficient practical knowledge of men and affairs to know what is conventionally moral in any given case. Socrates, on the other hand, means abstract, philosophical knowledge of the nature of justice. There is also underlying the argument the "vicious intellectualism" of Socrates. The Platonic Gorgias fails to object to the Socratic thesis that if students of rhetoric knew the nature of justice, they would never commit an injustice. To Gorgias the teaching of justice was not a heavy responsibility, because the just or unjust actions of his pupils did not depend upon any ethical theories taught by him. The just rhetorician was just because he sought to live in a manner which his common sense told him would win the approval of his fellow men, and not because he had been taught to be virtuous.[54] It is difficult to believe that the real Gorgias would have been so easily entrapped by the argument that the injustices committed by pupils of the rhetoricians proved the ignorance of the teachers.

Polus indignantly attempts to rescue his master, but he also falls an easy victim to the Socratic dialectic. Since both Gorgias and Polus have been more apt at praising rhetoric than at defining it, Socrates proceeds to attack their claims and to establish the point that *rhetoric is not of much use in the world*. There are four arguments to substantiate this: (1) Rhetoric is not an art; (2) rhetoric does not confer power; (3) rhetoric as a protection against suffering wrong is of little importance; and (4) rhetoric as a means of escaping a deserved punishment is not to be commended. The philosophy developed in support of these points loses little of its significance when separated from its immediate purpose of refuting the claims of rhetoric; but the unity of the dialogue is not perceived until it is understood that the philosophical theses are part of a consistent argumentative plan.

Rhetoric was not an art, Plato believed, because it did not rest on universal principles. It was really only a knack, a routine, or experience. Aiming at persuasion, it cared only for appearance. It did not aim at justice, but only at a semblance of justice. By an art, Plato meant more nearly what we should call a science, that is, a body of knowledge organized on universally valid principles. The dispute as to whether or not rhetoric was an art was of great practical significance to the rhetoricians. If it was not an art, and rested upon no principles, then the attempt to teach it must be futile. There has always been considerable scepticism as to the possibility of teaching rhetoric profitably. Its rules have often been multiplied in order to have something more to teach. Plato, in common with other writers of genius, was fond of minimizing the importance of technique, just as teachers as a class are fond of overemphasizing it.

Aside from the immediately practical effect upon the teaching of the subject, it was injurious to the prestige of rhetoric to deny it a scientific character. As Gomperz observes of the age:

All the business of mankind, from cooking a dinner to painting a picture, from going a walk to waging a war, was guided by rules and, wherever possible, reduced to principles.[55]

Plato's charge that rhetoric was not an art, then, was somewhat analogous to the denial of a place among the sciences to sociology or psychology. Such a charge, even if unaccompanied by any implications concerning the doubtful morality of persuading ignorant multitudes, was enough to injure the subject.

In denying that rhetoric is an art, Plato gives it a place among the pseudo-arts. In the hierarchy of arts and pseudo-arts, the higher arts aim at the production, real or apparent, of permanent conditions; the lower, at the removal, real or apparent, of temporary derangements. Sophistry is distinguished from rhetoric and placed above it. Sophistry is an imitation of the statesman's art, which is higher than the art of the pleader, because the pleader only remedies miscarriages of justice, while the statesman has the opportunity to create permanent institutions which give society an organization based upon justice. We probably agree today in paying more honor to the statesman than to the trial lawyer. In the *Gorgias,* the sophist is the sham statesman; the rhetorician is the pleader who "makes the worse appear the better reason," and forgets justice in the winning of his case.

The second argument against rhetoric in the dialogue with Polus is that rhetoric, in spite of appearances, does not really confer power. People who do not know, in the philosophical sense (and Plato believed that very few could know anything in the philosophical sense), what is really good for them, have no power, for they are unable to do what they will. When they do evil, they are not doing what they will, for no one really wills to do evil; he only makes a mistake in the art of measuring. The Socratic belief that no man errs voluntarily is again the basis of the argument. The minor premise, that rhetoricians have not the philosophical insight to know what is really good for them, Plato believes may safely be assumed.

The third and fourth assertions about rhetoric which Socrates established against Polus gain significance when considered in relation to the conditions of Athenian court procedure. With a jury of five hundred—somewhat predisposed to convict any wealthy man, since his goods would be at the disposal of the state—innocent persons were liable to be convicted on the flimsiest of charges. The size of the jury made oratory a much more important matter than evidence. This would make it quite as possible for the guilty to escape punishment, as for an innocent man to suffer at the hands of his enemies. Any practical-minded person would therefore conclude that rhetoric was of great importance to the innocent as a protection against injury, and to the guilty as a means of avoiding a just penalty. Socrates, however, denies both of these claims, and advances his famous paradoxes in support of his argument. Rhetoric is not of great importance as a protection against suffering wrong; the really important thing is to keep oneself from doing wrong, for doing wrong is a greater evil than suffering wrong. The dialectic by which Socrates establishes this is hardly as noble as the conclusion which he reaches, but Polus is not able to offer any effective opposition. Again, rhetoric as a means of escaping punishment is of no great service, for the man who is punished for his injustice is happier than he who is not punished. This Socratic thesis is a matter of feeling and belief rather than of logical proof, but against Polus it was not difficult to establish dialectically. If it is honorable to inflict punishment on a guilty person, then it must be honorable to receive it. Punishment, as a deliverance of the soul from evil, should be welcomed by the guilty as a medicine.

When Polus seems to be hopelessly defeated, Callicles takes up the argument. In the discussion with him the argument turns more directly to the contrast of philosophy and rhetoric as ways of life. In the words of Socrates:

> We are arguing about the way of human life; and what question can be more serious than this to a man who has any sense at all: whether he should follow after that way of life to which you exhort me, and truly fulfill what you call the manly part of speaking in the assembly, and cultivating rhetoric, and engaging in public affairs, after your manner; or whether he should pursue the life of philosophy, and in what this differs from the other.[56]

Callicles vigorously attacks philosophy, upholds rhetoric, and offers in its support the doctrine that might makes right, that justice is but an artificial convention invented by the many weak to protect themselves against the few strong, that the law of nature decrees that the strong should take what they can get, and that in a society full of conventions, rhetoric offers the strong man the means of getting what he wants. The Socratic argument in reply to this passes into the realm of ethics, and deals with the self-seeker as such, rather than merely with the rhetorician.

Socrates is disposed to admit that there might conceivably be a true and noble art of rhetoric. The true rhetorician would attempt to improve the people, rather than to please them. He would attempt this, not only for the moral benefit of the people, but also because any process which does not improve souls is not really an art; it is an ignoble flattery. Among such flatteries are music, poetry, drama, and painting. They may occasionally improve the people, but for the most part they are to be viewed with distrust.

Although there might be a noble rhetoric, and true rhetoricians, none such have ever existed. All statesmen and rhetoricians of the past, even the best, such as Themistocles, Cimon, Miltiades, and Pericles, have failed to make the citizens any better.[57] The proof of this is that the citizens treated these men very ungratefully and unjustly, which they would not have done if they had been taught justice by the statesmen. The professional teachers of rhetoric, even though the teaching of justice should be a part of the instruction in rhetoric, dare not trust their own pupils to treat them justly, for they exact a fee instead of leaving it to the pupil's sense of honor.

Socrates is further offended at the pretentiousness of rhetoric and rhetoricians. If rhetoric occasionally saves a life in courts of law, there are other life-saving arts which are equally important, and much more modest. A swimmer may save many lives, but he is not likely to boast that he practises the greatest of the arts. Or a pilot, if swimming seems to be a contemptible example, is also a great life-saver. But he keeps his modesty. If he has any philosophy in him, he knows that some of the lives he has saved were probably not worth saving; but a rhetorician never seems to indulge himself in such sobering reflections.

Rhetoric destroys the integrity of a man's soul, for it involves conformity to the ways of the multitude. The philosopher, on the other hand, sees further:

The noble and the good may possibly be something different from saving and being saved, and that he who is truly a man ought not to care about living a certain time; he knows, as women say, that none can escape the day

43

of destiny, and therefore he is not fond of life; he leaves all that with God, and considers in what way he can best spend his appointed term.[58]

The dialogue closes with a myth of the after-world, in which the judgment that bestows rewards and punishments is not based upon appearances, as are the judgments won by the rhetoricians, but upon the true nature of the soul. The myth sums up the whole argument of the dialogue. The fundamental contrast is between appearances and reality; the rhetorician deals with appearances, the philosopher with reality.

In the *Gorgias,* the rhetoricians appear to be men bent upon getting on in the world. They seem to believe that an unjust man who escapes punishment, and practises his injustice on such a large scale that he is conspicuously successful, is a man to be envied and imitated. It is easy for us, made familiar with the doctrine that injustice is an evil, through the teachings of Plato, of the Stoics, and of Christianity, and accustomed at least to pay lip-service to it as a truism, to suppose that Plato was upholding the traditional righteousness against a peculiarly corrupt set of public teachers, the sophists and rhetoricians. It should be remembered, however, that public opinion in Athens was not with Plato. Instead of regarding Gorgias and Polus and Callicles as especially corrupt, we should regard Plato as the reforming philosopher, attacking public opinion through its prominent representatives. That Plato himself took this view is shown by his remark in the *Republic* that the youth are not corrupted by individual sophists, but by the public.[59]

It is also worthy of note that this attack upon rhetoric is itself a rhetorical triumph. The rhetoricians are ridiculed for their inability to reason closely, and to defend themselves against the dialectic of Socrates; but the triumph of the Platonic Socrates is not a triumph of logic over oratory. John Stuart Mill has put this clearly:

This great dialogue, full of just thoughts and fine observations on human nature, is, in mere argument, one of the weakest of Plato's works. It is not by its logic, but by its ἦθος that it produces its effects; not by instructing the understanding, but by working on the feelings and imagination. Nor is this strange; for the disinterested love of virtue is an affair of feeling. It is impossible to prove to any one Plato's thesis, that justice is supreme happiness, unless he can be made to feel it as such. The external inducements which recommend it he may be taught to appreciate; the favorable regards and good offices of other people, and the rewards of another life. These considerations, however, though Plato has recourse to them in other places, are not available in the *Gorgias*. . . . It is the picture of the moral hero, still *tenax propositi* against the hostility and contempt of the world, which makes the splendor and power of the *Gorgias*. The Socrates of the dialogue makes us *feel* all other evils to be more tolerable than injustice in the soul, not by proving it, but by the sympathy he calls forth with his own intense feeling of it. He inspires heroism because he shows himself a hero. And his failures in logic do not prevent the step marked by the *Gorgias* from being one of the greatest ever made in moral culture.[60]

VII

The *Phædrus*, which has been described as a dramatized treatise on rhetoric, contains three speeches upon the general subject of love; one of which Plato introduces as the work of Lysias, a noted rhetorician of the day, and two of which are put into the mouth of Socrates. It is in a comparison of these speeches that Plato's ideas about rhetoric are expressed. At the close of the final speech upon love, delivered by Socrates, Phædrus expresses his admiring approval; he fears that Lysias, whose speech he had just read to Socrates, could not produce anything as good; [61] indeed, he had already been reproached for his speech writing. Socrates remarks that it is not writing speeches, but writing them badly, that is disgraceful. This opens the way for a discussion of the entire practice of speaking and writing.

Socrates enunciates as the first rule of good speaking:

The mind of the speaker should know the truth of what he is going to say. . . . There never is nor ever will be a real art of speaking which is unconnected with the truth.[62]

This rule of Socrates is contrasted with the prevalent conception of rhetoric. Rhetoric is usually considered to be an "art of enchanting the mind by arguments"; it has no concern with the nature of truth or justice, but only with opinions about them. Rhetoric draws its persuasive power, not from truth, but from harmony with public opinion. This conception of rhetoric, however, Plato thinks inadequate. The objection here is not, as is often stated, from high moral motives. In the *Gorgias* and elsewhere it is stated that the genuine rhetorician must be a true and just man. And from many sources we know how Plato abhorred the "lie in the soul." But here the ground is simple expediency. The art of persuasion is the art of winning the mind by resemblances. The speaker goes by degrees from that which is accepted to that which he wishes accepted, proceeding from one resemblance to another. If the difference between two resemblances is small, there is an excellent opportunity for making the audience believe that one is the other.

This rule, that "the mind of the speaker should know the truth of what he is going to say" and not "catch at appearances," may seem to be a commonplace. But it is not mere faithfulness to fact that Plato has in mind; it is that Truth which only philosophers know. All others dwell in a darkened cave.[63] The moving figures they behold are not realities; they are shadows, phantoms. Only the philosopher has ascended into the clear light of day. Only he has beheld Ideas in their Absolute form. Only he it is who is able to see "unity and plurality in nature." Hence the exclamation of Socrates:

> Come out, children of my soul, and convince Phædrus, who is the father of similar beauties, that he will never be able to speak about anything unless he be trained in philosophy.[64]

These Platonic conceptions are not new to Phædrus, and no time is wasted in explaining them. Having secured acceptance of the first rule of good speaking, Socrates proceeds to lay down two corollaries. First, rhetoric has greater power in discussions where men disagree and are most likely to be deceived. The rhetorician ought therefore to have in mind a clear distinction between debatable and nondebatable subjects. Secondly, particulars must be carefully observed, so that they may be properly classified. In other words, careful definitions must be drawn, and mere matters of opinion separated from matters of scientific knowledge.

A lack of any definition of the subject of love is the first criticism of the speech of Lysias. This is particularly reprehensible as love is used in two different senses. Socrates, however, was careful in both speeches to start from a definition of the love he was treating. Again, there is no principle of order in the speech of Lysias. He is accused of beginning at the end, and his topics follow one another in a random fashion.

> I cannot help fancying that he wrote off freely just what came into his head. . . . Every discourse ought to be a living creature, having its own body and head and feet; there ought to be a middle, beginning, and end, which are in a manner agreeable to one another and to the whole.[65]

From this study of the speeches on love, two fundamental principles of composition emerge:

> First, the comprehension of scattered particulars in one idea; the speaker defines his several notions in order that he may make his meaning clear. . . .

46

Secondly, there is the faculty of division according to the natural ideas or members, not breaking any part as a bad carver might.[66]

But these processes of generalization and division, which the speech of the famous rhetorician failed to employ, are principles that Socrates has hitherto held to belong to dialectic, and not to rhetoric.

I am a great lover of these processes of division and generalization; they help me to speak and think. And if I find any man who is able to see unity and plurality in nature, him I follow, and walk in his steps as if he were a god. And those who have this art, I have hitherto been in the habit of calling dialecticians.[67]

Phædrus acknowledges that these principles rightly belong to the dialecticians, but persists in inquiring about the principles of rhetoric; he mentions a number of prominent rhetoricians together with some characteristic elements of their systems. Socrates admits that in addition to the really fundamental principles of composition to be found in dialectic, there may be in rhetoric some "niceties of the art." Theodorus, Evenus, Tisias, Gorgias, Prodicus, Hippias, Polus, Protagoras, and the other rhetoricians spend much time upon proems, statements of fact, witnesses, proofs, probabilities, confirmations, superconfirmations, refutations, diplasiology, gnomology, and other technicalities. These theories and practices of the rhetoricians, however, are not really principles of the art of rhetoric. They are mere preliminaries, as the tuning of strings is preliminary to playing upon an instrument. But no one would call the tuning of strings the art of music. The contemporary rhetoricians have no more real claim to be practitioners of the art than a man who knows a few drugs, but does not know how to use them, could claim to be a physician. Since all these teachings of the rhetoricians are not true principles of the art, and are altogether useless except when used in conjunction with the principles of dialectic, Socrates proceeds to give what might be called an outline of a true art of rhetoric.

Oratory is the art of enchanting the soul, and therefore he who would be an orator has to learn the differences of human souls—they are of so many and of such a nature, and from them come the differences between man and man. He will then proceed to divide speeches into their several different classes. Such and such persons, he will say, are affected by this or that kind of speech in this or that way, and he will tell you why; he must have a theoretical notion of them first, and then he must see them in action, and be

47

able to follow them with all his senses about him, or he will never get beyond the precepts of his masters. But when he is able to say what persons are persuaded by what arguments and recognize the individual about whom he used to theorize as actually present to himself, This is he and this is the sort of man who ought to have that argument applied to him in order to convince him of this; when he has attained the knowledge of all this, and knows also when he should speak and when he should abstain from speaking, when he should make use of pithy sayings, pathetic appeals, aggravated effects, and all the other figures of speech, when, I say, he knows the times and seasons of all these things, then, and not until then, is he perfect and a consummate master of his art.[68]

Such an outline of rhetoric, Socrates feels, may be discouraging to the young Phædrus. The road to the mastery of such an art is obviously long and hard. The sophists, on the other hand, are represented by Plato as offering promises to impart culture quickly and easily.[69] Here, then, is an opportunity for Socrates to compare the true way of mastering the art of rhetoric with the sophistic short cut. The rhetoricians succeed in imparting a certain skill in making plausible speeches because they content themselves with creating an appearance of probability. They teach that "in speaking the orator should run after probability and say good-by to truth." [70] The teaching of Tisias on the topic of probability, which enabled a man quickly to make a case either for the defense or the prosecution, regardless of the evidence, is cited as typical of the rhetoricians. To show the superiority of the true rhetoric over such trickery, Socrates repeats his former statement:

Probability is engendered in the minds of the many by the likeness of the truth, and he who knows the truth will always know best how to discover the resemblance of the truth.[71]

The rhetoric of Tisias, then, is deficient in two respects. First, it is not even effective, for it is not quick at perceiving likenesses of truth; and secondly, such a rhetorician is as likely to deceive himself as his audience. Further, the true rhetorician masters his art after much labor:

Not for the sake of speaking and acting before men, but in order that he may be able to say what is acceptable to God and in all things to act acceptably to Him so far as in him lies.[72]

Rhetoric, then, like all the arts, is to be an instrument of righteousness. After stating that enough has been said of the true and false art of

48

rhetoric, Socrates feels that something remains to be said of the propriety and impropriety of writing. He proceeds to speak of writing, but only to condemn the practice.[73] Concerning the invention of letters he cites a myth in which the prophecy is made that the art of writing will create forgetfulness and a pretense of wisdom. Contrasted with this futility of writing is "an intelligent writing which is graven in the soul of him who has learned, and can defend itself, and knows when to speak and when to be silent." [74] This expression of opinion about writing concludes Plato's theory of rhetoric as found in the *Phædrus.*

That these suggestions of Plato for the organization of rhetoric into a scientific body of knowledge may be more clearly in mind when we come to contrast the *Phædrus* with Aristotle's *Rhetoric,* we shall here summarize them.

1. "The first rule of good speaking is that the mind of the speaker should know the truth of what he is going to say." This cannot be interpreted as an injunction to speak the truth at all times. It is rather to *know* the truth in order (a) to be persuasive by presenting to the audience something which at least resembles truth, and (b) to avoid being oneself deceived by probabilities. In order to know the truth, the rhetorician must be a philosopher.

2. The rhetorician must define his terms, and see clearly what subjects are debatable and what are not. He must also be able to classify particulars under a general head, or to break up universals into particulars. The rhetorician, then, must be a logician.

3. Principles of order and arrangement must be introduced. "Every discourse ought to be a living creature, having its own body and head and feet; there ought to be a middle, beginning, and end, which are in a manner agreeable to one another and to the whole."

4. The nature of the soul must be shown, and after having "arranged men and speeches, and their modes and affections in different classes, and fitted them into one another, he will point out the connection between them—he will show why one is naturally persuaded by a particular form of argument, and another not." In other words, the rhetorician must be a psychologist.

5. The rhetorician must "speak of the instruments by which the soul acts or is affected in any way." Here we have the division under which comes practically all of rhetoric when viewed more narrowly and technically. The "instruments" by which rhetoric affects the soul

49

are style and delivery. Plato believed style to be acquired, however, as Pericles acquired it, by "much discussion and lofty contemplation of nature."

6. The art of writing will not be highly regarded; nor will continuous and uninterrupted discourse be regarded as equal to cross-examination as a means of instruction. This is Plato's way of saying that any method of attempting to persuade multitudes must suffer from the very fact that it is a multitude which is addressed, and that the best of rhetoric is unequal to philosophic discussion.

7. The rhetorician will have such a high moral purpose in all his work that he will ever be chiefly concerned about saying that which is "acceptable to God." Rhetoric, then, is not an instrument for the determination of scientific truth, nor for mere persuasion regardless of the cause; it is an instrument for making the will of God prevail. The perfect rhetorician, as a philosopher, knows the will of God.

VIII

De Quincey says that rhetoric has, in general, two connotations: one of ostentatious ornament, and the other of fallacious argument. That part of Plato's attack upon rhetoric which we have considered, largely concerns itself with rhetoric as "ostentatious ornament" (although the two aspects can seldom be completely separated). And it was this attack which led Plato to the constructive theory of the *Phædrus*. But there was a later assault upon the sophists which concerned rhetoric as an art of fallacious argument.[75] The sophists of Plato's earlier dialogues are declaimers and rhetoricians who can overwhelm opponents with long speeches, but they are tyros in the art of argumentation. In the *Euthydemus, Sophist,* and *Statesman,* Plato caricatures the imitators of Socrates, who practise argumentation by question and answer, but who resemble Socrates as the wolf does the dog.

The *Euthydemus* is the earliest known attempt to exhibit a variety of fallacies. In it Plato desired to make clear the distinction between truly philosophical argumentation and that eristical disputation which served no purpose except to display a certain type of cleverness. A young man, Cleinias, is cross-examined by two sophistical teachers of argument, Euthydemus and Dionysodorus. They conduct their examination in a spirit of horse-play, and soon have the youth hopelessly confused. Socrates then rebukes them, and offers to examine Cleinias in a truly philosophical fashion. His kindly questions (much more kindly here than in other dialogues, but they serve Plato's purpose in emphasizing the contrast), which lead Cleinias to the conclusion that wisdom is the only good, and ignorance the only evil, are an example of the way in which a philosopher conducts an argument—for the enlightenment, and not the confusion, of youth.

Having distinguished the philosopher from the sophistical teachers of fallacious argument, Plato in an epilogue contrasts the philosopher and the orator-statesman. Here Plato is probably thinking of Isocrates and his "philosophy," which was a mixture of rhetoric and politics. Philosopher-politicians and speech writers, Socrates is made to say, imagine themselves to be a superior sort; they think they have a certain amount of philosophy, and a certain amount of political insight; thus they keep out of the way of all risks and conflicts and reap the fruit of their wisdom. Socrates asserts, however, that philosophy and political action tend to such different ends that one who participates in both achieves little in either. The Isocratean ideal of the orator-statesman, which had so great an influence upon Cicero, was objectionable to Plato for at least three reasons. In the first place, the true statesman was a philosopher rather than an orator; he ruled arbitrarily through his wisdom rather than through persuasion. Secondly, if the statesman was forced to stoop to the use of oratory, it was to be clearly understood that oratory was a subordinate instrument. The ideal of the orator-statesman only helped to confuse the superior art of politics with rhetoric. Thirdly, the orator-statesman falsely imagined that the ideas which he used in the persuasion of the public constituted his philosophy; whereas in reality he was so tied to particulars in all his speaking and thinking that he never approached the wisdom of the true philosopher.

In the *Euthydemus*, then, we have pictured a later development of the older sophists. Imitators of Socrates had appeared who taught the art of argumentation for pay: Isocrates had enlarged and dignified the instruction of the rhetoricians by allying it more closely with pan-Hellenic politics, and had become much more popular and successful than Plato. Plato insists that true philosophy is a different sort of thing, and indulges in caricature and satire to make it evident.

In the *Sophist*, we have an abstract and methodical discussion of that which is dramatically pictured in the *Euthydemus*. Plato planned a trilogy of dialogues, the *Sophist*, the *Statesman*, and the *Philosopher*, in which the man of the world and the man of wisdom should be contrasted. The *Philosopher* was never written, but from the *Sophist* and the *Statesman* we get the Platonic discussion of the false art of argumentation known as eristic.

The sophist, in the dialogue of that name, is discovered by a preliminary study of the angler, which suggests a method of search, and also furnishes an implied analogy, for the sophist is found to be a fisher of men who finally destroys them. By a series of homely figures the sophist is revealed in his various aspects. He is (1) a paid hunter after youth and wealth, (2) a retail merchant or trader in the goods of the soul, (3) he himself manufactures the learned wares which he sells, (4) he is a hero of dispute, having distinctly the character of a disputant, (5) he is a purger of souls who clears away notions obstructive to knowledge. In the last-named characteristic, Plato seems about to admit that the sophist serves a great educational purpose, for he has previously admitted that "refutation is the greatest and chiefest purification." But the sophist, as the supposed minister of refutation, is related to the real purger of souls as "a wolf, who is the fiercest of animals, is to the dog, who is the gentlest." [76] Here Plato does not seem to see that a given logical procedure is as a method essentially the same, whether used by a sophist or a philosopher. For Plato, even the *logical* nature of cross-examination seems to be changed by the *moral* nature of the examiner. No sophist ever employed greater fallacies than the Socrates of the Platonic dialogues; yet fallacies in the arguments of a philosopher seemed somehow elevated by their moral purpose. Aristotle followed Plato in this error. Probably no fallacy is more persistent than the judgment of logical method by the standard of moral purpose.

The eristical sophists, as the rhetorical, profess a knowledge which they do not have. They profess that the art of disputation is a power of disputing about all things. Plato puts the sophists in the position of teaching that a mastery of form gives also a mastery of substance. The sophists delight in the discovery that a certain facility in logical method, accompanied by entire unscrupulousness, can make almost any proposition appear to be plausible. With no standard of consistency looking farther than the immediate discussion, method can so arrange any small group of facts, or alleged facts, that any thesis may be made to appear tenable. The sophists *seem* to teach young men to argue about all things because "they make young men believe in their own supreme and universal wisdom." They are enabled to do this by their readiness

in offering "conjectural or apparent knowledge of all things" as a substitute for truth. They are like painters who profess "by one art to make
all things." [77] What the sophist makes is a resemblance, but it is easy
to deceive the less intelligent children, by showing his pictures at a
distance, into believing that he has the absolute power of making
what he likes. In the same way there is an imitative art of reasoning,
and by the use of this art the sophist passes himself off as a philosopher.
There are two types of these imitators: the popular orator, who makes
long speeches to the multitude and who appears to be a statesman, and
the sophist, who teaches argumentation and pretends to be a philosopher.

The *Statesman* is an attempt, by the same method of division used in
the *Sophist*, to discover the true statesman. Here we have an introductory analogy concerning the weaver. As the weaver has the auxiliary
arts of the fuller, the carder, and the maker of the warp and woof, so
the statesman has the auxiliary arts of the rhetorician, the general, and
the judge. There is always the danger, however, that the rhetorician
may be mistaken for the statesman. Politics is the science that tells us
when to persuade, and of what; rhetoric merely tells how to persuade.
If the rhetoric be a noble rhetoric, however, and does really persuade
men to love justice, it may be regarded as a useful instrument in our
second-best state, where persuasion is an unfortunate necessity in
government. Rhetoric, however, should never lose its instrumental
character, and should never aspire to be more than one of the several
subordinate arts which the statesman weaves together into the whole
which is the state.

In these two dialogues, then, the *Sophist* and the *Statesman*, we are
warned against the rhetorician, who appears in different guises. In
the *Sophist*, he appears as the dialectician who purges the soul of false
knowledge, but he is really an eristical disputant. In the *Statesman*,
he appears as the persuader of the public who is quick to seize power
as a demagogue unless he be kept strictly under the direction of the
true statesman.

IX

To summarize briefly our whole discussion of Plato: we have shown
that his treatment of rhetoric is based upon his feelings toward certain
rhetoricians, and upon his dislike of the rhetorical tendency of all
Athenian life. Plato never viewed rhetoric abstractly, as an art of

composition, as an instrument that might be used or abused; he always considered it a false impulse in human thought. He therefore attacked in published dialogues the more prominent contemporary teachers and the art they professed to teach. The evidence seems to show that the sophists of the earlier attacks were intellectually respectable, and that they made significant contributions to the thought of their time. At the conclusion of his earlier attacks (if we may trust the attempts to arrange Plato's dialogues in approximately chronological order) Plato offers an outline of a reconstructed rhetoric. Here, too, he shows his inability to conceive of rhetoric as a tool; the ideal rhetoric sketched in the *Phædrus* is as far from the possibilities of mankind as his Republic was from Athens. In later life, a new generation of teachers that patterned its methods after Socrates, aroused the wrath of Plato, and he wrote other dialogues to distinguish the false art of argumentation from the dialectical processes of the true philosopher.

X

In turning to Aristotle,[78] we shall be chiefly interested in his relation to Plato. To explain the relation of any one of Aristotle's treatises to Plato is, according to Sir Alexander Grant, almost a sufficient account of what it contains. Familiarity with the Platonic dialogues and their Athenian background, makes it possible to proceed more rapidly with the systematic work of Aristotle upon any particular subject under investigation. It is not our purpose here to present an exposition of the *Rhetoric*,[79] and the preceding discussion should make it possible to condense the account of Aristotle, although his contribution to rhetoric is greater than that of Plato or the sophists.

It is obvious that as Plato's pupil, Aristotle must have had his attention called to those aspects of Athenian life which interested his master. As a reader of Plato's dialogues, Aristotle found a wealth of concretely pictured material ready for classification into various compartments of knowledge. Aside from the magnificent gesture of the *Phædrus*, Plato apparently gave little constructive thought to rhetoric. He did not teach its practice, nor lecture upon its theory. Aristotle, however, during the first period of residence at Athens, and while still a pupil of Plato at the Academy, opened a school of rhetoric in competition with Isocrates. We have here an instance of the way in which rhetoric in Athens, as in other times and places, has offered men whose minds could not be confined to a single field, an opportunity to establish themselves as teachers and thinkers. The works upon rhetoric which have been lost were probably composed during this earlier period. There seem to be adequate grounds for attributing three such works to Aristotle: a history of rhetoric, a dialogue upon the subject, named for Gryllus, a son of Xenophon, and the *Theodectea*, mainly devoted to style, composition, and arrangement, and which probably contained in greater detail the subject matter of the third book of the extant *Rhetoric*.[80] It is not known when the *Rhetoric* was composed, but it was not published until Aristotle's second period of residence and teaching in Athens (336 B.C. is the most generally accepted date of publication). It is believed that the third book, which deals with style and arrangement, was not written until some time after the first two books. The *Poetics* was written before the third book of the *Rhetoric*, but probably after the earlier books. From this it is sometimes inferred that Aristotle's interest in style as a part of rhetoric was of late development. This is hardly consistent with his earlier treatment of the subject in the *Theodectea*. A more probable explanation of the greater interest which Aristotle seems to have felt in the subject of proofs and their sources is that this part of rhetoric represented most distinctly his own contribution to the subject. In writing of style and arrangement he was dealing with questions already fully treated by many writers, for most of whom he had little regard. In the first two books, however, he was organizing a new unity out of material drawn from logic, psychology, ethics, and politics. It may have been an additional source of pleasure to him to be able to draw from his own treatment of these special fields such material as was needed to give rhetoric a more philosophical character. It is significant that Aristotle, having taught rhetoric in his early youth, and having waged war with both preceding and contemporay rhetoricians, should, in his age, after having surveyed all the fields of knowledge, return to the treatment of the same subject. It seems to be one of the ironies of history that that portion of rhetoric which was most particularly his own, and which owed most to his previous work in other fields, should be forever slipping back into its component parts of logic, psychology, ethics, and politics; and that style and arrangement, regarded by both himself and Plato as mere preliminaries to the art, rather than the art itself, should fix more permanently the character of rhetoric.

XI

While Aristotle agreed with Plato in his contempt for the unscientific nature of the instruction given by other teachers of rhetoric,[81] and in applying the term sophist to false pretenders to knowledge,[82] his approach to rhetoric was affected by certain philosophical and temperamental divergences from Plato. It is an oft-quoted remark of Friedrich Schlegel's that every man is born either a Platonist or an Aristotelian. This is generally interpreted to mean that the tribe of Platonists are poets and mystics, seeking a truth above the truth of scientifice knowledge, while the Aristotelians rely upon methodical experience and classified observations. It cannot be said that Aristotle paid greater attention than Plato to the facts of experience in the creation of a philosophical rhetoric, for he constructed the entire art from the general principles of dialectic, psychology, and ethics, referring to any existing examples of eloquence only most casually for the sake of illustration. But it is, perhaps, a safe generalization to say that Plato sought to reform life, while Aristotle was more interested in reorganizing theory about life. For this reason Aristotle's *Rhetoric* is largely detached from both morality and pedagogy. It is neither a manual of rules nor a collection of injunctions. It is an unmoral and scientific analysis of the means of persuasion.

We have seen that Plato was predisposed to feel a contempt for rhetoric and rhetoricians by certain of his political ideas—his belief in a government of philosophers, administered by experts; his desire for a permanent stratification of society, free from attempts of men to rise out of their class; and his profound contempt for public opinion. Aristotle had no enthusiasm for what has been called Plato's "pedantocracy." He realized that expert knowledge and professional training have their limitations, and that in political matters the judgment of the people may be superior to that of those who have special knowledge.[83] Although Aristotle shared Plato's belief that a laborer could hardly possess a virtue which should entitle him to citizenship, he never expected ranks and classes to be permanently fixed, as in the *Republic*. In the *Politics* he suggests that final power should rest with the multitude, which, of course, would make rhetoric a universal political instrument. And Aristotle's attitude toward public opinion—the common sense of the majority—is distinctly different from that of Plato. This is most marked, perhaps, in his *Ethics*,[84] although it is difficult to distinguish ethical from political thinking in the speculation of the period. But one impulse which set Plato to writing was his intense dissatisfaction with the empirical and prudential morality of his countrymen. The constant contrast in his dialogues is between unreflective, chaotic public opinion, and reasoned, philosophic knowledge. He did not care to organize public opinion, subject it to definitions, and extract from it its modicum of truth. The mind must not only reason about the good; it must contemplate the Idea of the Good in the heavens above until conformed to it. Aristotle attacked the Platonic doctrine of ideas, separated ethics from metaphysics, and took as his guiding principle a practical good, happiness. In discussing happiness, Aristotle did not limit himself to the doctrines of the philosophers; he often accepted generally received opinions, and where he rejected them he at least paid them the honor of refutation. The lists and divisions of goods presented in the *Ethics* were largely derived from current Athenian discussion, and many ideas which Aristotle accepts as authoritative were common property. In the *Topics*,[85] when he discusses the uses of dialectic, he explicitly recognizes the value of a wide acquaintance with public opinion. There was little danger that a Socrates, discoursing freely in the market place with anyone he chanced upon, would be unfamiliar with the beliefs of "the man in the street." But the growth of schools, the habit of scientific study, and the production of written compositions tended to make of the philosopher a man apart. Aristotle recognized the dangerous effect of this upon the public influence of the learned; he recommended the practice of dialectical discussion as a means of keeping in touch with the opinions of men. He himself drew up a collection of current proverbs. Even his more scientific works have been criticized for his willingness to accept common opinion where accurate observation was called for. We may say, then, that Aristotle approached the subject of rhetoric with a belief in its necessity as a political instrument, and a conviction that both the trained thinker and the multitude would benefit by making a common stock of their wisdom for the guidance of the state.

XII

The effect of these philosophical divergences upon the treatment of rhetoric becomes clearly evident when we compare the Platonic discussion between Gorgias and Socrates on the nature and functions of rhetoric with the statements upon the same subject in the early part of Aristotle's *Rhetoric*. Aristotle states clearly what Gorgias seemed to be groping for, and unmistakably sides with Gorgias against Plato in practically all controverted points. In the *Gorgias*, Socrates asserts that teachers of rhetoric know nothing of justice, and that the art of rhetoric is inimical to justice. Aristotle, in the first chapter of the *Rhetoric*, expresses his belief that rhetoric makes for the prevalence of truth and righteousness.

> Rhetoric is useful because things that are true and things that are just have a natural tendency to prevail over their opposites, so that if the decisions of judges are not what they ought to be, the defeat must be due to the speakers themselves, and they must be blamed accordingly. . . . Further, we must be able to employ persuasion, just as strict reasoning can be employed, on opposite sides of a question, not in order that we may in practice employ it both ways (for we must not make people believe what is wrong), but in order that we may see clearly what the facts are, and that, if another man argues unfairly, we may on our part be able to confute him. No other of the arts draws opposite conclusions: dialectic and rhetoric alone do this. Both these arts draw opposite conclusions impartially. Nevertheless, the underlying facts do not lend themselves equally well to the contrary views. No; things that are true and things that are better are, by their nature, practically always easier to believe in.[86]

It is worthy of note that Aristotle, although he does remark parenthetically that the rhetorician should not make people believe what is wrong, does not base his faith in the benefits of rhetoric upon the moral training of the rhetorician, but rather upon the nature of things. Rhetorical effectiveness does not add equally to the strength of a just and an unjust cause. To use an imperfect analogy, we may say, perhaps, that skilful presentation of a just cause strengthens its appeal geometrically, while an unjust cause is aided only arithmetically. The inherent superiority of just and true things is thus increased by the universal use of rhetoric. This is a broader and sounder view than Plato was able to take. As a reformer Plato had no patience with the evils which inevitably accompany all good things. Aristotle is quite cognizant of the evils of rhetoric, but is content that the good shall, on the whole, outweigh it.

> And if it be objected that one who uses such power of speech unjustly might do great harm, that is a charge which may be made in common against all good things except virtue, and above all against the things that are most useful, as strength, health, wealth, generalship.[87]

In the *Gorgias,* Socrates establishes the point that the power of rhetoric is only an apparent power, because it rests upon the ignorance of the multitude addressed. The persuasion of the ignorant many is a rather unseemly occupation for a philosopher. As to the essentially popular function of rhetoric, Aristotle agrees, but without condescension.

Moreover, before some audiences not even the possession of the exactest knowledge will make it easy for what we say to produce conviction. For argument based on knowledge implies instruction, and there are people whom one cannot instruct. Here, then, we must use, as our modes of persuasion and argument, notions possessed by everybody, as we observed in the *Topics* when dealing with the way to handle a popular audience.[88]

The Platonic Socrates argued against Gorgias and Polus that the persuasion of multitudes was not properly an art at all, but only a knack or routine or experience. The first claim that Aristotle makes for rhetoric is that it may properly be considered as an art.

All men attempt to discuss statements and to maintain them, to defend themselves and attack others. Ordinary people do this at random or through practice and from acquired habit. Both ways being possible, the subject can plainly be handled systematically, for it is possible to inquire the reason why some speakers succeed through practice and others spontaneously; and every one will at once agree that such an inquiry is the function of an art.[89]

One of the Platonic reasons for refusing to admit that rhetoric was properly an art was the difficulty of discovering its proper subject matter. Gorgias is exhibited to us as struggling with this question, and as insisting that persuasive discourse is the proper subject-matter of rhetoric; but when Socrates presses him with analogies from the other arts, and asks him if instruction in music and geometry and arithmetic is not persuasive discourse, Gorgias is unable to make a satisfactory statement. This interested Aristotle; it led him to distinguish between rhetoric and the special sciences, but it did not lead him to deny that rhetoric was a discipline in itself.

Rhetoric may be defined as the faculty of observing in any given case the available means of persuasion. This is not the function of any other art. Every other subject can instruct or persuade about its own particular subject-matter; for instance, medicine about what is healthy and unhealthy, geometry about the properties of magnitudes, arithmetic about numbers, and the same is true of the other arts and sciences. But rhetoric we look upon as the power of observing the means of persuasion on almost any subject presented to us; and that is why we say that, in its technical character, it is not concerned with any special or definite class of subjects. . . . The duty of rhetoric is to deal with such matters as we deliberate on without arts or systems to guide us, in the hearing of persons who cannot take in at a glance a complicated argument, or follow a long chain of reasoning. . . . But the more we try to make either dialectic or rhetoric not, what they really are, practical faculties, but sciences, the more we shall inadvertently be destroying their true nature; for we shall be refashioning them and shall be passing into the region of sciences dealing with definite subjects rather than simply with words and forms of reasoning.[90]

The argumentative purpose of the Socratic thesis in the *Gorgias,* that it is better to suffer wrong than to do it, was to disparage the claim made for rhetoric that it was useful for purposes of defense. Aristotle agrees that a man may well be eulogized for choosing to suffer wrong rather than to do it.[91] Such a choice, however, is a *moral* problem for the individual, and is quite irrelevant to a consideration of the uses of any art—rhetoric or boxing or generalship. Aristotle insists that the use of speech and reason as a method of protection against injustice is distinctively human.[92]

XIII

It is not surprising that Aristotle, as a writer on rhetoric, should disagree with the passionately hostile treatment of his subject in the *Gorgias.* Most writers who have compared the *Rhetoric* with Plato's sketch in the *Phædrus* content themselves with indicating the similarities of the two works.[93] Aristotle's indebtedness to Plato is pointed out, and it is suggested that Plato, in lectures or conversation, may have given Aristotle a pretty complete outline for his work. When we consider the specific suggestions of the *Phædrus* for a philosophical rhetoric, however, the differences between the Platonic and the Aristotelian conception of the subject are at least as manifest as the likenesses.

Taking up first the relationship of rhetoric to Truth, we note a wide divergence. Plato held that the rhetorician must know the Truth, because probability was engendered by a likeness to Truth. Here Plato seems hardly consistent with himself, for a public so depraved as Plato felt all multitudes to be, would never care so much for a resemblance to Truth, as for a probability based upon a consonance with its own interests and tastes. Such a probability, however, could not, according to Plato, form the basis for any art.

For Aristotle, however, probability forms the very groundwork of rhetoric. Rhetoric is frankly an art of appearances. Its function is to enable a man to see quickly what are the available means of persuasion *on either side of any proposition.* The whole plan of the *Rhetoric* bears out this conclusion. Consider first the topics, or commonplaces, or, as Roberts translates the term, lines of argument. The topics, according to some critics, represent Aristotle's determined effort to classify the essentially unclassifiable.[94] Aristotle himself seems hardly clear in his own mind whether the topics were to be regarded as premises or methods of argument, whether they were indicative or imperative. At any rate, they were collections of brief statements with which the rhetorician was to be familiar in order to call to mind immediately all the available arguments for either side of the case. If, for example, a written law is adverse to one's case, one can impugn its authority by an appeal to a higher and more universal law. On the other hand, if the law favors one's case, it can be urged that the attempt to be wiser than the law increases the bad habit of disobeying authority. It is noteworthy that as aids to invention the topics were not axioms, propositions universally true, but were often less than half-truths. For almost any Aristotelian topic, which was to serve as a reminder of or a basis for an argument, another topic could be found which would serve equally well for a contrary argument. The topics, then, constituted a sort of rhetoricians' first aid. They were to assist him in producing immediately, and perhaps without any special knowledge of the subject, a plausible argument upon either side of a debatable proposition.

Additional evidence of the merely contingent and probable nature of rhetoric, as opposed to the Platonic conception, is to be seen in the distinct method of reasoning which Aristotle elaborated for popular persuasion. Realizing, with Plato, that a general audience cannot be *instructed* by close reasoning, but must be *persuaded* by an easier procedure, he substitutes in rhetoric the enthymeme for the syllogism, and the example for the more careful induction of scientific reasoning. The enthymeme was a rhetorical syllogism; that is, a syllogism drawn, not from universal principles belonging to a particular science, but from probabilities in the sphere of human affairs. In proceeding hastily with a subject before an audience, it would usually happen that one of the three members of the formal syllogism would be omitted. Whether or not the essential distinction between the enthymeme and the syllogism is in the merely probable nature of the premises or in the suppression of one of the parts,[95] the enthymeme is to be regarded as the principal method of popular presentation of thought. For the persuasive use of examples (less conclusive but more persuasive than a logical induction) Aristotle offers the astute advice, "If you put examples first, you must use many; if at the end, even one is enough." [96]

A study of the topics, of enthymemes and examples, makes it evident that the rhetorical *processes* of invention and logical formulation were designed for quick plausibility. Turning from processes to *content*, this impression is heightened. For each of the three branches of rhetoric—deliberative, epideictic, and forensic—an outline of the usual subject-matter treated by the speaker is offered. A student of each of the special sciences represented would probably say that Aristotle has given us as the subject-matter of deliberative rhetoric a superficial political science; for epideictic rhetoric a conventional ethics; and for forensic rhetoric a very loose and inexact criminal jurisprudence.

The subjects suggested as the content of deliberative speeches are all much more fully treated in the *Politics*. The *Rhetoric* takes from the *Politics* a brief sketch of political matters upon which speakers must be persuasive. The rhetorician should be familiar with the various forms of government—democracy, oligarchy, aristocracy, monarchy—not that he shall determine which is best, or shall speak as a political philosopher, but in order that he may gain persuasiveness by being able to adapt himself to the political beliefs of his audience. It is, of course, perfectly possible for the student of rhetoric to be a political scientist, as Aristotle himself was, but as a rhetorician his task is to use whatever political commonplaces are most likely to win approval. That Aristotle was fully conscious of the differences between his scientific and his rhetorical treatment of the same subject, is indicated by the statement with which he concludes his section on the forms of government in the *Rhetoric:*

We have also briefly considered the means and methods by which we shall gain a good knowledge of the moral qualities and institutions peculiar to the various forms of government—only, however, to the extent demanded by the present occasion; a detailed account of the subject has been given in the *Politics.*[97]

The epideictic speaker, as his function is to praise or blame, finds that his subject-matter lies largely in the field of ethics. We have in the *Rhetoric*, therefore, a summary view of the needed ethical material —happiness, goods, virtue and vice, wrong-doing and injustice, pleasure, equity, laws, and friendship. These subjects are given a much fuller exposition in the *Ethics,* and some of the rhetorical definitions, notably that of pleasure, are there repudiated. While neither ethics nor politics were exact sciences in Aristotle's eyes, and while he repeatedly insisted that the exactness of the physical sciences should not be expected in them, he nevertheless put forth a much greater effort in those fields than in rhetoric to arrive at conceptions that would bear searching criticism. The ethical conceptions of the *Rhetoric* are the conceptions of the man in the street—current popular notions that would supply the most plausible premises for persuasive speeches.

Aristotle remarks in the opening of the *Rhetoric* that forensic oratory, more than political, is given to unscrupulous practices. But the oratorical jurisprudence which he offers as the material of the forensic speaker would not go far to elevate the argumentation of the courtroom. This section of the rhetoric most clearly indicates that Aristotle's was a scientific and not a moral earnestness; the dialectician is here in the ascendant.

In dealing with the evidence of witnesses, the following are useful arguments. If you have no witnesses on your side, you will argue that the judges must decide from what is probable; that this is meant by "giving a verdict in accordance with one's honest opinion"; that probabilities cannot be bribed to mislead the court; and that probabilities are never convicted of perjury. If you *have* witnesses, and the other man has not, you will argue that probabilities cannot be put on their trial, and that we could do without the evidence of witnesses altogether if we need do no more than balance the pleas advanced on either side. . . . So, clearly, we need never be at a loss for useful evidence.[98]

The entire section on forensic rhetoric recognizes that each pleader's loyalty is to his case, and that as a skilful rhetorician he must be quick to discern all the persuasive possibilities of any situation. Aristotle professed a dislike for the business, but once engaged in the classification of arguments he is concerned with rhetorical effectiveness and not with moral justifiability.

The explicit statement which shows that Aristotle regarded rhetoric as an instrument of persuasion quite detached from the moral nature of the rhetorician, occurs in the third book, in connection with the discussion of delivery.

Besides, delivery is—very properly—not regarded as an elevated subject of inquiry. Still, *the whole business of rhetoric being concerned with appearances,* we must pay attention to the subject of delivery, unworthy though it is, because we cannot do without it.[99]

Turning now from the general problem of the relationship of the *Rhetoric* to Platonic Truth, we take up the second of Plato's suggestions in the *Phædrus,* that the rhetorician must be a dialectician, a man who can distinguish between particulars and universals, who can define his terms, and who can distinguish debatable from undebatable questions. With this Aristotle seems to be in agreement. He opens his *Rhetoric* by declaring that it is the counterpart of dialectic. Elsewhere he refers to rhetoric as parallel to, an offshoot or branch of, dialectic.[100] He also says that the master of dialectic will be the true master of rhetoric. But it is impossible to make clear the relation between dialectic and rhetoric without explaining the Platonic contrast between the two, and the great advance made by Aristotle in relating both of them to demonstrative science.

After all, the sum and substance of Plato's suggestions for rhetoric is that rhetoric, if it is really to be an art, must coincide with philosophy. When Plato said that the rhetorician must be a dialectician, he meant that he must be a philosopher. So far as he differs from the philosopher, he is an impostor; so far as he coincides with him, his art of rhetoric is superseded. But Aristotle gave to the term dialectic such a different significance that it is another thing entirely to say that the rhetorician should be a dialectician. For Plato, dialectic was the whole process of rational analysis by which the soul was led into the knowledge of Ideas. It had both a positive and a negative aspect. In the earlier dialogues the negative function was most prominent, and the principal contribution which the Socratic dialectic made to the wisdom of those who underwent his cross-examination was to disabuse them of their false knowledge. As Plato developed his own doctrine of Ideas, dialectic became the instrument of awakening by which the soul recollected the eternal Ideas which it had known in a pre-existent state. Dialectic became a means of positive instruction, as well as of refutation. As Plato grew old and became more dogmatic in exposition, he found the dialectical form somewhat inconvenient, but he did not develop a new form for didactic procedure. The teachings implanted by dialectic represented reasoned and tested conclusions, carrying with them the certainty of philosophical knowledge, as opposed to the superficial opinions which constituted the material of rhetoric, and which persuaded without giving any real instruction. In Plato's later life, mathematical reasoning came to represent the type of demonstrated knowledge, but at the time of the attacks upon the sophists and rhetoricians, certainty and exactitude were to be found through the dialectical process.

Aristotle had even more clearly in mind the antithesis between opinion or common sense and scientific knowledge or real instruction. He had, however, no sympathy with the Platonic doctrine of Ideas, and was free from any sense of a mystical significance for dialectic. Observing the didactic elements of the Platonic dialectic, he perfected the syllogism as the instrument of scientific knowledge and teaching. In the two books of the *Analytica Priora* he developed the functions and varieties of the syllogism and suggested that it could be applied both to scientific demonstration and to the process of argumentation in the realm of opinion. There is, however, such a difference of matter and purpose in scientific and nonscientific discussion that the use of the syllogism in the one and in the other is to be governed by a distinct body of theory. The *Analytica Posteriora* develops the use of the syllogism for demonstrative reasoning, and the *Topica*, together with the *Sophistici Elenchi*, for dialectic. The material for the *Topica* and the *Sophistici Elenchi*—which is really the last book of the *Topica*—is drawn from that type of argumentation pilloried by Plato in the *Euthydemus, Sophist,* and *Statesman*. Aristotle in his classification of fallacies cites the *Euthydemus* frequently. Plato drew a vivid picture of the fallacious disputers and excited the feelings of the reader against such arguments without really analyzing the fallacies. But Aristotle, in the *Sophistici Elenchi*, analyzed and classified fallacies with the purpose of enabling the reader to use them more skilfully. That type of disputation which Plato made a variety of false rhetoric, the very antithesis of true dialectic, is for Aristotle an integral part of dialectic. Thus it is evident that Aristotle has allowed dialectic to descend into that realm of opinion inhabited by sophists and rhetoricians. Where Plato had been chiefly impressed by the contrast between rhetoric and dialectic, Aristotle noticed the similarities. The realm of opinion, which Plato had regarded as unworthy the attention of the philosopher, is thus accorded by Aristotle two distinct disciplines, dialectic and rhetoric. There are differences between the two, but the more fundamental contrast is between rhetoric and dialectic, on the one hand, and scientific reasoning, on the other.[101]

Scientific procedure, for Aristotle, starts with universal or necessary principles and proceeds to universal and necessary conclusions. Both dialectic and rhetoric, however, take as their premises current popular opinions, or perhaps the opinions of dissenters. Any probable or plausible assertion will serve. The fundamental principles of a science cannot be proved within the bounds of that science; they are therefore assumed. The only way of questioning them is in dialectical debate. A few fundamental principles, as axioms, are common to all or to several of the sciences; but by far the larger part of the principles employed are special to the sciences concerned. As against this, rhetoric and dialectic are not limited to the propositions of any particular field. They may regard the ultimate assumptions of any science as mere probabilities and discuss them as such. In dialectic, the number of special propositions, corresponding to scientific laws peculiar to one field, is small. On the other hand, the number of general propositions, called topics (corresponding to the comparatively few axioms of science), is large. In science, again, we do not have matter to be settled by debate, but rather by impartial investigation. Dialectic and rhetoric can argue as easily upon one side of the question as another. They may employ any material conceded by an opponent. They may be indifferent to the truth of a conclusion if the form and method have been accurately followed.

From all this it is evident that, as contrasted with scientific knowledge, dialectic and rhetoric are much alike. There are certain differences, however, which Aristotle regarded as sufficiently fundamental to justify their treatment as separate disciplines. The most obvious difference, and one which accounts for several others, is that dialectic is an argument conducted by two speakers with a small audience of interested listeners who will see that the argument is fairly conducted. Such a method of argument is best fitted for speculative questions, although it can be applied to anything. It will be concerned with logical processes and not with the feelings of an audience. It is aimed not so much at persuading the opponent as at defeating him by involving him in contradictions. The method of reasoning employed is the syllogistic or inductive, the only difference from genuinely scientific reasoning being that the materials are taken from the realm of the merely probable. Rhetoric, on the other hand, because of the fact that one speaker is continuously addressing a large audience of untrained hearers, cannot use the form of scientific reasoning. In place of the syllogism and induction it uses the enthymeme and example. Since the feelings of the hearers will probably be more influential than the logic of the speaker, rhetoric must include an account of the emotions and characters of men. While rhetoric is not necessary to the dialectician, the rhetorician will be better for a thorough knowledge of dialectic.

One additional contrast between rhetoric and dialectic is of significance. Theoretically, Aristotle regarded rhetoric and dialectic as applicable to the same range of subjects. Theoretically, anything could be discussed by either method. But practically, as we see when we compare the topics of the *Topica* and the *Rhetoric*,[102] rhetorical discussion is limited to human actions and characters. The subject-matter of rhetoric is for practical purposes limited to ethics and politics. There is a mention of the popular exposition of scientific subjects as one of the uses of rhetoric, but the system as Aristotle develops it is much more limited than the system of dialectical argument.

Analytics (logic), dialectic, and rhetoric form the organon of thought and expression for the ancient world. Aristotle, as much indebted to the Platonic dialogues, perhaps, as to his own observations of Athenian life, observed scientific thought, systematized it, and gave us logic; observing the sport dear to all Athenians—argumentation by question and answer—and systematizing it, he gave us dialectic; observing and systematizing the art of persuading crowds, he gave us rhetoric. Thus, although Aristotle agrees with Plato that the rhetorician should also be a dialectician, it is evident that the dictum has a very different meaning for the two writers.

Another suggestion in the *Phædrus* concerned order and arrangement. This suggestion is developed by Aristotle in the second half of the third book of the *Rhetoric*. He attacks as unnecessarily complex the numerous divisions of the contemporary rhetoricians, and treats arrangement under the heads of Proem, Narrative, Proofs, and Epilogue. As our purpose is to compare Aristotle with Plato, rather than to give an exposition of his *Rhetoric*, we need observe only that this Platonic

67

suggestion is carried out by Aristotle, although he was probably much more indebted to other rhetoricians than to Plato for his discussion of arrangement.

The Platonic requirement that the nature of the soul must be shown, and arguments adapted to the different kinds of people addressed by the speaker, is the basis of the oft-repeated assertion that the *Rhetoric* is an expanded *Phædrus*. There are two reasons for this. In the first place, that part of the second book of the *Rhetoric* which treats of the emotions and characters of men is the part which has the greatest interest and significance for the modern reader.[103] Secondly, it is, perhaps, the most distinct addition Aristotle made to the work of his predecessors in the field. But even here, where Aristotle has apparently carried out the suggestions of his master most brilliantly, it must be observed that his treatment is only a popular and inexact discussion of the external manifestations of character and emotions, and not the sort of treatment he would have given the doctrine of the affections, had he developed it in his *De Anima*. It is also to be noted that while the classification of the emotions is as complete as the rhetorician would desire, Aristotle did not share Plato's notion that a true art of rhetoric would enable a speaker to adapt himself to each of the persons of an audience as the dialectician adjusts himself to one deuteragonist. He expressly disclaims such a belief.

The theory of rhetoric is concerned not with what seems probable to a given individual like Socrates or Hippias, but with what seems probable to men of a given type.[104]

Nor does Aristotle suppose that even the best of rhetoricians will always succeed with his audience. The function of rhetoric is not simply to succeed in persuading, but rather to discover the means of coming as near such success as the circumstances of each particular case allow.[105]

Style and delivery, Plato stated, were necessary preliminaries to the art of rhetoric. An elevated style, however, was to be attained, not by technique, but by contemplation of lofty subjects. Aristotle seems to have shared his master's feeling that style and delivery should be subordinate matters, as spectacle was the least artistic element of the drama. His classifying mind, however, was much better able than Plato's to resist the tendency to place all subjects in a hierarchical order of moral dignity and to slight all the lower orders. He dismisses delivery briefly with the explanation that not enough is yet known about it to treat it scientifically; but he does regard both delivery and diction as means of persuasive discourse.

Plato's dislike for writing, which in our day would so limit the province of rhetoric, does not seem to have disturbed Aristotle. He wrote several times as much as Plato, and upon subjects which Plato would probably have regarded as unsuitable for literary presentation. It is only on the heights of learning that truth and beauty are always compatible, and for the most part Plato kept to the heights. Aristotle saw his own writing, not as moral truth to be graven on the soul of a reader, but as an instrument by which his thought was systematized and preserved. Had he agreed with the Socrates of the *Phædrus,* he would not have devoted twelve chapters of the *Rhetoric* to style.

XIV

In comparing Aristotle with Plato, we have seen that the *Rhetoric* discusses most of the questions of rhetorical theory raised by Plato in the *Gorgias;* it agrees with the rhetoricians that rhetoric is an art, that the universality of its applications does not mean that it has no subject matter of its own, that the evils arising from rhetoric are no greater than the evils that arise from the abuse of all good things, that truth and righteousness are, on the whole, more prevalent because of a general knowledge of rhetoric, and that the persuasion of multitudes of relatively ignorant people, instead of being merely a vulgar task, fit only for demagogues, is a necessary part of education and government in a stable society.

A contrast of the *Rhetoric* with the *Phædrus* makes it evident that even here Aristotle is closer to the rhetoricians than to Plato. Rhetoric *is* an art of appearance; and this fact prevents it neither from being an art nor from serving the ends of truth and righteousness. Rhetoric, instead of being a sham dialectic, is the *counterpart* of dialectic, a dialectic fundamentally different from the Platonic conception of it. The analysis of the emotions, which seems to follow Plato, is, after all, of a loose, inexact, and external character, as Aristotle thought was suitable for rhetoric. Aristotle agreed with Plato that the rhetorician should be virtuous and intelligent, that he should be a keen logician, that he should understand the ordering and arranging of material, and that he should know many things beyond the principles of rhetoric. They were also agreed that contemporary rhetoricians fell far short of these ideals. But the fact that Aristotle and Plato agreed upon the deficiencies of Athenian rhetoricians seems to have blinded us to the equally significant fact that Aristotle's rhetorical theory bears more resemblance to that of Protagoras and Gorgias than to that of Plato.

XV

The significance of a study of rhetoric in Athens is not entirely historical. However indifferent we may be to Protagoras and Gorgias, we live in a world of journalists, publicists, advertisers, politicians, diplomats, propagandists, reformers, educators, salesmen, preachers, lecturers, and popularizers. When in Platonic mood we condemn them all as sophists and rhetoricians. And the Platonic attitude is supported by the growth of specialization and "research." To large classes of specialists the rest of mankind is made up of ignorant laymen. These scholars and experts share Plato's contempt for the masses; they apparently are as blind as he to the limitations of the academic mind; they dwell so securely in the well-mapped areas of knowledge that they decline to venture into the uncharted realms of opinion and probability. The modern sophists may justly be reproached for their habit of offering mere opinion when knowledge is obtainable; but it may be questioned whether theirs is a greater error than the specialists' habit of mistaking knowledge for wisdom. In the problem of the relation of Plato to Protagoras, of philosopher to sophist and rhetorician, are involved the issues which we debate when we discuss the aims of a liberal education, the desirability of government by experts, the relation of a university to the state, the duty of a scholar in a democracy, the function of public opinion in a popular government, the difference between a conventional and a rational morality, to say nothing of more speculative questions.

We cannot agree with Bishop Welldon's statement that Aristotle's *Rhetoric* is "a solitary instance of a book which not only begins a science, but completes it," but we do not regard the *Rhetoric* as of merely historical interest. It is the one treatment of the subject which raises clearly the problem of the relation of rhetoric to psychology, ethics, politics, jurisprudence, and literary criticism. If we have made any progress in these subjects since Aristotle, in so far his *Rhetoric* may be inadequate for modern needs. But for a sense of proportion and a grasp of relations, we do well to acquaint ourselves with the survey of the subject made by the great classifier of knowledge.

Classical Rhetoric and the

Mediaeval Theory of Preaching[1]

HARRY CAPLAN

AMONG the sculptures on the *portail royal* of Chartres Cathedral, that mediaeval *summa* of chiseled stone, one may see the seven liberal arts personified in female forms. And under these one may perceive the outstanding representatives of all the arts. There, symbolized in its place in mediaeval life is rhetoric, and at her feet is Cicero. From Carolingian times well into the Renaissance, rhetoric as one of the liberal arts was figured in church sculptures, murals, mosaics, manuscript miniatures, the ornamentation of library rooms, fountains, tabletops, bronze vessels, windows, tapestry, altars, and gravestones; in one form or another at Auxerre, Bourges, Clermont, Laon, Rheims, Rouen, St. Omer, Sens, Soissons, Freiburg Münster, the Abbey of St. Gall, Rimini, Florence, Siena, the Vatican; the handiwork in the earlier period most often of unknown artists, but later also of Giotto, the brothers Pisani, Pollaiuolo, Botticelli, Melozzo da Forli, Pinturrichio, and Raphael.[2] Cicero is almost always her attendant, and she appears with attributes that vary with the imagination of the artist. At times she holds a pose perhaps intended to be faithful to Capella's striking portrait[3] of the omnipotent queen, a woman of sublime and radiant beauty and regal poise, helmeted, and bearing her flashing weapons in her hands; her robe, girt about her shoulders in the Latin way, embroidered with a multitude of figures, and her breast bejeweled in

71

most exquisite colors. Thus she appears with a sword and shield; or, again, she makes an oratorical gesture, or carries a scroll, a tablet and stilus, or a golden nugget. The motive was persistent in the fine art of the period.

This prominence of rhetoric in art is a reflection of her importance in literature. Almost consistently throughout the Middle Ages—from the works of Capella to those of Vincent of Beauvais, from the fifth century to the thirteenth and beyond—rhetoric as one of the liberal arts played a significant part in mediaeval life. The classical rhetoric survived in many forms. In the first place, manuscripts of some of the chief classical authors themselves were plentiful in European libraries. Secondly, there were the works of the minor rhetoricians [4] of later date, who, following the relatively compendious fashion of an isagogic work or encyclopedia, preserved the general principles and terminology of the ancient rhetoric—writers like Fortunatianus, Marius Victorinus, Martianus Capella, Cassiodorus, Isidore, Alcuin, Notker, and Anselm of Besate. Thirdly, there were commentaries on, and translations of, Cicero, commentaries on and adaptations of the *Rhetorica ad Herennium*, and several commentaries on Capella, notably by John Scot, Dunchad, and Remigius of Auxerre. In the tradition of Alcuin and others that rhetoric is fundamentally a juridical art,[5] concerned with speaking well in civil questions, there arose a group of works like the *Ecclesiastica rhetorica* [6] of the second half of the twelfth century, virtually a forensic rhetoric for canon law, and professedly developed in accordance with rhetorical doctrine. Also in this tradition, and maintaining the alliance of rhetoric and law in the schools, there grew up from Carolingian times well into the later period a huge mass of tracts, *Artes dictaminis,* devoted to letter-writing and legal administration. These were designed to prepare students for positions in the ecclesiastical and state chanceries; the *artes* [7] assumed the name of rhetoric, and the teachers often called themselves "rhetors." Almost universally such tracts borrowed their *introductio* and stylistic from rhetoric, added *salutatio* and *petitio* to the Ciceronian divisions of *exordium, narratio,* and *conclusio,* frequently used the principles of invention, disposition, and *captatio benevolentiae,* and discussed *clausulae,* colors, and the modes of expanding material. Boncampagni pictures [8] this kind of rhetoric as empress of the liberal arts, adorned with gold and precious stones, moving among roses and lilies of the valley. His fancy at least reflects the high esteem in which the rhetors held their art. And, finally, there were many special tracts on rhetorical colors.

Rhetoric then, as always, was in close kinship with grammar, and with that other member of the trivium, of which she is traditionally the ἀντίστροφος, dialectic. The rhetorical use of the dialectical τόποι, developed by Aristotle, the *Auctor ad Herennium,* and Cicero, and for the Middle Ages especially by Boethius, in his *De differentiis topicis,* became of particular importance with the increased interest in dialectic that after the year 1200 attended the growth of scholasticism. To Alcuin,[9] Roger Bacon,[10] and Gerson,[11] rhetoric was a branch of logic; while Brunetto Latini,[12] Dante's teacher, places rhetoric under politics. And lastly, there was the usual interaction between rhetoric and poetry. In his study of the theories of poetry [13] of the twelfth and thirteenth centuries, Professor Edmond Faral includes works just as properly belonging to the field of rhetoric, for example, the *Ars versificatoria* of Matthew of Vendôme and the *Poetica* of John of Garland.

Now, while there are signs that in the tenth and eleventh centuries the interest in rhetoric had in some places somewhat abated, in the period we are now considering, from the twelfth century on into the fifteenth, its popularity is again unquestionable. The rhetorical education flourished in the schools [14] of Europe, and especially France. With grammar it was a fundamental subject in cathedral schools, monasteries, and city schools, although in the new universities it had not yet won the influence that a great deal later it was to enjoy. And as one of the *artes sermocinales* it was included in the *studium artium* of the religious orders. Late in this period an anonymous rhetorician can with bold assurance maintain that "rhetoric is the science which refreshes the hungry, renders the mute articulate, makes the blind to see, and teaches one to avoid every lingual ineptitude." [15]

What I consider significant in mediaeval literature, as in the cathedral sculptures, is the theological environment of rhetoric. It is not strange that men of vision, like Roger Bacon, saw the value of rhetoric in moral philosophy. Nor is it surprising that William of Auvergne should write a *Rhetorica divina,*[16] a rhetoric of prayer. I paraphrase slightly an introductory poem addressed to William:

When you teach suasion to the lowly, how to pour out words to God, the Creator becomes gentler toward the sin, and for your guidance grants pardon to the sinner. Quintilian, these are not your oratorical colors, nor are they

73

yours, Marcus, glory of eloquence. Nor did he give them forth, the admired of Athens. Lost, vain, and treacherous was your wisdom, which taught only how to move the heart of a human judge. Whereas our lofty art teaches by prayer to mollify the just wrath of that great Judge, even God. Ah, how much better with words to placate the puissant and eternal Father than to dispense the words of human law!

This preface is an echo of chapter I, in which the author establishes an art of "spiritual oratory in causes and affairs of the soul. . . . If secular *oratio* has deserved so many works of laborious care, how much more worthy and just that sacred *oratio*, with which in fruit and utility the secular cannot compare, should have its artists and scholars?" William's art of prayer, like the Roman oration, embraces *exordium, narratio, petitio, confirmatio*, and *conclusio*.

But obviously the widest field for rhetoric in the Middle Ages was in preaching, the dissuasion from vice, and the persuasion to virtue, the winning of souls to God. With the spread of scholasticism and the rise of the great preaching orders, the Dominicans and the Franciscans, preaching flowered in practice and theory. In the twelfth century for the first time, and continually thereafter, the theory received treatment in special manuals—the *Quo ordine sermo fieri debeat* of Guibert de Nogent (*saec.* xii),[17] the *Summa de arte praedicatoria* of Alain de Lille (end *saec.* xii),[18] the *De instructione praedicatorum* of Humbert de Romans (*saec.* xiii),[19] the Franciscan *Ars concionandi* wrongly attributed to St. Bonaventure,[20] *Artes praedicandi* professing falsely the authorship of Albertus Magnus [21] or of Henry of Hesse (*fl. saec.* xiv),[22] or claiming the influence of St. Thomas Aquinas,[23] and *Artes praedicandi* by the following: [24]

THIRTEENTH CENTURY	FOURTEENTH CENTURY	FIFTEENTH CENTURY
Alexander of Ashby (?)	Symon Alcok	St. Antoninus of
William of Auvergne [25]	Fr. Astazius, O.M.	Florence, O.P.[27]
Arnoldus de Podio, O.P.	John Avonius, Carm.	Thomas von Cleve,
Jean de la Rochelle,	Robert of Basevorn	O.P.[28]
O.M.	Alphonsus Bononiensis	John Felton(?)
Richard of Thetford,	Franciscus Fabrianensis,	Jacques le Grand, O.S.A.
O.S.B.	O.M.	John of Guidernia
John of Wales, O.M.[26]	Philippus Florentinus,	Gozewijn Haeks, Carm.
	O.M.	Stephanus Hoest [29]
	John Folsham, Carm.	Magister Koburck

FOURTEENTH CENTURY	FIFTEENTH CENTURY
Jacobus Fusignani, O.P.[30]	Paul Kölner of Ratisbon
Ranulph Higden, O.S.B.	Martinus Alphonsus of Cordova, O.S.A.
Robert Holcoth, O.P.	Michael of Hungary,[32] O.M.
Hendrik Aeger van Kalkar, Carth.	Fridericus de Nuris
Henry of Langenstein (Henry of Hesse, the elder) [31]	Thomas Penketh, O.S.A.
	Ludovicus de Rocha, O.M.
Jean de Châlons	Silvester de Marradio, O.P.
Raymond Lull, O.M.	
Martin of Amberg	Hugo de Sueth, O.P.
Nicolas Oresmius	Thomas of Salisbury
Hermannus Teutonicus, O.P.	
Thomas de Tuderto, O.S.A.	
Baldo degli Ubaldi	
Thomas Waleys, O.P.	
Olivier de Went, O.P.	

and others. Add a goodly number of anonymous *Artes praedicandi* or *sermocinandi*, and as well numerous small tracts on methods of expanding a sermon. These systematic, carefully developed treatises are quite different from the rare, sketchy, and rudimentary attempts of the earlier period to give outline to the art. For example, a ninth-century manuscript (Cod. Lat. Monac. 22053, fol. 93) progresses as far as to list seven *modi* of preaching: (1) by teaching disciples; (2) by persuading people; (3) by chiding the haughty; (4) by refuting the contrary-minded; (5) by terrifying the lukewarm; (6) by assuaging the wrathful; (7) by promising life everlasting to the good and torments everlasting to the wicked. The manuals were scattered plentifully over the libraries of Europe. A catalogue of the year 1500 of the library of Tegernsee Abbey (Benedictine),[33] numbering from fifteen hundred to two thousand manuscripts, lists over fifty on rhetoric, and twelve *Artes praedicandi;* but this is perhaps a special instance. Tracts on rhetoric and preaching were indeed extremely popular, though I cannot prove that an art of preaching was ever so highly esteemed as the two *artes dictaminis,* by Peter de Vineis and Thomas of Capua, which the usurious wardrobe clerk, John of Ockham, lent to a friend—at a charge of a goose per week.[34] These tracts are perhaps over two hundred in number, the great majority still in manuscript form, unpublished.[35] I have examined only a fair proportion of them, but feel confident that the general conclusions of this paper will be borne out when this attractive and unplowed field of research has been exhaustively worked. Further study of these documents is bound to throw light on a great cultural activity.

Having reviewed the different aspects of mediaeval rhetoric, I shall now indicate the attitude of theologians and preachers to rhetoric, consider briefly the acknowledged dependence of these *Artes* on classical rhetoric, and from a brief survey of their technique point out the general lines of the inheritance.

Even when regarded as different from preaching in origin, material, or purpose, rhetoric has been admitted to close kinship with it. In their view of pagan learning the Middle Ages show differences of opinion that warn us against generalization, but it is safe to say that the distrust of rhetoric as a profane study was not as anxious in the later period [36] as often in earlier times. One is tempted even to decide that the repeated expression of antipathy to secular learning was often more a convention than a proof of genuine belief or feeling.

Let us select for a spokesman that fierce opponent of the liberal arts, the Spaniard Paulus Albarus of the ninth century:

"In the beginning was the Word and the Word was with God and God was the Word. The same was in the beginning with God (John 1:1)." This the learned Plato knew not, of this the eloquent Tully had no thought, into this fiery Demosthenes never inquired. The tortuous briar-bushes of Aristotle have it not, nor is it found in the sinuous subtleties of Chrysippus. The art of Donatus has not searched into this by the rules of art, nor yet the rank discipline of all the grammarians. The geometricians, named after the earth, follow what is earthly and dusty. The rhetoricians, wordy and redundant, have filled the air with empty wind. The dialecticians, bound fast by rules and entangled on all sides by syllogisms, crafty and cunning, are deceitful spinners of words rather than builders of the art of speech.[37]

The state of mind herein exposed must not be regarded as by any means universal. To be sure, St. Augustine, former teacher of rhetoric, in his *Confessions* looks back with misgivings upon the days when, as he says, he "used to sell the talkativeness that emphasizes victory [*victoriosam loquacitatem vendebam*]"; furthermore, one learns how flagrant he judged this offense to be from the fact that his next words refer to the lustful passion of his early years—so that the editors of a recent book of selections from this work are quite justified in stressing the collocation when they head the chapter as follows: "In my teaching of rhetoric and keeping a mistress I yet showed traces of faith in Thee." [38] But the more significant tradition was set by St. Augustine in the *De doctrina Christiana,* Book IV, in which he depends heavily on Cicero's *Orator,* joins eloquence to religion, and proclaims the value of such profane wisdom for theology. This point is echoed by countless writers through the Middle Ages. Three quotations expressing the dominant attitude to pagan erudition recur: Prov. 9, 1: "Wisdom has builded her house; she hath hewn out her seven pillars [of the liberal arts]"; from St. Augustine: "It is no sin to despoil pagan thought of the gold of wisdom and the silver of eloquence, as by God's precept the Hebrews despoiled the Egyptians"; [39] from the marriage law in Deut. 21:12–13: "If the hair of the beautiful captive woman [pagan learning] shall be shorn and her nails pared, after that 'thou shalt go unto her, and be her husband, and she shall be thy wife.'" [40] In the influential *De clericorum instructione,*[41] Rabanus in effect writes: "Rhetoric, by which I understand the art of speaking well in civil questions, which seems to belong to mundane science, still is not extraneous to ecclesiastical discipline, for skill in this art is useful to the preacher for fluent and proper teaching, as well as for apt and elegant writing, and for delivering a sermon. He does well who learns it fully, and so fits himself to preach God's word." Then, borrowing from St. Augustine (*De doctr. Christ.,* IV, 2): "For although rhetoric can sway to either truth or falsehood, who dares say that truth should be unarmed and defenseless, that only the false persuader should make his hearer *benevolus, intentus,* and *docilis,* should speak briefly, clearly, with verisimilitude, and, on the other hand, dares condemn the speaker of truth to a tedious, unintelligible, and incredible discourse?" To be sure, Robert of Melun (*saec.* xii), inspired by Plato, bids philosophers spurn rhetoric, which makes the false appear true and the true false, which emphasizes the *inanis suavitas verborum* instead of the *fructuosa virtus sententiarum,* which aims to delight rather than profit, and feeds the ear rather than the soul.[42] Yet in the same century John of Salisbury, praising eloquence, declares that he who condemns so great a good is manifestly a fool.[43] "Honorius Augustodunensis" (*saec.* xii) in the striking work, *De animae exilio et patria,*[44] conceives the soul, which is traveling in search of the fatherland, the wisdom of scripture, as first passing through the ten cities of the liberal arts, the third of which is Rhetoric, where Tully teaches the Roman virtues by ornate speech. The suburbs to this metropolis are History, Fable, and Books on Oratory and Ethics. Vincent of Beauvais (*saec.* xiii), who outlines well the traditional rhetoric in civil questions, using Cicero's *De oratore,* Quintilian, Isidore, and Boethius, would not in his *Speculum doctrinale* pass over the dignity and excellence of rhetoric; in preaching, however, he prefers the Christian, who acknowledges Holy Writ is paramount, to the Ciceronian.[45] St. Thomas Aquinas (*saec.* xiii): "Eloquence and learning can profitably be used by a preacher." [46] In the same century, Ranulphe d'Hemblières,[47] and in the next, John Bromyard,[48] oppose secular literature when read for pleasure's sake, for the delight in poetic adornments and verbal ornamentation, but approve it when the useful therein is turned to Holy Writ. The "Aquinas"-tract, echoing William of Auvergne: "So many works have been written by rhetors on their art. How much worthier that the art and doctrine of sacred rhetoric should receive attention from the preacher-company."

The preacher does well to consider the cock, we read in a thirteenth-century manuscript of Bruges (546, fol. 42vb), if he would learn his various duties, and chiefly the duty he owes the liberal arts. The cock and the good preacher have seven qualities in common:

1. Before crowing, the cock beats his sides. Before preaching, the preacher must mortify himself.
2. To crow, the cock stretches his neck. So must the preacher lift his head; he must preach of heavenly things, and not mundane.
3. The cock crows only at certain hours. So does the preacher preach.
4. The cock shares his grain with his hens. The preacher must willingly communicate his wisdom to others.
5. The cock attacks his rivals. The preacher should attack all heretics.
6. The cock shuts his eyes before the sun. The preacher must shut his eyes to the blaze of success.
7. At nightfall the cock mounts to his wooden roost, and comes down only at daybreak. The preacher must at time of temptation climb to his perch—that is, consider the cross and the passion of Christ, and descend only when all danger has vanished.

But the cock possesses another "virtue." Before lifting his head to crow he bends a bit. So at times the preacher must incline to the liberal arts—not always, for he must lift his head—that is, must climb towards the higher wisdom, must *ad universitatem vel theologiam ire,* and not do as those who are so charmed by logic of grammar as never to be able to part from it, in the manner of the husband who knows not how to leave his wife.

Thus, even though we remember that in some cases rhetoric found a welcome place in civil matters but was not admitted in theology; even though occasionally the Psalter was considered sufficient to train a monk for his career; [49] and even though at times there was legislation within the religious orders against recourse to the profane arts, yet rhetoric clearly had an accepted place in theology and preaching. To be sure, the art did not in the Middle Ages attain to the full flower of its great days in classical civilization, when there existed a free environment for deliberative oratory. When scholars pass this judgment,[50] they cannot be gainsaid. Yet it is equally true that rhetoric in the mediaeval period flourished far more than is generally believed. It is incorrect to say, as Gröber does, that the Middle Ages were averse to it,[51] or to say, as Specht does,[52] that the art of speaking well could not concern a clerk or monk because his interest did not rest in this world.

What distrust there was for rhetoric was distrust for embellished style, because rhetoric was an art of adornment. *"Ornatu florum sermonem reddo decorum,"* speaks rhetoric in a mediaeval chart of the liberal arts.[53] Elegance is neither necessary nor fitting for truth; elegance is reserved for *dictamen*. Alain opposes scurrilous and puerile words, and rejects rhythmic melodies, and metric consonances, because they soothe the ear rather than inform the mind; he would steer a middle course between purple trappings and bloodless words.[54] "Albertus" has no faith in the sublimity of words, nor in the learned words of human science, as so much meretricious adornment, but desires verbal simplicity.[55] The preacher's discourse should be neither scorned for rusticity nor suspected for a counterfeit grace and beauty. Humbert emphasizes content; to seek adornment is to prefer the beauty of the salver in which food is carried rather than the food itself.[56] The Franciscan *Ars concionandi:* "Use ordinary words; do not coin words, or you will be ridiculous." William of Auvergne: "The more simple and unadorned a sermon is, the more it moves and edifies." [57] Even Surgant,[58] in 1502: "Divine Rhetoric has no need for polished language."

What is noteworthy in these judgments is the rhetorical nature of the critique. Style was indeed studied, even *clausulae* were not neglected, and special tracts on rhetorical colors for use in sermons were common; but, as in classical theory, λέξις did not have equal importance with εὕρεσις. Style was subordinate to content.

Now what influence of the ancient rhetoric do we find acknowledged in these tractates? The "Albertus"-tract uses Isidore's rhetoric. The Franciscan author of the *Ars concionandi* uses St. Augustine and Cicero, adopting their rhetorical aims—*docere, delectare, flectere,* and finding that divisions, through *proprietas,* fulfilled the purpose *docere,* that distinctions through *lenitas* served the aim *delectare,* and expansions through *utilitas* achieved the end *flectere.* He thus sets the thematic form of preaching, the unique contribution of mediaeval theory, squarely upon the basis of classical rhetoric. The "Aquinas"-tract, using Cicero's name, but really paraphrasing a passage in Aristotle's *Rhetoric,* Book III, insists that it is not enough to have something to say, but it is necessary also to know how to say it. Humbert uses Seneca, Horace, and Cicero, and suggests that pagan history as well as Christian should be read by preachers. Alain, who in the treatment of rhetoric in *Anticlaudianus* cites Cicero, Quintilian, Sidonius, and Symmachus, in the *Summa de arte praedicatoria* quotes from Cicero, Plato, Seneca, Lucretius, and Persius; he approves of inserting the sayings of Gentiles. The dependence, then, on ancient authors and classical rhetoric is often highly conscious, and we are not in all cases left to infer the subtle effects of indirect influence. Indeed, the studies of Cruel, Linsenmayer, and Lecoy de la Marche would lead a reader to believe that in the actual practice of preaching recourse to the classics was more general a habit than even the theories indicate. For one example, Ovid is extensively used for moralization, even though, so far as I now know, the name of Ovid is absent from these *Artes.* The preacher would learn so to use Ovid from consulting the moralities, the tracts on vices and virtues, the collections of *sententiae, exempla,* and the like mediaeval books designed expressly for his aid, themselves rich in classical lore. With these I am not here concerned.

When we look at the pertinent classical works that were available for the formation of a theory of preaching, we find the logical works of Aristotle, which were the strongest basis of scholastic science, and lent themselves to rhetorical application; the *Categories* and *Topics,* directly or indirectly, seem to have contributed most. Add such rhetorical and dialectical works as Cicero's *Topics, De inventione,* and *De oratore,* Horace's *Ars poetica;* the *Rhetorica ad Herennium* (regarded as Cicero's *Rhetorica nova*), which had a wide influence, as did the *Commentaries* of Boethius [59] on Aristotle's *Categories* and *Topics*, and his own *De differentiis topicis*. Quintilian was perhaps used to a lesser degree.[60] One should note that in these classical works the emphasis is upon invention. And, indeed, I would say that the richest legacy bequeathed to mediaeval rhetoric from the ancient period was the principle of the inventional use of the *topos* or commonplace, the artistic finding of the right argument communicable to the right audience in the right circumstances. Developed in ancient theory for the three types of secular oratory—judicial, epideictic, and deliberative—it was admirably suited to the scholastic method and to the fourth kind of oratory, preaching. In accordance with classical doctrine the method was used in selecting the text and materials of discussion; further, as the peculiar sermon form demanded, in applying the very weighty principle of amplification; and, finally, in the study of the audience.[61] Neither before nor since has the method been carried out in such a systematic yet varied way.

The topical method operated at once in the enumeration of the proper materials of preaching—usually ten, as with "Aquinas" and "Albertus": God, the devil, the heavenly city, hell, the world, the soul, the body, sin, penitence, and virtue. "Albertus" (William of Auvergne, *De faciebus*) studies each of these by seven *loci* of disputation. In his *Ars praedicandi* [62] William devotes twenty chapters to repertories of ideas which should serve the preacher as themes for artistic development.

The tracts are not all concerned with only one type of preaching; they vary in content, treatment, and, occasionally, point of view. They vary, too, in their definitions. Alain's is often quoted: "Preaching is open and public instruction in faith and morals, devoted to the informing of men, based on divine science, and confirmed by authorities." The "Aquinas"-tract borrows this and offers also: "Preaching is the fitting and appropriate dispensation of God's word." "Henry of Hesse" supplies the following curious sentence: "The art of preaching is the science which teaches how to say something about something," but proceeds to explain that the subject of the art is the Word of God. And John of Wales provides this: "Preaching consists in invoking God's aid and then suitably, clearly, and devoutly expounding a proposed theme by means of division and concordance; its aim being the catholic enlightenment of the intellect and the enkindling, with grace, of emotion." [63] Guibert's treatise is an inner

81

psychological study of the preacher rather than a technical manual. The author of the "Henry"-tract knows four kinds of preaching: the *postillatio* (by mystic interpretation of the terms of a text), the modern method (thematic), the *antiquus* (homily), the *subalternus* (a mixture of homily and modern). "Albertus" discusses three: the *tractatus* (homily), preaching through syllogisms and distinctions (equivalent to the modern and thematic), and preaching through poetic fictions. John of Wales treats four variations of the type developed by concordances. The author of the "Aquinas"-tract knows three kinds: The *antiquus* (called also the laical, beautiful, and popular); the smooth and simple, a variation of the thematic, with divisions but without distinctions; and the modern or thematic. And St. Antoninus offers seven methods of procedure.

Despite the outstanding opposition of such tracts as Humbert's, the thematic, in its varied forms and modifications, was the most popular method. It comprised a theme from Holy Writ; a protheme,[64] also from the Bible, which should lead to a prayer invoking God's aid, and yet recall the theme; and divisions and subdivisions of the theme, by means of authoritative passages, from the Bible, the Church Fathers, and the philosophers, arranged largely in a skilful syllogistic order. This scheme was of course not inherited from classical rhetoric, which could not have had such special needs in view. The Middle Ages are to be credited with inventing it. But the contribution of the principles of Aristotelian logic is evident in its form, so that a title of a tract may, like Jean de Châlons', read *De modo praedicandi et sylogizandi*,[65] and preaching be defined as an "exposition of Holy Writ by division and subdivision." Were the modern student, fortified by a knowledge of Aristotle's *Rhetoric*, to contend that the rhetorical enthymeme, not the syllogism, is proper to the art of rhetoric, the mediaeval preacher would perhaps reply that sacred eloquence differs from secular in that its subject matter lies not in the realm of opinion and probability, but in truth and divine science; that it is as sound a procedure to use a dialectical method in the demonstration of truth as in the investigation of it; and, further, that in Aristotle and Cicero and Quintilian he had precedents for the policy of adapting to rhetorical purposes the methods of the allied art of dialectic. Petrus Cantor (*saec.* xii) makes clear this relationship of dialectic and rhetoric, so peculiar to scholasticism, in his idea of the edifice of the spirit. This is formed of *lectio*, the foundation, and *disputatio,* the wall, supporting *praedicatio,* the roof, which protects the faithful from the surge and whirl of vices.[66]

In these tracts the part played by what one might term "purer" rhetoric was in the means of division and subdivision, namely, amplification, as a principle of both invention and disposition.

In examining a number of *artes* I note the following topics of expansion: [67] (1) Concordance of authorities, Biblical, patristic, philosophic. (2) Questioning and discussion of words and terms, often with division—*Dominus illuminatio mea et salus.* Ask, why *dominus,* why *illuminatio,* why *mea?* (3) Discussion of the properties of things. Ps. 55:7: "God hath anointed thee with the oil of gladness." Oil betokens grace, for it has a sanative virtue. (4) Analogies and natural truths. You love your parents. Your parents come from God. Therefore you must love God. (5) Ratiocination and argument. This might be from simile, example, the topic of the greater and less, or from opposites, often with confirmation, refutation, and conclusion. In the later period argument could be presented by any of the following means: *syllogizando, inducendo, exemplificando,* or *enthymematizando.* In the favorite argument from opposites, vices might be set against virtues. St. Antoninus offers also an epideictic method of expansion, the praise or blame of the matter in hand. (6) Comparison, a play upon adjectives or verbs. A play on the topic of the greater and less: Judas' sin was great in that he was greedy; it was greater in that he betrayed his master; it was greatest in that he despaired of God's mercy. Or, following Richard of Thetford, the preacher could ring the changes upon *qu(a)eritur, requiritur, exquiritur, inquiritur.*[68] (7) Similitudes. Among the mediaeval books which "Henry of Hesse" advises for supplementary use by the preacher is the *Book of Similitudes,* the *Summa de exemplis et rerum similitudinibus libris decem constans* (*ca.* 1300) of Joannes Gorinus of San Gemignano, which supplies the preacher with every kind of material for moralistic comparison. (8) Explication by hidden terminology. Here perhaps may be found the source of the practice still operative today, of orating by the interpretation of initials—to which, no doubt, we must ascribe the high success of an alumni secretary who pleads with all elements that make up the university to hold FAST: *F,* the faculty; *A,* the alumni; *S,* the students; and *T,* the trustees! (9) Multiplication of synonyms. Ah, men's woes! He is oppressed by cares, surrounded by worries, vexed by adversity, and choked by perils.

(10) Any or all of the dialectical topics like species and genera, whole and parts, and the categories: *quid, de quo, quare, quale, quantum, quando, ubi.* (11) Explication of scriptural metaphors. (12) Cause and effect, in the moral realm. (13) Anecdotes. The place of *exempla* in these tracts is yet to be investigated. (14) Observation of the end or purpose of a thing. (15) Setting forth the essential weight of a word. Sermons devoted to the mere word *et* were not unknown. (16) Interpretation of Hebrew names. (17) Etymology. Since *mulier = molliens herum* (William of Auvergne), one may see how unlimited was the service to tropology of this science. Yet of such fancies was born the beautiful legend of Veronica [69]—not Berenice ($\phi\epsilon\rho\epsilon\nu\iota\kappa\eta$), victory bearer, but Vera Icon, true image. (18) Parts of speech. (19) Rhetorical colors, as with Surgant,[70] at the end of this period (1502). (20) The use of the four senses of scriptural interpretation—historical or literal, allegorical, tropological—which is especially important in preaching because it looks to the correction of morals—and anagogical, which is explication from the point of view of heavenly things. A great proportion of the anonymous tracts, and also Bromyard, Guibert, the "Aquinas"- and "Henry"-tracts, and the *Ars concionandi* employ these senses as a means of prolonging a sermon in developing a theme; I have elsewhere discussed the history and popularity of the "four senses." [71] The method is perhaps not quite lost to us even today,[72] and apparently was still popular in England well into the eighteenth century. I here offer what I fear is an unworthy illustration, from an account [73] of a sermon allegedly delivered by the notorious Dr. Dodd of Samuel Johnson's day, which I coalesce with a seventeenth-century version, somewhat different, in a letter of Sir John Suckling.[74] It will be noticed that this sermon illustrates also explication by hidden terminology, and, at the end, the principle of multiplying synonyms:

Certain drunken students of Cambridge, returning from a merry meeting at a country alehouse, by the way overtook Dr. Dodd, who in a sermon he had lately made on temperance, among other reproofs, as the sweet-sugared fellows constructed it, had termed them "malt-worms." Wherefore they by violence took him and compelled him to preach a sermon upon the theme "Malt." The reverend gentleman commenced: "Let me crave your attention, my beloved. I am a little man, come at a short warning, to preach a short sermon, upon a short subject, to a thin congregation, in an unworthy pulpit. Beloved! My text is 'Malt.' There is no teaching without a division. I cannot divide my text into syllables, it being but a monosyllable. Therefore I must divide it into letters, which I find in my text to be four: *M-A-L-T*. *M,* my beloved, is moral; *A* is allegorical; *L* is literal; *T* is theological.

"First, the moral teaches such as you drunkards good manners; wherefore *M,* my masters, *A,* all of you, *L,* listen, *T,* to the theme; and therefore, *M,* my masters, *A,* all of you, *L,* leave off, *T,* tippling.

"Secondly, the allegorical is when one thing is spoken, and another meant. The thing here spoken is malt, the thing meant the oil of malt, which you rustics make *M,* your masters, *A,* your apparel, *L,* your liberty, *T,* your treasure.

"Thirdly, the literal sense hath ever been found suitable to the theme, confirmed by beggarly experienc: *MA,* much ale, *LT,* little thought.

"Fourthly, the theological is according to the effects it works, which are of two kinds: the first in this world, the second in the world to come. The effects it works in this world are *M,* murder, *A,* adultery, *L,* looseness of life, and *T,* treason. In the world to come the effects of it are *M,* misery, *A,* anguish, *L,* lamentation, *T,* torment. And thus much for my text, 'Malt.'

"A word of caution, take this: A drunkard is the annoyance of modesty, the spoiler of civility, the destroyer of reason, the brewer's agent, the ale-wife's benefactor, his wife's sorrow, his children's trouble, his neighbor's scoff, a walking swill-tub, a picture of a beast, a monster of a man. But I much fear that I lose my labor, my theme showing that it is *M* to *A,* a thousand pounds to a pot of ale, that one knave of *L,* fifty, will ever leave to love potting."

By this time the ale and his persuasion had so wrought as they fell asleep, and the preacher closely crept away.[75]

The *doctrina localis* is employed throughout in *dilatatio.* To the author of the *Ars concionandi* it is a *clavis* method, a "Key to the Scriptures," for it opens and closes the sense of a scriptural passage.

It is clear, then, that the sermon was studied from the point of view of *elocutio, inventio,* and *dispositio.* The preacher and the hearer were likewise not neglected.

The saying of Gregory, that whose life is despised so is his preaching, is often quoted. The "Aquinas"-tract recognizes preaching by deed as well as by word. Much attention is paid to the speaker's personality and habits. For example, St. Bonaventure sets down nine desirable qualities. He must be of the right age, not far from thirty; he must not be boyish either in appearance or in habits; he must have no bodily deformities; he must be strong, and of competent eloquence, well trained at least in grammar and Holy Writ, and able to speak without error or confusion; for his persuasive purpose he must be irreproachable in life and habits, industrious, prudent, and not contentious.[76] Evidently these sacred rhetors had a lively consciousness of the power of ethical persuasion.

These divine rhetors give as much thought to *pronuntiatio* as did the Roman authorities. A Berlin manuscript (Theol. Fol. 287 [*saec*. xv], fol. 310) offers, in verse form, the following aids to delivery: regulate your gestures; neither drag along nor run too fast; be very patient; keep the people in order happily; avoid shouting; suppress a cough; refrain from spitting; let your words be clear, not harsh, and never vile. The "Henry"-tract suggests a *vox acuta* in exposition, a *vox austera* in correction, a *vox benevola* in exhortation. The "Aquinas"-treatise sets forth specific gestures to express the emotions appropriate to different Biblical verses: admiration, horror and excitement, irony and derision, elation, weariness and indignation, joy and hate. *Venite ad me omnes* must be uttered with gracious countenance and holding up of the hands. And the preacher should imitate the gestures he thinks Christ used in a given case. William's *Divina rhetorica* (chap. xxv) considers even the gestures of prayer and the part played in prayer by such *adjutoria* as blushing, weeping, groaning, and sighing. Among the preacher's vices listed in the "Henry"- and "Aquinas"-tracts are ignorance, lack of facility, excessive pointing of the fingers, tossing of the head, closing of the eyes, too much noisiness, remote digression.[77] The "Aquinas"-treatise also sets forth precautions: proper reverence, the clear and intelligible enunciation of every syllable; the avoidance of tedium and laughter by avoiding repetition or a deviation from the original plan of the sermon; an adequate summary to aid the hearer's memory; the comporting of one's self as if in Christ's presence; watching the hour and shunning prolixity, lest the people do not return.

The soundness of rhetorical judgment in these precepts arises from the close study that the theorists made of their audiences. But for the profound treatment of the emotions in Aristotle's *Rhetoric*, I would say that the classical rhetoricians never so thoroughly analyzed affections as the mediaeval theorists did the vices and virtues. Numberless tracts on this subject were purposely designed for the preacher's aid. Humbert has one hundred chapters on different audiences (*ad varios status*) with topical hints as to what they should be told—scholars, nobles, paupers, boys, harlots. St. Bonaventure studies the commonplace vices of certain audiences: if you address merchants, you must discuss fraud and mendacity; if soldiers, rapine and arson.[78] With audience in mind, he protests against involved sentences, and demands easy words within the capacity of the hearers to understand.[79] Jacques de Vitry had 120 categories of hearers.[80] The *Ecclesiastica rhetorica* reminds the speaker that there are seven primary emotions: fear, pain, sadness, shame, indignation, wrath, and hate of sin. Even the psychology of communication between speaker and audience is nicely imaged forth by "Albertus'" figure of preaching as a *desponsatio* or *matrimonium* of gospel truth; the bride is decked out with simple diction, and the witnesses to the alliance are arguments, examples, and parables.[81] But long before our period Gregory in his *Pastoral Rule* (Part III, Prologue) had asked the preacher to remember, when weighing the condition of his hearers, that certain herbs nourish some animals and kill others, that a soft whisper quiets a horse but excites a puppy, that bread which gives the strong their strength afflicts children, and that in the ideal state the hearer's attention resembles the tense strings of the cithara. The sick, the simple, the rich, the sad—all kinds of people and all affections were examined by these preachers, and a therapeutic by opposites artistically employed. They followed the rule: *sermo coaptandus qualitati auditorum,*[82] and therein they well followed ancient precept. ἦθος, πίστις, and also πάθος—all were studied in this "art of arts, and science of the sciences." [83]

The theory of thematic preaching had its critics. Humbert considers vicious the current multiplication of distinctions and authorities.[84] Gerson (*saec.* xiv–xv) calls the preachers of his day "sophists" because they use naught but crude logic, devoid of verbal adornment.[85] Obviously to him they were incomplete artists, and insufficient rhetoricians. Roger Bacon's (*saec.* xiii) opposition also rests on rhetorical grounds: in the divisions, consonances, and verbal concordances, he finds neither sublimity nor great wisdom, but an infinite childish dulness and a cheapening of God's word; "of which ostentatiousness may God himself rid his Church; . . . it is perverse vanity lacking every rhetorical ornamentation and persuasive virtue." [86] Bacon desired beauty, emotion, and the study of such works as Seneca *On Wrath;* this he recommended as a thesaurus for special persuasive topics. Joly, eighteenth-century historian of preaching, consistent with the spirit of his times, savagely attacks the bizarre and ridiculous taste of these scholastics, their false subtleties, the tissue of texts, the exaggerated allegories, the excessive divisions and minute reasonings, and the insipid monotony of thoughts.[87] But while acknowledging the pedantry and concentrated formalism, we can find much to praise in the method-ical ordering of the thematic sermon (the *arbor picta* is a favorite suf-fix to these tracts); [88] we can find much to laud, too, in the inventional scheme, and in the dexterity and practical variety of treatment, and can appreciate that the theory served its day well.

The influence of classical rhetoric on mediaeval preaching was there-fore definite and considerable. Furthermore, from the nature of the preacher's education, from the wide interest in rhetoric in this period, from the persistence of the rhetorical tradition, and from the quality of some elements that we have considered in the mediaeval theory, I regard it as legitimate to assume an even greater contact and influence than one finds expressed or recognized. This is a safe assumption, even when one allows for the possibility that need and experience often create the development of a practice which is not always to be identified with conscious art, nor is to be referred to rules derived from an alien source. But the Middle Ages never achieved that complete synthesis of homiletics and classical rhetoric that we begin to find in the Renais-sance. It is only in that period and later that manuscripts appear in which the classical authors are fully searched and carefully excerpted for the specific use of preachers.[89] Then, as in Chytraeus' *Praecepta rhetorica*, Cicero, Pericles, and Demosthenes are studied together with St. Basil and St. Paul.[90] Then appear such descriptions as Reuchlin's in his *Liber congestorum de arte praedicandi* (1503): [91] a preacher is a *vir religiosus dicendi peritus,* which converts the elder Cato's famous definition of the orator as a *vir bonus dicendi peritus;* and the matter of preaching is everything offering itself to make us daily better, on which the preacher knows how to speak well. Then appears the rhet-orically scientific division of the kinds of preaching into the didactic, epitreptic (devoted to inducing belief), and paraenetic (directed to persuading men to a course of conduct), which Melanchthon devised in a system of sacred rhetoric firmly based on classical rules.[92] It is much later when, in *Polyhistor,*[93] Morhof, a severe critic of what he terms the barbarous preaching of the scholastic period, insists there is no distinction between civil and sacred oratory except in subject mat-ter; that the precepts and method are the same in both, and all in-spiration is to be drawn from Aristotle. But, although the greatest of all oratorical theories, Aristotle's *Rhetoric,* was known in translation in the thirteenth century, mediaeval preaching had no demonstrable first-hand contact with it. The first direct quotation from this book that

I have thus far found in any of these *artes* is in Surgant (1502),[94] and it is more than a century later when Peacham in the *Compleat Gentleman* (1622) [95] refers offhand to the reputation enjoyed by Aristotle's *Rhetoric* as a book sufficient to make both a scholar and an honest man. So far as I know, it is only in modern times that to the three classical types of oratory, forensic, deliberative, and epideictic, the sacred has been added as a fourth,[96] thus gaining a rightful place among its fellows within the rhetorical art. And indeed, perhaps only in the nineteenth century was developed the systematic classification of the *ars praedicandi* itself into its genera, the *concio*, the *laudatio*, the *homilia*, the *enarratio sacrarum litterarum*, and the *oratio funebris*, as by the Jesuit Polcari.[97] The preaching of the Renaissance and modern times drank more deeply, yet mediaeval theory also tasted more than superficially at the fount of classical rhetoric.

Quintilian's Witnesses

HAROLD F. HARDING

SAMUEL JOHNSON was so deeply impressed with the merit of Roger Ascham's *Scholemaster* that he wrote in the Preface of James Bennet's 1761 edition of the book: "It contains, perhaps, the best advice that was ever given for the study of languages." A modern scholar writing on the place of this book in the history of education in the Renaissance concludes: "Had Ascham's own college, St. John's, Cambridge, founded a lectureship on education three hundred years ago, restricted to Quintilian and Ascham, the whole course of English education would have been powerfully influenced." [1] There is, indeed, good reason for joining the names of the Roman teacher and the English scholar in a review of the history of education; each wrote the most significant treatise of his age on the theory and method of teaching. Although, unfortunately, a chair such as the one proposed never was established, there is evidence enough that Quintilian's book, the *Institutio Oratorio*, or *The Training of the Orator*, has been studied and respected by English writers from the Renaissance to the present day. The proof is to be found in works on rhetoric and literary criticism, in treatises on educational theory, courtesy and manners, and in the curricula of the English schools and universities themselves. In this essay I shall attempt to summon a few of the more important witnesses to the value of the *Institutio*. Their testimony will be found of two kinds: direct praise of the book, and secondly, that more complimentary sign of preference—the appropriation of Quintilian's ideas, either knowingly or unknowingly.

Quintilian's Witnesses

Marcus Fabius Quintilian (A.D. c. 35–c.100), a Spaniard by birth, was probably the most distinguished teacher of public speaking in antiquity. His book, written after a highly successful career as a pleader and a teacher, was published in A.D. 96. Although its title implies that Quintilian writes on the training of the orator, the work is far more than a mere text-book on that subject. Rhetoric in the first century was a most comprehensive study; was in fact the organon for all learning, the principal course of statesmen and men of public affairs, embracing a knowledge of grammar, literature, reading, writing, philosophy, history, logic, persuasion, and speaking in public. Accordingly, Quintilian's twelve books, which consider the education of a boy from birth until as a man he begins to appear in public life, comprise a treatise on educational theory, on writing and speaking, on literary criticism, and in brief, what we might today call the making of a cultivated gentleman.

The *Institutio* was known and well regarded throughout the Middle Ages, even when it could be read only in fragments. Upon the finding of a complete copy by the Florentine scholar, Poggio, in the monastery of St. Gall in the year 1416, the treatise became one of the great books of the Renaissance. It profoundly influenced writers on pedagogy, rhetoric, and poetics; and a knowledge of its doctrine was deemed essential to the scholarly equipment of every learned man.

Although the scope of this essay will be limited to witnesses from the time of the Renaissance onward, there is evidence that the *Institutio* was known in England long before Poggio's important discovery of the manuscript in full. For example, in the year 849, that notable teacher, scholar, and humanist, Lupus of Ferrières, wrote to the Augustinian Abbot of York, Altsigus, asking if he might borrow to copy, and then return, the twelve books of the *Institutio*.[2] John of Salisbury (1120?–1180) has in his *Metalogicus*[3] left us an excellent account of how such teachers as Bernard, William of Conches, and Richard l'Evêque relied upon Quintilian at the great school of Chartres (about 1050–1150). Professor C. S. Baldwin has recently shown by parallel passages not only the similarity of ideas between the *Institutio* and the *Metalogicus*, but a frequent actual use of the same words.[4]

In the Wardrobe Accounts of King Edward I for the year 1289 there is a bill for expenses at Oxford of two nephews of Edward's royal architect. Along with other items the Exchequer paid for two copies of the *Institutio*.[5]

Among important English scholars of mediæval times who studied the *Institutio,* or owned copies of it, were Adelard of Bath; [6] Richard de Bury; [7] Humphrey, Duke of Gloucester; [8] and William Grey, Bishop of Ely.[9] There were at least three copies of Quintilian in the libraries of Oxford and Cambridge in the early part of the fifteenth century.[10]

With Poggio's discovery in 1416, the copyists at once set to work to produce complete editions of the *Institutio.* The first printed edition was published at Rome in 1470. From then until 1600 there were no fewer than 118 editions of the *Institutio* and the *Declamationes* issued in Italy, France, Switzerland, Belgium, Holland, and Germany.[11] It is true, books in these days were costly, and printings were not large, but this number of editions is proof that scholars, teachers, and pupils kept demanding the rhetoric of Quintilian. Moreover, the custom of students in the universities of taking full and detailed lecture-notes must have put into circulation a rather large number of abstracts and commentaries of the *Institutio.*

THE SIXTEENTH CENTURY

Let us now turn to some of the more important deponents to the value of Quintilian in the English Renaissance. Perhaps the most conspicuous figure was Erasmus. By his lecturing, his travels, his writing of books and letters, his constant communication with scholars of England and the Continent, he profoundly impressed the education of the Revival. While at Cambridge (1511–1514), Erasmus became greatly interested in the efforts of John Colet to re-establish St. Paul's School. Henry VIII had granted to Colet a royal license-in-mortmain for the school in 1510. In the following year Erasmus wrote and dedicated to Colet for his use in the school the *De Copia Rerum et Verborum.* Professor W. H. Woodward points out that the very title of the *Copia* comes from Quintilian and says:

It is a manual of "enrichment" and "variation" based mainly upon Quintilian [Book 8], with modern examples. . . . A student of the classical Renaissance, desirous to make a first-hand acquaintance with the art of expression as understood by humanist writers, cannot do better than make a careful analysis of the *De Copia,* reading side by side the *De Oratore* and the fourth and eighth books of the *Institutio Oratoria.*[12]

In his treatise on the curriculum, *De Ratio Studii* (1511), Erasmus again shows his dependence upon Cicero and Quintilian. Their works are prescribed for the advanced study of rhetoric. Many of the authors mentioned in Book 10 of the *Institutio,* Erasmus approves of for criticism. Finally, the exercise of turning Greek into Latin, which is recommended in the *Ratio,* is, of course, found in both Cicero and Quintilian. As further proof of a real devotion to Quintilian, we find Erasmus indicating in his letters that he himself intended to bring forth an edition of the *Institutio.*[13]

Next after Erasmus in importance, undoubtedly the leading figure in the scholarly world in England at this time, was the Spaniard, Juan Luis Vives. At the invitation of Cardinal Wolsey, he came to Oxford in the autumn of 1522; in the following year there was offered him a lectureship in humanity at the University. Later he was appointed tutor to Princess Mary. Foster Watson, who points out that Vives has been referred to as "the second Quintilian," considers the *De Tradendis Disciplinis* (1531), and the *Linguae Latinae Exercitatio* or *School Dialogues* (1539), as his great pedagogical works, "the first a most comprehensive theoretical work in education." "The *Exercitatio* is perhaps the most interesting school text-book of the age." [14]

The modern reader who carefully studies the translation [15] of the works of Vives can see at once the marked similarity between his theories and those of Quintilian.[16] The ideas contained in the four books of the *Disciplinis* on the value of group teaching,[17] the merit in a boy's imitation of the good,[18] the importance of right speaking,[19] the method of interpretation of authors,[20] the development of memory,[21] corporal punishment,[22] figures of speech,[23] the value of Homer,[24] and the use of the *Institutio* as a text [25]—all show a reliance upon the early master both in similarity of thought and in actual citation. Continuing, we may include the portions dealing with the use of models in speaking and writing,[26] the gift of the teacher,[27] the *Declamations* of Quintilian,[28] the cultivation of judgment,[29] the value of history,[30] the correction of written composition,[31] progress in learning,[32] the grammarian's standard,[33] the proper conditions for study,[34] and the noble purpose of eloquence; [35] all these portions quote from the precepts of the *Institutio.*

Although Sir Thomas Elyot probably is more indebted to Plato than to any other writer for the main concepts of *The Governour* (1531), yet his book in several places contains quotations or echoes from Quintilian; in particular, in the discussion of the proper age to begin studies,[36] the best type of student,[37] the study of Greek and Latin,[38] training in memory,[39] the great merit of Homer,[40] the use of the *Institutio* as a text,[41] the value of Livy,[42] poets and versifiers,[43] gentleness in discipline,[44] and the worth of ancient authors.[45] In his first book,

Elyot discusses "for what cause at this day there be in this realme fewe perfecte schole maisters." Thus, after setting up Quintilian's grammarian as his ideal, he concludes in despair: "Then beholde howe fewe grammariens after this description be in this realme." [46]

In *The Scholemaster* (1570), Roger Ascham reveals a somewhat mistaken and prejudiced notion of the *Institutio,* accusing Quintilian in one place of having "a lust to dissent from Tully." [47] But, evidence of respect for Quintilian's ideas is not lacking. Indeed, one might say that a large part of the doctrine of Imitation, for which *The Scholemaster* has so often been praised, is derived from Quintilian.[48] Ascham says that he regards the writings of Johann Sturm on Imitation "farre best of all"; but, of course, the German scholar was himself a borrower from the ancients, and especially from Quintilian.[49] And so, while it is true that Ascham seldom seeks out the Roman teacher for praise,[50] it is patent that much of the humanistic doctrine of the *Institutio* has found itself again in *The Scholemaster.* Specifically, Ascham's views on discipline, on praise and gentleness in teaching, on the exercise of writing in learning to prepare speeches, on the importance of memory, on the effects of companions on children, and on the use of rhetoric as an organon, may all be traced to our writer of the late first century A.D. Whereas Quintilian would have his youth trained to speak well, Ascham simply changed the emphasis to writing; he insists that the best way to perfection in the mother tongue is to be found in the mastery of the Latin.

Richard Mulcaster, the first headmaster of Merchant Taylors' School, displays a remarkably wide acquaintance with the classics in his two books, *Positions* (1581) and *The Elementarie* (1582). The actual references to the *Institutio* in *Positions* are few, but sufficiently show Mulcaster's respect for Quintilian. For example, in speaking of the value of public schools, Mulcaster says:

> Use common schools to the best, join a tutor to your child, let Quintilian be your guide; all things will be well done where such care is at hand, and that is much better done, which is done before witness to encourage the child. Comparisons inspire virtues, hearing spreads learning; one is none; and if he do something at home, what would he do with company? [51]

In *The Elementarie* we find Quintilian called upon under the subjects of a plan of studies,[52] custom in writing,[53] the grammarian,[54] how young children are to be taught,[55] the value of good examples,[56] and how to inspire a boy.[57]

The Arte of English Poesie, probably written by Richard Puttenham, and published in 1589, was one of the notable works on poetic theory of the century. In his third book, "Of Ornament," the author gives us a most elaborate inventory of rhetorical terms. Not content with repeating the Greek and Latin technical names of the figures, he attempts an English translation of them. For instance, *aposiopesis* is called the "Figure of Silence," *ironia* becomes the "Drye Mock," *enigma* is the "Riddle," and *epitheton* is the "Qualifier." And what is the source of this great list of terms? Although the author makes no acknowledgment of his indebtedness, there can be no doubt that he has helped himself from the *Institutio.* In a dozen or more instances the illustrations used are direct translations from the very ones used by Quintilian. In all, some one hundred and twenty rhetorical terms are discussed. Ninety-two of these are quickly found in the *Institutio.*[58] Some twenty-eight are not so readily traceable, but I suggest that terms like *auxiexis, pragmatographica, epizeuxis, hypozeuxis, enallage, sillepsis, liptote,* and others come from Henry Peacham's *Garden of Eloquence* (1577).

The Arte of English Poesie also gives us an interesting sidelight on the intellectual diversion of a statesman of the day, Sir Nicholas Bacon (1509–1579), the father of Francis Bacon. From him, we are told, came "more grave and natural eloquence than from all the orators of Oxford or Cambridge."

I have come to the Lord Keeper, Sir Nicholas Bacon, and found him sitting in his gallery with the works of Quintilian before him; indeed, he was a most eloquent man, and of rare learning and wisdom, as ever I knew England to breed, and one that joyed as much in learned men and men of good wits.[59]

There is proof that the study of Quintilian was not neglected at the English universities during the Renaissance. By the statutes of Edward VI of 1549, a professor of dialectics and rhetoric was appointed at Cambridge. He was to lecture on the *Elenchi* of Aristotle, Cicero's *Topics,* Quintilian, and Hermogenes.[60] At Oxford, legislation for the betterment of learning was enacted somewhat earlier. By the foundation-statutes issued to Bishop Fox for Corpus Christi College in 1517, the lecturer on humanity was to expound, among other prose writers, Cicero, Sallust, Pliny, Livy, and Quintilian.[61] Cardinal College was founded in 1525. By its statutes, issued shortly afterward, and revised in 1527, the Professor of Humanity was to give daily lectures on Cicero, Trapezuntius, and Quintilian.[62]

Historical Studies of Rhetoric

In the seventeenth century, Quintilian's chief supporter is Ben Jonson. His important prose work, *Timber, or Discoveries,* was written at some time between 1620 and 1635, and published in 1641. Maurice Castelain has marked out the leading parallels between Jonson's thoughts and those of his predecessors in an excellent critical edition of *Discoveries.*[63] Of the thirty authors from whom Jonson, according to Castelain, borrows in this work, Quintilian heads the list with no fewer than twenty-seven extracts. Twelve passages or allusions come from Book I of the *Institutio,* five from Book X, and the remainder from Books II, IV, VIII, and XII. In some instances Jonson has merely appropriated the thought of the *Institutio;* in others he has made an almost literal translation; in a few he has actually taken over the Latin phraseology intact.[64] A comparison of these passages from *Timber* with the Latin originals leads the reader to agree with Castelain that Jonson "must have known by heart whole chapters from Quintilian and Seneca, the Rhetorician." [65]

This marvelous capacity of Jonson's mind to utilize classical patterns of thought for his immediate purpose is also evident in the celebrated *Conversations* with William Drummond of Hawthornden. Here, it will be recalled, Jonson advised the reading of the *Institutio,* saying, as Drummond records the remark, that Quintilian "would tell me the faults of my verses as if he had lived with me." [66] There are at least four instances in the *Conversations* of Jonson's applying critical phrases of Quintilian to other authors.[67]

We see the growing importance that attaches to a speaker's study of delivery in Jonson's day in the appearance of John Bulwer's *Chirologia and Chironomia* (1644). The author calls himself a "Philochirosophus," and says that he has investigated the "Canons, Lawes, Rites, Ordinances, and Institutes of Rhetoricians, both Ancient and Moderne, Touching the artificial managing of the Hand in Speaking." [68] Throughout Bulwer's treatise, the *Institutio,* and especially Book XI, is cited again and again. It is true, Cicero's utterances are not overlooked. But Bulwer calls Quintilian "the most cleare Interpretour of all the ancients"; [69] and the *Chironomia* is indeed very largely a recast of the Roman professor's observations on *actio.*

Obadiah Walker is likewise a writer of text-books that show respect for Quintilian. Walker's two books are: *Some Instructions Concerning*

the Art of Oratory, collected for the use of a Friend, a young Student
(1659); and *Of Education, especially of a young Gentleman* (1673).[70]
In the former work, Cicero and more frequently Quintilian seem to
be the only authorities relied upon. Walker extracts sentences and
ideas from the *Institutio* in practically every one of his sections, all
told, in about twenty instances. It frequently appears that the phrases
of Quintilian are so well-known to Walker that he sees no need of
citing the places where they may be found.

The diplomat and poet, Sir Henry Wotton, who late in life became
provost of Eton, was the author of a curious little essay of twenty
pages called *A Philosophicall Survey of Education, or Moral Architecture*, posthumously published in 1651. Wotton displays a fondness for
Quintilian in several complimentary passages, and in the parenthetical
remark, "whom I have ever thought, since any use of my poor judgment,
both the elegantest and soundest of all Roman pens." [71]

At some time in the early part of the seventeenth century, the study
of rhetoric as an academic discipline began to suffer a reaction. The
concept of "exorning the matter" caused many people to regard rhetoric as an affected and artificial instrument for misleading men by a
deceitful method. Towards the end of the century, the philosopher,
John Locke, clearly showed his distrust of rhetoric. He said in his
Thoughts Concerning Education (1693) that he had "seldom or never
observed any one to get the skill of reasoning well, or speaking handsomely, by studying these rules which pretend to teach it." [72] In his
Essay on Human Understanding (1690) Locke wrote that rhetoric and
eloquence "are for nothing else but to insinuate wrong ideas, move the
passions, and thereby mislead the judgement, an so, indeed, are perfect cheat." [73]

Despite his strictures on the study of rhetoric, however, there is
a strikingly sympathetic relationship between Locke's two essays and
Quintilian's *Institutio*. Laurie, who believes that both essays should
be read together, considers the *Thoughts* "the best treatise on education which has ever appeared with the (doubtful) exception of Quintilian." [74] A reader who has the main doctrine of the *Institutio* in mind
is at once impressed with the humane reasonableness of Locke's
theories. Nor can we escape the general similarity of the *Thoughts* and
the *Institutio* on the subject of the early training of children. Locke is
opposed to corporal punishment; sees the importance of the influence
of companions; believes that lessons should not be tasks; and thinks

that a few sensible rules bring better results than an unnecessary many.[75] In neither of these two works, apparently, does Locke name Quintilian. In fact, as for Locke's sources, Laurie holds that: "Not withstanding his debt to Rabelais and still more to Montaigne, his educational conceptions are in the truest sense his own." [76] As I have intimated, however, either knowingly or otherwise, "the English Rationalist" has several ideas that, historically viewed, have proceeded from Quintilian.[77]

THE EIGHTEENTH CENTURY

From about the year 1750 to some time in the early nineteenth century there was a tremendous interest in England in the art of speaking —in lectures by professors of the subject, in their books, and in parliamentary speeches themselves. John Ward, who in 1720 had been appointed Professor of Rhetoric at Gresham College, taught there continuously until his death in 1758. John Lawson was made lecturer in oratory and history at Trinity College, Dublin, in 1753. His *Lectures Concerning Oratory* were first published in 1758, and quickly gave him a considerable reputation. While Aristotle is clearly Lawson's master, throughout his book we find much to indicate a debt to Quintilian. In Lawson's fourth lecture, Quintilian and Longinus are treated in full and in terms of high praise. Ward's two-volume work, *A System of Oratory*, published in 1759, undoubtedly represents the best synthesis of ancient rhetorical theory to be found in English. The first chapter mentions the contributions of Aristotle, Hermogenes, and Cicero. Then Ward reveals his favorite:

> But Quintilian himself outdid all who went before him, in diligence and accuracy as a writer. . . . [His] *Institutions* are so comprehensive, and written with that great exactness and judgment, that they are generally allowed to be the most perfect work of this kind.[78]

A study of the lectures plainly shows that nearly forty years of teaching have made Ward a master of Cicero and Quintilian. He quotes or refers to one or the other on almost every other page of the two volumes, in all, some two hundred and thirty times. The citations to the *Institutio* are in a slight majority.

A more detailed treatise is the two-volume work by the Scottish clergyman, John Ogilvie, called *Philosophical and Critical Observa-*

tions on the Nature, Character, and Various Species of Composition (1774). The acknowledgment of the author to the mastery of Quintilian is found in the first book, under the section, "Introductory Observations on the Nature of Composition":

> Of Roman writers who have treated of the present subject, the judicious and elegant Quintilian is by far the most copious and particular. In his well-known work, entitled *Instutiones Oratoriae* (of which the reader will find much use in the following essay, and whose excellence is equal to almost any eulogium), the present subject is discussed by itself.[79]

Perhaps the most popular text of this great age of classicism was that of the professor of *belles-lettres* at Edinburgh University, Hugh Blair. His *Lectures on Rhetoric and Belles-Lettres* were first issued in 1783. They reached a tenth edition in 1806, and have since been many times reprinted. In his chapter entitled "Means of Improving in Eloquence," Blair contends:

> But of all the ancient writers on the subject of oratory, the most instructive, and most useful, is Quintilian. I know few books which abound more with good sense, and discover a greater degree of just and accurate taste, than Quintilian's *Institutions*. Almost all the principles of good criticism are to be found in them. He has digested into excellent order all the ancient ideas concerning rhetoric; and is, at the same time, himself an eloquent writer. Though some parts of his work contain too much of the technical and artificial system then in vogue, and for that reason may be dry and tedious, yet I would not advise the omitting to read any part of his *Institutions*. To pleaders at the bar, even those technical parts may prove of much use. Seldom has any person of more sound and distinct judgment than Quintilian applied himself to the study of the art of oratory.[80]

Cicero, and more frequently Quintilian, are Blair's principal authorities. He selects ideas from the *Institutio* with such care and effect that Colson is obliged to say: "His quotations would make a very respectable 'florigelium' to illustrate Quintilian's sense and incisiveness." [81] In all, there are about forty citations, including allusions to the Roman teacher's words on the study of grammar,[82] perspicuity of style,[83] the structure of sentences,[84] metaphors,[85] similes,[86] instructions for good writing,[87] Cicero's oratory,[88] and the proper division in an oration.[89] Much as some may condemn or belittle Blair's originality or judgment as shown in the *Lectures*, we should recall that the tremendous vogue of his teaching and the use of his book until the middle of the next century were potent forces in keeping alive the beauty and soundness of Quintilian's opinions.

The writer who, possibly more than any other, has made Quintilian's name familiar in English literature of the Augustan Age is, of course, Pope. His *Essay on Criticism,* published in 1711, when he was but twenty-two years old, attracted endless attention. The lines which praise the *Institutio* read:

> In grave Quintilian's copious work, we find
> The justest rules and clearest method joined:
> Thus useful arms in magazines we place,
> All ranged in order, and disposed with grace,
> But less to please the eye than arm the hand,
> Still fit for use, and ready at command.[90]

Aside from the fact that Pope took pains to indicate his debt to Quintilian in his own published notes on the *Essay,* we know from his conversations with the Rev. Joseph Spence that he regarded Quintilian "as an old favourite author." [91]

When, some years later, Joseph Warton published his *Essay on the Genius and Writings of Pope* (1756–1782), he took occasion to express his own estimate of the *Institutio* by saying:

To commend Quintilian barely for his method, and to insist merely on this excellence, is below the merit of one of the most rational and elegant of Roman writers. Considering the nature of Quintilian's subject, he affords copious matter for a more appropriated and poetical character. No author ever adorned a scientifical treatise with so many beautiful metaphors.[92]

Elsewhere in the *Essay,* Warton distributes his praise with such phrases as "perhaps the most judicious and elegant critic among the ancients"; "whose knowledge of human nature was consummate"; "the admirable tenth chapter of the twelfth book of Quintilian"; and "who speaks of the ancient painters and statuaries with so much taste and sentiment." [93]

The publication of Pope's *Essay* started a series of bitter quarrels. Addison praised the work in the *Spectator;* John Dennis denounced it in a "critical and satyrical" essay; and Lady Mary Wortley Montagu said she at first admired it very much until she read the ancient critics and found "that it was all stolen." As a result of this controversy, the eighteenth-century literary man must have been virtually forced to read or re-read Quintilian.

There are several instances of Samuel Johnson's liking for the *Institutio* in the *Lives of the Poets* [94] and in the *Rambler*.[95] In the first edition of Robert Dodsley's *Preceptor* (1748), Johnson outlined a rather strenuous program of training for children, and when he arrives at the advanced stage of the study of rhetoric, he advises thus: "For a farther progress in these studies, they may consult Quintilian and Vossius's Rhetoric." [96] P. H. Houston has recently pointed out that, although the actual references to the *Institutio* by Johnson are few in number, yet they are sufficient to prove it had been the object of his careful study. Houston also reminds us that Quintilian and Johnson performed similar services in criticism for their respective ages, and concludes that "Quintilian's writings must have become a part of Johnson's intellectual being." [97]

The popular interest in literary criticism in the middle of the eighteenth century is illustrated by the offer of the Edinburgh Society for the Encouragement of Arts of a gold medal for the best essay on the subject of taste. In 1756 the award was made to Alexander Gerard, professor of moral philosophy at Mareschal College, Aberdeen. In his *Essays on Taste*, published in 1759, Gerard gives this opinion:

> Longinus, Dionysius of Halicarnaceus, and Aristotle, all possessed fine taste. But it will scarce be denied that the first peculiarly excelled in *sensibility*, the second in *refinement*, and the last in *correctness* and *enlargement*. There is none of the ancients in whom all the four appear to have been equally, or in a higher degree, combined than in Quintilian.[98]

Altogether there are some half-dozen useful adaptations from the *Institutio* in Gerard's essay.[99]

There remain three other important witnesses of the eighteenth century whose testimony is worth quoting. While serving as a captain in the South Hampshire militia at Ringwood, Edward Gibbon wrote in his journal for June 6, 1762:

> I formed a design (but I doubt whether I shall find time to execute it) to give part of my day to Homer, and part to Quintilian; that is, to unite the example with the precept. Accordingly, I began with Quintilian, in Burman's edition; read his article in Bayle's *Dictionary*, the preface of Burman. Burman was a mere critic, without being (in my opinion) a good one, since a good

critic must reason well; and Burman never could reason at all. I began likewise the *Annales Quintilianaei* of Dodwell, and read C. 1–3.[100]

Lord Chesterfield, whom Boswell called the best speaker in the House
of Lords, paid his respects to Quintilian several times in his writings.
In a letter to his son from London, dated June 21, 1748, Chesterfield is
much exercised over a report of bad enunciation and admonishes:

> Good God! If this ungraceful and disagreeable manner of speaking had,
> either by your negligence or mine, become more habitual to you, as in a couple
> of years more it would have been, what a figure you would have made in
> company or in a public assembly! Who would have liked you in the one, or
> attended to you in the other? Read what Cicero and Quintilian say of enuncia-
> tion, and see what stress they lay upon the gracefulness of it.[101]

The advice must have been followed, for on November 24, 1749, we
find Chesterfield again writing:

> You have read Quintilian, the best book in the world to form an orator;
> pray read Cicero *De Oratore,* the best book in the world to finish one. Trans-
> late and re-translate, from and to Latin, Greek, and English. Make yourself
> a pure and elegant English style; it requires nothing but application.[102]

The last book I shall quote from for the eighteenth century is not
well known. It is called *Personal Nobility: or, Letters to a Young Nobleman on the Conduct of his Studies, and the Dignity of the Peerage.*
This was published in 1793 by the Rev. Vicesmius Knox, and was
dedicated to Charles James Fox. It is characterized by a respectful
admiration for the classics, and reads as from a man of unusual good
judgment. Cicero is the author's approved model for the English nobleman, and the assiduous imitation of his speeches is the way to perfection. But, for the study of rhetorical theory, Knox unreservedly
prescribes the *Institutio,* saying:

> But I recommend Quintilian; he is indeed a most excellent writer, and
> worthy of your study for his goodness of heart and his general good sense,
> independently of his instruction as a master of rhetoric.
> As a master of rhetoric, he is the best qualified of any I know to introduce
> you to a knowledge of the excellencies of Cicero and Demosthenes. . . .
> If I should tell you how greatly I admire Quintilian, you would attribute
> my praises to the prejudice of an unreasonable partiality. I have long made
> him my companion; and I know no author in didactics that equals the merit of
> Quintilian. If you anxiously desire improvement, read Quintilian repeatedly.[103]

Quintilian's Witnesses

Noteworthy books on public speaking and composition in the nineteenth century are relatively few. An interest in eloquence was a logical and proper outgrowth of the age of classicism of the preceding century. But with the passing of that age, and indeed, almost with the death in 1797 of Burke, its last great representative, we find a decreasing number of works on rhetoric and eloquence. It is true that popular treatises like the lectures of Ward, Lawson, and Blair continued to be published and used well into the eighteen hundreds. But, for the most part, the new productions are neither numerous nor significant.

Included in that amazing list of books which Lord Byron says he read before he was fifteen is the Reverend Gilbert Austin's *Chironomia, or a Treatise on Rhetorical Delivery* (1806). Exhibiting a detailed knowledge of Cicero and Quintilian, Austin refers to the *Institutio* over a hundred times. In Chapter IV, "Of Gesture," there is an evaluation of the two ancient authorities as follows:

Cicero has said something upon it [Delivery], valuable indeed, as everything must be from him, but extremely short. To Quintilian we are indebted for the most extensive, and the best, treatise which antiquity has left us; he has devoted nearly a whole book of his *Institutes* to the subject of delivery, and has given many excellent precepts.[104]

After explaining the wide range of subjects which the study of oratory comprised in the days of Domitian, Austin comments:

The education of the British youth seems to have been modeled upon the very plan of Quintilian. All the learning of the ancients is their study; they read their historians, their poets, their orators, their philosophers; they comment upon them, they commit them to memory, they write expressly in imitation of their most beautiful passages.[105]

As proof that Quintilian was studied in the universities, we find Bishop Copleston, in his famous *Reply to the Calumnies of the Edinburgh Review*, explaining the content of the examination in Rhetoric and Ethics at Oxford in 1810:

Besides these treatises of Aristotle, Quintilian as belonging to Rhetoric, and the philosophical works of Cicero, especially the *De Officiis* as belonging to Ethics, are admitted.[106]

I suppose the most unwitting admirer of Quintilian's doctrine in recent times was the poet, Algernon Swinburne. He devoted almost a third of his book, *A Study of Ben Jonson*, to critical praise of *Discoveries*—of which a part of section 114, on the training of children, receives special commendation. Swinburne says of this:

> If the nineteenth century has anything on this subect as well worth hearing —as wise, as humane, as reasonable, as full of sympathy and of judgment— as these reflections and animadversions of a scholar living in the first half or quarter of the seventeenth, I have never chanced to meet with it.[107]

Although he mentioned Quintilian on the preceding page, clearly Swinburne was unaware that much of the thought of his favorite excerpt is to be found in the *Institutio*, 1.3.7, and 1.3.13.[108] Nor was he conscious of the cento-like character of *Discoveries* with its very pronounced indebtedness to Quintilian. Otherwise the encomium: "A single leaf of his *Discoveries* is worth all his lyrics, tragedies, and epigrams together," [109] might not have been written.

Perhaps the most distinguished English prose-writer to admire the *Institutio* was Thomas De Quincey. In his essay, *Rhetoric*, published in *Blackwood's Magazine* for December, 1828, De Quincey held that rhetorical method was best taught by the Greeks, but adds:

> In reality, for a triumph over the difficulties of the subject, and as a lesson on the possibility of imparting grace to the treatment of scholastic topics naturally as intractable as Grammar or Prosody, there is no such *chef-d'œuvre* to this hour in any literature as the *Institutions* of Quintilian. Laying this one case out of the comparison however, the Greek superiority was indisputable.[110]

Both Lord Macaulay [111] and Lord Beaconsfield [112] were fond of Quintilian. And so was John Stuart Mill. In his *Autobiography*, Mill relates his studies at the age of twelve:

> At this time I also read the whole of Tacitus, Juvenal, and Quintilian. The latter, owing to his obscure style and to scholastic details, of which many parts of his treatise are made up, is little read and seldom sufficiently appreciated. His book is a kind of encyclopædia of the thoughts of the ancients on the whole field of education and culture; and I have retained through life many valuable ideas which I can distinctly trace to my reading of him, even at that early age.[113]

RECENT YEARS

Among the university scholars of recent years who have highly praised the critical opinions of Quintilian, are, to name only three,

Professors George Saintsbury,[114] S. S. Laurie,[115] and John Churton Collins. When Sir Edmund Gosse published his badly conceived and inaccurate book, *From Shakespeare to Pope,* in 1885, Collins attracted attention with his brilliant review, *English Literature at the Universities.*[116] Here he vigorously defended the study of classical rhetoric by saying:

> How can a teacher deal adequately even with the subject which these regulations profess to include—the history of criticism—who need have no acquaintance with the *Poetics* and the *Rhetoric,* the *Treatise on the Sublime,* and the *Institutes of Oratory?*[117]

A few years later, Collins even more forcibly deplored the state of affairs at Oxford and Cambridge:

> We have absolutely no provision for systematic critical training. Rhetorical criticism as a subject of teaching is confined to what is known in elementary schools as "analysis." Aesthetic and philosophical criticism is a branch of teaching without recognition at all. It has been killed by philology. Fifty years ago such works as the *Institutes of Oratory,* the *De Sublimatate,* and the *Rhetoric* were studied as thoroughly and methodically as the *Ethics* and *Republic* are now. And till that study is revived and extended—till, in addition to the treatises of the ancients, such treatises as the *Laocoön,* and Schiller's *Letters and Essays on Aesthetic Education* have a place in our Universities—there is small hope of sound principles in exegesis.[118]

In the same volume the writer cites the tenth book of the *Institutio,* along with four other works, as the "foundation of a sound critical education." [119] In the judgment of Professor Collins "the only door to the teaching of Milton lies through Quintilian and Longinus." [120]

Conclusion

The *Institutio Oratoria* of Quintilian was known in England long before Poggio's discovery of the manuscript in 1416. The work attained high favor and great reputation in the Renaissance, and again in the eighteenth-century age of classicism. At intervals, and sometimes for long periods, the *Institutio* has remained in the background. But, as our study shows, for well over five hundred years students and scholars have been able to approach and to apply the great Roman teacher's precepts on public speaking, literary criticism, educational theory, and the philosophy of a cultivated gentleman. That the educated Englishman has amply profited from the study of Quintilian and of the other great masters, Aristotle, Plato, and Cicero of course, is attested and reflected in his literature, his educational system, and his culture generally. We of this generation, immersed as we are in a confusion of purposes, misled by the fallacious judgments of our educational specialists, and lost in our efforts to seek a correct method, should find as Erasmus, Vives, Elyot, Ben Jonson, Pope, Samuel Johnson, De Quincey, and Blair found, a stimulating, clarifying, and substantial help in the advice of the first public Professor of Rhetoric of Rome.

Thomas Wilson's Contributions

to Rhetoric

RUSSELL H. WAGNER

WILSON'S *Art of Rhetorique*, 1553, has received attention from scholars because it is the first complete work in English on the subject. Cox, in his *Arte or Crafte of Rhethoryke*, 1531, aimed to treat invention alone. Sherry's *Treatise of Tropes and Schemes*, 1550, is confined to figurative language. A lesser reason for interest in Wilson is the fact that his *Rhetorique* was popular in its day; it was published eight times between 1553 and 1585. Another is Wilson's own prominence, for he was not only the author of the first *Logic*, and the first translator of Demosthenes in English, but also Secretary of State under Elizabeth.

These facts, however, only raise the question: "How significant, if significant at all, is Wilson's *Rhetorique?*" The answer, to be complete, would be not only difficult but long. But if we pose a narrower question: "What distinctive contributions to rhetorical theory, especially to the theory of public address, did Wilson make?" we may be able to suggest some answers to the larger query.

By contributions, let us understand not absolutely original ideas, of which there are few in any age, and very few in such a period as Wilson's. Let us understand principles from whatever source derived, but which bear, in formulation, those marks of originality we ourselves accept today—selection, assimilation, change in concept, in application, or in emphasis. If we can also observe the persistence of these concepts among later writers, we may reinforce our answer.

The first and the most important contribution of all has already been mentioned—the completeness of Wilson's treatise. Wilson was the first to re-assemble, in English, the lost, strayed, or stolen doctrines of rhetoric. For some centuries before Wilson wrote, the possessions of rhetoric had been absorbed, for the most part, by sister arts or sciences, or lost entirely. *Inventio* had been recaptured by logic, *dispositio* figured little except in arts of preaching, *elocutio* was partially enveloped by grammar and poetics. *Memoria* and *pronuntiatio* had almost completely disappeared. Cox, in his truncated work, attempted to interpret *inventio* as a rhetorical doctrine to school children. But Sherry's *Tropes and Schemes,* also a school text-book, reveals the more typical sixteenth century conception of rhetoric.

Exceptions can be found, of course. Trapezuntius and Caesarius, for example, treat all the departments of rhetoric, though more in the manner of mediaeval writers who are bent on preserving antique doctrine than as functional contributors to the needs of a new age. The supposed exception of Talaeus is a doubtful one, for, until after Wilson's *Rhetorique* appeared, Talaeus' *Rhetoric* contained nothing of invention or disposition. Erasmus would be by far the greatest exception, were it not for the fact that his re-discoveries and contributions are not made under the title of rhetoric, but are sparpled through other works, philological and homiletic, and are, even taken as a whole, an incomplete reconstruction. Moreover, Erasmus, like Talaeus and Trapezuntius, wrote in Latin.

Thus, it was Wilson's task to re-assemble, under the head of rhetoric, all the scattered principles which in ancient times had been thought indispensable to the complete art of the orator. He added to this task another, that of making his rhetoric useful to men in his time by writing it in their native language and by adapting it to their needs. Moreover, he wrote his book for the use of all—not merely school boys but, as he says, "For all such as are studious of eloquence"—for men of affairs and of state, for lawyers and preachers. Croll, in his *Introduction to Lyly's Euphues,* observes that Wilson's book "was too advanced for use in schools or even in colleges." [1] It appears, therefore, that Wilson's is the first rhetoric since Quintilian's to give a full and unified treatment of the best of the classical doctrines and to make them really useful in the world of practical affairs.

Thomas Wilson's Contributions

The concept underlying this complete treatment of his subject is in itself important. Wilson conceives rhetoric as the art of discourse. First, it is art, or method—principles derived from observation of effective speakers, principles for use in real situations. It is not a faculty, nor a science of speaking well, nor a set of static, artificial conventions, but a pragmatic, dynamic body of principles. Thus he imprints upon our subject the hand of Cicero, the orator-statesman-philosopher of the *De Aratore,* not that of Hermagoras or of Aphthonius or of Mosellanus. That imprint it has borne ever since.

Moreover, it is oral discourse, mainly and typically. Rhetoric is recalled from its close association with grammar, poetics, school composition, and letter writing, to its ancient position as, first of all, the art of the orator. It is true that in his first sentence Wilson defines rhetoric very generally—"the art of setting forth matter at large, by utterance of words." We may believe that "utterance" here covers written and spoken language, and we note that written persuasion receives much attention, mainly under the head of deliberative oratory, but also in other sections. But the second sentence begins: "An Orator must be able to speak fully . . . ." And the orator is mentioned continuously thereafter. Nor is "orator" to Wilson merely a conventional term for any user of rhetoric, for example, a writer of rhetorical prose or verse, as we find it in some works of the time. The lawyer and the preacher—these are the orators meant, and their problems are much in Wilson's mind. They are reflected, for instance, in the frequent references to methods of keeping audiences awake and sympathetic with the speaker; and the sections on memory and delivery, which conclude the book, have meaning only for the speaker. Rhetoric, then, though it ministers to the needs of writers, is to Wilson, as to the Greeks, the art of the speaker; and so it has remained, consistently in British thought, less so in American.

At this point it is proper to ask why a work so thoroughly conceived as the art of the speaker, and devoting itself so consistently, with one exception, to the problems of speech-making, should be so continuously misrepresented by scholars generally? From Warton to Mair, literary historians and critics have regarded Wilson's *Rhetorique* as a book on style, mainly the style of written prose. Thus Warton, in 1778, called it "the first book or system of criticism in our language," [2] and commentators generally have chiefly regarded it as an antiquarian curiosity in the field of literary history. There is more than one reason for this mistaken view. Wilson's famous blast against "ink horn terms" has linked his work with the study of written composition. The style of the book seems difficult and archaic; the type and spelling of available editions magnify these impressions. Mair frankly confesses that for him the principles set forth make "no more cheerful reading" than in other writers.[3] In sum, we may conjecture that the misrepresentation has arisen from sheer failure to read the whole work with more than perfunctory attention. The fact remains, however, that our first rhetoric in English is a treatise dealing almost wholly with the art of public oral address.

Two or three special doctrines of Wilson's may be selected to exhibit the nature of his contributions to that art. The first concerns the importance of winning attention. On this Wilson is emphatic. Early in the book Wilson says that not only must the orator, early in his speech, "utter his mind in plain words, such as are usually received, and tell it orderly, without going about the bush," [4] but that he must speak so that "the ears may find much delight . . . for except men find delight, they will not long abide; delight them and win them; weary them and you lose them forever . . . therefore even these ancient preachers, must now and then play the fools in the pulpit . . . or else they are like sometimes to preach to the bare walls. . . ." [5] Later, under disposition, he begins by offering the usual classical advice on the best methods of "entrance" or exordium, but goes on to stress such other methods of capturing attention early as novelty ("strange news"), humor ("foolish tales"), the desirability of getting on common ground, oblique, tactful, methods of securing favorable consideration, arousing curiosity, and anticipation.

Closely associated with the unique stress on getting attention is the even greater emphasis on holding attention. One can hardly exaggerate the importance of this theme in Wilson's book. The very first sentences make rhetoric the art of amplifying—"of speaking largely." There is no doubt that Wilson was more impressed by Cicero's and Quintilian's praise of amplification as the peculiar and distinctive and highest quality of oratory, than by any other one precept in ancient rhetoric. "Among all the figures of Rhetoric," he says, "there is no one that so much helpeth forward an oration . . . as amplification." [6] Erasmus had taken the same view in De Copia and Ecclesiastes, and in both books had heavily emphasized amplification. Wilson with even more reason gave it stress in his English rhetoric for English speakers.

Thomas Wilson's Contributions

For this was the outstanding need of the age—skill in expressing ideas in a language which was just coming into general use—not alone skill in elaborating and enlarging the bare statement, but skill in intensifying, making more striking and effective what one had to say. The result is that throughout his work Wilson takes as his objective "copie" —amplification by examples, by sententious utterances, by variety of expression, by figurative language; to amplification he devotes almost one-fifth of the book, not counting topics closely related though not actually subordinated to this subject; emotional proof itself is made a sub-category of amplification; and Wilson's own style demonstrates what he seeks to teach.

Wilson, therefore, makes getting and holding attention the essential principle of effective oral discourse, and, with emotional proof, into which it rapidly fuses, the grand principle of persuasion. This concept and emphasis, differing from that of all his predecessors, is, of course, largely conditioned by the peculiar needs of the times. And whether right or wrong, whether Wilson has been directly influential or not, the principle persists in rhetorical theory today.

I have elsewhere [7] pointed out the lack of logical and ethical proof in Wilson's *Rhetorique*. In the main, Wilson's distinctions between logic and rhetoric, as those between rhetoric and poetic, and grammar, are so carefully made as to deserve special notice: far more than any previous writer in English, and more than almost all sixteenth century writers in any language, he restored and to some extent improved on the boundaries and lines of demarcation. In this one respect, however, his judgment may be questioned. His omission of ethical proof, whether influential or not, is probably to be deplored. His omission of logical proof—the apparatus of reasoning—which may have resulted from the well established hold which logic had on that topic—is less easily condemned. Modern theorists have long debated the subject, but the tendency has been, as in Wilson, to leave the logic of proof to logic, or to the applied logic of argumentation.

To an even greater extent, Wilson's emphasis on emotional proof marked a new departure and established a modern trend. Though emotional proof is nominally subordinated to amplification, it tends to become the chief method of securing and holding attention, and its image is visible in almost every page of the treatise. The methods of delighting and moving to pity early in the book are made the guiding principles of securing attention. Most of the long treatment of amplifi-

cation consists of suggestions on arousing varied emotions. And throughout the rest of the work, the methods of appealing to the feelings are
liberally interspersed. This concentration on emotional proof is unique
in rhetorical theory up to this time. Nor is Wilson reflecting contemporary practice, for, as Sir Thomas Elyot says, in respect of forensic
eloquence at least, "the sterynge of the affections of the mynde in this
realme was neuer used. . . ." [8] And this conception of persuasion and
of oral discourse generally, as, essentially, the securing of the desired
emotional response, has wide acceptance with us today.

The most famous contribution of Wilson—his strongly expressed
preference for plain, English words as opposed to "ink horn terms"—
strange, Latinate, Italianate, or Gallic importations—should not fail
to remind us of another signal contribution in the field of style: in an
age when rhetoric itself, quite generally, and *elocutio*, almost without
exception, meant adornment and beautifying by figurative terms, Wilson recalled style to its former status by insisting on plainness, aptness,
and sound composition, as indispensable qualities to be achieved *before* attention should be paid to the heightening of style by use of
figurative language.

There is significance too in Wilson's conception of composition. To
the ancients, *compositio* had meant word-combination for the sake of
rhythm and modulation; it had included no concepts of composition in
the large, as Baldwin justly observes.[9] But Wilson, under the head
of composition, gives only brief treatment to the subject of word-
joining, and proceeds to discuss such stylistic faults as prolixity, obscurity, crabbedness, pedantry, lack of variety and especially lack of
good order and coherence generally. For example, he says, "Some
burden their talk with needless copie, and will seem plentiful when
they should be short. . . . And some use so many interpositions, both
in their talk and in their writings, that they make their sayings as dark
as hell." Here we have, in embryonic form, a statement of those broad
and pervasive qualities of style with which we have become so familiar
—unity, coherence and emphasis,—with clearness and brevity added
for good measure. This may be the first statement of the principles of
composition, in English, as we today conceive them.

Enough has been said of the novelty in Wilson's presentation of
rhetorical doctrine to lay the ghost conjured up by Hallam in 1843
and re-evoked by Jebb, Saintsbury, and others: "Wilson embodied
rules chiefly from Aristotle, with help from Cicero and Quintilian." [10]

Thomas Wilson's Contributions

In re-uniting, selecting, and adapting the classical principles of public address, Wilson restored the body and, to some extent, reformed the concepts of rhetorical theory. In recalling rhetoric from the museum to the market-place, he not only re-established the ancient conception of rhetoric as the art of the speaker, but, because of his own self-imposed purpose of adapting old doctrines to new times and new needs, he effected far reaching changes which have greatly influenced the theories of public address we hold today.

Bacon's Conception of Rhetoric

KARL R. WALLACE

THE esteem in which scholars hold Francis Bacon is tribute to his penetrating intellect. Historians of logic and of science usually examine his contribution to the method of scientific investigation. His entire system of thought finds a place in every history of modern philosophy. He claims respect from the historiographers of psychology and of ethics. Even the literary historians have regarded Bacon as among the first to suggest the real scope and method of literary history.[1] In brief, Bacon's utterances on many subjects, both in their content and their felicity of expression, have had an enduring quality. In view of his place in intellectual history, then, it would appear that his thoughts on the art of public address, as on other subjects, merit study. The purpose of this essay, accordingly, is to set forth in general Bacon's rhetorical theory, its special function and province, and some of the more important topics with which it must deal. To set out in detail Bacon's views on rhetorical address would require a volume; the present study aims to be merely an introductory chapter.

For such a study the most valuable of Bacon's writings are *The Advancement of Learning* and its expanded Latin version, *De Augmentis Scientiarum*. In these cyclopedic works Bacon deals with rhetoric and its essential nature more fully and accurately than elsewhere. This investigation, accordingly, regards the view of rhetoric as presented in the *Advancement* and the *De Augmentis* as the *sine qua non* of rhetorical discourse, takes the rhetorical allusions garnered from Bacon's other writings, and attempts to harmonize them with the rhetoric of the cyclopedia.

114

Bacon's Conception

The rhetorical remarks in the cyclopedia unfortunately do not form a well-developed, nicely-proportioned survey of rhetoric; rather, they pick out and throw into relief those elements which Bacon thought had been neglected. For the most part, the *Advancement* tells us, "the science which we call Rhetoric, or Art of Eloquence" has, in the past, been "excellently well laboured." [2] Hence, Bacon declares, he will write rather of the deficiencies which may "as handmaids attend the art, than in the rules and use of the art itself." [3] He will, however, particularly note the duty and function of rhetoric as it differs from the duty and office of logic and ethics, and will "open and stir the earth a little, according to my custom, about the roots of this subject." [4] We may expect, then, not a systematic exposition of theory, but merely a number of suggestions, some practical, some philosophical; and from these we may infer Bacon's conception of rhetorical address.

With penetration and dispatch, Bacon himself characterizes rhetoric in two sentences that may well comprise the core of his entire theory. "The duty and office of Rhetoric," Bacon asserts in the *Advancement*, 1605, "is *to apply Reason to Imagination* for the better moving of the will." [5] Eighteen years later, in the *De Augmentis,* he saw no reason for altering materially the earlier statement, still satisfied to express it in terms of a faculty psychology: "The duty and office of Rhetoric, if it be deeply looked into, is no other than to apply and recommend the dictates of reason to imagination, in order to excite the appetite and the will." [6]

Such a definition suggests that the end of rhetorical endeavor is persuasion, that is, the influencing of conduct; and to some extent the function of the faculties of the mind, as they appear in the Baconian psychology, bears out this interpretation. Although, according to Bacon, we may know very little concerning the *substance* of the mind, with its *faculties* we are well acquainted: they comprise the "understanding, reason, imagination, memory, appetite, will; in short, all with which the logical and ethical sciences deal." [7] It is in accordance with the use and function of these faculties that Bacon distinguishes two important parts of philosophy: ethics, and what he terms the Four Intellectual Arts, or logic. And logic, we perceive, "discourses of the Understanding and Reason; Ethics of the Will, Appetite, and Affections: the one produces determinations, the other actions." [8] In Bacon's view, then, the mind employs its faculties either as instruments of knowing or as means of action; and when he says that rhetoric operates to excite the appetite

115

and the will, it appears that although not, like Aristotle,[9] specifically employing in his definition the word *persuasion*, Bacon intends to say that rhetorical address is pre-eminently the art which directly influences human behaviour. Indeed, wherever Bacon alludes to a rhetorical situation, he customarily describes it as persuasive. When he refers to the means of resolving the bitter debate between Anglican and Puritan, he warns the government that "consciences are not to be forced, but to be won and reduced by the force of truth, with the aid of time and the use of all good means of instruction and persuasion." [10] At another time he recommends to William Cecil that the English religion is the most effective means of restoring the affection of the Irish toward England, the method of "advancing religion" to be principally "the sending over of some good preachers, especially of the sort which are vehement and zealous persuaders, and not scholastical, to be resident in principal towns. . . ." [11] Again, in a little treatise entitled *Helps for the Intellectual Powers*, Bacon holds that the will, a most obedient faculty, may be readily swayed by "Opinion and Apprehension; whether it be infused by tradition and institution, or wrought in by disputation and persuasion." [12] It seems manifest, therefore, that in Bacon's view rhetorical address is that species of discourse which seeks to persuade.

Bacon recognizes as other species of discourse, the didactic and the scientific, each having an end somewhat different from that of exciting the appetite and the will. The *Advancement* and the *De Augmentis* suggest, under the head of "Method of Discourse" or Disposition, a classification of prose according to the nature of the audience addressed and the purpose intended.[13] Broadly considered, audiences are either general—the common run of men and learners, or select—critical men of some learning, particularly those interested in the advancement of knowledge. The first group gives rise to didactic discourse, the second to scientific or aphoristic writing. Such a classification is explicity stated in an early work, *Of the Interpretation of Nature*, in which Bacon represents himself as teacher and scientist:

There are forms and methods of tradition wholly distinct and differing, according to their ends whereunto they are directed. . . . there are two ends of tradition of knowledge, the one to teach and instruct for use and practice, the other to impart or intimate for re-examination and progression. . . . the former of these ends requireth a method not the same whereby it was invented and induced, but such as is most compendious and ready whereby it may be used and applied. . . . the latter of these ends, which is where a knowledge is delivered to be continued and spun on by a succession of labours, requireth a method whereby it may be transposed to another in the same manner as it was collected, to the end it may be discerned both where the work is weak, and where it breaketh off.[14]

It is probable, therefore, that Bacon does not wish to include rhetoric as a branch of didactic or of scientific discourse, but reserves for rhetoric the function of exciting the will.

Within the genus of rhetorical discourse Bacon distinguishes a number of species: the deliberative or political speech, aiming to establish the good or evil of a course of action; the forensic speech, aiming at justice; and the occasional speech, determining the praise or blame due to a person or his actions.[15] Bacon, it is apparent, preserves the traditional kinds of rhetorical address first set forth by Aristotle. In addition, by referring to the preachers as "zealous persuaders,"[16] Bacon seems to include preaching as a kind of rhetorical endeavor, although he does not explicitly name it as a type. Finally, it appears probable that he regarded private conversation, particularly that occurring in diplomatic negotiations, as a form of persuasive discourse, since he recommends the study of private discourse as a means of giving the speaker facility in adapting his speech to his auditor:

The application and variety of speech, in perfection of idea, ought to extend so far, that if a man should speak of the same thing to several persons, he should nevertheless use different words to each of them; though this political and familiar part of eloquence in private discourse it is certain that the greatest orators commonly want; while in observing their well graced forms of speech, they lose that volubility of application, and those characters of style, which it would be better to use in addressing different individuals.[17]

Bacon therefore suggests a fresh inquiry, to be called *The Wisdom of Private Discourse*, and adds that "whether it be placed in rhetoric or in policy, is a matter of little moment." [18]

As Bacon understands it, rhetorical discourse thus has as its end the moving of men to action. But to this statement of the function of rhetoric, Bacon adds a significant qualification. He believes that rhetoric lives up to its true function only by presenting pictures of conduct that is virtuous and good. He extends scant sympathy to Plato for condemning rhetoric merely because some men, by skillful application of its principles, make the worse appear the better reason, while others, through bungling attempts at artistry, manage only to destroy the natural force of reason:

It was a great injustice in Plato (though springing out of a just hatred of the rhetoricians of his time) to place rhetoric among arts voluptuary; resembling it to cookery, which did as much to spoil wholesome meats, as by variety and delicacy of sauces to make unwholesome meats more palatable. But God forbid that speech should not be much more conversant in adorning that which is good, than in colouring that which is evil; for this is a thing in use everywhere; there being no man but speaks more honestly than he thinks or acts.[19]

Bacon adds that Plato said most elegantly and truly " 'that virtue, if she could be seen, would move great love and affection' "; consequently, "it is the business of rhetoric to make pictures of virtue and goodness, so that they may be seen." [20] When virtue cannot be shown by human example, or, as Bacon expresses it, "cannot be shewed to the Sense by corporeal shape, the next degree is to shew her to the Imagination in lively representation." [21]

Beyond perceiving the end of rhetorical discourse, its species and its ethical function, we must understand what Bacon means when he writes that rhetoric should "apply Reason to Imagination." Here he seems to have in mind a special function for the imagination. This aspect of mental activity acts as a messenger between the reasoning faculty on the one hand and the will on the other:

The Imagination is an agent or *nuncius* in both provinces, both the judicial and the ministerial. For Sense sendeth over to Imagination before Reason hath judged: and Reason sendeth over to Imagination before the Decree can be acted; for Imagination ever precedeth Voluntary Motion: saving that this Janus of Imagination hath differing faces; for the face towards Reason hath the print of Truth, but the face towards Action hath the print of Good. . . .[22]

What Bacon seems to mean is that the use of language is always accompanied in some degree either by a picture of the objective world or by a picture of the words themselves. If one is engaged in scientific inquiry, the imaginative accompaniment of language has the face of truth, for the end of science is the discovery of truth; if one is concerned with human conduct and behaviour, with the influencing of men in society, the imaginative picture evoked by language has the face of Good, for the goal of ethics is right action. In short, without the aid of the imagination, human reason cannot operate and the human will cannot decide upon a line of action.

By making the imagination a messenger, Bacon forsakes his first classification of knowledge, in which the imagination is related to poetry. As he began to write the *Advancement*, he had specified the imagination, along with reason and memory, as one of the three rational faculties: "The parts of human learning have reference to the three parts of Man's Understanding, . . . History to his Memory, Poesy to his Imagination, and Philosophy to his Reason." [23] Later in the same work, however, occurs the observation that "the knowledge which respecteth the Faculties of the Mind of man is of two kinds: the one respecting his Understanding and Reason, and the other his Will, Appetite, and Affection. . . ." [24] The imagination has disappeared from the list of faculties to which the chief divisions of knowledge are referred, and along with it, poetry. Bacon's motive for withdrawing the imagination from the list of faculties is reasonably clear. His entire system of thought, founded on the assumption that progress constitutes the gradual extension and dominance of reason over emotion, is incompatible with the irrational function of the creative imagination in its production of poetry. The imagination in its creative capacity obeys no law:

Poesy is a part of learning in measure of words for the most part restrained, but in all other points extremely licensed, and doth truly refer to the imagination; which, not being tied to the laws of matter, may at pleasure join that which nature hath severed, and sever that which nature hath joined. . . .[25]

The lawless action of the creative imagination is again apparent when Bacon contrasts the two imitative arts, poetry and history:

Poesy . . . is . . . concerned with individuals; that is, with individuals invented in imitation of those which are the subject of true history; yet with this difference, that it commonly exceeds the measure of nature, joining at pleasure things which in nature would never have come together, and introducing things which in nature would never have come to pass; just as Painting likewise does. This is the work of Imagination.[26]

Thus we can understand why Bacon distrusts the imagination and why his final word on the subject somewhat scornfully dismisses poesy from serious consideration: ". . . imagination hardly produces sciences; poesy (which in the beginning was referred to imagination) being to be accounted rather as a pleasure or play of wit than a science." [27]

Such a conception of the imagination is of extraordinary significance to rhetoric, for it means that the *creative* imagination—that which joins at pleasure things which in nature would never have come together—has no place in rhetorical address. The sole function of the imagination in speaking or writing is to render logical argument attractive and pleasing; the imagination merely translates logical inference into pictures. Thus when Bacon writes that rhetoric applies reason to imagination, he means that rhetorical address must be, always and foremost, logically sound; imaginative dress, although highly desirable, is not fundamental. The true rhetorician, in Bacon's view, therefore does not teach his pupil to use *any* idea which may prove "effective" on a given occasion, for if a speaker justifies the means by the end only, he will be tempted by what Bacon picturesquely calls "the jugglers of words," [28] a practice that, subtly assailing the government of reason, is "well compared by Seneca to the feats of jugglers in which though we know not how the thing is done, yet we know well it is not as it seems to be." [29]

Some people speak of rhetoric today as that study which deals with the art of *spoken* address. But Bacon apparently intends that the medium of rhetorical discourse may be written language as well as oral, a conclusion that clearly emerges from a proper appreciation of the position of rhetoric in the cyclopedia. An important branch of philosophy is called the "Four Intellectual Arts"; the Arts are divided, Bacon declares, "according to the ends whereunto they are referred; for men's labour is to *invent* [30] that which is *sought* or *propounded;* or to *judge* that which is *invented;* or to *retain* that which is *judged;* or to *deliver over* that which is *retained.* So . . . the arts must be four: Art of Inquiry or Invention; Art of Examination or Judgment; Art of Custody or Memory; and Art of Elocution or Tradition." [31] The Arts of Invention and of Memory, as we shall observe later, are necessary to rhetorical address. So also is the Art of Judgment, which deals with proofs and demonstrations. But in the Art of Elocution—called in the *De Augmentis* the Art of Transmission—we at last locate rhetoric. The Art of Elocution, we observe, is for Bacon the art of communication:

Let us now proceed to the Art of Transmitting, or of producing and expressing to others those things which have been invented, judged, and laid up in the memory; which I will call by a general name the Art of Transmission. This art includes all the arts which relate to words and discourse. . . . The art of transmission I will divide into three parts; the doctrine concerning the Organ of Discourse, the doctrine concerning the Method of Discourse, and the doctrine concerning the Illustration or adornment of Discourse.[32]

The Illustration of Discourse, Bacon explains, is rhetoric. Thus, in regarding rhetoric as one of the three parts of the Art of Elocution, he intends it to share the function of communicating knowledge with the other arts of transmission; namely, the Organ and the Method of Discourse.

The Organ of Discourse deals with a theory of language. The language employed may have considerable similarity in sound, in sign, or in movement with the notions expressed, or it may operate by conventional characters whose meanings have been agreed upon. In the first class fall speech, hieroglyphics, and gesture; in the second, written language whose symbolic meaning may be either emblematic or representative.[33] The science of speech and words, the *De Augmentis* explains, is customarily called Grammar, "the harbinger of other sciences; an office not indeed very noble, yet very necessary. . . ."[34]

The Method of Discourse, Bacon's second division of the Art of Transmission, constitutes a "principal" part of the communication or "delivering over" of knowledge.[35] By "Method" is meant primarily a way or technique of organizing and expressing subject matter according to the end sought and the audience addressed. One method is by dichotomy, another by assertions and proofs, and yet another by questions with determinations, or, in other words, by dialectic. Some methods depend upon the type of subject-matter handled and upon the auditors, whether they be the speaker's critics or his pupils; other methods, as has already been observed, are determined by the author's purpose, whether his discourse be designed to explain or to win consent.

Such a division of the Art of Transmission into the Organ, Method, and Illustration of Discourse, we notice, does not result in mutually exclusive parts, nor in parts co-ordinate in value; the divisions clearly overlap. Bacon makes the partition thus, because he wishes to emphasize that the process of communication involves correct choice of the medium to be employed, order and arrangement to be followed, and the selection and adornment of ideas according to the purpose at hand. It follows, accordingly, that rhetoric as the art of persuasive discourse may properly be said to employ any language-medium it sees fit, providing reason is recommended to the imagination of the audience. This assertion, together with the omission in Bacon's works of any statement specifically limiting rhetoric either to the spoken word or to the written symbol, implies that rhetorical discourse operates through language, oral or written. Bacon's ultimate division of discourse, we remember, is tri-partite: the didactic, the scientific, and the rhetorical; at no time does he suggest a classification of prose according to the medium of communication. In fact, the only evidence that would seem to limit rhetoric to oral discourse is Bacon's tendency, when writing of rhetoric somewhat at length, to refer to the "orator" and to "speech."

The end of rhetoric, as we have seen, is the influencing of right action through the medium of oral or written discourse. In the Baconian conception of rhetoric there is included, furthermore, explicit means whereby persuasive discourse is to achieve its end. Bacon clearly recognizes that the speaker who recommends the dictates of reason to imagination in order to excite the appetite and the will ought, above all, to regard logical reasoning as his cardinal means of proof. Like Plato and Aristotle, he feels that reason is "the soul of discourse." [36] Especially in the deliberative type of address, as distinguished from the forensic and the epideictic, topics of good and evil may be developed most soundly by "true and solid reasons." [37] Accordingly, rhetoric may legitimately consider the types of argument known as the syllogism and the example, although by right they belong to logic. A second means of proof, intrinsically related to the special function of rhetoric, may be called "imaginative appeal"; the chief problem of rhetorical address is to render logical argument vivid, and hence any language-symbols which will engage the imaginative faculty of an audience will make acceptable the logic of the discourse. By "imaginative appeal," then, is meant in part ideas whose *content* incites the imagination and in part a style of expression which translates passionless reason into vivid terms.

Of the two kinds of proof that find a place in the Baconian idea of rhetorical address, the more important is clearly logical argument or reasoning. Public address, in urging virtuous actions upon men, should make reason the basis of its plea, and imaginative appeal therefore becomes only a servant. Bacon thus evaluates the types of proof, because, in the first place, he distrusts the power of the imagination when uncontrolled. In his psychology the imagination, as we have hitherto observed, properly fulfills one of its functions by acting as a messenger between the reason and the affections. Normally the imagination is under the restraint of reason, but occasionally it slips off its shackles and springs up, free and powerful:

Neither is the imagination simply and only a messenger; but it is either invested with or usurps no small authority in itself, besides the simple duty of the message. For it was well said by Aristotle, "That mind has over the body that commandment which the lord has over a bondman; but that reason has over the imagination that commandment which a magistrate has over a free citizen," who may come also to rule in his turn. . . . It is no small dominion which imagination holds in persuasions that are wrought by eloquence; for when by arts of speech men's minds are soothed, inflamed, and carried hither and thither, it is all done by stimulating the imagination till it becomes ungovernable, and not only sets reason at naught, but offers violence to it, partly by blinding, partly by incensing it. . . .[38]

Man's conduct, consequently, ought ever to be governed by reason; but as society is constituted, Bacon points out, the proper functioning of the reasoning faculty is disturbed by three agencies: sophistical reasoning, vehement and ambiguous catch-words and phrases, and unbridled passion.[39] To combat these agencies and to promote the rule of reason is the grand social purpose of logic, ethics, and rhetoric:

For the end of logic is to teach a form of argument to secure reason, and not to entrap it; the end likewise of moral philosophy is to procure the affections to fight on the side of reason, and not to invade it; the end of rhetoric is to fill the imagination with observations and images, to second reason, and not to oppress it.[40]

Rhetoric, then, like its psychological counterparts, becomes an instrument of reason, and in the exposition of his theory, the rhetorician must recommend and explain the theory of logical proof as applied to persuasive discourse. We are not surprised, therefore, to discover that most of the passages in which Bacon treats of rhetoric explicitly deal with the invention of arguments. With rhetorical invention, however, we shall deal later.

Bacon insists on the primacy of logical proof, in the second place, because in his psychology the reason is long-sighted, the emotions short-sighted. Both the affections and the reason in their normal activity naturally impel the individual to do good. The affections, however, are inferior guides to conduct, for they regard only immediate or *present* action. Reason, on the other hand, looks to *future* actions, and hence is the superior guide. The imagination, standing between the affections on the one side and reason on the other, may ally itself with either. If to the passions, then the individual is impelled to short-sighted acts; if to the reason, then the individual moves with better direction, for the imagination mirrors the future as though it were the present. Or, in Bacon's concise phraseology:

The affections themselves carry ever an appetite to good, as reason doth; the difference is, that *the affection beholdeth merely the present; reason beholdeth the future and sum of time;* and therefore, the present filling the imagination more, reason is commonly vanquished; but after that force of eloquence and persuasion hath made things future and remote appear as present, then upon the revolt of the imagination reason prevaileth.[41]

Reason would become captive and servile, Bacon continues, "if Eloquence of Persuasions did not practice and win the Imagination from the Affection's part, and contract a confederacy between the Reason and Imagination against the Affections." [42] In Bacon's view, then, rhetoric provides a body of rules whereby the dictates of reason are applied to the imagination for the better moving of the will.

The enlistment of rhetoric in the cause of rational living is of course an integral part of Bacon's scheme to advance learning. If true knowledge is unearthed, according to his great method of scientific inquiry as presented in the *Novum Organum,* eloquent men must aid in its communication. Scientists and learned men may dig profound truths "out of the hard mine of history and experience," but such knowledge, "except it be delivered with strange advantages of eloquence and power, may be likely to appear and disclose a little to the world and straight to vanish and shut again." [43]

Perhaps Bacon's activity as a lawyer, the logical bent of his nature, and his desire to reform scientific inference all contribute to the emphasis that is given to reason as it appears in rhetoric. But whatever the forces at work, the emphasis is clear and unmistakable. In fact, Bacon is not content with merely asserting that rhetorical proof ought to be fundamentally logical; at one time he actually classifies rhetoric as a part of logic. In the cyclopedia, logic is used to describe the Four Intellectual Arts: the arts of Invention, of Judgment, of Memory, and of Transmission. According to this conception of logical activity, then, rhetoric as part of the Art of Transmission is also part of logic. Bacon's works, it is to be observed, contain many evidences of disapproval that certain sixteenth century theorists should have limited the scope of rhetoric to the "garnishing" of language and speech,[44] and it is perhaps in protest that the *Advancement* brings rhetorical address within the field of logic.

Bacon recognizes as kinds of logical proof open to rhetorical discourse the syllogism and the example, but discusses neither form systematically. He is much more interested in the errors of inference against which rhetorical discourse, as well as logic and science, must ever be on guard if the speaker is to apply reason to imagination for the better moving of the will. Three main classes of fallacy emerge from Bacon's logic; sophistical fallacies, fallacies of interpretation, and the famous Idols.[45] The sophistical fallacy is an inference which on the surface appears correct, but upon examination does not prove to be so. Sometimes "the more subtle sophisms not only put a man beside his answer, but many times seriously confound his judgment." [46] Consequently, Bacon offers to the deliberative speaker or writer as an aid in detecting sophistical reasoning the little tract, *Colours of Good and Evil*,[47] a compilation of generalizations that have become commonplace in discussion as ultimate premises of an argument. They consist for the most part of propositions whose fallacies rest on faulty induction and faulty connections. Fallacies of interpretation are errors caused by ambiguous meanings inherent in common and general notions. To them rhetorical discourse should pay special attention:

For common and general notions enter necessarily into every discussion; so that unless care be taken to distinguish them well at the outset, all the light of disputations will be strangely clouded with darkness by them, and the matter end in disputes about words. For equivocations and false acceptations of words (especially of this sort) are the sophisms of sophisms.[48]

As for the Idols, Bacon never specifically connects them with rhetoric, but it is possible that, if he had worked out a comprehensive theory of rhetorical address, their utility would have been indicated. Since the Idols deal with the errors to which the mind by its very constitution is prone, it is obvious that a speaker or writer whose function is to move men to action may select and adapt his arguments most advantageously if he is keenly aware of such errors, and can circumvent them, although he may be unable to expose and refute them as he might sophisms and ambiguities. To know, for example, that men tend to rationalize beliefs already held (an idol of the Tribe); that men's minds are conditioned by custom, education, and habit (idols of the Den); that ordinary men can comprehend new notions only when expressed in familiar terms (an idol of the Market-Place); that an audience, public or private, holds opinions and dogmas no nearer reality than a romantic play (idol of the Theatre); to know these is a necessary condition to their circumvention.

Beyond the necessity of logical proof as means of accomplishing the social end of rhetorical discourse, Bacon recognizes that rhetoric, if it is to apply reason to imagination, must treat of another technique: the adaptation of logical proof to the audience, consisting primarily in rousing the imagination to activity. "When by arts of speech men's minds are soothed, inflamed, and carried hither and thither, it is all done by stimulating the imagination. . . ."[49]

Skill in the application of reason to one's auditors, Bacon appears to hold, depends first upon a knowledge of human nature, and second upon expressing ideas so as to appeal to the imagination. For a knowledge of human motives and of traits of character rhetoric is undoubtedly indebted to ethics as Bacon understands that study.[50] One of the aims of ethical study, according to him, is to examine the nature of the good, because the highest motive of human activity is the good life. Consequently, the speaker or writer who considers what course men ought to follow in meeting the problems of everyday affairs obviously will base many arguments upon the nature of the good. In fact, Bacon asserts that in all deliberative speaking and political discourse the orator must consider what is good or evil with respect to the action he is urging: "The persuader's labour is to make things appear good and evil, and that in higher or lower degree."[51] Accordingly, a treatise on rhetoric such as Bacon might construct would include some material belonging by right to ethics, and adapted to the needs of persuasion. Certainly therein would appear one of Bacon's early works, *The Colours of Good and Evil*, inspired by the ethical remarks in Aristotle's *Rhetoric*[52] and intended by Bacon to supply the deficiencies of contemporary rhetorical theory.

It is from ethical theory, furthermore, that rhetorical discourse will derive a knowledge of character types. One function of ethics, Bacon explains, is not only to examine the nature of the good, but also to present the "sound and true distributions and descriptions of the several characters and tempers of men's natures and dispositions," and in general the knowledge of man's affections.[53] In other words, the Baconian ethics assumes many of the duties of modern psychology, for Bacon felt that traditional ethics had neglected character analysis. Moral philosophy cannot rest content with speculation on goodness and virtue; it must train the mind, mould the affections, and in general regulate character. Hence, if its training is to be effective, it must study human nature. The *De Augmentis* therefore commends Aristotle for discussing the abstract nature of good and evil in the *Nicomachean Ethics*. Bacon finds it strange, however, "that Aristotle should have written divers volumes of ethics, and never handled the affections, as a principal portion thereof; yet in his Rhetoric, where they are considered but collaterally and in a second degree (as they may be moved and excited by speech), he finds a place for them, and handles them acutely and well, for the quantity thereof." [54] Manifestly, then, Bacon feels that a treatise on rhetoric will make use of the knowledge of good and evil and of human character that ethics makes available, probably in a manner similar to Aristotle's *Rhetoric*. If Bacon had written a rhetorical treatise, perhaps many of his essays, or at least parts of them, would have found a place in it, for they were intended to be an integral part of his ethical system.[55]

Besides treating of the types of human character and of the nature of the good in so far as they are useful to persuasion, rhetoric performs the function most peculiar to it by showing how abstract ideas may be transformed into imaginative terms, for rhetoric is properly concerned with the "adornment" of discourse. In Bacon's eyes rhetorical address would be impossible without imagery and without words that stir up the imagination. Reason is of course essential, but reason and imagination work hand in hand; each in the proper functioning of rhetoric depends upon the other. So essential is this relationship that Bacon at one time cites as the subject-matter of rhetoric, "Imaginative or Insinuative Reason." [56] But in spite of the necessity of imagery and in spite of the statement that "the application and variety of speech . . . ought to extend so far, that if a man should speak of the same thing to several persons, he should nevertheless use different words to each of them," [57] Bacon disdains to discuss style as such, apparently motivated by contempt of the Schoolmen and the habit of some contemporary orators of trafficking in words rather than matter. Elocution or style, he scornfully suggests, is associated with a pedant making a speech. His works, however, contain many remarks that indicate certain attributes of style. Three of them may be designated as perspicuity, appropriateness to content, and a certain beauty of language that Bacon connects with the "Accidents of Grammar": the sound, measure, and accent of words. The fourth and chief attribute of rhetorical style is the quality of rousing the imagination to fight on the side of reason. Thus the speaker is warned to avoid using "barbarous words, of no sense, lest they should disturb the imagination" and move it in the wrong direction; he will try, on the contrary, to employ "words of similitude, that may second and feed the imagination," as well as "Scripture words; for that the belief that religious texts and words have power, and may strengthen the imagination." [58] The persuasive writer or speaker, moreover, is encouraged to invent ideas that employ comparison and contrast, such as the parable, fable, allegory, and analogy. Of considerable significance to the function of rhetorical discourse, furthermore, are those ideas that merely stir up or rouse the imagination, as distinguished from those ideas that carry specific images. Bacon therefore suggests to the speaker or writer that the Colours of Good and Evil, beyond helping in the discovery of fallacious reasoning, may constitute an aid for recommending reason to the imagination; they serve "to quicken and strengthen . . . opinions and persuasions . . . : for reasons plainly delivered and always after one manner . . . enter but heavily and dully: whereas if they be varied and have more life and vigour put into them by these forms and insinuations, they cause a stronger apprehension, and many times suddenly win the mind to a resolution." [59]

Bacon's theory of rhetorical address, it is clear, emphasizes the place of logical proof and imaginative appeal, and indicates in general how reason may be applied to imagination for the better moving of the will. But the Baconian theory of persuasive discourse does more than this; Bacon recognizes that there must be included in rhetorical theory considerable practical advice concerning the invention or discovery or arguments and material appropriate to the peculiar function of rhetoric. How, in other words, is the speaker or writer to find logical means of proof and ideas that rouse the imagination? Furthermore, how will the prose artist arrange his material, when discovered, into continuous discourse? Finally, when the speaker comes to deliver orally the material that he has invented and arranged, are there ways to aid his memory and to assist in managing his voice and gesture? Bacon's works clearly acknowledged these problems, and offer suggestions which I shall group under the heads of invention, disposition, memory, and delivery.

"Invention," writes Bacon, "is of two kinds, much differing; the one, of Arts and Sciences; and the other, of Speech and Arguments." [60] The first type of invention is that method of scientific inquiry which in the *Novum Organum* is designated as the "new logic," or, in other words, an inductive scheme of invention that, when applied to the observation of natural phenomena, yields universally valid knowledge previously unknown to mankind. The method that produces this new knowledge is a system of observations so managed that the investigator may readily draw general conclusions from tabulated particulars.[61] It is hardly probable, therefore, that a scheme of inductive search designed to yield universal truth can be of utility in persuasive discourse, for, as Bacon indicates, the speaker deals with probabilities, not universals:

The end which this science of mine proposes is the invention not of arguments but of arts; not of things in accordance with principles, but of principles themselves; not of probable reasons, but of designations and directions for works. And as the intention is different, so accordingly is the effect; the effect of the one being to overcome an opponent in argument, of the other to command nature in action.[62]

The second type of invention, as distinguished from the procedure of scientific inquiry, pertains to the discovery of arguments. Somewhat loath to admit that this process may be properly called invention, Bacon carefully explains that the finding of arguments by a speaker or writer means essentially the recall and recovery of ideas; it is "no other but *out of the knowledge whereof our mind is already possessed, to draw forth or call before us that which may be pertinent to the purpose which we take into our consideration . . . it is . . . but a Remembrance or Suggestion,* with an application." [63] The technique of discovering arguments is accomplished in part by using the topics of conventional logic, consisting of phrases and questions which not only serve "to prompt and suggest what we would affirm and assert, but also what we should inquire or ask. For a faculty of wise interrogating is half a knowledge." [64] Bacon divides *Topica* into two species, the general and the particular. The general topic, Bacon explains, "has been sufficiently handled in logic, so that there is no need to dwell on the explanation of it," [65] but although the subject is thus dismissed, it is probable that he is here alluding to those traditional "places" of invention first set forth in Aristotle's *Analytics* and found in one form or another in most subsequent logical treatises down to Bacon—the topics, namely, of the Like and Unlike, Equal and Unequal, the Greater and the Less, the Subject and the Adjunct, along with the topics suggested by such questions as What is the Cause? the Effect? the Definition? the Genus? and the Species? If the political orator, for example, finds occasion to discuss Elizabeth's failure to marry, he may discover arguments by asking himself such queries as What is the Cause? What is the Effect? What is the nature of the difficulty? Does her conduct find an historical parallel? Such topics are mentioned, in

Bacon's system of knowledge, in connection with the First Philosophy where a few of them are cited: the topics of "Much, Little; Like, Unlike; Possible, Impossible; likewise Being and Not-Being, and the like." [66] Thus Bacon holds that the use of topics drawn from logic will help the prose artist to discover logical proof. He is willing, therefore, to commend Aristotle for placing "Rhetoric as between Logic on the one side, and moral or civil knowledge on the other, as participating of both. . . ." [67]

The particular topic, like the general topic, aids the investigator or searcher by recalling to mind ideas and arguments which he had previously unearthed and by prompting lines of inquiry which will bring forth new material appropriate to the purpose at hand. Particular topics, however, are unlike the general, in that they are special lines of inquiry applicable to a special subject and to no other. They are "places of invention and inquiry appropriated to particular subjects and sciences . . . they are a kind of mixture of logic with the proper matter of each science." [68] Bacon separates his *Topica* into the species general and particular because no one scheme of invention, no single formula, can be applied to all subjects and to all phases of their growth and development. Each science, as it pursues its special inquiries, will develop its own art of invention:

He must be a trifler and a man of narrow mind who thinks that the perfect art of invention of knowledge can be devised and propounded all at once; and that it needs only to be set at work. Let men be assured that the solid and true arts of invention grow and increase as inventions themselves increase; so that when a man first enters into the pursuit of any knowledge, he may have some useful precepts of invention; but when he has made further advances in that knowledge, he may and ought to devise new precepts of invention, to lead him the better to that which lies beyond.[69]

Although Bacon never explains precisely what the particular topic means to rhetoric, the inference, I think, is clear: a speaker, if he wishes to discover true and solid reasons, cannot rest content with the lines of argument suggested by general topics; if the occasion demands it, he must push his investigation into a special subject-matter until he learns what problems are peculiar to it. Indeed, Bacon would probably counsel the young speaker not to wait upon the occasion before undertaking the study of special subjects, but to delve into the natural and social sciences, into ethics, psychology, and politics, and to frame for himself question-topics that would facilitate the invention of technical arguments, should an occasion require them. This interpretation seems to be partially borne out by Bacon's assertion that of all the methods of invention, particular topics "are to be accounted most useful." [70]

Other aids to the invention of both logical proof and of ideas that stir up the imagination are the Colours of Good and Evil, Antitheta, Formulae, and Apothegms. The nature and purpose of these helps to invention are first described in the *Advancement* under the name of "Preparation":

Preparation . . . seemeth scarcely a part of Knowledge, consisting rather of diligence than of any artificial erudition . . . the ancient writers of rhetoric do give it in precept, that pleaders should have the Places whereof they have most continual use ready handled in all the variety that may be; as that, to speak for the literal interpretation of the law against equity, and contrary; and to speak for presumptions and inferences against testimony, and contrary. And Cicero himself, being broken into it by great experience, delivereth it plainly, that whatsoever a man shall have occasion to speak of . . . he may have it in effect premeditate, and handled *in thesi;* so that when he cometh to a particular, he shall have nothing to do but to put to names and times and places, and such other circumstances of individuals. We see likewise the exact diligence of Demosthenes; who, in regard of the great force that the entrance and access into causes hath to make a good impression, had ready framed a number of prefaces for orations and speeches.[71]

The nature of the Colours is suggested by the heading to the first collection, published in 1597: "A table of colours or appearances of good and evil, and their degrees, as places of persuasion and disuasion, and their several fallaxes, and the Elenches of them." [72] Preceding this caption is Bacon's first sentence of the preface to the *Colours:* "In deliberatives the point is, what is good and what is evil, and of good what is greater, and of evil what is the less." [73] In brief, the Colours are generalizations concerning good and evil, though the *De Augmentis,* containing an amplified version of them, calls them the sophisms of rhetoric. Through careful analysis of such generalizations, a speaker or writer learns to distinguish in what cases they are sound, in what false, and is able, as a result, to employ them both in direct argument and in refutation. By means of such analysis, to be carried out to the point of writing short essays on each generalization, the speaker can arrive at true and safe judgments. For the work cannot be done, Bacon declares, "but out of a very universal knowledge of the nature of things, so being performed, it so cleareth man's judgment and election, as it is the less apt to slide into any error." [74] This, of course, is in line with his wish that rhetoric should aid reason rather than suppress it. Bacon also points out that a very important use of the Colours lies, as we have already seen, in their power to impress and move the hearer.

Antitheta find a place in Bacon's rhetoric as valuable aids to the invention of arguments. In the *De Augmentis* they comprise a series of forty-seven tables which contain arguments *pro* and *con,* arranged in parallel columns and classified according to subjects such as a speaker or writer often has occasion to handle. Similar in nature and form to the modern affirmative and negative briefs, they list some main heads on both sides of a popular question, the heads being described as arguments that function "as skeins or bottoms of thread, to be unwinded at large when they come to be used. . . ." [75] Under the stimulus of a speech-situation, the speaker finds himself with a few general arguments ready at hand, to which he needs only add authorities and examples appropriate to the audience and the occasion.

Besides Antitheta and the Colours of Good and Evil, Bacon has other aids to rhetorical invention, the next in order being what he identifies in the *Advancement* as Formulae, in the *De Augmentis* as Lesser Forms. In the two works mentioned, enough is said about Formulae to indicate that they are small parts of a speech, fully composed and ready for use; they are phrases or sentences—a ready introductory phrase or a stock transitional sentence—such as there is frequent occasion to employ. They are "those parts of speech which answer to the vestibules, back doors, ante-chambers, with drawing-chambers, passages, etc., of a house; and may serve indiscriminately for all subjects. Such are prefaces, conclusions, digressions, transitions, intimations of what is coming, excusations, and a number of the kind." [76] Whereas Antitheta resemble "a shop of pieces unmade up," Formulae are like "a shop of things ready made up; both to be applied to that which is frequent and most in request. . . ." [77] Doubtless Bacon believes that the Formulae so far as they add finish and ornament to discourse, assist in recommending reason to imagination: "For as in buildings it is a great matter both for pleasure and use that the fronts, doors, windows, approaches, passages, and the like be conveniently arranged, so also in a speech these accessory and interstitial passages (if they be handsomely and skillfully fashioned and placed) add a great deal both of ornament and effect to the entire structure. . . ." [78] If arguments constitute the skeins or bottoms of thread, then the Lesser Forms, binding together the grosser elements and giving to the pattern smoothness and finish, render the tapestry as a whole readily perceptible and interesting.

One other aid to invention is mentioned in Bacon's works. Besides the Colours, Antitheta, and Formulae, Bacon sees considerable utility in a collection of Apothegms, or "pointed speeches"; they are words which act as goads, "words with an edge or point, that cut and penetrate the knots of business and affairs." [79] The Apothegms, moreover, like the Colours and the Formulae, serve to recommend reason to imagination, for they work not only for use and action but also for pleasure and ornament, and because "former occasions are continually recurring, that which served once will often serve again, either produced as a man's own or cited as of ancient authority." [80] Bacon himself, by way of example, made a collection of the deft repartees attributed to famous persons, always supplying enough of the narrative to give point to the clever rejoinder. Here is one of Bacon's examples, the Apothegm being italicized:

Alcibiades came to Pericles, and stayed a while ere he was admitted. When he came in, Pericles civilly excused it, and said: *I was studying how to give my account.* But Alcibiades said to him: *If you will be ruled by me, study rather how to give no account.*[81]

Concerning the use of the Apothegms, Bacon declares that "you may extract the salt out of them and sprinkle where you will." [82]

Of schemes of invention—Colours, Antitheta, Formulae, and Apothegms—the *Advancement* and the *De Augmentis* provide extended examples. As a result, they take on a prominence in Bacon's works somewhat disproportionate to their real value. Actually, however, they represent only the deficiencies which as handmaids attend the art of rhetoric. They are not to be regarded as substitutes for wide and deep knowledge of a subject, for "to him who has little or no knowledge on the subject proposed, places of invention are of no service; and on the other hand, he who is ready provided with matter applicable to the point in question will, even without art and places of invention (although perhaps not so expeditiously and easily), discover and produce arguments." [83]

After invention, the next step in rhetorical discourse is disposition, or the art of determining the order and sequence of ideas that have been invented and are ready for use. Bacon feels that disposition, like invention, is of such importance to the dissemination of knowledge that he removes it from its traditional place under rhetoric and logic, and makes it a special study in its own right. As a distinct study it comprises two parts, "the one relating to the disposition of the whole work or argument of a book; the other to the limitation of propositions." [84] The first part classifies patterns that are useful in organizing discourse as a whole; the second relates to the limitation of propositions. The second, however, need not detain us long. Like Ramus Bacon has in mind the restriction of a work or book to its own professed subject, for it must not "intermeddle within the province of another"; [85] and "repetition, excursion, and all confusion" [86] must be avoided. Here he has in mind also the need for determining "unto what degree of particularity a knowledge should descend"; [87] writers and speakers, in the judgments they offer, must avoid being *Cymini Sectores* and refrain from discoursing on generalities that are too remote to be useful to men. Under "limitation of propositions," then, Bacon is considering questions of unity, of scale and proportion, of degree of comprehensiveness and detail in treatment; and he thinks of them as involving not the plan of a discourse in general, but the propositions that make up the discourse.

In classifying the forms of disposition that pertain to discourse in general as distinguished from rhetoric specifically, Bacon distinguishes sixteen kinds,[88] some having no name at all, others having such special names as Initiative, Magistral, Exoteric, Enigmatical, Aphoristic, Analytic, and Homeric.[89] Some are plans that obviously apply to rhetorical discourse, but what is more important to rhetoric is the principle of classification underlying the methods of arrangement. In all plans the principle of division is determined by the *purpose* of the author, governed in part by the audience addressed and in part by the subject-matter. Fundamentally, then, Bacon is dominated by the notion that the form or order or arrangement of discourse is governed by the *function* of communication. This means, of course, that the *form* of persuasive speaking and writing, like discourse in general, is also functional, and that the form of a speech is organic with its end. Since the true function of rhetoric is to recommend reason to imagination, the speaker or writer will present his ideas in the order and sequence that seems best suited to rouse the imagination. It is significant that Bacon, although not neglecting to utter wise advice concerning introductions and conclusions, has abandoned the method of classical disposition as represented by Cicero and Quintilian.

Besides treating of invention and disposition, rhetoric must also offer advice on the *retention* of ideas that are to be spoken before an audience. The technique of remembering ideas, suggests Bacon, finds application in persuasive discourse. Because memory is a mental operation which comes into play whenever the mind functions, Bacon believes that it ought, like the other rational processes of invention and disposition, to attain the dignity of a separate art which would treat of the nature of memory and the means of its improvement. Incorporated in the *De Augmentis* [90] and in the *Novum Organum*,[91] accordingly, we discover short discussions on memory, containing helpful suggestions for the extemporaneous speaker. Some of the observations concerning the improvement of the memory Bacon seems to have derived from rhetorical theory or from his own experience as a Parliamentary speaker.

The chief problem in recall, Bacon points out, is "cutting off of infinity of search," [92] to get the mind to range within a narrow compass, "like the hunting of a deer within an enclosure." [93] This may be greatly promoted by arranged ideas into patterns and sequences, particularly when the form employed is congruous with the content. Thus it is that poetry is "more easily learned by heart than prose; for if we stick at any word, we have prenotion that it must be such a word as fits the verse." [94] A digest of good commonplaces also aids the memory, for they contract "the sight of the judgment to a point." [95] Finally, the habit of associating abstract conceptions with concrete objects, particularly applicable to the function of rhetoric, helps the memory considerably. Anyone, says Bacon in a neat illustration, "will more easily remember the image of a hunter pursuing a hare, of an apothecary arranging his boxes, of a pedant making a speech, of a boy repeating verses from memory, of a player acting on the stage, than the mere notions of invention, disposition, elocution, memory, and action." [96]

To that aspect of persuasive address known as delivery Bacon does not accord explicit and extended discussion. This omission is in part explained by his comment on Demosthenes' judgment that the chief attribute of the orator consists in action, that is, in voice and gesture: "A strange thing, that that part of an orator which is but superficial, and rather the virtue of a player, should be placed so high, above those other noble parts of invention, elocution, and the rest. . . ." [97] For one who holds that imaginative discourse is the province of rhetoric such a judgment is probably not final. In fact, seven consecutive entries in the *Promus of Formularies and Elegancies,* a kind of commonplace book, suggest that Bacon may have contemplated a short treatise on delivery.[98] The entries indicate an art of declamation in which sincerity and directness of utterance are recommended, along with proper control of the breath and of emotion, an enunciation that is neither slovenly nor forced, and action that is suited to the word.

If our exposition of Bacon's theory of rhetorical address has been sketched with due emphasis and proportion, it is manifest that rhetoric as it emerges from the cyclopedia has a broad social function of promoting the ascendance of reason over emotion in human affairs. In this respect rhetoric of course shares the end of logic, of ethics, and for that matter of the entire program for the advancement of learning. In the cyclopedia Bacon has endeavored to see human knowledge in perspective, to relate the fields of learning to one another, as well as to notice their deficiencies. As a result, he perceives that the common divisions of the arts and sciences are artificial; all knowledge is really a unity. The rhetorical theorist, consequently, would do well, in Bacon's view, to perceive "the mutual consent and light which one part (of knowledge) receiveth of another." [99] The arts of speech, for example, would be greatly improved by a study of Grammar, which underlies them all. "So likewise," Bacon continues,

in this same logic and rhetoric, or arts of argument and grace of speech, if the great masters of them would but have gone a form lower, and looked but into the observations of Grammar concerning the kinds of words, their derivations, deflexions, and syntax; specially enriching the same with the helps of several languages, with their differing proprieties of words, phrases, and tropes; they might have found out more and better footsteps of common reason, help of disputation, and advantages of cavillation, than many of these which they have propounded.[100]

The student of rhetoric should perceive what Bacon calls the communities of knowledge:

A man should be thought to dally, if he did not note how the figures of rhetoric and music are many of them the same: The repetitions and traductions in speech and the reports and hauntings of sounds in music are the very same things. . . . The figure that Cicero and the rest commend as one of the best points of elegancy, which is the fine checking of expectation, is no less well known to the muscians when they have a special grace in flying the close or cadence. And these are no allusions but direct communities, the same delights of the mind being to be found not only in music, rhetoric, but in moral philosophy, policy, and other knowledges, and that obscure in the one, which is the more apparent in the other, yea and that discovered in the one which is not found at all in the other, and so one science greatly aiding to the invention and augmentation of another.[101]

Hence Bacon urges that the continuity of knowledge be preserved.

For the contrary hereof hath made particular sciences to become barren, shallow, and erroneous; while they have not been nourished and maintained from the common fountain. So we see Cicero the orator complained of Socrates and his school, that he was the first that separated philosophy and rhetoric; whereupon rhetoric became an empty and verbal art.[102]

It becomes apparent, then, that Bacon would condemn the rhetorician who studies rhetoric and nothing else.

The habit of viewing knowledge as a whole, although leading Bacon to respect the continuity and unity of all knowledge, does not prevent him from evaluating separately the arts and sciences so far as they contribute to the advancement of learning. As a consequence, rhetorical address, because it deals with popular opinions and disputations, and because it makes its appeal to the multitude, becomes a somewhat inferior science. Though excellent in purpose and "excellently well laboured," "truly valued . . . eloquence is doubtless inferior to wisdom. For what a distance there is between them is shown in the words spoken by God to Moses, when he declined the office assigned him on the ground that he was no speaker: 'There is Aaron, he shall be thy speaker, thou shalt be to him as God.' Yet in profit and in popular estimation wisdom yields to eloquence; for so Solomon says: 'The wise in heart shall be called prudent, but he that is sweet of speech shall compass greater things'; plainly signifying that wisdom will help a man to a name or admiration, but that it is eloquence which prevails most in action and common life." [103]

The science which discovers new knowledge is that which Bacon esteems most. All other studies must rank below it, for they can only begin their discussion when scientific research has supplied the facts and materials. Yet, so far as popular arts are concerned, logic and rhetoric "rightly taken are the gravest of sciences, being the arts of arts, the one for judgment, the other for ornament; besides they give the rule and direction how both to set forth and illustrate the subject matter." [104]

Francis Bacon's theory of rhetorical address, then, by virtue of its reference to the imaginative faculty of man's mind and the peculiar function of the imagination in relation to the reason and the affections is essentially social. Conceived of as the most effective means of communicating knowledge for persuasive ends, rhetoric at the same time carries the social obligation of helping reason to prevail over passion, of establishing, on the level of popular knowledge, the just and good cause. To this end the orator, abjuring the vain scholastical manner of utterance, should speak "soundly indeed, ordering the matter he handleth distinctly for memory, deducing and drawing it down for direction, and authorizing it with strong proofs and warrants. . . ." [105] More concretely, the conception of the speaker who honors Bacon's rhetorical rules may well be that which Ben Jonson had in mind when he applied a passage from Seneca to the Lord Chancellor himself:

There happened in my time one noble speaker who was full of gravity in his speaking; his language, where he could spare or pass by a jest, was nobly censorious. No man ever spake more neatly, more pressly, more weightily, or suffered less emptiness, less idleness, in what he uttered. No number of his speech but consisted of his own graces. His hearers could not cough or look aside from him without loss. He commanded where he spoke, and he had his judges angry and pleased at his devotion. No man had their affections more in his power. The fear of every man that heard him was lest he should make an end. [106]

Sources of the Elocutionary Movement in England: 1700-1748

WILBUR SAMUEL HOWELL

I

HISTORIANS of English rhetoric concur in saying that the elocution-ary movement originated in England around 1750.[1] By the term "elocutionary movement" they mean, of course, the historical trend in which rhetoric as a formal discipline not only renounced her previous interest in the classical doctrines of invention, arrangement, and style, but undertook also to confine herself to the study of oratorical delivery and its twin aspects of voice and gesture. Sandford, one of the earliest of these historians, begins his account of the elocutionary movement by discussing Thomas Sheridan's *Course of Lectures on Elocution* (1762) and his introductory *Discourse* which preceded the *Lectures* by three years.[2] Twenty-two years after Sandford defined these limits, Guthrie enlarged them somewhat by placing John Mason's *Essay on Elocution, or, Pronunciation* (London, 1748) at the beginning of the list of "the great English works on elocution," and by saying later that "Mason seems to have been the first writer to justify the use of the term 'elocu-tion' in the sense of delivery."[3] Thus when Parrish remarked in 1957 that John Mason "might be regarded as the originator of the elocution movement in England,"[4] he endorsed in effect the conclusion that Guthrie had expressed, and he suggested no English writers earlier than Mason as ones to have had a direct and demonstrable influence upon Mason's pioneering work.

It is now possible to establish the English origins of the elocutionary movement at a considerably earlier date than Sandford, Guthrie, or Parrish has indicated, and to declare that our historians as a whole have overlooked several important authors and works which Mason and Sheridan themselves would have regarded as their true and direct predecessors.

When I say this, however, I do not mean to accept Sandford's statement that Robert Robinson's *The Art of Pronuntiation* (London, 1617) was a native English influence behind the elocutionary movement of the eighteenth century, or that it has any claim whatever to be regarded as "probably the first book written in English devoted exclusively to the subject of delivery." [5] Robinson's work has nothing directly to do with the classical or elocutionary doctrine of oratorical pronunciation. It is instead a description of the art by which "the true pronuntiation of languages might be learned." [6] This art is set forth by Robinson under two headings, "*Vox Audienda,* Or The Elements of Mans *Voice*," and "*Vox Videnda,* Which is writing, or the Characters of Mans voice." Here is his own summary of these two parts:

In the first by certaine propositions applying my selfe to set foorth the elements and parts of the voice: In the second part appointing for euery simple sound in mans voice sundry letters and characters, that the voice being thereunto once committed may by any (who shall know the vse of them) without any other expositor or instructor be aptly and truly pronounced vpon view of the writing, how strange soeuer the language be.[7]

Needless to say, Robinson is as good as his word. His work is thus a treatise on phonetics, not rhetoric, and any attempt to associate it with the English elocutionists, except as they were generally interested in phonetics, is unjustifiable. Even in the field of phonetics, Robinson's work does not apparently have value in terms of the influence it exerted upon later phoneticians; its chief claim to recognition consists in its being "a witness to the pronunciation of the first half of the seventeenth century." [8]

My purpose in this essay is to sketch in outline the history of the elocutionary movement between 1700 and 1748 and thus to identify certain authors and works as the direct forerunners of Mason and Sheridan. In my story there will be some matters of date and authorship that have not yet been completely established beyond all doubt. But the documents with which I shall deal are solid evidences that the elocutionists had evolved their terminology and marked out their special field of activity in England almost a half-century before the date when they are supposed to have launched their movement upon its astonishing but controversial course.

II

Before I turn to the early writers in this movement, it might be well to remind ourselves that they did what they did not only as a result of the attacks made upon English Neo-Ciceronian rhetoric of the seventeenth century but also because of the tendency of English logic in that same period to monopolize functions formerly shared between herself and rhetoric. Thus a few words upon these matters will best set the stage for the developments to be explained in the central sections of this essay.

As we know, the Neo-Ciceronian school of rhetorical theory gradually supplanted that of the Ramists in the period between 1620 and 1700 and re-established as the four components of rhetoric the classical doctrines of invention, arrangement, style, and delivery.[9] The word style in this sequence was an English equivalent of the Latin term *elocutio*, and, to the Neo-Ciceronians as to the ancients, *elocutio* referred to the problem of wording a discourse, whereas they designated the problem of oral presentation by the Latin terms *pronuntiatio* or *actio*. The chief English members of the Neo-Ciceronian school were Thomas Vicars, Thomas Farnaby, William Pemble, and Obadiah Walker, all of whom dealt with the four components just mentioned. Lesser figures were John Smith, Thomas Blount, William Prideaux, and John Bulwer, who contributed treatises on separate components of the whole Neo-Ciceronian system, Smith, Blount, and Prideaux being authors of works on style, and Bulwer, of a work on gesture or "the Art of Manvall Rhetoricke." [10] All together, these eight major and minor figures were the dominant rhetoricians of their century, and for a large part of the era they had things more or less their own way.

But, as the century advanced, powerful opposition began to develop against certain traditional elements in logic and rhetoric. The Port-Royalists in their vastly popular *Logique* (1662), and Bernard Lamy in his *Rhétorique* (1675), attacked the classical system that provided for the invention of ideas by a resort to the commonplaces.[11] When these two works became popular in England soon after their publication in France, they caused English logicians and rhetoricians to lose some of their confidence in the traditional machinery of *inventio* as it had been stated and taught by Vicars and Farnaby.[12] This crisis in confidence was intensified by Locke's influential theory that our knowledge comes to us from sensation and reflection, and that the study of objective reality is therefore the true source of ideas in the acquisition or transmission of learning and opinion.[13] Meanwhile, powerful spokesmen of the new science like Robert Boyle and Thomas Sprat subjected the doctrine of *elocutio* or style to a scorching attack. Boyle convincingly declared that the classical Roman conception of style had been uncritically accepted as the only standard of eloquence in the modern world, whereas that standard did not wholly explain the eloquence of the Scriptures or of other works in the non-Roman tradition.[14] Somewhat later, Sprat pointed out with caustic emphasis that the traditional tropes and figures of rhetoric were of little value in solving the problem of communication between scientist and scientist or between scientist and public, and thus would have to be abandoned in scientific exposition.[15]

While the late seventeenth century was making these devastating criticisms of traditional invention and style as concepts in rhetoric, the theory of rhetorical arrangement was being taught by logic. Ramus, it will be recalled, had transferred the theory of arrangement from rhetoric to dialectic, and in the great reaction against him towards the end of the seventeenth century, this was one of his reforms which English logicians allowed to remain in force.[16] Method or disposition or arrangement became a standard part of logical doctrine between 1600 and 1700, and in all logics of the period method meant in large part the theory of organizing discourses for the communication of ideas. This trend continued during the eighteenth century. One has only to read the logics of Aldrich, Crousaz, Watts, and Duncan, who best represent the major trends in English logical theory for the first half of that period, to see that the classical doctrine of rhetorical disposition was to a large extent being superseded and made obsolete by what logic had to say upon the subject of arranging treatises for the purpose of exposition and argumentation.

Faced with open attacks upon two important aspects of their doctrine and with the threat of having a third aspect stolen completely, some eighteenth-century rhetoricians through inertia or indifference pretended that nothing had happened and that the traditional doctrines were still valid. Thus they constructed rhetorics upon the four chief terms of Ciceronian theory, as did John Holmes in *The Art of Rhetoric Made Easy*,[17] or they wrote treatises which covered *elocutio* and thus dealt with the tropes and figures, as did Nicholas Burton, Thomas Gibbons, Daniel Turner, and Anthony Blackwall.[18] These writers did not have a great influence in their time, but they have to be mentioned as unreconstructed followers of the conservative doctrines of the seventeenth-century Neo-Ciceronians.

Meanwhile, other rhetoricians of the eighteenth century sought to revise and reinterpret Ciceronian theory so as to answer on the one hand the criticisms that had been leveled at the traditional systems of invention and style, and on the other to preserve the precepts of rhetorical arrangement against further encroachments by logic. These writers produced the great rhetorical works of their time, and chief among them are Ward, Priestley, Campbell, and Blair. They were by no means in conformity with each other in regard to the main divisions and the contents of their rhetorical doctrine, but they were basically agreed that much in the great tradition of Cicero and Quintilian was worthy of preservation and capable of adaptation to the needs of the modern world.

The English elocutionists chose still another direction. Feeling that the classical theory of invention had been largely replaced by the new theories of knowledge, that contemporary logics were doing an adequate job with the doctrine of arrangement, and that the day of the tropes and figures was probably over so far as schoolroom instruction in style was concerned, the elocutionists decided to concentrate their energies upon *pronuntiatio*, which was the only part of the traditional scheme to have been spared from attack in the seventeenth century. Thus they occupied what appeared to be the strongest defensive position that remained to classical rhetoric.

But they decided to give that position a new name, and the name that they chose was elocution. Even before the formal beginning of their movement, however, there was an English precedent for calling oral presentation in rhetoric by this new name rather than by the more obvious and more traditional name of pronunciation or action. So far as a treatise on rhetoric is concerned, that precedent was at least as old as John Wilkins's *Ecclesiastes, or, A discourse concerning the Gift of Preaching*. Originally published at London in 1646, and given six later editions before 1700, this treatise divided its doctrine into three headings, that is, Method, Matter, and Expression, and when it came to speak of Expression, it first discussed Phrase, and secondly, Eloquution.[19] There can be no doubt that Phrase designates for Wilkins what the ancient rhetoricians had called *elocutio,* and that Eloquution designates for him what the ancients had called *pronuntiatio* or *actio,* and what we today call rhetorical delivery. "The *phrase,*" he says, "should be plain, full, wholesome, affectionate," [20] and these four terms provide the framework for his discussion of the problem of wording in sermon-making. As for the problem of oral presentation, Wilkins briefly develops the single thesis that "in the elocution there are two extremities to be avoided: too much Boldnesse, Fear," [21] and these two qualities as Wilkins explains them refer to the speaker's attitude as it is reflected in his voice and bearing. Wilkins concludes his discussion of these qualities by saying, "In brief, the most proper manner of eloquution is with modesty and gravity, which will best sute with our calling and businesse." [22]

III

The English elocutionary movement thus received its distinctive English name from native sources, but it borrowed its first doctrines from a Frenchman. This Frenchman is to be identified as Michel Le Faucheur. Born in Geneva in the late fifteen hundreds, Le Faucheur became a Protestant preacher and theologian, and for much of his life occupied pulpits with considerable distinction at Montpellier and Charenton. At the time of his death at Paris in 1657, he had already published a few religious works, and was the author of an unpublished essay, the *Traitté de l'action de l'orateur, ou de la Prononciation et du geste,* which was seen through the press that very year by Valentin Conrart.[23] This work received several editions in French before the end of the seventeenth century, and in 1690 at Helmstedt it was published in Melchior Schmidt's Latin version, thus being made available to the entire European world of learning. Some dozen years after this latter event, it was given an anonymous English translation and was published at London under the title, *An Essay Upon The Action of an Orator; As To His Pronunciation & Gesture. Useful both for Divines and Lawyers, and necessary for all Young Gentlemen, that study how to Speak well in Publick.*[24] In 1727 this same translation was given another printing at London, its title being altered to read *The Art of Speaking in Publick: or an Essay on the Action of an Orator; As to his Pronunciation and Gesture. Useful in the Senate or Theatre, the Court, the Camp, as well as the Bar and Pulpit. The Second Edition Corrected. With an Introduction relating to the Famous Mr. Henly's present Oratory.*[25] Twenty-three years later, in 1750, this translation was given a third edition and was now called *An Essay upon Pronunciation and Gesture, Founded Upon the Best Rules and Authorities of the Ancients, Ecclesiastical and Civil, and Adorned with the Finest Rules of Elocution.*[26]

The date of the first publication of this English translation is the date when the English elocutionary movement formally began, and the name of the translator is that of the English founder of the movement. It is exasperating, therefore, to be forced to confess that the translator does not identify himself and that the first edition does not proclaim its date of publication. To be sure, John Henley is credited with being the author of the edition published in 1727,[27] but a mere reading of "The Editor's Introduction and Apology for this Edition," as contained in the work, promptly dispels any thought that Henley had anything to do with it, except as the unwilling victim of the editor's hostility. So far as I know, there is at present no firm clue to the identity of the editor of the second edition, or of the single translator of the three editions. But there is a way to be sure that the first edition was published early in the eighteenth century, probably in the year 1702, although this statement contradicts the accepted belief that it appeared around 1680.[28] Here are the chief items of evidence to support the eighteenth-century date.

For one thing, the second edition, which, I repeat, was published in 1727, speaks of the first edition as "having been buried upwards of twenty Years in the most profound *Silence* and *Oblivion*." [29] This statement points to the first decade of the eighteenth century as the date of publication of the first edition, and leaves us only the problem of deciding whether some one year in that decade has any special claim above another as the time when the work appeared. For another thing, the first edition is dedicated "*To the Honoured* Christopher Rawlinson, *Esquire*," and the dedicatory letter compliments Rawlinson on the honorable part he has played in the commonwealth of learning.[30] It plainly appears that this compliment is a reference to Rawlinson's only literary endeavor, his edition of King Alfred's Old English version of Boethius's *Consolationis Philosophiae Libri V*, which was published at Oxford in 1698; and if it is such a reference, then the dedicatory letter was probably written not more than three or four years after Rawlinson's own work came out. For still another thing, the translator's Preface to the Reader, as contained in the first edition, confesses "that this *English Translation* of that *Tract*, is wholly owing to the extraordinary character, which the Incomparable Sir Roger L'Estrange and the Reverend Dr. Wake have been pleased to give it"; [31] but "The Editor's Introduction and Apology," as contained in the second edition, changes this particular passage to read "the incomparable Sir *Roger L'Estrange,* and *his Grace the present Arch-bishop of Canterbury,* when Preacher to the *Honourable Society of Gray's Inn.*" [32] Dr. Wake is the person indicated along with L'Estrange in both of these references. He was preacher at Gray's Inn between 1688 and 1695; he was canon of Christ Church between 1689 and 1702; he became dean of Exeter in 1703, and held that office until 1705; and after that, he was successively Bishop of Lincoln and Arch-bishop of Canterbury.[33] The printed reference to him as "the Reverend Dr. Wake" would most probably have been made only at that time in his career when he did not have any special title that the public mention of him should in propriety include; and that time may be identified as the latter part of the year 1702, when the sole office he held was that of rector of St. James's in Westminster. No doubt as a young preacher at Gray's Inn between 1688 and 1695 he had recommended Le Faucheur's *Traitté* to one of his friends as being something that should be translated into English; and that friend in the course of a few years did the translation and published it, mentioning Dr. Wake only by the title that applied to him at the moment of its publication. Thus there is a strong probability that the first edition came from the press in 1702. The rival date, 1680, is impossible on all counts, and agrees with none of the available pieces of evidence that I have pointed out. For example, the Christopher Rawlinson to whom the first edition is dedicated, and who is mentioned as a person of some learning at the time when the dedication is being written, would have been only three years of age in 1680, and thus at that moment ineligible for special claims to erudition.[34]

Le Faucheur's *Traitté* is one of the most respectable works of scholarship in the whole elocutionary movement and one of the finest treatises on delivery in the history of rhetorical theory. The same comments apply to the English version, which unfortunately can receive only a brief description in this essay.

Early in his first chapter Le Faucheur remarks that "the *Great*

Masters of *Rhetorick* have set up *Invention, Disposition,* and *Elocution* for the three first parts of Oratory," [35] but that later, in recognition of the influence of the passions in human affairs, they added a fourth part, action, "which consists of *Speaking* and *Gesture*," and which Demosthenes rated as the first, the second, and the third of the important parts of oratory, as did Cicero.[36] In making action the subject of his own treatise, Le Faucheur devotes his first three chapters to general considerations affecting it. Then he turns to speaking or using the voice, and for the next eight chapters he successively analyzes the problems of being heard without difficulty, of being heard with delight, and of varying the voice in respect to the necessary degree of loudness, vehemence, and speed, in respect to the different kinds of subjects, to the different passions, to the different parts of the classical oration, to the various important figures of rhetoric, and to the different kinds of sentences and words. His next two chapters discuss gesture first in general and then as it relates to the various parts of the body, particularly the head, face, eyes, and hands. In dealing with the latter topic, he enumerates seventeen rules for the use of the hand in gesturing. He concludes his work with a fourteenth chapter on the application of all the preceding precepts to the speaker's actual practice. Throughout the entire treatise, Le Faucheur keeps ancient illustrations and ancient doctrine continuously before his readers' eyes, except for the mention of a few modern parallels. Thus Demosthenes, Cicero, Quintilian, and St. Augustine provide examples of difficulties overcome, or their doctrines are quoted to teach the proper management of voice and body, while Philostratus, Plutarch, Aristotle, Isocrates, and others are mentioned from time to time.

It is curious to see in the first edition of this translation that the English terminology gives the translator a certain amount of trouble. In general he uses the word elocution to mean style, and the word pronunciation or action to mean delivery, as we gather from the passage quoted just above.[37] Indeed, these terms are authorized by Le Faucheur's French text, even if the translator had not had Latin theory in mind. But every now and then, as if to offer evidence that the word elocution, as used in the context of the theory of rhetoric, is transferring itself from the realm of style to the realm of delivery, the translator uses it in this latter sense. Thus in speaking of the habit of articulating words with an open mouth, he reproduces Le Faucheur's advice about correcting the fault, adding, "And where's the Elocution of unintelligible

Gibberidge?" [38] Thus also, in beginning the chapter on varying the voice according to the different kinds of subjects, he makes the French text say that the speaker must be able not only to manage his voice in general but also to follow particular rules "for all the *changes* and *variations* of the Voyce that are necessary to set-off his Discourse with a *taking Air* of Elocution, according to the quality of the *Subjects* he treats of, the nature of the *Passions* he would shew in *himself* or raise in *others,* the several parts of his *Discourse,* the different *Figures* he makes use of, and the *variety* of his *words* and his *Phrase.*" [39] In these two passages, elocution means delivery rather than style, and there are other examples of the same kind in this translation, [40] despite its tendency to preserve the older usage.

IV

Le Faucheur had intended his *Traitté* to be useful primarily to the pulpit and the bar, and this fact is stressed on the title page of its first edition in English. But in its second edition in English, the title page enlarges its sphere of usefulness to include the senate, the theatre, the court, and the camp as well. Lest these new-found beneficiaries be regarded merely as the brain children of promoters bent upon improving the sale of their product, I should like to say that long before 1727 the English version of the *Traitté* had been adapted to the uses of the theatre. In fact, in the book which I am about to discuss, it had been paid the compliment of having been extensively plagiarized and applied to the art of acting.

That book, published at London in 1710, is by Charles Gildon, and its title I shall quote in full, precisely because the first part of it seems to indicate that a distinguished actor rather than the art of acting is under consideration in the ensuing pages. The title reads thus:

The Life of Mr. *Thomas Betterton,* The late Eminent Tragedian. Wherein The Action and Utterance of the *Stage, Bar,* and *Pulpit,* are distinctly consider'd. With The Judgment of the late Ingenious *Monsieur de St. Evremond,* upon the *Italian* and *French* Music and Opera's; in a Letter to the Duke of *Buckingham.* To which is added, The Amorous Widow, or the *Wanton Wife.* A Comedy. Written by Mr. Betterton. Now first printed from the Original Copy. . . . London: Printed for Robert Gosling, at the *Mitre,* near the *Inner-Temple Gate* in *Fleetstreet.* 1710. [41]

Despite the opening words of this title (and they are the words that become in bibliographical abridgments the only clue to the contents of the work), we have here no proper life of Thomas Betterton. We do have the text of his play, *The Amorous Widow*. Before that, exclusive of front matter, we have a work of 176 pages made up as follows: there is first a four-page introduction promising a biography of Betterton and a set of his precepts on acting; [42] there is next a six-page sketch of Betterton's life; [43] then there is a 163-page work devoted to the precepts of action and utterance on the stage, and to some critical observations on dancing, music, and opera, these two sections being faintly modeled upon Cicero's *De Oratore;* [44] and finally there is a three-page list of plays in which Betterton had acted.[45] I shall deal here only with that part which concerns action and utterance; but even so, I shall be concerning myself with some 126 pages of the work.

The precepts on action and utterance grow out of a dialogue represented to have taken place at Betterton's country house in Reading between the distinguished actor himself and two friends who had called upon him.[46] The dialogue opens as the three men retire to the garden after having dined together. They fall into a discussion of famous actors and actresses and of the art of the stage, and Betterton is soon prevailed upon to deal at length with this latter subject. He consents only because he happens to have on hand a manuscript on acting by a friend of his; and he proceeds to read aloud what the friend had written,[47] and to incorporate into this reading two shorter papers by two other friends.[48]

After some comment upon the conduct of actors and actresses in their private lives, the first manuscript takes up a player's conduct upon the stage and discusses his gesture and his speaking. Hamlet's advice to the players is mentioned several times in the following pages, and is quoted and admired; [49] moreover, Francis Bacon and a person identified only as a learned countryman are noticed; [50] but by and large this manuscript is made up of doctrine gathered from the English version of Le Faucheur's *Traitté*, from Julius Pollux's *Onomasticum Graece & Latine*, and from Louis Crésol's *Vacationes Autumnales*, which is a 706-page Latin treatise on the subject of oratorical pronunciation and gesture.

In a way, Gildon acknowledges that his treatise on acting is founded upon these sources. Thus when Betterton interrupts his reading of the first manuscript to introduce a few comments written by another friend, it is he who acknowledges that these latter come from Pollux.[51] Thus when he interrupts himself on an earlier occasion to introduce a special section written by still another friend, he identifies it as having come from the pages of "a learned Jesuit," [52] and it is this author who can be positively identified as Crésol.[53] Moreover, Gildon takes the trouble to tell his readers that he would not have bothered them with a preface except "to prevent an Objection, which may be made, and that is, that I have been a *Plagiary*, and deliver'd Rules for my own, which are taken out of other Authors." He adds:

I first allow, that I have borrow'd many of them from the *French*, but then the *French* drew most of them from *Quintilian* and other Authors. Yet the *Frenchman* has improv'd the Ancients in this Particular, by supplying what was lost by the Alteration of Custom, with Observations more peculiar to the present Age.[54]

Thus it could be argued that Gildon does not indulge in unacknowledged borrowing, and that even his use of Le Faucheur is acknowledged far enough to prevent a charge of plagiarism against him.

But in actual fact Gildon makes heavy and unacknowledged borrowings not from Le Faucheur's *Traitté* but from the English translation of it.[55] Some of his borrowings can be identified as verbal echoes of the translation; [56] some, as the adaptation of the translation's doctrine to the particular needs of the actor; [57] and some, as the outright use of passages copied from the translation almost verbatim. Here are examples of this last kind of borrowing:

GILDON: *Pericles*, tho 'tis said he had the Goddess Persuasion on his Lips, and that he thundred and lightned in an Assembly, and made all *Greece* tremble when he spoke, yet would never publish any of his Orations, because their Excellency lay in the Action.[58]

LE FAUCHEUR'S TRANSLATOR: *Pericles*, for all the *Poets* said that the *Goddess of Persuasion* sat upon his *Lipps;* that he *thunder'd* and *lighten'd* in an Assembly, and made all *Greece* tremble again when he *Spake;* never made any of his *Orations* Publick: For why, *says one*, their Excellency lay in the Action. . . .[59]

GILDON: The *Mouth* must never be writh'd, nor the *Lips* bit or lick'd, which are all ungenteel and unmannerly Actions, and yet what some are frequently guilty of.[60]

LE FAUCHEUR'S TRANSLATOR: As for the *Mouth*, you must never *wry* it at all; for that's very *disagreeable*. . . . As for your *Lips*, you must take care not to *bite* 'em, nor to *lick* 'em with your *Tongue;* as I have seen some People do sometimes; Which is very *Ungenteel* and *Unmannerly* in an *Orator*.[61]

GILDON: There are, in short, two things to make the Speaker heard
and understood without Difficulty; first, a very distinct and
articulate Voice, and next a very strong and vigorous Pronunciation. The first is the most important; for an indifferent
Voice, with a distinct Pronunciation, shall be far more
easily understood, than one, that is stronger and more
audible, but which does not articulate the Words so well.[62]

LE FAUCHEUR'S   *First,* there are two things requisite to qualify a Man for
TRANSLATOR: this Work: That is, a very *Distinct* and *Articulate Voyce,*
and a very *Strong* and *Vigorous Pronunciation;* but the
former is the more important and necessary of the *Two.*
For a Man that has only an *indifferent Voyce,* if his *Pronunciation* be but Distinct, he shall be understood with far
more ease than another that has a stronger and more
Audible Faculty of *Speaking,* but does not *articulate* his
words so well.[63]

Before we take leave of Gildon's *Life of Mr. Thomas Betterton,* we
must observe that some of what it says on stage history, and much of
what it says on stage gesture, appear almost verbatim later in the
eighteenth century in a work called *The History of the English Stage*
(London, 1741), attributed on its title page to Betterton, but more
properly regarded as a miscellany compiled by Edmund Curll. This
work runs to 167 pages, 66 of which can be positively identified with
pages that Gildon had written himself or borrowed from the English
version of Le Faucheur.[64] With his eye fixed upon human weaknesses,
Curll distributed these 66 pages in such fashion that sections of doctrine on stage action preceded and followed sections devoted to episodes in theatre history or to accounts of the lives and loves of famous
actors and actresses. Curll omits almost everything that Gildon had
said on utterance or voice,[65] which had been Le Faucheur's most
important topic, and which Gildon had treated as subordinate to
gesture. But Curll gives most of Gildon's (and many of Le Faucheur's)
precepts on gesture, thus making it possible for us to say that well
before 1750 elocutionary doctrine in England had appeared twice in
the context of the art of acting.

V

The next episode, and a crucial one, in the early history of this doctrine in England concerns an anonymous pamphlet entitled *Some Rules
for Speaking and Action; To be observed At the Bar, in the Pulpit, and*

the Senate, and by every one that Speaks in Publick. This work was first published at London in August or September of 1715, and had an immediate run of popularity, with the result that it reached a third edition by the following February, and had two later editions by 1750.[66] I do not know where a copy of its first edition can be located. My present discussion is based upon the third edition, a copy of which is held by the Huntington Library. That copy contains 32 pages, and is made up of a short Preface, a section called "The Portraiture of a Compleat Orator," a passage "Out of Bishop Sprat's Charge to his Clergy," another passage "Out of Bishop Burnet's Pastoral Care," and an unsigned Letter dated Feb. 4, 1715–1716, and headed "Some Rules for Speaking and Action." The Preface is brief enough to be quoted in full:

This Letter was writ and printed about Six Months ago at the Request of a *Friend;* and the *Bookseller* being now about Publishing another Edition, and desiring me to give him what farther *Collections* I have made; I have prefix'd to it, *The Portraiture of a Compleat Orator,* which is agreeable enough to the Letter, as taken from *Quintilian,* and an *Epitome* of what the Bishops *Sprat* and *Burnet,* the one the *English Cicero,* the other one of the greatest Orators of the Age, have written upon this Subject. What other *Observations* I have since made, are inserted in the Letter; and indeed I should have digested what is prefix'd into the same Method, but only I thought there was no Occasion to be nicely Methodical in such a short Discourse, and which consists wholly of Hints and Sketches. I *submit* it to the World as it is, and shall be glad to see it *mended.*

As these words indicate, the author of the pamphlet considers that his own contribution to his subject is contained in his Letter on speaking and action. When we turn to it, we find that it begins on a note of apology for the author's unfitness, and that it declares his intention of relying only upon what others have said.[67] He later adds that his Letter is an epitome of volumes.[68] Despite this amiable pretension, however, he depends completely upon the first edition of the English version of Le Faucheur's *Traitté,* as a reading of the two works will reveal to anyone interested.

Perhaps the most significant aspect of *Some Rules for Speaking and Action,* apart from its connection with Le Faucheur's influence upon the early history of the elocutionary movement in England, is that it gets cited in John Mason's *An Essay on Elocution, or, Pronunciation,*[69] and thus it can be established as a source of what has hitherto been regarded as itself the main foundation and source of English elocutionary theory. That Mason relies upon the first or second edition of the English version of Le Faucheur can also be demonstrated. For example, Mason's discussion of the problem of varying the voice according to the passions and according to the parts of an oration has a clear source in Le Faucheur and his translator,[70] but it is not supported by anything in *Some Rules for Speaking and Action*.

VI

The closing episode of my present story concerns John Henley, who attracted more attention to the elocutionary movement than did anyone else of his time. Henley styled himself, in fact, the *"restorer of the ancient elocution,"* as Ephraim Chambers noted in 1738 in the second of many editions of his vastly popular *Cyclopaedia;* but, adds Chambers, Mr. Henley is confused when he uses the term elocution in this sense, and he means rather to call himself the restorer "of the ancient *pronunciation*." [71] Henley was still living when Chambers thus recognized and corrected his title to fame, and it is no small accomplishment for a living man to be mentioned in this special way in an important reference work, even with a rebuke implied in the notoriety.

Henley is also known to fame as Orator Henley.[72] Son of the vicar of Melton Mowbray and grandson of the vicar of the same parish on his mother's side, Henley was born in 1692 and educated at St. John's College, Cambridge. He became a schoolmaster in his native village, where, says his biographer, Mr. Welstede, he established the "Practice of improving Elocution by the publick Speaking of Passages in the Classicks, Morning and Afternoon, as well as Orations, &c." [73] During this time he began an extensive work on universal grammar, refused an invitation to apply for a fellowship at his college in Cambridge, wrote a historical poem called *Esther,* was ordained deacon by Dr. Wake (who figures earlier in this present essay), and, after receiving his M.A. in 1716, was admitted into the clergy of the Anglican Church. Successful at once as a preacher, and ambitious to succeed in this new career, he went to London equipped with thirty letters of recommendation, "and preach'd more Charity-Sermons about Town, was more numerously followed, and raised more for the poor children at those Sermons than any other Preacher, however dignify'd, or distinguish'd." [74] In delivering these sermons, Henley placed open stress upon proper utterance and gesture, influenced no doubt by the popularity of such treatises as the English translation of Le Faucheur, Gildon's misnamed *Life of Mr. Thomas Betterton,* and the anonymous pamphlet, *Some Rules for Speaking and Action.* At this same era of his life, Henley did a considerable amount of literary work. He published translations of Pliny the Younger's *Epistles* and *Panegyric,* of various works of René Vertot, of Montfaucon's *Diarium Italicum,* of Jean Pierre de Crousaz's *Logique,* and of Addison's Latin poems. He also edited *The Works of Sir Philip Sidney* (London, 1724–1725).[75]

But his growing reputation as preacher, his obvious concern for success, his introduction of elocutionary techniques into his sermons, and his literary exertions, began to tell against him. Mr. Welstede says that Henley's "Popularity, with his enterprizing Spirit, and introducing regular Action into the Pulpit, were the true Causes, why some obstructed his rising in Town, from Envy, Jealousy, and a Disrelish of those who are not qualify'd to be compleat Spaniels." [76] There is also a possibility, not mentioned by Welstede, that Henley's career in the Anglican establishment was impaired by rumors of his having been forced to leave Melton Mowbray because of a scandal linking him to a married woman, Mrs. Tolson, who was subsequently alleged to have followed him to London and to have passed as his wife.[77] At any rate, about the year 1724 Henley was relieved of his ecclesiastical duties in London and tossed "into a country-Benefice by the Way of the Sea, as far as *Galilee* of the *Gentiles.*" [78] Not in the mood to endure this exile from town, Henley gave up his country benefice and his career in the established church, returning to London to open on July 3, 1726, in quarters above the market house in Newport Market, an institution which he called The Oratory.

The Oratory had two aspects, one religious and the other secular.[79] On the former side its practices rested upon the legal right of private judgment in religion, and upon the liturgy of the primitive Christian church. As a secular institution, it was declared to be an academy of the sciences and languages to supply the want of a university in London. Thus Henley preached sermons on Sunday; and on week days he conducted public conferences, or had others conduct them, on a variety of subjects.[80] He widely advertised himself as a preacher who applied the proper rules of voice and gesture to the presentation of his sermons; and in describing the educational aims of The Oratory in the first sermon he preached there, he said: "Above all, what shall most strongly engage our attention, shall be the beautiful, and long neglected science of rhetoric and elocution." [81] He attracted so much attention with this concern for elocution that by 1727 the publisher of the first edition of the English version of Le Faucheur decided that a second edition would be a profitable enterprise, and commissioned an unidentified editor to see it through the press and to supply, as its title page declared, "an Introduction relating to the Famous Mr. *Henly's* present Oratory."

That introduction indicates at once the intensity of the public interest in Henley and the controversies that were surrounding his elocutionary techniques. It begins:

The Town having been of late very much alarm'd at the *Reverend* and *ingenious* Mr. *Henly's* extraordinary Performances and Attempts, to revive the antient Manner of Speaking in Public, upon all Occasions; several Pamphlets have appear'd in the World, and particularly one, written by Mr. *Wood*, which mightily condemns Mr. *Henly's* Gestures, comparing them to the absurd and indecent Gesticulations of a *Merry-Andrew* or *Harlequin*. Mr. *Wood* lashing the *Newport Market* Orator's Gestures so satyrically, and at the same time referring his Readers to the following Sheets, whereby they might judge how different Mr. *Henly's* Gestures were from the Rules laid down in them; great Demands were made for them, which is the real and true Occasion for their appearing abroad once more in public Print. . . .[82]

Having thus justified the republication of the English version of Le Faucheur, the editor goes on to speak of the circumstances under which it was first published in England and composed in France. Then he discusses speaking and action in oratory, and at length returns to the subject of Henley:

To Conclude. Notwithstanding the great Pains and Industry, of the *Reverend* Mr. *Henley,* and his under Strapers to collect Passages from Authors upon *Elocution;* Yet it is very much feared he will have but little longer Success, because his own Gestures are thought by many experienc'd *Orators* not conformable to the Precepts he lays down, and if they were, as they really in Fact are not; yet his Auditors cou'd never attain it, without a diligent and constant Practice.[83]

As for Henley's actual contributions to the doctrine of the elocutionary movement, we have space here only to mention one of his sermons. Indeed, it is his chief publication in this field, and it circulated widely in its time. But we should bear in mind that among the voluminous Henley manuscripts in the British Museum and the Guildhall Library,

London, there are other writings on this subject,[84] and that someday they too ought to be discussed, along with all of his scattered pronouncements of the same kind.

On Sunday, November 15, 1724, when he was still the rector of his country benefice, and had not yet broken with the Anglican establishment, Henley preached in the Church of St. George the Martyr, in London, a sermon on his theory of elocution. It was published the following year at the request of many in the audience under the title *The History And Advantages of divine Revelation, with the Honour, that is due to the Word of God; especially in regard to the most Perfect Manner Of delivering it, form'd on the antient Laws of Speaking and Action: Being an Essay to restore them.*[85] It was given a second edition in 1727, appearing as one of the units in Henley's *The Appeal of the Oratory to the First Ages of Christianity;* [86] and the same second edition was included as a part of one of Henley's later works, *Oratory Transactions, No. II.*

The sermon is on the text of I Samuel 3.1: "And the word of the Lord was precious in those days; there was no open vision." Henley lays down three purposes for his discourse, and proceeds to fulfill each. The first is that of commenting upon the several methods God used in the period between the Creation and the writing of the Gospels to reveal his will to mankind. The second is that of showing what honor and happiness came to men as a result of these revelations. And the third, which concerns Henley's theory of elocution, is that of weighing the respect to be paid to God's word in general and particularly in preaching upon it. Thus Henley speaks "of sacred eloquence, or the oratory of the pulpit; with regard to the publick exercise of it." [87] He presupposes, he says, that the preacher is qualified for his task by nature and by training, and that he has "a well weigh'd composition, or, a discourse in the mind, and a ready mastery of it in speaking." [88] What, then, should be the preacher's chief concern in utterance and gesture?

Henley's answer to this question sounds familiar to anyone who has followed Le Faucheur's ideas into their first English version and through their subsequent use by Gildon and the anonymous author of *Some Rules for Speaking and Action.* Indeed, in the second edition of the sermon now under consideration, Henley inserts a note which refers to what Bishops Ken, Burnet, Sprat, and Gibson had said in recommending greater attention to delivery on the part of clergymen,[89] and, as we know, Henley could have found in *Some Rules for Speaking and Action* the very passages in question, so far as Bishops Burnet and Sprat are concerned. Moreover, the following passage from Henley's sermon parallels the philosophy of Le Faucheur's *Traitté:*

In proper speaking and gesture, the nature of the thing spoken, strongly imprinted on the mind, and present feeling of the orator, is the only guidance; and as things are, in their own nature, various, they necessarily require a variation of the voice, and of the deportment, that is conformable to each of them: and the precise fitness of one certain sound and movement of the whole person, even to a line of the countenance, to one certain thing, most properly and perfectly express'd, and the consequent unfitness of any other, to it, are as demonstrable, as any proposition in the Mathematics.[90]

And the same parallelism becomes even more apparent when Henley recommends varying the voice in relation to the parts of the oration and the kinds of passions involved in it. He adds:

These, and all other subjects, claim a diversity of pronunciation, and of the conduct, agreeable to the distinct and true nature and merits of them. And this should be carefully study'd, in reading the offices of those churches, where prayers are to be read, as well as in the discourses.[91]

There is much else in this sermon to remind us of the part played by the English version of Le Faucheur in focusing attention upon delivery as a separate problem in rhetoric, and upon the extensive classical doctrine connected with that problem. But enough has been said to indicate Henley's debt to Le Faucheur's translator and to suggest that Henley himself contributed to the understanding of what he describes as "the nature of sacred elocution, the rules, the advantages, and history of it, the causes of our defects in it, the proper remedies, and the right treatment of objections to it." [92] But a further elaboration of his contribution is impossible at this time.

VII

In bringing this essay to a conclusion, I feel justified in saying that Henley, Gildon, Curll, and the unknown translator of Le Faucheur, as well as the anonymous author of *Some Rules for Speaking and Action,* should not be allowed henceforth to suffer the neglect that has been their lot since their own generation perished. They have much to teach us about the genesis of the elocutionary movement in England. And they have much to teach us about the merits and the shortcomings of that movement. No subsequent elocutionist in England was more firmly grounded in the classics than Le Faucheur proved himself to be, and no one of them understood better than he the other parts of the whole Ciceronian doctrine of rhetoric. He teaches us that voice and gesture are important in the total problem of oral communication, and he gives us a critical interpretation of the best classical thinking upon these matters. But also he makes us uneasily aware, as he himself was, that voice and gesture seem much more trivial when studied by themselves than they are when studied within the context of the best possible conceptions of invention, arrangement, and style. It was the solidest virtue of Cicero's and Quintilian's rhetorical writings that they saw delivery as an activity allied with, but never separable from, the speaker's need to know his subject, to arrange it properly, and to give it effective expression. Indeed, Cicero and Quintilian had learned this virtue from Aristotle, and the lesson should never be forgotten, even if we can safely forget some of the means provided by the ancients for guaranteeing knowledge of subject matter and for defining adequate standards of organization and style in discourse. Despite his other virtues, however, Le Faucheur forgot this lesson or saw it only as a pious formulation to which he must subscribe while he proceeded to do what the formulation forbade. Thus he and the other authors with whom I have here been occupied sought to save classical rhetoric by rediscovering its precepts of delivery and by emphasizing them by themselves, whereas in reality classical rhetoric could best have been saved by modernizing those precepts and by teaching them only within the context of a philosophically reconstituted theory of the other basic procedures of discourse.

Whately and His Rhetoric

WAYLAND MAXFIELD PARRISH

IF one accepts Aristotle's statement that rhetoric is "an off-shoot of Dialectic and of that Ethical science which may fairly be called Politics," then Richard Whately was unusually well qualified by taste, temperament, and training for the composition of a text on rhetoric.[1]

He published in 1826 a textbook on logic, which he several times revised in the course of its eight later editions, he served as Professor of Political Economy at Oxford from 1829 until his elevation to the Archbishopric, and he founded and endowed in the University of Dublin a chair of political economy. The influences surrounding him as student and tutor at Oriel College reacted favorably upon a temperament already strongly disposed to disputation, and his entire life was spent in an atmosphere of theological controversy. Whately's *Rhetoric* is essentially a textbook on argumentation. It was this phase of rhetoric which was of primary interest and importance in his mind, and which received from him the most attention in the five revisions of the work.

A. FORMATIVE INFLUENCES

THE INFLUENCE OF COPLESTON

Little is known of Whately's undergraduate years at Oxford except that he early attracted the favorable notice of his tutor, Edward Copleson, and the two formed a strong attachment which lasted as long as the latter lived. It is easy to imagine that Whately's taste for controversy may have been whetted by familiarity with the satirical and argumentative works which his tutor was at this time publishing. The first of these, *Advice to a Young Reviewer,* appeared in 1807, one year before Whately came up for honors. His *Examiner Examined, or Logic Vindicated* appeared two years later. It is a spirited, and at times brutal, attack upon Kett's *Logic Made Easy.* His furious controversy with the *Edinburgh Review* raged through the years 1811 and 1812. It is inconceivable that the young Whately, who must have known their authorship though they were all published anonymously, should not have been deeply stirred by these glorious battles of his beloved tutor, and it is quite likely that they did much to stimulate his interest in logic and in the technique of controversy. His indebtedness to Copleston for materials in his own treatise on logic is freely acknowledged, in his dedication and preface to that work, and in various places in his later correspondence with Copleston.[2]

Copleston's views on the nature and province of rhetoric, particularly in its relation to logic, are stated in one of the closing paragraphs of his attack on Kett:

Logic regulates. This may be placed at one extremity of the series. At the other extremity is Poetry, where language, as well as thought, is made subservient to the production of a refined pleasure. The several gradations of the scale between these extreme points are occupied by the various branches of Rhetoric, taking Rhetoric in its most extensive signification as the art of good writing. To demonstrate the reason of those principles which conduce to the end of good writing, to shew how they depart, and why they depart, from the rigid laws of Logic, is one of the most grateful services which philosophy can render to polite literature. When we measure these anomalies, as they may be called, by that standard, we better know how to estimate their propriety, their congruity, their relative force, and their utility. The doing of this, I admit, belongs to the province of Rhetoric, but without Logic it cannot be done. *The Examiner Examined,* p. 52.

A fuller account of the place of rhetoric in Whately's education may be found in Copleston's account of the "Course of Studies pursued at Oxford," which forms Chapter IV of his first *Reply to the Calumnies of the Edinburgh Review against Oxford.* In both the preliminary and the final examinations, candidates for honors were examined in logic (p. 140). In the later case:

The Examination then proceeds to Rhetoric and Ethics. Upon these subjects the celebrated treatises of Aristotle are chiefly used: and whoever is master of them knows what an exercise of the mind it is to acquire a thorough insight into the argument, and what a serious discipline the student must have undergone, who has accomplished this point. The accurate method observed in each treatise renders it not a perplexing, but merely an arduous task: the precision of the language, the close connection of the reasoning, the enlarged philosophical views, and the immense store of principles and maxims which they contain, point them out as the best calculated perhaps of any single works for bringing into play all the energies of the intellect, and for trying, not merely the intelligence of the scholar, but the habit of discrimination he has formed, the general accuracy of his thoughts, and the force and vigor of his mind. If it be at all of use to divide, to distinguish, and to define, to study clear arrangement and order, to discern connection, and to comprehend a plan composed of many widely separated parts, hardly any works can be named, so well adapted to these purposes. To these is often added, at the option of the student, the treatise on Politics, which is in fact a continuation and completion of the Ethical System.

Besides these treatises of Aristotle, Quintilian as belonging to Rhetoric, and the philosophical works of Cicero, especially that De Officiis, as belonging to Ethics, are admitted. And these last, as being of easier attainment, are of course the choice of many candidates. But neither of them are strictly indispensable (pp. 140–141).

This passage shows not only the content of a part of Whately's education, but also something of the aim and method of his tutor in teaching. It should be remembered that this content and this method were in all probability continued in Whately's own teaching during the years when the *Rhetoric* was taking form in his own mind and on paper. It is significant that the relative importance in Copleston's mind of the works here mentioned is almost exactly echoed in the number of references to each in Whately's *Rhetoric*.

The high esteem in which Aristotle's *Rhetoric* was held by Copleston is further shown in that portion of the first *Reply* devoted to a defense of Aristotle:

The Treatise on Rhetoric is a magazine of intellectual riches. Under an arrangement the most accurate perhaps and the most luminous ever marked out, the diversified elements of thought, of feeling, and of taste, are presented in due order to the reader's mind. Nothing is arbitrary, nothing gratuitous. Long experience with mankind, attentive observation of human nature in public and private life, the political history of past times, and the occurrences of his own age, furnished him with the materials of his great work. In the course of the enquiry, nothing is left untouched, on which Rhetoric, in all its branches, has any bearing. His principles are the result of extensive original induction. He sought them, if ever man did seek them, in the living pattern of the human heart. All the recesses and windings of that hidden region he has explored: all its caprices and affections, whatever tends to excite, to ruffle, to amuse, to gratify, or to offend it, have been carefully examined. The reason of these phaenomena is demonstrated, the method of creating them is explained. The third Book contains a body of rules for good writing, traced to these natural principles, out of which they all grow, and illustrated by examples, which his own intimate acquaintance with the best poets and orators of Greece readily supplied. The whole is a textbook of human feeling; a storehouse of taste; an examplar of condensed and accurate, but uniformly clear and candid, reasoning (pp. 26–27).

It would lead me too far, if I were to do justice to my own feelings on this subject (pp. 26–27).

Small wonder then that Whately should have been deeply influenced by Aristotle, and especially by the *Rhetoric*. Whately's biographer says,

He was perhaps the leader among those who rendered the ethics and rhetoric of the Stagirite for many years the class-book of his University, and who studied to unite them, by comparison and analysis, with all that they esteemed most valuable in modern philosophy. For the enthusiastic and exclusive Aristotelian tendency of Oxford minds, for a whole generation after his introduction to tutorial life, no man was so responsible as Whately.[3]

Of a somewhat later period John Morley wrote, "Whately's common sense had set a new fashion, and Aristotle was studied as the master of those who know how to teach us the right way about the real world." [4]

THE ORIEL COMMON ROOM

A very important formative influence of a later period was the Oriel Common Room. "Oriel College at that time," says a student of the period, "contained some of the most distinguished personages, the most vigorous minds, and the most attractive characters in Oxford. From the provost, Dr. Copleston, to the youngest undergraduate they had been carefully selected, for to get a son into Oriel was a great thing in those days. Keble, Whately, Tyler, and Hawkins were tutors." [5] He continues later (p. 21), "There was something more than a morbid intellectual restlessness in the so-called Oriel School of that day." This was the period "when Copleston and Whately ruled the college and threatened to dominate over the University" (p. 23).

"Copleston, Whately, Keble, Davison, Hawkins, Hampden, and Arnold," says another student,[6]

formed in Oxford what was known as the *Noetic* School, maintaining around them a continuing dialectical and mental ferment. Tommy Short used to say that Davison and Whately habitually crammed for after-dinner talk; and unfortunate outlanders whose digestion of the dinner and enjoyment of the port wine was spoiled by it, complained that Oriel Common Room *stunk* of logic. A country gentleman once, after listening to Whately's talk throughout the evening, thanked him formally for the pains he had taken to instruct him. "Oh, no," said Whately, "not instruct; I did not mean to be didactic; but one sometimes likes having an anvil on which to beat out one's thoughts."

Bishop Hinds, his pupil and lifelong friend, wrote that the "Common Room was to him not a mere place of resort for relaxation and recreation, but a school for sharpening his argumentative powers, and for training him to make that use of them in his social intercourse, in Parliament, and in other public assemblies, which was so striking and effective. It is hardly too much to say, that he was not less indebted to Oriel Common Room than to the college lectures in the earlier portion of his life." [7] Mark Pattison said the Noetics "called everything in question; they appealed to first principles, and disallowed authority as a judge in intellectual matters. There was a wholesome intellectual ferment constantly maintained in the Oriel Common-room." [8]

Such an environment would tend to stimulate Whately's natural independence and originality in thinking. He had in addition a blunt uncompromising honesty which, fostered in this circle of brilliant and sympathetic friends, led him to be at times more outspoken and tactless than was good for his own reputation. Mozley says,[9] "It would not be possible now to describe the terror his presence was sure to infuse among all who wished things to remain such as they were in their own lifetime. Instead of being comforted and built up in the good old fashion they were told they were altogether wrong, and must first retrace all their steps and undo all they had been doing. What was worse, the efficacy of the cure which had become necessary consisted in the hearers thinking it out for themselves." His biographer admits [10] that "Whately was never a popular man in the ordinary sense of the word. His opinions clashed too decidedly with those which prevailed in the Oxford society of his day to render him so in general life." The *Edinburgh Review*, in an obituary notice reviewing his *Commonplace Book*, and Fitzpatrick's *Memoirs of Richard Whately*, says,[11] "With younger men he had great influence through the generous and expansive nature of his political liberalism, and (it must be added) not a little of the Johnsonian tendency to argue down, trip up, and domineer over, antagonists in controversy."

No understanding of the *Rhetoric* can be complete which does not reckon with the vigor and originality of Whately's mind. He prided himself upon the independence of his thinking, and attempted to impart the same independence to his pupils. He was a master of the Socratic dialectic (though strangely indifferent to Plato [12]) and insisted always that his pupils think for themselves. Bishop Hinds gives an excellent example from his early Oxford days (1813) of his employment of the Socratic method upon a stranger encountered in a stage coach.[13] "Do not adopt my opinions because they *are mine*," he said to one of his pupils, "but judge for yourself." [14] To Lady Osborn he wrote,

And is it getting up a faction for me you are after? No, I'll have no Whately-ites! . . . I wish people to believe all the facts which I state on my own knowledge—because I state none which I have not ascertained to be true; and to listen to the reasons I give for my conclusions—because I never use any arguments which do not appear to me sound. And that is all the conformity I covet. Any one who tries to imitate me, is sure to be unlike me in the important circumstance of being an imitator; and no one can think as I do who does not think for himself.[15]

But while urging his pupils to think for themselves he sometimes, like the Platonic Socrates, insisted that they should reach the same conclusions as himself. While Newman acknowledges freely that Whately "opened his mind, and taught him to think and to use his reason," he adds, "When I was diverging from him in opinion (which he did not like) I thought of dedicating my first book to him, in words to the effect that he had not only taught me to think, but to think for myself." [16] Mozley is probably not far wrong in saying that Newman "would have been ready to love and admire Whately to the end, but for the inexorable condition of friendship imposed by Whately—absolute and implicit agreement in thought, word, and deed." [17]

As a partial consequence perhaps of this intolerance of opposition, he was frequently caught as his biographer observes,[18] "quoting, with much approbation, expressions of this or that follower, which in truth are mere 'Whateleiana,' consciously or unconsciously borrowed from him." It is certainly true that his religious works, as well as the *Rhetoric*, contain frequent appeals to the writings of his lifelong friends and followers: Hinds, Hampden, Senior, and Dickinson. On this point the *Edinburgh Review* observes,[19] " 'What people most readily and cordially approve,' he somewhere says, 'is the echo of their own sentiments'; and he does not seem to have been in the least aware how truly he was characterizing himself."

In this connection should be noted the comment of J. S. Mill that "he was the least equipped with books among any of the great thinkers of his time." [20] "His favorite authors were few," says his biographer. "Aristotle, Thucydides, Bacon, Bishop Butler, Warburton, Adam Smith; these were, perhaps, his principal intimates among great writers; and it will be easily seen that they are among the most 'suggestive'; among those who could furnish the most ready texts on which his ruminating powers might be expended." [21]

This meagre acquaintance with books was perhaps not so great a handicap in the composition of his *Rhetoric* as in the composition of some of his other works. He was well grounded in the rhetorical works of Aristotle, Cicero, Quintilian, Bacon, and of his immediate predecessors, Blair and Campbell. However, he evidently lacked acquaintance with, or interest in, the orations of Demosthenes, Cicero, and Burke,[22] and when he needs an illustration he turns, not to standard oratory, but to some theological essay of his own, or to the sermon of one of his pupils or friends.

Though Whately was independent and liberal in his religious opinions, so liberal that many questioned the wisdom of his elevation to the archiepiscopacy,[23] and the Commissioner of Stamps refused to exempt his *Thoughts on the Sabbath* from the Pamphlet Duty on the ground that it was not a religious work,[24] yet in fundamental matters he was sound and conservative, and a staunch champion of his church and creed.[25] So in the *Rhetoric*, though he states frankly all the objections that have been raised to the study and practice of rhetoric, and even claims that only second-rate minds can expect high success in oratory (p. 31), yet he takes Aristotle as his master, claiming that his treatise, though the earliest on the subject, is also the best (p. 7), since it is not *an* art of rhetoric, but *the* art of rhetoric (p. 16) and so follows in the main the traditional methods and teachings in the subject.

Guizot, then ambassador to England, who met him in London in 1840, has left an admirable summary of his character:

Parmi les prélats anglicans avec lesquels je fis connaissance, l'archevêque de Dublin, M. Whately, correspondant de notre institut, m'intéressa et me surprit; esprit originel, fécond, inattendu, instruit et ingénieux plutôt que profond dans les sciences philosophiques et sociales, le meilleur des hommes, parfaitement désintéressé, tolérant, libéral, populaire, et, à travers son infatigable activité et son intarissable conversation, étrangement distrait, familier, ahuri, dégiggandé, amiable et attachant, quelque impolitesse qu'il commette et quelque convenance qu'il oublie." [26]

HIS METHOD OF COMPOSITION

Whately's method of working out his ideas is described by his biographer:

As in the early school and Oxford days, of which we are now writing, so down to his latest times, the daily occupation of his brain was to seize on some notion of what he considered a practical order, belonging to any one of the various subjects with which his mind occupied itself; to follow it out to its minutest ramifications, and to bring it home with him, turned from the mere germ into the complete production. And this perpetual "chopping logic with himself" he carried on not less copiously when his usually solitary walks were enlivened with companionship. His talk was rather didactic than controversial; which naturally rendered his company unpopular with some, while it gave him the mastery over other spirits of a different mould. "His real object, or his original objects," (*sic*) writes one of his earliest and ablest friends, "was to get up clearly and beat out his ideas for his own use. Thus he wrote his books." *Life*, I, pp. 10–11.

It was thus that he worked out the principal parts of the *Logic* with his friend and tutor, Copleston.[27] And in a similar manner was evolved his early satire, *Historic Doubts Relative to Napoleon Bonaparte*.[28] Fitzpatrick records a letter from Newman in which he says, "It was one of his peculiarities at that time to hammer out his thoughts (if I may so speak) by means of other minds, and he conversed so well and so profitably, that it was a pleasure to be so employed by him." [29] Newman is here writing of his part in the composition of Whately's *Logic*. It is regrettable that no such direct testimony is available as to the composition of the *Rhetoric*. But presumably it was "hammered out" in much the same way, the anonymous "young friends" mentioned in the Preface serving as anvils.

As early as 1809 Whately began jotting down his thoughts in a Commonplace Book.[30] "He always considered this practice to have been highly beneficial to his own mind," [31] said his daughter. "It contributed undoubtedly to the clearness and correctness of his style; and by thus working out, correcting, and revising the results of his own reflections and studies, a vast body of materials was prepared for future works." The entries in the Commonplace Book are brief essays of one to ten pages each. It is significant that the notes to his edition of Bacon's *Essays* (1856) are not textual criticism or exposition, but similar brief essays on thoughts suggested by Bacon. Many of his longer writings, including the *Rhetoric*, as will be shown later, are made up of just such brief original essays, connected into a more or less coherent structure by short transitonal passages.

HIS INTEREST IN POLITICAL ECONOMY

Whately's interest in political economy may well have been derived from the studies of his undergraduate days. Copleston records that the subject was introduced into the lectures on modern history. To him, as to Whately, it was more a treatment of economy than of politics, though he deplores the fact that the study often narrowed the student's views, and "made him regard every public measure simply in the relation it bears to national wealth." [32] Whately's fondness for puzzles, problems, and "logical traps," [33] and his unsuitability for political philosophy of Burkian breadth, would lead one to expect in him a greater interest in speculation over economic problems, than in the application of political principles to a criticism of the British Constitution. It follows that for him political economy had little relation to rhetoric. He conceived rhetoric more as an art of theological disputation than as a science of influencing voters, legislators, and judges. The *Rhetoric* contains four references to Adam Smith's *Theory of Moral Sentiments*, but none to his *Wealth of Nations*. It contains one reference to Burke *On the Sublime*, but none to his speeches. It has frequent references to the then current theological controversies, but it contains no reference at all to the oratory of Pitt, Fox, Erskine, Canning, Brougham, or O'Connell. Oxford in Whately's day (1805–1831) might well have been a religious cloister, completely insulated from all political ideas. When later Whately sat with the bench of bishops in the House of Lords, he took an active interest in only three political problems: the transportation of criminals, Jewish disabilities, and the Irish poor laws. Lord Holland's remark to Guizot is significant: "'Je ne suis pas sûr', me dit Lord Holland, 'que dans son indiscrète sincérité il ne dise pas qu'il ne sait point de bonne raison pour qu'il y ait, à la Chambre des Lords, un banc des évêques.'" [34]

Historical Studies of Rhetoric

SUMMARY

Out of this milieu then was Whately's *Rhetoric* formed. The factors contributing to it may be summarized thus: a natural fondness for dialectic (in the Platonic sense of discussion by dialogue) and disputation, fostered by early training in logic, and in Aristotle's *Rhetoric,* and by the ferment of the Oriel Common Room; a long experience as a tutor in teaching both logic and rhetoric; a vigorous and independent mind, coupled with a blunt uncompromising honesty; an early acquired habit of using others as an anvil on which to hammer out his own thoughts, which were then recorded in essay form in his Commonplace Book; a tendency to depend too much upon a few congenial friends and a few familiar books; an ability to examine most questions with candid and unprejudiced mind while clinging tenaciously, almost intolerantly, to fundamental premises; a deep interest in political economy coupled with a curious indifference to politics.

B. Probable Date of the Composition of the *Rhetoric*

Of the exact date of the composition of the *Rhetoric* it is impossible to speak with accuracy. The finished work was published in 1828, probably early in the year, as it was reviewed in the *Monthly Review* for February of that year. De Quincey's well-known review appeared in the December number of *Blackwood's.* Of the history of the work prior to its publication we know little more than is stated in its Preface:

A brief outline of the principal part of the following work was sketched out several years ago for the private use of some young friends; and from that MS. chiefly, the Article "Rhetoric" in the *Encyclopaedia Metropolitana* was afterwards drawn up. I was induced to believe that it might be more useful if published in a separate form, and I have accordingly, with the assistance of some friends revised the treatise, and made a few additions and other alterations which suggested themselves, besides dividing it in a manner more convenient for reference.

The identity of the "young friends" is unknown, but they were doubtless Whately's pupils at Oxford during the period between 1811, when he was elected fellow of Oriel College, and 1822, when he married and left Oxford to take a pastoral living at Halesworth.

The *Encyclopaedia Metropolitana, or Universal Dictionary of Knowledge, on an Original Plan,* projected by S. T. Coleridge, began to appear in 1817, and continued by "parts" until 1845. Volume I, containing the

Rhetoric and *Logic,* seems to have been published complete for the first time in 1829. Coleridge's Introduction, attempting a methodical organization of the whole field of knowledge, makes no mention of rhetoric, but Whately's article on that subject follows immediately after his article on Logic. Whately's two contributions are preceded by Grammar, and followed by Geometry, Arithmetic, Algebra, etc.—all of which (rhetoric omitted) are classified in Coleridge's curious Prospectus as Formal Sciences, in the general division of Pure Sciences.[35]

The *Quarterly Review* for October, 1817, lists under "New Publications" Volume I, Part I of the new encyclopaedia. *Blackwood's* for May, 1818, notes the publication of Part II. And from then on for many years there are in various reviews announcements of the publication of successive "parts" of the work. Just what each part contained it seems impossible now to determine. There is, however, a hint in the *Gentleman's Magazine* for May, 1818, which notes under works nearly ready for publication, "The Third Part of the *Encyclopaedia Metropolitana,* containing the continuation of Grammar, in the Pure Sciences; the conclusion of Hydrodynamics, as including Hydrostatics and Hydraulics in the mixed and applied sciences; sections of the early History of Egypt, Assyria," etc. One may infer from this that the various articles were published piecemeal, and that a part of the *Rhetoric* was composed and published perhaps ten years before the publication of the entire work in 1828. But there is one factor which points to a later date. Cardinal Newman, in a letter to W. J. Fitzpatrick written in 1864,[36] says, "My part in Whately's Logic was small indeed. He wrote it originally in 'Analytical Dialogues,' as he called them. In this shape I first saw it in 1822. At the same date he employed me to draw it up in synthetical form; and when he wrote his article for the *Encyclopaedia Metropolitana* he made use of this rough draft of mine as a sort of basis for his own work." It is apparent then, if Newman's memory is accurate over this period of 42 years, that the article "Logic" was composed after 1822. And it seems likely that the *Rhetoric* was composed after the *Logic.* It was certainly second in Whately's interest, it follows the *Logic* in the *Metropolitana,* and as a separate work it appeared two years after the *Logic* was published.

It would seem to be a safe assumption, then, that though Whately may have made notes on rhetoric during his first years of teaching, and doubtless did at that time make numerous entries on the subject in his Commonplace Book, yet the finished work as it appeared in the

Metropolitana was probably not put together until the years of his pastoral service at Halesworth (1822–1825), or possibly even after his return to Oxford as Principal of Alban Hall.

C. Growth of the *Rhetoric*

The *Rhetoric* received a share of Whately's attention during at least twenty years of his life; that is, from its first conception, probably during his tutorial service at Oxford, till its final revision in 1846, after he had served for fifteen years as Archbishop of Dublin. During this period it went through eight editions: its first appearance in the *Metropolitana* and seven editions as a separate work. It was five times revised: in the first,[37] third, fifth, sixth, and seventh editions, and in the course of these revisions grew to considerably more than double its original dimensions. It would seem that to Bishop Whately to revise meant to enlarge. It is true that there are frequent changes in wording, aiming generally at increased clarity, but the bulk of the changes are additions, often of single phrases and sentences, but more often of whole paragraphs, or even of longer passages of one to twenty pages.

There are only three important excisions. One was a note to a part of the preface in which he took to task a writer in the *Westminster Review* for some criticism of Oxford. This note appeared in the first two editions, and thereafter was omitted. The second was a part of a note (cf. p. 158) defending himself from some criticism on his *Logic*. It too appeared only in the first two editions. The third was a passage of three long paragraphs (cf. p. 208) in criticism of Bentham's *Book of Fallacies*, which appeared originally in the text of the *Metropolitana* article, was reduced to a footnote in the first two editions, and thereafter omitted. It would seem that at about the time of his elevation to the See of Dublin, Whately made it a settled rule to abstain from personal controversy.

Of the 271 pages in that portion of the *Rhetoric* here under consideration, approximately 109 were in the *Metropolitana* article. A total of about 16 pages was added in the first edition, 33 in the third, 10 in the fifth, 19 in the sixth, and finally 84 in the seventh. The figures do not include additions placed in the appendix. Of the total of 162 pages added from first to last, 11 went to form a Preface, 25 were added to the Introduction, 78 to Part I, on Conviction, and 48 to Part II, on Persuasion. If we exclude from Part II the lecture on "The Intellectual and Moral Influences of the Professions," the additions to this Part total only 22 pages. To Part III, on Style, barely 6 pages were added to the original 75, and to Part IV, on Elocution, a similar amount was added. It is plain that Whately's primary interest was in Conviction, that part of rhetoric which lies closest to logic.

It is obvious from an examination of these changes that twenty years of revision made little alteration in the basic plan of the work. There is not one change in the order in which the items are presented, and there are only a few changes in the location of illustrative material. Neither are any important new topics introduced, if one excepts the discussion in the Introduction of composition exercises and debating societies. The most extensive additions are those on testimony and authority, analogy, and burden of proof and presumption, in Part I, and on the employment of appeals to the feelings and on inconsistency, in Part II. None of these, unless it be the last, is strictly speaking a new topic. The additions are in the main either slight variations on themes discussed in the original publication, or further illustration of such matter.

D. Sources of the *Rhetoric*

It is time now to inquire as to the sources from which Whately drew his materials. As he was scrupulously honest in acknowledging all his borrowings, this is a relatively easy task. As hinted above, his principal indebtedness is to Aristotle's *Rhetoric,* no less than 39 specific references to that work being made. There are besides several references to the *Poetics, Politics,* and *Ethics.* It would be difficult to find in Whately (or for that matter in *any* sound work on rhetoric) anything that is not stated or at least suggested in Aristotle, and yet he makes not a single quotation of any length from his acknowledged master. This is especially surprising since he does quote at length from Cicero, from Thucydides, from Campbell, and from others. But Aristotle seems merely to have furnished him with texts on which his own ruminative powers might work.

WHATELY'S DEFINITION OF RHETORIC

Whately's definition of rhetoric is unique. He does not follow Aristotle in limiting rhetoric to persuasion. This he thinks is too narrow a province. On the other hand he rejects the conception which he finds current in his day that rhetoric includes all composition in prose. Between these two he intends to steer a middle course, and to treat of rhetoric as "argumentative composition, generally and exclusively"

(p. 4). Instead of accepting the traditional or the current definition of the term, he uses "rhetoric" arbitrarily to cover the particular activity in which he is most interested. Then instead of justifying under such a definition the inclusion of a dissertation on persuasion, he remarks at the beginning of his treatment of that subject that "the *Conviction* of the understanding . . . is an essential *part* of Persuasion" (p. 175). He does not deplore appeals to the "passions" as extraneous to rhetoric, but quotes with approval Campbell's defense of such appeals as right and necessary (pp. 176–177), and claims that Aristotle deplored only "the excitement of such feelings as *ought not to influence* the decision of the question in hand" (p. 177). But he makes no attempt to justify his inclusion of rules for persuasion in a treatise which is to consider "argumentative composition exclusively." Indeed, in introducing the subject he says (p. 188) that he intends to give a few rules for "those parts of any Composition which are designed to influence the Will," as if he were treating here of a different kind of composition. His definition applies properly to his Introduction and Part I, but not to his treatment of Persuasion, Style, and Elocution, as he practically concedes in the first two paragraphs of Part I, Chapter II. All of these could have been included under Aristotle's definition.

It should be noted that Whately avoided the confusion of rhetoric with poetic which prevailed generally after Aristotle down to Campbell. Whately was evidently unacquainted with mediaeval rhetoric, and was not in this matter of definition influenced by his immediate predecessors, Blair and Campbell. His distaste for poetry was also perhaps an advantage.

THE SUBDIVISIONS OF RHETORIC

Whately's fourfold division of rhetoric into Conviction (the invention of arguments), Persuasion, Style, and Elocution, is distinctly his own. It does not parallel Aristotle's division of all proofs into artificial and inartificial, which Whately definitely rejects,[38] nor to the division of artificial into ethical, pathetic, and logical proofs. Whately, however, includes all these forms of proof, giving them his own arrangement, making ethical proof subsidiary to pathetic (Pt. II, iii). He ignores also Aristotle's division of rhetoric into three species, deliberative, forensic, and epideiktic. This is to be expected since he had little interest in either legal or legislative procedure, and eulogistic oratory was rare in his day. Neither does he follow the traditional fivefold division of classical rhetoric: *inventio, dispositio, elocutio, pronuntiatio,* and *mem-*

oria. His Part I treats of the "invention" of arguments, and in the same Part, Chapter III, sections 4, 5, 7, and 9, in Chapter IV, and in Part II, Chapter II, section 5, there are discussions of "disposition." The traditional *elocutio* is treated in his Part III, Style; *pronuntiatio* and *memoria,* in Part IV, Elocution. Whately was the first important writer to transfer the term "elocution" from style to delivery.

SOURCES OF PART I

Whately's indebtedness to Aristotle for his treatment of "Conviction," his page heading for this Part, is readily apparent. His division of all arguments into *a priori* and "the other class" (he rejects the term *a posteriori,* p. 52) is derived from Aristotle,[39] though he departs from Aristotle's subdivision when he classifies arguments from sign not with probabilities, but with example, under what are generally called *a posteriori* arguments. His discussion of probability (p. 47 ff.) borrows from both the *Rhetoric* and *Poetics* of Aristotle, and acknowledges indebtedness also to Campbell. On Testimony his debt to Aristotle is less evident. He borrows from Locke, Paley, and Campbell, and here as throughout the *Rhetoric* makes frequent reference to his *Elements of Logic.*[40] The section on the calculation of chances (pp. 76–81) is typically Whateleian in its presumably original observations based upon common sense and common experience, and in its evidence of a fondness for problems, and skill in inventing examples. The same may be said for the section on the argument from "progressive approach."

The treatment of example and induction (pp. 85–108) owes more to Aristotle, though he again makes frequent reference to his own *Logic.* He draws illustrative material from theology, chemistry, political economy, history, medicine, and common experience. He quotes from or refers to his own works on logic, on political economy, his *Lessons on Reasoning,* his speech on the Jewish Relief Bill, and cites also the Bible, Thucydides, Cicero, Mandeville, Bacon, Adam Smith, Copleston, and the *Edinburgh Review.*

The section distinguishing arguments of confutation from those which aim only to satisfy a candid mind (pp. 108–112), is again largely original, though it borrows paragraphs from Adam Smith and Paley, and refers once to Aristotle's *Ethics.* Whately's ruminative habits are further evident in the long section on Presumption and burden of proof (pp. 112–132). There is no clue as to what caused him to insert this topic in the third edition, and amplify it in subsequent editions. It owes no indebtedness to Aristotle or Campbell, but seems to be characteristically the product of Whately's own mind. The sources of his illustrations are as usual diverse. He cites his own *Logic* and several of his theological works, and draws material from Horace, Shakespeare, Milton, Bacon, Hooker, Johnson, and the Bible, as well as from his experiences with Parliament, and the popularity of his work on logic.

In treating of arrangement, too (pp. 137–146), he follows in the main his own mind, expressing regret that Aristotle and Cicero did not furnish more precepts on this topic. He returns to Aristotle for a text for his treatment of refutation (146–150), citing his division of refutation into counter-syllogism and objection, and his statement that there is no distinct class of refutatory arguments. Much of the discussion of this topic is somewhat technical, being drawn largely from the *Logic,* but it is unusually rich in illustrative material, drawn as usual from a wide range of reading and observation. Chapter IV on Introductions and Conclusions draws again from Aristotle and Cicero, but is characteristically original in treatment and illustration.

SOURCES OF PART II

In his treatment of persuasion Whately again takes his texts in the main from Aristotle and Campbell. The subject invites him to typical brief essays on the prejudice existing against excitement of the feelings, on the necessary indirectness of appeals to the feelings, on the dangers of practicing rhetoric on oneself, etc. Following the teachings of eighteenth century "Moral Philosophy" he conceives of reason and will as existing in separate compartments, and so not to be moved by the same means. He accepts Dugald Stewart's division of the "Active Principles of our nature" into appetites, desires, and affections, to which he adds self-love, and the "Moral-faculty" (Adam Smith's "sense of propriety"), but in the ensuing discussion of the conduct of appeals to the feelings, he makes no use of this division. Such an analysis of the various feelings as Aristotle gives, he does not feel called upon to make.

His brief caution against exhortation (pp. 190–192) seems to be his own, but in discussing the advantages of copious detail he borrows from Cicero, Quintilian, and Campbell. His only reference to Cicero's orations occurs in his treatment of climax (p. 197). Comparison, climax, and amplification are all considered in relation to their effect on the feelings, though Whately recognizes that they are "connected in some degree with style" (p. 199). The modes of heightening an impression, suggested in Aristotle's treatment of style, are by Whately included in this general discussion of the conduct of appeals to the feelings (p. 199). In lieu of Aristotle's analysis of the emotions and description "of the prevailing Characters of men of different ages and situations," Whately inserts at this point (p. 204) a reference to his lecture on the professional dangers to which ministers, physicians, and lawyers are subject.

In introducing the subject of "ethical" persuasion Whately frequently acknowledges his indebtedness to Aristotle, and quotes twice again from Campbell. He gives the subject an original turn by discussing the speaker's character chiefly in terms of the varying taste and intelligence of his hearers. His remarks on the disadvantages of being thought eloquent (pp. 210–215) are largely original. The basis of this discussion throughout is Aristotle's threefold division of character into intelligence, virtue, and good-will, and he found Aristotle especially rich in texts for his discussion of "authority derived from experience," "allaying of unfavorable impressions," and "ridicule."

In summary, then, it may be said that Aristotle's *Rhetoric* furnished the bulk of the texts from which Whately developed his thoughts on rhetoric. The whole treatise bears evidence of his preoccupation with logic. He borrows frequently from Campbell, and gets occasional thoughts from Cicero and Bacon. His thinking is colored throughout by his close familiarity with the writings of Butler, Paley, Adam Smith, and Copleston.

SOURCES OF HIS ILLUSTRATIONS

His illustrations are drawn from a somewhat wider range of reading. Among the ancients he refers frequently to Thucydides, and less often to Horace and Tacitus. He is familiar with Shakespeare. He draws more from eighteenth century literature than from his contemporaries. He refers frequently to the Bible, and very frequently to his own theological writings, and those of his friends, Copleston, Hinds, and Dickinson.

It may be well to tabulate the number of his references to or quotations from his principal sources. They are as follows: Aristotle's *Rhetoric*, 39; *Poetics*, 2; *Ethics*, 4; *Politics*, 1; Whately's *Elements of Logic*, 32; his various volumes of essays on theological subjects, 10; his charges, speeches, sermons, and other works, 15; the Bible, 16; Cicero's *De Oratore*, 8; *De Officiis*, 2; *Oration on Verres*, 1; Campbell's *Rhetoric*, 9; Bacon, 9; Thucydides, 8; Paley, 6; Shakespeare, 5; Adam Smith's *Theory of Moral Sentiments*, 4; the *Edinburgh Review*, 4; Butler's *Analogy*, 4;

Dugald Stewart, 3; Horace, 3; Tacitus, 3; Warburton, 2; Burke *On the Sublime,* 1; *Vindication of Natural Society,* 1; Milton's *Paradise Lost,* 1; *Tractate of Education,* 1; Swift, 2.

The Lowndes *Bibliographical Manual* lists ninety-seven published works by Richard Whately. These, so far as I have examined them, contain numerous quotations from and cross references to each other. The *Rhetoric* (i.e. excluding the portions on Style and Elocution) has no fewer than fifty-seven references to his other published works. It is hardly inaccurate to say that Whately's chief source was his own other works. Well might his biographer say, in commenting upon his comparative want of reading, that

he continually stumbled upon the thoughts of others, and reproduced them in perfect honesty as his own. This was one of his characteristics through life. It is singular to read one of his earlier critics commenting on his tendency to reproduce the "commonplace of other writers, not unfrequently, without any apparent consciousness of their ever having seen the light before"; while one of his latest, Mr. Stuart Mill, speaking of his philosophical investigations, says that "of all persons in modern times, entitled to the name of philosophers, the two, probably, whose reading was the scantiest, in proportion to their intellectual capacity, were Archbishop Whately and Dr. Brown. But though indolent readers they were both of them active and fertile thinkers." [41]

A word should be added concerning the facility with which Whately found illustrations from common observation of life, and the felicity with which he used them. For instance, in defending the necessity for having names for rhetorical terms, he asks us to consider the inconvenience to a carpenter of "having no names for the several operations of *sawing, planing, boring,* etc." (p. 19). In discussing the selection of subjects for school compositions, he says (p. 23), the student "may freely transplant indeed from other writers such thoughts as will take root in the soil of his own mind; but he must never be tempted to collect *dried specimens.*" He recommends (p. 142) that an unpopular thesis be kept out of sight as much as possible "because men listen with prejudice, if at all, to arguments that are avowedly leading to a conclusion which they are indisposed to admit"; and "if we thus, as it were, mask the battery, they will not be able to shelter themselves from the discharge." In recommending moderation in combating deep-rooted prejudice he says (p. 165), "Laborers who are employed in *driving wedges* into a block of wood, are careful to use blows of no greater force than is just sufficient. If they strike *too hard,* the elasticity of the wood will *throw out the wedge."*

In conclusion it may be said that inasmuch as the field of rhetoric is somewhat limited, and was completely surveyed by Aristotle, no new principles are to be expected in a modern work on this subject. Whatever claim to originality may be made for Whately, must consist chiefly in his novelty of illustration and of arrangement. As to his point of view it should be noted that throughout his treatment of the subject he looks primarily to the establishment of past fact, rather than to the determination of future policy. Even in his discussion of persuasion, he seems more concerned with an abstract moving of the will, than with a practical incitement to present action. Rhetoric for him has little to do with the legislature, charged with the determination of a wise future policy. It is rather the instrument of the theologian, bent upon proving the soundness of his doctrines, or the authenticity of his beliefs.

Whately on Elocution

JAMES A. WINANS

IN Bishop Whately's *Elements of Rhetoric,* which Jebb pronounces "undoubtedly the best modern book on the subject," the part most significant in the history of rhetoric deals with the topic he knew least about. I refer to Part IV, which he entitles "Of Elocution." Few of us consider his treatment adequate and many consider it unsound; but by his insistence that delivery should spring from thought and feeling rather than from rules and imitation he exerted a far-reaching and wholesome influence. The idea had been suggested before, but apparently waited for Whately to work it out and make it the core of a method of teaching.

The subject is not without present-day interest; for, as I believe, the majority of teachers of speaking still are Walkerites, though some of them may not know it and though many of this majority pay lip service to Whately's teachings. It may, therefore, be worth-while to clear up one's ideas of what Whately actually taught and what he was warring against.

His strictures on earlier writers lead one to turn to some of them, and especially to Sheridan, Walker, and Blair, whose works were in Whately's mind as he wrote.

Thomas Sheridan was an actor. Perhaps his greatest contribution to the world was fathering Richard Brinsley Sheridan; but he may have considered his greatest contribution to be his *Lectures on Elocution,* first published in book form in 1763. Fritz tells [1] us that this book was "the most popular work of the time."

178

Whately on Elocution

Sheridan laments the low state of English delivery, both in reading and speaking. This low state, he says, cannot be due to any inability in the English people, for if you listen to Englishmen conversing earnestly you will note that they deliver their sentences well. But if you write down their remarks and ask the same men to read their own words, they will do so in an artificial manner.

Sheridan blames the faults of English elocution on faulty teaching and false notions of what good delivery is. The true standard he finds in conversation, the natural standard of men conversing in earnest. So if you have a passage to read, he advises, think how you would say it if you were expressing the same ideas and sentiments in conversation, and say the passage that way. Moreover, "here is the sure standard for force and propriety in public speaking, which is to make use of the same manner" in public speaking as in conversation.

It seems evident that this fundamental rule of Sheridan's will tend to produce conversational style, mode, or manner, but not conversational quality. As I understand him, you are to go on the platform and imitate yourself as you speak in conversation. He does not say speak in public with the same mental action, or in the same spirit as in conversation, or with the same purpose of communication. His thought is always of manner, a manner consciously adopted, which will have the air of genuineness. Perhaps a natural thought for an actor.

There are, to be sure, passages in Sheridan which, read hastily and out of their contexts, might lead one to suppose his doctrine to be quite other than what it really is. Some of these have to do with persuasion, though persuasion receives but slight attention in the *Lectures* as a whole. For example:

When we reflect that the end of public speaking is persuasion . . . and that in order to persuade others to belief in any point, it must first appear that the person who attempts it is firmly persuaded of the truth of it himself; how can we suppose it possible to affect this unless he delivers himself in the manner which is always used by persons who speak in earnest? How shall his words pass for the words of truth when they bear not the stamp of truth?

These words sound like gospel, but a careful reading reveals that Sheridan calls only for the appearance of sincerity. "The speaker should at least appear himself to believe what he utters . . . but this can never be the case where there is any evident mark of affectation or art." So Sheridan advises the speaker who cannot have an ideal training:

Let him give up all pretensions to art, for it is certain that it is better to have none than not enough; and no man has enough who has not arrived at such a perfection of art as wholly to conceal his art; a thing not to be compassed but by the united endeavors of the best instruction, perfect patterns, and constant practice.

The passages just quoted remind one who has studied the lectures as a whole that they are addressed to adults who cannot hope to have proper instruction and to whom he is offering suggestions to enable them to do tolerably well. If they are still awkward and their tones are ill-regulated, well, after all, if they follow Sheridan's suggestions, they will probably do better than most English speakers. But he makes it clear that the ideal training is quite different; only unfortunately there is a lack of skilled masters to give such training. Ideally the masters would be equipped with elaborate rules in which they would train their pupils until the pupils had the art which conceals art; and presumably the masters would be "perfect patterns."

How thoroughly mechanical was Sheridan's method of reading is shown by his repeated lament that there is no established system of symbols by which an author could indicate in print, not only emphases, pauses, and inflections, but also tones and gestures. But still the case is not hopeless. When you are to read in public, either the words of another or your own, Sheridan suggests that you should go over the passage and decide on emphases, pauses, inflections, tones and gestures, marking them in some manner intelligible to yourself; and then you should go on the platform and give your mind wholly—to what? The content? No, to the manner of delivery.

If you speak extempore, continues Sheridan, you cannot, of course, follow this method; but if you will forget all those bad reading tones and the affectations common to English speakers, and try to speak in the same manner as in conversation, you will, let us hope, do pretty well.

Sheridan had done some thinking, and his insistence on "natural manner" probably contributed to the development of Whately's ideas. Whately refers to him as one of the best writers on the subject, "though he differs from me on the main question—as to the system to be followed with a view to the proposed object."

Contemporary with Sheridan was John Walker, another actor, whose *Elements of Elocution* (1781) has greatly influenced the teaching of delivery. One who takes no account of the temperaments of authors might suppose that Sheridan welcomed this book, for it seems to supply just that system of rules and that basis for the training of masters the lack of which Sheridan had lamented; but, as a matter of fact, Sheridan and Walker came to be looked upon as leaders of two hostile schools of elocution.

Walker's great pride was in his "discovery" of the upward and downward "turns" of the voice, and later of the circumflex. He tells us by definite rules how to use the turns for simple emphasis, double emphasis, and general emphasis. He lays down an appalling number of rules, many loaded with exceptions. For example:

Direct periods [i.e., periodic sentences] which commence with participles of the present or past tense, consist of two parts; between which must be inserted the long pause and the rising inflection.

But when the last word of the first part of these sentences requires a strong emphasis, the falling inflection must be used instead of the rising.

Walker treats of the modulation and management of the voice, of gesture, and of the passions. He tells us how to depict by voice, attitude, and gesture seventy-six different emotions. He thinks it is better when the reader feels the emotion, but since often he cannot feel a given emotion to order, Walker tells him how to show it anyhow.

It is interesting to note that some years after Walker published his *Elements* Sheridan published a book in which he also told how to express emotions. A comparison of the two treatments shows how close these two rivals were in their thinking. For instance, Walker says:

Modesty bends the body forward, has a placid, downcast countenance, levels the eyes to the breast, if not to the feet, of the superior character; the voice is low, the tone submissive, the words few.

While Sheridan says:

Modesty, or submission, bends the body forward; levels the eyes to the breast, if not to the feet, of the superior character. The voice low, the tone submissive; and words few.

Were both copying from the same actors' manual?

I am not here concerned with the correctness of Walker's rules. I was trained in some of them and they give me nostalgia for college days. They may have done me some good as a sort of voice training; but I am sure they did me much more harm. I have brought Walker in chiefly to say that I find no fundamental difference between him and

Sheridan. Sheridan takes for his standard conversation; Walker does not say what his standard is. Probably it is the way he, a trained actor, delivered sentences. The methods of both are thoroughly mechanical and tend to take the speaker's mind off meaning and audience.

My second reason for bringing in Walker is that his system is one of those, perhaps the chief one, that Whately objects to and ridicules.

The Reverend Hugh Blair devoted one discourse of his *Lectures on Rhetoric* (1783) to Pronunciation or Delivery. In great part his ideas seem to be derived from Sheridan, with perhaps an admixture from Walker. While he puts more stress on a "just conception of the force and spirit of those sentiments which you are to pronounce," the methods he suggests are as mechanical as theirs. For example, take these two bits of pure Sheridan doctrine:

The capital direction is to copy the proper tones for expressing every sentiment from those which Nature dictates to us in conversation with others.

In all prepared discourses it would be of great use if they were read over and rehearsed in private, with this particular view, to search for the proper emphases, before they were pronounced in public, marking at the same time the emphatical words in every sentence . . . and fixing them well in memory.

It is very difficult to see how Blair gets from such directions as these to his concluding words:

When a speaker is engaged in Public Discourse, he should not then be employing his attention about his manner, or thinking of his tones and his gestures. If he be so employed, study and affectation will appear. He ought then to be quite in earnest, wholly occupied with his subject and his sentiments, leaving nature and previously acquired habits to prompt and suggest his manner of delivery.

Plainly Blair had not thought out clearly a theory of delivery. He is mentioned here only because his concluding words may have had a part in setting to work the more logical mind of Whately.

In his *Elements of Rhetoric*, first published in 1828, Whately writes about Elocution with a fervor which indicates that he does not include the subject merely because it was customary to treat delivery in works on rhetoric. He roundly condemns all the systems of instruction that have been brought forward; and he doubts that they have helped anyone to attain a really good delivery.

But there are many, probably nearly as many as have fully tried the experiment, who have by this means been totally spoiled;—who have fallen irrecoverably into an affected style of *spouting*, worse, in all respects, than their original mode of delivery. Many accordingly have, not unreasonably, conceived a disgust for the subject altogether; considering it hopeless that Elocution should be *taught* by any rules; and acquiescing in the conclusion that it is to be regarded as entirely the gift of nature, or an accidental acquirement of practice. It is to counteract the prejudice which may result from these feelings, that I profess in the outset a dissent from the principles generally adopted, and lay claim to some degree of originality in my own. Novelty affords at least an opening for hope.

Admitting that previous writers have made some valuable remarks on elocution generally, Whately asserts that

there is one principle running through their precepts which . . . must vitiate every system founded upon it. The principle I mean is, that in order to acquire the best style of Delivery it is requisite to study analytically the emphases, tones, pauses, degrees of loudness, &c. which give the proper effect to each passage that is well delivered—to frame rules founded on the observation of these—and then, in practice, deliberately and carefully to conform the utterance to these rules, so as to form a complete artificial system of Elocution.

Before proceeding to argument Whately attempts to forestall some criticisms that are still being made upon his contentions; first by saying:

When however I protest against all artificial systems of Elocution, and all *direct* attention to Delivery, *at the time,* it must not be supposed that a general inattention to that point is recommended . . . though it may safely be affirmed that even this negative plan would succeed far better than a studied modulation. But it is evident that if any one wishes to . . . deliver a written composition with some degree of the manner and effect of one that is extemporaneous, he will have a considerable difficulty to surmount; since, though this may be called, in a certain sense, the *Natural Manner,* it is by no means what he will naturally, i.e. spontaneously, fall into. It is by no means natural for any one to read as if he were *not* reading, but speaking.[2]

Here we can see the difficulties in the term *natural manner,* which Whately has taken over from Sheridan. It has too many meanings, requires too much explanation, and leads to the absurdity, as here, of saying that it is not natural to be natural. Besides, it involves the fallacy of assuming that whatever is natural is good, an assumption that might be stretched to cover stammering, mumbling, cleft palates, thievery, and murder.

Whately also tries to forestall another objection by saying that it is not enough that the reader should actually understand the composition to be read, nor that he should be impressed with its force. He may still read as if he did not understand and were not impressed. He continues:

> The remedy that has been commonly proposed for these defects, is to point out in such a work, for instance, as the Liturgy, *which* words ought to be marked as emphatic,—in what places the voice is to be suspended, raised, lowered, &c. One of the best writers on the subject, Sheridan, . . . adopts a peculiar set of marks for denoting the different pauses, emphases, &c. . . . recommending that the habit be formed of regulating the voice by his marks. . . . To the adoption of any such artificial system there are three weighty objections. . . .
>
> First, such a system must necessarily be imperfect. No variety of marks that could be invented,—not even musical notation,—would suffice to indicate the different *tones* which the different emphatic words should be pronounced.

Among other examples Whately uses Macbeth's reply to the witches when they call his name three times: "Had I three ears I'd hear thee." Although emphasizing the right word a reader may give the absurd meaning, "Since I have but two ears I cannot hear you." Probably Walker would have said that with his marks for slides and turns he could indicate the proper reading of Macbeth's sentence; but Whately holds that the infinite possibilities of emphasis, pause, rate, and tone make an adequate system of marks impossible.

> 2ndly, But were it even possible to bring to the highest perfection the proposed system of marks, it would still be a circuitous road to the desired end. . . . The learner might ask, "but *why* should this tone suit the awful,—this the pathetic,—this the narrative style? . . . The only answer that could be given, is, that these tones, emphases, &c. are a part of the language;—that nature, or custom, which is second nature, suggests spontaneously these different modes of giving expression to the different thoughts, feelings, and designs, which are present to the mind of any one who, without study, is speaking in earnest his own sentiments. Then, if this be the case, why not leave nature to do her own work? Impress but the mind fully with the sentiments, &c. to be uttered; withdraw the attention from the sound, and fix it on the sense; and nature, or habit, will spontaneously suggest the proper Delivery. That this will be the case is not only true, but is the very supposition

184

on which the artificial system proceeds; for it professes to teach the mode of Delivery *naturally* adapted to each occasion.

It is surely, therefore, a circuitous path that is proposed, when the learner is directed, first to consider how each passage ought to be read; i.e. what mode of delivering each part of it would *spontaneously* occur to him, if he were attending exclusively to the matter of it; then to observe all the modulations, &c. of voice; then, to note these down, by established marks, writing; and, lastly, to pronounce according to these marks. This seems like recommending, for the purpose of raising the hand to the mouth, that he should first observe, when performing that action without thought of anything else, what muscles are contracted,—in what degrees,—and in what order; then, that he should note down these observations; and lastly, that he should, in conformity with these notes, contract each muscle in due degree, and in proper order; to the end that he may be enabled, after all, to—lift his hand to his mouth; which by supposition, he had already done.

Whately's analogy here is the probable source of Nathan Shepard's more spicy comparison in his *Before an Audience:* "Finding that when eating, every time your elbow bends your mouth flies open, therefore this rule: When your elbow bends, open your mouth."

3. Lastly, waiving both of the above objections, if a person could thus learn to read and speak, as it were, by *note,*—still the desired object of a perfectly *natural* as well as correct Elocution, would never be in this way attained. The reader's attention being fixed on his own voice . . . the inevitable consequence would be that he would betray more or less his studied and artificial Delivery.

Whately does not explicitly recognize as a fourth the most serious objection of all: that thinking how one's voice goes interferes with one's attention to meaning. But that objection is plainly indicated in later passages; for example:

The practical rule then to be adopted . . . is, not only to pay no attention to the voice, but studiously to *withdraw* the thoughts from it, and to dwell as intently as possible on the Sense; trusting to nature to suggest spontaneously the proper emphases and tones.

This natural manner, i.e. the manner which one naturally falls into who is *really speaking,* in earnest, and with a mind *exclusively* intent on what he has to say.

Whately will not compromise and agree with many who acknowledge that "it is a great fault for a reader to be *too much* occupied with

185

thoughts respecting his own voice," and think to steer a middle course between opposite extremes. "A reader is sure to pay *too much* attention to his voice, not only if he pays *any at all,* but if he does not strenuously *labor to withdraw* his attention from it altogether."

This does not mean, Whately points out, taking no pains. It is not easy to keep attention on meaning to the degree he proposes. One's mind tends to wander to other matters, or to leap forward to the next sentence. He also points out that his method precludes the easy way of imitation.

So far Whately has been treating of reading and mostly of reading the words of others, for he, like Sheridan, was particularly interested in improving the reading of the church service. He also takes up the reading of one's own compositions, and his treatment of this topic may be passed with the statement that it is just what one would expect from the foregoing. The aim in such reading is to approach as nearly as may be to extempore style; and while it is impossible to reach extempore style when reading, one may approach indefinitely near. If Whately's ideas are carried out, he says, the reader will not seem, as most do, to be saying as a running commentary, "I do not mean, think, or feel all this; I only mean to recite it with propriety."

Bishop Whately seems to think no difficulties arise in carrying out his ideas when speaking extempore. He ignores the fact that at times it is very difficult to keep one's mind from straying even when extemporizing.

Passing over much in Whately's discussion and also over the criticisms [3] that have been made upon it, I now proceed to some comments of my own upon his doctrine.

1. While Sheridan, Blair, and Whately all agree that thinking and feeling prompt adequate expression in wide-awake conversation and in extempore speechmaking, Whately was the only one of these to state clearly, and to make the statement an article of faith, that the same cause will prompt adequate expression in reading. There should be no rules, no marks for emphasis, pause, inflection, tone, or gesture. One should speak with "a mind exclusively intent on what he has to say" and trust entirely to thought, feeling, and speech habits.

2. Whately pays little attention to voice training and the like. He does say (following Blair in this) that if one has habitually ungraceful gestures, or if in common discourse one has indistinct, hesitating, dialectal, or otherwise faulty speech, he should endeavor to remedy

the defect, "not in public speaking only, but in ordinary conversation. It is in these points, principally, that the remarks of an intelligent friend will be beneficial."

If the Bishop should today look over the battlements—presumably of heaven—he would be amazed to see the expensive laboratories and the corps of specialists who now take the place of his intelligent friend. It would hardly have occurred to a cultivated Englishman who did his teaching in Oxford that speech defects were problems. Had his teaching been done in one of our city or state universities, with students reared under all sorts of influences, he might have given the topic more than a page. Nevertheless in that page he did open the door for remedial work. I imagine he would say now, "Very well, so long as you keep your training strictly as training and do not cause considerations of phonetics, intonation and the like to become a part of your student's speechmaking consciousness; so long as you do not cause your students to think of these matters when on the platform."

3. While the teachings of Sheridan and Blair would tend to produce conversation *style* or *mode*, through imitation of delivery in conversation, I doubt that Whately's teaching would do even that, or tend to the natural manner they all aim at. Whately says many will object to what they will call a "colloquial style of delivery" and say it is "indecorous and unsuitable to the solemnity of serious, and especially of religious discourse." He says also that the natural manner even when most elevated and solemn, will remind the hearers of the *tone* of conversation. All this indicates that he aimed at public delivery which *sounds* like conversation. But I fail to see how he could get that out of his teaching, for he puts all the stress on *exclusive* attention to matter.

Now *exclusive* is a strong word, and Whately uses it over and over and stresses it with italics. But it seems evident that if one gives all his attention to subject matter, he cannot give any to the audience. Think the thought, feel the sentiment, says Whately, and all will be well. But I suppose that is precisely what Hamlet was doing when he exclaimed in solitude, "Oh, what a rogue and peasant slave am I!" and when he gave vehement thought to suicide. Yet surely it would take a dull auditor, listening to a poor actor, to miss the difference between Hamlet's soliloquies and his direct speeches. Whately's teaching misses a half or two-thirds of the truth, and leads straight to soliloquy.

Soliloquy may be a natural manner, and it is natural for some to stand up in public and talk with themselves; but soliloquy is certainly not the kind of speaking Whately is advocating, which is delivery that sounds like conversation. Sheridan might attain conversational style by imitating conversation; but Whately's teaching will not lead even to that. And certainly his teaching will not lead to conversational *quality*, for soliloquy lacks the essential element of conversation, communication with others.

It is surprising that the keen Whately never came through to recognize the other necessary element in delivery, what I like to call "a sense of communication." The idea seems to have been lurking in the back of his mind, and he comes so near to it that at times one feels like crying out, as in the game of button, button, "He's getting warm!" One of his warmest spots is where he says that one not used to the "natural manner may be embarrassed at finding himself, as it were, stripped of the sheltering wall of a conventional delivery—delivering his thoughts as one man *speaking* to other men"; and also that the audience may give greater attention "from their perceiving themselves to be personally *addressed,* and feeling that he is not merely reciting something before them, but saying it to them." Whately is warm here!

But probably because he is intent on combating mechanical methods and enforcing the belief that thinking should prompt delivery, he never quite comes through to say that the feeling of contact with the audience has a definite effect upon delivery, and he never urges that the learner should cultivate this feeling. His nearest approaches to the idea are rather incidental. When he is really telling us how to acquire the "natural manner," his stress is all on exclusive attention to subject matter.

Nevertheless, although Whately missed a trick, we owe him much, even those who do not agree with him in the main. It was wholesome to have his ideas vigorously pressed upon us, for we are all prone to get lost in technicalities.

John Thelwall: His Life,

His School, and

His Theory of Elocution

FREDERICK W. HABERMAN

PERHAPS the most remarkable professor of oratory and elocution in London early in the nineteenth century was John Thelwall. "Citizen" John Thelwall had not always been a professor of rhetoric. In fact, the announced decision of John Thelwall in 1801 to open a school of oratory and elocution created a minor sensation. A revolutionary patriot had turned professor. A demagogue stood revealed as a pedagogue.

I

Like most demagogues and even some pedagogues, Thelwall had not followed a single road to fame. In the course of a life that extended from 1764 to 1834, he had changed directions more than once.[1] By the time he was fourteen years old, Thelwall had attended several schools where (in his opinion) he underwent various degrees of physical and intellectual injury. He was apprenticed in turn in the family dry goods store and then in a tailor shop, but, disliking both the needle and the counter, he turned to law. For three-and-a-half years, Thelwall read the law, but with only half an eye. He spent most of his time reading the poets and the philosophers, and in selling the manuscripts of pieces he himself composed. Thelwall found law repugnant because, as he said, it made the fee "the major and minor of moral proposition." He discovered that he wanted to know what was true, not how best to support his client—a ruinous prejudice.

Aged twenty-two, Thelwall began his literary career, publishing first a volume of poetry which was moderately well received. Within five years, his annual income from sundry literary engagements and publications had risen to something between two and three hundred pounds, a respectable sum, despite the remark of an eminent nobleman that it took forty thousand pounds a year "to jog along."

Meanwhile, Thelwall had been carrying on a secondary career in public life. He first came forward in the debating society at Coachmaker's Hall in 1783 when he was nineteen. His interest in public questions became so concentrated under the potent excitement of the French Revolution that he spent the seven years from 1791 to 1798 as a reforming zealot. Imprisoned for seven months by the Pitt government in 1794, Thelwall, along with Horne Tooke and Thomas Hardy, was acquitted of treason by Lord Erskine's celebrated plea.

Violence and contumely finally drove Thelwall into voluntary retirement. For two years he devoted himself to farming, but his was not a nature to thrive on silence and solitude. Returning to London in 1801, he founded his school of oratory and elocution. The school prospered. For three decades it attracted considerable attention because of Thelwall's lectures and because of the interest shown in the school by some of the contemporary men of letters, among them Coleridge, Southey, Hazlitt, Lamb, Thomas Noon Talfourd, and Henry Crabb Robinson.

Although Thelwall never achieved historical eminence, he was nonetheless one of the outstanding speakers of his day. His speeches lack academic polish, but they contain a full complement of ardor and pungency; they are humorless, but honest; inflammatory, but practical; discursive, but energetic. The qualities of the man himself are epitomized in a statement by Coleridge: "John Thelwall is a very warmhearted, honest man, and we like each other uncommonly well. . . . He is intrepid, eloquent, and honest, perhaps the only acting democrat who is honest." [2]

II

Thelwall's announcement in 1801 of the founding of his school caught immediate attention. "This bold and daring scheme," one writer remarked, "alarmed some of Mr. Thelwall's friends, astonished and mortified his political enemies, and created no small speculation in literary and scientific circles." [3]

Thelwall aimed to provide, as he said, "a proper system of oratorical education" in a land that is "an exhaustless mine of oratorical capability." [4] Thelwall's establishment, in reality, developed into a combination of "clinic" for the cure of impediments of speech, of private school for instruction in the traditional subjects of the day, and of professional tutorial school for adults who sought aid in certain speech and oratorical problems.

A publication called *Terms of Instruction* gives us some information about the school.[5] Three age groups were eligible for enrollment: junior pupils, young gentlemen and ladies, and adults. For instance, gentlemen designed for the pulpit, bar, or senate, and desirous of "being accomplished in the science and practice of Elocution" were accommodated with board, room, and instruction at 200 guineas a year. Thelwall also maintained a consultative service by appointment. Thus, a clergyman could make an appointment for a certain time, when, in one sitting, Thelwall would go over with him the entire morning and evening service. Fee, five guineas.

Thelwall was proud of his library of 4000 volumes, but even prouder of the Historical and Oratorical Society, a school organization that met every Monday evening. At these meetings, there were disquisitions, debates, declamations, and orations. Since the subjects of debates and orations were drawn from past events in English history, safely removed from the passions of the day, the Society was but a pale reflection of that turbulent Coachmaker's Hall where the master first discovered his power.[6]

Thelwall himself lectured to distinguished audiences at the Institution, his listeners including John Britton, Godwin, Holcroft, Dr. Wolcot, Major Cartwright, Kenny, Robinson, Lamb, Quin, Cline, Taylor, and many other eminent men. Sir Thomas Noon Talfourd remarks that Thelwall's lectures were delivered with much enthusiasm, adding,

Sometimes, indeed, his fervour animated his disquisitions on the philosophy of speech with greater warmth than he reserved for more attractive themes; the melted vowels were blended into a rainbow, or dispersed like fleecy clouds; and the theory of language was made interesting by the honesty and vigour of the speaker.[7]

In short, behind the pedagogue, there still stood the ghost of the demagogue.

III

Thelwall called himself an elocutionist; he called his institution a school of elocution; and he called his doctrine a theory of elocution. In 1800, what did those labels mean? Their meaning may best be explained by a brief examination of the fifty-year-old tradition of the elocutionary movement. For Thelwall was a part of that movement; much of his theory and practice may be most readily understood by referring to the theories and practices of the movement itself.

Elocution was an offshoot of rhetorical study. It was an exhaustive and systematic analysis of delivery. The elocutionary movement, which began about 1750, was a response to the demands of the age. This widespread and intense study of delivery was an answer to the eighteenth-century denunciations of oratorical frigidity, to the pressure for professional and educational training in speech, to the new consciousness of the need for standardization of spoken language, to the desire of the people to obtain facility in speaking a language of which they were becoming proud, and to the demands of those who dealt with democratic movements. The elocutionary movement, however, was more than a simple renaissance of a particular canon of rhetoric. It was, rather, a new ordering of an old subject.

This new ordering resulted from the application of the tenets of science and of rationalism to the physiological phenomena of spoken discourse. The new study of delivery was affected by the impact of science and of rationalism in precisely the same way that the study of history, of economics, of politics, of poetry, and of prose style was affected. The spirit of elocution, like that of science, was one of independence and originality. The elocutionist looked forward to a golden age, not backward. The methodology of the elocutionary movement, like that of science, was a combination of observing and of recording. Just as the astronomer observed the movements of the planets and recorded them in special symbols, so the elocutionist observed certain phenomena of voice, body, and language and recorded them in systems of symbolic notation. The philosophy of the elocutionary movement, as of rationalism, was a conception of man controlled by natural law. The rationalist believed that the nature of man was governed by the same order and law which seventeenth-century science discovered in the nature of the universe. Implicit in the minds of the elocutionists was the sense of a mechanical order in nature. Thus their rules and their systems, of which they were so vain, were claimed to represent the order that is found in nature; they were "nature still, but nature methodized."

Animated by this spirit, philosophy, and methodology, the elocutionists investigated various phases of delivery. Their diverse contributions to the study may be grouped into four divisions: gesture, voice management, vocal production, and pronunciation.

The division of gesture included all physical action. James Burgh, in his important book, *The Art of Speaking*, analyzed the proper and universal actions to be used in expressing certain emotions.[8] His assumption, shared by other elocutionists, of a natural determinism in emotional expression persisted through much of the nineteenth century.

The division of voice management included accounts of accent, pitch, pause, rhythm, force, and emphasis. John Walker formulated the inflective system of voice management, developing it from an exhaustive analysis of the interplay of vocal elements and grammatical forms.[9] Joshua Steele analyzed vocal elements on musical principles, and applied musical notation to printed discourse, so that one might sight read an oration as he would a sheet of music.[10]

In the division of vocal production, the elocutionists made attempts to find consistent phonetic principles and to understand the physiology of speech, but the first important investigations in this division did not take place until the nineteenth century.

The division of pronunciation was concerned with the correct phonation of words, knowledge of which was vital to graceful elocution. Sheridan produced the first pronouncing dictionary of the English language in 1780;[11] but Walker's dictionary,[12] published eleven years later, supplanted it, and became the "statute book of English orthoëpy."[13]

IV

In 1800, after fifty years of existence, elocution had a temper and a subject matter. John Thelwall's work is a faithful reflection of this elocutionary tradition. The spirit he brought to his work was eager, inventive, and daring, though reduced in effectiveness in his case by a haphazard scholarship. In methodology, he stayed in step with the movement. As an observer, he brought to his work the results of twelve years' experience in popular oratory and the knowledge gained by attending the anatomical lectures of two distinguished London physicians. He did not invent any system of symbolic notation, but he used those systems that were now becoming public property. His philosophy, identical to that of the movement, held implicitly that man, like the universe, is governed by the mechanical laws of nature, and that the task of the investigator is to discover those laws.

That Thelwall touched upon each division of the subject matter of elocution in the school is indicated by his published list of 30 lectures.[14] But his four published rhetorical works are almost exclusively concerned with the divisions of voice management and of vocal production.[15] He published nothing on pronunciation, and allocated only a portion of one essay to gesture.[16]

Thelwall's personal conception of elocution, the fundamental principle of voice management and of vocal production which he formulated, and the application of this principle to the teaching of elocution in his institution are inseparably connected.

Thelwall conceived of elocution as a science. He based elocution on the science of physiology which demonstrates the anatomy of the vocal organs and the laws of physical necessity in speech, on the science of music which explains the rhythm and harmony of speech, and on the science of philology which settles disputed questions of accent, pronunciation, and quantity.

The utility of the science of philology to the division of pronunciation in elocution is self-evident. It was from an interaction between the science of physiology and the science of music that Thelwall constructed his distinctive doctrine of voice management and of vocal production. He called this doctrine the principle of rhythmus. He learned from physiology that there is a rhythm in the production of speech sounds by the vocal organs, a pulsation and remission, an action and reaction, an ebb and flow, and that this pendulum-like action is from heavy stress to light stress. He called this action the law of vocal progress from heavy to light. He learned from musical science that there is an identity in rhythm between music and literary composition, that the rhythm of prose and of poetry is cadential, that these cadences can be measured into musical bars, and that this rhythmic action is regularly recurrent. He called this rhythmic action the law of measured cadences. The principle of rhythmus is, then, the combination of the law of vocal progress from heavy to light and the law of measured cadences. The principle asserts, in other words, that the rhythm of vocal production must be synchronized with the rhythm of literary composition in order to produce proper speaking. If the gears do not mesh, then at its best, the speaking will be unpleasant, and at its worst, be stammering. The principle of rhythmus, therefore, is at once a technique for curing speech defects, and a technique for teaching a just and pleasing speaking style.

The law of vocal progress from heavy to light is eccentric. Thelwall states unequivocally that heavy and light accents alternate. Clearly, however, alternate heavy and light accents do not occur in some three-syllable words such as *honestly, murmuring,* and *wishfully;* nor in some four-syllable words such as *beautifully* and *honorably.* Thelwall did not adhere to this alternation in his own scansions, for he frequently has dactyls, anapests, and spondees, and in one horrible example has a cadential foot composed of five unaccented syllables. Absurd as this law appears to be, it survived in elocutionary writing for over three-quarters of a century.

The law of measured cadences, however, is of some importance in the history of elocution, of oral interpretation, and especially, of prosody. Amplifying this law, Thelwall says that "in all harmonious utterance, the time occupied by each cadence, in a given sentence or passage is to be the same, whether the cadence contain one syllable or several. . . ." [17] Thelwall here states that the essential prosodial element in verse or prose is *time*. Metre is equated with its etymological meaning of *measure*. He disavows syllable counting as the key to rhythm. Unfortunately, his conception of stress was vague, and his knowledge of oratorical effect constantly interfered with his prosodial practice. For instance, he puts as many cadences in a single line of poetry as he pleases. Thus he scans Milton's "Paradise Lost" into lines of four feet, five feet, eight feet, and one into ten feet; yet Milton was under the impression that he constructed pentameters.

The idea of cadential measure in speech was derived in large part from Joshua Steele's book *Prosodia Rationalis,* published in 1775. Steele's ideas were carried on in the early nineteenth century by Thelwall, Roe, Odell, and Chapman; in the mid-nineteenth century by the poet Coventry Patmore; and in the early twentieth century by the distinguished scholar, T. S. Omond. Omond, though recognizing the absurdities of Thelwall's work, yet finds much to admire. "Surely it is discreditable to English prosody," he writes, "that work like Odell's and Thelwall's remained almost entirely unnoticed; unanswered not because unanswerable, but because unread. So it was however; we shall find the high priests of criticism sublimely unconscious of their contributions to metrical science. . . ." [18] Now George Saintsbury is a high priest of criticism, but not one who is unconscious of Thelwall. Far from it. Saint George rides to destroy the dragon. After reading Thelwall's *Illustrations of English Rhythmus*, Saintsbury concludes that Citizen John Thelwall might have been "none the worse for a hanging." [19] But Saintsbury is less discriminating in his censure than Omond in his praise.

These laws of cadential utterance were not, in Thelwall's mind, divorced from practical application. His pedagogy was rooted in the principle of rhythmus. On the utility of scanning, for instance, he insists that theory should coincide with practice. He admonishes the student in these words:

In working out these exercises, the student is expected to scan every cadence into its correct quantity; to score out every passage into its proper bars, with all the regularity of a piece of music; and to read them over, reiteratedly, under the regulation of the time-beater,—sometimes solo, and sometimes in chorus; sometimes accompanied by the voice of the tutor, and sometimes without such guidance;—while the critical ear of that tutor, watches every tone and every quantity. . . . [20]

We might characterize these time-beating doctrines as "metronomic elocution."

This metronomic doctrine was applied to the reading of prose as well as of poetry. "As soon as the rhetorical rhythmus begins to be understood [by means of scanning prose]," he says, "animated recitation should, occasionally, relieve the more tame and sedentary practice of cadential reading; and should, also, at first, be practiced under the regulation of the time-beater; the pauses being as regularly measured as the sounds. . . ." [21] The orator may eventually break free of the fetters of the time-beating tutor, but he must always obey the law of rhythmus, which, even in oratory, is dependent upon "metrical proportions of cadences and feet."

Thelwall developed the theory and the application of the principle of rhythmus in intricate detail. Yet it is clear that he erected too high a structure upon too narrow a foundation. Thelwall took both his strength and his weakness from the elocutionary movement itself. He, along with the other elocutionists, planted the seeds or stimulated the growth of many modern speech subjects, such as oral interpretation, voice training, phonetic science, and speech therapy. But Thelwall,

196

along with the other elocutionists, suffered the limitations of a mechanistic philosophy. He was concerned with only the externals of delivery, with physiology and not with psychology, with light waves and sound waves and not with the power plant. He studied measurable things: the volume of a voice, or the time of a cadence, or the quantity of a vowel; and shunned the immeasurable things, such as the personality of a speaker or the context of a passage. In his quest for the universal law he passed by the individual man.

Despite his eccentricities and his limitations, Thelwall was the outstanding speech therapist and the foremost lecturer and teacher of elocution in his day. If we are to characterize his career, we can do no better than to quote the words of Sir Thomas Noon Talfourd. Speech was, in Thelwall, said Talfourd, "his all in all, his delight, his profession, his triumph."

De Quincey on Rhetoric
and Public Speaking

HOYT H. HUDSON

WHEN the schoolmaster at Bath said of thirteen-year-old Thomas De Quincey, "That boy could harangue an Athenian mob better than you or I could address an English one," he singled out one of the interests which De Quincey maintained throughout his long life of study—an interest in public speaking and rhetoric, rooted in a knowledge of the Greek masters. True, he never himself faced the perils or sought the prizes of public address; and in scattered passages he attacks, or at least discounts, wielders of rhetoric. Those familiar with the criticism of oratory need not be told that it is contemporary orators he discounts, in favor of the "giants" of a generation or two previous, and that he uses a skilful rhetoric to make his attack upon the art.

One or two of De Quincey's reminiscent anecdotes relate to quelled orators. "Ah! what a beautiful idea occurs to me at this point," he exclaims on one page of his burlesque novel, *The Spanish Military Nun.* "Once, on a hustings at Liverpool, I saw a mob orator, whose brawling mouth, open to its widest expansion, suddenly some larking sailor, by the most dexterous of shots, plugged up with a paving-stone." At this point the veil is drawn.

More revealing, perhaps, is an incident of his childhood. Thomas' elder brother had taken it upon himself to give lectures in physics to the other children of the family and their playmates. His "habit of

De Quincey on Public Speaking

lowering the pitch of his lectures with ostentatious condescension to the presumed level" of his hearers' understandings, however, so irked his sister Mary that she planned an insurrection. When the speaker came to say, as was his custom, that he flattered himself he had made the point under discussion tolerably clear, gratuitously adding "to the meanest of capacities," there was a feminine voice raised protesting, "No, you haven't; it's as dark as sin." This was followed by a second voice—Thomas' we may presume—saying, "Dark as night," and still another with, "Dark as midnight,"—"and so the peal," writes De Quincey, "continued to come round like a catch, the whole being so well concerted, and the rolling fire so well maintained, that it was impossible to make head against it." The disconcerted lecturer finally fell back upon a phrase of Burke's, then current, and addressed his audience as a "swinish multitude," adding something about pearls.

Alert observation, multifarious knowledge, and critical acumen, together with the lively interest already noticed, served to make De Quincey a keen student of the oratory of all ages, including his own. He was one of those who rediscovered, as someone in each generation must, it appears, rediscover, that literary prose had its origins in public speaking; that the persuasive impulse—that is, an impulse not only to communicate but also to attract and influence a more or less clearly defined audience—underlies stylistic devices and effects; and that by taking into account the factors of changing methods of publication, changing polities, and changing standards of taste, the story of literary prose can be written in terms of speaker and audience.

Such are the important and inescapable conclusions left in one's mind after reading De Quincey's "Elements of Rhetoric," [1] an excursive review suggested by Whately's book of that title, together with his essay entitled "Style," and the section on orators in his "Brief Appraisal of the Greek Literature in its Foremost Pretensions." [2] Yet when one attempts to go further and to ascertain De Quincey's concepts of rhetoric, eloquence, and style, and the interrelation of these, one is baffled by the author's continual discursiveness and occasional inconsistency. Such an ambitious attempt was originally the purpose of this study. Let it now be stated that the writer has rather chosen from the teeming mass of De Quincey's ideas a few which appear specially significant, considered in relation to rhetorical tradition and recent stylistic theory and practice; and illustrations from our author's own practice of the salient points of this theory. After these major considerations were decided upon, a number of additional observations and suggestions from De Quincey's overflowing bounty were found to be too valuable or too interesting to omit.

I

What, for example, are we to make of such a statement as this, set down early and prominently in De Quincey's essay on rhetoric: "And, in fact, amongst the greater orators of Greece there is not a solitary gleam of rhetoric"? [3] It follows upon an accurate and important distinction between rhetoric as an *ars docens,* or theoretical study, and as an *ars utens,* or practical accomplishment; with the admission that "the theory, or *ars docens,* was taught with a fulness and an accuracy by the Grecian masters not afterwards approached." [4] The statement cited, then, has to do with rhetoric in practice. But why such a gap between theory and practice? The Greeks were the greatest of all teachers of rhetoric, the science; but in their best rhetorical discourse there is to be found no application of the principles of this science. Such is De Quincey's argument. Rhetoric, says Aristotle, is "the faculty of finding, in any subject, all the available means of persuasion." Granting that such is the *ars docens,* one must say that rhetorical discourse, the *ars utens,* consists in the employment of all available means of persuasion in speech. Yet, says De Quincey, "there is not a solitary gleam of rhetoric" in the orations of Demosthenes or Lysias or Aeschines, though a little of it may be found in the unspoken ones composed by Isocrates.

The truth is that De Quincey, heeding his private genius, is for the moment disregarding every previous concept of rhetorical discourse in favor of one which apparently has just swum into his consciousness, with all the dazzle of novelty playing about it. To be sure, he had made a show, at the beginning of his essay, of disposing of previous explanations of rhetoric. But so ill-considered is his treatment of them that Professor Masson finds it necessary to write a fifteen-hundred-word note designed to set the reader right, a note beginning with the suggestion that De Quincey suffers from "an imperfect recollection of the contents and substance of Aristotle's Treatise on Rhetoric." [5] But De Quincey is in a hurry to set down his own delightful ideas—his bombshell theory concerning rhetorical enthymemes and his touchstones of rhetorical discourse—so that he has not time enough to be wholly fair to his predecessors. And what is his own conception of rhetoric? Here is something like a definition (p. 92): [6]

> But Rhetoric is the art of aggrandizing and bringing out into strong relief, by means of various and striking thoughts, some aspect of truth which is of itself supported by no spontaneous feelings and therefore rests upon artificial aids.

This alone does not appear to be strikingly different from the Aristotelian conception, and certainly does not justify the statement concerning Greek orators with which we began. It is from various comments, and from his illustrative material, that we learn what De Quincey is driving at. We find, for instance (p. 93), that rhetoric "aims at an elaborate form of beauty which shrinks from the strife of business, and could neither arise nor make itself felt in a tumultuous assembly." Again it appears that the essence of rhetoric is (p. 97) "to hang upon one's own thoughts as an object of conscious interest, to play with them, to watch and pursue them through a maze of inversions, evolutions, and harlequin changes." The modern French writers are found to be "never rhetorical" because in their work (p. 121) "there is no eddying about their own thoughts; no motion of fancy self-sustained from its own activities; no flux and reflux of thought, half-meditative, half-capricious." From these passages a fairly consistent definition emerges, a definition worded by the indispensable Masson (p. 92n.) as "the art of intellectual and fantastic play with any subject to its utmost capabilities, or the art of enriching any main truth or idea by inweaving with it the largest possible amount of subsidiary and illustrative thought and fancy."

Now if we allow ourselves to dwell upon the elements of "play" and "fancy" in this conception, and to draw from these the suggestion of a love for ornament, we are likely to conclude that, in classical terms, De Quincey limits rhetoric to the epideictic, or demonstrative, branch, and this only in its decadent phases. He favors the Asiatic against the Attic. He makes it a game rather than a business. It belongs, as he says more than once, to ages of leisure rather than to those of stress and turmoil. It is the maneuvering of troops for display, in the gold braid of dress uniforms, rather than their mobilization for warfare or their deploying for battle. And to say that there is not a solitary gleam of rhetoric in the best Greek orators is somewhat like saying that there was not a solitary gleam of soccer football in the battle of the Marne.

One must be aware that De Quincey's taste favored this playing with ideas, this "eddying about one's own thoughts," and with the sure instincts of a gourmet he went through the literatures of the world, smacking his lips over the choicest morsels. He would himself have admitted that his taste in this was a cultivated, highly civilized, taste; perhaps an exotic taste. But it is a legitimate one, and it is not strange that he hastened to exhibit it, just as one who possesses a discriminating taste for artichokes or even an undiscriminating taste for daily cold baths rarely attempts to conceal the possession. De Quincey's defense is sound (p. 101): "The artifice and machinery of rhetoric furnishes in its degree as legitimate a basis for intellectual pleasure as any other; that the pleasure is of an inferior order, can no more attaint the idea or model of the composition than it can impeach the excellence of an epigram that it is not a tragedy."

But to leave De Quincey here, thinking of rhetoric as a game, its end-product the "intellectual pleasure" of a few connoisseurs, and pointing to Ovid, Petronius Arbiter, the Senecas, Sir Thomas Browne, and Jeremy Taylor as its greatest players, would be to do him injustice and to miss the best part of his contribution upon the subject. We can appeal from De Quincey drunk with the heady rhythms of *rhetoriqueurs* to De Quincey the sober critic and craftsman; from the De Quincey who says (p. 94), "All great rhetoricians in selecting their subject have shunned the determinate causes of real life," [7] to the De Quincey who honors Edmund Burke as supreme—if not supreme as a "pure rhetorician," then as something unnamed (an impure rhetorician, perhaps), but of a higher order. The soldier who plays at sham battles and who parades in review may also fight, even without changing his uniform; and though there may not have been any soccer at the battle of the Marne, we have it upon good authority that there were some gleams of cricket at Waterloo.

What is needed to convert rhetorical play into earnest is a persuasive purpose. Given this, De Quincey's art of play becomes Aristotle's art of war. It is a matter of taking the buttons off the rapiers. True, the presence of the persuasive impulse will tend to rein a bit the rhetorician's fancy; he will not eddy about his thoughts so freely, he will be less capricious; he will not, to refer to Masson's interpretation of De Quincey, necessarily inweave with his idea "the *largest possible amount* of subsidiary and illustrative thought and fancy," but rather such amount as serves his purpose and suits his audience. Yet the general tactics remain the same. And upon these tactics, which we know as rhetorical invention and rhetorical style, De Quincey is sound and helpful. "Like boys who are throwing the sun's rays into the eyes of a mob by means of a mirror," he writes in "Style," "you must shift your lights and vibrate your reflections at every possible angle, if you would agitate the popular mind extensively." Here are the "inversions, evolutions, and harlequin changes," beloved by the rhetorician, carried on not for their own sake, but for the sake of producing a certain desired result in the minds of hearers. Still more explicit is this passage (p. 140):

Time must be given for the intellect to eddy about a truth, and to appropriate its bearings. There is a sort of previous lubrication, such as the boa-constrictor applies to any subject of digestion, which is requisite to familiarize the mind with a startling or a complex novelty. And this is obtained for the intellect by varying the modes of presenting it—now putting it directly before the eye, now obliquely, now in an abstract shape, now in the concrete; all which, being the proper technical discipline for dealing with such cases, ought no longer to be viewed as a licentious mode of style, but as the just style in respect of those licentious circumstances. And the true art for such popular display is to contrive the best forms for appearing to say something new when in reality you are but echoing yourself; to break up massy chords into running variations; and to mask, by slight differences in the manner, a virtual identity in the substance.

Here is a fair synopsis of two branches of rhetoric, invention and style; and here, as elsewhere in De Quincey, we are made to see that invention and style are two phases—an inner and an outer phase—of the same process.

One heresy into which De Quincey never fell is that rhetoric has to do primarily with the disposition of words or the application of verbal embellishment. Even when he thought of it as fanciful play, the objects played with, as may be seen in passages already quoted, were ideas. He contrives to make clear throughout that the process of rhetorical invention is a mode of thinking. In his tribute to Burke the climax is capped in this sentence: "His great and peculiar distinction was that he viewed all objects of the understanding under more relations than other men, and under more complex relations." What is this but a tribute to Burke's powers of rhetorical invention—and incidentally to rhetorical invention as mental discipline?

We have just gone over De Quincey's prescriptions for handling an idea which is to be presented rhetorically: "varying the modes of presenting it—now putting it directly before the eye, now obliquely, now in an abstract shape, now in the concrete." Readers familiar with Winans' *Public Speaking* will recall the many pages of that book which treat of this process,[8] for which Professor Winans finds a psychological basis in such statements as these, which he quotes from Angell and James:

"To keep a thought alive . . . keep turning it over and over, keep doing something with it"; "roll it over and over incessantly and consider different aspects of it in turn." "Ask questions of it; examine it from all sides." (P. 79)

And readers familiar with Aristotle's *Rhetoric* may see in that author's formidable lists of "topics" an ambitious attempt to provide a complete technique for this process of examining from all sides an idea "up" for rhetorical treatment.

Newman, in his address entitled "Literature,"[9] quotes from *Macbeth:*

> Canst thou not minister to a mind diseased,
> Pluck from the memory a rooted sorrow,
> Raze out the written troubles of the brain,
> And, with some sweet oblivious antidote,
> Cleanse the foul bosom of that perilous stuff,
> Which weighs upon the heart?

and then proceeds, "Here a simple idea, by *a process which belongs to the orator* rather than to the poet. . . ." Yes, this process which Aristotle examined so acutely and so minutely, this process which arose in the "licentious circumstances" of the public assembly, is one of the contributions of rhetoric to poetry. We meet it in Shakespeare and Milton and Shelley; we see a bravura exhibition of it when Cyrano heaps up a cumulation of possible jests about his nose; but what we are likely to forget, unless a De Quincey comes along to remind us, is that the place of its nativity and early culture was the law court, the *bema,* or the forum; or, perhaps better, the battlefield where the prehistoric general harangued the drawn lines of his troops. Rhetorical invention is a mode of thinking; and if the school rhetorics of the nineteenth century had followed De Quincey, Whately, and Newman, instead of Blair and Bain, we should not now find rhetoric so far from the minds of educators when they are looking about for "some way to make students think."

It is almost unnecessary to enforce the point by calling attention to our author's insistence that a speaker's or writer's diction, sentence structure, and figures (in short, what is loosely called his style) constitute the *incarnation*, not the *clothing* or *dressing*, of his thought. A less obvious wing of the main position here described is to be found in De Quincey's theory of the rhetorical enthymeme as treated in Aristotle's *Rhetoric*. Although at first sight the passage dealing with this subject may seem to be merely the facetious stirring up of a mare's nest, there is more in it than that. Briefly, De Quincey called attention to the idea, advanced before him by Facciolati (and before him by one Pacio), that the rhetorical enthymeme, as treated by Aristotle, is not, like the logical enthymeme, merely a syllogism with one part omitted. A rhetorical enthymeme, in this view, is a syllogism (whether completely or partially expressed, it does not matter) of which the premises are drawn from probable rather than from demonstrated knowledge. In the light of this theory, which a close study of the *Rhetoric* seems to support, we see that the difference between rhetorical and other forms of discourse is an essential rather than a superficial one. It is in the subject matter itself. The mode of thinking which is rhetorical invention demands a methodology of inference different from that of rigorously logical thinking. And whether or not this difference is recognized by Aristotle, every working rhetorician, whether statesman or writer of advertisements for tooth paste, utilizes it. This it is that makes the scientist fight shy of rhetoric or of a "popular" presentation of his science; and conversely, this it is that makes the lay audience dread the scientist. No matter how lucidly and intelligibly the scientist may speak, we do not feel that he has made a speech—unless perchance he has used an abundance of analogy, a form of inference unsatisfactory to logic but honored by rhetoric.

To sum up our observations thus far: De Quincey teaches that the rhetorical process, the process of *presenting an idea attractively*, whether as a display of power, in play, in poetic exuberance, or for a persuasive purpose, involves an inner and an outer activity. The inner activity we may call rhetorical invention; the outer, rhetorical style. The first is a mode of thinking about one's subject, turning the subject over in one's mind, and viewing it in as many relations as possible. The second is the incarnation in speech of the thoughts (or of a selection from the thoughts) engendered by the preceding mental activity.[10] No one has shown so well the organic union of these two.

II

Let us turn briefly to De Quincey's rhetorical practice. Here again we have a bewildering variety from which to choose. We shall be on safest ground, perhaps, if we avoid the heights, where De Quincey produces something *sui generis,* and confine our examination to such writing as we find in his book reviews and literary essays. Here he is aiming primarily at interest—that favorable interest, we might say, which is persuasion in the first degree. How does he attain it? A specimen or two will show that he attains it precisely by that process which we have already found him analyzing.

Suppose we turn to a paragraph of his review of Schlosser's *History of the Eighteenth Century.*[11] Reduced to the headings of a brief, this paragraph would appear:

> A. Schlosser's statement that Pope's translation of the "Odyssey" was the work of hired help is an exaggeration, for
>   1. Pope translated twelve books of the "Odyssey" himself.

Now let us choose from De Quincey's paragraph the clauses which embody this minimum of idea—the logical or factual skeleton. These are the "massy chords" which he must break up into "running variations":

> Of Pope's "Homer" Schlosser thinks fit to say . . . "that Pope pocketed the subscription of the 'Odyssey,' and then left the work to be done by understrappers." Don't tell fibs, Schlosser. . . . Pope personally translated one-half of the "Odyssey." . . . This is the truth of the matter.

But that is not enough to satisfy the rhetorically minded De Quincey: if he is to think this thought at all, he must think it in more relations than appear in this skeleton; and if the reader is to be interested, the thought must be exhibited from more angles and must be related to other interesting ideas. So with the addition of concessions, analogies, and repetitions, the paragraph appears as follows:

> Of Pope's "Homer" Schlosser thinks fit to say,—amongst other evil things, which it really *does* deserve (though hardly in comparison with the German hexametrical "Homer" of the ear-splitting Voss),—"that Pope pocketed the subscription of the 'Odyssey,' and left the work to be done by his understrappers." Don't tell fibs, Schlosser. Never do *that* any more. True it is, and

disgraceful enough in itself without lying, that Pope (like modern contractors for a railway or a loan) let off to sub-contractors several portions of the undertaking. He was perhaps not illiberal in the terms of his contracts. At least I know of people now-a-days (much better artists) that would execute such contracts, and enter into any penalties for keeping time, at thirty per cent less. But *navvies* and bill-brokers, that are in excess now, then were scarce. Still the affair, though not mercenary, was illiberal in a higher sense of art; and no anecdote shows more pointedly Pope's sense of the mechanic fashion in which his own previous share of the Homeric labour had been executed. It was disgraceful enough, and needs no exaggeration. Let it, there-fore, be reported truly. Pope personally translated one-half of the "Odyssey" —a dozen books he turned out of his own oven; and if you add the "Batra-chomyomachia," his dozen was a baker's dozen. The journeymen did the other twelve; were regularly paid; regularly turned off when the job was out of hand; and never once had to "strike for wages." How much beer was al-lowed I cannot say. This is the truth of the matter. So no more fibbing, Schlosser, if you please.

Anyone interested may find it an instructive pastime to analyze De Quincey's method in detail, noticing at what points the analogies are applied, to what degree they are elaborated, and how often some phases of the thought are repeated. By my count, the idea "Schlosser is exaggerating (or fibbing)" is stated or broadly implied no less than six times. Well, it is the main idea of the paragraph, and hence the axis, or point of reference, of the whole. Yet the question may be raised, is the rhetorical process overdone in this paragraph? For a reader whose sole purpose is to learn the exact truth about Pope's share of the translation, yes. But for the reader to whom it is addressed, the reader who must be kept interested, no. Let anyone begin reading, without prejudice, the review from which this is taken; he is likely to continue to the end of its forty-five pages and lay it down with the prayer that all book reviews might be as interesting and as cogent. He may decide, incidentally, that H. L. Mencken learned something from De Quincey.

Is there any gain, besides interest, resulting from the process exem-plified in De Quincey's paragraph? There is some casual information, such as that concerning Voss's German translation of Homer. But more than that, the finished paragraph leaves us with some rather definite emotional attitudes—slight scorn for Schlosser, somewhat lessened respect for Pope, and perhaps grateful confidence in De Quincey who has set us right. None of all this appears in the brief; and it is such disparity between the content of a speech or argument, as briefed, and its content as spoken or written, that encourages some observers to emphasize the separation of matter and manner. The emotional attitudes conveyed result from the *Manner*, they argue. And with that we are back again in the doctrine that rhetorical style is something *added* to the thought of a speaker or writer. But such a view assigns too essential a value to that portion of one's subject matter which can be briefed. Is it not true that the brief, far from being the skeleton of the finished argument, is likely to be something less than a picture of the skeleton? We have perfected no instrument for reducing to heads the matter of rhetorical discourse—that complex of ideas, images, and emotional attitudes associated under stress of impulses from the audience and occasion and under the curb of the speaker's purpose.

The second paragraph chosen for illustrative purposes, I find, is likewise one of refutation. It may be interesting to compare this with our first, noticing that while some additional methods of rhetorical invention are utilized, the general structure is similar and the maneuver of making a concession and then returning strongly to the attack reappears. The argument may be briefed thus: [12]

> A. Gilfillan's charge that Dr. Johnson was indolent is obviously a mistaken one, for
>   1. Johnson's voluminous and painstaking literary work refutes it.

De Quincey's paragraph follows:

Another paradox of Mr. Gilfillan's under this head is that he classes Dr. Johnson as indolent; and it is the more startling because he does not utter it as a careless opinion upon which he might have been thrown by inconsideration, but as a concession extorted from him reluctantly: he had sought to evade it, but could not. Now, that Dr. Johnson had a morbid predisposition to decline labour from his scrofulous habit of body is probable. The question for us, however, is not what nature prompted him to do, but what he did. If he had an extra difficulty to fight with in attempting to labour, the more was his merit in the known result,—that he *did* fight with that difficulty and that he conquered it. This is undeniable. And the attempt to deny it presents itself in a comic shape when one imagines some ancient shelf in a library, that has groaned for nearly a century under the weight of the doctor's works, demanding "How say you? Is this Sam Johnson, whose Dictionary alone is a load for a camel, one of those authors whom you call idle? Then Heaven preserve us poor oppressed book-shelves from such as you will consider active." George

III, in a compliment as happily turned as any one of those ascribed to Louis XIV, expressed his opinion upon this question of the Doctor's industry by saying that he also should join in thinking Johnson too voluminous a contributor to literature were it not for the extraordinary merit of the contributions. Now, it would be an odd way of turning the royal praise into a reproach if we should say: "Sam, had you been a pretty good writer, we, your countrymen, should have held you to be also an industrious writer; but, because you are a *very* good writer, therefore we pronounce you a lazy vagabond."

Now a teacher of rhetoric can hardly make as an assignment to a student: "Present the facts concerning Pope's own share in the translation of the 'Odyssey,' relating these facts with railway contractors, bill-brokers, navvies, an oven, beer, and striking for wages"; or, "Refute the charge against Johnson of indolence, bringing in book-shelves and making them talk, comparing the wit of George III with that of Louis XIV, and ending with a jocular apostrophe to Johnson, addressing him as 'Sam.'" Yet is it not the ability to do just that sort of thing which the teacher tries—by hook or crook, by fair means or foul, by pleas to "use your imagination" and to "make it concrete"—to develop? As to actual means of instruction, our precious pedagogical devices, we can hardly look for them in De Quincey. He gives us some models and helps to clarify our aims. And he does more: he points us away from that sort of rhetoric which is largely an *ex post facto* critical apparatus, emphasizing nomenclature, classification, and theme *correction*, to the older discipline (never wholly extinct, but certainly under a cloud for some generations) which was largely a mode of procedure for the *preparation* of a theme or speech.

Our suggestion that De Quincey gives us models needs some qualification. His faults are obvious—and they are the faults resulting from an excess of the very faculty we have noticed in him. Or perhaps we may say that he has one fault—that of digression.[13] Such pleasure does he take in turning an idea over and over and relating it to other interesting ideas, that he frequently extends the process beyond use or reason. "De Quincey, however, offends beyond the possibility of justification," writes Professor Minto, "overloading his sentences in a gossiping kind of way with particulars that have no relevance whatever to the main statement." It is the fault of the rhetorician who forgets the limits set by the patience and docility of his audience, and who, in the elaboration of minutiae, even forgets his theme. Such a one is a familiar figure: he was familiar in Rome, as is evidenced by Martial's epigram to the lawyer Postumus (VI, xix), which has been translated thus:

My action is not for assault, or wounding, or poisoning: it concerns my three she-goats; I complain that they are lost by my neighbor's theft; this is the fact which the judge prescribes to be proved to him. You, with a mighty voice and every gesture you know, make the court ring with Cannae, and the Mithridatic war, and insensate Punic perjuries, and Sullas, and Mariuses, and Muciuses. Now mention, Postumus, my three she-goats.

And Martial was only rewriting, in terms of Roman history, an older epigram of the Greek Anthology.

So with De Quincey. When, in the midst of "Style," we find ourselves involved in a long discussion of the hypothesis that great men appear in galaxies, with quotations from C. Velleius Paterculus and comparisons of the age of Leo X with that of Louis XIV and that of Shakespeare, we feel like saying, "Now mention, De Quincey, *style.*" As we have seen, De Quincey in one of his moods made a virtue of fanciful vagaries. He thought that one was only a *pure* rhetorician when he gave his fancy free rein to wander where it would. But we can hardly grant that one is a good rhetorician, or even a mediocre one, when he forgets his audience and his theme and his purpose, prime factors, all of them, in the rhetorical equation. Perhaps this one defect was all that barred De Quincey from being supreme in persuasive art—the lack of that will, always manifest in great orators, which sternly subordinates means to ends, making the speaker forego indulgence in fanciful or playful or even eloquent digressions in the interest of the persuasive victory to be won. Yet when all is said, we can still go to him for models of rhetorical invention, as a process in itself, regardless of his use or abuse of the process. He is among the greatest tacticians, however weak he may be in major strategy.

III

But we have not exhausted so much as a tithe of De Quincey's ideas on rhetoric and public speaking. So fertile is his thinking and so voluminous his information that many an unconsidered fragment, thrown in by the way, is worth gathering into our basket. We cannot gather them all, for there are more than twelve baskets full. We have said nothing of his treatment of the influence of national or racial characteristics, as present in audiences, upon rhetorical style. Under this heading his description of the Athenian audience and its effect upon the style of Demosthenes is probably most suggestive. But it should be read only in connection with his similar treatment of the Roman audiences addressed by Cicero and of the audience of Fox and Burke in the House of Commons.

Perhaps still more striking, as more original, is De Quincey's thesis concerning the effects upon style of methods of publication. "Did the reader ever happen to reflect on the great idea of *publication?*" he asks, and is off for a dozen pages. And there is more in these pages than a clever "botanico-mechanical interpretation [of Greek style] in the lack of linen rags in the ash barrels of ancient Greece." [14] Here are clues to a whole branch of rhetorical study, a branch dealing with the technique of publicity in its relation to the rhetorical and literary expression of a given period. Sporadic attempts at such investigations have been made by literary critics and by sociologists, but there is much to be done. Literary tendencies are usually analyzed in terms of earlier literary tendencies, with historical events, such as wars and revolutions, coming in for a vague share; such factors as freedom or censorship of speech and the press, the rise of cheap printing, the convenience of assembly or communication, are too often overlooked. The oration and the drama reached a high degree of perfection in Greece, says De Quincey, because the chief means of publication were oral. He might have added that the Greeks were also rather fond of carving inscriptions on stone or metal and hence perfected the epigram to an equal degree. Could not one, following such clues, explain why the modern novel was developed when and as it was? In such light, is there not added significance in the fact that the great stories of the world survived the Middle Ages chiefly in the form of *exempla* used in sermons? Or in the renascence of drama in the same period in connection with services of the church? To follow De Quincey's clue, one would have to take into account the size and architecture of auditoriums, stages, theatres, and pulpits. Or coming to recent phenomena, one might study the vogue of pamphleteering, the rise of the newspaper, and the significance of radio broadcasting as a means of publication. Is there a "Chautauqua style," and if so, is it determined largely by the audience, or are both audience and style controlled by the physical aspects of Chautauqua? Will the English of headlines and the devices of billboard advertising invade poetry and uncommercial rhetoric?

What of the appalling multiplication of pictures in recent publicity, and of pictorial communication—will all this have its effect upon the speaker and writer? These are a few of the questions suggested by De Quincey's twelve pages.

In another section of De Quincey's "Style" we find the following passage, thrown in by way of illustration, which embodies a suggestive application of a principle drawn from such study as we have been considering:

Punctuation, trivial as such an innovation may seem, was the product of typography; and it is interesting to trace the effects upon style even of that one slight addition to the resources of logic. Previously a man was driven to depend for his security against misunderstanding upon the pure virtue of his syntax. Miscollocation or dislocation of related words disturbed the whole sense; its least effect was to give *no* sense,—often it gave a dangerous sense. Now, punctuation was an artificial machinery for maintaining the integrity of the sense against all mistakes of the writer; and, as one consequence, it withdrew the energy of men's anxieties from the natural machinery, which lay in just and careful arrangement.[15]

The passage is reinforced by a footnote too extended for quotation. Incidentally, the point of this passage supports the position of those of us who hold that the norm of good writing is good speaking. And it is to be observed that never does one realize the artificality of punctuation so much as when one attempts by reading aloud to translate writing into speaking.

Nothing De Quincey has to say directly about the organic nature of style is so convincing as is his treatment of the styles of Herodotus, Thucydides, and Plato. His discussion of Herodotus may be said to set a model for the most fruitful type of rhetorical criticism. He considers the character of the historian, his audience, and his method of publication. With reference to the audience, De Quincey is most full on the topic of the state of mind of the Greek public at the time when the work of Herodotus appeared. But he enters still more thoroughly into the subject matter of his author, evidently considering that the controlling factor. The result of it all is that, without De Quincey's having directly characterized or described the style of Herodotus, the reader finds himself, at the end of three pages, thoroughly familiar with it. And in connection with this, or elsewhere in the essays we are considering, one may find sketches, at least, for similar treatments of Plato and Isocrates, of Francis Bacon, Fox, Sheridan, Burke, and others.

De Quincey on Public Speaking

We are reduced to cataloguing. That discerning injunction to listen to the speech and read the letters of cultivated women, in order to apprehend the best possibilities of a living language—who will gainsay it? The several pages, scattered here and there, on French eloquence—where is there better criticism of its kind? And that part of a paragraph which contrasts the forensic with the deliberative speaker—how well it says what many of us grope for when we attempt to contrast English and American debating! And how many of our most important recent developments of rhetorical theory are to be found, in germ, in the following passage at the end of "Conversation":

Many other suggestions for the improvement of conversation might be brought forward within ampler limits; and especially for that class of conversation which moves by discussion a whole code of regulations might be proposed that would equally promote the interest of the individual speakers and the public interests of the truth involved in the question discussed. Meantime nobody is more aware than we are that no style of conversation is more essentially vulgar than that which moves by disputation. This is the vice of the young and the inexperienced, but especially of those amongst them who are fresh from academic life. But discussion is not necessarily disputation; and the two orders of conversation—*that,* on the one hand, which contemplates an interest of knowledge and of the self-developing intellect; *that,* on the other hand, which forms one and the widest amongst the gay embellishments of life—will always advance together. Whatever there may remain of illiberal in the first (for, according to the remark of Burke, there is always something illiberal in the severer aspects of study until balanced by the influence of social amenities) will correct itself, or will tend to correct itself, by the model held up in the second, and thus the great organ of social intercourse by means of speech, which hitherto has done little for man, except through the channel of its ministrations to the direct *business* of daily necessities, will at length rise into a rivalship with books, and become fixed amongst the alliances of intellectual progress, not less than amongst the ornamental accomplishments of convivial life.

Strange indeed is the fate that has made generally known, of all De Quincey's fertile and prophetic ideas in literary criticism, only that questionable distinction between literature of knowledge and literature of power.[16] And it is sad to reflect that, copious as we find his "Style," the essay is but a fragment. The enticing prospectus placed near the middle of it, in which the author promises to mark out "for subsequent cultivation and development all the possible subdivisions and sections amongst the resources of the rhetorician, all the powers

which he can employ, and therefore all the difficulties which he needs
to study"—this is never fulfilled. "Were this done," says De Quincey,

> we should no longer see those incoherent sketches which are now circulating
> in the world upon questions of taste, of science, of practical address, as ap-
> plied to the management of style and rhetoric; the public ear would no longer
> be occupied by feeble Frenchmen—Rollin, Rapin, Batteux, Bouhours,
> De Bos, and *id genus omne;* nor by the elegant but desultory Blair; nor by
> scores of others who bring an occasional acuteness or casual information to
> this or that subsection of their duty, whilst (taken as general guides) they
> are universally insufficient.

"Were this done"—alas, it was not done; and his description of rhetorical instruction (with the addition of the numbing system of dryasdust
Bain) holds good for the latter half of the nineteenth century as well
as for the earlier. Yet, as has been suggested on another page, in reading De Quincey, fragmentary and desultory as he is, we catch a spirit
which, allowed to operate, would transform all this; we hear echoes of
a great past, and prophetic whispers of a return, in education, to that
rhetoric which can be and should be "the *organon* of all studies."

IV

So the last word is, read De Quincey. For an eloquent enunciation of
this word I am turning to a page in one of those little volumes which
treasure up for us the "life-blood of a master spirit," Hiram Corson.
To him all who in recent years have concerned themselves with the
oral expression of literary content, felt deeply and mastered thoroughly,
owe a great debt. Corson says:

> For range of power, for great diversity of subject, for poetic, philosophic,
> and logical cast of mind, for depth of feeling, for an *inspiring vitality of think-
> ing,* for periodic and impassioned prose which, running through the whole
> gamut of expression, is unequalled in English Literature, no more educating
> author could be selected for advanced students than Thomas De Quincey. A
> good education in the language as a living organism, could be got through
> his writings alone; and his wealth and vitality of thought and feeling could
> hardly fail, unless opposed by extraordinary obtuseness, to excite and enliven,
> and strengthen the best faculties of thought and feeling in any reader. How
> much a student might do for himself, by loyally reading all of De Quincey's
> Works, as they are presented in Dr. Masson's edition! [17]

RHETORICAL PRACTICE

Some Differences between Literary Criticism and Rhetorical Criticism

HERBERT A. WICHELNS

LITERARY critics are all, in various ways, interpreters of the permanent and universal values they find in the works of which they treat. Nor can there be any quarrel with this attitude—unless all standards be swept away. The impressionist and the historian of the evolution of literature as a self-contained activity may deny the utility or the possibility of a truly judicial criticism. But the human mind insists upon judgment *sub specie aeternitatis*. The motive often appears as a merely practical one: the reader wishes to be apprised of the best that has been said and thought in all ages; he is less concerned with the descent of literary species or with the critic's adventures among masterpieces than with the perennial freshness and interest those masterpieces may hold for him. There is, of course, much more than a practical motive to justify the interest in permanent values; but this is not the place to raise a moot question of general critical theory. We wished only to note the common ground of literary criticism in its preoccupation with the thought and the eloquence which is permanent.

If now we turn to rhetorical criticism, we find that its point of view is patently single. It is not concerned with permanence, nor yet with beauty. It is concerned with effect. It regards a speech as a communication to a specific audience, and holds its business to be the analysis and appreciation of the orator's method of imparting his ideas to his hearers.[1]

Rhetoric, however, is a word that requires explanation; its use in connection with criticism is neither general nor consistent. The merely depreciatory sense in which it is often applied to bombast or false ornament need not delay us. The limited meaning which confines the term to the devices of a correct and even of an elegant prose style— in the sense of manner of writing and speaking—may also be eliminated, as likewise the broad interpretation which makes rhetoric inclusive of all style whether in prose or in poetry. There remain some definitions which have greater promise. We may mention first that of Aristotle: "the faculty of observing in any given case the available means of persuasion"; [2] this readily turns into the art of persuasion, as the editors of the *New English Dictionary* recognize when they define rhetoric as "the art of using language so as to persuade or influence others." The gloss on "persuade" afforded by the additional term "influence" is worthy of note. Jebb achieves the same result by defining rhetoric as "the art of using language in such a way as to produce a desired impression upon the hearer or reader." [3] There is yet a fourth definition, one which serves to illuminate the others as well as to emphasize their essential agreement: "taken broadly [rhetoric is] the science and art of communication in language"; [4] the framers of this definition add that to throw the emphasis on communication is to emphasize prose, poetry being regarded as more distinctly expressive than communicative. A German writer has made a similar distinction between poetic as the art of poetry and rhetoric as the art of prose, but rather on the basis that prose is of the intellect, poetry of the imagination.[5] Wackernagel's basis for the distinction will hardly stand in face of the attitude of modern psychology to the "faculties"; yet the distinction itself is suggestive, and it does not contravene the more significant opposition of expression and communication. That opposition has been well stated, though with some exaggeration, by Professor Hudson:

> The writer in pure literature has his eye on his subject; his subject has filled his mind and engaged his interest, and he must tell about it; his task is expression; his form and style are organic with his subject. The writer of rhetorical discourse has his eye upon the audience and occasion; his task is persuasion; his form and style are organic with the occasion.[6]

The element of the author's personality should not be lost from sight in the case of the writer of pure literature; nor may the critic think of the audience and the occasion as alone conditioning the work of the composer of rhetorical discourse, unless indeed he include in the occasion both the personality of the speaker and the subject. The distinction is better put by Professor Baldwin:

> Rhetoric meant to the ancient world the art of instructing and moving men in their affairs; poetic the art of sharpening and expanding their vision. . . . The one is composition of ideas; the other, composition of images. In the one field life is discussed; in the other it is presented. The type of the one is a public address, moving us to assent and action; the type of the other is a play, showing us [an] action moving to an end of character. The one argues and urges; the other represents. Though both appeal to imagination, the method of rhetoric is logical; the method of poetic, as well as its detail, is imaginative.[7]

It is noteworthy that in this passage there is nothing to oppose poetry, in its common acceptation of verse, to prose. Indeed, in discussing the four forms of discourse usually treated in textbooks, Baldwin explicitly classes exposition and argument under rhetoric, leaving narrative and description to the other field. But rhetoric has been applied to the art of prose by some who include under the term even nonmetrical works of fiction. This is the attitude of Wackernagel, already mentioned, and of Saintsbury, who observes that Aristotle's *Rhetoric* holds, "if not intentionally, yet actually, something of the same position towards Prose as that which the *Poetics* holds towards verse." [8] In Saintsbury's view, the *Rhetoric* achieves this position in virtue of its third book, that on style and arrangement: the first two books contain "a great deal of matter which has either the faintest connection with literary criticism or else no connection with it at all." [9] Saintsbury finds it objectionable in Aristotle that to him, "prose as prose is merely and avowedly a secondary consideration: it is always in the main, and sometimes wholly, a mere necessary instrument of divers practical purposes," [10] and that "he does not *wish* to consider a piece of prose as a work of art destined, first of all, if not finally, to fulfil its own laws on the one hand, and to give pleasure on the other." [11] The distinction between verse and prose has often troubled the waters of criticism. The explanation is probably that the outer form of a work is more easily understood and more constantly present to the mind than is the real form. Yet it is strange that those who find the distinction between verse and prose important should parallel this with a distinction between imagination and intellect, as if a novel had more affinities with a speech than with an epic. It is strange, too, that Saintsbury's own phrase about the right way to consider a "piece of prose"—as a work of art destined "to fulfil its own laws"—did not suggest to him the fundamental importance of a distinction between what he terms the minor or suasive rhetoric on the one hand, and on the other poetic, whether or not in verse. For poetry always is free to fulfil its own law, but the writer of rhetorical discourse is, in a sense, perpetually in bondage to the occasion and the audience; and in that fact we find the line of cleavage between rhetoric and poetic.

The distinction between rhetoric as theory of public address and poetic as theory of pure literature, says Professor Baldwin, "seems not to have controlled any consecutive movement of modern criticism." [12] It has not controlled the procedure of critics in dealing with orators; yet in their writings one can find many suggestions of a better method, and some few critical performances against which the only charge is overcondensation.

Rhetorical criticism is necessarily analytical. The scheme of a rhetorical study includes the element of the speaker's personality as a conditioning factor; it includes also the public character of the man—not what he was, but what he was thought to be. It requires a description of the speaker's audience, and of the leading ideas with which he plied his hearers—his topics, the motives to which he appealed, the nature of the proofs he offered. These will reveal his own judgment of human nature in his audiences, and also his judgment on the questions which he discussed. Attention must be paid, too, to the relation of the surviving texts to what was actually uttered: in case the nature of the changes is known, there may be occasion to consider adaptation to two audiences—that which heard and that which read. Nor can rhetorical criticism omit the speaker's mode of arrangement and his mode of expression, nor his habit of preparation and his manner of delivery from the platform; though the last two are perhaps less significant. "Style"—in the sense which corresponds to diction and sentence movement—must receive attention, but only as one among various means that secure for the speaker ready access to the minds of his auditors. Finally, the effect of the discourse on its immediate hearers is not to be ignored, either in the testimony of witnesses, or in the record of events. And throughout such a study one must conceive of the public man as influencing the men of his own times by the power of his discourse.

What is the relation of rhetorical criticism, so understood, to literary criticism? The latter is at once broader and more limited than rhetorical criticism. It is broader because of its concern with permanent values: because it takes no account of special purpose nor of immediate effect; because it views a literary work as the voice of a human spirit addressing itself to men of all ages and times; because the critic speaks as the spectator of all time and all existence. But this universalizing of attitude brings its own limits with it: the influence of the period is necessarily relegated to the background; interpretation in the light of the writer's intention and of his situation may be ignored or slighted; and the speaker who directed his words to a definite and limited group of hearers may be made to address a universal audience. The result can only be confusion. In short, the point of view of literary criticism is proper only to its own objects, the permanent works. Upon such as are found to lie without the pale, the verdict of literary criticism is of negative value merely, and its interpretation is false and misleading because it proceeds upon a wrong assumption. If Henry Clay and Charles Fox are to be dealt with at all, it must not be on the assumption that their works, in respect of wisdom and eloquence, are or ought to be sources of perennial freshness and interest. Morley has put the matter well:

> The statesman who makes or dominates a crisis, who has to rouse and mold the mind of senate or nation, has something else to think about than the production of literary masterpieces. The great political speech, which for that matter is a sort of drama, is not made by passages for elegant extract or anthologies, but by personality, movement, climax, spectacle, and the action of the time.[13]

But we cannot always divorce rhetorical criticism from literary. In the case of Fox or Clay or Cobden, as opposed to Fielding or Addison or De Quincey, it is proper to do so; the fact that language is a common medium to the writer of rhetorical discourse and to the writer in pure literature will give to the critics of each a common vocabulary of stylistic terms, but not a common standard. In the case of Burke the relation of the two points of view is more complex. Burke belongs to literature; but in all his important works he was a practitioner of public address written or uttered. Since his approach to *belles-lettres* was through rhetoric, it follows that rhetorical criticism is at least a preliminary to literary criticism, for it will erect the factual basis for the understanding of the works, will not merely explain allusions and establish dates, but recall the setting, reconstruct the author's own intention, and analyze his method. But the rhetorical inquiry is more than a mere preliminary; it permeates and governs all subsequent interpretation and criticism. For the statesman in letters is a statesman still: compare Burke to Charles Lamb, or even to Montaigne, and it is clear that the public man is in a sense inseparable from his audience. A statesman's wisdom and eloquence are not to be read without some share of his own sense of the body politic, and of the body politic not merely as a construct of thought, but as a living human society. A speech, like a satire, like a comedy of manners, grows directly out of a social situation; it is a man's response to a condition in human affairs. However broadly typical the situation may be when its essential elements are laid bare, it never appears without its coverings. On no plane of thought—philosophical, literary, political—is Burke to be understood without reference to the great events in America, India, France, which evoked his eloquence; nor is he to be understood without reference to the state of English society. (It is this last that is lacking in Grierson's essay: [14] the page of comment on Burke's qualities in actual debate wants its supplement in some account of the House of Commons and the national life it represented. Perhaps the latter is the more needful to a full understanding of the abiding excellence in Burke's pages.) Something of the spirit of Morley's chapter on Cobden, and more of the spirit of the social historian (which Morley has in other parts of the biography) is necessary to the literary critic in dealing with the statesman who is also a man of letters.

In the case of Burke, then, one of the functions of rhetorical criticism is as a preliminary, but an essential and governing preliminary, to the literary criticism which occupies itself with the permanent values of wisdom and of eloquence, of thought and of beauty, that are found in the works of the orator.

Rhetorical criticism may also be regarded as an end in itself. Even Burke may be studied from that point of view alone. Fox and Cobden and the majority of public speakers are not to be regarded from any other. No one will offer Cobden's works a place in pure literature. Yet the method of the great agitator has a place in the history of his times. That place is not in the history of *belles-lettres;* nor is it in the literary history which is a "survey of the life of a people as expressed in their writings." The idea of "writings" is a merely mechanical one; it does not really provide a point of view or a method; it is a book-maker's cloak for many and diverse points of view. Such a compilation as the *Cambridge History of American Literature,* for example, in spite of the excellence of single essays, may not unjustly be characterized as an uneven commentary on the literary life of the country and as a still more uneven commentary on its social and political life. It may be questioned whether the scant treatment of public men in such a compilation throws light either on the creators of pure literature, or on the makers of rhetorical discourse, or on the life of the times.

Rhetorical criticism lies at the boundary of politics (in the broadest sense) and literature; its atmosphere is that of the public life,[15] its tools are those of literature, its concern is with the ideas of the people as influenced by their leaders. The effective wielder of public discourse, like the military man, belongs to social and political history because he is one of its makers. Like the soldier, he has an art of his own which is the source of his power; but the soldier's art is distinct from the life which his conquests affect. The rhetorician's art represents a natural and normal process within that life. It includes the work of the speaker, of the pamphleteer, of the writer of editorials, and of the sermon maker. It is to be thought of as the art of popularization. Its practitioners are the Huxleys, not the Darwins, of science; the Jeffersons, not the Lockes and the Rousseaus, of politics.

Of late years the art of popularization has received a degree of attention: propaganda and publicity have been words much used; the influence of the press has been discussed; there have been some studies of public opinion. Professor Robinson's *Humanizing of Knowledge* [16] is a cogent statement of the need for popularization by the instructed element in the state, and of the need for a technique in doing so. But the book indicates, too, how little is known of the methods its author so earnestly desires to see put to use. Yet ever since Homer's day men have woven the web of words and counsel in the face of all. And ever since Aristotle's day there has been a mode of analysis of public address. Perhaps the preoccupation of literary criticism with "style" rather than with composition in the large has diverted interest from the more significant problem. Perhaps the conventional categories of historical thought have helped to obscure the problem: the history of thought, for example, is generally interpreted as the history of invention and discovery, both physical and intellectual. Yet the history of the thought of the people is at least as potent a factor in the progress of the race. True, the popular thought may often represent a resisting force, and we need not marvel that the many movements of a poet's mind more readily capture the critic's attention than the few and uncertain movements of that Leviathan, the public mind. Nor is it surprising that the historians tend to be occupied with the acts and the motives of leaders. But those historians who find the spirit of an age in the total mass of its literary productions, as well as all who would tame Leviathan to the end that he shall not threaten civilization, must examine more thoroughly than they as yet have done the interactions of the inventive genius, the popularizing talent, and the public mind.

Thomas Wilson's Speech against Usury

RUSSELL H. WAGNER

ON April 19, 1571, Thomas Wilson, a member of the English House of Commons, made a speech in that assembly against usury.[1] This is not a highly significant speech, from some points of view. It did not prevent the bill to which Wilson was opposed from being passed. It was not the first or last speech in the House on this subject. Though to our knowledge it is by far the most extended and carefully prepared speech Wilson made in Parliament, it is not the best one.

Nevertheless, there are some reasons which may justify careful study of this address, especially for those interested in Wilson or in sixteenth century public address in Britain. The fame of the speaker in his own day, and ours, as scholar, author, religious reformer, politician and statesman, and the fact that this was his only attempt in the House at defending an unpopular cause in rough-and-tumble debate, give it some importance. Moreover, its subject and purpose, together with the long dialogue on usury which he had already written and which he published the next year, conspire to justify attention to this speech, on a special topic of great significance in its day and in the centuries preceding, and one long neglected by students of public address.

In speaking against usury Wilson was espousing an ideal long and vigorously advocated by almost all religious authorities but violated in practice by almost everyone. He was attempting not only to stem a tide which was as inexorable as that which invaded the lowlands of his native Lincolnshire each spring, but to restore a state of affairs which had not existed for centuries.

For any close study of this speech we must first attempt a definition of usury. The concept of exorbitant interest, common today, is quite inadequate. But to arrive at a completely satisfactory definition which will serve all pronouncements and arguments on this subject is well-nigh impossible, for this definition was a leading issue in this controversy and had been for over a thousand years.

The chief sources on which the ecclesiastical opponents of usury based their objections are passages in the Old Testament, especially in Exodus and the Psalms, which plainly denounce a practice having to do with lending. But whether the Hebrew words used refer to the lending of money, or of goods, or the like, and whether they forbid interest of any kind or merely excessive interest, was the main cause of contention in the medieval and Renaissance debates. Thus *usury*, the world selected by the earliest translators as the English term nearest to the Hebrew *neshekh* and the Latin *usura* of the Vulgate, meant, until late in the sixteenth century an emolument or something to the advantage of a lender or primitive capitalist. It was something secured without effort, merely because of permitting someone to make use of a possession, such as money or goods; but whether the force of the word, and of the practice, depended on extent, kind, or time, or other conditions, was in dispute.

The meaning of this term, then, especially in the late medieval Christian theocracy, was never really settled and the controversy over it flamed anew in the Reformation when Calvinists and other Protestant leaders, attempting to build their heavenly cities on earth, tried to reconcile early Christian principles with secular practice.

Beyond this slight incursion into the muddy waters of this historico-theological controversy we cannot now go.[2] Fortunately, Wilson's position on the question and the subsequent development of the practice and of the controversy about it are such as to simplify somewhat our problem in understanding it.

Wilson was against usury of any type; that is, he was against the taking of interest whether in specie, in kind—goods, grain, domestic animals—in property or bills, "dry exchange," discounts, or any other sort of advantage to be gained by lending. Like other austere moralists he quite approved of rents, fees for hire, ventures, etc., where depreciation and risks of loss were involved. He was simply against the taking of interest, in our sense, no matter how small. In opposing it, he plainly had in mind a practice defined in his book on the subject: "Usurye is also said to be the price of tyme, or of the delaying or forbearing of moneye. . . . And usurye is not onely in moneye, but also in wares and merchandises, such as maye be consumed or spent by usinge of them." [3]

In taking this position Wilson, though a layman, was in good ecclesiastical company. He took the same attitude toward usury, or interest, (as he conceived it and as we shall define it hereafter) as the Schoolmen and theologians of the medieval period; he took the same position as Bishops Jewel and Sandys, as Latimer, Becon, Crowley, and the other ecclesiastical reformers of his own acquaintance had taken; he opposed Bucer (who had been influenced by the Calvinists), though with evident regret since the two of them had been closely associated in the early reform movement during the reigns of Henry VIII and Edward VI. We should remember that this strict definition of usury and this uncompromising opposition to it "continued well into the seventeenth century to be the orthodox teaching of the Church of England." [4]

But the gap between preaching and practice, statute and enforcement, canon law and common law, which existed in late medieval and early modern England, cannot be better illustrated than in the case of usury. Time was, as Wilson says in his book on usury (but far back before the Conquest), that public opinion, culminating in the massacre of five hundred Jews in England, forced the enactment of laws against interest-taking. And grievances against usurers continued, sporadically at least, to encourage theologians and ecclesiastical reformers in high political places to cause the enactment of severe laws against all forms of usury. But most of these violent expressions of public opinion against interest-taking occurred well in the past and were mostly forgotten by 1571. At all times, the necessity of borrowing to harvest a crop, to erect a mill, to enter trade in even a small way, and the inadequacies of such legal resources as existed—the guilds, monastic funds, and the rare individuals who would lend without interest—had made a mockery of the statutes. Laws were passed to stop loopholes and evasions, such as the substitution of payment of interest in kind for payment in specie, but lawyers found ways of evading them in most cases.

In order to legalize the existing practice, laws permitting and controlling interest were sometimes passed. Thus the law of 1545 sanctioned an interest rate of ten per cent. But the thunderings of Latimer and other clerical reformers, and the inability of the authorities to enforce the limitation of the rate in a period of depression and financial stringency combined to cause the enactment in 1552 of laws prohibiting usury or interest-taking of all kinds, thus affecting all financial enterprises from private lending to foreign exchanges and public loans. But this law, which was expected to stamp out usury once and for all, was, by 1571, so unsatisfactory to the majority of the population represented in Parliament that the amendment, which Wilson opposed, was passed without real difficulty.

As Tawney says, ". . . there had been a revolution in the social and economic life of England, and indeed of Europe, which was bringing the capitalist class into their own, and it was no longer as easy as it had been to put a hook in their jaws." [5] Socio-religious reformers like Latimer and Wilson were thoroughly sincere in their desire to build a Christian state composed largely of a middle class of small land owners and artisans free from debt and the temptations of speculation. They remind us of Jefferson, two centuries later, dreaming of a landed society in America—of free, independent, self-sufficient, educated citizens, requiring little aid from laws or government or money marts. But England in the third quarter of the sixteenth century had no time for such dreaming. The economic opportunities created by exploration, the breakdown of the guilds, the disestablishment of the medieval church—especially its monastic orders—but also the vastly increased opportunities for trade with the Continent, the rise of a strong merchant class, the entrance of former serfs and bound men into the artisan and commercial ranks, the rise of banking and exchanges on the Continent, especially in Protestant centers—all strengthened the determination of the hard-headed business men of the day to throw off churchly interference with business and finance.

The existence of the law of 1552 was obnoxious to many groups, especially the rising commercial class, for many reasons. Though it was commonly evaded, the stigma of illegality still attached to the capitalist-banker-lender. Now and then an unlucky lender was disgraced by being caught red-handed in the iniquitous practice of taking interest or trading on the exchange. At all times such persons were regarded as socially inferior, thundered at by preachers, and harried by all who had no need to borrow. Moreover, interest rates, in a system where all interest was illegal, were often truly exorbitant. Loan sharks would sometimes charge a poor peddler as much as four hundred per cent interest; fifty to one hundred per cent was not uncommon in agricultural communities; and the leading merchants, forced to borrow or to sell to those who must borrow, were hampered by a rate much higher in England than in Antwerp or Rouen, where interest was legal—and regulated.

This "Act Against Usury" was one of a number proposed during Elizabeth's time to mitigate the evils described, and it was the first to be enacted. Out of respect for the strong clerical opposition which was no doubt responsible for defeating, earlier in this session, a proposal to establish banks in seven cities of the kingdom to lend money at six per cent, this bill was relatively modest. As its title implies, it attempted to make the term *usury* mean "exorbitant interest," and was ostensibly designed to prevent such excesses. It provided for the repeal of the act of 1552 which forbade interest. It revived the act of 1545 which made the taking of more than ten per cent interest punishable by forfeit of three times the principal and interest received and by imprisonment. And it established certain new rules, complicated and somewhat specious, in effect weakening the security of loans and strengthening the position of a wily creditor.

When the bill was read in the House for the second time, there "ensued divers Arguments and Speeches," which D'Ewes transcribes as he found them reported in the "Anonymous Journal" he so often uses. It is to be noted that of these thus reported, four, including Wilson's, are against the bill, and the same number are in favor of it. (I do not count Mr. Dalton, who, in the reporter's words, "endeavored to prove, that Mr. Fleetwood mistook the Bill, but in fancy he mistook his Arguments" and whose speech is not further reported.[6]) Thus Tawney, who says only one other besides Wilson opposed the bill, is apparently in error.

The first speaker, a Mr. Clarke, opposed the bill on two grounds, viz.: 1. The provisions for punishment were unenforceable, since civil law allowed usury, the canon law was abolished, and the temporal law ignored the problem. 2. Usury was condemned by both Christians and pagans, as shown by the writings of the Psalmist, St. Augustine, Plato, and Aristotle.

The second speaker, Mr. Molley, denied that the taking of moderate interest was ungodly, but only the taking of excessive interest; that borrowing was necessary, and interest was indispensable to that practice; that it is better to permit moderate interest than to prohibit it and to have to endure immoderate usury; that many things advised in the Scriptures, such as never uttering a vain word, are no doubt desirable admonitions but cannot be punished by temporal laws since so few can be expected to obey them; and, finally, that learned men, such as Beza and Bellarmine, supported his belief that not interest but excessive usury is prohibited in the Scriptures and that the true interpretation of the Hebrew word is not *Usura* but *Morsus*.

It was at this point that Thomas Wilson entered the debate. Before we consider his speech, it may be well to say a few words about his audience and about Wilson as a speaker.

It seems probable that most of the members of the House, at least in this early period of Elizabeth's rule, were of the middle class, merchants, lawyers, self-made men like Wilson, but lacking his education, and inarticulate, rarely speaking more than a few sentences in public (and those not always clearly or correctly). Most of them were barely emancipated from a deep and almost inherited reverence for clerical and kingly authority but were keenly aware of the burgeoning of new social and economic trends, of England's rapid rise to power and importance in European affairs. Almost all were imbued not only with national pride in her political and cultural prominence but also with a shrewd sensibility of the opportunities for improving their own social and economic position in the rapidly changing world of their day.

These were the majority—the ones who are rarely mentioned by D'Ewes, or by the writers of the Journals he used. There were others, of greater education or higher birth or political prominence, many of them aspiring to high positions in state or church, members of the Privy Council or, as in Wilson's case, soon to become members, masters of colleges, doctors of divinity or law, wealthy adventurers expecting to command armies or naval vessels or to head diplomatic or commercial missions or exploratory and colonizing expeditions in other parts of the world. These were the ones who made most of the speeches and engaged in the running debates. They were the articulate audience which might be expected to speak, sometimes "at large," but often to the point, on any subject touching their interests and to debate freely and extemporaneously the claims made in a prepared speech such as Wilson's.

The more one studies the speaking in the early Elizabethan parliaments, the more one is impressed with the courage of many of the speakers, the insistence on freedom of speech, the readiness and eloquence of the speakers, and the apparent general appreciation of eloquence that prevailed. On the first point, we should not forget the heroic example set by Mr. Strickland, who in this particular session courted and received the punishment of imprisonment for daring to propose a law the introduction of which was expressly forbidden by her Majesty through her Lord Keeper. Nor should we overlook the contemptuous disregard of warnings from Speakers of the House to desist from speaking on certain subjects or to confine their remarks on them to plain and few words; or the stoutness of heart of men like Sir Nicholas Arnold and Mr. Yelverton, who in this year vehemently argued that it was the duty of the members to run the risk of offending the Prince, in order to preserve their own self-respect and the privilege of free speech for their successors and to prevent the Prince from thinking she could either make or break the laws of the realm. We should not forget that it was also in this session that the "still small voice" of Peter Wentworth, that cantankerous old Puritan, no doubt the "hot gospeller" so heartily disliked by Wilson, was first raised to denounce Sir Humphrey Gilbert for flattering and fawning on the Prince and for his ability to change himself to all fashions save honesty, "comparing him to the Cameleon, who can change himself into all colours, saving white," to denounce Mr. Bell for misreporting the House to the Queen for the purpose of making them afraid to speak freely, and to desire the members to take vigorous measures to preserve free speech and the liberties of the House, especially by censuring all liars and laying the curse of David upon them.[7]

The readiness and eloquence of certain of the members and their respect for effective speech is attested by the quality of the speeches themselves in the setting provided by D'Ewes, and by their references to eloquence and the problems of impromptu debate. The reporters, whose accounts D'Ewes made use of, frequently describe speakers as eloquent, or "having a natural eloquence." Members were well aware that effective speaking was indispensable in any important debate and that careful planning and preparation were desirable. We read that "Mr. Norton, a man, wise, bold and Eloquent, stood up next, and said, he was not ignorant, but had long since learned what it was to speak on a sudden, or first, before other men in Parliament; . . ."[8]

Mr. Strickland, that grave and highly respected elder statesman and austere moralist, also on one occasion "prayed he might be excused, for that he was to speak on a sudden and unprovided."[9]

231

A recent authoritative reappraisal of the oratory of the Commons in this period asserts that "The standard of speaking in Elizabethan parliaments was very high; indeed parliamentary oratory may be said to have begun its resplendent history in this reign. The set speeches were artificial in the purer sense of the word." [10] The careful perusal of D'Ewes' *Journal* fully confirms this opinion. Both the members and the reporters comment on the orderliness of arguments, of speakers who moved the House by the force of eloquence and by "intrapments" of oratory. The reporter says of Mr. Pistor's speech: "And so did set it forth with vehemency, that there lacked no modesty, and with such Eloquence, that it neither seemed studied, nor too much effected, but well approved of." [11]

Poor speaking was also not uncommon—and suffered due reproof. The House "had a short way with bores or with speeches that annoyed them. They hawked and they spat, they shuffled and they hissed." [12] The reporter speaks thus of the speaker who followed Mr. Pistor: "And after him Mr. Snagge, and far after him indeed, either for order, proof, or matter. . . ." [13]

In fact we read that at least one member, Mr. Alford, wished to insure even higher standards of eloquence by a rather unusual means:

He was of this mind, that Moses and Aaron should be conjoined together [in the choosing of burgesses], and that there should be one of their own, or some Gentleman near them, who had knowledge of the State of the Country, and the other a man Learned, and able to utter his mind and opinion, since the knowledge locked up in the breast, not being orderly opened, is to no purpose; and this part (he said) was as requisite for consultation as the other.[14]

It seems probable, then, that Wilson's audience consisted mainly of men who, while they themselves rarely spoke in public, had an opportunity to hear eloquent deliberative speakers, both well-prepared and impromptu or extempore, and very probably coveted greatly the facility they so sadly lacked. They probably admired, secretly and timidly, the courage of those who spoke on forbidden subjects. They were no doubt much influenced by powerful oratory on matters of broad policy in public and private affairs which did not closely relate to their own lives. No doubt they were mainly moved, in their voting, by facts and reasons which were in line with their own interests and ambitions, chiefly economic, so long as such votes did not bring upon them, personally, the wrath of the Prince, the Star Chamber, or their religious leaders. In matters affecting their own personal interests they were no doubt impressed by the speaking of learned men who opposed their commercial interests, but usually not much influenced thereby in their voting. Finally, like all such audiences, they were probably often wearied by long speaking and sympathetic to the appeal of Mr. Speaker who, on Tuesday the 10th of April, of this session, "recited a Commandment from the Queen's Majesty, to spend little time in Motions and to avoid long Speeches."

The speaker who rose to make the principal attack on the "Act Against Usury" was well and favorably known to this House for many reasons. His part in establishing the reformed church and the new learning under Edward VI, as the youngest member of the famous Cambridge group composed of Sir John Cheke, Sir Thomas Smith, Roger Ascham, Walter Haddon, Martin Bucer, and others, was familiar to all. His flight to Italy, his romantic intrigues with other Protestant refugees, involving reputed attempts on the life of a cardinal, and his narrow escape from martyrdom at the hands of the Inquisition at Rome, were common knowledge. Twenty years earlier he had written the first logic in English, eighteen years earlier the first rhetoric—both very popular books, the latter having reached five editions by this time. It is quite possible that some of the members of Parliament had studied these books and owed their positions in life to the lessons they had learned in them. It was for just such persons that Wilson had written them. Who would be more "studious of eloquence," for example, than this generation of self-made men who, in Protestant England, entered the Parliaments of Elizabeth?

Few, at least, would have been unfamiliar with the fact that Wilson was a learned man, a graduate of Cambridge with an LL.D. from an Italian university; for example, he is always referred to by the reporters of the House as "Doctor" Wilson. And none but would know that he was a prominent Civilian Advocate, Master of Requests, Master of St. Katherine's Hospital, and the brother-in-law of Admiral Sir William Winter, that he was frequently sent abroad on special diplomatic and commercial missions, and that he was considered the best informed man in England on Portuguese affairs. All would know that he was a man of great industry, unusual memory, wide knowledge, and varied talents, and certain of high political preferment.[15]

In his favor also was the fact that he had spoken briefly but well in a speech only four days earlier on a bill against vagabonds, and that he was largely instrumental in the bill's being passed. We have no record of his having made other speeches before this in Parliament although he had been a member in 1563 as well as this session.

But Wilson was not an inexperienced orator. Of his speaking, in Latin or English, at Cambridge, in Italy, and in England after his return in 1560, we have but an incomplete record. His Latin speeches (manuscripts of which are in the British Museum) especially those in behalf of Sir William Winter, given at Lisbon, and those in favor of clemency, given before Queen Elizabeth in 1566, attest his mastery of Cicero's language and rhetoric. His commemorative Latin sermon in honor of Edward Courtney, Earl of Devonshire, delivered in St. Anthony's Church in Padua during Wilson's exile, is an excellent model of the demonstrative speech, illustrating all of Wilson's doctrine on this type of speech. This address, indeed, surpasses in loftiness of thought, sublimity of diction, sincerity and earnestness of feeling, any of his examples in the *Rhetorique*.

Such was the speaker, "Doctor Wilson, Master of the Requests," who rose to attack the "Act Against Usury," following Mr. Molley's defense of it. He began by saying that in a matter of so great weight he could not speak shortly; he acknowledged that he had studied the matter thoroughly; and he begged the patience of the House. Following this exordium, he may have stated his proposition and have partitioned the subject and his speech, but the reporter does not so indicate. Instead, it would seem that he proceeded at once to points in confirmation as follows:

1. The common state may exist without usury.
2. The pagans prohibited it.
3. It is forbidden by Christian doctrine and canon law.
4. It is economically harmful to both Queen and Commonwealth.
5. It has properly been condemned by common law.

Thereafter, in the version we have, some miscellaneous points are given, mainly examples and precedents related to the preceding main heads of arguments. And the speech ends with the statement that "the offence in his Conscience should be judged a Felony."

The speech as reported in D'Ewes consists of only four paragraphs of normal length, a severe compression of an obviously long address and a slender basis for extended comment or criticism. In Wilson's

A *Discourse Upon Usurye*, written two years before this speech, and first published a year later, 1572, we have, of course, excellent assistance in exegesis; but we have no warrant for supposing that he amplified and phrased the points of the speech as in the book.

In his first point, however, that the common state may be without usury (and this is all that D'Ewes reports on this argument), Wilson no doubt expounded the ideal Christian state, much as Ockerfoe, the preacher, did in his first oration in the book on usury: "Love God above all things and thy neighbor as thyself. This is the proper and natural state of the true Christian and in it there will be neither borrowing or lending, for love is the perfection of the law; and usury the negation of all love and Christian charity."

On the second point, that the pagans had forbidden usury, Wilson, as his speech is reported, instanced laws by the Athenians and Lycurgus which forbade usury. As for the third point, Christian condemnation, he gave the familiar argument from definition—that usury is the taking of any reward, price, or sum, over and above a due debt or principal. He then quoted Ezekiel and other prophets and parts of Scripture in support of this definition and of the prohibition of such practices. He also cited St. Augustine's statement that to take but a cup of wine is usury and damnable. This, says the reporter, was apparently in refutation of Mr. Molley's claim that not moderate but excessive interest was the usury condemned by Holy Writ; but apparently Wilson made no direct reference to his opponent and did not depart from his prepared and no doubt perfectly memorized speech.

The argument that usury is economically harmful to Queen and Commonwealth rests upon the claim that men, not using their own money, but putting it out to hire, cease to practice legitimate business activity and normal occupations, causing prices to rise and reducing the export trade and the taxes available for the Queen's use.

To prove that usury is condemned by common law, a point in utter contradiction of the claim of Mr. Clarke who spoke first and on Wilson's side, he says only that "an Usurer was not admitted to be a Witness, nor after his Death to the common Sepulchre of Christians."

At this point in his speech, Wilson said:

And for that his Discourse had been long, he inserted (as he said) this Tale for recreation of the Hearers.

In *Italy,* Quoth he, a great known Usurer being Dead, the Curate denied him the common place of Burial; his Friends made Suit, the Priest would not hear; in fine, the Suitors, bethought them of a Policy to bring it to pass, that he might be Buried in the Church; which was this. The Parson of the Church did accustomably use to carry his Books daily from his House to the Church on his Ass; and the Ass by often going needed not to be driven, but knowing his Journey, as soon as he was laden, would of himself go to the Church Door; they desired the Parson, his Ass might carry the dead Body and where it should stay, the Body to be Buried. To so fond a request the Priest agreed, the Body was laid on the Ass, who feeling a greater burthen than he was used to bear, did run towards the Town, never staying until he came to the common place of Execution.

The tale was "merrily told," the reporter says. It was followed, apparently, by a variety of attacks on usury; the speaker reminded his hearers that the early Church Councils had forbidden it, that various theologians had called it a spider, a canker, an asp, a snake, and a devil, and that they had compared it to murder. The speaker charged that it had caused the downfall of Rome, that it was the reason for the suspicion that Edward the Third of England practiced magic or alchemy, and that, through the Fuggers, and others of the Low Countries and Germany, it had beggared many mighty princes. He ended his arguments by citing Sir John Cheke and ancient English legal authorities to prove that the offense of taking interest is punishable by canon law during life and by civil law (through confiscation of goods and estate) after death.

That the speech made a considerable impression, as Tawney believes, is borne out by the fact that Mr. Bell, a member of the Privy Council, a leading merchant, one of the most prominent and popular speakers of the session, and the party Whip of his day, saw fit to make the principal answer. Mr. Bell began by saying that "This matter being so ample had occasioned much Speech, and was for cunning men a fit theme to shew their Wits and skills upon." He proceeded to show the lack of a satisfactory definition of usury among theologians, the impossibility of prohibiting all things criticized by the Scriptures, and the necessity of reasonable legislation in all such cases.

Other speakers dealt with the economic necessity of legalizing interest, reiterated the controversial theological arguments on the question, and disputed its status in current law and in legal history.[16] Thereafter the Bill was ordered to be committed and eventually was enacted. For all the respect paid to Wilson and to his speech, it is evident that this extended effort of his was ill-adapted to his audience and purpose and

236

had little practical effect on the voting of the members. Most important, Wilson violated at least two principles he had strongly urged in his *Rhetorique:* First of all he did not attempt to secure good will from this audience in his "Entrance" or Introduction but rather chilled them by saying that "in a matter of such weight he could not shortly speak"; and, secondly, he proceeded in fact to make what he himself realized was an intolerably long speech—which was in direct opposition to the strong admonition, in his *Rhetorique,* not to do one's cause harm by long and tedious speaking, especially when the audience is in opposition.[17] Moreover, the speech is not well adapted to stirring the appropriate emotions of this audience—the principle of persuasion most strongly stressed in his *Rhetorique*—since it makes no appeal to the economic interests of the majority of the House on a subject closely related thereto.

Other obvious defects are these: Wilson did not meet the very important issues of enforceability, of the evils of exorbitant illicit usury, of the necessity of borrowing by the increasing number of small capitalists, the lack of available funds, and the general financial situation of the English mercantile class. He rested his case entirely too much upon theological pronouncements and legal precedents drawn from times long past and wholly unrelated to the peculiar conditions of his day; he failed to refute successfully the relaxations in continental Protestant theological doctrine on the subject, which had infected the merchant class through their contacts and rivalries with Flemish and German traders and bankers.

The speech conforms closely to Wilson's emphasis on and varied methods of amplification, including the use of humor. But it illustrates and perhaps makes more evident certain defects of his *Rhetorique,* especially his emphasis on topical and verbal amplification. The doctrines of his *Rhetorique,* highly valuable to the inarticulate young lawyers and preachers for whom he wrote in the days of Edward VI, were inadequate guides for a debater on such a subject in Parliament in the thirteenth year of Elizabeth's reign.

It is, of course, highly probable that Wilson knew the futility of attempting to persuade this audience on this subject at this time. He may well have desired to speak for the record; he may have been mainly concerned with advocating doctrines consistent with the ideas of his book on usury (already written and soon to be published); or, he may have made the speech he did, and the book as well, to advance his own political fortunes, rather than with any hope of turning the tide of rampant mercantilism.

At any rate, he continued to grow in favor with state and church, becoming a minister to Antwerp, Dean of Durham—one of very few laymen to achieve an ecclesiastical position of this stature—and, with Sir Francis Walsingham, Principal Secretary (of State). His speech against usury, no matter how improved, could probably not have halted the rise of modern capitalism in England. As given, it probably added much to his reputation as an uncompromising conservative and austere religionist—a reputation which won him high favor with the ruling party in his own day.

Milton's Rhetoric on the

Tyranny of Kings

WILBUR E. GILMAN

FROM 1640 to 1660, or from the thirty-second to the fifty-second year of his life, John Milton devoted most of his time and energy to debating public questions and holding public office. During this period he composed and published more than a score of pamphlets intended to influence public opinion in favor of greater religious and civil liberty.

To scholars interested in rhetoric these pamphlets are significant as examples of persuasive writing in the seventeenth century—a period when the circulation of pamphlets was the chief means of reaching the public mind. An analysis of these writings reveals not only Milton's points of view on the important public controversies of his age and the rhetorical principles he followed, but also some aspects of the composition of the poetry he delayed writing until circumstances forced him to give up the struggle against the prelates and the Stuarts, particularly of the speeches in *Paradise Lost* and *Paradise Regained*.[1]

The Tenure of Kings and Magistrates (1649), though published after the death of Charles, is a plea for the trial, deposition, and punishment of tyrants, and is intended to support the cause of the regicides. Milton maintains that a king or a magistrate who has become a tyrant may be as lawfully deposed and punished as he was at first elected.[2]

BACKGROUND

In the spring of 1648, under the leadership of Fairfax, Ireton, and Cromwell, the army officers resolved that Charles Stuart must be

239

tried and punished on their indictments. On November 16, their demands for justice finally culminated in the Grand Army Remonstrance charging the king with the highest treason. On December 1, acting upon that charge, the army imprisoned Charles, and the next day Fairfax used his troops to force the acquiescence of Parliament. After Pride's Purge on December 6, followed by the voluntary withdrawal of nearly thirty members, Parliament consisted of only fifty members. On January 20, 1649, a court of one hundred thirty-five commissioners appointed by this fraction of the legal Parliament began the trial of the king, and just a week later, on January 27, sixty-seven sentenced him to death as a tyrant, a murderer, and an enemy of the nation.

The specific object of this determined Parliamentary group was the death of Charles—an idea so extreme as to shock even those in the nation who thoroughly hated the highhanded monarch. Of all the clergy, only two Independent ministers openly approved the trial of the king. In spite of their former bitter hostility to him, the Presbyterians directed their efforts toward saving Charles from the army and the Independents, largely because they wanted to rescue Presbyterianism itself. From August, 1646, to November, 1648, throughout Charles's imprisonment by the Scots, they had tried to obtain from the king a treaty guaranteeing their form of church government, in return for his restoration to full power. The Presbyterians were unanimous in condemning Cromwell and his supporters in Parliament.[3]

This defection of the group whose views Milton had defended less than a decade before, aroused his indignation and his contempt. Finding himself one of the few men in the country who believed that the king should be put to death, he set forth the reasons for his position in the pamphlet entitled *The Tenure of Kings and Magistrates: Proving, That it is Lawfull, and hath been held so through all Ages, for any, who have the Power, to call to account a Tyrant, or wicked King, and after due conviction, to depose, and put him to death; if the ordinary Magistrate have neglected, or deny'd to doe it. And that they, who of late, so much blame Deposing, are the Men that did it themselves.*

Five years later, Milton justified his participation in the controversy with the following explanation:

The civil species of liberty, the last which remained, I had not touched, as I perceived it drew sufficient attention from the magistrate. Nor did I write any thing on the right of kings, till the king, pronounced an enemy by the parliament, and vanquished in war, was arraigned as a captive before judges, and condemned to lose his head. But, when certain presbyterian ministers, at first the bitterest foes to Charles, unable to endure that the independent party should now be preferred to them, and that it should have greater influence in the senate, began to clamour against the sentence which the parliament had pronounced upon the king (though in no wise angry at the deed, but only that themselves had not the execution of it) and tried to their utmost to raise a tumult, having the assurance to affirm that the doctrine of protestants, that all the reformed churches shrunk with horror from the atrocity of such a sentence against kings—then indeed, I thought it behoved me openly to oppose so barefaced a falsehood. Yet even then, I neither wrote nor advised any thing concerning Charles; but simply showed, in general, what may be lawfully done against tryrants; adducing, in confirmation, the authorities of no small number of the most eminent divines; inveighing, at the same time, almost with the zeal of a preacher against the egregious ignorance or impudence of those men, who had promised better things. This book was not published till after the death of the king, being intended rather to compose the minds of men, than to settle any thing relating to Charles; that being the business of the magistrates instead of mine, and which, at the time I speak of, had already been done.[4]

According to Edward Phillips, *The Tenure of Kings and Magistrates* was written after the execution of Charles, but both Milton's own statement quoted above and evidence within the pamphlet itself prove that Phillips was mistaken.[5] Its publication, to be sure, occurred just two weeks after Charles had been put to death: Charles died on January 30, and the pamphlet was issued on February 13. But Allison shows that Milton must have written it in less than three weeks: between the eighth and the twenty-seventh of January. Hence it was hastily composed while England was tense with the excitement of unusual events.[6] This first apology for the Commonwealth bore Milton's initials on the title page, as well as the name of the publisher.

IDEAS AND STRUCTURE

Although in the passage quoted above Milton sought to give the impression that *The Tenure of Kings and Magistrates* did not apply specifically to the tyranny of Charles Stuart, his obvious purpose in writing the pamphlet was to justify the trial of the king. The issue, however, is not the superiority of a republic over a monarchy; it is simply the justice of deposing and punishing tyrants.

The pamphlet exemplifies the use of deliberative rhetoric to support the political course of the group in power. Milton's case rests primarily upon political theory, historical instances, and religious authority. The major ideas fall into the following organization:

Introduction

Only reasonable, virtuous, and courageous men can be depended upon to go so far as to demand the death of a tyrant.

Proposition

A king or a magistrate who has become a tyrant may be as lawfully deposed and punished as he was at first elected.

Discussion

I. He has no claim to absolute sovereignty.
   A. He derives his power from the people.
   B. His power is entrusted to him for the common good of all.
   C. The power remains fundamentally in the people.
   D. The power cannot be taken from the people without a violation of their natural birthright.
   E. A king is one who governs to the good and profit of his people and not for his own ends.
   F. The best emperors and kings do not assume absolute authority.
   G. Both the Jewish Church and that of the ancient Christians disapproved of absolute rule, even though the Jews and the Asiatics approved of slavery.

II. The assumption that title to the crown is a hereditary right is merely a courtesy or a convenience; but even if the assumption is valid, the king, when convicted of high crimes, can, like a subject, be deprived of his title and inheritance.
   A. To say that the king has as good right to his crown and dignity as any man to his inheritance, is to make the subject no better than the king's slave.
   B. To deny the justice and legality of such forfeiture is to commit treason against the dignity of mankind.

III. The declaration that kings are accountable to none but God, being at variance with all law and government, must be rejected.
   A. If they may refuse to give account, then all covenants with them at coronation are in vain.
   B. If the king does not fear God, the people hold their lives and estates by the tenure of his mere grace and mercy.
   C. Aristotle writes that monarchy unaccountable is the worst sort of tyranny, least of all to be endured by free-born men.
   D. The testimony of good kings and emperors shows that they held themselves accountable to law.

IV. The people by their right as free-born men to be governed as seems to them best, may choose or reject a monarch, retain or depose him, whether he is a tyrant or not.

    A. Reason substantiates this tenet.

    B. Scripture supports this view.

V. A tyrant must be considered a common enemy deserving to be punished.

    A. Regarding neither law nor the common good, he reigns only for himself and his faction.

    B. He is frequently guilty of oppression and atrocities.

    C. Examples from history, not only among the heathen, but also among the Jews and among the Christians down into Protestant times, furnish precedent for treating a tyrannous ruler as a felon.

    D. The treatment of Charles by the Presbyterians is an especially pertinent instance.

    E. The people of a free nation must have the power to dispose and economize in the land which God hath given them, as masters of family in their own house and free inheritance.

VI. A tyrant may be not only justly deposed, but like a private citizen, arraigned for his transgression.

    A. If wise and religious men have done immediate justice upon tyrants, it is surely much more mild and humane to give them fair and open trial.

    B. It is not, nor ought to be, the glory of a Protestant state never to have put their king to death; rather it is the glory of a Protestant king never to have deserved death.

    C. Regardless of the absence of a precedent, the Parliament and Military Council have the responsibility of performing their duty.

    D. History shows that a tyrant even if restored to power under stipulated conditions cannot be trusted to keep his promises.

    E. Illustrious Protestant divines have favored not only the removal, but also the death of tyrants.

    F. The logical consequences of the statements and activities of the clergy support both the deposing and the punishing of a tyrant.

Conclusion

The Presbyterian ministers who are responsible for the deposing of Charles seek vainly to prove that it is illegal to try the king, only because they are interested in selfish ends.

Suspense is not a part of Milton's technique in this discussion, since the title-page itself clearly reveals the nature of the whole argument, even including the responsibility of the Presbyterian clergy. Likewise, the rhetorical plan is the straight-forward procedure from the general to the specific, although in places observations precede the inferences to which they point.

The pamphlet may be divided into the traditional rhetorical parts, which are quite well proportioned. The whole treatise occupies fifty-eight and one-half pages in the Columbia edition. After a vigorous exordium of about six pages, directed especially toward the Presbyterians and the faltering Independents, comes a page devoted to the exclusion of irrelevant matter, to the partition, and to the statement of the proposition. Definitions of king and tyrant are postponed until they are needed in the discussion. A narration, which in about three pages sets forth the origin and nature of the power of a king and the history of the relation he bears to his subjects, forms an excellent transition to the discussion, which begins with inferences drawn from the derivative nature of the power of kings and magistrates. The discussion extends over forty-seven pages. The conclusion, which is devoted chiefly to flaying the Presbyterian ministers, requires only two pages.

Such slight digressions as there are may be attributed to Milton's overpowering desire to reproach the Presbyterians for their inconsistencies and their selfishness. But the main theme is never long obscured. Milton's usual fault of requiring the reader to grasp large units of thought is again conspicuous. The development of the reasoning is three times retarded: once for a survey of Scriptural passages; once for a long list of specific instances; once for an impressive display of quotations from theologians.

LOGICAL PROOF

Logical proof begins with a restatement of the idea brought out in the narration that the people always retain as their fundamental possession the power they entrusted to kings and magistrates for the common good. As his second basic idea, Milton cites the Aristotelian definition of a king as one who governs to the good and profit of his people, and not for his own ends. Four inferences follow from the acceptance of these premises: (1) such titles as sovereign lord applied to the monarch are either arrogancies or flatteries; (2) either the assumption that title to the crown is a hereditary right is merely a courtesy or a convenience, or the king, like a subject, can be deprived of his title and inheritance when convicted of high crimes; (3) the declaration that kings are accountable to none but God, being at variance with all law and government, must be rejected; (4) the people, by their right as free born men to be governed as seems to them best, may choose or reject a monarch, retain or depose him, whether he is a tyrant or not. These inferences are further supported by Scriptural and historical authority, by enthymematic reasoning, by refutation, by specific example. Much space is devoted to the interpretation of Scriptural passages so that their implication will favor Milton's position. One of his objects is to furnish conclusive proof that kings "cannot show the time when God ever set on the throne them or thir forefathers, but onely when the people chose them." [7] His Scriptural evidence also shows that God did not hesitate to dethrone princes. His reasoning on the problem presents an effective dilemma: if the people originally conferred power upon their king, they may, for just causes, lawfully take it away; if the people were the instrument of God in placing a king upon the throne, they are likewise the instrument of God in removing him from the throne.

After a recapitulation of the case thus far, Milton proceeds to the consideration of what a tyrant is, and what the people may do against him. He defines a tyrant, on the authority of St. Basil, as one who "regarding neither Law nor the common good, reigns onely for himself and his faction." [8] With examples ranging from the summary action of the Greeks and Romans to the carefully judged cases of Protestant times, Milton amply demonstrates that there are all sorts of precedents for deposing and sometimes executing tyrants. In the course of citing these instances, he pauses for an elaborately reasoned interpretation and defense of a Biblical case, and he frequently uses enthymematic argument to support his particular use of concrete illustrations. His trump card is the blending of example and argument in maintaining that contemporary Presbyterians in England have given the best demonstration of what to do about tyranny. He declares:

The Presbyterians, who now so much condemn deposing, were the men themselves that deposed the King, and cannot with all thir shifting and relapsing, wash off the guiltiness from thir own hands. For they themselves, by these thir late doings have made it guiltiness, and turn'd thir own warrantable actions into Rebellion.[9]

To establish the assumption here, Milton works out a long and intricate chain of reasoning, covering nine pages, based upon the violation of the two oaths of allegiance and supremacy. In the course of this argument he urges that during the civil wars the Presbyterians several times endangered the very life of Charles, and that by taking him captive, figuratively they killed the king.

In further justification of drastic action to free the country of tyranny, Milton reasons that if England is really a free nation, the people must have the power "to dispose and *oeconomize* in the Land which God hath giv'n them, as Maisters of Family in thir own house and free inheritance." [10] Using the *a fortiori* argument, Milton maintains that if the people have the right to abrogate a good government, they have much more right to overthrow a tyrant. Under this power not only can they depose a tyrant but they can try him as a private man for crimes committed; Milton contends:

> It is not, neither ought to be the glory of a Protestant State, never to have put thir King to death; It is the glory of a Protestant King never to have deserv'd death.[11]

He argues that Parliament and the Military Council should dare to set a precedent in the present circumstances. Both by reasoning and by citing examples of similar situations, Milton shows that the Presbyterians will be disappointed if they expect that Charles ever will keep promises made to them, and that it is to their interest to support the Independents. Devoting six pages to the vigorous testimony of such illustrious predecessors as Luther, Zwingli, Calvin, Peter Martyr, and Knox, and of such well-known Puritan apologists of the previous century as Cartwright, Fenner, Gilby, and Goodman, Milton proves that the reluctance of contemporary divines to sanction the punishment of the king is in sharp contrast to the pronouncements of those distinguished clergymen favoring not only the removal but the death of tyrants. Refutation of the contemporary clergymen by showing the full consequences of their own statements completes Milton's logical proof. Their inconsistency Milton brings out quite well in the following statement:

> To Warr upon a King, that his instruments may be brought to condigne punishment and therafter to punish them the instruments, and not to spare onely, but to defend and honour him the Author, is the strangest peece of justice to be call'd Christian, and the strangest peece of reason to be call'd human, that by men of reverence and learning, as thir stile imports them, ever yet was vented.[12]

246

Milton on the Tyranny of Kings

PATHETIC PROOF

Pathetic proof generously colors the logical proof just summarized. Several of the emotions are deeply stirred. Milton seeks to arouse the anger and indignation of his fellow citizens against those who opposed Charles while he was in power but are now trying to bargain with him to their own advantage. His attitude toward the Presbyterian ministers in particular is strikingly revealed in the following passage:

Divines . . . have thir postures, and thir motions no less expertly, and with no less variety then they that practice feats in the Artillery-ground. Sometimes they seem furiously to march on, and presently march counter; by and by they stand, and then retreat; or if need be can face about, or wheele in a whole body, with that cunning and dexterity as is almost unperceavable; to winde themselves by shifting ground into places of more advantage. And Providence onely must be the drumm, Providence the word of command, that calls them from above, but always to som larger Benefice, or acts them into such or such figures, and promotions.[13]

Quite consistently with the attempt to arouse anger against the Presbyterians, Milton endeavors to stir fear in the Presbyterians themselves. He exclaims:

But if they be the Ministers of Mannon in stead of Christ, and scandalize his Church with the filthy love of gaine, aspiring also to sit the closest & the heaviest of all Tyrants, upon the conscience, and fall notoriously into the same sinns, wherof so lately and so loud they accus'd the Prelates, as God rooted out those wicked ones immediately before, so will he root out them thir imitators: and to vindicate his own glory and Religion, will uncover thir hypocrisie to the op'n world; and visit upon thir own heads that *curse ye Meroz*, the very *Motto* of thir Pulpits, wherwith so frequently, not as *Meroz*, but more like Atheists they have blasphem'd the vengeance of God, and traduc'd the zeale of his people.[14]

Those who have weakened and become unwilling to sanction the trial and execution of Charles, particularly Whitelocke (the lawyer), Elsyng (the clerk of the House), and Fairfax (commander of the troops), he tries to make ashamed of their cowardice. He observes:

Another sort there is, who comming in the cours of these affaires, to have thir share in great actions, above the form of Law or Custom, at least to give thir voice and approbation, begin to swerve, and almost shiver at the Majesty and grandeur of som noble deed, as if they were newly enter'd

247

into a great sin; disputing presidents, forms, and circumstances, when the Commonwealth nigh perishes for want of deeds in substance, don with just and faithfull expedition.[15]

Fundamental interests are the basis of a number of Milton's strongest appeals. The following passage shows Milton's skill in combining appeals founded upon religion and patriotism:

> But God, as we have cause to trust, will put other thoughts into the people, and turn them from giving eare or heed to these Mercenary noise makers, of whose fury, and fals prophecies we have anough experience; and from the murmurs of new discord will incline them to heark'n rather with erected minds to the voice of our Supreme Magistracy, calling us to liberty and the flourishing deeds of a reformed Common-wealth; with this hope that as God was heretofore angry with the Jews who rejected him and his forme of Goverment to choose a King, so that he will bless us, and be propitious to us who reject a King to make him onely our leader and supreme governour in the conformity as neer as may be of his own ancient goverment; if we have at least but so much worth in us to entertaine the sense of our future happiness, and the courage to receave what God voutsafes us: wherein we have the honour to precede other Nations who are now labouring to be our followers.[16]

More than once Milton appeals to the People's sense of justice. For example, he says:

> And certainly if men, not to speak of Heathen, both wise and Religious have don justice upon Tyrants what way they could soonest, how much more milde & human then is it, to give them faire and op'n tryal? To teach lawless Kings, and all who so much adore them, that not mortal man, or his imperious will, but Justice is the onely true sovran and supreme Majesty upon earth.[17]

Another instance follows:

> They tell us that the Law of nature justifies any man to defend himself, ev'n against the King in Person: let them shew us then why the same Law, may not justifie much more a State or whole people, to doe justice upon him, against whom each privat man may lawfully defend himself; seing all kind of justice don, is a defence to good men, as well as a punishment to bad; and justice don upon a Tyrant is no more but the necessary self-defence of a whole Common-wealth.[18]

Milton does not lose the opportunity in this pamphlet to associate his favorite theme of liberty with the necessity of punishing tyrants. He declares:

248

None can love freedom heartilie, but good men; the rest love not freedom, but licence; which never hath more scope or more indulgence then under Tyrants.[19]

Fear of the loss of liberty he brings to play upon the Presbyterians:

Let them not oppose thir best friends and associats, who molest them not at all, infringe not the least of thir liberties; unless they call it thir liberty to bind other mens consciences, but are still seeking to live at peace with them and brotherly accord. Let them beware an old and perfet enemy, who though he hope by sowing discord to make them his instruments, yet cannot forbeare a minute the op'n threatning of his destind revenge upon them, when they have servd his purposes. Let them, feare therfore if they be wise, rather what they have don already, then what remaines to doe, and be warn'd in time they put no confidence in Princes whom they have provok'd, lest they be added to the examples of those that miserably have tasted the event.[20]

ETHICAL PROOF

Ethical proof in this pamphlet is of the indirect or implied type. Milton has no occasion to talk about himself. His character becomes evident to the reader from his criticisms and appeals. The very fact that he frankly sides with the Independents, who are bent on taking the life of the English king, establishes his decision and courage. His love of virtue, justice, and liberty asserts itself several times. The opening sentences of the pamphlet stamp him as a man earnestly endeavoring to attain self-discipline and self-control:

If men within themselves would be govern'd by reason, and not generally give up thir understanding to a double tyrannie, of Custom from without, and blind affections within, they would discerne better, what it is to favour and uphold the Tyrant of a Nation. But being slaves within doors, no wonder that they strive so much to have the public State conformably govern'd to the inward vitious rule, by which they govern themselves.[21]

His keen sense of loyalty and honor stand forth in the accusation:

Most men are apt enough to civill Wars and commotions as a noveltie, and for a flash hot and active; but through sloth or inconstancie, and weakness of spirit either fainting, ere thir own pretences, though never so just, be half attain'd or through an inbred falshood and wickednes, betray oft times to destruction with themselves, men of noblest temper joyn'd with them for causes, whereof they in their rash undertakings were not capable.[22]

His scorn of shame and insincerity brings out his strength of character in the denunciation:

If we consider who and what they are, on a suddain grown so pitifull, wee may conclude, thir pitty can be no true, and Christian commiseration, but either levitie and shallowness of minde, or else a carnal admiring of that worldly pomp and greatness, from whence they see him fall'n; or rather lastly a dissembl'd and seditious pity, fain'd of industry to begett new discord.[23]

His familiarity with Scripture and his identification of most of his thinking with religious principles mark him as a strongly religious person. Likewise his command of the ideas of historians, philosophers, and theologians elicits respect for his erudition. Most important, perhaps, his frequent references to the power of the people and the welfare of the English nation impress the reader with his patriotism and love of democracy. He doubtless increases good will by making clear that he does not condemn all forms of monarchy; he denounces only tyranny.

NON-ARTISTIC PROOF

Authority, though less important than in *Of Civil Power*, plays an unusually large part in this pamphlet. The authority of Scripture is abundantly used to justify extreme measures to free the country from tyranny. In several instances this authority is used to refute the supporters of Charles, and sometimes Milton reinterprets passages which have been used to uphold the position of his opponents. Since he is arguing primarily against Presbyterian divines, Scripture is the most acceptable authority he can adduce. Next to Scripture, however, the writings of the leading Protestant clergymen have greatest weight. As was pointed out in the consideration of logical proof, Milton draws support from a large number of the most important of these theologians. A third class of especially significant authorities is that composed of emperors and kings. Such a statement as the following is unusually persuasive:

And not *Trajan* onely, but *Theodosius* the yonger, a Christian Emperor and one of the best, causd it to be enacted as a rule undenyable and fit to be acknowledg'd by all Kings and Emperors, that a Prince is bound to the Laws; that on the autority of Law the autority of a Prince depends, and to the Laws ought submitt. Which Edict of his remains yet in the *Code* of *Justinian. 1.* I. *tit.* 24. as a sacred constitution to all the succeeding Emperors.[24]

Not content merely to state an authority, Milton emphasizes his importance and virtue as well. For definitions he turns to Aristotle, whom he calls "one of the best interpreters of nature and morality." [25]

Near the close of the pamphlet, in the process of maximizing and minimizing arguments, Milton makes some significant remarks about authorities:

The best and chief of Protestant Divines, we may follow them for faithful Guides, and without doubting may receive them, as Witnesses abundant of what wee heer affirme concerning Tyrants. . . . if they were divided in opinion, yet greater then these here allg'd, or of more autority in the Church, there can be none produc'd. If any one shall goe about by bringing other testimonies to disable these, or by bringing these against themselves in other cited passages of thir Books, he will not only faile to make good that fals and impudent assertion of those mutinous Ministers, that the deposing and punishing of a King or Tyrant, *is against the constant Judgement of all Protestant Divines*, it being quite the contrary, but will prove rather, what perhaps he intended not, that the judgement of Divines, if it be so various and inconstant to it self, is not considerable, or to be esteem'd at all.[26]

CONCLUSION

This pamphlet, noteworthy for its striking use of forceful political philosophy developed with considerable historical, Biblical, and theological support, employs an elaborate logical case to justify the deposing and punishing of a tyrannical king. In spite of being overshadowed by logical proof, pathetic proof stands out occasionally by contributing several effective appeals, particularly those which arouse indignation against the bargainers and the cowards, and those which stir fear of the consequences of allowing a tyrant to continue in power.

Although *The Tenure of Kings and Magistrates* is an interesting example of Milton's persuasion, its rhetorical significance is not nearly so great as its political significance. It secured for Milton the position of Latin Secretary. Masson comments as follows:

Open and bold, beyond what may now appear, had been Milton's own conduct in publishing this pamphlet. Written mainly while the King was yet being tried, or was under sentence, and only touched here and there with additions after his death, so that throughout we are never quite sure whether the King is not still alive as we read, what did the publication of the pamphlet, a fortnight after the fact it defended, really imply? It implied not only that Milton had thrown in his lot with the Commonwealth, but also that he avowed himself a partisan of the Regicides, and was willing to abide all the consequences of that connexion. Actually, by his *Tenure of Kings and Magistrates,* he had attached himself more closely than any other person in England to the group of about sixty men, with Cromwell in their midst, who had constituted themselves the real Regicides by signing the Death-warrant or executing it. He had declared that, had it been necessary, his signature also would have been given to that Warrant.[27]

George Whitefield:

Commoner Evangelist

C. HAROLD KING

I

STANDING at 1800 and looking back over the previous century, an historian might have remarked, "When shall we see their like again!" He would have been referring both to great men and to the sweeping power of movements. The eighteenth century was brought to climax by two earth-shaking events, the American and French Revolutions, and each of these had brought forth leaders of such calibre as to be at once individual and representative.

Contributing to the doubled climax of the American and French Revolutions were more subtle forces that, stirring the depths of human nature itself, worked powerfully in areas more basic than symptomatic revolution and war. Two forces especially were thus determinant of the more frequent and constant problems of life and truth, the Enlightenment and its antithesis, known vaguely as Romanticism. If every man is born an Aristotelian or a Platonist, it may be assumed with equal confidence that a child born between 1750 and 1850 would be influenced, directly or indirectly, by rationalistic or romantic guides.

We all know that thinking men in the early eighteenth century had made reason the standard for judging all values. Reason was king and to its bar of judgment were brought all things in Heaven and earth. It was not indeed secular matters alone which were thus evaluated, for religion, the last refuge of the mystical, was made to conform to non-mystical norms.[1] *The Reasonableness of Christianity* by John Locke[2] indicated in what manner Christianity would stand or fall and the *Analogy* by Bishop Butler claimed as its triumph over rational skepticism that it had established Christianity on a firm basis of probability.[3] Clergymen in America too—and not Anglican alone—now spoke of reason more often than faith, and such also was the trend in Catholic France and Lutheran Germany.

It is not that the standard of reason was new. The Greeks had broken from mystical explanations of nature to found a rational science. Even Christianity, holding high the banner of faith, had come to accept reason as a respectable partner by the synthesis of Aquinas, and Erasmus, inspired by Greeks, went only a little further on the highway of reasoned piety. What then was new about the Age of Reason?

Emphasis on reason in the eighteenth century was not so much new as more insistent. And what had made it more insistent? Newtonian science was the compelling difference. In the seventeenth century, rational science had extended its sway over greater and greater areas of more and more scientific fields until Newton's secular synthesis challenged that of the medieval theologians.[4] If the physical universe was so simply rational, it must be that human life could be so judged and so determined. Rationalism itself became a faith as men strewed their books and conversations with such terms as *Nature* and *Nature's Laws.*[5]

Reason's kingship is observable in areas less obvious than those which dealt directly with human values. In literature, in the arts and in some more practical affairs of living, rationality was worshipped by inference. French authors revealed their admiration for the balance and decency of Roman literature; German writers, as if hurriedly expiating the sin of Germany's non-Roman past, managed a belated Classicism; while the English Alexander Pope, delighting those whose frequent thoughts were not so well expressed as his, fashioned tributes in couplet and in substance to the Rule of Reason.

The more tangible affairs of everyday living felt the contagion of reason's spell. Even if indifferent to the language of philosophers, Robert Walpole read common sense as caution that would prevent any whisper of disturbance of the comfortable *status quo.* Nor was reason always a dull thing. The courtly manners of society, the strains of Mozart or Handel, the comely lines of Hepplewhite or Sheraton would delight future generations with images of reason's charm.

But, it seemed, the spell of reason was too exacting—even the light bonds of Mozart and Sheraton. Reaction appeared—not for the first or last time, taking form on this occasion in a broadly gauged Romanticism. On almost every front, rebellion appeared, sometimes unconscious, sometimes conscious without hostility, but, very often, both rebellious and hostile. Whatever the degree of conscious revolt, intuition—or, in religion, faith—was elevated and reason degraded as a fallen Lucifer. Writers began to speak of the impulses of their hearts more often than the discipline of their minds; music became a wilder thing, and formal gardens were deliberately dishevelled; the long bleak Age of Walpole, designated by J. R. Green as "almost without a history," [6] gave way to the abrupt outburst of patriotism under William Pitt; and slowly and excruciatingly, the lines of Sheraton, Duncan Phyfe and McIntire gave way to the undoubted reaction of Victorian furniture.

As already noted, these shifts of power were not always charitably managed. Reason, arrogant in its claims, found language of derision for man's non-rational impulses. No epithet of mid-twentieth-century scorn—unless "Communist"—could approach the concentrated contempt of the eighteenth-century "Enthusiasm" and "An Enthusiast." [7] Romanticism replied with equal defiance, finding rationalists and their dogma inadequate.[8] Men scarcely paused in the heat of extremes of denunciation to realize that human nature draws sustenance from both rational and non-rational springs.

Nowhere was the general reaction of romanticism against reason so marked and so hostile as in religion. In France, the Jansenists found a new lease of life; in Germany, Pietists rebelled against Lutheranism now become formalistic; in Scotland, hot-blooded Presbyterians castigated more conservative members of the same persuasion; in Wales, Calvinism was united with religious fervor; in England, Methodists drew apart from Anglicans in spite of Wesley's insisting, "I live and die a member of the church of England"; in America, revolts against the old way sprang up with rapid sequence in Pennsylvania, New Jersey and Massachusetts.[9]

Less obviously than some but as surely, George Whitefield played a part in this massed revolt on many fronts against the pretensions of reason. He was not a Wordsworth or a Shelley, a Goethe or Lessing, a Brahms, an architect of structure or of statesmanship. His field was religion, narrowed to revivalism. And even there, his place is uncertain or obscured. Sober history has recorded Whitefield's immediate and spectacular triumphs, the social importance, as movements, of Methodism and the Great Awakening, but has left it to be inferred that Whitefield's contributions to each were ambiguous or ephemeral. In popular memory, he is remembered, if at all, as a kind of assistant to Wesley or perhaps as a vague associate of Jonathan Edwards. Here and there a church [10] or a rise of ground [11] from which he spoke is associated with his name. He is represented by only one statue,[12] and seemingly condemned to oblivion by the melancholy epitaph quoted by an historian of Gloucester,[13] "Whitefield is then forgotten in his native place."

Yet in his time, Whitefield was more prominent than any other religious figure. He was so noteworthy that he was a subject of letters traversing colonial boundaries [14] and the Atlantic barrier.[15] A report of his approach excited the English or American populace,[16] absorbed the attention of divines who opened or closed their churches to him,[17] evoked the disdain or deference of public officials who discouraged his entrance into their communities or extended official welcome.[18] His fame was so high in 1739–1740 that he was often referred to as the leader of the Methodists; [19] 82 out of 110 anti-Methodist publications were directed against him as their villain,[20] while one whole issue of the *New York Gazette* was devoted to reports of his doings.[21] It is evident therefore that George Whitefield's power with the multitude, even if leading to no more than impermanent fame, is worthy of analysis.

II

The disparity between Whitefield's contemporary and later reputations has made perspective especially difficult to achieve. Popular orators are often dismissed contemptuously in their time, and, when they begin to lose face in the records, their declining renown is speeded by indifference or carelessness. Popular orators become increasingly the victims of fragmentary and irrelevant epithet.

Whitefield has been victimized by fragmentary comment. So "speckled a bird" [22] aroused the anger of defenders of neo-classic restraint. Samuel Johnson, uttering quarter-truths overwhelmingly, ascribed the evangelist's popularity to "the peculiarity of his manner," and, warming to this theme overmuch, added, "He would be followed by crowds were he to wear a night-cap in the pulpit, or were he to preach from a tree." [23] Years later, two respected historians, troubling themselves little, reported, in unison, that Whitefield "danced about the pulpit, roared and ranted," [24] as if that were a full analysis of technique.

Whitefield has been a speckled bird to those who wish their heroes to be literary. Tyerman found "much that is familiar, a little that is coarse," and "no genius, no poetry," and "no embellishment of language." [25] Turberville objected that the evangelist could be "maudlin and vulgar as well as finely inspiring." [26] To professional critics, the loosened proprieties of a field situation and the mixture of ordinary and sublime, which appealed to the average man, were subjects for disapproval rather than explanation.

If, on occasion, the irritation of professional critics is revelatory, protest of another sort may be equally worthy of notice. Whitefield's friends objected strongly to one picture, showing the orator in a hands-raised-in-benediction pose, and, since the likeness, one would think, is not unfavorable, the grounds of objection are especially significant. Perspective was violated, the friends infer, because "the attitude was very transient, and always accompanied by some expressions which would justify it." [27]

Fragmentary explanations are indeed inapplicable to the question of Whitefield's power over the multitude. Fortunately the limited testimony of those who were offended by "frightful gestures" [28] or charmed by "celestial animations" [29] is supplemented by the more comprehensive comments of Hume, Franklin, and other discriminating contemporaries. For these sophisticates to be caught up in the magic of a Whitefield spell, there must have been, at least, a cohesiveness—almost a propriety—in the orator's extravaganza.

Previous articles by this author have brought out that in thirty-four years, George Whitefield preached 18,000 sermons in England, America, Scotland, Ireland and Bermuda; [30] that hurried preparation and impromptu settings encouraged extempore preaching; [31] that the evangelist initiated, or revived, several features which broadened the appeal of both Methodism and other segments of the eighteenth-century revivalist surge, and that this perception of when to do "a new thing" marked him as representative of the character of that surge; [32] that field preaching, his greatest contribution to revivalist technique, reached masses who otherwise would not have been reached; that his crowds, assembling in "prodigious number," [33] comprised "persons of every rank and condition, high and low, rich and poor"; [34] that his most responsive auditors were the humble,[35] who, often coming under difficulties, remained, sometimes in inclement weather,[36] to praise with effusive emotional display; [37] that these conditions, both of setting and reaction, affected doctrine, delivery and the nature of the evangelist's harvest.

This study will review Whitefield's doctrine and technique, adding new lights to old, and inviting attention to the problem of long-term impetus beyond immediate result.

III

Whitefield's doctrines deserve attention—but not because of their novelty. His perceptible tenets—original sin, justification by faith, election—were not new at all; they can be traced back to the origins of Christianity and the focusing of doctrine by the early Fathers. They were not only all-Protestant but all-Christian doctrines.[38]

The ancient lineage of Whitefield's doctrines did not prevent their having been stated anew from time to time. Because, as the Christian world, once new, grew old, original tenets seemingly lost their pristine freshness, and new prophets arose to proclaim with new vigor the principles which had become dim through perfunctory usage. The Reformation and the Catholic Counter-Reformation were but more mighty reassertions, with ground of dispute between, to be sure, but these differences loomed larger at the moment than in the perspective of time. While there continued to be wars of words over ritual and principle, the doctrinal tenets of eighteenth-century revivalists, including Whitefield, were reassertions rather than newly formed doctrine.

In most of what he said, Whitefield's doctrinal assertions were consistent with tradition. So far as original sin was concerned, nothing was lost of traditional emphasis. "Remember, I beseech you to remember, that you are fallen creatures." [39] Nor was justification by faith slanted away from what it had always been. "When we are once convinced of our need and helplessness . . . a poor soul throws himself upon this Jesus, believes the word. . . ." [40]

On the more controversial third doctrine, election, there was still no variation by Whitefield from the traditional line, or alternative, which he chose to follow. "God intends only to give a certain number saving grace . . . and . . . the rest of mankind are left to perish under the imputation of Adam's guilt, and will be damned for their actual sins." [41] Whitefield, rejecting the Arminian position of Wesley, committed himself in pamphlets fully to what he called the "comfortable doctrine of election." [42] Even with respect to disputed election, readers of pamphlets were not cheated of their Christian heritage.

But election did not always reach the listening audience with the pamphlet, or traditional, emphasis. An atmospheric or editorial change often occurred in between. The loosening effects of the field-preaching situation modified this doctrine most—particularly in view of another factor, which we might call a fourth doctrine. Into the picture there enters a most powerful dissolvent of habitual attitudes, conversion. All other tenets were subjected to its needs and demands.

The history of conversion too has been a barometer of both the erosive effects of human frailty and resurgence of high purpose. Since Christ had said, "Ye must be born again," very nearly every generation had witnessed a relaxation of that credential because seemingly too difficult for the commonality of men. It was tempting to admit citizens of good standing as members of the saved, even though without clear evidence of the special experience of conversion. And such respectables had been admitted to the membership elite of established churches.[43]

But if nearly every generation had felt a slackening of original fire, every other generation had given birth to resurgence. The history of monasticism is a parallel. The formation of the original monastic communities and the emergence of individual monastic persons has been termed "a second chapter in the history of Christian renunciation," thus drawing attention to the ascetic ideal of Christianity itself. But the first monastic ascetic fervor became dim, was renewed—within the same or seceding bodies—gave way to slackness, was again renewed, et cetera.[44] And so in the milder, but essentially similar, world of secular Christianity, "Ye must be born again" became once more the first requisite for salvation by the standards of eighteenth-century revivalists.[45]

And yet the stringent demands of conversion appeared so unlikely of fulfillment in the eighteenth century because of the unheroic nature of the revivalist's clientele! Of whom was this metamorphosis demanded? Of the eighteenth-century inept, whose incompetence was very nearly a leading characteristic; of the social outcast, repugnant to those who rode high with fame; of the moral and financial disreputables, designated by the Duchess of Buckingham as "the common wretches that crawl the earth." [46]

Nevertheless—and, in fact, for reasons given above—conversion was eagerly grasped by the eighteenth-century inept. Their exclusion from material satisfactions whetted their appetite for substitutes. Their being told that God preferred the likes of them afforded some hope for redemption. Hence with avid desperation, the eighteeth-century have-nots grasped at the panacea within their reach. Not only were their sins forgiven. If hounded by debt, riches would be waiting in Heaven; if clothed in rags, fine raiment would be theirs on the other shore; if blighted by man's contempt, they would become God's Elect, destined for royal favor.[47]

But the sinner must do something before receiving the boon of salvation, must take action himself, and, under such conditions, there stole into the Calvinist garden the insidious serpent of free will. One can find statements by Whitefield, to be sure, in which he manfully denies any virtue of action by man, maintaining that God will bring his faithful home when He—not man—chooses.[48] But still another inference is possible from those remarks of Whitefield which were made in the heat of persuasion. When, for instance, the listener was told that if he threw himself upon the mercy of God, and then "by venturing on this promise" of salvation, he would receive the reward,[49] non-intellectual listeners could readily conclude that they were being offered a reward if they made the right choice.

Whitefield's conscious, or unconscious, urging of choice is apparent also in appeals at the ends of sermons. "Come, dear souls, in all your rags . . . come, thou poor, distressed woman; you, who think God will never forgive you . . . ; come, thou doubting creature. . . ." Action was not only broadly implied here, but directly urged. Then too, action should not be put off. "What if a fit of apoplexy should seize you? And your souls be hurled away before the awful judge of the quick and the dead?" In fact there was the hesitant young woman within Whitefield's memory who was in good health one hour and then had "an inflamation of the bowels—and is now a breathless corpse." [50] Delay in accepting Whitefield's offer might be, in fact, dangerous.

Whitefield's adaptation of doctrine to his humble clientele did not consist, therefore, in proclaiming new tenets of Christianity, or in introducing what we would now call a "social gospel." His was, on the contrary, the old-time religion. Adaptation consisted of orienting all exposition, all pleas, all doctrine to the demands and needs of conversion. In such adaptation, Whitefield apparently did not notice that, while he thought he was preaching determinism, his audience understood him to be advocating free will.[51]

IV

In what manner did Whitefield convey his message, and, especially, how did he make it intelligible and convincing to a general audience whose most responsive element was the humble? What was the nature of his sermon material? In what rhetorical form was this material expressed? What part did Whitefield's rhetoric play in the composite technique by which potential was transformed to active acceptance of his doctrine?

The nature of Whitefield's sermon material is revealed by themes as indicated by his titles. According to Cornelius Winter, who heard Whitefield as often as any man, the most representative sermons were those on such subjects as "Saul's Conversion," "The Conversion of Zaccheus," "The Resurrection of Lazarus," "The Seed of the Woman and the Seed of the Serpent [Temptation of Eve]," and, especially, "Abraham's Offering Up His Son Isaac." [52] Sermons on such topics offer opportunities indeed for conveying the doctrines of Whitefield.

To get the full impact of the message, the characteristic listener wanted simplicity of treatment. *Simplicity* is, of course, a relative term. We are concerned here quite naturally with what would be simple to the audience in question. That kind of simplicity would, in this instance, require identification with what—or what little—the listeners knew. Whitefield aimed particularly at the lowest common denominator of his audience when he said, "I would cloathe my thought in such plain language that the meanest negro or servant may understand me." That he was not blind to more universal appeal is shown by the rest of his remark, "for I am certain, if the poor and unlearned can comprehend, the learned and rich must." [53]

Whitefield put the humble mind at ease by lapsing into the colloquial. He made more natural the introduction of Biblical and Heavenly experience by such passages as "Who would have thought of this; probably Jacob did not," [54] or he made certain that a supposedly obvious fact was not overlooked, as in "A ladder, you know, is something by which we climb from one place to another." [55] It was this lapse into the ordinary which irritated the sensibilities of some readers of his sermons.

Whitefield's colloquial insertions cleared up any possible ambiguity of Biblical phraseology, e.g. "It is easier for a camel (or a cable rope) to go through the eye of a needle, than for a rich man to enter into the kingdom of God." [56] He did not bother with the tortuous explanation that a needle does not mean a needle but means a gate. He was quite certain that his hearers' experience would recognize threading a needle with a cable more readily than threading a needle with a camel, and that citation would illustrate well enough the rich man's difficulty of getting into Heaven. Similarly he did not hesitate to give a free translation of Eve's conversation with the serpent, i.e. "[Satan] said unto the woman, ye shall not surely die. Surely God will not be so cruel as to damn only you for eating an apple." [57]

Whitefield was not merely simple; he was vivid. The nearer an audience approaches the primitive, the more it is inclined to "think" in images. The meanest servant would require imagery as the price of his attention. Whitefield had, of course, a rich source of imagery in the Bible. Using a Biblical image already at hand, the evangelist accentuates a few details so that a simple yet vivid picture results. For instance, when Jacob has his adventure with the ladder, Whitefield emphasizes that Jacob looked up, while God looked down.[58] When Zaccheus climbed the tree, Whitefield drew attention to the leaves which concealed the curious but modest one from all but divine observation.[59]

Whitefield did not always lower high drama into colloquial terms. He knew that the humble wished to be lifted up occasionally to plains of sublimity. Winter describes the rendition of a vivid passage:

You may be sure from what has been said, that when he treated upon the sufferings of our Saviour, it was not without great pathos. He was very ready at that kind of painting which frequently answered the end of real scenery. As though Gethsemene were within sight, he would say, stretching out his hand—"Look yonder!—what is that I see! it is my agonizing Lord!" —And, as though it were no difficult matter to catch the sound of the Saviour praying, he would exclaim, "Hark! hark! do not you hear?"—You may suppose that as this occurred frequently, the efficacy of it was destroyed; but, no; though we often knew what was coming, it was as new to us as though we had never heard it before.[60]

Whether in visualized touches or in building more substantial visual combinations, Whitefield reminds us of the Arabian proverb, "He is the best orator who can turn men's ears into eyes."

V

The elements of Whitefield's voice and action were as remarkable as those of his speech composition. His resources of delivery must have been tremendous, not really reconstructible for us as we realize at once from the significantly intense disapproval by Whitefield's friends of the hands-up-in-benediction picture that lost so much from being taken out of the total perspective. We must isolate nevertheless the elements before we can observe how they functioned ensemble.

Whitefield's voice, first of all, was an instrument of great power and beauty. Nearly all comments on other attributes imply unusual vocal range.[61] Still more precisely on this point is the testimony of one of his Philadelphia listeners that when the evangelist preached from the gallery of the courthouse in Market Street, three blocks from the Delaware River, he could be heard on the Jersey shore, and every word distinctly understood on board a shallop at Market Street wharf.[62]

Franklin said that Whitefield's voice was loud and clear, especially since he "articulated his words and sentences so perfectly that he might be heard and understood at a great distance." [63] Indeed Franklin, always the scientist, estimated by an ingenious experiment that the orator could be understandably heard by "more than 30,000." [64]

Whitefield's voice was not merely extraordinarily audible; its quality was equally exceptional. That he made full use of his magnificent instrument may be gathered from Garrick's alleged remark that he, as an actor, would give a thousand guineas if he could "say 'Oh!' like Mr. Whitefield." [65] Franklin, both factual and discriminating, testified, "Every accent, every emphasis, every modulation of voice, was so perfectly turned and well plac'd, that, without being interested in the subject, one could not help being pleas'd with the discourse, a pleasure of much the same kind with that receiv'd from an excellent piece of musick." [66]

Whitefield's action was comparable with vocal power and skill. By "action," we do not, of course, limit ourselves to gestures—even the full quiver whence came the occasional benediction-raising of hands. Hume's comment, "animated, yet natural, action" [67] is corroborated by many instances, but the totality and synchronization of action is nowhere better epitomized than by the tribute of an eyewitness: "He uses much Gesture, but with great Propriety. Every Accent of his Voice, every Motion of his Body *Speaks,* and both are natural and unaffected. If his Delivery is the product of Art, 'tis certainly the Perfection of it, for it is entirely concealed." [68]

It is most significant, as noted before, that discriminating critics of Whitefield's time rarely fix on voice or gesture alone. Almost invariably they bring out the blend of voice and action, and, more significantly still, pay direct, or indirect, tribute to the convincingness of the whole performance. We are therefore directed in our study toward the quality in Whitefield which—from a secular standpoint, at least—gave unity and synthesis to his extraordinary and well-rounded technique as a revivalist orator. This quality was his dramatic sense.[69]

VI

In previous articles, this author has pointed out that the story of Whitefield's life reveals opportunities, from early boyhood, to observe the elements of drama in the life around him; that he showed talent in school dramatics; that, on a stop-over in Lisbon, his Prostestant disapproval of the festival to commemorate Lent waned before his growing interest in the colorful pageantry of the occasion; [70] that, indeed, there was constant warfare within him between his piety and dramatic instincts, none the less ironic because unconscious; and that he owed a large measure of his success before audiences to the quality and talent which theologically he denounced.

Whitefield's dramatic sense was revealed in the sermons which came to be his favorite productions. Those which Winter said were repeated most often and with the best effect had dramatic, as well as theological, possibilities. Saul was torn by conflict before his issuance on the right road; Zaccheus, the modest doubter, was struck with living fire in his place of concealment; Lazarus' rising from the dead was a most intriguing reversal of the laws of nature.

These Biblical dramas are redolent with suspense. Will Saul accept the benefits of conversion in spite of an unpromising upbringing and its resultant adult prejudices? Will Zaccheus be discovered in the tree? Will Eve yield to the persuasions of the serpent and eat the forbidden fruit? What will happen when, as we hope, the wicked Pharisee gets what is coming to him? And the Abraham-Isaac story is an example of progressively mounting action toward the climax of near-death and deliverance.

Descriptions abound of precious bits of acting before appreciative audiences for whom Garrick was too removed in price and substance. Winter tells of Whitefield's frequently putting on a judge's black cap at the end of a sermon, and then pronouncing sentence with the excoriation, "Depart from me, ye accursed, into everlasting fire"; [71] the *Gentleman's Magazine* relates the execution of "Robert Tilling, who, for robbing a house . . . received the sentence of death," an opportunity not lost by Whitefield, who "in a declamatory way . . . showed that the Wages of Sin is Death. . . ." [72] Many contemporaries tell of persons in the audience answering Whitefield's rhetorical questions—too compelling, it seemed, for pallid colloquies with the inner mind—of sailors, upon hearing, "What next?" (following Whitefield's visualization of a storm at sea), shouting, ". . . take to the long boat!" and of Chester-field's feeling so identified with one of Whitefield's characters, de-scribed as approaching the edge of a cliff, that the realistic lord of sophistication exclaimed, "Good God! he is gone!" [73]

VII

The manner in which the various elements of Whitefield's revivalist technique were co-ordinated can be illustrated—to some extent, at least —by giving an account of the manner in which the evangelist presented one of his favorite themes. That was the story of Abraham and Isaac. It is evident from the Biblical account alone that any narrative of near-tragic test of faith contains inherent drama; Whitefield's dramatic sense is thus revealed immediately by his choice of subject.

Whitefield begins this fair sample of the common man's drama by reading the scriptural text, interpolating colloquial clarifications of the sort we have noted. We learn that the main character will need fortitude; hints in this direction arouse our curiosity and delicious dread of the coming ordeal.

The theme, when disclosed, is startling. Abraham must take his son to an appropriate place for sacrifice. Whitefield brings out the astound-ing nature of such a command.[74] "Had God said, 'take now a firstling, or choicest lamb, or beast of the flock, and offer it up as a burnt offering,' it would not have appeared so ghastly: but for God to say, 'take now thy son, and offer him up as a burnt offering' one would have imagined was enough to stagger the strongest faith." The problem is thus placed care-fully within the experience of the average man—or of Everyman. To make certain that the average person will have every drop wrung in his presence, Whitefield goes on to say,

But this was not all: if it must be a son, and not a beast, that must be offered, why will not Ishmael do, the son of the bond woman? No, it must be his *only son*, the heir of all, his Isaac, by interpretation *laughter*, the son of his old age, in whom his own was wrapped up. And this son, this only son, this Isaac, the son of his love, must be taken now, even without delay, and be offered by his father, for a burnt offering, upon one of the mountains of which God will designate.

Then follow the astonished objections of Abraham. He has served God faithfully for years, in fact so well that he shines "as a light . . . in the midst of a crooked and perverse generation." The neighbors will surely call this blasphemy. And, "above all, what will Sarah my wife say. How can I ever return to her again, after I have imbued my hands in my child's blood?" This sharp, though distressing, skirmish between Abraham's faith and natural inclinations is soon settled, however, in favor of faith. But, will faith carry him through yet more tragic episodes?

Incidents during the journey add to the mounting action and suspense. Abraham and Isaac start off. The scriptural account is supplemented by Whitefield's comments on the virtue of Abraham's early rising, the humility shown by Abraham's saddling his own ass, and the restraint of keeping the secret from Isaac and others who are travelling with them. Disconnected ramblings as they might appear to the sophisticate, these interjections would build suspense for eighteenth-century have-nots, reminding them of their own pitiful clutchings of small matters in hours of trial. Through it all, Everyman wonders what will happen when Isaac learns his fate.

The sufferings of Abraham on the three-day journey become poignant as the destination draws near. "Methinks I see the good old man walking with his dear child in his hand, and now and then looking upon him, and then turning aside to weep. And, perhaps, sometimes, he stays a little behind to pour out his heart before God; for he had no mortal to tell his case to." Abraham's lonely grief continues thus until "on the third day, he lifted up his eyes and saw the place afar off."

But what of Isaac, the intended victim? We should know soon what a fully grown man will do when his doom can no longer be kept from him. To add to our anxiety, he is made to carry the firewood for his own sacrifice, while Abraham bears "the fire in his hand, and the knife." At this point we are relieved from supposing Isaac stupid by his saying, "My father . . . behold the fire and the wood; but where is the lamb for a burnt sacrifice?"

Our revived confidence in Isaac's intelligence only heightens our dread of other human reactions on his part. It would be too bad to end this story in unfilial violence. But he has asked a direct question which should not be evaded. It is not evaded. Isaac is told the truth. And what does Isaac do? He does nothing. "He made no resistance at all . . . though he was near thirty years of age, and, it is plain, was capable of carrying enough wood for a burnt offering." This meek submission is hardly expected. But can it be real? Perhaps the young man is stunned, only to react the more violently when the message penetrates his consciousness. The big moment must come pretty soon.

The big moment does come. Not that we are hurried along the last few steps. Whitefield, with apparently exasperating deliberation, sets the stage at the place of sacrifice, emphasizing the calmness of the principals and their omitting no items that would have attended the usual ceremony.

We are lured on by the unexpected, instantly recognizable as consistent with the developing story. The question of what Isaac will do when the last moment comes is answered; again he does nothing at all. The question of whether Abraham can go through with his inhuman assignment is answered by his proceeding calmly, even ruthlessly, toward the unnatural act of taking the life of his son. Isaac is bound on the altar like any animal. Abraham takes the knife in his hand—as he has done countless times before in conventional sacrifices. He raises the knife to strike. Then, with arm and knife in mid-air, his attention is riveted by the voice from Heaven which calls to him, "Abraham! Abraham!"

Then comes the denouement. The voice from Heaven tells Abraham that he has met the test of faith, that his son may now be released. And to corroborate this happy turn of events, yet to prevent disintegration of what still remained a sacred ceremony, a ram, by entangling his horns in the underbrush, submits himself as a substitute for Isaac.

It is understandable that Whitefield should say immediately after the climax of his story, "I see your hearts affected, I see your eyes weep." [75] Though, as Winter said, no description could possibly reconstruct the spell by words alone,[76] one can perhaps glimpse why Hume said of a comparable moment during a Whitefield sermon, "This address was accompanied with such animated, yet natural, action, that it surpassed anything I ever saw or heard in any other preacher," [77] and why the eye-witness, already quoted for discriminating comments, testified, "I never saw nor heard the like." [78]

VIII

Such was George Whitefield, almost certainly the greatest evangelist of the contemporary English-speaking world.[79] Rarely—among people of any time—has there been, one may venture, so remarkable an example of rapport between speaker and audience, between listeners who craved much and an orator superbly equipped to satisfy their immediate cravings. The generous tributes of his listeners have been treasured as the acme of audience acclaim.

But what of results beyond the immediate moment? He was surely not easy to forget, and the momentum of the force he had evoked continued in the wake of his departure from a community.[80] The Presbyterian Church in Wall Street, New York, had to be enlarged to accommodate its magnified membership,[81] and Franklin said of his after-effects in Philadelphia in 1739 that "one could not walk thro' the town in an evening without hearing psalms sung in the different families of every street."[82] These echoes testified to the power of the original Whitefield impulse. But more was needed for sustained and permanent results.[83]

The powers of the awakener did not include equal gifts of organization. Though representative of various eighteenth-century revivals, Whitefield did not truly lead them. He was a poor consolidator of his own efforts and those of his disciples. He formed societies at haphazard intervals. He gave but careless administration to churches built for him.[84] He was surrounded by assistants who were indifferently supervised.[85] He accepted the moderatorship of the Welsh Calvinists, but gave up that onerous task at the first opportunity.[86] He founded a minor orphanage whose financial demands kept him on the rack for thirty years.[87] He was content to pass from one immediate triumph to another, indifferent—or, at least, not sufficiently attentive—to the patient chores of organization.[88] In these respects, alas, he was representative of the common man's inability to protect himself against the shocks of changing circumstance.

If weak, he was also strong in his commonality. Whitefield was the common man's fulfillment, an extension in grander proportions. He was of humble birth, raised high by Oxford and the vestments of a clergyman. The account of his conversion by himself repelled the man of taste by its attempted forcing of mean materials into heroic mold, but the common man was uplifted as he heard his own petty adventures rendered sublime. From the evangelist's mounting the pulpit [89] until descent, there was the same mixture of ordinariness and sublimity. For these reasons, the common man saw in the great orator himself writ large.

Affinity with the common man prompted Whitefield's most tangible results beyond the moment and the day. In early advocacy of conversion, religious journalism, use of lay preachers, contact with existent religious societies, and, especially, inauguration of field preaching, he was the pioneer among eighteenth-century revivalists. Whitefield's initiative was not so much in new design as in a reassertion of old practices,[90] which, at critical junctures, released more fully the revivalist surge. With the aid of these devices—old and new—the Methodist Movement and the Great Awakening were swept from by-waters into wider channels.

Whitefield's influence beyond these tangibles must be certified more carefully. The problem of awarding some portion of credit for social effects differs with respect to Methodism and the Great Awakening. Because the general picture of Methodism is so clear, Halévy asserts confidently that its influence on the social structure of nineteenth-century England "would be difficult to overestimate." [91] But the shadow of John Wesley has dimmed Whitefield's share in this picture. For this and other reasons, the Whitefield impetus in England should be reviewed—not here but on some other occasion.

Social effects on the other side of the Atlantic should also be reviewed on some later occasion. When historians discuss social aspects of the Great Awakening, they appear at least to have Whitefield in mind. His impetus is assumed to have had something to do with separatist movements—in Connecticut, for example—and one may infer that he is not disconnected from the widening of missions, education and humanitarianism.[92] It may be that further study will merely corroborate the image of Whitefield as a brilliant meteor which glowed and dimmed, or a similar image of one who was destined to sow for others to reap. But this negative picture should not be assumed until all the evidence is in.

Historiography has become increasingly conscious of its wider and deeper opportunities. Social history is as old as Herodotus, of course, and no one can pose any longer as ignorant of its inclusion in the works of Thucydides, von Ranke, Macaulay and, indeed, of every true recorder of civilization. The newest history is only a little more determined to conquer the more difficult areas of a recognized and familiar world. Its many eyes, technological and otherwise, will accept fewer denials than ever before. For such a dedication, the discipline must be not less but more scrupulous, more rather than less determined to find answers if they exist.

One should review critically the larger hypotheses concerning the Methodist Movement and the Great Awakening. Lecky suggested that, by draining off the surcharged and baffled emotion of the have-nots, Methodism may have saved England from a French Revolution.[93] Becker, Osgood and other responsible scholars of eighteenth-century

American lore have inferred that the Great Awakening, by dissolving psychological barriers, prepared a major step toward nationalism and independence.[94] But if these larger vistas are viewed with caution, they can also be regarded as beckoning the disciplined adventurer.

Will the disciplined adventurer explore further the deeper tides and currents, on whose surface there appear, now and then, symptomatic revolution and war? Will such adventurous scholarship look further into the power of the common man, for whom our evangelist was a faithful representative? What indeed of those gray and faceless masses, who serve as the back-drop for news of the past, who are the recipients of benefits handed or thrown them by famous benefactors, who starve and die for leaders associated with movements and crises, who constitute armies led by brilliant or incompetent generals, and who win battles, lose them, and, in either instance, submit themselves to be slain. These may very well be tides drawn by inconstant moons—but they are a force.

The enigmatic and inconstant masses may teach us little. Beneath inarticulateness we may find insensate dullness rather than mysterious wisdom. Perhaps nothing more may be learned than that the mob killed the Gracchi, forced continuance of bread and circuses, moved for the execution of Louis XVI—tales already known, lacking grandeur. But then again, the newest history may illumine recesses hitherto beyond the reach of caution. Will the newest history notice more fully that common men carried great stones for pyramids; braved the thirst of deserts, the hazards of mountain trail, the lurking danger of forest thicket, the terror of darkness in unfamiliar regions; settled a continent by twos and threes and families; uprooted plantations that they might be replanted in the wilderness; mastered the intricacies of twentieth-century technology? If the newest history follows these, and other bold paths, with the hardy discipline of the adventurous, such a commoner as George Whitefield may yet be remembered with honor in his native place.

The Contemporary Reception of Edmund Burke's Speaking

DONALD CROSS BRYANT

FROM his own day to this, Edmund Burke has been praised by responsible critics as the greatest English orator of the eighteenth century, if not of all time; yet he has as often been dismissed—and by some of the same persons—as the "dinner-bell" of the House of Commons. His oratory has been lauded for vast knowledge, for penetrating analysis and vivid, stirring composition, for flights of the highest imagination and passages of the most affecting pathos; yet it has been described in the same paragraphs as emptying the benches of the British Senate. The masterpieces of his written eloquence are granted a position second to none in the English language; yet the oral versions of the same performances are treated with a grudging indulgence only a little short of contempt.[1]

These disparate appraisals can be assessed only by reference to Burke's contemporaries. The basis of this essay, therefore, lies in two hundred or so different critiques and observations, formal and casual, from over fifty different persons, great and small, in and out of Parliament, friend and foe. There is no other satisfactory kind of source for an answer, concerning a speaker in the past, to one of the key questions of rhetorical history: How did this man affect those who heard him?

Other critics of Burke and some of his biographers have, after a fashion, followed this procedure. Since, however, as H. A. Wichelns has pointed out,[2] their interests and their biases have been primarily written and literary, rather than rhetorical and oral, they have been content with a few of the more spectacular estimates from great or prominent men. They have neglected, perhaps naturally enough, the run-of-the-mill comments of the lesser persons who also heard Burke and recorded their observations. And even among the great, the biographers and critics have tended to quote deprecatory comment and to omit praise. They have quoted Goldsmith but have omitted Johnson, they have reported Sheridan's dicta but not Boswell's, they have drawn upon Wraxall and Horace Walpole while they have overlooked Sir Gilbert Elliot and Edward Gibbon and Edmond Malone.

Why critics and commentators on Burke should have chosen to elevate a neat epithet, founded upon the undeniable fact that at times Burke's listeners howled him down or walked out when he was speaking, into a summary characterization of his oratory is something of a puzzle. Perhaps a partial explanation may be suggested. Persons whose prime interest was in Burke's writings have been aware, perhaps subconsciously, that magnifying Burke's tendency to "empty the house" by the spoken word only tended to heighten the impression of the excellence and power of his writing and to render it more remarkable. Furthermore, people like Mrs. Carter, Goldsmith, and Hazlitt, who had little patience with public affairs, would find in the "dinner-bell" theory confirmation of their belief that Burke was too good for politics, that he was wasting his time and effort on "that motley crew of knights, citizens, and burgesses" in the House of Commons, when he was "eminently qualified to shine as a man of genius, as the instructor of mankind, as the brightest luminary of his age." [3]

To get down to the cases, the following are examples of later perpetuations of the "dinner-bell" theory of Burke's speaking. Wrote Bliss Perry, "[Burke's] oratory was praised . . . beyond that of any man of his time, yet, as everybody knows, he was called 'the dinner-bell of the House,' from his power of emptying the benches." And Hobhouse, the biographer of Charles James Fox: "[Fox] could fill the House of Commons at a time when Burke was known as the dinner-bell." [4] Finally, Thomas H. D. Mahoney, an historian now making valuable contributions to Burke scholarship, still feels justified in offering the following apparently paradoxical appraisal:

As he grew older, . . . [Burke's] temper became more ungovernable, and many of the younger members delighted in baiting him before trooping noisily out of the chamber while he delivered one of his long orations. He became known as the Dinner Bell of the House.

Although he was a skilled and seasoned debater, Burke was not a good speaker. He spoke with a pronounced Irish brogue and frequently employed awkward gestures which often seemed ludicrous. His flow of language was so rapid, as one observer noted, that it was almost impossible to take him down, a fact which probably accounts for the injustice done to his speeches by Hansard. Burke's speeches had a marked literary flavour and were designed largely to be read. They were impressive in their mastery of subject matter, seriousness, earnestness, sincerity, and in depth and variety of allusions. But theirs was a message which was too rich for the ordinary listener.[5]

Unquestionably Burke was called the "dinner-bell" in his own day, though when the epithet was coined, by whom coined, and what currency it enjoyed, I am unable to say.[6] It is not with Burke's contemporaries, subject as they were to the asperities of immediate conflict, that I would quarrel, but with those later critics who, having once heard the phrase, could think of no other way of characterizing Burke's speaking. It is probably true that Burke, because of his habit of speaking often and long, merited more properly than some others of the Opposition speakers some such reproach, for he might well keep the Commons in session at times when everyone had known what the final vote would be long before the question had been opened for debate. The tendency of members of a legislative assembly to leave their seats during a speech, however, has no necessary relation to the quality of the entertainment or the cogency of the arguments which the speaker is providing. It is more often governed by the knowledge that some important action is or is not going to be taken when the speaker is through.

Preliminary to further discussion, it must be understood that if the question whether Burke's speaking was effective in Parliament is made to depend upon his success in carrying the vote of the House on major questions, we must admit him to have been usually ineffective.[7] If, however, the question is whether his contemporaries listened to him with attention, interest, even enthusiasm, the answer is quite different.

But now, let us turn to the evidence, and first to that from the chief promulgators of the "dinner-bell" theory. First Goldsmith's lines in *Retaliation*, written in 1773:

> Who, born for the Universe, narrow'd his mind,
> And to party gave up what was meant for mankind.

Though fraught with all learning, yet straining his throat
To persuade Tommy Townshend to lend him a vote;
Who, too deep for his hearers, still went on refining,
And thought of convincing, while they thought of dining.

Neat, suggestive, and cutting; and *Retaliation,* as its title implies, was
Goldsmith's last counter-thrust at all his friends who for years had made
him the butt of their jokes. Then there was Thomas (later Baron) Erskine, one of whose anecdotes seems to have been spread far and wide,
until it has become a standard illustration, and sometimes the only illustration, used to characterize Burke's oratory. The following is Bliss
Perry's version:

Lord Erskine used to say that on one occasion he grew so tired of hearing
Burke in a debate on the India Bill, that, not liking Burke should see him
leave the House of Commons while he was speaking, he crept along under
the benches and got out and went to the Isle of Wight. Afterwards that
very speech was published, and Lord Erskine found it "so very beautiful
that I actually wore it to pieces by reading it." [8]

Here is the epitome of the criticism of Burke's rhetoric which has
been taken, uncritically, to tell the whole story. An equivalent episode
also persists. After Burke's famous speech on the Nabob of Arcot's debts
(which was perhaps the speech Erskine recalled when he told his story)
the ministerial leaders whispered together a moment, and decided that
it was not worth while to answer Burke's speech, "so little practical
impression," add the recounters, "had it made upon the audience." [9]
A different conclusion is at least possible: Since the ministry were merely
awaiting the conclusion of the debate in order to come to a vote the
result of which was already assured, the fact that they consulted at all
might be taken as evidence of the force of Burke's speech rather than
proof of its weakness. Another popular witness is Nathaniel Wraxall,
traveller, minor diplomat, Tory member of Parliament, whose *Historical
and Posthumous Memoirs* constitute a standard source-book of contemporary parliamentary comment. To quote one or two of his judgments:

Burke, who wanted Sheridan's nice tact, and his amenity of manner, was
continually coughed down. . . . [Barré was] more attentive than Burke
not to fatigue the patience of the House when he saw them eager to
rise. . . . Scarcely indeed could he [Burke] obtain a hearing from an

audience whose patience, it must be confessed, he frequently put to severe trials.[10]

Early in his career Burke himself was perfectly well aware of this sort of adverse judgment, but characteristically was disinclined to let it deflect him from the mode which he had adopted. In one of the newly discovered letters to his Irish friend Charles O'Hara, March 1, 1766, Burke wrote:

Those who dont wish me well, say I am abstracted & subtile; perhaps it is true; I myself dont know it; but think, if I had not been known to be the Author of a Book somewhat metaphysical, the objections against my mode of Argument would be of another nature, & possibly more just. However until I know better, I intend to follow my own way. Observe when I say so much of myself it is for your private ear. . . . My argument to night has I think hurt me. Not for the matter but for the propriety. The house was teezed to Death & heard nobody willingly.[11]

There is no need of further witnesses. All they prove is that Burke, who spoke frequently over a period of nearly thirty years, was not always at his best, and was not always listened to with interest and attention, especially when he was obviously arguing in opposition to the preponderant opinion of the House. One of Burke's faults, it must be confessed, lay in his unwillingness to refrain from speaking when success was patently hopeless. In extenuation of this fault, or at least in explanation of it, Burke himself may be quoted, in conversation with Sheridan at a meeting of the Literary Club on April 3, 1778. Said Sheridan: "I don't mean to flatter, but when posterity reads one of your speeches in Parliament, it will be difficult to believe that you took so much pains, knowing with certainty that it could produce no effect, that not one vote would be gained by it." Burke replied:

Waiving your compliment to me, I shall say in general, that it is very well worth while for a man to take pains to speak well in Parliament. A man, who has vanity, speaks to display his talents; and if a man speaks well, he gradually establishes a certain reputation and consequence in the general opinion, which sooner or later will have its political reward. Besides, though not one vote is gained, a good speech has its effect. Though an act which has been ably opposed passes into law, yet in its progress it is modelled, it is softened in such a manner, that we see plainly the Minister has been told, that the Members attached to him are so sensible of its injustice or absurdity from what they have heard, that it must be altered.

At this point Johnson joined in, jocularly, no doubt, but with aptness: "And Sir, there is a gratification of pride. Though we cannot out-vote them, we will out-argue them. They shall not do wrong without its being shown both to themselves and to the world." [12]

And for the most part Burke seems to have governed his speaking on this principle throughout his career. In 1770 Johnson had said that though, as was commonly observed, Burke spoke too often in Parliament, nobody could say that he did not speak well. And even Wraxall could say of Burke years later that, "like Dr. Johnson, he always *spoke his best*, whether on great or small occasions." [13]

On the other side, it will suffice to show that, though Burke had his ups and downs, from day to day and from year to year, and though he tended to decline somewhat in oratorical repute after 1783, many people heard him gladly throughout his life. I shall select from among the many witnesses enough to establish their characteristic opinions, including such qualifications as they present from time to time.

Burke entered Parliament in December 1765 in the Rockingham interest. Previously, during his service with William Gerard Hamilton in Ireland, he appears to have had some experience in Irish parliamentary management on Hamilton's behalf. It is doubtful, however, that there is sufficient warrant for the statement by an anonymous writer in the *Annual Register* for 1797 that "his eloquence produced much effect in the Irish Senate." [14]

For his earliest speeches in the House of Commons, however, there was uniform praise.

When and under what circumstances did Burke make his maiden speech in the House? The biographers had settled on January 27, 1766, just a month after his election and about two weeks after the opening of the session. The evidence was Horace Walpole's assertion that a "new speaker, whose fame for eloquence soon rose high above the ordinary pitch," Edmund Burke, first appeared in the debate on an American petition against the Stamp Act that day.[15] Dixon Wecter first established an earlier date, January 17, on the basis of a letter of Garrick to Burke among the Burke papers at Wentworth-Woodhouse.[16] He, however, without the advantage of acquaintance with the O'Hara correspondence, rather misconstrued the circumstances.

A new member's maiden speech in the eighteenth-century House of Commons could be a formidable experience, especially since great importance was attached to a man's beginning to be heard in the House and continuing to be heard.[17] Burke, apparently, was no exception. His family, his friends in London, his associates in the Club, his colleagues in the Rockingham circle, and especially his host of well-wishers in Ireland were eager to have their rising friend, on the threshold of a great career, speak and speak well in the House. Dean William Markham of Rochester, an old friend formerly of Westminster School, wrote in the tone of father and schoolmaster that he wished Ned "to appear at once on some important question. If he has but that confidence in his strength which I have always had," Markham continued, "he cannot fail of appearing with lustre. . . . One splendid day will crush the malevolence of enemies as well as the envy of some who often praise him."[18] Other letters of the few weeks after Burke's election glow with bright predictions and encouragement. A tone of nervous apprehension, however, sounds in the background of some of them, which changes, in the Irish letters, after that first speech, to pride that Ireland has a new luminary lighting the British Senate.

Perhaps Burke had suggested in advance to some of his friends that he proposed to take the plunge and speak on the evening of the 17th, only three days after the opening of the session, for Garrick was in the gallery, and perhaps Arthur Murphy also.[19] The next morning Garrick wrote the note which Wecter discovered:

Last Night . . . [in] the house of Commons . . . I had the honour and Pleasure of Enjoying Your Virgin Eloquence! I most sincerely congratulate you upon it—I am very Nice and very hard to please and where my friends are concern'd most Hyper-critical— I pronounce that you will answer the warmest Wishes of your Warmest friend—I was much pleas'd—I have much to say, which you will politely listen to, and forget the next moment, however you shall have it— [20]

This sounds as if Burke burst with splendor upon an astonished House on a major question. Here, perhaps, was another Colonel Barré out-Pitting Pitt on his first day in Parliament. Very soon, that was the situation. Referring to the *Parliamentary History* for that day, therefore, Wecter found that the business had been a petition from the London merchants begging that something be done to save their dying trade with America. He inferred that Burke spoke on that question, and added: "Although no minutes of the debate which evidently followed are given, it is easy to conjecture what side the future great champion of the American colonist took." Burke's letter to O'Hara the next day, however, shows that the facts were significantly different.

The *Journal of the House of Commons,* from which the account in the *Parliamentary History* was abstracted,[21] shows that besides the main petition from the merchants of London, a dozen minor petitions from the other trading cities and towns were presented, including one from the "Merchants, Manufacturers, and Traders, of the Town of *Manchester,* and the Neighbourhood, thereof. . . ." This petition, at the request of one of the important Rockingham members from Liverpool, Burke presented, and on it, quite unnecessarily, he decided to speak.

His letter, in the reportorial vein which by then had become his habit in writing to O'Hara, is mostly a spirited account of the opening of the session three days before: Pitt's melodramatic appearance in the House on the first day, his exasperating speech both for and against the ministers, Conway's adulation of him, the three-days' trouble over printing the American papers. Then he turns to himself, with depreciation perhaps, but with frankness none the less:

That day I took my first trial. Sr Wm Meredith desired me to present the Manchester Petition; I know not what struck me, but I took a sudden resolution to say something about it, though I had got it but that moment, & had scarcely time to read it, short as it was; I did say something; what it was, I know not upon my honour; I felt like a man drunk. Lord Frederick Campbell made me some answer to which I replied; ill enough too; but I was by this time got pretty well on my Legs; Mr Grenville answered & I was now heated, & could have been much better; but Sr G Saville caught the Speakers eye before me; & it was then thought better not to proceed further, as it would keep of [off?] the business of the day. However I had now grown a little stouter, though still giddy, & affected with a swimming in my head; So that I ventured up again on the motion, & spoke some minutes, poorly but not quite so ill as before. All I hoped was to plunge in, & get off the first horrors; I had no hopes of making a figure. I find my Voice not strong enough to fill the house; but I shall endeavour to raise it as high as it will bear. This is prattling like a Child to a father. Whenever I enter into these minutiae about myself I beg you throw my Letter into the fire.[22]

It sounds as if Burke spoke to two different purposes that day, the virtue of the Manchester Petition, and the general question of receiving petitions about America.

O'Hara replied post haste, reassuring Burke, and warning him at the same time:

Give me leave to know you, tho' I know nothing else so well, better than you know yourself; your voice will form from practice, your manner will improve, the great point you are to attend to is temper. Was it not Jephson that used to tell you that in some circumstances you had an air of anger? Get rid of that air.[23]

His acclaim, however, was instantaneous. Early in 1766 Samuel Johnson wrote to Bennet Langton:

We have the loss of Burke's company since he has been engaged in publick business, in which he has gained more reputation than perhaps any man at his appearance ever gained before. He made two speeches in the House for repealing the Stamp-act, which were publickly commended by Mr. Pitt, and have filled the town with wonder.[24]

On March 1 Burke himself is witness to his initial success. He wrote to O'Hara: "As to myself I work on, & I thank God not without some encouragement. Mr. Pitt has been very kind & generous in protecting me by very strong & favourable expressions, twice or thrice in publick, & often in private conversation."[25] On February 22, 1766, Mrs. Elizabeth Montagu wrote to her friend and Burke's, Mrs. Vesey:

The stamp act was repeal'd by a majority of one hundred and eight, and our friend Mr. Burke spoke divinely, yes divinely, dont misunderstand me, and report he spoke as well as mortal man could do, I tell you he spoke better. The great Commoner praised him highly in the Senate, and all people join in the chorus. Indeed Mr. Burke has every day acquired great praise but yesterday crowned all.

After the fall of the Rockinghams, Mrs. Montagu commented thus on one of Burke's early passages at arms with the Chatham ministers: "Mr. Wedderburn and Mr. Burke attackd the Ministry on Tuesday with great witt, eloquence, and spirit"; and a year or so later she could still write: "Our Friend Burke speaks better and better."[26] The satisfaction of Burke's prominent Irish friends may be represented by a passage from a letter of Lord Charlemont to Henry Flood (March 13, 1766):

I some time ago sent Leland [Dr. Thomas Leland, the Trinity College historian] a short account of our friend Burke's unparallelled success, which I suppose he has communicated to you. His character daily rises, and Barré is totally eclipsed by him; his praise is universal, and even the Opposition, who own his superior talents, can find nothing to say against him, but that he is an impudent fellow.[27]

The comparison to Colonel Isaac Barré, the celebrated lieutenant of Shelburne and Pitt, would mean much at this point. Dr. Leland's great relief at the news of Burke is exhibited in his letter of March 11 to Charlemont.[28] In October we find the Duke of Grafton describing Burke to Lord Chatham as "the readiest man upon all points perhaps in the whole house." [29] In December one of Chatham's correspondents described the finest piece of oratory on a certain occasion as Burke's; [30] and the following spring Lord George Sackville wrote to General Irwin: "Mr. Bourke has made himself very considerable. He is the most ingenious debater I ever heard, and at least as strong in the reply as in the opening." [31] About a year later General Charles Lee wrote to Prince Czartoryski:

An Irishman, one Mr. Burke, is sprung up in the House of Commons, who has astonished every body with the power of his eloquence, his comprehensive knowledge in all our exterior & internal politics & commercial interests. He wants nothing but that sort of dignity annexed to rank & property in England, to make him the most considerable man in the Lower House.[32]

Burke, himself, though he obviously recognized and enjoyed his successes, was not so sanguine as his friends and was as well aware as General Lee of the limitations under which he worked. In a letter to O'Hara in December 1766 he mentioned the debate on Beckford's motion for the East India papers and added:

You desire to know something in particular of my conduct. I spoke a long time, upwards of an hour I believe. I was well heard; and have had some Credit out of Doors on the occasion. But I had not the good fortune to please your Secretary Aug. Harvey, who called me to order while I was pouring out some humble and warm supplications to Ld Chatham, to implore him not to destroy the National Credit to which he owed the glories of the late war. The marine Secretary had however no reason to pride himself on the reception his point of order met with from the house; and he did not in the least embarrass me. It rather gave me an opportunity for some explanations, that I was not sorry to bring out. Conway seemed hurt at what I had said of the situation of the ministers. I got up a second time, and satisfied him as to his own particular. It was on the whole a good day for me.[33]

Earlier in the same letter, however, Burke had indulged in some remarks about himself of a rather different tone. After the fall of the Rockingham administration, many of his friends had been sure that his splendid performances in speaking and in other parliamentary business would gain him an offer from Pitt. Negotiations had actually taken place, and Burke had toyed with the idea of going over. Finally, however, he had decided to stay with the Marquis. It was upon that decision that he was commenting to O'Hara:

Not that I am enamourd of adversity, or that I love opposition. On the contrary it would be convenient enough to get into office; & opposition never was to me a desirable thing; because I like to see some effect of what I am doing, & this method however pleasant is barren & unproductive, & at best but preventive of mischief; but then the walk is certain; there are no contradictions to reconcile; no cross points of honour or interest to adjust, all is clear & open; & the wear & tear of mind, which is saved by keeping aloof from crooked politicks, is a consideration absolutely inestimable.[34]

A year later Burke's discouragement and perhaps also his realism were more pronounced as he confessed to O'Hara:

For myself I really have no hopes. Every body congratulated me on coming into the House of Commons, as being in the certain Road of a great & speedy fortune; & when I began to be heard with some little attention, every one of my friends was sanguine. But in truth I never was so myself. I came into Parliament not at all as a place of preferment, but of refuge; I was pushed into it; & I must have been a Member, & that too with some Eclat, or be a little worse than nothing; Such were the attempts, made to ruin me when I first began to meddle in Business. But I considered my situation on the side of fortune as very precarious. I lookd on myself, with this New Duty on me, as on a man devoted; & Thinking in this manner, nothing has happend that I did not expect, & was not well prepared for.[35]

Burke's prominence and his reputation, however, continued to grow. The following testimony from the pen of Will Burke, prejudiced though he may be, bears directly upon the notorious failure to consider his audience, which is often charged against Burke. The occasion mentioned was one of the county meetings held in the summer of 1769 to instigate petitions against the Government's handling of Wilkes and the Middlesex election. Wrote Will:

There was a meeting at Ailesbury, among others Ned spoke, but with great modesty, declaring that the smallness of his property and the shortness of his time in the County made it a reluctant thing to him to speak, but, as was said by the Men of Sense (for the others were undistinguishing praise) He adapted himself to his Audience. The fact is that everybody till he spoke, was heard, well indeed, but patiently, but when he had done, there was a thunder, & I who had kept myself in the Crowd heard the fellows say, damn it, He has explained it, & they all understood their Grievances quite plain.[36]

The following June, Will wrote to O'Hara that because of the *Present Discontents* (Burke's celebrated political testament for the Rockingham party) and because of his speech on American affairs at the end of the session, Burke now "certainly stands higher than ever He did in his Life. I had almost said the highest of any man in the Country." [37]

Next we come to the time when Goldsmith composed his lines in *Retaliation*, and when the "dinner-bell" theory seems to have had some original currency—the period of the middle seventies, when Burke's two famous American speeches were made. In December 1772, Viscount Townshend, in commenting on the way the opposition had abandoned the nation "entirely to this wicked Ministry," wrote that "even Burke, the mouthpiece of the party, was reduced to a mere speech of entertainment on that serious subject" of the India business.[38] In the following April, James Boswell was "fortunate enough to hear Mr. Edmund Burke speak twice." "It was a great feast to me," he wrote, "who had never heard him before." Boswell continued, remarking upon one characteristic of Burke's speaking which impressed most of those who heard him, as it has struck those who have read his speeches and writings:

It was astonishing how all kinds of figures of speech crowded upon him. He was like a man in an Orchard where boughs loaded with fruit hung arround him, and he pulled apples as fast as he pleased and pelted the ministry. It seemed to me however that his Oratory rather tended to distinguish himself than to assist his cause. There was amusement instead of persuasion. It was like the exhibition of a favourite Actor. But I would have been exceedingly happy to be him.[39]

A few days earlier Burke had written to O'Hara about the unpopular position which he and the Rockinghams had taken on the East India Company, and then had added: "The dissenters affair diversified the scene a little, and gave me an opportunity of saying something which was not against the universal feeling of the house." [40] Apparently he did not always *covet* the unpopular position.

The following description of Burke the so-called "dinner-bell," composed by Chauncey Goodrich, from the accounts in Prior's *Life* and other sources, on the occasion of the delivery of his speech on American taxation (1774) may be taken as sympathetic but just:

The opening of the debate was dull, and many of the members had withdrawn into the joining apartments or places of refreshment. [Burke apparently had not driven them there.] But the first few sentences of his stinging exordium awakened universal attention. The report of what was going on spread in every quarter; and members came crowding back, till the hall was filled to the utmost, and resounded throughout the speech with the loudest expressions of applause. Highly as they had estimated Burke's talents, the House was completely taken by surprise. Lord John Townshend [who had come into the gallery] exclaimed aloud, at the close of one of those powerful passages in which the [printed] speech abounds, "Heavens! what a man this is! Where could he acquire such transcendent powers!" The opening of his peroration, especially, came with great weight on the minds of all. . . . The moment Mr. Burke closed, his friends crowded around his seat, and urged him to commit his speech to writing.[41]

Of Burke's speech on conciliation a year later, the *Universal Magazine* carried the following comment in its account of the occasion: "There was a remarkable full attendance of the Members. . . . It was confessed on all hands, that it was the most finished piece of oratory ever delivered in a British Senate." [42] And the *Gentleman's Magazine* reported: "The House was remarkably attentive and serious. It is thought this speech, if not the best, was at least inferior to none, which Mr. Burke ever delivered." [43] Concerning this same speech Henry Flood, the Irish politician, wrote to Lord Charlemont in terms which we have seen before and will see again:

His performance was the best I have heard from him in the whole winter. He is always brilliant in an uncommon degree, and yet I believe it would be better he were less so. I don't mean to join with the cry which will always run against shining parts, when I say that I sincerely think it interrupts him so much in argument, that the house are never sensible that he argues as well as he does. Fox gives a strong proof of this, for he makes use of Burke's speech as a repertory, and by stating crabbedly two or three of those ideas which Burke has buried under flowers, he is thought almost always to have had more argument.[44]

An unfinished and undated note from Rockingham to Burke among the Rockingham papers at Sheffield was written, apparently, immediately after Burke had concluded the speech on conciliation. The Marquis was at home waiting for word from Burke of the outcome of the night's session. It may be that Burke's arrival with the news interrupted the writing and enabled him to receive the praise in person.

I left the House of Commons after the Conclusion of Your Speech—I just staid long enough to see Jenkinson get up to answer you, & I went out with a Crowd, who seemed to shew by their Conduct that they had no Expectation of an adequate Reply, at least not from that Gentleman. . . .

I never felt a more Complete Satisfaction on hearing any Speech, than I did on hearing Yours this day. The Matter & the Manner were equally perfect, & in spite of Envy & Malice & in Spite of All Politicks, I will venture to prognosticate that there will be but one opinion, in regard to the wonderful ability of the Performance.[45]

Both these speeches, it should be recalled, failed to obtain the votes of the Commons for the propositions they supported.

Further evidence that Burke's speaking was enjoyed, and to some extent appreciated, may be found in the trouble some persons took to remark those occasions when he fell below himself. Thus on October 27, 1775, Lord George Sackville wrote that Burke was "passionate, long, and not so entertaining as usual," and again on November 18, "[Burke] did not speak so well as usual." [46]

Evidences of the effectiveness of wit in Burke's speaking come from various parts of his career. In 1777, for example, George Johnstone wrote to the Marquis of Granby on November 29: "Burke attacked Wedderburn with repeated flashes of wit like the forked glare of lightning in a thunderstorm under the line. He was shrivelled under it like a blooming tree after a hurricane." [47]

Thus during the first ten years of Burke's parliamentary career he established a great consequence for himself. Though he was not often on the winning side, and though at some points his party became so weak in voting power that its members practically withdrew from the fight, Burke was listened to. Though the government's voters may at times have walked out, he was often enjoyed and often feared. Of this period Fox's biographer, Hobhouse, one of the subscribers to the "dinner-bell" theory, wrote, "But he terrorised the House while he bored it, and could intimidate his opponents even when he was making himself ridiculous." [48] These are attractive paradoxes whose meaning is hard to pin down.

As we approach the 1780's, the decade during which Burke enjoyed his highest point of influence and power and then, perhaps, his lowest, the witnesses to the quality and effect of his speaking are more numerous and on the whole fuller in their comments. His speech of

February 6, 1778, on using Indians against the Americans in the war, though three hours and a half long, was thought by some of those who heard it as the best he had ever delivered. Colonel Barré, himself no mean speaker, was so excited by it that he offered enthusiastically to nail it to every church door in England by the side of the proclamation of a general fast. George ("Governor") Johnstone said he thought it fortunate for North and Germaine that there were no visitors in the galleries to hear the speech, for they might have rushed down and done violence to the responsible ministers. Sir George Savile exclaimed: "He who did not hear that speech, has not witnessed the greatest triumph of eloquence within memory." The vote which followed showed the largest minority yet obtained against the ministry on the continuance of the American War.[49] But the foregoing picture of the occasion is in all the books. Here is yet another testimony about the same speech, written by one W. Moore to his father:

Mr. Burke never displayed the powers of oratory so strongly as the other day when the affair of the contracts with the Indians was agitated. His speech drew tears from the whole house, particularly that part of it where he described the murder of Miss McReay. I had not the pleasure of hearing him, as it is at present a standing order that nobody is to be admitted into the gallery.[50]

The testimony of Edward Gibbon, the historian, himself a silent member of the House with a lucrative sinecure on the Board of Trade, is explicit on the reception of Burke's speech on economical reform in 1780. Wrote Gibbon in his autobiography: "Mr. Burke's bill of Reform was framed with skill, introduced with eloquence, and supported by numbers. . . . I can never forget the delight with which that diffusive and ingenious Orator was heard by all sides of the House, and even by those [like Gibbon himself] whose existence he proscribed."[51] Sir Gilbert Elliot, later Earl of Minto, and long one of the most loyal young supporters of Burke and Fox, said that it was this same speech which "captivated all his [Elliot's] sympathies" and decided him on "taking an active part in that business."[52]

The testimony of Nathaniel Wraxall, already mentioned, applies in its detail to a period of some fifteen years, beginning about 1780. Wraxall was a member of the party opposed to Burke. Furthermore, his great idol and special favorite among parliamentary speakers was Sheridan. We should expect him, therefore, to be thoroughly aware of those elements which may be called faults in Burke, and we should expect him to report and to analyze them. This he does. On the whole Wraxall is indulgent to Burke, though his recognition of Burke's abilities is usually tempered by an attitude of "We should all like to remember him in his better moments which were, after all, comparatively rare." Wraxall's general estimates of Burke acknowledge his learning, his information, his energy, his great eloquence and passion, and his intense seriousness; but they emphasize even more pointedly his long-windedness, his bad temper, his irascibility, his intractability, his lack of judgment and moderation, and the absence in him of any sense of boring or wearying the House with the length and the frequency of his speeches.

In Wraxall's incidental remarks, however, and in his specific observations on individual occasions, the details of another portrait of Burke show through. "If," he wrote, "Fox occupied the first place in the ranks of Opposition, Burke might be pronounced without contest, the second person in that powerful body." [53] Barré, as a speaker, Wraxall observed, "was not carried away by those beautiful digressions of genius or fancy, with which Burke *captivated and entertained his audience.*" [54] Wraxall complimented highly the effectiveness of Burke's "Shearing the Wolf" speech after Yorktown; [55] and he was apparently delighted with the way Burke routed the new Secretary of State, Mr. Ellis, who was defending the continuance of the American War in 1782.[56] On Burke's speech on Fox's India Bill in December 1783, Wraxall wrote:

The most ignorant Member of the House, who had attended to the Mass of Information, Historical, Political, and Financial, which fell from the lips of Burke on that occasion, must have departed with a rich knowledge of Indostan. It seemed impossible to crowd greater variety of matter applicable to the subject, into a smaller compass; and those who differed most widely from him in opinion, did not render the less justice to his gigantic range of ideas, his lucid exposition of events, and the harmonious flow of his periods.[57]

On March 8, 1784, Burke (according, again, to Wraxall) "spoke with great animation, and with equal eloquence; [but] no exertions could sustain a declining, as well as unpopular Party, or infuse new vigour into its component parts." [58] This, one might observe, was Burke's all-too-usual situation.

Wraxall's notes on Burke's famous speech on the Nabob of Arcot's debts, in February 1785, are especially characteristic of his response to Burke. When Dundas sat down, Wraxall observed:

The house appeared ready to divide; but Burke, rising with evident marks of strong emotion, delivered an oration which lasted nearly five hours; and which neither Demosthenes nor Tully could have excelled in energy, eloquence, or animation. I speak with perfect impartiality, as I by no means coincided in opinion with Burke, whose prejudices and animosities almost always blinded his judgment, or obscured his superior intelligence. But, even when he most failed in producing conviction, he excited not less admiration for his resplendent talents. . . . But Burke, in 1785, however sublime were his endowments, had by his intemperate abuse of them, sunk greatly in general estimation.[59]

In commenting on Burke's opening of the charges against Warren Hastings in the House of Commons in February 1786, Wraxall observed that "no individual knew better than Burke how to enlist and marshall the finest emotions and passions of the human mind, in whatever cause he undertook"; and then Wraxall added, "sometimes perhaps in violation of truth, frequently in opposition to reason." [60] A further measure of the "dinner-bell" theory is the following note by Wraxall on a speech of Burke's on March 22, 1786: "But the principal attention was justly directed on that evening towards Burke, who poured out the accumulated stores of his indignation in a tone of such violence as excited astonishment even in him." [61] And another is the following remark upon Burke's defense of himself in the Regency debates of February 1789: "This elegant and ingenious apology, cloathed in the language of Scripture, which, with the single exception perhaps of Erskine, Burke alone could have applied with so much felicity and promptitude to the case, produced its full effect." [62]

Before calling another major witness to the general effect of Burke's speaking, I wish to turn back to the opening of the impeachment charges against Hastings in the House of Commons on February 17, 1786, and to show what James Boswell and Edmond Malone, both friends of Burke, thought of that speech. In his journal, Boswell recorded that Courtenay took him to the House that day to hear Burke arraign Hastings. "He did it," wrote Boswell, "with extraordinary ability, but now and then lessened the solemn effect by oratorical sallies." [63] Malone, in writing the next day to Lord Charlemont, offered a comment on the response of the audience: "Burke made his charge yesterday against Mr. Hastings in a most masterly manner. He was up an hour and fifty minutes and kept his temper well, and was heard with great attention." [64]

Sir Gilbert Elliot, already mentioned as a young man converted to the Foxite Whigs by Burke's speech on economical reform in 1780, kept the mails to Scotland busy throughout his long career as member of Parliament, Cabinet Minister, and statesman, carrying diary-like letters home to his wife. From these intimate and frank accounts of current affairs, many interesting comments on Burke's speaking may be had. It will be obvious from what I shall quote that Sir Gilbert's ideal was Burke and that he was by no means in agreement with the fashionable idolatry of Sheridan. Even so, his estimates of Burke are no more prejudiced than Wraxall's. Like everyone else, including Burke, Elliot was delighted with Sheridan's first notable speech, the one on the "Begum's" charge against Hastings in February 1787. "You will conceive how admirable it was," he wrote to his wife, "when I tell you that he surpassed, I think, Pitt, Fox, and even Burke, in his finest and most brilliant orations." [65]

When the actual trial of Hastings began, however, a year later, Burke was again in first place. On February 15, 1788, Sir Gilbert wrote: "Burke has done nobly, and with the most universal admiration, and they say also with great effect and impression." [66] (There can be no question of the effect and impression of that speech, as I shall show later.) On the eighteenth Sir Gilbert reported again: "Burke has exceeded his former excesses today, and in one of his excesses he did not, I believe, leave a dry eye in the whole assembly. Mrs. Sheridan had a fit on the occasion." [67] Sheridan suffered by comparison, for he seemed artificial and studied:

[Sheridan's speech of June 3] was strewed very thick with more brilliant periods of eloquence and poetical imagination, and more lively sallies of wit, than could be produced probably by more than one other man in the world, with whom, however, they spring up and shoot out with all the luxuriance and grace of spontaneous nature. This certainly cannot be said of Sheridan's flowers, which are produced by great pains, skill, and preparation, and are delivered in perfect order, ready tied up in regular though beautiful bouquets, and very unlike Burke's wild and natural nosegays.

Elliot goes on pursuing the comparison of Burke and Sheridan:

As you see, I cannot help still comparing him with my *own hero*, and as I am known to be more particularly a worshipper of *another deity*, it might

and certainly would expose Burke to the imputation of envy and perhaps
even of envious detraction, if his friends should be found disparaging
Sheridan. . . . Burke also abounds with these fine passages, and he soars
also as much out of the lower regions of discourse, and infinitely further
into those of imagination and fancy; but no man could ever perceive in him
the least trace of preparation, and he never appears more incontestably inspired by the moment, and transported with the fury of the god within him,
than in those finished passages which it would have cost Shakespeare long
study and labour to produce.[68]

This is significant in view of a "Sheridanolatry" which had converted
everyone, even Burke himself. The following year, during the bitter
Regency debates, when Burke is often said to have reached one of his
lowest ebbs, Sir Gilbert could still write: "Burke has come forward in
the debate since Fox's departure to Bath, and made a speech yesterday
[February 2, 1789] thought one of the best ever heard by anybody on
all sides; so that we should not be without a great leader even if we
were to lose Fox." [69]

Apparently the contemporary impressions of Burke's greatness as a
speaker were current and immediate, in spite of moments of eclipse,
throughout his life, and were not derived from memories of his early
successes or from the reading of his printed works. Many other and
better known persons than Sir Gilbert Elliot, for example, were moved
to enthusiasm by his opening speeches in the Hastings trial. Fanny
Burney, a member of the Court of the Queen, a Tory, and an admirer of
Hastings, was one. As I have written elsewhere: "When she heard Burke,
on the 16th [of February], she was *almost* carried out of her Tory
sympathies by his eloquence. For this day her *Diary* records one of the
most flattering descriptions of Burke's oratorical powers ever penned.
Admiration for Hastings, however, overcame her as it did the Lords
themselves; and when Burke approached her after the speech and
bowed, her curtsy was 'most ungrateful, distant, and cold.' " [70] Hannah
More also was impressed: "Such a splendid and powerful oration" she
never heard. The very power of it angered her, because it put Hastings
in so bad a light.[71] Boswell, the guest of Courtenay in the Manager's
Box on February 18, heard Burke speak "astonishingly well"; [72] and of
these same speeches, Edmond Malone wrote to Lord Charlemont:

I suppose you have heard much of Burke's astonishing performance on the
business of Hastings. I had the good fortune to hear him on the first, second,

and fourth day, but could not get a ticket on the third, when he gave so pathetic a description of the tortures that had been practised in India. All the papers have made sad stuff of his most delicate touches, on a point of so nice a nature that nothing but the most consummate art could have guarded him against ridicule.[73]

Citations to much the same effect—the continued vitality of Burke's speaking—could be piled up for the remaining six years of his speaking career. I shall, however, present but three. Malone wrote to Charlemont on February 4, 1789: "Burke made one of the best speeches ever made in Parliament, on Monday evening, that in which he so happily applied the lines of Prior: 'And handles the rope,' etc." [74] The following analysis, by Hobhouse, the biographer of Fox, is significant especially as applying to a time when Burke is said to have been most violent and uncontrollable, the time when tension between him and his colleagues over the French Revolution was reaching a peak. Hobhouse asserts that, in answer to Fox's sophistical defense of the French army in the debates on the army estimates in February 1791,

Burke's speech was as carefully argued and conciliatory as Fox's had been confused, dogmatic, and provocative. The effect of such mature opinions, and such a mass of information, brought to bear upon a question about which other men had scarcely begun to think, was overwhelming. Fox's little glib epigram about the soldier and the citizen evaporated before Burke had said a few sentences. The contrast between the far-fetched optimism of the first and the solemn, solid warning of the second was a mortifying blow to Fox's usual superiority in debate. He felt called upon to make some sort of explanation: but it was not a great success.[75]

Even in the late and bitter years, Burke was listened to, and even then he could overturn the idol, Fox. Futhermore, as late as April 16, 1794, during his last session in Parliament, there were still those who found his speaking good. On that day the Duke of Portland wrote to William Windham about Burke's speech on the immigrant bill: "From what I hear of it, you have had a very great loss indeed, in missing Burke's speech . . . last Friday. There is not a Jacobine who pretends to taste who dares for his own sake to withhold from it his full tribute of applause, and I understand it was given in Burke's best manner." [76] This, of course, was on a subject on which Burke had for some time been speaking the thoughts of a great many of the English people.

Now, finally, before presenting certain generalizations about the effects Burke's speaking produced on those who heard him, let me set down without comment two general estimates of Burke's speaking as a whole. The first is, again, from Wraxall:

Nature had bestowed on him a boundless imagination, aided by a memory of equal strength and tenacity. His fancy was so vivid that it seemed to light up by its own powers, and to burn without consuming the aliment on which it fed; sometimes bearing him away into ideal scenes created by his own exuberant mind, but from which he, sooner or later, returned to the subject of debate. . . . He always seemed to be oppressed under the load and variety of his intellectual treasures; of which he frequently scattered portions with a lavish hand, to inattentive, impatient, hungry, and sleepy hearers, undeserving of such presents. Nor did he desist though warned by the clamorous vociferation of the House, to restrain or to abbreviate his speeches. . . . Though he instructed, delighted, and astonished, he frequently fatigued, because his faculties were not controlled and chastened by a severe judgment.[77]

The second excerpt is from the analysis of Burke's American speeches by one of their more recent editors, H. Clay Harshbarger:

What effect did . . . his well-ordered topics have upon the audiences which heard and read them? . . . The normal emotional and intellectual reactions of men had been unbalanced; blind patriotism had supplanted reason; desire for punishment of the colonial offenders had displaced goodwill. . . . In such situations philosophical assumptions leave men undisturbed, while phrases, slogans, and party war cries impel men to action. When Burke preached that the end of government was happiness, the Tories thought only of their dignity; when Burke lectured the House on the nature of the English constitution, the ruling party called for unanimity; when Burke urged conciliation as a means for bringing peace, the ministry condemned all who wished for moderation in dealing with the colonies; and when Burke set up the wisdom of the ancestors as the criterion of their actions, the majority cried for the punishment of its factious children. It is no wonder that Burke was unsuccessful.[78]

How, then, does the "dinner-bell" theory stand, in view of the available testimony? It has a significance—a certain critical value—as, indeed, it must have, since at times it was indubitably applied to Burke by some of his contemporaries. It does represent, therefore, one phase of the response to Burke among some persons at certain times in his career—a response which is a real part of the picture. Furthermore, it epitomizes one of Burke's great faults as a parliamentary speaker, or perhaps more exactly as a parliamentary debater and strategist: he talked too much (as Samuel Johnson early observed) and he talked when prudence might have bidden him be silent. He is reported at one time to have said that the habit of not speaking at all in Parliament grew on some men as fast and was as difficult to break as the habit of speaking ill grew on others, and that he was not sure which was the greater misfortune.[79] Burke himself was apparently as incapable of falling into the first habit as into the second. In mid-career—in the middle and late seventies—when Burke's party was hopelessly in opposition and in command of the smallest of minorities, even then Burke could not allow a matter of any apparent importance to go unargued, and he was usually unwilling to content himself with brief statements of his opposition to measures whose passage by overwhelming odds was a foregone conclusion. Furthermore, he would often begin long speeches at a late hour, when the House was eager to adjourn, and he would seem to pay no attention to his auditors' weariness and impatience. This was by no means always or usually so, as we have seen. Nevertheless, it must be admitted that it became a fault, and a serious one. When this much has been said, however, the significance of the "dinner-bell" theory is exhausted. The temptation, because it is couched in a neat and convenient figure, to expand it into a characterizing generality leads to serious misrepresentation. Many other qualities of Burke's speaking attracted his contemporaries and produced strong effects upon them.

Two qualities appeared almost at once to most of his listeners, both friend and foe: an uncommon extent and depth of knowledge and thought, and a remarkable prodigality of imagination. His speeches, not merely as read (and only a few of his speeches were ever printed), but as heard, appeared not as compendia of tremendous quantities of dry facts, but as the most complete, thorough, orderly, and exhaustive treatments of whole subjects, livened and made vivid and powerful by a natural profusion of imagery and emotional fervour which left listeners astonished. As Sir W. W. Pepys once wrote to Hannah More: "You and Burke are the only *two* persons I know who can safely be trusted with a metaphor. . . . I once heard a man say of him, while he was pouring forth torrents of eloquence in the House of Commons, 'How closely that fellow reasons in metaphor!' " [80] These two qualities, however, affected people differently. Many persons delighted in them and admired Burke the more for them; others, especially the stupid, inferior, and uneducated (of whom there were not a few in the House of Commons), were bored, confounded, or annoyed by them. Among the more brilliant contemporaries, however, Flood, it will be recalled, thought that Burke sometimes obscured his reasoning by his figurative expression; and Wilkes and others were of similar opinion.[81]

Burke, however, for fully half his long career, was the voice of the Rockingham party in the Commons and was, not without reason, counted on by that party to put forward its case in the most powerful form. And during the last half of his active parliamentary life, he shared with Fox that same spear-head position in the ranks of two short-lived administrations and a long siege of opposition. He remained, as he was called at the beginning, the readiest man on all subjects in the whole house; and though Fox was perhaps the better debater, Burke was no mean opponent or supporter in the rough and tumble of the daily sessions. His wit was biting and devastating; the clothing of his speeches, as we are repeatedly told, was delightful and entertaining; and if his platform appearance was unprepossessing and his voice and Irish accent annoying to some English and Scottish ears, the "torrents" of his "eloquence," and the "force" of his "oratory," awed and frightened his hearers even when it did not win their votes.

The violence and intemperance of his behavior and his contempt for delicacy, often observed by his critics, appeared in his speeches and did him harm, especially in the later, bitter years from the fall of the coalition in December 1783 through the French Revolution. Founded, as these attitudes were, in a deep, sincere, passionate, almost fanatic earnestness which precluded moderation and compromise on matters to which Burke's soul had become devoted, and supported as they were by a fund of knowledge, a power of thought, and a faculty of high imagination unequalled in the House of Commons while he was there, they were uncontrollable. And they were at least as important in keeping Burke from cabinet office as was the fact that he had not been born into that little aristocratic Whig oligarchy which considered itself appointed to rule England.

When, however, Burke's purpose moved, as it did on many notable occasions, in the same direction as the will and sympathy of his audiences, the very magnitude of his materials and the fire of his imagination carried all with them. No "dinner-bell" then, or "cutting Blocks with a razor," but the voice of free Englishmen being oppressed in the colonies, of slaughtered settlers in the forests of North America, of enslaved peoples and of desecrated gods in the temples of ancient India, or of the terrified island-dwellers aghast at the rabble-noises of revolutionary France.

Lord Thomas Erskine:

Modern Advocate

CARROLL C. ARNOLD

ON January 10, 1750,[1] Thomas Erskine was born in Edinburgh, the youngest son of Henry David, tenth Earl of Buchan. He was fortunate in family, health, and natural intelligence, but unfortunate in being the third son of a "good family" whose patrimony had been wasted by previous generations. His parents had only meager funds for the education of their eldest and second sons and little but affection and guidance for the youngest.[2] Still, the accepted chronicle of Erskine's first fifty-six years is remarkably filled with fortunate coincidences and examples of determination and talent demanding and earning their proper rewards.

Erskine displayed apt scholarship and high spirits as a grammar school student, first in Edinburgh and then in St. Andrews. At the age of thirteen, he briefly attended lectures on science and mathematics at the University of St. Andrews, but could not afford to matriculate. For the same too-familiar reason he was unable to purchase the army commission he coveted; and so, assisted or perhaps pressed by friends and family, he enlisted as a sailor on the man-of-war, the *Tartar*, in the spring of 1764.

Thus entered upon service in His Majesty's forces, Erskine was probably expected to move through the ranks, carving for himself the standard naval career of an impecunious scion of good family. But fortune had better things in store. At eighteen, with a small inheritance from his father, he managed to purchase an ensign's commission in the First Royal Regiment of Foot. At twenty, and still without clear prospects, he foreclosed a common path to personal advancement by marrying for love a girl as poor as he. When his regiment was moved to Minorca for a period of two years, Erskine used his leisure to develop an extensive knowledge of English literary classics. Back in England, at twenty-three and with the rank of lieutenant, he is said to have visited, almost casually, a courtroom presided over by Lord Mansfield. On this day, so the story goes, he was invited to sit beside the distinguished jurist on the bench and later to dine with him, in consequence of which Erskine fixed his hopes upon a career at the bar. Whatever the genesis of Erskine's interest in the law, Lord Mansfield does appear to have encouraged it, and, receiving approval but virtually no aid from his family, Erskine enrolled as a student at Lincoln's Inn in April 1775. His chief source of support for himself, his wife, and his children was money realized from the sale of his lieutenancy.

A university degree reduced from five to three years the required period of enrollment at an Inn of Court; therefore, since university and law terms could be kept concurrently and since Erskine was entitled by rank to a degree without examination, he also matriculated at Trinity College, Cambridge. During the same period he regularly attended and engaged in debates and harangues at Coachmakers' Hall [3] and elsewhere in London. By thus telescoping his formal education, by living in what was at best embarrassing poverty, and by studying law, literature, and public life assiduously, Thomas Erskine secured an honorary A.M. from Cambridge in June 1778 and was called to the bar the following July. He was twenty-eight. He had been midshipman, army officer, university student, law student, and now he was a barrister without a brief.

Good fortune and evident intelligence brought Erskine from his ordinary station to the prospect of a great career in a single, giant stride. An invitation to dinner gave him the occasion to defend in conversation one Captain Baillie, formerly Lieutenant Governor of Greenwich Hospital but now under suit for libel against those responsible for the institution's support and administration. Captain Baillie, or it may have been the Captain's brother, was also at the dinner, heard Erskine's talk, and next day the young lawyer received his first fee and an invitation to serve as a junior counsellor in Baillie's trial. Erskine did the unexpected. He exercised his counsellor's privilege during the trial, despite his junior status, and delivered to Lord Mansfield and the other judges what Lord Campbell called, "all the circumstances considered, . . . the most wonderful forensic effort of which we have any account in our annals." [4] Baillie was acquitted, and Erskine's argument was credited with contributing greatly to the outcome. Thus the course of his career was settled; he would rise from success to success in pleading until, having once served as Lord Chancellor, he could no longer practice in the courts. Only then would his star slowly begin to set.

It is with the quality of Erskine's forensic pleas that this essay has to do. His courtroom arguments have been universally praised; but in this century, at least, we are in some danger of submerging his claim to greatness as a forensic *artist* beneath our enthusiasm for the political ideals into which his art breathed new life and vigor in an important but limited series of trials.

There is unquestionable nobility and significance in Erskine's iterated propositions that subversive *intent* must be shown before convictions for treason or libel can be just, and that *juries* must be allowed to judge *both* fact and intent where libel is charged. But others, before and after, spoke on these and equally noble themes without comparably influencing the course of law and without adding to our permanent literature. We shall err, therefore, if we suppose that Erskine's claim to continued attention springs primarily from the political position he took in a few momentous state trials. He was not, after all, a one-man Civil Liberties Union; neither was he a Clarence Darrow irrevocably committed to the cause of the underdog, though Stryker's biography and the foci of other recent studies might seem to imply that he was. [5]

Whether Erskine defended John Stockdale's publication of a pamphlet critical of the Government or prosecuted Thomas Williams for publishing Paine's *Age of Reason*, whether he prosecuted Benjamin Boddington for eloping with his cousin's wife or defended Richard Bingham who had eloped with the wife of Bernard Howard, Erskine's rhetorical artistry gave to each client his fullest, rightful claim to judicial attention and sympathy. It was by art more than by choice of briefs that he served the cause of justice, for in a wide variety of causes he gave full effect to the honorable tradition that if liberty and justice are to be wedded in the courts, each litigant must have the most persuasive representation the limits of fact and law allow. There is, I think, no other English-speaking pleader who, in the service of this tradition, achieved more completely the degree of creative excellence to which Cicero has Crassus allude in his question: "What is so admirable as, that, out of an infinite multitude of men, there should arise a single individual, who can alone, or with only a few others, exert effectually that power that nature has granted to all?" [6]

If we take Erskine's published forensic addresses as a whole, the leading and distinctive quality of his discourse is the congruity of the rhetorical forces he loosed in each persuasive effort. The most striking elements in this consonance of matter and manner seem to me to be three: his ability, within a single speech, to direct effective persuasion toward the predispositions of judges and jurors even when these two classes of auditors were differently inclined; the entire harmony of language, thought, and purpose which marks all his pleas; and, above all else, his ability to discover and make inescapable the *public* significance of each case for which he accepted a brief. These, I believe, are the features of pleading which set Erskine apart from the advocates who were his contemporaries and raise his addresses above those of the advocates who have followed. They are features the more striking because they appear in the speeches of one who spoke at a time when much English oratory was cluttered with vestiges of a rhetoric shorn of *inventio* and *dispositio* and burdened on the one hand by digression and ornament and on the other by dull detail.

Henry Roscoe asserted that the care and nicety with which Erskine joined fact, reason, and feeling to central principles of justice was "the most remarkable" of all the qualities that contributed to the success of his addresses. Roscoe continued:

In every case he proposed a great leading principle to which all his efforts were referable and subsidiary, which ran through the whole of his address, arranging, governing, and elucidating every portion. As the principle thus proposed was founded in truth and justice, whatever might be its application to the particular case, it necessarily gave the whole of his speech an air of honesty and sincerity which a jury could with difficulty resist.[7]

Such centricity in composition has merit in almost any oral discourse but it contributes special force and effect to forensic argument, where facts of human actions and their relations to accepted systems of rules and policies are the bases of judgment. Harry Caplan has used the phrase, "the complete economy of the entire speech," to suggest this degree of centricity required in effective pleading.[8] This is precisely the degree of unity and systematic emphasis Erskine achieved. He created in each address a "complete economy" of thought and feeling in which a principle of truth or of justice became the adductive force and the decision called for became a necessary intermediate step in accepting the still more attractive central proposition.

The broad principles to which the rhetorical resources of Erskine's pleas had unbroken relationship were not usually rules of law. They were propositions about justice or the way to justice, about truth or the way to truth. They focused attention on the ends and methods of social organization. If they were also administrative rules or guides to legal interpretation, this was incidental. Characteristically, they suggested strongly but indirectly that judge and juror ought to *make* law, ought to refashion social patterns by *creating* precedents.

There were at least two strong reasons for the favor with which these subtly developed invitations to form or conserve social practices were received: (1) the "Point to Adjudicate," being relatively nontechnical and therefore readily comprehensible, was inescapable, for it was central to everything in the entire plea; (2) jurors almost always, and judges very often, actively desire to influence the future, even though they know, intellectually, that they are expected to render decisions according to law and precedent alone. To put the matter another way, Erskine tempted his courtroom "deciders" to become policy makers too, a temptation few men even desire to resist.

Almost all of Erskine's defenses and prosecutions exemplify what has been said of the nature and function of pivotal propositions in his forensic addresses, but the defenses of Bingham [9] and Hadfield [10] furnish convenient illustrations unencumbered by the themes with which Erskine's name has been so exclusively associated in twentieth-century studies.

First to be noticed are the gradual, cautious, but always directly relevant stages by which Erskine advanced toward the principle of justice on which he would rest his plea. In Bingham's behalf the principle to be established was that forced, loveless marriage is prostitution. Through the first two thirds of the speech the coldness and degradation of the Howards' marriage are hinted at, asserted, vivified, and finally traced to their source: "the legal prostitution of parental choice in the teeth of affection." There follows the familiar social application of the principle: the jury's decision must resoundingly condemn marriages of arrangement and must teach the aristocracy to abandon practices so morally reprehensible and so dangerous to established order. The jury was only too willing to teach the lesson, and *The Times* did Erskine the honor of copying out his homily.[11]

Erskine's plea for Hadfield was built around a basic principle of justice too. He stated it in rather negative fashion at the close of the first third of his address:

He alone can be emancipated . . . [from criminal responsibility] whose reasoning and corresponding conduct, though governed by the ordinary dictates of reason, proceed upon something which has no foundation or existence.

Lord Kenyon endorsed this proposition and made it a principle of law by interrupting the presentation of defense evidence to suggest a directed verdict of acquittal by reason of insanity.[12] But Erskine had not taken the jurist's mind by storm. His principle was a proposition of law as well as justice, and he had woven the web of his discourse cautiously. By rhetorical necessity he had to instruct the judges without seeming to invade the realm of their privileged judgment, for he was not, as in the Bingham case, addressing chiefly the less self-conscious jurors.[13]

The argument for Hadfield began conventionally enough. The advocate praised the caution and generosity of English justice; he protested that the case was not entirely as the prosecutor, Sir John Mitford, had represented it. But even here he inserted the first hints of the psychological problem the court must resolve: the prisoner's obligation to British institutions, "if he had the consciousness and reason to reflect upon [them]," was deftly mentioned before the pleader passed on to explore the special difficulties of interpreting the legal responsibilities of the insane under British law. Having thus laid open the inadequacies of existing law, Erskine hastened to reassure his listeners that he had no revolutionary judicial interpretation in view; he would never, he insisted, apply in a criminal case such liberal definitions of insanity as Coke and Hale had applied in civil cases. Who could refuse fair and favorable attention to the case analysis that would follow from such conservative doctrine? [14]

Only after such cautious preparation did Erskine dare to assault directly Mitford's legal orthodoxy:

If a total deprivation of memory was intended by these great lawyers to be taken in the literal sense of the words . . . [Mitford had so taken it] then no such madness ever existed in the world. It is idiocy alone which places a man in this helpless condition; where from an original mal-organization there is the human frame alone without the human capacity.

By now his argument clearly showed that Hadfield's ability to reason and plan could not be taken as proof of his *general* sanity, but Erskine did not rest content with this factual and theoretical invalidation of traditional views. He set about to justify his own theory of mental disease by illustrating from familiar cases at law the restricted character of insanity in some of its forms. It was thus that he cleared the way for his summary observations that "insane persons frequently appear in the utmost state of ability and composure" and that Hadfield's act was the "immediate, unqualified offspring of the disease." With the minds of the judges prepared by this chain of suggestion, direct refutation, and affirmative reasoning and evidence, Erskine felt secure enough to assert, in the most reserved language, the pivotal judicial principle I have already quoted. He did not neglect to add that the monarch's safety would be better served by justice to Hadfield than by an effort "to stretch the laws" to convict him.

When Erskine at last revealed the principle of justice for which he was arguing, one may suppose judges and jurors found it plausible and sanctified by reason and authority (though no authority had been adduced to support it directly). They received the new doctrine without shock, for the speaker had done nothing abruptly; from first to last his proofs were rendered acceptable by the method of *insinuatio* before being directly argued. Even Sir John Mitford appears to have been convinced by Erskine's argument, once evidence had established that Hadfield actually suffered from special and recurring delusions.[15]

Though one of the pleas just reviewed recommends a revolutionary interpretation of the marriage contract and the other extends the principles of civil law to a limited class of criminal cases, their general rhetorical design is the same. The arcs of discourse, as it were, rise gently and suggestively toward the proposition that sustains the plea, then inflect through an application of the principle, finally coming to rest on an aspect of Erskine's favorite topic of persuasion—the decision to be rendered must be that which best promotes the public good.[16]

When one remembers that judges in the late eighteenth century claimed authority to sit in judgment on fact as well as law and that juries were often restless under such judge-imposed restrictions on their powers, Erskine's subtle urgings that *both* classes of auditors assume deliberative authority seem especially well adapted to the sometimes conflicting inclinations of his two audiences. By so carefully clearing the way for his central propositions, he made it easy for even conservative judges to assume lawmaking functions, almost without realizing it. And since he asked that decisions be rendered on principles having considerable public significance, it became easier and seemingly justifiable for jurors to act upon the bases of their common sense and their impressions of society's needs.[17]

In selecting and structuring persuasive materials Erskine exhibited a fuller apprehension of the scope of forensic discourse and of the psychological process we call suggestion than did the rhetorical theorists of his own or earlier times.[18] By unifying direct and indirect persuasion in the service of central purposes that reached beyond the confines of existing law and isolated cases, he almost imperceptibly raised his courtroom arguments to that level of thought which Aristotle considered "nobler and more statesmanlike than the branch that is concerned with the everyday relations between man and man." [19] His forensic addresses are, thus, subtle blends of forensic and deliberative elements in which, contrary to the advice of most rhetorical theorists, he extended to all parts of the discourse the method of *insinuatio*. These qualities were rare in eighteenth-century pleading and, I suggest, their presence in Erskine's pleas contributed greatly to the high proportion of unexpectedly favorable verdicts he obtained from juries and judges alike.

Not only did Erskine select and develop subtle arguments clustered closely but unobtrusively about principles of policy and justice, he exercised equal care and purposefulness in selecting the language that was to bear his thought. So far as I have been able to discover, only Sergeant William Draper Best and Sir Robert Dallas, among his contemporaries at law, even resembled him in these respects; and they resembled him but weakly. Certainly among his colleagues there was no other who succeeded in making history, law, and literature while pleading.[20] Best was thought "one of the principal ornaments" of the common law courts, but it was also said of him that, being superficial in both legal and general knowledge, he needed an able "junior" to handle the more formal aspects of difficult cases.[21] In his defense of E. M. Despard against charges of treason, Best had a splendid opportunity to emulate Erskine in thought development and style but fell far short of Erskine's artistry in both respects.[22] Sir Robert Dallas, who,

like Erskine, had practiced debate at Coachmakers' Hall, could isolate pivotal principles on which to rest a case and could bring circumstances within the vicarious experience of jurors; but beside Erskine's,
his style is flat and wanting in vitality.[23] There is certainly little similarity between the bright efficiency of Erskine and Sir John Scott's
"detail of facts, mixed up with protestations of his own honesty and
good intentions," or Scott's carelessness "as to the structure of his
sentences, or the order of his discourse." [24] Bearcroft's verbose cir-
cumlocutions clearly mark him as Erskine's inferior. It was with Edward
Law that Erskine divided most of the business of the common law
courts so long as Law remained in active practice, but Law's dry re-
citals of facts, his abruptness in argument, and his overly "cautious
and calculating spirit" [25] deny him favorable comparison with Erskine.

The fact seems to be that in Erskine's day courtroom pleading was
more often than not acute but dull; yet even those pleaders who were
not dull usually exhibited a rhetoric less functional and hence less
persuasive than Erskine's. James Macintosh's great address in the
trial of Jean Peltier is justly famous; but in it Macintosh adopted a
grand, discursive manner such as Erskine never used in court. In
striking but diffuse fashion the plea for Peltier magnifies the domestic
and European need for a free English press, it turns aside for extended
condemnation of Bonaparte and the Jacobin spirit, it is threaded with
literary allusion, analogy, and quotation, often more impressive than
persuasive. The judges and jurors must be excused for finding much
of the discourse irrelevant to the actions of Macintosh's client and the
specific libel charged against him, so evocative and so generalized are
the leading arguments for freedom of political expression.[26]

The Irish advocate John Philpot Curran was seldom if ever dull
in pleading, yet Erskine's superiority in invention and style is at once
apparent on comparison. Happily, very close comparison is possible,
since Curran, with one Bartholomew Hoar, prosecuted a criminal conversation case almost exactly like the famous *Markham v Fawcett*
cause in which Erskine appeared. In each instance a clergyman's wife
had been seduced by one to whom her husband had extended his
personal friendship. In 1802, Erskine sought damages for the Reverend George Markham, against John Fawcett, on such charges; and
in 1804, Curran and Hoar represented the Reverend Charles Massy
in a similar action against the Marquis of Headfort. Both cases were
tried in county courts, the former in Middlesex and the other in County

Lord Thomas Erskine

Clare, Ireland. In each case it was imperative that the prosecutors magnify the offensiveness of the undeniable adultery by impressing upon their hearers that the wrong was the greater for being also a violation of friendship.

Hoar's treatment of this forensic commonplace is fairly represented by the following passage from his opening for Massy:

The Cornish plunderer, intent on the spoil, callous to every touch of humanity, shrouded in darkness, holds out false lights to the tempest-tost vessel, and lures her and her pilot to that shore upon which she must be lost forever—the rock unseen, the ruffian invisible, and nothing apparent but the treacherous signal of security and repose. So, this prop of the throne, this pillar of the State, this stay of religion, the ornament of the Peerage, this common protector of the people's privileges and of the crown's prerogatives, descends from these high grounds of character to muffle himself in the gloom of his own base and dark designs; to play before the eyes of the deluded wife and the deceived husband the falsest lights of love to the one, and of friendly and hospitable regards to the other, until she is at length dashed upon that hard bosom where her honor and happiness are wrecked and lost forever. The agonized husband beholds the ruin with those sensations of horror which you can better feel than I can describe. Her upon whom he had embarked all his hopes and all his happiness in this life, . . . sunk before his eyes into an abyss of infamy, or if any fragment escape, escaping to solace, to gratify, and to enrich her vile destroyer.[27]

As Snyder says, "the striking parallel . . . with the treachery of the Cornish pirates . . . presents a graphic picture," [28] but one must also add that the compensable anguish of the husband twice betrayed is enshrouded in words better calculated to sustain the orator's rhythmic flight than to mirror the poignancy of his client's suffering.

Curran's closing plea for the same plaintiff illustrates a similar sacrifice of sharp persuasiveness in favor of embellishment:

There is another consideration, gentlemen, which, I think, most imperiously demands even a vindictive award of exemplary damages, and that is the breach of hospitality. To us peculiarly does it belong to avenge the violation of its altar. The hospitality of other countries is a matter of necessity or convention; . . . but the hospitality of an *Irishman* is not the running account of posted and legered courtesies, as in other countries; it springs, like all his qualities, his faults, his virtues, directly from his heart. The heart of an Irishman is by nature bold, and he confides; it is tender, and he loves; it is generous, and he gives; it is social, and he is hospitable. This sacrilegious intruder has profaned the religion of that sacred altar so elevated in our worship, so precious to our devotion; and it is our privilege to avenge the crime. You must either pull down the altar and abolish the worship, or you must preserve its sanctity undebased. There is no alternative between the universal exclusion of all mankind from your threshold, and the most rigorous punishment of him who is admitted and betrays. The defendant has been so trusted, has so betrayed, and you ought to make him a most signal example.[29]

The profusion of religious symbols and the appeal to national pride make it easy for the listener to lose sight of the immediate issue before the court; the Reverend Mr. Massy ceases to be a husband-friend betrayed and becomes an abstraction, an artifact of Irish character and custom. The invocation of deliberative ends is so complete that "the everyday relations between man and man" are almost lost from view.

Erskine had the same argument to make in the Reverend Mr. Markham's behalf, but the manner of its making was profoundly different:

Invited into the house of a friend—received with the open arms of affection, as if the same parents had given them birth and bred them—in this situation this most monstrous and wicked defendant deliberately perpetrated his crime, and, shocking to relate, not only continued the appearances of friendship, after he had violated its most sacred obligations, but continued them as a cloak to the barbarous repetitions of his offence; writing letters of regard, whilst, perhaps, he was the father of the last child, whom his injured friend and companion was embracing and cherishing as his own. What protection can such conduct possibly receive. . . ? A passion for a woman is progressive; it does not, like anger, gain an uncontrolled ascendency in a moment, nor is a modest matron to be seduced in a day. Such a crime, can not, therefore, be committed under the resistless dominion of sudden infirmity; it must be wilfully, and wickedly committed. The defendant could not possibly have incurred the guilt of this adultery without often passing through his mind (for he had the education and principles of a gentleman) the very topics I have been insisting upon before you for his condemnation. . . . He was a year engaged in the pursuit; he resorted repeatedly to his shameful purpose, and advanced to it at such intervals of time and distance, as entitle me to say that he determined in cold blood to enjoy a future and momentary gratification, at the expense of every principle of honor which is held sacred amongst gentlemen, even where no laws interpose their obligations or restraints.[30]

Curran and Hoar could not have claimed that their client must doubt the parentage of a child he had thought his own, and it is true that Headfort devoted but four months to his nefarious business. But Massy's advocates might, like Erskine, have focused attention more clearly upon the deliberateness of the deceit, the trust of the husband for his friend, and the impossibility of excusing the Marquis on grounds of sudden weakness.[31] Erskine's development of these standard topics of degree in wrongdoing is stronger than the developments furnished by either of his Irish contemporaries because, proceeding with economy and rigid relevancy, he vividly "furthered the magnification of the crime against his client by creating a hierarchy of loss: one item after another . . . added to the structure of the argument until the crime became the worst of its kind and the loss suffered by Erskine's client, the deepest." [32]

Other ways in which Erskine's art excelled that of his contemporaries are also illustrated by the passages just quoted. In contrast to the practice of Curran, Hoar, or Macintosh, Erskine admits to his discourse no allusion that might draw the mind of a hearer from the quality of the human action he examines. His language contains scarcely a hint of copy-book polish; yet he is at great pains that the amplification of his topics shall recreate in the vicarious experience of each auditor the most acute sensations of his client. Figures of speech and thought, allusions, quotations—all the beautifying and evocative resources of language—are cleanly functional; the presence of each symbol is justified by its contribution to the sum of the advocate's *proof*.

But when Erskine stepped from the bar to the floor of the House of Commons or, later, delivered his opinions in the House of Lords, it was as if his wonted unity of thought, harmony of methods, and functionalism in style had been left among his briefs and law books. In Parliament he cluttered his speechs with *ad hominem* arguments, sprinkled them with lumbering quotations from Dr. Johnson, with commentary to match, and only now and then revealed his real powers in a telling proof of expediency or inexpediency. He who, as Goodrich observed, never digressed in the courtroom without bringing back from his excursion something important to his central theme,[33] treated parliamentarians to so many autobiographical semi-relevancies that he fairly justified the taunt in the suggestion that he be raised to the title "Baron Ego, of Eye, in the county of Suffolk." [34] The texts of his legislative addresses are at some points studded with parentheses, those printers' accommodations to involved constructions and unmanaged qualifications of thought.

Clearly Erskine was not a brilliant pleader because he possessed

305

some divine general gift of persuasive speech; had it been so, his deliberative speaking must surely have been quickened. Though from the beginning he was able to solve the rhetorical problems of court-room discourse, he seems never to have understood fully the ultimate ends and methods of advisory or occasional speaking. Had he, then, only a special, limited knack? Or had he studied and learned the art on which his profession depended? One may speculate, but no clear answer is to be found.

Quite possibly poverty and ambition drove the highly intelligent Erskine to induce the elements of the pleader's art from independent observation and study.[35] Since he was already successful in his profession when he entered Parliament, he was probably not similarly motivated to analyze the new rhetorical problems that confronted him there, after 1783. Almost certainly, too, legislation interested him less than advocacy.

If we were to judge from his deliberative oratory alone, we might suppose him a child of the tradition that saw rhetoric as style or as delivery, but his forensic principles could never have been derived from such sources. The rhetorical works published in England during the period of his formal and self-education offered little advice that would make for the qualities of oratory he displayed in the courtroom.[36] It would be far easier to believe that his achievements at the bar drew some guidance from that branch of rhetorical theory which, during his earlier years, was beginning to move "out of the intellectual vacuum in which Ward [and others] had kept it, and . . . into line with contemporary developments in psychology, epistemology, and literary criticism." [37]

Erskine's forensic practice might have derived from thoughtful application of the theoretical doctrines published by George Campbell in his *Philosophy of Rhetoric,* particularly those found in Book I, Chapters VII through IX.[38] There is no evidence that Erskine read this book by a fellow Scotsman, but Campbell stated the psychological premise that underlay all of Erskine's distinctive methods when he wrote, "It must be allowed there are certain principles in our nature, which, when properly addressed and managed, give no inconsiderable aid to reason in prompting belief." [39] Again, Campbell's concern with rhetorical adaptation to listeners, collectively and particularly, is an emphasis remarkably consistent with Erskine's principles of practice.

But to try to erect an hypothesis connecting Erskine's art with Campbell's body of theory would certainly strain the scattered bits of circumstantial evidence. Campbell's *Philosophy* was, after all, only one of a number of signs of rising interest in psychological principles, including those of communication. An alert and ambitious barrister-in-training, with even a general impression of the scientific and critical speculations emanating from his native Edinburgh, might well see for himself how completely the principles of persuasion derive from the natures of men in general and men in particular. The supposition that Erskine formulated his principles of pleading independently of contemporary theory and practice is strengthened by the fact that he extended the range of forensic thought and feeling considerably beyond the bounds Blair or Campbell prescribed.[40] At the same time, he was more rigid than they or his more systematically educated fellow barristers in measuring both substance and language by the test of *immediate* relevance.

Thus, the sources of Erskine's principles of advocacy remain obscure and uncertain; but whatever their derivation, his practice was distinctive. I have suggested as the essence of his forensic art the convergence of all the forces of discourse—as though this were their nature and not the orator's design—toward a clear and expedient rule for decision in a given case. In his forensic addresses there are no digressions inspired by models of another age or by a rhetoric confused with poetic. There are no vagrant thoughts; even vagrant words are few, considering the habits of the age. There is much that is striking and beautiful but it is as *proof,* not as formula, that style arrests or excites: consider the idyl on conjugal love in the plea for Bingham or the description of Hadfield's battle wounds.[41] Even when he rose to deliver his first plea, for Captain Baillie, on November 24, 1778, Erskine gave notice that his was a fresh, broad-gauged theory of argument in which the structuring of listeners' predispositions, perceptions, and emotional energies was the end of all persuasive effort. His artistic command over the complex ideational and motivational resources of advocacy came to its full development in the last decade of the eighteenth century and reached its zenith, I believe, in the later treason and libel trials, in his defense of Bingham, and in his defense of Hadfield.

Almost without exception, Thomas Erskine's speeches at the bar illustrate that the best persuasion is unitary, that forensic rhetoric is neither reason on a work detail nor parade-ground polish on review. His rhetoric was an artistic integration of reason, suggestion, and functional symbols, organized to form a complete and dynamic economy. In this he was, and remains, a thoroughly modern practitioner of the art of rhetoric—though in one of its branches only. In the manner of the classical forensic orator, he perceived that "there is indeed no cause in which the point that falls under dispute is considered with reference to the parties to the suit and not from arguments relating to questions in general." [42] In the modern manner he applied the method of *insinuatio*, "the subtle approach," in all the parts of his discourses. Again exhibiting his modernity, he found the topics of forensic discourse not only in places having reference to particular and general questions of fact and justice, but in those reaches of popular thought where questions of expedient public policy are found and resolved. Finally, more than the ancients or his contemporaries, he devoted his rhetorical efforts to the end of evoking *and controlling* strongly motivated reason through rigorously organized and sharply relevant substance and symbols.

Immediate influence, not beauty or profundity, was Lord Erskine's goal in the courtroom; in consequence, he achieved all three. In the process he left his mark on Anglo-American law, advanced the general cause of political liberty, and, at so unlikely a place as the counsel's bench, he enlarged the store of imaginative literature in the English language. His life of influence through consummate art closed on February 7, 1806, when he accepted the seals of the Lord Chancellor's office and thereby closed his career as an advocate. He died on November 17, 1823. The intervening years were years of slow but steady decline, for the artist was denied the practice of his special, single art. His culture was denied the further contributions to law, politics, and literature that the challenge of courtroom advocacy might have inspired in Lord Thomas Erskine, Baron of Restormel Castle, whose motto was, "Trail by Jury."

Samuel Taylor Coleridge in
Lecture-Box and Pulpit

RAYMOND F. HOWES

BETWEEN 1794 and 1820 Coleridge delivered approximately one hundred fifty lectures and more than a dozen sermons.[1] From his lectures, which included the notable courses of 1808, 1811–1812, 1812–1813, and 1818 in London and several courses in Bristol, he received a larger financial return than from the sale of his books, and to them more than to his books and essays he owed his contemporary fame as a critic and philosopher.[2] Yet he contemptuously called them "employment for the bread and beef of the day," and expressed gratification that they could not (as he supposed) be reconstructed and printed.[3]

On the surface, this seems a strange attitude for one so thoroughly at home in oral discourse, but Coleridge was well aware that informal talk, no matter how brilliant, may fail to satisfy an audience that has assembled to hear a lucid, unified discussion of a particular theme. His carefully prepared prospectuses [4] attest his knowledge that when he spoke for pay he assumed certain definite obligations toward his listeners—that he might reasonably be expected to speak on the topic announced and to do it methodically, thoroughly, and in such a way as "to keep the audience awake and interested during the delivery, and to leave a *sting* behind—i.e., the disposition to study the subject anew, under the light of a new principle." [5] Public speaking has restrictions, no less than prose and verse. William Wordsworth was right when he told J. P. Collier that Coleridge's "thoughts as well as his words flow spontaneously. He talks as a bird sings, as if he could not help it." But Wordsworth was wrong when he inferred that lectures had therefore been "to him no effort." [6] The correct inference is that the lectures, so far as they represented conscious attempts to fulfill promises to his audience, were a great effort indeed. The struggle to control the living fountain of his mind was difficult in public speaking, as in writing.

If the struggle was often unsuccessful, it was not for lack of good intentions. Writing to Sir Humphry Davy concerning the proposed lectures of 1808 at the Royal Institution, Coleridge declared, "I have all my materials ready, and can rapidly reduce them to form (for this is my solemn determination, not to give a single lecture till I have in fair writing at least one half of the whole course)." [7] Even after experience had convinced him that his audiences were better pleased when he spoke without manuscript or notes,[8] he assured Britton that he took "far, far more pains than would go to the set composition of a lecture, both by varied reading and by meditation," because during a course he employed "*all* the intervening days in collecting and digesting the materials" and devoted the day of the lecture "to the consideration, what of the mass before me is best fitted to answer the purposes." [9]

That he did actually spend a considerable amount of time and energy in preparation is proved by the mass of fragments and notes now in print.[10] It has been established that he wrote a number of complete original lectures,[11] pieced others together from notes and marginalia,[12] and sometimes offered long translations from German sources.[13] At other times, however, he seems to have improvised from the sketchy jottings in his commonplace books,[14] and frequently to have arrived at the hall empty-handed, with less idea of the subject than his audience, who had at least looked at the announcement.[15] Depending somewhat on his method of preparation, his delivery ranged from formal reading of a manuscript through various stages of extemporizing to entirely impromptu rhapsody.

It is quite unsafe, however, to draw even a tentative conclusion about the quality of a lecture (or sermon, because there was little difference between them) after ascertaining merely how Coleridge prepared and delivered it. On many subjects his memory was so well stored that no specific research was necessary; and so thoroughly had he mastered the art of impromptu discourse in private that when he forgot he was speaking in public his delivery might be highly effective. He seems never to have had sufficient knowledge of the popular mind to be able to predict whether his treatment of a subject would seem intelligible or abstruse; yet so strong was the force of his personality—"that electric power of genius," Miss Mitford called it [16]—that he could sometimes blind every auditor to defects in thought, arrangement, and diction.[17] His knowledge of the subjects, his adaptation of material to the audience, and the force of his personality were all variable factors, the first varying with his interest, the second by sheer chance, and the third with his health and mood.[18]

Hence arise the extreme discrepancies in the judgments of contemporary critics, most of whom heard him only a few times. We might accept them all at face value, disregarding the obvious personal bias of some, without departing very far from an accurate picture, because Coleridge as a lecturer evidently deserved both admiration and censure. Even if this were not true, we would still be forced to rely on such first-hand accounts as those of Cottle, Collier, Gillman, De Quincey, and Crabb Robinson in forming our own judgment, since no printed record of what Coleridge said can tell us anything about the other factors essential to effective speaking. Certain typical combinations of these factors recur in the lectures and lecture-sermons as reported.

Cottle has told at length how in 1796 he accompanied Coleridge to Bath to hear him preach his first two sermons. The material had been carefully prepared—had indeed been used in previous lectures. The delivery was animated. But Cottle wanted to slink out of the church in shame when his young friend, peremptorily refusing the conventional sable gown, mounted to the pulpit in a vivid blue coat and white waistcoat and harangued the congregation on the Corn Laws and the Hair-Powder Tax.[19] Several years later another carefully prepared lecture, based on Herder's *Kalligone* and completely unfit for presentation to a popular audience, drew from Crabb Robinson the laconic comment, "At Coleridge's lecture, where I slept." [20]

Lack of preparation often had precisely the same effect of making his lectures unadapted to the audience. Robinson notes in his diary, December 1, 1812, "Evening, at Coleridge's lecture, Surrey Institution. Three-fourths of the lecture a declamation on atheism. He meant to introduce by a reference to religion the German antithesis between paganism and Christianity, which was itself to be merely an introduction to the contrast between classic and romantic poetry; but, as usual, he wasted his time on the introduction to the introduction!" [21] Imagine Robinson's disgust a week later when the lecturer, attempting to atone for this error, apologized profusely and then "spoke of nothing but Christianity" with "not even a single word on the subject of polite literature in any way." [22]

Even when Coleridge made adequate preparation and talked intelligibly on the subject announced, his delivery might be adversely affected by ill health.[23] This happened frequently during the lecture course at the Royal Institution in 1808. S. C. Hall, after attending one in this series, wrote, "There was little animation; his theme did not seem to stir him into life; the ordinary repose of his countenance was rarely broken up; he used little or no action; and his voice, though mellifluous, was monotonous. He lacked, indeed, that earnestness without which no man is truly eloquent." [24] It may have been of this lecture that Coleridge himself wrote Mrs. Morgan, "I went from my bed to the R. Institution on Friday last, and having with great difficulty read thro' my lecture with my eyes never off the book, I returned from thence again to my bed." [25]

The lectures of 1818 in the rooms of the Philosophical Society, London, should, by all the usual criteria, have been Coleridge's best. He wrote most of them before delivery,[26] but used only notes on the platform so that he might speak extemporaneously.[27] He gave every lecture on the date promised, kept to the announced subjects, and was in good health except for intermittent hoarseness.[28] Some of his most penetrating literary criticism is preserved in the printed manuscripts. Robinson, however, jotted down the following series of comments in his diary: [29]

The lecture was heavy . . . seemed to give general satisfaction . . . more entertainment than instruction . . . like his other lectures in most particulars, but rather less interesting . . . on Shakespeare and as usual interesting . . . convinced me that his circle of favorite ideas he is confined within as much as any man . . . more than usually prosing . . . much obscurity and metaphysics in the long introduction and not a little cant and commonplace in the short criticisms . . . digressed less than usually and really gave information and ideas about the poets he professed to criticize.

On the whole, the lectures seem not to have been extraordinary.

Coleridge did give extraordinary lectures, but they were not dependent upon inspiration from the audience or on any special method of preparation. They burst forth unheralded when theme and occasion and mood happened to form the right pattern. Robinson speaks of the lecture on education in 1808 as "most excellent, delivered with great animation and *extorting* praise from those whose prejudices he was mercilessly attacking. And he kept his audience on the rack of pleasure and offense two whole hours and ten minutes." [30] Of the seventh lecture in the course of 1811–1812, the same reporter says, "C. declaimed with great eloquence on *Love* without wandering from his subject, *Romeo and Juliet*. He was spirited; for the greater part intelligible, tho' profound; and he was methodical." [31] The twelfth lecture, on *Richard II* and *Hamlet*, he pronounced "perhaps his very best," [32] and he also praised highly the final lecture on Milton in the series of 1812–1813 at the Surrey Institution,[33] concerning which Coleridge himself wrote his wife, "I concluded my Lectures last night most triumphantly, with loud, long, and enthusiastic applauses at my entrance, and ditto in yet fuller chorus as, and for some minutes after I had retired. It was lucky that (as I never once thought of the Lecture till I had entered the Lecture Box) the two last were the most impressive and really the best." [34]

On such themes as education, love (especially as illustrated in *Romeo and Juliet*), moral unbalance (as in the character of Hamlet), and moral grandeur (as in the poems of Milton), he could speak effectively without specific preparation. If the occasion called for one of these themes, if his health was good, and if he was in the mood to establish a bond of sympathy with his hearers, he could give a performance that even the most unfriendly critic had to call splendid. Coleridge was still, as in his less coherent rhapsodies, giving out his "whole soul and spirit" and bathing the audience in the "spray of the outpouring"; [35] but the outpouring conformed more closely to the accepted pattern of a lecture.

Despite these occasional triumphs, Robinson's summary is fair: "Coleridge's lectures . . . are discreditable to him (perhaps I might use without injustice a stronger word) as a man who has a duty to discharge. . . . They are not a scientific or instructive course of readings on any one subject a man can wish to fix his attention on." [36] Judged as a fulfillment of his promises to the public, they were rightly received with bewilderment and disappointment.

To say this is not to deny, as Robinson hastens to point out, that these same discourses abounded in "brilliant thoughts, fine flashes of rhetoric, ingenious paradoxes, occasionally profound and salutary truths." [37] Listeners more interested in the man than in the specified subject, who came, like Mary Russell Mitford, merely to be "Coleridgeified," were quite content to hear about "Milton and Shakespeare, and criticism and poetry, and poets and critics, and whipping little boys, and love and philosophy, and every other subject that ever entered the head of man," [38] without any reference to a prospectus. They made no complaint about digressions, nor did they expect every passage to be crystal-clear, because they applied the standards of informal talk rather than the more rigid criteria of public speaking. To Cottle the lectures "were all of a conversational character, and were little more than the earnest harangues with which on all possible occasions, he indulged his friends." [39] Gillman judged them on precisely the same basis. "Coleridge's eloquence," he said, "when he gave utterance to his rich thoughts, flowing like some great river . . . so arrested his listeners, as at times to make them feel almost breathless. Such seemed the movement of Coleridge's words in lecture or in earnest discourse." [40] Even Robinson occasionally adopted this point of view and arrived at conclusions radically different from those he held when describing the lectures' effect on a general audience. Enrolling himself among the "small circle of friends who . . . listen with delight to his effusions," Robinson said that he seldom left Coleridge's lecture room without "the satisfaction which the hearkening to the display of truth in beautiful form always gives." [41]

Thus far we have looked at Coleridge's lectures primarily from the point of view of actual listeners. It is only fair to consider also what the speaker himself was trying to do, so that we may understand something about the working of Coleridge's mind as he attempted to present a subject orally to an audience.

There are several reasons why the seventh lecture in the series of 1811–1812, on *Romeo and Juliet*,[42] is well adapted to analysis. Collier's report, based on careful shorthand notes, is especially good, and has a double value because it is one of the few full-length transcripts of a Coleridgeian monologue.[43] Professor Raysor has discovered and printed a set of marginal notes that seem to be Coleridge's preliminary plan.[44] And we have Crabb Robinson's newspaper report for the *Morning Chronicle* [45] and one printed by James Amphlett in the *Rifleman*.[46]

Robinson, as has been indicated, called this lecture methodical. What he meant is clear from his summary in the *Chronicle*. So far as he could determine, Coleridge's purpose had been to discuss the characters of the play in the order of ascending importance: first Tybalt and Capulet, then Mercutio, then the Nurse, and last Romeo and Juliet. However, "Mr. C. postponed the examination of the hero and heroine of the

piece, but prefaced his inquiry by remarks on the nature of love. . . .
[He gave only a] partial illustration of this in the characters of Romeo
and Juliet." [47] Perhaps the notation in Robinson's diary after the word
"methodical" indicated his intention later to qualify the adjective.[48]

Amphlett discerned the presence of general principles beneath the
surface, but as a mere listener, debarred from studying a printed
record, he could not determine what they were. He therefore concluded that Coleridge wandered in a maze of digressions "till love
was lost in the boundless wilds of thought; and Shakespeare himself
disappeared in the ocean of human nature." [49]

Coleridge's actual plan for a lecture was so unlike that of the ordinary speaker that even a modern editor may be pardoned for failing
to suggest a connection between the jottings in Morgan's copy of Shakespeare and this lecture in the series of 1811–1812. Coleridge did not
make a logical analysis, as one might do in preparing an argument, nor
did he list a series of characters to be discussed or of topic sentences for
consecutive paragraphs. He made a list of general critical dicta which
he purposed to exemplify in *Romeo and Juliet;* and it may as well be
said at once that the same list might have been used, and certainly was
used in part, as the basis for discussing other plays.[50] Perhaps it is mere
coincidence that nearly all the dicta find expression and illustration in
this one lecture. At any rate, the juxtaposition of the list and Collier's
report will throw light on Coleridge's method of communication. The
marginal notes follow: [51]

1. [Characters] drawn from the . . . [?] faculties of the human mind,
the idea always *a priori,* tho' incarnated by observation *a posteriori et ab
extra.*

2. No appeals to appetites, but to the passions.
3. In the high road of nature.
4. The only poet, except Milton's Eve, who drew women as they are in
their incorruptible nature.
5. The only modern English poet who was both a poet and at the same
time a dramatic poet.
6. The only one who supplied all the beauties of the ancient chorus
without its defects and limitations; first, by the exquisite lyric inter-mixtures,
and second, by making general truths the outburst of passion.
7. Reverence for all the professions and established ranks and usages of
society—friar, physician, etc.
8. In very few instances mere monsters introduced, as in Goneril—and
then with what judgement.

9. Moral and prudential wisdom.
10. Comparative purity.

Let it be said again that these are not topic sentences but general critical judgments. We shall be led astray if we look for a paragraph concerning Number 1 and then a paragraph on Number 2. What Coleridge did was to keep them all in mind and to apply them whenever they seemed appropriate as he went along. The notion that Shakespeare drew his characters primarily from his own imagination rather than from accurate observation (No. 1) is carried through approximately half the lecture, whereas the generalization that he had reverence for all the professions (No. 7) calls forth a single paragraph on Friar Laurence. Similarly, many details throughout the lecture support the statement with which Coleridge began, that Shakespeare was both a poet and a dramatist (No. 5), while Shakespeare's appeals to passion rather than to appetites (No. 2) needed only brief specific mention in the long discussion of love. In this discussion are fused Shakespeare's comparative purity (No. 10), his delineation of women in their incorruptible nature (No. 4), and his use of the characters themselves, instead of a chorus, to incarnate moral truths (No. 6). When Coleridge has finished with love, however, he carries forward the discussion of Shakespeare's comparative purity (No. 10) and his method of supplanting the chorus (No. 6) into paragraphs on avarice and envy, and uses the same paragraphs to illustrate the dramatist's moral and prudential wisdom (No. 9). Only one item in the outline, the introduction of monsters (No. 8), fails to appear in the lecture, and the most general dictum, that Shakespeare was in the high road of nature (No. 3) permeates the whole.

It must be obvious that Coleridge, with his attention focused on a set of critical judgments applicable to all of Shakespeare's dramatic works, had a standard of relevance quite different from that of his audience, who had come to hear him analyze *Romeo and Juliet*. Powerful forces operated, especially since he spoke extemporaneously, to pull him away from the specific drama. He could find more effective illustrations of some of his dicta in other plays of Shakespeare, in works by other authors, and in his own observation of life. The temptation to use such material was doubly strong because he had propounded the same theses before and could remember excellent examples used in other contexts. It was much easier to restate the old than to search for new examples in the particular play before him. When he yielded to temptation he was often still within the confines of his own plan, though to the audience he seemed to be digressing.

For instance, the audience must have felt an abrupt leap from the relevant to the irrelevant when, toward the end of the lecture, Coleridge remarked that Shakespeare "never introduced the passion of avarice," and developed the paragraph by citing the Miser of Molière and Plautus, making no reference whatever to *Romeo and Juliet*.[52] Yet this passage, as has been suggested, carried forward two of the critical ideas on which the entire lecture was based, and paved the way for further discussion of a third in the next paragraph. This paragraph, dealing ostensibly with Greek tragedies, must have seemed to listeners a further departure from the main road.[53] How were they to perceive that during a considerable portion of the lecture Coleridge had been building toward the conclusion that in *Romeo and Juliet* Shakespeare used traits of the characters themselves to take the place of the Greek chorus? The general idea is nowhere clearly stated, and the clinching illustration, in a still later paragraph, comes from *Julius Caesar*.[54] The audience would probably have been even more puzzled if Coleridge had found time to complete the lecture as planned by declaring that Shakespeare rarely introduced monsters, and using as his example the character of Goneril in *King Lear* (No. 8).

One begins to understand H. N. Coleridge's insistence that the charge of habitual digressing, made particularly against Coleridge's talk, often implied lack of comprehension on the part of the listener rather than lack of purpose in the speaker's own mind.[55] In the best of his monologues Coleridge followed a plan. But his method was so subtle that only those long accustomed to his mental processes were able to apprehend it. Furthermore it was a method which called for firm control in order to suppress the centrifugal force that constantly threatened its disruption. If, as frequently happened, Coleridge did not have a set of general dicta firmly in mind before he began to speak, there was little to prevent the lecture from flying apart into a series of separate items without coherence or unity.

The sixth lecture of the same series [56] of 1811–1812 is an excellent example of one in which Coleridge, for a time at least, lost control. According to Robinson, the advertisements announced *Romeo and Juliet* and Shakespeare's female characters as the subject.[57] What Coleridge actually discussed has been outlined above by Miss Mitford. Robinson's outline is somewhat more detailed:

He began with a defense of school-flogging, at least in preference to Lancaster's mode of punishing. . . . Afterwards he remarked on the character of the age of Elizabeth and James 1st at the commencement, in which intellect predominated, over that of Charles 1st, in which moral feeling prevailed. He distinguished between wit and fancy . . . ; he discoursed on the character of the different languages of Europe, attacked the fashionable notion concerning poetic diction. . . . And he commented on the alleged impurity of Shakespeare and vindicated him against the charge with warmth!!!!! [58]

Anyone who paid for a ticket to learn something about *Romeo and Juliet* might have approved the exclamation points, and would probably have shared Robinson's pessimistic conclusion, "The man is absolutely incorrigible." [59]

Certainly the opening paragraphs on corporal punishment and on reading poetry with intonation are irrelevant, resurrected from previous lectures to amuse the audience while Coleridge tried to make up his mind what to say about Shakespeare. Then comes an interlude, perhaps caused by expressions of bewilderment and disgust on the faces before him. Coleridge assures his listeners that if he seems dogmatic, he is merely paying tribute to their intelligence; and he goes on to inform them that he really speaks better without preparation: "It is true that my matter may not be so accurately arranged: it may not dovetail and fit at all times as nicely as could be wished; but you shall have my thoughts warm from my heart, and fresh from my understanding." [60]

The remainder of the lecture is neither incoherent nor irrelevant by Coleridge's own standards. *Romeo and Juliet* must be discussed in the light of certain critical judgments on Shakespeare as a writer. It happened that the particular judgments at the head of the list could best be explained and enforced in general terms.

He begins by saying that men of genius confer transcendent benefits upon mankind. Two paragraphs later he is approaching his goal from another angle: "I have looked at the reign of Elizabeth, interesting on many accounts, with peculiar pleasure and satisfaction, because it furnished circumstances so favourable to the existence, and to the full development of the powers of Shakespeare." [61] But the times of Elizabeth cannot be thoroughly understood without glances at the times of Charles I and of Cromwell. The seeming digression leads to the paradoxical conclusion that the age of Elizabeth was not so favorable as others to the production of literature by men of talent, but that for a genius, for Shakespeare, it was helpful because it forced him to rely on his imagination. "He had only to imitate certain parts of his own character, or to exaggerate such as existed in possibility, and they [the characters he created] were at once true to nature, and fragments of the divine mind that drew them." [62]

With the development of this theme, Coleridge has classified Shakespeare as a genius, has placed him in his setting, and has explained by the interaction of genius and environment his "miraculous powers" of creating personages who seem to live lives of their own.[63] Next, quite logically, the lecturer discusses Shakespeare's medium, "the language of our country." [64] Since Coleridge is the lecturer, such a discussion inevitably includes the special qualities of French, German, Greek, Spanish, and Italian; but these are paragraphs of amplification, not digression. "In truth," he concludes, "English may be called the harvest of the unconscious wisdom of various nations. . . . Hence, the number of its passionate phrases—its metaphorical terms, not borrowed from poets, but adopted by them." [65] And to make the application directly to Shakespeare, the so-called "conceits" are not, as some critics have said, unnatural, but quite natural in Shakespeare's time. "Read any part of the works of our great dramatists, and the conviction comes upon you irresistibly, not only that what he puts into the mouths of his personages might have been said, but that it must have been said." [66]

There follows a long passage on the principles underlying wit and fancy, but all directly concerned with proving that Shakespeare had not the "talent which gives a sort of electric surprise by a mere turn of phrase" but "that higher ability which produces surprise by a permanent medium, and always leaves something behind it, which satisfies the mind as well as tickles the hearing." [67] The lecture ends with a brief defense of Shakespeare against the charges that his writings are indecent and immoral and that he could not portray women—items to be discussed at greater length on a future occasion.

The bulk of this lecture, from Coleridge's point of view, did not lack method. But his method took no account of the passage of time, and, as has been said, it tempted him to draw material from sources other than the play immediately before him. To his audience the discourse therefore seemed to have little if any relation to the subject announced. Other lectures, in this respect, were even worse. The quality of unexpectedness, so often remarked in Coleridge's monologues, might be caused either by subtlety of plan or by lack of plan.

There were likewise two possible causes for the same quality in Coleridge's sentences. To a shorthand reporter who complained that with the ordinary lecturer he could usually foretell from the first part of a sentence what the last part would be but that Coleridge continually surprised him, H. N. Coleridge replied, "It is the uncommonness of the thoughts or the image which prevents your anticipating the end." [68] His analysis applies well enough to examples like this:

Then lived Bacon, Burghley, Sir Walter Raleigh, Sir Philip Sidney, and a galaxy of great men, statesmen, lawyers, politicians, philosophers, and poets; and it is lamentable that they should have degraded their mighty powers to such base designs and purposes, dissolving the rich pearls of their great faculties in a worthless acid, to be drunken by a harlot.[69]

But there are other sentences, illustrating how Coleridge's mind worked when less rigidly controlled, that would try the ability and patience of the most efficient modern stenographer. Here is one:

O, when I think of [the] inexhaustible mine of virgin treasure in our Shakespeare, that I have been almost daily reading him since I was ten years old, that the thirty intervening years have been not fruitlessly and unintermittingly employed in the study of Greek, Latin, English, Italian, Spanish, and German *belle lettrists,* and for the last fifteen years far more intensely to the analysis of the laws of life and reasons as they exist in man, and that every step I have made forward in taste, number of facts, from history or my own observation, and in the knowledge of [the different laws] and the apparent exceptions [from] accidental collision [of] the disturbing forces of them, and know that at every new accession of knowledge, after every successful exercise of meditation, every fresh presentation of experience, I have unfailingly discovered a proportionate increase of wisdom and intuition in Shakespeare—when I know this, and know too that by a conceivable and possible, tho' hardly to be expected, arrangement of the British theatres, so large—*not* all indeed—but so large a proportion of this indefinite *all* (which no comprehension has yet drawn the line of circumscription so as to say to itself, I have seen *the whole*), might be sent into the heads and hearts, into the very souls, of the mass of mankind, to whom except by this living comment and interpretation it must remain for ever a sealed-up volume, a deep well without a wheel or windlass—it seems to me a pardonable enthusiasm to steal away from sober likelihood and share so rich a feast in the faëry world of possibility! [70]

This type of sentence structure occurs frequently in Coleridge's prose.

Although there is value in studying Coleridge's lectures as printed texts, it must never be forgotten that they were offered as courses of oral instruction on specific subjects, and that many of them which delight the reader today, and would also have delighted the informal gatherings at Lamb's, profoundly disappointed the ticket-holders at the Scots Corporation or the Crown and Anchor Tavern. Even Coleridge's friends who attended his best lectures considered him less effective on the platform than in the drawing-room. "I had heard the same things from Coleridge in private conversation," wrote Robinson, "and frequently in a better style than in the lecture itself." [71] Coleridge recorded a similar observation concerning his efforts in the pulpit. After a sermon he told Tom Poole, "One fellow remarked that he would rather hear me *talk* than *preach*." [72] Perhaps for the reason that De Quincey heard only a few lectures, most of them generally conceded to be among Coleridge's worst, he stated flatly that Coleridge "never once recovered that free and eloquent movement of thought which he could command at any time in private company." [73]

To the reasons De Quincy advanced—ill health and mental depression—must be added a third, the consciousness of attempting self-expression in unfavorable circumstances. Reports of numerous lectures contain apologies for repetition and digression and pleas that the audience will overlook other defects in material and presentation.[74] Coleridge's sense of failure to fulfill the promises of his prospectuses, intensified by the disapproval of his listeners, whether shown passively or, as sometimes happened, by heckling and other kinds of disturbance,[75] made it difficult for him to give his best.

William Godwin was too severe when he called the lectures "infinitely below his conversation in private company," [76] but he was merely exaggerating an opinion held by many of Coleridge's closest friends. With Cottle, who had heard him preach, lecture, and talk during many years, they concluded that "the parlour was the element for Mr. Coleridge." [77]

Matthew Arnold:

The Critic as Rhetorician

EVERETT LEE HUNT

MATTHEW ARNOLD'S reputation now rests upon his poetry and upon his criticism of literature. To his contemporaries he may have appeared to be, as Professor Garrod suggests, a successful writer upon educational, political and theological subjects who had once written poetry which nobody read, and who from time to time wrote literary criticism which not very many people read. But no one takes this view now, and Professor Garrod is the only contemporary critic I have found who seems to recognize the truth that the *Essays in Criticism* were by-products of a talent interested primarily in something else. And even Professor Garrod writes:

Most of the questions in which Matthew Arnold was interested no longer interest anybody. His theological writings are, save so far as he is our only artist in theology, no longer vital. When he first wrote on education, there was none—it is perhaps not his fault that there is now too much. How changed is the face of politics and society I need not say; if there is any real break in the continuity of English political history, it falls between Matthew Arnold and ourselves. . . . A hundred years hence Arnold's writings will be interesting from their readability and from their temper, the temper of a man of letters consistently looking at the world in the manner which literature had taught him.[1]

I cannot agree with this dictum that most of Arnold's prose now possesses historical interest only, and it does not come within the limits

322

of this essay to dispute with those critics who insist that the significance of Arnold's poetry and literary criticism has now also become historical. I am content with citing Professor Garrod's view as the typically literary one that permanence is a *sine qua non* of value, that the glory of literature is that it endures, while scientific hypotheses and social theories become transformed and absorbed. It is not strange, then, that most of Arnold's prose is dismissed by critics as mere rhetoric, and is ascribed to those lamentable weaknesses which lead genius to waste its abilities.

To the student of rhetoric, apparently, most of Arnold's prose is consigned, and such a student will have his reward; but beyond that I shall show, I think, that the literary critic may have a better understanding of Arnold and of the art of criticism if he will be less careful of his literary boundaries.

De Quincey, who had given some days and nights to Aristotle, classifies rhetoric into an *ars utens* and an *ars docens*.[2] For the purpose of this essay I should like to add a third type which De Quincey also discussed in an introductory paragraph, namely, the abuses of writing and speaking which in general are adequately condemned when referred to as mere rhetoric. These distinctions will be clear, I believe, if they are here treated (in reverse order) as the rhetoric which Arnold attacked, the rhetoric he taught, and the rhetoric he used in his own appeals to the public.

The Aristotelian conception of rhetoric, so familiar to De Quincey, has largely disappeared from contemporary criticism, but to most readers of this book it will not be necessary to amplify the statement that in studying Arnold as a rhetorician it is primarily the Aristotelian rhetoric I have in mind. This rhetoric was not in Arnold's mind, apparently, for all his evident familiarity with Plato, with Aristotle's *Ethics* and *Politics*, and for all his father's love of the *Rhetoric*.[3] In considering Arnold's attacks on rhetoric it is his own, the prevalent and popular conception, that we are discussing. In the other divisions the connotations of the term change to the Aristotelian. I should use the term criticism in a general sense if I could rest upon any such clear conception as we have of the Aristotelian rhetoric, but this unfortunately is not the case. It will be safer to limit ourselves to the Arnoldian criticism, and to say that the relation of Aristotelian rhetoric to Arnoldian criticism will be fairly clear if it is recognized that the study of the means which the critic takes to commend to the public the best that has been said and thought in the world belongs to the province of rhetoric. A rigorous intellectual discussion of whether what is commended really is the best that has been said and thought belongs to criticism, or in Aristotelian terms, to dialectic.[4] Where, as in Arnold's case, the critic freely employs what Aristotle calls the topics, or commonplaces of rhetoric, it will be necessary to separate the rhetoric from the criticism and attempt to relate them.

How great a part rhetoric plays in Arnoldian criticism is clear from the conclusion of "Sweetness and Light."

> The great men of culture are those who have had a passion for diffusing, for making prevail, for carrying from one end of society to the other, the best knowledge, the best ideas of their time; who have laboured to divest knowledge of all that was harsh, uncouth, difficult, abstract, professional, exclusive; to humanize it, to make it efficient outside the clique of the cultivated and learned, yet still remaining the *best* knowledge and thought of the time.[5]

Arnold apparently felt that the men who carry the best knowledge from one end of society to the other might also be the men to determine whether or not it was the best knowledge. The processes of discovery and of persuasion were often, to Arnold, identical. He was quite capable of defending an unsystematic method of presentation by an appeal to the intuitive method of discovering truth. But he was also willing to acknowledge his indebtedness to scholars when he was popularizing their work, insisting only that he transformed their results with his literary tact and a quick perception, the result of wide, humane reading. With the growth of specialization the contributions of "literary tact" to any study are viewed with suspicion, and the Arnoldian critic is accused of being a purveyor of literary loose talk, a practitioner of the higher charlatanry.[6] This essay, then, is only a beginning of a more general study of the relations of criticism, rhetoric, and scientific method.

I

It was the fact that Arnold did appeal to the public that gives us the opportunity to study him as a rhetorician. For Walter Pater, the critic was a scholar writing for scholars; the cultivation of his readers, if not his own taste, would forbid his use of the more obvious tricks of rhetoric; he removed himself entirely, or liked to think that he did, from the realms of the charlatan. But Matthew Arnold, like Gilbert and Sullivan, addressed the "lower middle classes"; like Socrates, he talked in the market place about conduct; and like Socrates, too, he was in danger of being called a sophist. It is not strange that Plato's distinctions between the philosopher and the rhetorician were constantly in Arnold's mind. He competed with Cobden and Bright, Spurgeon and Gladstone, Moody and Sankey, even, for the attention of the British Philistine; but he wanted it understood that he did it with a difference. He liked to quote Plato's remark that Socrates was the only true politician in Athens. This applied to himself, Arnold seems to have felt; but he preferred to be known as a critic.

The basis of Arnold's attacks upon the rhetoricians, among whom he included most of the contemporary journalists and political leaders, was the Platonic conception of rhetoric as a flattery.[7] He summarizes Plato for his readers in his *Higher Schools and Universities in Germany.*[8]

Nay, as Socrates amusingly said, the man who defers to clap-trap and the man who uses his intelligence are, when they meet in the struggle of active politics, like a doctor and a confectioner competing for the suffrages of a constituency of schoolboys; the confectioner has nearly every point in his favor. The confectioner deals in all that the constituency likes; the doctor is the man who hurts them, and makes them leave off what they like and take what is disagreeable. And accordingly the temptation, in dealing with the public and with the trade of active politics, the temptation to be a confectioner is extremely strong, and we see that almost all leading newspapers and leading politicians do in fact yield to it.

This Arnold develops further as one of the reasons why journalistic comparisons of domestic and foreign institutions can rarely be trusted. The journalist is a confectioner intent on pleasing his own readers; all comparisons must and do flatter the home country and the truth is not in them. Various critics have suggested that Arnold was not above rhetoric in pointing his own comparisons the other way, and he might, I think, have admitted this, but with the Platonic reply that if there was some deception in his rhetoric it was for the good of his countrymen.

The national habit of self-deception by laying a flattering unction to the soul is, by a rather peculiar use of the term *pedantic* (borrowed from Goethe), attributed to the English people as characteristic of their treatment of the Irish.

No, the English are pedants, and will proceed in the way of pedantry as long as they can. They will not ask themselves what really meets the wants

of a case, but they will ask what may be done without offending the prejudices of their classes and parties, and then they will agree to say to one
another and to the world that this is what really meets the wants of the case,
and that it is the only thing to be done.[9]

The systematic development of the baneful effects of rhetoric as a
flattery is to be found in *Culture and Anarchy*. It is true that the habits
and instincts of the British do not tend to make them spontaneous
lovers of sweetness and light, but they might be brought to it with
the aid of a few effective critics, if it were not that the rhetoricians
constantly flatter them into contentment with their imperfect condition.
The critic gives us what we need so lamentably in these anarchic times,
a real principle of authority in the state as the affirmation of our best
selves, of national right reason. Such a state knows no classes and
operates to encourage the pursuit of perfection. It overlooks and over-
comes the very ordinary selves of the Barbarians, the Philistines and
the Populace, who, when acting at the dictates of the ordinary self,
struggle to govern the state in the interests of class. But rhetoricians
keep themselves in power by flattering the weaknesses of each of the
classes, their natural dislike of any authority but their own, their natural
leaning toward lawlessness and bathos. Because of these rhetoricians,
and Arnold often names them,

the Barbarians remain in the belief that the great broad-shouldered Englishman may well be satisfied with himself; the Philistines remain in the belief
that the great middle class of this country, with its earnest common-sense
penetrating through sophisms and ignoring common-places, may well be
satisfied with itself; the Populace, that the working man with his bright
powers of sympathy and ready powers of action, may well be satisfied with
himself. . . . Thus everything in our political life tends to hide from us
that there is anything wiser than our ordinary selves, and to prevent our
getting the notion of a paramount right reason.[10]

Not only are the weaknesses of particular classes and organizations
flattered by the rhetoricians, but those weaknesses which extend
through all classes of society are made the common topics of patriotic
oratory to the great increase of national complacency. Doctrines and
pursuits entirely unworthy of a place as ends in themselves receive
the blesssings of the rhetoricians. All of those discouraging phenomena to be classed under the heading of machinery—worship of irre-
sponsible freedom, the pursuit of wealth, of bodily health and vigor,
of increase of population, the energetic activities of religious and

political organizations—all these come to be valued as ends in themselves because of the rhetoricians, some of whom know no better, but many of whom are industriously grinding axes of their own.

As Arnold proceeds in his attack upon the enemies of culture it becomes more and more apparent that every one of these enemies receives aid and comfort from the rhetoricians, that Arnold regards the critic as a sort of Socratic gad-fly to sting the national complacency, and that the contrast between the rhetorician and the cultured critic had its prototype in Plato's contrast between the rhetorician and the philosopher. The citation of Socrates as the exemplar for the critic, at the conclusion of *Culture and Anarchy,* would seem to warrant the belief that Arnold was quite consciously drawing his criticism of the British from Plato's indictment of the Athenians. I do not understand why he chose Pericles as the orator when he might have heightened the contrast by choosing an obviously sophistical speaker, unless in his enthusiasm he meant to condemn all oratory.

Pericles was perhaps the most perfect public speaker who ever lived, for he was the man who most perfectly combined thought and wisdom with feeling and eloquence. Yet Plato brings in Alcibiades declaring that men went away from the oratory of Pericles, saying it was very fine, it was very good, and afterwards thinking no more about it; but they went away from hearing Socrates talk, he says, with the point of what he had said sticking fast in their minds, and they could not get rid of it. Socrates has drunk his hemlock and is dead; but in his own breast does not every man carry about a possible Socrates, in that power of a disinterested play of consciousness upon his stock notions and habits, of which this wise and admirable man gave all through his lifetime the great example, and which was the secret of his incomparable influence? And he who leads men to call forth and exercise themselves in this power, and who busily calls it forth and exercises it in himself, is at the present moment, perhaps, as Socrates was in his time, more in concert with the vital workings of men's minds, and more effectually significant, than any House of Commons orator, or practical operator in politics.[11]

Macaulay always seemed to Arnold to carry the spirit of the "practical operator in politics" into literature, and the references to him are usually by way of deprecating his influence as a rhetorician. He was unfair to Macaulay at times, but in his discussion of the famous essay on Milton the distinction between rhetoric and criticism transcends the attack upon any particular writer, and asserts that flattery in the realm of culture is quite as powerful as in the sphere of political action.

Human progress consists in a continual increase in the number of those, who, ceasing to live by the animal life alone and to feel the pleasure of sense only, come to participate in the intellectual life also, and to find enjoyment in the things of the mind. The enjoyment is not at first very discriminating. Rhetoric, brilliant writing, gives to such persons pleasure for its own sake; but it gives them pleasure, still more, when it is employed in commendation of a view of life which is on the whole theirs, and of men and causes with which they are naturally in sympathy. The immense popularity of Macaulay is due to his being preëminently fitted to give pleasure to all who are beginning to feel enjoyment in the things of the mind. It is said that the traveler in Australia, visiting one settler's hut after another finds again and again that the settler's third book, after the Bible and Shakespeare, is some work by Macaulay. Nothing can be more natural. The Bible and Shakespeare may be said to be imposed upon an Englishman as objects of his admiration; but as soon as the common English, desiring culture, begins to choose for himself, he chooses Macaulay. Macaulay's view of things is, on the whole, the view of them which he feels to be his own also; the persons and causes praised are those which he himself is disposed to admire; the persons and causes blamed are those with which he is out of sympathy; and the rhetoric employed to praise or blame them is animating and excellent. Macaulay is thus a great civilizer. In hundreds of men he hits their nascent taste for the things of the mind, possesses himself of it and stimulates it, draws it powerfully forth and confirms it. But with the increasing number of those who awake to the intellectual life, the number of those also increases, who, having awoke to it follow where it leads them. And it leads them to see that it is their business to learn the truth about the important men, and things, and books, which interest the human mind. For thus is gradually to be acquired a stock of sound ideas, in which the mind will habitually move, and which alone can give to our judgments security and solidity. To be satisfied with fine writing about the objects of one's study, with having it praised or blamed in accordance with one's own likes or dislikes, with any conventional treatment of it whatever, is at this stage of growth seen to be futile. At this stage, rhetoric, even when it is as good as Macaulay's, dissatisfies. And the number of people who have reached this stage of mental growth is constantly, as things are now, increasing. . . . So that while the number of those who are delighted with rhetoric is always increasing, the number of those who are dissatisfied with it is always increasing, too.[12]

Macaulay, Arnold regards as a "born rhetorician" who lacks all the qualities of a critic. There are critics, however, and good ones, who, though not born rhetoricians, have hurt their criticism by speaking the language of rhetoric. This is as much an indictment of the British people as it is of the critics. In France it is not necessary for a critic to adopt the rhetorical violence of the "provincial spirit":

M. Planche's advantage is, that he feels himself to be speaking before competent judges, that there is a force of cultivated opinion for him to appeal to. Therefore he must not be extravagant, and he need not storm; he must satisfy the reason and the taste, that is his business. Mr. Palgrave, on the other hand, feels himself to be speaking before a promiscuous multitude, with the few good judges so scattered through it as to be powerless; therefore, he has no calm confidence and no self-control; he relies on the strength of his lungs, he knows that big words impose on the mob, and that, even if he is outrageous, most of his audience are apt to be a great deal more so.[13]

This might be a characterization of the methods of Mr. Mencken rather than those of a gentle anthologist; the description of the results of this style is even more applicable to the Mencken school. The cause in both cases is the same, a critical intelligence, speaking on issues of criticism, but using the rhetorical language of the hustings. Such a style

does not persuade, it makes war; it has no urbanity, the tone of the city, of the centre, the tone which always aims at spiritual and intellectual effect, and not excluding the use of banter, never disjoins banter itself from politeness, from felicity. . . . Even if its view is right, the note is violence; for abandoning the true mode of intellectual action—persuasion, the instilment of conviction,—it simply astounds and irritates the hearer by contradicting without a word of proof or preparation, his fixed and familiar notions; and this is mere violence.[14]

But even worse than the lack of persuasiveness is the critic's loss of ability to see things as they are when he rushes into practical affairs with the vehemence of the rhetorician.

A polemical practical criticism makes men blind even to the ideal imperfection of their practise, makes them willingly assert its ideal perfection, in order better to secure it against attack.[15]

Cobbett, "blackened as he is with the smoke of a life-long conflict in the field of political practice," Carlyle, "after his furious raid into the field with his *Latter Day Pamphlets*," and Ruskin, "after his pugnacious political economy," have sacrificed their power to see things as they are, and would be generally misunderstood if they even attempted to return to the method of sweet reasonableness.

Rhetoricians, then, as practical men of action, are so given to flattering the ordinary selves of the Barbarians, Philistines and Populace, that the voice of the critic, urging them to the pursuit of perfection, is hardly heard. But the critic, with his more sensitive audience, must not adopt the tone and manner of the rhetorician, lest he lose both truth and persuasiveness.

II

Indignant at the victories of flattery, many honest souls have denounced persuasion and all its works. Plato has made Socrates a hero in the eyes of the generations by a rhetorical account of the bravery with which the philosopher, at his great trial, denounced the methods of the rhetoricians and irritated an Athenian jury into sentencing him to death. But even Plato afterward admitted that there might be a noble rhetoric by which people could be persuaded of that which was acceptable to God and the philosophers. This nobility of purpose explains the seriousness with which Arnold regarded his own persuasiveness, or as I shall call it, his rhetoric.

Arnold was singularly free from pose and affectation in his letters to his family, and I shall cite two letters to show the seriousness of his purpose in attempting to influence public opinion in England. These and similar utterances are taken by some contemporary critics as an indication of a Messiah complex in Arnold's mind, but I am not now so much concerned with contemporary attitudes toward high seriousness as I am with establishing the basis of what I shall call Arnold's rhetorical purpose. In January, 1865, when most of his reputation was still to be achieved, Arnold wrote his sister, "K":

Indeed, I am convinced that *Science*, in the widest sense of the word, meaning a knowledge of things as the basis of our operations, becomes, as it does become, more of a power in the world, the weight of the nations and men who have carried the intellectual life farthest will be more and more felt; indeed, I see signs of this already. That England may run well in this race is my deepest desire; and to stimulate her and to make her feel how many clogs she wears, and how much she has to do in order to run it as her genius gives her power to run, is the object of all I do.[16]

In November of the same year, Arnold wrote another sister, "Fan":

I have a conviction that there is a real, an almost imminent danger of England losing immeasurably in all ways, declining into a sort of greater Holland, for want of what I must call ideas, for want of perceiving how the world is going and must go, and preparing herself accordingly. This conviction haunts me, and at times overwhelms me with depression; I would rather not live to see the change come to pass, for we shall all deteriorate under it. While there is time I shall do all I can, and in every way, to prevent its coming to pass.

Sometimes, no doubt, turning oneself one way after another, one must make unsuccessful and unwise hits, and one may fail after all; but try I must, and I know that it is only by facing in every direction that one can win the day.[17]

Beside these expressions of serious resolve should be placed certain earlier expressions of doubt and dissatisfaction with his direct assault upon public opinion. A year earlier he had written Grant Duff:

One is from time to time seized and irresistibly carried along by the temptation to treat political, or religious, or social matters, directly; but after yielding to such a temptation I always feel myself recoiling again, and disposed to touch them only so far as they can be touched through poetry.[18]

Two years before this, in 1862, he had written his mother:

I had much rather avoid all the sphere of dispute. One begins by saying something, and if one believes it to be true one cannot well resist the pleasure of expanding it when it is controverted; but I had rather live in purer air than that of controversy, and when I have done two more things I must do—an article on Middle Class Education and one on Academies (such as the French Academy) both of which will raise opposition and contradiction—I mean to leave this region altogether and to devote myself wholly to what is positive and happy, not negative and contentious, in literature.[19]

And in 1861, he wrote:

I must finish off for the present my critical writings between this and forty, and give the next ten years earnestly to poetry. It is my last chance. It is not a bad ten years of one's life if one resolutely uses it, but it is a time in which, if one does not use it, one dries up and becomes prosaic altogether.[20]

Toward the end of his life, when it had become evident that he would not add to the production of his earlier years in poetry, and that the energy remaining to him after his retirement from his school inspectorship would continue to be spent in addressing the public on general questions, how did he feel about it? In 1887, when he was sixty-four, and had expressed various premonitions that he had not much longer to live, he wrote Charles Eliot Norton:

I do not know whether I shall do any more poetry, but it is something to be of use in prose, and by coming out from time to time as the organ of "the body of quiet, reasonable people," I believe I do some good.[21]

This conflict in Arnold's mind, with the progressive victory for persuasive prose, is not adequately explained nor sympathetically treated by the literary critics, and it is not a problem that calls for discussion here except to say that Arnold would not have devoted so much energy to his social, political and theological criticism if he had agreed with the scholars of his day, and many of the scholar-critics of ours, on the unimportance of persuading the public of anything. The sense of what he was losing in poetry may have strengthened his tendency to see himself saving England with his prose, but his view of persuasion as an aspect of character and an instrument of truth, in which he was virtually taking up the cause of Isocrates against Plato,[22] is needed by critics who regard their function as purely aesthetic.

The rhetoric which Arnold taught in this campaign for culture in England, he taught chiefly to himself in his reflections upon persuasion and persuasiveness. The Letters continue to be the chief source. In October, 1863, shortly after he had had some evidence that his essay on Heine had been well received, he wrote his mother:

> It is very animating to think that one at last has a chance of *getting at* the English public. Such a public as it is, and such a work as one wants to do with it! Partly nature, partly time and study have also by this time taught me thoroughly the precious truth that everything turns upon one's exercising the power of *persuasion, of charm;* that without this all fury, energy, reasoning, power, acquirement, are thrown away and only render their owner more miserable. Even in one's ridicule one must preserve a sweetness and good humour.[23]

In November of the same year he writes his sister, Mrs. Forster, that he will do what he can in literature to further the movement her husband is supporting in Parliament "with the risk always before me that if I cannot charm the wild beast of Philistinism while I am trying to convert him, of being torn to pieces by him." [24]

Again in January, 1864, he wrote her:

> I have the second part of my *French Eton* in this next *Macmillan*. It will take a third part to finish it. In this part I am really labouring hard to *persuade,* and have kept myself from all which might wound, provoke or frighten, with a solicitude which I think you will hardly fail to perceive, and which will perhaps amuse you; but to school oneself to this forbearance is an excellent discipline if one does it for the right objects.[25]

This disciplinary aspect of the attempt to be persuasive recalls the view of Isocrates that in the attempt to be persuasive one becomes virtuous. Arnold repeats his idea in a letter written the same month to his mother, replying to her compliments on his *Joubert:*

I would far rather have it said how delightful and interesting a man Joubert was than how brilliant my article is. In the long run one makes enemies by having one's brilliancy and ability praised; one can only get oneself really accepted by men by making oneself forgotten in the people and the doctrines one recommends. I have had this much before my mind in doing the second part of my *French Eton*. I really want to *persuade* on this subject, and I have felt how necessary it was to keep down many and many sharp and telling things that rise to one's lips, and which one would gladly utter if one's object was to show one's abilities. . . . I think such an effort a moral discipline of the very best sort for one.[26]

The moral discipline of the attempt to be persuasive is the first of Arnold's important generalizations about persuasion. The second is that the intuitive as opposed to the logical method of persuasion is best both for discovering and for teaching truth. Writing to his mother in December, 1864, Arnold discusses a vigorous attack made upon his "Function of Criticism" by Fitzjames Stephen.[27]

His complaint that I do not argue reminds me of dear old Edward, who always says when any of his family do not go his way, that they do not reason. However, my sinuous, easy, unpolemical mode of proceeding has been adopted by me, first, because I really think it the best way of proceeding if one wants to get at, and keep with, truth; secondly, because I am convinced that only by a literary form of this kind being given to them can ideas such as mine ever gain any access in a country such as ours.[28]

Another statement of this method, often quoted, is at the conclusion of the introduction to *Culture and Anarchy*.

Therefore I propose now to try to inquire, in the simple unsystematic way which best suits my taste, what culture really is.

When Frederic Harrison took Arnold to task in the best of satires on culture for his want of systematic reasoning,[29] Arnold took a malicious pleasure in lamenting frequently and ironically his want of what Harrison had rather pretentiously called "a system of philosophy with principles coherent, interdependent, subordinate and derivative."

Arnold's preference for his method of composition, as for his method of thought, though often expressed in bantering mood, represented a deep-seated conviction. In the Preface to his *Essays in Criticism*, he writes:

It is not in my nature—some of my critics would rather say, not in my power—to dispute on behalf of any opinion, even my own, very obstinately. To try and approach Truth on one side after another, not to persist in pressing forward, on any one side, with violence and self will—it is only thus, it seems to me, that mortals may hope to gain any vision of the mysterious goddess, whom we shall never see, except in outline. He who will do nothing but fight impetuously toward her in his own, one, favorite, particular line is inevitably destined to run his head into the black robe in which she is wrapped.

But the truth is, I have never been able to hit it off happily with the logicians, and it would be mere affectation in me to give myself the airs of doing so. They imagine truth something to be proved, I something to be seen; they something to be manufactured, I something to be found. I have a profound respect for intuitions, and a very lukewarm respect for the elaborate machine-work of my friends the logicians. I have always thought that all which was worth much in this elaborate machine-work of theirs came from an intuition, to which they gave a name of their own. How did they come by this intuition? Ah! if they would tell us that. But no: they set their machine in motion and build up a fine showy edifice, glittering and unsubstantial like a pyramid of eggs; and then they say: "Come and look at our pyramid!" And what does one find in it? Of all that heap of eggs, the one poor little fresh egg, the original intuition, has got hidden away far out of sight and forgotten. And all the other eggs are addled.[30]

These intuitions, though non-rational in origin, are not revelations, they do not come to the untrained and unlettered mind. They come from literary tact, the result of wide reading in the best books. This is a favorite doctrine of Arnold's. It is his justification for faith in his own conclusions in religion against those of the theological specialists; for trusting his own taste rather than that of highly specialized Greek scholars in questions relating to the translation of Homer; and for believing that he was really a better politician than contemporary men of affairs. So many passages might be cited that selection is difficult; I quote the conclusion of the introduction to *Literature and Dogma:*

For the good of letters may be had without skill in arguing, or that formidable logical apparatus, not unlike a guillotine, which Professor Huxley speaks of somewhere as the young man's best companion. . . . But the valuable thing in letters . . . is, as we have often remarked, the judgment which forms itself in a fair mind along with fresh knowledge. . . . For this judgment comes almost of itself; and what it displaces it displaces easily and naturally, and without any turmoil of controversial reasonings. . . . So that minds with small aptitude for abstruse reasoning may yet, through letters, gain some hold on sound judgment and useful knowledge, and may even clear up blunders committed, out of their very excess of talent, by the athletes of logic.

The numerous other references to persuasion in the letters and prose works show how much the subject was in Arnold's mind; their chief addition to the theory is the almost complacent belief in charm, mildness, sweet reasonableness as a method.[31] In January, 1866, he wrote his mother:

The best of this country is that if you say truth as it ought to be said it is sure with time to take effect.[32]

In citing the example of Jesus to those bitter religious controversialists whose spirit seemed to be devoid of the mildness and sweet reasonableness appropriate to Christian character and Christian rhetoric, Arnold, strangely enough, makes an important exception to his principle of persuasion by charm:

Now, there can be no doubt whatever, that in his invectives against the Scribes and Pharisees Jesus abandoned the mild, uncontentious, winning, inward mode of working which was his true characteristic, and in which his charm and power lay; and that there was no chance at all of gaining by such invectives the persons at whom they were launched. . . . What may fairly be said is, that the Pharisees against whom Jesus denounced his woes . . . were the people whom there could be no hope of gaining; and that not *their* conversion but a strong impression on the faithful who read or heard, was the thing aimed at, and very rightly aimed at.[33]

This rhetoric of "a strong impression on the faithful" by a denunciation of opponents was a common phenomenon of democratic life before the time of Paul and Jesus; it will probably continue to flourish with or without the sanction of their example, and it is just what Arnold lacked. Arnold never "spoke out." [34]

Arnold's growing faith in the power of mildness and charm may have been responsible for his surprising docility in attempting to learn the art of public speaking during his American tour,[35] after so many years of scorning the orator. In November, 1883, he wrote his sister from Boston:

I wrote last from New York, before my last lecture. I was badly heard, and many people were much disappointed; but they remained to the end, were perfectly civil and attentive, and applauded me when I had done. It made me doubtful about going on with lecturing, however, as I felt I could not maintain a louder pitch of voice than I did in Chickering Hall. . . . There is a good deal to be learned as to the management of the voice, however, and I have set myself to learn it, though I am old to begin. Last night I gave my New York lecture here. I spoke much better than at New York and shall improve much further, I hope.[36]

A week later he wrote again to Mrs. Forster:

The night before last I dined and slept at Barnum's. He said my lecture was *grand*, and that he was determined to belong to the *remnant;* that term is going the round of the United States, and I understand what Dizzy meant when he said I performed a "great achievement" by launching phrases. My love to William. Tell him it is curious to find how one is driven here to study the "technique" of speaking, and how one finds it may be learnt like other things. I could not make myself heard at first, but I am improving. A Professor Churchill, said to be "the best elocutionist in the United States," came twice from Andover to Boston on purpose to try and be of use to me, because, he said, he had got more pleasure from F. Robertson, Ruskin, and me than from any other men. This will give you a good notion of their kindness.[37]

Three weeks later he was quite sure of himself, and wrote to Charles J. Leaf:

The papers in England seem, by what you say, to have made too much of the failure in audibility at the first lecture; it never really endangered my success, as every one who read the report of the lecture was interested; I had no doubt that I could be heard with a little trouble. The "elocution lessons" were merely that a theological professor here, who is a capital speaker himself, and who is interested in me from my writings, went twice for twenty minutes to the hall with me when it was empty, heard me read, and stopped me when I dropped my voice at the end of sentences, which was the great trouble. I get along all right now, and have never failed *to draw* for a moment.[38]

Other criticisms led Arnold to realize that he had not quite mastered the "technique" of speaking in two twenty-minute sessions. Nearly a year later, some time after he had returned to England, he wrote his sister:

How very right you were about what you called my "too solemn," and poor Mr. Carnegie my "ministerial" manner in speaking. Since I have spoken so much, I perceive that it is my great defect, inasmuch as it strikes every one. Harper's Magazine goes so far as to say that just because I am irresistibly agreeable to read, I ought never to speak, because speaking is a line in which

I am imperfect. I was talking about this to Huxley, and he said that for years he had made the mere manner of speaking his perpetual study; but then, he said, he regarded speaking as to be his business in life.[39]

But all this willingness to learn the art of public speaking—or in his case, really, public reading—does not mean that he was willing to become a speech-maker in the ordinary sense. On his return from America he was in demand as a speaker, and might have spent his time addressing audiences, but he wrote to Sydney Buxton, M. P.:

I am refusing every invitation to lecture and make addresses this year or I shall never establish my freedom. It is the duty of a public man to appear in public, and he has many compensations; but I am not a public man, and the "saying a few words" which to a public man seems the most natural thing in the world, is to me an artificial and unnatural performance, quite out of my line.[40]

III

In Arnold's own time the irritation caused by his manners and mannerisms, and the hostility of the non-conformist theologians, liberal politicians, and conservatives who feared state action in education, led to the creation of a stereotype of an ineffectual reformer of the "kid-glove persuasion," a characterization about as far from the truth as Arnold's famous phrase on Shelley as the beautiful and ineffectual angel. In our time the criticism of Arnold is conducted by scholars writing for scholars. If we regard him for the time being simply as a rhetorician, and ask who it was that he was trying to persuade, and of what, we shall come to a better understanding of his purposes, the first requisite for intelligent criticism.

When Arnold referred to his efforts with the great English public, he meant ultimately, of course, the whole nation; but his direct influence he knew would be limited to a small portion of it, the saving remnant, the small group of intelligent folk to be found in all three classes, the Barbarians, the Philistines, and the Populace. In discussing political measures he often talked of the power of the opinion of the quiet folk, who did not rush into public meetings, but whose opinion in the long run carried great weight. An idea of this audience may be gained by reading the articles of contemporary contributors to *Macmillan's*, the *Edinburgh Review, Fortnightly, Quarterly Review, Nineteenth Century, Cornhill, Contemporary Review,* and others. Such essays, I think, represent a higher standard of thought and expression than the magazine articles of today, and largely because they were written for different readers. The subjects that the nineteenth century critics wrote upon are discussed today in technical journals in technical language. The growing specialization of scholarship with an accompanying growth in the organizations of scholars has produced a large number of small, highly specialized groups of readers very different from the general reader of the nineteenth century. These technical essays are doubtless necessary to the advancement of thought and learning; but writing for such specialized groups has its unfortunate effects upon style and thought. The path from criticism to scholarship to pedantry is short and easy.

The point of this apparent excursus is that it has become difficult for our critics to place Arnold. He was more learned than our journalists, and not so learned as our professors. His style was admirably adapted to a group of readers that seems to have disappeared; his function now seems to be to introduce college freshmen to culture. Even here we edit him carefully. It is well to read *On Translating Homer* edited by a classical scholar and learn that Arnold's theory of the unity of the authorship of Homer is not held by present-day scholars. It is well to be cautioned against rash generalizations in *Celtic Literature* by the learned editor. It would also be well to have it pointed out that Arnold was not writing or speaking as a professor,[41] that these topics in which he was in error were incidental to his main purpose, which was to persuade an audience of the general readers of the nineteenth century of the wisdom of certain general ideas usually relating to conduct. His real subject matter was in the realm of Aristotelian rhetoric, of probability, of ethics and politics, and not in the realm of scholarship. This, of course, does not mean that his errors should be overlooked. He was himself anxious that the knowledge he commended should be the best knowledge. But look for a moment at the rhetorical purposes of the works which chiefly interest scholars today.

On Translating Homer is, I suppose, the most scholarly of his works, the one in which he was most competent to deal with his subject, and with a theme which was chiefly interesting to scholars. It is the book which usually comes off best when in the hands of critics. It is not surprising, then, that it has the smallest element of rhetorical purpose. And yet there were two rhetorical aims, I believe, that animated Arnold in these lectures. They were, first, to show that the critic, by whom he means such generally well-read, sensitive and cultivated persons as himself, is a different and often better judge of poetry than the professional scholar; and, secondly, to exalt the grand style as an instrument in forming character.

Arnold's attacks on scholars are almost as numerous and vigorous as the attacks on rhetoricians. In this middle ground of the critic he again calls to mind Isocrates contending with both philosopher and sophist. But it will not do to suggest that the Arnoldian critic is a mere middleman. He has too great a source of authority in his own intuitions for that. He is quite willing to accept the products of the scholars when they serve his purposes, but he is more than willing to point out the limitations of their work. Numerous passages from *On Translating Homer* might be cited to show that scholarship is not enough, that the philological view is likely to be insensitive and uncreative, but I take only the most famous sentences:

Much as Mr. Newman was mistaken when he talked of my rancour, he is entirely right when he talks of my ignorance. And yet, perverse as it seems to say so, I sometimes find myself wishing, when dealing with matters of poetical criticism, that my ignorance were even greater than it is. To handle these matters properly there is needed a poise so perfect that the least overweight in any direction tends to destroy the balance. Temper destroys it, a crotchet destroys it, even erudition may destroy it. . . . Little as I know, therefore, I am always apprehensive in dealing with poetry, lest even that little should "prove too much for my abilities." [42]

The other great concern of Arnold's, the ethical value of the grand style, is not fully developed here; indeed Arnold nowhere develops it adequately, but it is stated about as fully as Arnold puts it anywhere; its frequent repetition indicates that it was a favorite notion.

The grand style, which is Homer's, is something more than touching and stirring; it can form the character, it is edifying. The old English Balladist may stir Sir Philip Sidney's heart like a trumpet, and this is much; but Homer, but the few artists in the grand style, can do more; they can refine the raw natural man, they can transmute him. So it is not without cause that I say, and say again, to the translator of Homer: "Never for a moment suffer yourself to forget our fourth fundamental proposition, *Homer is noble*." [43]

In expressing this distrust of the authority of the scholar, and the belief in the formative power of great poetry, Arnold is not speaking on matters of scholarship at all, and it is an inadequate estimate which overlooks this element of what I have called rhetorical purpose.

The Study of Celtic Literature has suffered most from the critics,[44] and perhaps it is not a coincidence that here the element of rhetorical purpose is much greater. The critics of these lectures do not usually mention the plain and repeated statements in which Arnold says that he is not writing on Celtic literature as a scholar. Any unprejudiced reader of the introduction will agree, I think, that Arnold could not have done more to make his position clear. He submitted his text to the best scholar of the times in the field, and printed his comments as footnotes. He nowhere poses as a scholar in Celtic literature. The scholar, of course, will say that if Arnold could not treat his subject as a scholar he should have left it alone. This is, I think, typical of scholastic blindness to rhetorical purpose. Why did Arnold write about Celtic literature when he knew little about it? Simply to plead effectively for more study of Celtic and to rebuke the prejudices of Philistine journalists who were attacking such studies and making themselves and all Englishmen odious in the eyes of the Celts. An editorial in the London *Times* which denounced the Chester Eisteddfod, began, "The Welsh language is the curse of Wales," and ended, "The sooner all Welsh specialties disappear from the face of the earth the better." This gave Arnold the opportunity he so often took of assailing what was unamiable in the English character, of pointing out why they had failed so lamentably in their relations with the Irish and the Welsh. One effective way of rebuking such narrowness was to emphasize the indebtedness of English literature to Celtic elements. In doing this Arnold made some errors which have been fully and fairly dealt with by Mr. Alfred Nutt in his annotated edition of the *Celtic Literature,* but such corrections should not lead us to forget Arnold's main purposes, which are stated many times, and emphasized again in the conclusion.

At such a moment it needs some moderation not to be attacking Philistinism by storm, but to mine it through such gradual means as the slow approach to culture, and the introduction of chairs of Celtic. . . . Let us reunite ourselves with our better mind and with the world through science; and let it be one of our angelic revenges on the Philistines, who among their other sins are the guilty authors of Fenianism, to found at Oxford a chair of Celtic, and to send, through the gentle ministrations of science, a message of peace to Ireland.[45]

Mr. Nutt's criticisms are searching, and should be read as a protection against Arnold's errors, but his tribute to Arnold's success in achieving his real purposes is not affected by his scholarly criticism.

Matthew Arnold

Matthew Arnold's Oxford Lectures on the Study of Celtic Literature are a masterpiece of critical insight and suggestive power, but they are far more than this: they inaugurate a new period in the relation between England and Ireland, between Teutonism and Celticism, as animating ethical and æsthetical conceptions, they herald a new attitude of the Celtic peoples toward their national literature; they suggest and adumbrate problems, political, racial, æsthetic upon the solution of which much thought and intellectual labor and self-sacrificing zeal have been expended in the last forty years; they are still, in a most effective sense, a quickening ferment in the Neo-Celtic Revival.[46]

At the particular time and in the circumstances Arnold's lectures did more for the study of Celtic literature than any technical treatment could have done; scholars then had little reliable knowledge; Arnold made no false pretensions; the results, I think, justified him in the pleasure with which he wrote his mother:

The Celtic papers are producing an effect far beyond what I had ventured to hope. This is a great pleasure to me, and a proof how much there is in the way of presenting a subject, for certainly a more hopeless subject in itself to approach the British public with one could hardly imagine.[47]

Not all the *Essays in Criticism* are concerned with literature, and it can hardly be claimed that those studies in which Arnold is, as Professor Saintsbury says, sticking to his own field, have less of rhetorical purpose than the political, theological, and social criticism, nor do they differ essentially in method. Arnold apparently had two audiences in view in these essays, neither of them composed of scholars. First, there were the possible writers of the future, who were to be persuaded that the present low estate of English literature, its inferiority to contemporary French and German work, was due to its lack of ideas, and its lack of restraint. Here we have one of the many cases in which the falsity of Arnold's premises seem to do so little damage to his conclusions. English literature at the time was not in a low estate, and it was not inferior to the French or German, but more ideas and more restraint are usually needed by young writers, and this advice, apparently, is safe from the slings and arrows of outraged scholarship.

The other audience, that of the general readers, was largely instructed in the sources of virtuous conduct. The ethical bias of Arnold's criticism has been dealt with by so many writers that it need not be discussed at length here. Byron shows us the value of sincerity and strength, Wordsworth the joy in common things. Shelley's life offers the critic the opportunity to mark the odious and yet preserve the beautiful, and Tolstoy gives us "sound and saving doctrine." Amiel's *Journal* is instructive as a warning against the pathological, and an example of the need of a writer or a doer of any task to limit himself. As Arnold knows that "a merely senuous man cannot either by promise or performance be a very great poet," he goes through Keats's letters looking "for signs of character and virtue." Gray wrote good letters of consolation and had seriousness, character. Milton is good for us. He counter-acts the Anglo-Saxon and particularly American glorification of commonness. His great style refines and elevates us, even if we cannot explain how, and he gives us the inspiring example of a man who worked hard to keep himself worthy of the grandeur of his vocation. Heine, with all the culture of Germany, and all the ideas of modern Europe, only gave us a half result, for want of moral balance, and of nobleness of soul and character. Goethe was for Arnold, as for Carlyle, not so much an artist as "a strong tower into which the doubter and despairer might run and be safe."

I do not offer these judgments as a complete or even thoroughly representative summary of Arnold's literary verdicts; I merely emphasize the hortatory, rhetorical character of the essays in which, if anywhere, Arnold is writing within the field of his special knowledge. It was Arnold's rôle to appear to be a moralist among aesthetes and an aesthete among moralists. His devotion to truth was, in spite of all his praises of disinterestedness, as pragmatic as that of most reformers. The truth he spoke at any particular time was always colored by the need of his audience. The English should be told the French were superior because French qualities ought to be cultivated by Englishmen. The Italians should not be told of French superiority because the Italians were too much like the French already. Whether Hebraism or Hellenism was to be prescribed depended entirely upon the ills of the audience. Viewing culture as harmonious development, as the pursuit of perfection, truth was merely the emphasis of the particular defect which most stood in the way of perfection at the moment. "This is the truth for you, now," he would say. Arnold never admitted the right of a people to the defects of their qualities, and in his counsels of perfection he never hesitated to urge a union of incompatibles. Such a critic will be always and everywhere a rhetorician. If he is free from self-seeking, refuses to become tied to organizations, and preserves his free play of ideas, he may be fortunate enough to be absolved from sophistry, but he belongs to the company of the rhetoricians, whether he call himself philosopher or critic.

Arnold's literary criticism, then, is as rhetorical as his political and social writing. And the examination of his political and social criticism (which has to be omitted here, for lack of space) shows it to be essentially literary in quality. This fact, I think, shows the looseness with which the term "literary criticism" is used. I shall not attempt to define it or even to enumerate all the various meanings, but I want to distinguish the Arnoldian conception of it as set forth in "The Function of Criticism," and modified by a study of his practice, from a usage which is perhaps more current now. We ordinarily think of literary criticism as the criticism of literature, that is, the term takes its meaning from its subject matter. We may be illiterates writing a jargon of pseudo-science, but if we are talking about literature, it passes as literary criticism, no matter how unliterary in tone and method. In so far as this criticism rests upon organized principles of recognized validity taken from a special field of thought, and reaching conclusions within that field, it does not come within the province of rhetoric, if we take rhetoric in its Aristotelian sense of the faculty of persuasion in the field of probability. Of course the battle over the existence of any organized principles of literary criticism with recognized validity is an eternal one, and it is probable that criticism at its most intellectual and scientific level has a considerable element of rhetoric in it. But when we look at the Arnoldian conception, we see how nearly identical it is with the Aristotelian rhetoric. Literary criticism is not necessarily criticism of literature at all. It may be the criticism of anything if it has a literary flavor. To be more exact, it is criticism of all branches of knowledge—theology, philosophy, history, art, science, to use Arnold's list— if the tone and temper and method, and oftentimes the scale of values, are taken from literature. That is, literary criticism takes its meaning from its method and tone, not its subject matter.

Most of the writing and speaking which Arnold condemned as rhetoric was lacking in the tone and temper of literature, but by this Arnold did not mean chiefly that it was not "elegant" or "literary," he meant that it lacked the tolerance and detachment and wisdom that come from a wide acquaintance with the best that has been said and thought. Disinterestedness for Arnold was not what we understand by scientific or even aesthetic detachment. Neither of these varieties is compatible with Arnold's emphasis upon persuasion. We often say, indeed, that detachment and persuasion are antithetical. Arnold's earnest, disinterested persuasion was for him criticism. I think we may also call it one of the branches of Aristotelian rhetoric.

This does not mean that Arnold's attack upon the rhetoricians was not valid, or that we should be blind to the differences between the noble and ignoble rhetoric. Such attacks as Arnold's looking backward to Plato, and forward to Mencken or Sinclair Lewis, or practically any social critic of the moment, are of the permanent stuff of the criticism of life, even if not subject to the laws of poetic truth and beauty. The struggle with such rhetoric is perpetual. On the other hand, criticism which is vital, which is vital as Arnold's was and is, will always have a large element of noble rhetoric in it, and rhetorical analysis will be useful in understanding it. We may agree with Max Eastman in his attack upon the literary mind so far as to admit the need of more science in the training of the critic, and we may sympathize with his irritation at the lofty, anti-scientific attitude of "literary gentlemen"; but to say that the judgment based upon Arnold's culture is merely loose talk, that psychology and sociology are about to take all the old questions of criticism out of the realm of probability and put them in the realm of science, is as loose talk as the most literary of literary critics can indulge in. The taste and judgment which are the products of our culture will differ from Arnold's taste and judgment. And the verdicts of our judgment will always be undergoing modifications at the hands of science and the taste of future generations. The critics of the future will doubtless have more humility forced on them than Arnold possessed. But the intuitions of a disciplined spirit and the persuasion of an accomplished rhetorician will always have their place in criticism.

The Gladstone-Huxley

Controversy on Genesis

C. K. THOMAS

IN 1909 the Houghton Mifflin Company published a collected edition
of the writings of Mrs. Humphry Ward, to which she contributed a
series of introductions. In her introduction to *Robert Elsmere*, the book
on which her reputation as a novelist chiefly rested, Mrs. Ward recalled
the theological and scientific unrest of the 1880's, of which both the
novel and the first Gladstone-Huxley controversy were symptomatic.
Midway through the introduction she reported a conversation with
Gladstone on the occasion of the first publication of *Robert Elsmere* in
1888. Gladstone had undertaken to write a review of the unorthodox
book; only three years had passed since his controversy with Huxley;
and he was still as vigorous a defender of theological orthodoxy as
ever.

After noting that Gladstone was forty years her senior, Mrs. Ward
wrote, "It was impossible that there should be any equal give-and-
take between us, even on subjects—such as German theological criticism—where I might have honestly felt that I had a better right to an
opinion than he. I was awed by his personality, and only too glad to
listen and follow. Only once, in the second day's conversation, did we
really come to close quarters."[1] Then Gladstone thundered. "It was as
though some great eagle hovered, ready for battle; and feminine courage gave way."[2] Though awed, Mrs. Ward remained unimpressed.

Thomas Huxley was neither awed nor impressed. He and Gladstone

345

had long known each other through the Metaphysical Society, a kind of informal debating organization in which all shades of political and religious belief were represented, from Gladstone and Cardinal Manning at their extremes to Huxley and the even more combative John Tyndall at theirs. Gladstone had written the lead article in the first number of *The Nineteenth Century* and remained a frequent contributor. For several years Huxley contributed a monthly department on science to the same magazine, which was to become one of the most influential of its day, and the scene of the verbal tilts between the two champions of orthodoxy and of science.

To understand the atmosphere in which the controversy took place, one must look back to the publication of Darwin's *Origin of Species* in 1859, perhaps as far back as Sir Charles Lyell's *Principles of Geology* a generation previously. By insisting that geological processes in the past had been much like those in the present, Lyell had put the orthodox geologists on notice that their theories of catastrophic change, like, for instance, the story of Noah's flood, would remain unchallenged no longer. When the publication of Darwin's *Origin of Species* transferred the challenge from the relatively abstract field of geology to the very concrete field of biology, with all its implications regarding the ancestry of man, the orthodox storm broke.

The storm reached its first climax at the meeting of the British Association for the Advancement of Science held at Oxford in 1860. Here the *Origin of Species* and the theory of evolution were violently attacked and as violently defended. For Huxley the climax came when Bishop Wilberforce asked him if he were descended from a monkey on his grandfather's or his grandmother's side. Huxley instantly retorted:

I asserted—and I repeat—that a man has no reason to be ashamed of having an ape for his grandfather. If there were an ancestor whom I should feel shame in recalling it would rather be a man—a man of restless and versatile intellect—who, not content with an equivocal success in his own sphere of activity, plunges into scientific questions with which he has no real acquaintance, only to obscure them by an aimless rhetoric, and distract the attention of his hearers from the real point at issue by eloquent digressions and skilled appeals to religious prejudice.[3]

Of course the Oxford meeting settled nothing, and the battle between the scientists and the orthodox theologians continued to rage for years thereafter. It was still raging when Gladstone and Huxley conducted their first controversy twenty-five years later.

Gladstone entered the lists with "Dawn of Creation and of Worship," the lead article in *The Nineteenth Century* for November, 1885.[4] Ostensibly this was a review of a book, entitled, in English translation, *Prolegomena to the History of Religions,* by Albert Réville, D.D., Professor of the Science of Religion at the Collège de France, whose theology did not impress Gladstone.

After several pages of compliments to his opponent, ethical proof, and definition of the issues, Gladstone came to the heart of the matter. Réville, he said, has specified three scientific errors in Genesis:

His charges are that (1) it speaks of the heavens as a solid vault; (2) it places the creation of the stars after that of the earth, and so places them solely for its use; (3) it introduces the vegetable kingdom before that kingdom could be subjected to the action of solar light. All these condemnations are quietly enunciated in a note, as if they were subject to no dispute. Let us see.[5]

For several pages Gladstone discussed the German and Greek analogues of the English verbs *make* and *create,* in an effort to show that Réville had mistaken the intent of the Biblical passage. Then [6] he stated his own interpretation of the order of creation as outlined in Genesis: first, the water population; second, the air population; third, the land population; and, finally, the land population consummated in man. Not content with this bare statement, he went on to say, "Now this same four-fold order is understood to have been so affirmed in our time by natural science, that it may be taken as a demonstrated conclusion and established fact." [7] This sentence, by the way, was the bait to which Huxley rose. Gladstone devoted the rest of the article to enlarging upon and polishing his conclusion. The entire twenty pages bristle with learning, including no less than 55 citations ranging from Homer to Dante, Luther, Milton, Goethe, English bishops, German theologians, and even Sir Walter Scott's *The Heart of Midlothian.*

Earlier in 1885, because of increasing illness, Huxley had regretfully decided to resign his professorship at the Royal College of Science, and had spent several months abroad in the hope that something would happen to improve his health. As reported by his son,

The lively fillip came in the shape of an article in the November *Nineteenth Century,* by Mr. Gladstone, in which he attacked the position taken up by Dr. Réville in his *Prolegomena to the History of Religions,* and in particular attempted to show that the order of creation given in Genesis i., is supported by the evidence of science. This article, Huxley used humorously to

say, so stirred his bile as to set his liver right at once; and though he denied
the soft impeachment that the ensuing fight was what had set him up, the
marvellous curative effects of a Gladstonian dose, a remedy unknown to the
pharmacœpia, became a household word among family and friends.[8]

The "lively fillip" resulted in Huxley's "The Interpreters of Genesis
and the Interpreters of Nature," which became the lead article in the
December, 1885, issue of *The Nineteenth Century*.[9] After a single page
of introduction, ethical proof, and limitation of the discussion to those
scientific details in which he felt himself competent, Huxley restated
Gladstone's "four-fold order" and his sweeping statement that this
"order is understood to have been so affirmed in our time by natural
science, that it may be taken as a demonstrated conclusion and established fact." [10] Huxley continued:

"Understood?" By whom? I cannot bring myself to imagine that Mr. Gladstone has made so solemn and authoritative statement on a matter of this importance without due inquiry—without being able to found himself upon
recognized scientific authority. But I wish he had thought fit to name the
source from which he has derived his information, as, in that case I could
have dealt with his authority, and I should have thereby escaped the appearance of making an attack on Mr. Gladstone himself, which is in every way
distasteful to me.

For I can meet the statement in the last paragraph of the above citation
with nothing but a direct negative. If I know anything at all about the results attained by the natural science of our time, it is "a demonstrated conclusion and established fact" that the "four-fold order" given by Mr. Gladstone
is not that in which the evidence at our disposal tends to show that the water,
air, and land-populations of the globe have made their appearance.

Perhaps I may be told that Mr. Gladstone does give his authority—that he
cites Cuvier, Sir John Herschel, and Dr. Whewell in support of his case. If
that has been Mr. Gladstone's intention in mentioning these eminent names, I
may remark that, on this particular question, the only relevant authority is
that of Cuvier. But, great as Cuvier was, it is to be remembered that, as Mr.
Gladstone incidentally remarks, he cannot now be called a recent authority.
In fact, he has been dead more than half a century, and the palæontology of
our day is related to that of his, very much as the geography of the sixteenth
century is related to that of the fourteenth. Since 1832, when Cuvier died,
not only a new world, but new worlds, of ancient life have been discovered;
and those who have most faithfully carried on the work of the chief founder
of palæontology have done most to invalidate the essentially negative grounds
of his speculative adherence to tradition.[11]

The rest of the article is an account of the findings of palaeontology in the geological strata: of the confusing complications in the order of appearance of birds, beasts, and fishes, of flying reptiles (pterodactyls), flying mammals (bats), and swimming mammals (whales), as well as the innumerable orders of winged and wingless insects and other invertebrates. In the end, Gladstone's "four-fold" order looks incredibly oversimplified. Thus the method of Huxley's argument was not to impress his audience with his learning, as many of Gladstone's readers must have been impressed, but to undermine his opponent's authorities, and to present the relevant evidence. Huxley did not rely on citations from a variety of sources; his single footnote is not a citation at all, but an expansion of a scientific detail which, like the other details, he gave on his own authority.

Gladstone returned immediately to the attack. His "Proem to Genesis: a Plea for a Fair Trial" appeared as the lead article in the January, 1886, issue of *The Nineteenth Century*.[12] In it he accused Huxley of shifting ground,[13] of exaggeration,[14] and of being high-handed with Gladstone's authorities and of taking the part for the whole.[15] Huxley, he wrote,

holds the [Mosaic] writer responsible for scientific precision: I look for nothing of the kind, but assign to him a statement general, which admits exceptions; popular, which aims mainly at producing moral impression; summary, which cannot but be open to more or less of criticism in detail. He [Huxley] thinks it is a lecture. I think it is a sermon. He describes living creatures by structure. The Mosaic writer describes them by *habitat*. Both I suppose are right. I suppose that description by *habitat* would be unavailing for the purposes of science. I feel sure that description by structure such as the geologists supply, would have been unavailing for the purpose of summary teaching with religious aim.[16]

Thus Gladstone, though conceding on some details, nevertheless maintained his original position in general, repeated his statement that the cosmology of Genesis agreed with modern textbooks of geology,[17] and found it significant that the over-all inspiration of the account was revealed to the Hebrews, not to the mightier civilizations of the period.[18]

Huxley concluded the formal controversy with "Mr. Gladstone and Genesis" in the February, 1886, issue of *The Nineteenth Century*.[19] He proceeded directly, in the manner of a rebuttal speech in a formal debate. In the original article Gladstone committed himself to three propositions: (1) the sequence of water population, air population, and land population in the creation; (2) the confirmation of this sequence by natural science; and (3) the proposition that the Mosiac writer was either "gifted with faculties passing all human experience, or else his knowledge was divine." [20] But, he pointed out, if Gladstone's second proposition had collapsed, the third had collapsed with it.[21] Then, turning to the classification of animals in the section of Leviticus which outlined the ancient dietary laws, he vividly showed that the Mosaic classification was not that of science.[22] Here he introduced a familiar device of rebuttal speeches when he wrote,

> I note, incidentally, that Mr. Gladstone appears to consider that the *differentia* between a lecture and a sermon is, that the former, so far as it deals with matters of fact may be taken seriously, as meaning exactly what it says, while a sermon may not. I have quite enough on my hands without taking up the cudgels for the clergy, who will probably find Mr. Gladstone's definition unflattering.[23]

Here the two antagonists rested until a later date, when a second controversy, this one on the ethics and authenticity of miracles reported in the New Testament, took place. In the meantime, however, three other writers had become involved in the first controversy.

In his original article, Gladstone had drawn some parallels between Genesis and Homeric mythology, which Huxley made no attempt to discuss. But in an article entitled "Solar Myths" in the December, 1885, issue of *The Nineteenth Century* [24] the great philologist Friedrich Max Müller took Gladstone mildly to task for some assumptions about Homeric mythology based on faults in etymology and phonetic theory, and in the same article spoke highly of Dr. Réville.

Réville himself entered the controversy in the January, 1886, issue [25] with an article entitled " 'Dawn of Creation'—An Answer to Mr. Gladstone." Lightly bantering in tone, the article supported both Huxley and Max Müller, and posed a new dilemma for Gladstone, who had accepted the figurative meaning of the "days" of creation. Wrote Réville,

> I know well that a lax interpretation has transformed the days of Genesis into periods of immense length, in spite of the mention of "evening" and "morning" which closes each of the creative acts. . . . Now, if the days of the creation should be understood as periods of thousands or millions of years, I beg Mr. Gladstone to explain how they can serve as an argument in support of the command to work for six days of our week and to rest on the seventh.[26]

Gladstone-Huxley Controversy

Finally Henry Drummond, in "Mr. Gladstone and Genesis II," a companion piece to Huxley's second article,[27] pointed out the unfairness of the whole controversy, in that although Huxley could speak authoritatively for modern science, Gladstone, whose theology was sadly out of date, could not speak authoritatively for modern theology. And there the matter rested.

The controversy is an indication of the healthy ferment that pervaded English life on the eve of Queen Victoria's first Jubilee. All sorts of new ideas were being cogently and vehemently expressed and discussed. Nobody evaded the arguments or called for legislative suppression of heretical ideas. Whatever we may now think of them, the Victorians were forthright and honest in their public utterances. Gladstone and Huxley would be at it again, Gladstone ponderous and impressive, Huxley buzzing around him like a gadfly and getting as much sardonic amusement from the encounter as H. L. Mencken, forty years later, at the sorry echo of this earlier encounter, in Dayton, Tennessee.

The Nazi Rhetorician

ROSS SCANLAN

SOON after Corporal Adolf Hitler joined an obscure little group of six men calling themselves the Central Committee of the German Workers' Party he sought and obtained control of the organization's propaganda.[1] His associates could busy themselves thinking up new planks to go into the Party's platform, but Hitler, as chief of propaganda, would be the speaker to stand on that platform before the public.[2] He knew that whoever directed the Party's propaganda would direct the Party itself.

The reasons for this were obvious and are set forth at some length in *Mein Kampf*.[3] No political movement of this sort could attain power without a broad base of mass support, and mass support could be achieved only by propaganda. But, again, no propaganda could succeed in winning mass support unless it was executed boldly, energetically, and in line with sound principles of propaganda. This last point had a special significance: Hitler was already convinced that in the Weimar Republic all parties, except the Communists,[4] were making a mess of their efforts to secure popular approval chiefly because they did not understand the popular mind and the right channels through which to reach it.

According to Hitler, the best channel was public speaking. This was one of his earliest and most enduring convictions, and none of his followers ever challenged it by word or action. Goebbels, Hadamovsky, Ringler, and others became master-minds of party propaganda technique, but their theories and operations always stayed within the basic prescriptions laid down by the Führer. That is why the

The Nazi Rhetorician

official party speaker system (*Rednerwesen der NSDAP*) always kept a central position in the Party's propaganda machinery, even after the Nazis came into complete power and took over other channels of public communication such as press and radio.[5]

Nazi belief in the superior effectiveness of public speaking explains the steady growth of the speaker staff. It shows why, at the height of Nazi power, an elaborate screening process operated to test the fitness of each individual, whether an "old fighter" from the early days or not,[6] to represent the National Socialist point of view on the platform. It explains why, first through courses of instruction offered by party units and auxiliary organizations,[7] and later in schools and institutions appropriated by the Nazis for the purpose,[8] the party speaker was trained in party doctrine and public speaking. It also explains the steady output of articles and essays on public speaking furnished the speaker through publications of the Party's propaganda headquarters.[9]

Although the Nazi rhetorician gave a great deal of instruction and advice about persuasive discourse, he made no pretense to scholarship in rhetoric. The oratorical achievements and rhetorical theories of other people with few exceptions received scant attention from him. Goebbels might comment, very incidentally and briefly, on the eloquence of Latin people but only to show that some nations have demonstrated a natural aptitude for speech.[10] It seems never to have occurred to any Nazi rhetorician to study classical treatises on rhetoric. Hans Krebs might refer to the speaker-training furnished by the Roman Catholic Church to its priests [11] and even recommend that Nazi speakers attend church services and study the technique of the sermon but only as an illustration of what could be done by proper training. He saw no need to study or make use of Church treatises on rhetoric. If the ages had gathered and refined a wisdom about persuasion in speech, that was a matter of no concern to the Nazi rhetorician.

Public speaking in America and England came in for considerable attention from Nazi commentators, as indeed from many other postwar Germans of various political faiths, for there was a prevalent theory in Germany at this time that American and British superiority in political speaking had enabled these countries to achieve a superior war effort. Friedrich Schönemann, a professor at the University of Berlin and a specialist in American affairs, published in 1924 a book entitled *Die Kunst der Massenbeeinflussung in den Vereinigten Staaten von Nordamerika,* which discussed at some length the wartime role of the public speaker in this country. I am not now prepared to say that Hitler knew of this work, either directly or indirectly, or that it influenced his own vehement opinions on this difference between Germany and her former enemies. But there is clear evidence that the contents of the book made a deep impression on other leading persons in the Nazi propaganda machine. Eugen Hadamovsky, for example, and F. A. Six, in books widely read by the party propagandists,[12] summarize in some detail material taken from Schönemann, and Schönemann's book itself appears in many selected reading lists issued by the Party. Other examples of the same kind of interest are to be found in such essays as H. Dietz's "Redekunst als Kampfmittel beim Engländer," [13] and Wolfgang Schmidt's "Die politische Rede in Entscheidungsstunden der Britischen Nation," [14] and of course Hitler's own scathing contrast of the oratorical powers of David Lloyd George and von Bethmann-Hollweg.[15]

Nazi interest here was political, not rhetorical. England and America were cited to support basic Nazi theories of leadership and propaganda. No man could be a true leader of his people if he did not have genuine ability to move them by his words. Especially in times of crisis the heads of government must possess the power to arouse the nation through public address. Even this was not enough to satisfy the needs of government; in addition, a government required the services of a large, well-organized corps of reasonably competent speakers operating as a constant channel from the government to the people.[16] England and America were thought to be excellent proofs of these propositions, but even so, there is no evidence that the Nazi looked to these countries for anything in the theory of rhetoric.[17]

We can better understand the Nazi's reference to England and America if we turn to his estimate of his own country's contribution to political oratory. From Hitler and Goebbels down to the least little district leader, Nazi writers on propaganda hammered away at the theme that Germany had rarely achieved anything in oratory commensurate with her political needs or her achievements in other fields. In the long stretch of German history from Martin Luther to Adolf Hitler the Nazis found few orators worthy of note. It was a standard practice among them to praise Johann Gottlieb Fichte for his ardently nationalistic lectures, *Reden an die Deutsche Nation;* [18] and in an essay already cited Goebbels briefly mentions Bismarck but only to say that, after Bismarck, the speaker's platform in Germany remained

The Nazi Rhetorician

devoid of talent until the advent of Hitler.[19] German studies in the theory of rhetoric offered the Nazi even less. German scholars customarily treated rhetoric as a branch of study in classical and mediaeval languages or as the material for a philosophy of prose literature. Had such studies as Wilhelm Wackernagel's *Poetik, Rhetorik, und Stilistik* ever come to the Nazi propagandist's attention—a meeting that seems most unlikely—they would have meant only one thing to him: further evidence of the futile and unreal pursuits of the German intellectual.

The only Germans outside his own party who could teach the Nazi any lessons in rhetoric that he would value were the Communists, because, in Nazi opinion, they were the only political force in Germany prior to National Socialism that made a genuine effort to reach the mass of the people. Nazi commentators took careful note of the fact that decades ago the followers of Karl Marx had undertaken the important task of translating the difficult language of Marx into terms that would be intelligible to the common man.[20] And now, in the Weimar Republic, the Communists were the only political party to exploit effective techniques of mass influence. To the Nazis this fact was a warning as well as an example. If any other political force was to succeed in opposition to Communism, it could be only such a force as understood and matched the Communist in the use of his own weapons.[21] That is why Hitler spends so much time in *Mein Kampf* on the subject of propaganda and the importance of the spoken word and why the Nazis regarded it as an historic mission of the Nazi Party to establish effective public speaking in a country that had long neglected the art.

The Nazi rhetorician undertook to furnish guidance and instruction for the Party's speaker organization. He, in turn, found within the productivity of National Socialism itself all the resources he seemed to need to give instruction to others. He had the speeches of Hitler, Goebbels, and other leaders of the Nazi Party. He had Hitler's discussion of propaganda and public speaking in *Mein Kampf*. He had the innumerable essays, articles, and published comments of Goebbels and other officials of the Party's propaganda machine, and the publications of his colleagues in the Party's speaker staff. And, finally, he could draw upon his own practical experience as a party speaker, for the Nazi rhetorician prided himself on having learned the fundamental principles of his skill in workshops, taverns, meeting halls, and the public square.

No man more thoroughly typifies the Nazi rhetorician whom I have

355

been describing than the Sudeten leader Hans Krebs. For that reason it may be worth while to outline his political career [22] before examining his specific contribution to the instruction of party speakers.

Krebs was born in 1886 in Iglau, a town about halfway between Vienna and Prague. According to testimonials with which the Nazi Party later honored him, Krebs was the son of a man himself noted throughout the community for the violence of his anti-Slav, pro-German sentiments. From the same sources we learn that young Krebs first distinguished himself for his own political sentiments at the age of ten in a classroom encounter with his Catholic Czech teacher. At that time, throughout its schools in Bohemia, the Catholic Church encouraged the collection of such objects as cork, tinfoil, and postage stamps to be sent as friendly offerings to children in foreign mission schools. On one occasion, the Nazis gleefully record, the pupil Krebs brought to school an impressively large collection of postage stamps. When his teacher innocently inquired if these were "for the Negro children," the boy dramatically answered, "No! I give nothing to your Czech collections, above all nothing for Negroes. These are for German children!" [23]

The town of Iglau was what the Pan-Germans liked to call "a German island in a Czech sea," "a German speech-island" (*Sprachinsel*), "a bastion of German art and culture in Bohemia." [24] In towns like these the Germans often outnumbered the Czechs five or six to one, but they were chiefly conscious of being a minority throughout the region as a whole, and they fought against their sense of insecurity by intense pro-German activities. It is, therefore, not surprising that Krebs was, to all intents and purposes, a practising National Socialist long before Hitler appeared in political life. The activities in which Krebs engaged in the first decade of this century are those which later made up the fundamental elements of Hitler's National Socialist movement: German nationalism, anti-Semitism, anti-Marxism, labor organization, youth organization. [25]

A German Worker's Party was established in Bohemia in 1904, and it was not long after that that Krebs became one of its most active members. In 1908 he contributed to *Volkswehr,* a weekly newspaper "dedicated to an intense fight against the Marxist distortion of the working-class movement and for the principles of a genuine National Socialism." [26] By 1910 he was the editor of *Volkswehr* [27] and also had won some prominence in organizing German workers in the railroads, the building trade, and the tobacco industry of the country. Between

1911 and 1914 he was head and chief organizer of a youth movement that had forty-seven branches throughout the country and more than two thousand members. During this period he found time also to be business manager of the Central Commission of the German Workers' Alliance, founder in Vienna of the publications *Deutsche Arbeiterpresse* and *Deutsche Arbeiterjugend,* member of the Austrian Parliament, general manager of the pan-Germanic convention in 1912, and of a similar convention of the German Workers' Party in 1913. Our State Department's Division of Biographic Information records him as "the last manager of the German Labor Party, a forerunner of the NSDAP, in Vienna" before World War I.

During the War he commanded a machine gun unit in the Austrian Army and won silver and bronze medals, first class, for bravery. Immediately after the War he went back into politics. He organized anti-Czech boycotts among the Sudeten Germans and promoted other activities against the new Republic of Czechoslovakia. But his most important enterprise at this time was to help in the foundation of a German National Socialist Workers' Party in Austria and Czechoslovakia. This movement was simultaneous with Hitler's in Germany, yet in the very beginning essentially independent of it. The names of the two parties were the same except for the order of words: in Austria and Czechoslovakia, DNSAP; in Germany, NSDAP. However, Krebs and the other Sudeten leaders quickly accepted the supremacy of the German party and Hitler's leadership, and rearranged their title to conform to Hitler's choice.[28]

From 1925 to 1933 Krebs represented this party in the Czech Chamber of Deputies. In 1932 he was co-founder of the *Sudeten Volkssport Verband,* a none-too-well disguised copy of the Storm Troopers of Germany. In 1933, after Hitler's accession to power, the Czech government became alarmed, outlawed Krebs's party, and placed him with other leaders under arrest. He soon escaped, however, and fled to the Reich where he received many honors and appointments. His membership card in Hitler's own party carried the comparatively low number, "86." He was a chief councillor in the propaganda ministry, press director of the Reich Ministry of the Interior, and an honorary state councillor. He was a member of the Reich Committee of German Homeland Organizations and chief signatory of an agreement whereby that committee pledged financial and political support to Konrad Henlein's Sudeten Germans Homeland Party. From 1936 on he was a member of the German Reichstag. Following the fall of Czechoslovakia at Munich, he returned to his old scene of operations but with new powers and new titles: Minister-Councillor for Czechoslovakia, District President of Aussig, Honorary Gauleiter, and SS-Brigade Leader.

In addition to all this, he was a rather prolific writer on National Socialist themes. The Reichstag directory lists among "other works" *Der Weltkampf, Kampf um die sudetendeutsche Selbstverwaltung, Deutsche Kampf in Böhmen, Katechismus der völkischen Arbeiterbewegung Österreichs, Macht und Recht, Paneuropa oder Mitteleuropa, Wir Sudetendeutsche.* Also he contributed to anti-Semitic publications such as *Die Weltfront.*

He earned his standing in the Party, however, not merely by his industry in organization and writing. The Nazis, especially the Sudeten Nazis, counted him one of the biggest guns in their battery of party orators. An admission card to a party rally bills Hans Krebs of Aussig as "one of our finest speakers." [29] The volume of testimony to him relates that "party rallies, with Krebs announced as the principal speaker, always drew enormous crowds; he filled the largest meeting halls in our Sudeten German towns." [30] The same source indicates that because of his eloquence the Czechs hated and feared him more than other German Deputies in the Czech parliament: "Never was the Chamber of Deputies so stirred up as on that historic occasion when Hans Krebs pronounced his unforgettable oration against President Masaryk." [31]

We have already seen that Krebs antedated Hitler as an active National Socialist. If we depend on dates of publication, the Sudeten Nazi also preceded the Führer in calling attention to the importance of public speaking for the good of the cause. *Mein Kampf* was written in 1924, while Hitler was serving a prison term; but in 1921 Krebs had published a guide for national socialist speakers entitled *Lerne Reden!* This little work was to enjoy wide and enduring use among speakers of the NSDAP. A Nazi publisher in Leipzig produced a second edition in 1930, and after Hitler's victory in 1933 the book appeared in a somewhat revised and expanded form under the title *Redner-Fibel.* Thereafter, it went through a series of editions, at least nine, the sixth being published in 1935.

At the beginning of his book Krebs joins the general chorus of Nazi rhetoricians in decrying Germany's previous accomplishments in political oratory:

We Germans have always cultivated the art of public speaking very poorly. Few of us have been masters of speech communication . . . at least to a degree that would enable us to employ it as an effective means of influencing the masses. [In Germany] the National Socialist Revolution first brought great speakers, like great statesmen, to the front. Even today the asset of effective public speaking is not frequently to be found among the German people.[32]

The deficiency can be largely overcome by a correct understanding of the needs of the Party and a correct understanding of the sources of competence in speaking. As to the needs of the Party:

Who could argue that even the National Socialist victory [of 1933] has made it no longer necessary to publish the ideas of the movement through talks, lectures and public meetings? No less a person than the Führer himself has shown—over and over again—how necessary it is to sustain close contact with the broad mass of people. Even today, when National Socialism has become master of the radio and the press, no one can doubt that, to extend an understanding of the NSDAP in its role as the governing power, innumerable meetings, even in the smallest workshops and tiniest villages, are still needed.[33]

Again, as to ability in speech, it is true that some persons exhibit a natural talent but these are "great exceptions"; most normally endowed people can develop competence through study and practice. There is an *angeborene Beredsamkeit* and an *erlernte Redekunst,* and the Party has need of both. "We must not forget that, in addition to party comrades who speak at the great public meetings, the Party needs many speakers who can clearly present the National Socialist standpoint at smaller meetings or at little gatherings in the workshops and factories."

But Krebs is perhaps most truly the rhetorician when he discusses in some detail the general and specific education of the speaker. The Nazi speaker is advised to study the German classics. "The speaker—not only the beginner but the expert—must continuously study the best works of our greatest poets. In this way he will amass a large treasury of words and the best forms of expression and, beyond that, a steadily widening sphere of knowledge." A little later Krebs returns to the same theme; the speaker must have "a knowledge of belles-lettres, especially a detailed acquaintance with the classic German writers— Goethe, Schiller, and Grillparzer—and also philosophers like Fichte and Schleiermacher." And it is well for him to know German history.

Great importance is given to knowledge of a kind of psychology.

This is a much-vaunted specialty of Nazi experts in propaganda. We must call it a "kind of psychology" because the Nazis handled it in their own way. The subject of this knowledge was the *Volksseele*, a term which, ever since the Romantic era, has been used by many Germans to hypostatize the mind and the heart of the people. To the Nazis the *Volksseele* was a single, definite, concrete reality, an object to be studied with great diligence by party speakers. But the Nazi rhetoricians seem generally to have been of the same opinion as Krebs, that this kind of knowledge did not come from book-learning. At least, one did not seek it in the published works of someone calling himself a social psychologist. True, the party speaker was directed to the writings of Hitler, Goebbels, and others on the subject; but he was constantly advised to depend mainly on his own close observation of the people to give him this resource.

The speaker's effectiveness will depend basically on a knowledge of the *Volksseele*. . . . Only the speaker who constantly studies the mind of the people will have that inner contact that is so necessary to effective speaking. Only one who knows the sufferings and struggles of the people will know how to coin expressions that are right for the people.

The careful observer can get his clearest view into the soul of the people when a party campaign, a national upheaval, an election, a plebiscite, or some other significant movement in the development of the people is taking place. . . . At every meeting the speaker should make note of especially effective expressions that he hears and should observe what arguments make the deepest impression on the audience. At such meetings one must closely study the psychological reactions of the audience, if he is himself to achieve the greatest effect.[34]

Thus German literature, German philosophy, German history, and the Nazis' own brand of psychology made up the general education of a party speaker. His specific education consisted of heavy doses of party ideology. Like all Nazi rhetoricians Krebs takes great pains with the political indoctrination of the speaker. Here apparently the eager learner cannot spend too much time reading. He needs, first of all, to have a "firm National Socialist philosophy," which comes from an extensive acquaintance with the "vast number of brochures and books" provided by the Party. Krebs's list of required reading includes: Hitler's *Mein Kampf* and his collected speeches; Rosenberg's *Nature, Principles, and Purposes of the NSDAP*, his *Blood and Honor*, and his *Structure of the [National Socialist] Concept*; Fritsch's *Handbook of*

the Jewish Problem; Schwartz-Bostunitsch's *Jewish Imperialism:* Dr.
Ley's *Germany Has Become More Beautiful,* and his *The Upsurge of
Social Integrity;* Goebbels' *Signs of the New Era,* and of course, issues
of *Der Angriff;* Frick's *We Build the Third Reich;* Darré's *Peasantry
as the Life-Source of the Nordic Race;* and a number of others on
Judaism, Catholicism, and Free-Masonry. The Nazi student is warned
that this list is far from exhaustive, and that he must assemble his own
library according to his particular needs, and must make every effort
to keep abreast of the current output. In later editions of the *Redner-
Fibel* there is a further warning that ever since Hitler came into power
there has been a flood of pseudo-National Socialist works against which
he must be on guard. To help protect him the NSDAP has established
an "Official Party Testing Commission for the Integrity of National
Socialist Literature," and every book approved by it bears on the fly-
leaf the notation "No Objection" (*Unbedenklichkeitsvermerk*). Moreover, "the speaker must not borrow these books—he should own them!
They must always be available to him." [35]

In addition to basic National Socialist philosophy the speaker must
have a precise knowledge of current political events, and for this he
will read at least one Nazi newspaper every day. Krebs cannot speak
too strongly in favor of the practice of taking clippings from newspapers.

Whoever wishes to speak with effect and to work evidence into his speech
can scarcely get along without a good collection of newspaper clippings.
Building up such a collection is a basic requirement for the speaker and
the speech. There is almost no talk in which the speaker can do without
such clippings. The more conscientious and exhaustive the collection, and
the more lucidly it is arranged, the more value it will have.[36]

Detailed instructions are given for the method of handling these clippings: pasting them on sheets of paper of uniform size; writing appropriate labels for them; filing them; etc. Some illustrative headings
are: "Winter Relief Work," "Race Questions," "Social Politics," "Jewry,"
"The German Labor Front," "Marxism"; there are sixteen in all, offered
as a possible over-all classification with suitable sub-heads. Krebs even
suggests that it will help if the folders containing these clippings are
of different and appropriate colors.[37] There is some ironical and thoroughly unconscious humor in his examples. Items on agriculture are
properly, if somewhat obviously, filed in a green folder, and items on

Communism in a red folder. We cannot be sure of the significance or propriety of blue for items on the self-determination of peoples or yellow for items on tenant-farming; but, in view of the very ambiguous attitude of Nazi leaders toward labor once the Party came into power, the choice of "rose" to represent the German Labor Front seems to be a stroke of unconscious genius.

Apart from this discussion of the general and specific education of a speaker, most of the *Redner-Fibel* is devoted to the standard themes of a textbook in public speaking: classification of speech-forms, development of confidence, organization, style, and delivery. However, since they give us an insight into the Nazi concept of the *vir dicendi*, they are worth notice. For Krebs the major distinction in speech-forms lies between the *Vortrag* and the *Rede*, essentially the distinction between exposition and persuasion. The *Vortrag* is

the exclusively factual exposition of a carefully limited subject. Here the speaker must follow a closely constructed outline. The speech must hold itself strictly to the subject in hand and be addressed primarily to the faculty of understanding. The speaker will avoid large gestures and other forms of emotional excitation. The *Vortrag* is brief and to the point.

The *Rede* works to other ends and with other means:

It must be spontaneous, without manuscript. At most the speaker permits himself only a few notes, keywords . . . that indicate his main thoughts. If the *Rede* is to achieve its purpose, it must be delivered in a stirring manner . . . it must reach beyond understanding to the feelings of the listeners.[38]

Stage-fright has no rational basis in the situation confronting the speaker, and, after explaining this, Krebs advises the speaker who suffers from it "to breathe deeply or to drink a few swallows of water."

But in no case make use of alcohol. The best thing is some mineral water. Spring water works extraordinarily well, both on the nerves and on the vocal chords. Alcohol produces congestion in the speech organs, brings about fatigue, and increases nervous tension. Soda water also is not recommended because it quickly dries up the mouth and throat.[39]

The speech has its standard division into three parts: introduction, body, and conclusion. First there must be an appropriate salutation: "Honored Assembly" (*Geehrte Versammlung!*), or "Comrades of the People" (*Volksgenossen*), "German Men and Women" (*Deutsche*

Frauen und Männer), "Dear Labor Comrades" (*Liebe Arbeitskammeraden*). Then the speaker begins, "as simply, plainly, engagingly as possible and *not too loud!*" [40]

The introduction must be well worked out; thereby the speaker gains absolute assurance. As soon as he has presented the introduction properly, he feels this sense of assurance. He looks the audience calmly in the eye, takes note of whatever factions there may be among the listeners, especially of opponents, and remains tranquil and undisturbed. Then he begins [the body of] his speech. . . . Under no circumstances should he open his speech with an apology of any kind.[41]

In discussing the body of the speech Krebs urges the speaker to be well prepared with all kinds of evidence and supporting material. At the same time he cautions the speaker to be discreet in the amount of statistical data he uses. When attacking the enemies of National Socialism, one should always try to turn their own statements against them. Whatever the purpose of the speech the speaker should always develop it so that "the most important and impressive part comes at the end." [42]

The standard Nazi talk always ends with a peroration. Thus Krebs advises his readers that "the conclusion is often the deciding part of the speech . . . it must aim not only at understanding but even more at the emotions . . . it must call up will and action." He cites the conclusions in Fichte's *Reden an die Deutsche Nation* as good specimens.[43] But the outstanding example of "an overwhelming conclusion" is that which Adolf Hitler delivered when he was on trial in a Munich court in April, 1924, after the famous *Putsch*.[44] Krebs also undertakes to get his speaker off the stage in the proper way. The exit must be conducted in a "serious and dignified" manner. "The speaker should never respond to applause by bowing; rather he should turn away with his head erect and a firm step. Inwardly and outwardly his behavior should be courteous, straight-forward, upright, and manly." [45]

With our attention focussed on the language favored by Hitler in his writings and speeches, and, we may add, by a host of lesser Nazis who imitated and sometimes even outdid him in the new jargon, it is interesting to see what a Nazi rhetorician has to say on the subject of style. Actually, Krebs's treatment is rather moderate and conventional. Style, like handwriting, we are told, is individual. Basically it cannot be learned, but it can be improved by growth of culture and education and by tireless effort in composition. It must be natural and unified, and not dressed up for the platform. "Let each one speak and write as he speaks and writes in daily life. Let him avoid the affected, the theatrical, the forced. Whoever puts too much artifice into his style thereby defeats his own purpose and rings hollow!"

There are four forms of style:

One dominated by the intellect, which is capable of great effectiveness through the power of logic and thought. This is the way professors and scholars speak. [*sic*]

A style ruled by imagination. Here the speaker seeks his effect through the beauty and loftiness of his language. This form of style is used especially by clergymen, eulogists, and other ceremonial speakers.

A style ruled by the will and by a strong sense of urgency. . . . This is the characteristic style of the true *Volksredner*.

The style in which the faculties of reason, imagination, and emotion are equally dominant.[46]

Hitler is cited as the outstanding exemplar of this final and culminating form of style in which all powers of the mind combine.

Anyone aspiring to the post of Nazi speaker is cautioned against certain common errors of style. He should avoid the excessive use of "patch-words" (*Flickwörter*), phrases thrown in to cover gaps and hesitations. Examples are: "so to speak," "to some extent," "namely," "in any case," and the repeated use of salutations in the text of the speech. According to Krebs, another bad practice is the use of foreign expressions. This is an old injunction in German rhetoric, with its roots deep in German nationalism. In our text the speaker is given the added warning that misuse of foreign expressions may cause him to be laughed at and that such laughter is fatal, especially to a political speaker. More startling is the statement that extravagant phrases of abuse must be avoided. Too many speakers are prone to exaggerate. Discreet and accurate speeches have a far better effect. To this category of exaggerations belong the so-called *Kraftausdrücke*, common labels that are often the "signs of a weak intellect and a weak case." Such phrases "only succeed in filling the better sort of people [in our audience] with a deep aversion to political and public life."

One note will suffice on Krebs's treatment of the subject of delivery. He is a great believer in the value of oral interpretation as a method of training.

The Nazi Rhetorician

Everything that [the speaker] reads in [German literature and poetry] he should read aloud. In this way he improves the quality of his voice, acquires greater vocal endurance and a better inflection. The student of public speaking should read the dramas, poems, comedies of our greatest writers aloud, as loudly as actors sometimes do. If there is no place for this activity in his home, let him go out of doors! [47]

To sum up, the *Redner-Fibel* is a work of very modest proportions, not only in length but in treatment. It makes no slightest pretense to a deep philosophical analysis of the problems of persuasive discourse. In the field of rhetorical theory it is an item for the historian rather than the philosopher. However, the prestige of its author within the Party and the extensive use of the book by party speakers give it the status of an approved description of the Nazi concept of the good speaker. Actually, *Redner-Fibel* offers nothing that is not intended as practical advice and instruction; but in so doing it makes clear to a large extent the principles and conceptions of rhetoric maintained by the Nazi writer and endorsed by the Party.

EPILOGUE

Rhetoric and Poetry

HOYT H. HUDSON

YOU will recall that James Russell Lowell, in his *Fable for Critics*, includes a passage of self-characterization, beginning with these lines:

> There is Lowell, who's striving Parnassus to climb,
> With a whole bale of *isms* tied together with rhyme.
> He might get on alone, spite of brambles and boulders,
> But he can't with that bundle he has on his shoulders.
> The top of the hill he will ne'er come nigh reaching
> Till he learns the distinction 'twixt singing and preaching.

It is this "distinction 'twixt singing and preaching" which is my theme in what follows. I wish to urge that the distinction is an important one in literary criticism; I would urge especially that we who claim to know something about preaching have as great an interest in making clear the distinction, and can contribute as much to this end, as the student of "pure literature," whose attitude toward preaching too often lacks both sympathy and understanding. Recently I found a journalistic critic referring, with an air of having said something important, to "rhetoric, that borderland between prose and poetry." I fancy that a large collection might be made of such vague impressionistic contributions to obscurity. But such is not our present task.

Rather let us turn to the words of one who thought clearly upon our subject, John Stuart Mill, in one of whose early essays [1] we find these sentences:

All poetry is of the nature of soliloquy. It may be said that poetry which is printed on hot-pressed paper and sold at a bookseller's shop, is a soliloquy

369

in full dress and on the stage. But there is nothing absurd in such a mode of soliloquizing. What we have said to ourselves we may tell to others afterward; what we have said or done in solitude, we may voluntarily reproduce when we know that other eyes are upon us. But no trace of consciousness that any eyes are upon us must be visible in the work itself. . . . When he [the poet] turns round and addresses himself to another person; when the act of utterance is not in itself the end, but a means to an end—viz. by the feelings he himself expresses, to work upon the feelings, or upon the belief, or the will, of another,—when the expression of his emotions, or of his thoughts tinged by his emotions, is tinged also by that purpose, by that desire of making an impression upon another mind, then it ceases to be poetry, and becomes eloquence.

Mill sums up his thought in the famous apothegm, "Eloquence is written to be heard, poetry to be overheard." I trust I do no violence to his thought when I substitute for "eloquence" the word "rhetoric." [2]

We have, then, on the one hand rhetoric, of which the most typical example is the persuasive public address; on the other hand poetry, represented in its purest form, perhaps, by the personal lyric. Mill has characterized, in the passage just quoted, the work of the poet. The rhetorician stands at the opposite pole. He composes his discourse with his eye upon his audience and occasion. The occasion may dictate his very subject; and it may well be a subject quite other than that he would have chosen if left to himself.[3] The audience is likely to be a certain limited group. The man of rhetoric must test himself at every step by such questions as, "What will this mean to them?" "Will they be ready for this step?" and "How can this be illustrated so as to show its connection with their interests?" Thus the structure, too, of his discourse will be determined by his audience. Taking the exordium as an illustration, we can see that its length, its subject-matter, and even the necessity for having any exordium at all, will depend upon the audience and occasion.

Moreover, the rhetorician wants actually to do something with the audience—and usually something quite specific. Lincoln's Gettysburg speech is sometimes described as if it were a poetical discourse by a man who had brooded much in solitude, and who disregarded or "rose above" the occasion in order to express universal truths and emotions. Without denying the element of universality in this speech, we must say that what Lincoln did was to seize the occasion, with its already deep emotional associations, and to utilize all the elements of it in the performance of his task of persuading the members of his audience to help carry on the war. From our point of view, now that the occasion for such persuasion is past, we can fit the speech into its historical and biographical setting and read it very much as we read a speech in a drama, and with a similar delight. But at the time it was a piece of persuasive discourse with a very specific end in view.

The poet, as Wordsworth reminds us, keeps his eye not on the audience or the occasion, but on his subject: his subject fills his mind and engrosses his imagination, so that he is compelled, by excess of admiration or other emotion, to tell of it; compelled, though no one hear or read his utterance. It is not only sorrow that must be given words; it is not only grief which, if it does not speak,

> Whispers the o'erfraught heart and bids it break.

And so we find Wordsworth defining poetry as "the spontaneous overflow of powerful feelings." And so we find Tennyson writing,

> I do but sing because I must,
> And pipe but as the linnets sing.

and Shelley: "A poet is a nightingale, who sits in darkness and sings to cheer its own solitude with sweet sounds; his auditors are as men entranced by the melody of an unseen musician, who feel that they are moved and softened, yet know not whence or why."

For the moment, then, we shall say that poetry is for the sake of expression; the impression on others is incidental. Rhetoric is for the sake of impression; the expression is secondary—an indispensable means.

As an example of how this distinction may be applied in literary criticism, I might point to A. A. Jack's very discerning estimate of Byron; Jack concludes that most of Byron's writing should be considered as rhetorical rather than poetical discourse. Following are a few sentences which suggest how he arrived at this conclusion: [4]

He [Byron] has his eye always on his audience and is always directly addressing someone. And this is the root difference between the poet strictly so called and the orator. Poetry is a record of feeling; oratory is an appeal, based of course on emotional experience, but meant to excite feeling. . . . Great oratory, and Byron's is superbly great, forces a contact between the emotions of the audience and the emotions of the speaker. Poetry displays its own heart. Oratory tears open the heart of the listener. . . . We have

371

not to say [of Byron], "How different from Wordsworth." We have to say, "How much better than Patrick Henry."

Again, we might notice the following interesting passage in Dorothy Canfield's *Raw Material:*

> My clergyman grandfather always said that he never enjoyed any sermons so much as the ones he preached to himself sitting under another clergyman's pulpit. When the text was given out, his mind seized on it with a vivid fresh interest and, running rapidly away from the intrusive sound of the other preacher's voice, wove a tissue of clear, strong, and fascinatingly interesting reasoning and exhortations. Grandfather used to say that such sermons preached to himself were in the nature of things much better than any he could ever deliver in church. "I don't have to keep a wary eye out for stupid old Mrs. Ellsworth, who never understands anything light or fanciful; I don't have to remember to thunder, occasionally at stolid Mr. Peters to wake him up. I don't have to remember to keep my voice raised so that deaf old Senator Peasley can hear me. I am not obliged to hold the wandering attention of their muddled heads by a series of foolish little rhetorical tricks or by a prodigious effort of my personality."

In other words, what Miss Canfield's grandfather was saying is that in him the poetical impulse was stronger and afforded more pleasure than the rhetorical impulse. To a man who was more completely a rhetorician the shortcomings of his audience would be a stimulus and a challenge; the manipulation of what he calls "foolish little rhetorical tricks" would be a pleasurable exercise of power.

But now, having enforced this distinction (which seems to me of primary importance) between poetry and rhetoric, we should not fail to take into account all possible qualifications of it. First we may recall that in the *Poetics,* when Aristotle discusses the element of *dianoia,* or thought, in tragedy, he says, "We may assume what is said in the *Rhetoric,* to which inquiry the subject more strictly belongs." He goes on: "Under Thought is included every effect which has to be produced by speech, the subdivisions being,—proof and refutation; the excitation of the feelings, such as pity, fear, anger, and the like; the suggestion of importance or its opposite." [5] We recognize that in poetry in its broad sense, especially in dramatic and narrative poetry, there are a great many occasions when the poet must picture a character as trying to produce an effect by speech. On such occasions the character will use rhetoric, and for the time being the poet is writing persuasive discourse. Familiar examples drawn from English literature are the speech of Mark Antony in Shakespeare's *Julius Caesar* and the speeches of the fallen angels in Books I and II of *Paradise Lost*. Yet we should not say that in these cases the poet is any less a poet, even though for the moment he is working in the field of rhetoric. He is producing what we properly may call imitative rhetoric. He is representing "men in action," and since persuasive address is a common form of action he must represent it. Thus many of the poets have shown themselves masters of the persuasive art, and their imitative rhetoric deserves to be studied for its own sake. Yet the presence of this kind of writing in poetry does nothing, as we see, to break down our distinction between poetry and rhetoric. Rather it shows the broad scope of the poet's art; it bears out Ben Jonson's account of the education of the poet, wherein he brings him "down through the disciplines of grammar, logic, rhetoric, and the ethics," and later says: "He must have civil prudence and eloquence, and that whole, not taken up by snatches or pieces in sentences or remnants when he will handle business or carry counsels." [6]

A fact harder to deal with, yet one which must not be left unconsidered, is that there is to be detected, in any extended poetical work, a rhetorical element. The poet does not always do as we have described him doing: he does at times consider his audience. Granting that our previous account may suffice for poetry in a very restricted meaning,— for the "touchstones," let us say, and for most subjective works such as personal lyrics, yet it certainly does not suffice for the drama. Except for what has come to be called "closet drama," the poet's work in this species is designed for an audience as surely as is the orator's. And in greater or less measure, the same holds true for other of the species of poetry—for narrative, for the ode, certainly for didactic and satirical pieces.

Yet there are differences plainly discernible between the poet's audience and the orator's, and between the poet's relation to his audience and the orator's to his. The poet thinks of a more general and more vaguely defined audience than the orator. The poet may even think of all mankind of the present and future as his audience; or if he writes to address a certain class of readers, at least he chooses his own audience instead of submitting to the dictates of an occasion. Where this is not true, where the poet is writing an ode for a special occasion, a tribute to the royal family upon the king's birthday or an address of greeting to a visiting celebrity, I think we shall not hesitate to apply our distinction rigorously and to say that he writes rhetorical discourse rather than poetical. A study of the duties of "public orator" at English universities in past centuries shows that the writing of Latin verse to be read at special occasions was one of the common tasks of this skilled rhetorician. Returning to the poet, we find that he is likely to think of himself as a fair representative of mankind and write to please himself, trusting thereby to please others—which is equivalent to taking no account of his audience at all.

One cannot hope to find better authority on this point than Wordsworth, who wrote in his preface to *Lyrical Ballads:* [7]

The poet writes under one restriction only, namely, the necessity of giving immediate pleasure to a human Being possessed of that information which may be expected from him, not as a lawyer, a physician, a mariner, an astronomer, or a natural philosopher, but as a Man.

We have here an important clue to follow in ascertaining the poet's relation to his audience, namely, his reason for taking the audience into account. He desires to please, or delight, his readers. We are now thrown back to the doctrine which we used as a starting-point; we were inclined to say at first that the poet's end is expression, and that impression enters only incidentally. Now we are told that the poet writes under "the necessity of giving immediate pleasure to a human Being." Perhaps, however, we can give due weight to his desire, or necessity, to delight his readers and still cling to our original doctrine. Let us analyze a simple case of the impulse to expression. We have had an exciting experience, perhaps with some comic elements; our experience fills our mind for some time after its occurrence. We say to ourselves, "I must tell some one about it!" We are impelled to tell the first acquaintance we meet. But perhaps we do not obey that impulse, thinking, "I'll wait and tell A. He'll enjoy it more than any one else." It seems to me that still the primary impulse is that to expression; our telling is "the spontaneous overflow of powerful feelings." But the impulse requires us to *share* our feelings, and we feel the need of a hearer who will find pleasure in what we have to tell. We should notice, however, that the impulse to express still arises from the subject; the subject, not the audience, fills the mind and quickens the imagination. Thus the poet tends to look for an audience suitable to his subject and the resultant discourse, rather than to seek, as does the rhetorician, a subject and discourse suitable to the audience.

374

Accepting pleasure as the effect (or kind of impression) peculiar to poetry, we may name persuasion as the effect peculiar to rhetoric. There is, however, another effect which has come to be associated, perhaps indissolubly, with rhetorical discourse; that is the effect produced by *display*. Historically, rhetorical display grew up in connection with the epideiktic branch of oratory, the delivery of eulogies, panegyrics, and denunciations. Epideiktic rhetoric originally had a genuine basis of persuasion, drawing upon the topics of honor and shame, praise and censure. But the conventionality of the occasions for its use and the factitious nature of the persuasive problems on these occasions led such speaking in the direction I have indicated. And in all ages when there have been few opportunities for political and religious discussion, oratory has tended to flow in this channel of display. Rhetoric becomes then a study of how to vary a phrase, how to turn a compliment, write certain kinds of letters, and declaim ornate speeches. Order of words, with regard to emphasis and balance, clever paradox and specious reasoning, beauty and variety of figures and tropes, dignity and sonorousness of language,—such become matters of greatest concern.

Such manifestations of rhetoric have done much to degrade the whole subject in the eyes of philosophic thinkers and in the common opinion of mankind; so that one of the commonest uses of the word is with the meaning, "artificial elegance of language, or declamation without conviction or earnest feeling." The tendency to epideiktic display at various times has infected prose style, producing such results as Euphuism. When this rhetorical tendency has invaded poetry, it has placed a premium upon the "conceit," upon intricate and rigid rhyme-schemes and metrical patterns, upon word-juggling (as in the anagrammatic and punning verses of the Elizabethan period), and upon bombast (as in the "heroic plays" of Dryden and others).

We should not deny, to be sure, that there is a legitimate pleasure to be experienced on the part of a reader or hearer in perceiving the skill of the poet or speaker. Yet this is always in a subsidiary relation to the other impressions we have noted, and does not necessarily rise to distinct consciousness. As has been said,[8] "The pleasure we take in poetry rarely rests on the conscious perception of technical skill, but usually on an unconscious perception of order like that of nature in which the rigid law of uniformity is modified by variations which suggest the law without following it slavishly." And whatever may be the pleasure of the reader, I believe we should agree that the desire

375

to make a display of skill should never enter into the poet's impulse. Even with a rhetorician such a process, as we know, is likely to result in a degradation of his art; and most of the products of epideiktic rhetoric we should place among the lowest orders of literature,[9] if indeed we admit them at all.

To return to our main line of thought, we have established, or perhaps granted, that there is a legitimate rhetorical element in poetry. It might be interesting to consider gradations in the strength of this element in the various species of poetical discourse. We can hardly hope to draw up a table of mathematical exactness, or to make any generalization which is not open to exception. But we should probably agree that most free from the rhetorical element, as being most purely expression and least concerned with impression, are the personal or subjective lyric and the rhapsodic poem. Next I should place the idyll, pastoral poetry, and after them the whole field of narrative poetry, including the romance and the epic. In these the consideration of the audience is generally less than in dramatic poetry. Of comedy and tragedy I should say that comedy is more rhetorical in its conception than tragedy. Comedy is much more likely to be local and topical, is more apt for propaganda and persuasion. Still further than dramatic poetry in the direction of rhetoric, we shall find didactic poetry, satire, odes for special occasions, and epigrams.

The question may occur whether our ranking of poetical species according to the strength of the rhetorical element corresponds (inversely, of course) to their ranking in poetic excellence. Can we say that the personal lyric, being least rhetorical, is the highest kind of poetry? I believe modern taste would incline to this view. Aristotle, as we know, placed tragedy highest. He demanded a certain grandeur in the action represented, a demand satisfied only by tragedy and the epic. Tragedy is greater than the epic because it has all the elements of the epic with others in addition. This suggests that Aristotle may have admired tragedy as some modern critics have admired grand opera, because it is a "union of all the arts." And from this we might draw the further suggestion that the presence of the rhetorical element, or rather of a rhetorical necessity in the very form of a poetical composition, may heighten rather than degrade the composition. The tragedian may write the better poetry for having to make his lines impressive as well as expressive. In composing an elegy upon the death of a friend, a poet is faced by a complex problem: he is writing a poem for an

376

occasion, and he is constrained to fall into the rhetorical conventions which have grown up about such occasions; on the other hand his feelings may be so strong that he will forget his audience and give vent to private grief, probably with incongruous and distasteful results. But where the difficulties are transcended and exactly the right proportions are maintained, the result is a *Lycidas* or *Thyrsis* or *Adonais*, and belongs to a high order of poetry. Of the three elegies named, I should say that *Thyrsis* leans toward the side of personal feelings, and errs, if at all, in being too subjective; *Adonais* leans toward the rhetorical to such a point at times we question the warmth and genuiness of the author's emotion; *Lycidas* avoids both pitfalls.

Turning to less disputable regions of our inquiry, we shall not find it difficult to cite works wherein a poet has got clear across the borderland into rhetoric, and has unmistakably written rhetorical discourse. First we might mention pieces written with a persuasive end, though claiming the style of imitative literature. Prose fiction in our generation has suffered from a flood of novels written by propagandists, rhetoricians who utilize the devices and factors of interestingness peculiar to imitative literature in the service of some project dear to their hearts.[10] This phenomenon is too well known to need discussion. It is found also on the stage. I believe that when we apply our findings regarding poetry and rhetoric to Bernard Shaw, we discover that in most of his work he belongs with the rhetoricians rather than with the dramatic poets. We should, of course, make the allowances due him, remembering that he is a writer of comedies and clever in the use of what we have called imitative rhetoric. But aside from these considerations, we find him, as revealed in his plays as well as in his prefaces, a preacher or reformer more often than a creative artist. This is not necessarily a condemnation of Shaw's work. The preacher has a high function. He is to be praised rather than blamed for using such means of publicity as are available to him. No one thinks less of William Morris for having written *A Dream of John Ball*, a socialist tract in narrative form. But criticism is at fault if the distinction between the rhetorician and the creative artist is lost; and when criticism fails of its duty there is a resulting confusion and loss in literature.

Again, we should call attention to metrical *tours de force*, which, as epideiktic displays, belong to rhetoric rather than to poetry. Without going back to the strained and quaint products of "metaphysical poets," I would cite Poe's "Bells" and Southey's rhymed description of

"How the Waters Come Down at Lodore" as cases in point. Many of Swinburne's stanzas, with their balanced alliteration and assonance, err in the same direction, suggesting a kind of Euphuism in verse.

We have been considering how a poet may get over into the field of rhetoric. We might now ask, does a rhetorician ever get into the realm of poetry? I believe he does. Though the orator's end is persuasion, it is not hard to believe that there are moments in his discourse when this end is forgotten in his delight or wonder before some image which fills his inner eye. In such moments he has his eye on the subject, not the audience; he is expressing "the spontaneous overflow of powerful feelings," unrestrained by considerations of the effect he is producing. Although it is hard to be sure when we have such passages in rhetorical discourse, since skilled rhetoricians sometimes feign raptures and give a very good pretense of being carried away by their subject when they are in reality working upon the emotion and will of their audience, I believe there are many sentences in the sermons of John Donne and Jeremy Taylor, to mention only two, where we can say, "Here the poet speaks, rather than the preacher." Such passages in rhetorical discourse might conceivably weaken it as persuasion, since in becoming a poet the orator, as we have said, turns his eye from the audience and occasion to his subject. Thus we treasure many speeches and sermons for reasons quite apart from their persuasive effect either in their own time or in ours.

The supreme example of a rhetorician who became a poet is another preacher of the seventeenth century, John Bunyan. Bunyan was first and last a rhetorician. He was one of the most powerful speakers of his century. He wrote many tracts. And in all his public utterances and his tracts, we are safe in saying, every sentence was informed with a persuasive purpose. Thus his chief work, *Pilgrim's Progress*, was written as a tract, a persuasion to men to be converted. In it he did as we have found some modern rhetoricians doing—he cast his tract into a story, though he used the frankest sort of disguise, that of allegory. But once he had raised his homily into the realm of imagination, so clear were the images before his mind, and such was his delight in them, that he remained throughout almost continuously in the realm of poetry. I say "almost continuously," for I believe that Bunyan's use of imitative rhetoric is so frequent that it fails of verisimilitude; so that the reader comes to feel that the author is directly addressing persuasion to him rather than representing men in action—as indeed is the case.

There is another way in which a rhetorician may approach the realm of poetry, if indeed he may not enter it. That is by conceiving of his audience as does a poet—not as a limited group gathered for some special occasion, but as all mankind, or as posterity, or as the choice spirits of his own and succeeding ages. This practice, again, is very likely to detract from the immediate persuasive effect of his work, while making it of enduring value. I should name Edmund Burke as a rhetorician of this kind. The orator may be carried still further in the direction of poetry if his subject is one of enduring and universal significance.

To summarize, I have tried to emphasize the distinction between pure poetry and rhetoric, and then to suggest that rarely do we find them pure; that poetry in some of its most usual forms is more or less strongly tinged with a rhetorical element; that criticism will walk with surer feet if it can learn to isolate and analyze this rhetorical element. Hence it follows that a part of the equipment of a literary critic, and, we may add, of an interpreter of literature, must be a knowledge of the devices for getting and holding attention, the technique of adaptation to audience and occasion, which are the stock in trade of teachers of public speaking—in other words those "foolish little rhetorical tricks" which Shakespeare and Milton did not disdain to use.

NOTES

The Study of Rhetoric

The excerpt on page vii is from Drummond's article, "Graduate Work in Public Speaking," *Quarterly Journal of Speech*, IX (April, 1923), 138.

The Field of Rhetoric

1. C. H. Woolbert's *Fundamentals of Speech*, pp. 1–2.
2. Readers of "What Teachers of Speech May Learn from the Theory and Practice of the Greeks" by Paul Shorey, *Quarterly Journal of Speech*, VIII (April, 1922), already have a better view of rhetoric in the classical period than I can hope to suggest here.

Plato and Aristotle on Rhetoric and Rhetoricians

1. George Grote, *Plato*, London, 1888, III, 63.
2. G. W. Hegel, *Lectures on Philosophy*, 2d ed., 1840, tr. E. S. Haldane, London, 1892.
3. G. H. Lewes, *Biographical History of Philosophy*, London, 1857, pp. 87 ff.
4. Grote, *History of Greece*, London, 1851, VIII, 67.
5. H. Sidgwick, "The Sophists," *Lectures on the Philosophy of Kant and Other Philosophical Lectures and Essays*, London, 1905.
6. J. S. Mill, "Grote's *Plato*," *Dissertations and Discussions*, New York, 1874, IV.
7. E. M. Cope, "The Sophistic Rhetoric," *Journal of Classical and Sacred Philology*, II (1855), 129–169, III (1856), 34–80, 253–288.
8. E. Zeller, *Pre-Socratic Philosophy*, tr. S. F. Alleyne, London, 1881, II, sect. iii. For still other points of view, see A. W. Benn, *The Greek Philosophers*, London, 1882, ch. 2. Also Sir A. Grant, *The Ethics of Aristotle*, London, 1874, I, 103–154.
9. A. E. Chaignet, *La Rhétorique et son histoire*, Paris, 1888, pp. 43, 44.
10. Introduction to his translation of Plato's *Sophist*.
11. Theodore Gomperz, *Greek Thinkers*, tr. L. Magnus, New York, 1901, I, 422.
12. For citations illustrating the various uses of the word "sophist" by Greek writers, see Gomperz, *op. cit.*, I, 579.
13. Isocrates, *Antidosis, Against the Sophists*. For translations of selected passages see Richard C. Jebb, *Attic Orators*, London, 1893, II, 124–147. See also W. H. Thompson, "On the Philosophy of Isocrates and his Relation to the Socratic Schools," in his edition of Plato's *Phædrus*, London, 1868.
14. See O. T. Navarre, *Essai sur la rhétorique grecque avant Aristote*, Paris, 1900.
15. Hegel, *op. cit.*, I, 352.
16. For Prodicus, see the following: Philostratus, *Lives of the Sophists*, tr. W. C. Wright, New York, 1922, pp. 37–39; F. Welcker, "Prodikos von Keos, Vorgänger des Sokrates," *Rheinisches*

Notes

Museum für Philologie, III (1833), 1–39; Gomperz, *op. cit.*, I, 425–430; Benn, *op. cit.*, I, 77–81; Bromley Smith, "Prodicus of Ceos," *Quarterly Journal of Speech Education*, VI, ii (1920), 51.

17. Pseudo-Platonic *Axiochus*, 360, D. Cited by Gomperz, *op. cit.*, I, 428.

18. Xenophon's *Memorabilia*, tr. E. C. Marchant, New York, 1923, II, ch. 1.

19. For Hippias, see Philostratus, *op. cit.*, p. 35; Gomperz, *op. cit.*, I, 431–434; Benn, *op. cit.*, I, 81–85.

20. For Protagoras, see the following: Philostratus, *op. cit.*, pp. 33–35; Diogenes Laertius, *Lives of the Philosophers*, tr. C. D. Yonge, London, 1853, bk. ix, ch. 8; Hegel, *op. cit.*, I, 372–378; Gomperz, *op. cit.*, I, 438–475; Benn, *op. cit.*, I, 85–95; E. Barker, *Greek Political Theory*, London, 1918, pp. 60–64; Bromley Smith, "Protagoras of Abdera," *Quarterly Journal of Speech Education*, IV (1918), 196.

21. Diogenes Laertius, IX, 51.

22. Schiller, *Studies in Humanism*, London, 1907, p. xiv.

23. Hegel, *op. cit.*, I, 373.

24. For Gorgias, see the following: Philostratus, *op. cit.*, pp. 29–33; Diodorus Siculus, bk. xii, ch. 7; *The Historical Library of Diodorus the Sicilian*, tr. George Booth, London, 1814, I, 465–466; F. Blass, *Attische Beredsamkeit*, Leipzig, 1864, I, ch. 2; Navarre, *op. cit.*, ch. 3; W. H. Thompson's introduction to his edition of Plato's *Gorgias*, London, 1871; Hegel, *op. cit.*, I, 378–384; Gomperz, *op. cit.*, I, 476–494; Benn, *op. cit.*, I, 95–100; Bromley Smith, "Gorgias: A Study of Oratorical Style," *Quarterly Journal of Speech Education*, VII (1921), 335.

25. Aristotle, *Sophistici Elenchi*, tr. Edward Poste, London, 1866, ch. 34.

26. As translated in Gomperz, *op. cit.*, I, 482.

27. G. H. Lewes has shown why the relationship between the solitary thinker and the public speaker tends to remain constant. "The Sophists were wealthy; the Sophists were powerful; the Sophists were dazzling, rhetorical, and not profound. Interrogate human nature— above all, the nature of philosophers— and ask what will be the sentiment entertained respecting the Sophists by their rivals. Ask the solitary thinker what is his opinion of the showy, powerful, but shallow rhetorician who usurps the attention of the world. The man of convictions has at all times a superb contempt for the man of mere oratorical or dialectical display. The thinker knows that the world is ruled by Thought; yet he finds Expression gaining the world's attention. He knows that he has within him thoughts pregnant with human welfare; yet he sees the giddy multitude intoxicated with the enthusiasm excited by some plausible fallacy, clothed in enchanting language. He sees through the fallacy, but cannot make others as clear-sighted. His warning is unheeded; his wisdom is spurned; his ambition is frustrated; the popular Idol is carried onward in triumph. The neglected thinker would not be human if he bore this with equanimity. He does not. He is loud and angry in lamenting the fate of a world that can be so led; loud and angry in his contempt of one who could so lead it. Should he become a critic or historian of his age, what exactness ought we to expect in his account of the popular idol?" *Op. cit.*, p. 88.

28. *Republic*, VI, 492.

29. *Op. cit.*, IV, 262.

30. *Apology*, 20; *Cratylus*, 384 and 391.

31. *Op. cit.*, IV, 245.

32. *Theætetus*, 173. Jowett's translation used for all the dialogues.

33. *Laws*, VII, 798.

34. *Laws*, XII, 950.

35. *Laws*, II, 662.

36. *Laws*, XI, 938.

37. See especially *Republic*, VI, 509 ff.

38. *Antidosis*, tr. J. F. Dobson, in his *Greek Orators*, New York, 1920, p. 142.

39. *Protagoras*, 318.

40. For the Platonic treatment of Protagoras, see the dialogue of that name, and also *Cratylus*, 386; *Euthydemus*, 286; *Theætetus*, 152–178; *Meno*, 91; *Republic*, 600; *Phædrus*, 267.

41. See *Hippias Major* and *Hippias Minor*. Only *Hippias Minor* is admitted into the Platonic canon by Jowett. Grote held to the genuineness of the *Hippias*

Major, and gives an exposition of it in his *Plato.*

42. *Laches,* 197.
43. *Charmides,* 163.
44. *Euthydemus,* 277.
45. *Cratylus,* 384.
46. Other characterizations of Gorgias are found in *Meno,* 70; *Phædrus,* 267; and *Symposium,* 198.
47. *Gorgias,* 466 ff.
48. *Gorgias,* 481 ff.
49. *Republic,* I.
50. *Euthydemus,* 272.
51. E. Barker, *op. cit.,* p. 133.
52. *Gorgias,* 485.
53. *Gorgias,* 513.
54. See *Meno,* 95.
55. *Op. cit.,* I, 386.
56. *Gorgias,* 500.
57. Ælius Aristides, a sophist of the second century A.D., replied to the charges made against rhetoric in the *Gorgias.* One of his discourses is devoted to a defense of the four statesmen here attacked. For a discussion of this see André Boulanger, *Ælius Aristide et la sophistique dans la province d'Asie au II° siècle de nôtre ère,* Paris, 1923.
58. *Gorgias,* 512.
59. *Republic,* 493.
60. *Op. cit.,* IV, 291, 292.
61. Plato had no doubt that a philosopher could easily outdo a rhetorician at his own art. He wrote the *Menexenus* in order to satirize the conventional funeral oration and to show how easily a philosopher could dash off such a speech.
62. *Phædrus,* 259.
63. *Republic,* VII, 515.
64. *Phædrus,* 261.
65. *Phædrus,* 264.
66. *Phædrus,* 265.
67. *Phædrus,* 266.
68. *Phædrus,* 271.
69. For a later, satirical development of this idea, see Lucian, "The Rhetorician's Vade Mecum," *Works of Lucian,* tr. H. W. and F. G. Fowler, Oxford, 1905, III.
70. *Phædrus,* 273.
71. *Phædrus,* 273.
72. *Phædrus,* 273.
73. Scholars have commented variously and at length on this attitude of Plato toward the art of writing. Schlei-

ermacher (*Introduction to the Dialogues of Plato,* tr. William Dobson, London, 1836, p. 67) argues from this attitude that the *Phædrus* was written in Plato's early youth. Such contempt for writing, he thinks, is inconceivable in a man who has already written very much. Lutoslawski (*Origin and Growth of Plato's Logic,* London, 1897, ch. 6) insists that Plato did not despise writing in general, but only bad writing, and the cult of mere literary erudition which substitutes opinion for knowledge, and leads men to put all their attention on the form, making it impossible to have a clear view of general ideas. Lutoslawski has an ingenious explanation of the passages which at the close of so wonderful a piece of writing seem to condemn writing. In Plato's time, and in his own opinion, oral teaching stood very much higher than written handbooks. Plato was very proud of his own eloquence. The purpose of these passages, therefore, is to raise the reader's expectation to the highest pitch by announcing that this beautiful sample of written eloquence is nothing compared with his oral teaching.

A different view is taken by S. H. Butcher in an essay entitled "The Written and Spoken Word" (*Some Aspects of the Greek Genius,* London, 1893). He cites the *Phædrus* in asserting that the Greek dislike for writing was general. In proof of this thesis he offers arguments which may be summarized as follows: (1) The Greeks gave a very cold reception to the discovery of letters; for centuries they employed it, not as a vehicle of thought, but almost wholly for memorial purposes, such as registering treaties and commercial contracts, preserving the names of Olympic victors, and fixing boundaries. (2) They shrank from formulæ; unvarying rules petrified action. To reduce laws to writing was to kill the spirit and exalt the letter. (3) Writing was inartistic, as the letters conveyed no images. (4) The Greeks had a high conception of the dignity of knowledge. True knowledge is not among the marketable wares, that can be carried about in a portable shape in books, and emptied from them into the mind of the learner. True knowledge is a hard-won possession, personable and inalienable. "Much learning does not teach wisdom," was a saying of Heraclitus, and even Aristotle declared that "much learning produces confusion."

For a further account of Plato's aversion to writing see Grote's *Plato*, I, 358.

74. *Phædrus*, 276.

75. Henry Sidgwick in his essays on the sophists was the first to point out this distinction. See his *Lectures on the Philosophy of Kant and other Philosophical Lectures and Essays*. For a discussion of Sidgwick's essays, see Sir A. Grant, *The Ethics of Aristotle*, Essay 2.

76. *Sophist*, 231.

77. *Sophist*, 233, 234.

78. For translations of Aristotle's *Rhetoric*, see those by Welldon, London, 1886; R. L. Jebb, Cambridge, 1909; and W. R. Roberts, in *The Works of Aristotle*, vol. XI, Oxford, 1924. Citations of the *Rhetoric* in this study are taken from Roberts.

79. For expositions of the *Rhetoric*, see E. M. Cope, *An Introduction to Aristotle's Rhetoric*, London, 1867; Gomperz, *op. cit.*, IV; Zeller, *Aristotle and the Earlier Peripatetics*, London, 1897; and C. S. Baldwin, *Ancient Rhetoric and Poetic*, New York, 1924.

80. See Cope's *Introduction to Aristotle's Rhetoric*, section entitled "Aristotle's Lost Works on Rhetoric."

81. See the concluding section of the *Sophistici Elenchi*; also the first chapter of the *Rhetoric*.

82. *Sophistici Elenchi*, ch. 1; and ch. 1 of the *Rhetoric*.

83. *Politics*, 1282.

84. For the contribution of public opinion to Aristotle's *Ethics*, see J. Burnet's introduction to his edition of the work, London, 1900. See also L. H. G. Greenwood's essay, "Dialectic Method in the Sixth Book," in his edition of the sixth book of the *Ethics*, Cambridge, 1909. Sir A. Grant's *Ethics of Aristotle* is also useful in this connection.

85. See Grote's *Aristotle*, London, 1872, for an exposition of the *Topics*.

86. *Rhetoric*, 1355a.

87. *Rhetoric*, 1355b.

88. *Rhetoric*, 1355a.

89. *Rhetoric*, 1354a.

90. *Rhetoric*, 1355b, 1357a, 1359b.

91. *Rhetoric*, 1364b.

92. *Rhetoric*, 1355b.

93. See Lutoslawski, *Origin and Growth of Plato's Logic*, p. 344. Also Gomperz, *op. cit.*, IV, 421. W. H. Thompson, in the introduction to his edition of the *Phædrus*, London, 1868, compares it with the *Rhetoric*, and emphasizes the likenesses of the two works. E. M. Cope recognizes the fundamental difference between Plato and Aristotle on the matter of probability. See the introduction to his edition of the *Gorgias*, London, 1883.

94. For discussions of the topics, see Grote's *Aristotle*; Edward Poste's essays in his translations of Aristotle's *Posterior Analytics*, Oxford, 1850, and *Sophistici Elenchi*; and Cope's *Introduction to Aristotle's Rhetoric*. See also Hoyt H. Hudson, "Can We Modernize the Theory of Invention?" *Quarterly Journal of Speech Education*, VII (1921), 325.

95. On this controverted point, see Cope's *Introduction to Aristotle's Rhetoric*, p. 103 and note. See also De Quincey's essay on rhetoric.

96. *Rhetoric*, 1394a.

97. *Rhetoric*, 1366a.

98. *Rhetoric*, 1376a.

99. *Rhetoric*, 1404a. See the translation of this passage by C. S. Baldwin in his *Ancient Rhetoric and Poetic*, p. 23. Professor Baldwin denies that Aristotle had a "philosophic contempt" for delivery.

100. *Rhetoric*, 1355 and 1356.

101. For the relations of science, dialectic, and rhetoric, see Cope's *Introduction to Aristotle's Rhetoric*, p. 67; Poste's introduction to his translation of Aristotle's *Analytica Posteriora*; Appendix D in his translation of the *Sophistici Elenchi*; and Grote's *Aristotle*.

102. For a comparison of the *Rhetoric* with the *Topics*, and with all the other works of Aristotle with which it comes in contact, see C. A. Brandis, "Über Aristotles' Rhetorik und die griechischen Ausleger Derselben," in Schneidewin's *Philologus*, IV (1849), I.

103. Gomperz, in his *Greek Thinkers*, IV, 435, seems to feel that those sec-

tions of the *Rhetoric* which are genuinely a part of the subject are of relatively little significance for a philosopher, while the parts for which he professes admiration are really out of place in rhetoric. Referring to the treatment of the emotions and characters of men, he says: "It is surprising to find this subject, which seems to belong much more properly to psychology or descriptive ethics, imported into a work on rhetoric, and there treated with an exhaustiveness that goes far beyond the end in view. That which moved Aristotle to this procedure was probably, in the first place, the Platonic ideal of the art as set forth in the *Phædrus;* and secondly, the wish, cherished no less warmly by him than by his master, to separate the new exposition of rhetoric as widely as possible from the old empirical methods and routine wisdom. It so comes about that we have before us foundations of much greater strength and depth than is justified by the superstructure which rests upon them. We shall, perhaps, be not far wrong in conjecturing that Aristotle was glad of the opportunity to raise the tone of that initiation into rhetorical fencing tricks which practical considerations forced upon him. Another cause operating in the same direction may have been a recollection of the fact that at the beginning of the work he had been unwilling to allow emotional effects any place at all in oratory. Now that he felt constrained to descend from that ideal height, he preferred to do so in such a manner that the subject proscribed at first might appear in strictly scientific garb, not as merely auxiliary to rhetorical success."

104. *Rhetoric,* 1356b.
105. *Rhetoric,* 1355b.

Classical Rhetoric and the Mediaeval Theory of Preaching

1. Part of this paper was read before the Classical Association of England and Wales at Cardiff on April 9, 1929.
2. Karl Künstle's *Ikonographie der christlichen Kunst* (Freiburg in B., 1928) supplies much of the information available in this field. See his Bibliography, pp. 145 ff., and also W. Molsdorf, *Christliche Symbolik der mittelalterlichen Kunst* (Leipzig, 1926).
3. *De nuptiis Philologiae et Mercurii,* sec. 426; ed. Dick (Leipzig, 1925), p. 211.
4. See Carolus Halm, *Rhetores Latini minores* (Leipzig, 1863).
5. "Qui Retoricque bien sauroit
   Il connistroit et tort et droit"
says Gossuin of Metz (*saec.* xiii) in *L'image du monde;* Ch.-V. Langlois, *La vie en France au Moyen Age* (Paris, 1927), III, 161.
6. E.g., Cod. Lat. Monac. 4555 (*saec.* xiii), fols. 87 ff.; 22271 (*saec.* xii), fols. 143 ff.; ed. Ludwig Wahrmund in *Quellen zur Geschichte des römisch-kanonischen Processes,* I, Heft 4 (Innsbruck, 1906). See Eilbert, *Ordo Judiciarius,* ed. Ludwig Wahrmund, in *Quellen zur Geschichte des römisch-kanonischen Processes* I, Heft 5 (Innsbruck, 1906); Heinrich Siegel, "Über den Ordo Iudiciarius des Eilbert von Bremen mit Berücksichtigung der *ecclesiastica rethorica,*" *Sitzungsb. der Kaiserl. Akad. der Wiss.* (Vienna), LV (1867), 531–553; Albert Lang, "Rhetorische Einflüsse auf die Behandlung des Prozesses in der Kanonistik des 12. Jahrhunderts," *Festschrift Eduard Eichmann* (Marburg, 1941), pp. 69–97.
7. The works of Ludwig Rockinger are the most important for this branch of learning. See especially his *Briefsteller und Formelbücher des 11ten bis 14ten Jahrh.* (Munich, 1863–1864); cf. also L. J. Paetow, *The Arts Course at Mediaeval Universities* (Urbana-Champaign, Ill., 1910); C. H. Haskins, *Studies in Mediaeval Culture* (Oxford, 1929), pp. 170–192; André Wilmart, "L'Ars arengandi de Jacques de Dinant," *Analecta Reginensia* (*Studi e Testi,* 59, Vatican City, 1933), pp. 113–154; E. H. Kantorowicz, "Anonymi Aurea Gemma," *Medievalia et Humanistica,* I (1943), 41–57; Helene Wieruszowski, "Ars dictaminis in the time of Dante," *Med. et. Hum.,* I (1943), 95–108, and "Arezzo as a center of learning and letters in the thir-

Notes

teenth century," *Traditio*, IX (1953), 351 ff.; P. O. Kristeller, "Matteo de' Libri, Bolognese notary of the thirteenth century, and his *Artes Dictaminis*," in *Miscellanea G. Galbiati*, II (Milan, 1951), 283–320.

8. Cf. Rockinger, *op. cit.*, pp. 128 ff.

9. See his treatise in Halm, *op. cit.*, pp. 525–550.

10. *Opera*, ed. J. S. Brewer (London, 1859), *Opus Tert.*, LXXV, 309.

11. *Opera* (Antwerp, 1706), IV, 214 ff. and 571–582.

12. Francesco Maggini, *La rettorica di Brunetto Latini* ("Pubblicazioni del R. istituto di studi superiori: sezione di filosofia e filologia," Vol. XXXVIII) (Florence, 1915), and also his *La "rettorica" Italiana di Brunetto Latini* (Florence, 1912), p. 65. See also Helene Wieruszowski, "Brunetto Latini als Lehrer Dantes und der Florentiner," *Archivo Italiano per la Storia della Pietà*, II (1957), 186–189.

13. *Les arts poétiques du xii⁰ et du xiii⁰ siècles* (Paris, 1924).

14. On rhetoric in mediaeval education see particularly Paetow, *op. cit.*; F. A. Specht, *Geschichte des Unterrichtswesens in Deutschland* (Stuttgart, 1885); F. H. Denifle, *Die Universitäten des Mittelalters bis 1400* (Berlin, 1885); F. A. Eckstein, *Lateinischer und griechischer Unterricht* (Leipzig, 1887); J. L. Clerval, *L'enseignement des arts liberaux à Chartres et à Paris* (Paris, 1889); Hastings Rashdall, *The Universities of Europe in the Middle Ages* (Oxford, 1895); Hilarin Felder, *Geschichte der wissenschaftlichen Studien im Franziskanerorden* (Freiburg in B., 1904); H. Holzappel, *Handbuch der Geschichte des Franziskanerordens* (Freiburg in B., 1909); Martin Grabmann, *Die Geschichte der scholastischen Methode* (Freiburg in B., 1909); Friedrich Paulsen, *Geschichte des gelehrten Unterrichts* (Leipzig, 1919); C. S. Baldwin, *Medieval Rhetoric and Poetic* (New York, 1928); Richard McKeon, "Rhetoric in the Middle Ages," *Speculum*, XVII, No. 1 (Jan. 1942), 1–32; E. R. Curtius, *European Literature and the Latin Middle Ages*, tr. W. R. Trask (New York, 1953); Dorothy Grosser, *Studies in the influence of the Rhet-*

orica ad Herennium and Cicero's De Inventione, unpublished doctoral dissertation (Cornell University, Ithaca, N.Y., 1953); R. R. Bolgar, *The Classical Heritage and its Beneficiaries* (Cambridge, 1954).

15. An anonymous *Rhetoric* published at Memmingen, 1490–1495; see *Gesamtkatalog der Wiegendrucke*, No. 2671.

16. The copy I have consulted is in the Bibl. Nationale, Paris, Rés. D. 15239 (Hain-Copinger 8305).

17. *Prooemium ad commentarios in Genesim* (Migne, *Pat. Lat.*, Vol. CLVI, cols. 21–32).

18. Migne, *op. cit.*, Vol. CCX, cols. 110–198.

19. *Max. Bibl. Vet. Pat.*, ed. M. de la Bigne (Lyons, 1677), XXV, 426–567.

20. *Opera omnia*, Suppl. III (Trent, 1774), cols. 385–417.

21. *Gesamtkatalog der Wiegendrucke*, Nos. 590–591. See R. Stapper, "Eine angeblich von Albertus Magnus verfasste *Ars praedicandi*," *Römische Quartalschrift*, Suppl. xx (Freiburg in B., 1913), pp. 388–402, and H. Kuhle, "Zur angeblich von Albert d.Grosse verfassten *Ars praedicandi*," *Röm. Quart.* (1928), pp. 324–328. The *incipit* is the same as that of William of Auvergne's *De faciebus* (*Veritas ewangelica predicatoribus*), and these incunabula are regarded as copies of that tract of William's; see Th. Charland *Artes Praedicandi* (listed in n. 24 below), pp. 21 f. In the present paper I refer to this tract as the "Albertus"-tract.

22. See Hain 8397, 8398, 8399, and Caplan, " 'Henry of Hesse' on the Art of Preaching," *Publications of the Modern Language Association*, XLVIII, No. 2 (June, 1933), 340–361.

23. See Caplan, "A Late Medieval Tractate on Preaching," in *Studies in Rhetoric and Public Speaking in Honor of J. A. Winans* (New York: Century Co., 1926), p. 71.

24. In the case of several names in the list the authorship of tracts is as yet not definitely certain. Until the problems are thoroughly investigated I tentatively accept the attributions of the MSS themselves, knowing full well from many of the cases above that have been studied

how often such assignments are false. Furthermore, as regards several others in this list, references to tracts of their authorship are known, but as yet no MSS have been found by me. The enumeration here is not exhaustive, especially as to the fourteenth and fifteenth centuries; and where I have not made a personal examination of the MSS I may have inadvertently included other than strictly technical treatises.

Father Th.-M. Charland, O.P., has been so kind as to send me the following names, not obtained by me, which might be added to the list above: (*saec.* xiii) Dionysius de Gilleyo, Cist., and Thomas of Pavia (?), O.M.; (*saec.* xiv) Franciscus Eximenis, O.M., Landulphus de Manzoriis, O.M., and Simon de Ragusa; (*saec.* xv) Aegidius (?), Christian Borgsleben, O.M., Galfridus Schale, O.S.A., Hugo Sunfeld (?), Nicolas Eyfeler, O.M., and Dionysius Brisenus, O.S.A.

[The above is part of a longer note which appeared in the original publication of this paper in 1933. For much fuller lists of authors, problems of authorship involved in certain instances, information about the many anonymous tracts, and other pertinent studies of mediaeval homiletical theory, now see: M. M. Davy, *Les sermons universitaires parisiens de 1230–1231* (Paris, 1931); Harry Caplan, *Mediaeval Artes Praedicandi: A Hand-List* (Ithaca, London, Oxford, 1934), and *Mediaeval Artes Praedicandi: A Supplementary Hand-List* (Ithaca, London, Oxford, 1936); Th.-M. Charland, *Artes Praedicandi* (Paris, Ottawa, 1936); W. O. Ross, "A brief Forma Praedicandi," *Modern Philology*, XXXIV, No. 4 (May, 1937), 337–344, and *Middle English Sermons* (London, 1940); Mary F. Boynton, "Simon Alcok on Expanding the Sermon," *Harvard Theol. Rev.*, XXXIV, No. 3 (July, 1941), 201–216; J. de Ghellinck, *L'Essor de la littérature latine au xiie siècle* (2d ed., Brussels, 1954), n. 35, pp. 206–208; Harry Caplan and Henry H. King, *Pulpit Eloquence: A List of Doctrinal and Historical Studies in English,* in *Speech Monographs,* XXII, No. 4 (1955), and *Pulpit Eloquence: A List of Doctrinal and His-*torical Studies in German, in Speech Monographs, XXIII, No. 5 (1956)— see p. 5, n. 1, and p. 7, for Latin, Italian, French, Spanish, Scandinavian, and Dutch lists; Dorothea Roth, *Die mittelalterliche Predigtthorie und das Manuale Curatorum des Johann Ulrich Surgant* (Basel, 1956); Heinrich Fichtenau, *Arenga,* in *Mitteilungen des Instituts für Österreichische Geschichtsforschung, Ergänzungsband,* XVIII (Graz-Cologne, 1957).]

25. A. de Poorter, "Un manuel de prédication médiévale," *Revue néo-scolastique de philosophie,* 1923, pp. 192–209. See also n. 21, above.

26. Published anonymously as *Ars praedicandi sive informatio notabilis et praeclara de arte praedicandi* and as *Ars praedicandi;* see *Gesamtkatalog der Wiegendrucke,* Nos. 2669 and 2670, and Pellechet, Nos. 313 and 314. The MSS are also anonymous, except two that are pertinent: Mazarine 569, fols. 80^v–86^v, bearing the name of John of Wales, and Troyes 1922, fols. 87–95, bearing that of Humbert of Prully. The ascription, then, of this tract to John of Wales (throughout the present study) is merely tentative.

27. *Summa moralis, Pars* III, *Tit.* XVIII, chaps. iii–vi (Venice, 1582), fols. 331–337^v.

28. See n. 60.

29. *Modus predicandi subtilis et compendiosus* (Strassburg, 1513); Brit. Mus. T. 1567. (1).

30. Hain 7399, 7400, 8162, 8168.

31. Erfurt (Amplon.) MS Qu. 151 (end *saec.* xiv), fols. 155–161^v, regarded as genuine by F. W. E. Roth, "Zur Bibliographie des Henricus Hembuche de Hassia dictus de Langenstein," in *Beihefte zum Centralblatt für Bibliothekswesen* (Leipzig, 1888), II, 15. Cf. n. 22 above.

32. *Evagatorium, modus predicandi* (Cologne, 1503); Brit. Mus., 843, c. 20.

33. Cod. Lat. Monac. 1925 (= 21).

34. T. F. Tout, *Chapters in the Administrative History of Mediaeval England* (Manchester, 1920), II, 226.

35. The MSS of which we have knowledge must number almost five hundred.

36. See Grabmann, *op. cit.,* II, 59 ff.,

Notes

"Wertung and Verwertung der antiken Klassiker in der Literatur des 12. Jahrhunderts," for a discussion of the position of scholasticism with regard to profane studies.

37. M. L. W. Laistner, *Thought and Letters in Western Europe, A.D. 500–900* (rev. ed., London, 1957), pp. 212–213. For an excellent discussion of education and the seven liberal arts in the Carolingian period one should read all of chap. viii in this book.

38. J. M. Campbell and M. R. P. McGuire, *The Confessions of St. Augustine* (New York, 1931), p. 116.

39. *De doctr. Christ.*, II, 60.

40. Doubtless through Jerome, *Epist.*, No. 70.

41. III, 19: *De rhetorica* (ed. A. Knoepfler [Munich, 1900], pp. 225–226).

42. Quoted from the *Sententiae* by Grabmann, *op. cit.*, II, 350.

43. *Metalogicus*, I, 7 (835a), ed. C. C. I. Webb (Oxford, 1929), p. 23.

44. Migne, *op. cit.*, Vol. CLXXII, cols. 1243–1244.

45. *Speculum majus* (Venice, 1591), II, 3, 99; IV, 1, 55; IV, 17, 52.

46. See J. Walsh, "St. Thomas on Preaching," *Dominicana*, V (1921), 6–14.

47. See Daunou in *Hist. litt. de la France*, XX, 14.

48. *Summa praedicantium*, Prologue and II, 12, 32.

49. Felder, *op. cit.*, p. 382.

50. E.g., Paetow, *op. cit.*, chap. iii.

51. *Grundriss der romanischen philologie* (Strassburg, 1902), p. 252.

52. *Op. cit.*, p. 115.

53. Cod. Lat. Monac. 2689 (xiv), fol. 173ᵛ.

54. *Op. cti.* (Migne, *Pat. Lat.*, CCX, 112).

55. Cf. Stapper, *op. cit.*

56. *Max. Bibl. Vet. Pat.*, XXV, 432.

57. De Poorter, *op. cit.*, p. 202.

58. Book I, *Consideratio* 19.

59. See Grabmann, *op. cit.*, I, 149–160, "Boethius als Vermittler des Aristotelismus an das abendländische Mittelalter."

60. For a *Fortleben* of Quintilian in this period, see F. H. Colson, *M. Fabii Quintiliani Institutionis oratoriae liber I* (Cambridge, 1924), Introd., pp. xliii–lvi; also Paul Lehmann, "Die Institutio oratoria des Quintilianus im Mittelalter," *Philologus*, LXXXIX (1934), 349–383; A. Mollard, "L'imitation de Quintilien dans Guibert de Nogent," *Moyen Age*, V (1934), 81–87; Priscilla S. Boskoff, "Quintilian in the late middle ages," *Speculum*, XXVII, No. 1 (Jan. 1952), 71–78.

61. See Caplan, "Rhetorical Invention in Some Mediaeval Tractates on Preaching," *Speculum*, II, No. 3 (July, 1927), 284–295.

62. Part II.

63. Mazarine MS 569, fol. 81ᵛᵃ, or Basel A VIII, 1. fol. 148ʳ. Florenz Landmann, *Das Predigtwesen in Westfalen* (Münster in W., 1900), p. 122, n. 1, gives this as also Thomas von Cleve's definition, Münster Paulin. MS 476, fol. 139. On p. 121, n. 8, he recognizes the close resemblance of the tract going under the name of Thomas von Cleve (*saec.* xv) and the anonymous treatise represented by *Gesamtkatalog*, Nos. 2669, 2670. This last is really a version of the thirteenth-century treatise now attached to the name of John of Wales (cf. n. 26). A study of Paulin. 476.139–155 would be desirable.

64. See Etienne Gilson, "Michel Menot et la technique du sermon médiéval," *Revue d'histoire franciscaine*, II, No. 3 (July, 1925), 301 ff. This paper provides an excellent treatment of sermon-method.

65. Cod. Lat. Monac. 17290 (xiv–xv), fols. 136–146 ("ars . . . . faciendi sermones secundum artem [formam] syllogisticam"); also Bibl. Nat. 173 (xiv), fols. 12–24ᵛ; Cod. Lat. Monac. 14580 (xv), fols. 152 ff.; Vat. Ottob. 396 (xv), fols. 14–29; Angers 324 (xv), fols. 128 ff.

66. *Verbum abbreviatum*, chap. i (Migne, *op. cit.*, Vol. XXV, col. 25).

67. There are several tracts outlining eight methods—the favorite number. "Henry of Hesse," on the other hand, offers only three: division, question, and digression. This list is rather a composite (superficial, I am aware) of topics of *dilatatio* that are not necessarily distinct and separate, but obviously overlap.

68. Paris, Bibl. Nat. Nouv. Lat. 280 (xiii–xiv), fol. 1; *Inc.:* "Octo modis potest aliquis habundare in themate."

69. Dante, *Paradiso,* XXXI, 104, and *Vita Nuova,* XLI, 2–5.

70. Ulrich Surgant, *Manuale curatorum* (Basel, 1506); cf. Roth, *op. cit.,* p. 173 ff.

71. See Caplan, "The Four Senses of Scriptural Interpretation and the Mediaeval Theory of Preaching," in *Speculum,* IV, No. 3 (July, 1929), 282–290. Since that paper was written, it has become abundantly clear that the principle of the use of these senses was extremely popular in the tracts on preaching. A very interesting treatise, *Compendium de sensibus Sacrae Scripturae,* by Hermann von Schilditz, O.S.A. (*saec.* xiv) appears in MS A VII. 45, fols. 133–147, of the Universitätsbibliothek at Basel.

72. The Jesuit Polcari, as late as 1859, gives careful attention to the four senses in his influential *Universae eloquentiae institutiones* (Naples), pp. 245 ff.

73. A. C. Bombaugh, *Gleanings for the Curious from the Harvest Fields of Literature* (Philadelphia, 1876).

74. *A Book of Seventeenth-Century Prose,* ed. R. P. R. Coffin and A. M. Witherspoon, pp. 456 and 457, from Bodl., Ashm. MS 826, fol. 102^v.

75. The story of a sermon recently delivered at Yale University is doubtless apocryphal. A student, deeply affected by an hour's varied exposition, in this style, of the true meaning of the monosyllable *Y-A-L-E,* is alleged to have piously expressed his thankfulness that he was not attending the Massachusetts Institute of Technology.

76. *Opusc.,* XIII, 360*b* ff.

77. Surgant (Book I, *Consideratio* 23) adds: voluntary baring of the teeth, uncontrolled features, indecent gestures, sleepy delivery, excessive briskness or speed. Petrus Cantor (*Verb. abbrev.,* chap. 1): "Excessive speed is the mother of oblivion and the stepmother of memory."

78. *Opusc.,* XIII, 359*b.*

79. *Ibid.,* No. XVI.

80. See the *Prooemium* to his *Sermones* (Antwerp, 1575).

81. See Stapper, *op. cit.*

82. E.g., so suggests the Franciscan author of the *Ars concionandi.*

83. So called in the "Aquinas"-tract (Caplan, p. 71); cf. Gregory, *Pastoral Rule,* chap. i.

84. *Op. cit.,* chap. vi.

85. *Lectio 2 super Marcum* (Antwerp, 1706), IV, 217.

86. *Op. tert.,* chap. lxxv.

87. J. M. E. Joly, *Histoire de la prédication* (Amsterdam, 1767), p. 201.

88. Such an *arbor* appears at the end of the "Aquinas"-tract in some editions (cf. Cod. Lat. Monac. 23865, fols. 19^v–20).

89. Cf. Cod. Lat. Monac. 18635, fols. 67–123 (*saec.* xv–xvi): "Tractatus de rhetorica ex Tullio, Quintiliano, aliis excerptus in usum praedicatorum."

90. Ed. Leipzig, 1562.

91. In *De arte concionandi formulae . . . . Ioanne Reuclino. anonymo quodam rhapsodo, Philippo Melancthone, D. Ioanne Hepino autoribus* (London, 1570), fols. 2–19^v; Brit. Mus. 4499.a.30.

92. *De officiis concionatoris,* in *De arte concionandi formulae,* fols. 54–61.

93. (Lübeck, 1747), I, 6, 4: *De rhetoribus atque oratoribus sacris.*

94. Book I, *Consideratio* 6.

95. Ed. G. S. Gordon (Oxford, 1906), p. 45.

96. E.g., D. Ferrari, *L'arte di dire* (Milan, 1907).

97. *Op. cit.,* pp. 217 and 239 ff.

Quintilian's Witnesses

1. S. S. Laurie, *Studies in the History of Educational Opinion from the Renaissance,* Cambridge, 1903, p. 83.

2. Epistle 62 of the *Lettres de Servat Loup,* ed. by G. D. de Duzert, Paris, 1888, pp. 148–149. See also C. H. Beeson, *Lupus of Ferrières as Scribe and Text Critic,* Cambridge, Mass., 1930, p. 4.

3. See Bk. 1, ch. 24 of the edition by C. C. J. Webb, Oxford, 1929.

4. C. S. Baldwin, *Mediæval Rhetoric and Poetic,* New York, 1928, pp. 169–172.

5. H. C. Maxwell Lyte, *A History of the University of Oxford,* London, 1886,

Notes

1.92–93, citing *Wardrobe Accounts, 16–18 Edw. I (4/8 Exchequer Q.R.)* and *Wardrobe Book, 18 Edw. I (Tower).*

6. Thomas Warton, *History of English Poetry,* ed. by W. Carew Hazlitt, London, 1871, 1.180.

7. During the time when Richard held the Privy Seal he defended the monks of St. Albans in their controversy with the townspeople over the ownership of certain tracts of land. In gratitude, the Abbot, Richard de Wallingford, presented to the famous collector four choice volumes, among them a copy of Quintilian. F. S. Merryweather, *Bibliomania in the Middle Ages,* New York, 1900, p. 121.

8. Shortly before he died, Humphrey, the uncle of Henry VI, gave to the library at Oxford, a large number of valuable books, including seven volumes of Cicero's works, and a copy of Quintilian. Maxwell Lyte, *op. cit.,* 1.321.

9. Grey willed over two hundred manuscripts to the library of Balliol College, "including hitherto unknown orations and treatises by Cicero and Quintilian." J. B. Mullinger, *A History of the University of Cambridge,* Cambridge, 1884, 1.397.

10. Besides the copies just mentioned, the cataloguer of Peterhouse College in 1416 listed a copy of the *Institutio.* See Rev. T. A. Walker, "English and Scottish Education" in *Cambridge History of English Literature,* 2.415.

11. A complete list of editions in Quintilian down to 1810 is included in Lemaire's edition of his works in *Bibliotheca Classica,* Paris, 1825, 7.277–300.

12. W. H. Woodward, *Desiderius Erasmus, Concerning the Aim and Method of Education,* Cambridge, 1904, p. 20.

13. See Epistles 115, 324, and 335 in *Epistles of Erasmus,* translated by F. M. Nichols, London, 1901, 1.238; 2.205; 2.215.

14. *Tudor School-Boy Life, The Dialogues of Juan Luis Vives,* translated by Foster Watson, London, 1908, Introduction, p. xvii.

15. See also *Vives: On Education,* a translation of *De Tradendis Disciplinis,* Cambridge, 1913.

16. S. S. Laurie says: "There is, I suspect, little in Vives that may not be found in Quintilian and Plutarch." *Op. cit.,* p. 144.

17. Watson, *Vives: On Education,* p. 66; cf. *Inst. Orat.* 1.2.17–29.

18. *Ibid.,* p. 79; cf. *Inst. Orat.* 1.3.

19. *Ibid.,* p. 90, note 2, and p. 91, note 1; cf. *Inst. Orat.* 1.1.

20. *Ibid.,* p. 106; cf. *Inst. Orat.* 10.1.

21. *Ibid.,* p. 109; cf. *Inst. Orat.* 1.3.1.

22. *Ibid.,* p. 120, note 1; cf. *Inst. Orat.* 1.3.13–17.

23. *Ibid.,* p. 134; cf. *Inst. Orat.* 9.3.

24. *Ibid.,* p. 145, note 2; cf. *Inst. Orat.* 10.1.

25. *Ibid.,* pp. 152, 153, 183.

26. *Ibid.,* pp. 189, 190; cf. *Inst. Orat* 1.2 and 10.2.

27. *Ibid.,* p. 192; cf. *Inst. Orat.* 1.2 and 2.2.

28. *Ibid.,* pp. 141, 193. Vives questions the mediæval custom of assigning authorship of the *Declamations to Quintilian.* He himself published an imitation of them in 1520.

29. *Ibid.,* p. 230; cf. *Inst. Orat.* 10.1.

30. *Ibid.,* p. 235; cf. *Inst. Orat.* 10.1.31–34.

31. *Ibid.,* p. 30; cf. *Inst. Orat.* 10.4.

32. *Ibid.,* p. 118; cf. *Inst. Orat.* 1.1

33. *Ibid.,* pp. 152, 154; cf. *Inst. Orat.* 1.8.21.

34. *Ibid.,* p. 186; cf. *Inst. Orat.* 10.3.

35. *Ibid.,* pp. 186, 292; cf. *Inst. Orat.* 12.1.

36. *The Boke Named the Gouernour,* ed. by H. H. S. Croft, London, 1908, 1.31; cf. *Inst. Orat.* 1.1.15–20.

37. *Ibid.,* 1.51; cf. *Inst. Orat.* 1.3.7.

38. *Ibid.,* 1.53–54, 131; cf. *Inst. Orat.* 1.1.12, 15.

39. *Ibid.,* 1.57; cf. *Inst. Orat.* 11.2.1.

40. *Ibid.,* 1.58; cf. *Inst. Orat.* 10.1.46.

41. *Ibid.,* 1.72–73.

42. *Ibid.,* 1.82; cf. *Inst. Orat.* 10.1.32.

43. *Ibid.,* 1.120; cf. *Inst. Orat.* 10.1.89.

44. *Ibid.,* 1.32; cf. *Inst. Orat.* 1.1.20.

45. *Ibid.,* 1.131 and 2.401; cf. *Inst. Orat.* 10.1.40.

46. *Ibid.,* 1.163–165; cf. *Inst. Orat.* 1.4.4.

47. Ascham, *Works,* ed. by J. A. Giles, London, 1864–1865, 3.176; see also 3.192 and 3.221.

48. See *Inst. Orat.* 1.3.1; 10.1.3. Here Quintilian outlines the qualifications for the training of the ideal orator: "For obviously, the power of speech is the first essential, . . . the power of imitation comes next, and third and last, diligent practice in writing." I quote from the translation of H. E. Butler in the Loeb series, London, 1920–1922. The doctrine of Imitation is fully considered in 10.2.

49. Sturm's principal educational work was *De Litterarum Ludis* (1538). J. E. Spingarn says: "According to Sturm, imitation is not the servile copying of words and phrases; it is 'a vehement and artistic application of mind,' which judiciously uses and transfigures all that it imitates. Sturm's theory of imitation is not entirely original, but comes through Agricola and Melanchthon from Quintilian." *A History of Literary Criticism in the Renaissance*, New York, 1899, p. 132.

50. "Then must the master come to Quintilian's goodly lesson *de emendatione.*" *Works*. 3.183. "Quintilian in his learned chapter *de compositione, . . .*" *Ibid.*, 3.250. Altogether there are about twenty references, plain or implied, in *The Scholemaster*.

51. *Positions*, ed. by R. H. Quick, London, 1888, p. 11.

52. *The Elementarie*, ed. by E. T. Campagnac, Oxford, 1925, p. 10.

53. *Ibid.*, pp. 104–106.

54. *Ibid.*, p. 56, and *Positions*, p. 161. 161.

55. *Ibid.*, pp. 40–41.

56. *Ibid.*, p. 23.

57. *Ibid.*, p. 17.

58. See the thorough article by LaRue Van Hook: "Greek Rhetorical Terminology in Puttenham's *The Arte of English Poesie*," in *Transactions of the American Philological Association*, 45 (1914), 111–128. It would seem that Van Hook is over zealous in stating Puttenham's debt to Quintilian. He finds, p. 116: "only fourteen terms unaccounted for, and it is quite probable that most of these 14 terms could be found, in some form or other, somewhere in Quintilian's great work, which bristles with technical terms."

59. *The Arte of English Poesie*, London, 1589, p. 107. W. L. Rushton in *Shakespeare and "The Arte of English Poesie,"* Liverpool, 1909, p. 1, says: "Shakespeare not only introduces in his plays many of the figures which Puttenham describes, but also frequently uses the same words which appear in the examples Puttenham gives of Figures."

60. Mullinger, *op. cit.*, 2.109–111.

61. Maxwell Lyte, *op. cit.*, 1.412. See also G. R. M. Ward, *The Foundation Statutes of Corpus Christi College*, London, 1847, p. 99 ff.

62. Maxwell Lyte, *op. cit.*, 1.453.

63. Paris, 1906. See also: Maurice Castelain, *Ben Jonson, L'Homme et L'Œuvre*, Paris, 1907.

64. The longer parts which Jonson makes his own from the *Institutio* are to be found in the following sections of *Discoveries:* 62, De vere argutis; 63, Censura de poetis; 65, Ingeniorum discrimina; 110, De pictura; 114, On Studies for Children; 115, De stylo et optimo scribendi genere; 116, Praecipiendi modi; 117, Fals. querel. fugienda; and 118 Praecept. element.

65. Ben Jonson, *Discoveries*, ed. by Castelain, Introduction, p. xxv.

66. *Conversations*, ed. by R. F. Patterson, London, 1923, p. 2.

67. *Ibid.*, Introduction, p. xxv. See also p. 13.

68. Title-page of *Chironomia*.

69. *Ibid.*, p. 125.

70. In Chapter XI of this work, entitled "Invention, Memory, and Judgment," Walker prescribes as "inventive" authors: Cicero, Quintilian, and Seneca.

71. Essay found in Wotton's *Reliquae Wottoniae*, London, 1651, pp. 315–335. References to Quintilian are on pp. 330–331.

72. *The Works of John Locke, Esq.*, London, 1740, 3.85.

73. *Ibid.*, 1.245.

74. Laurie, *op. cit.*, p. vi.

75. These may be found *passim* in R. H. Quick's second edition of *Some Thoughts Concerning Education*, Cambridge, 1889, and also in the three chapters on Locke in Laurie, *op. cit.*, pp. 181–234.

76. Laurie, *op. cit.*, p. 234.

77. Gabriel Compayré points out that the scheme recommended by Locke in

Notes

the *Thoughts,* section 160, of teaching children to write with the aid of a stencil, is the same as the one suggested by Quintilian. *The History of Pedagogy,* translated by W. H. Payne, Boston, 1892, p. 49. See Quick's edition of the *Thoughts,* p. 36.

78. John Ward, *A System of Oratory,* London, 1759, 1.15.

79. John Ogilvie, *Observations,* London, 1774, 1.8.

80. Hugh Blair, *Lectures on Rhetoric,* Philadelphia, 1846, pp. 386–387.

81. F. H. Colson, *Quintilian, Book I,* Cambridge, 1924, Introduction, p. lxxxvii, note 3.

82. Blair, *op. cit.,* p. 94.

83. *Ibid.,* pp. 102, 107.

84. *Ibid.,* p. 131.

85. *Ibid.,* p. 164.

86. *Ibid.,* p. 186.

87. *Ibid.,* pp. 213–214.

88. *Ibid.,* pp. 275–276.

89. *Ibid.,* pp. 348–349.

90. Lines 669–674 of the *Essay* in *The Works of Alexander Pope,* ed. by Elwin-Courthope, London, 1871, 2.76.

91. Spence, *Anecdotes, Observations, and Characters of Books and Men,* London, 1820, p. 234. Pope applied Quintilian's theory of Imitation in his own early training in composition. His practice he revealed to Spence, as follows: "In these rambles of mine through the poets; when I met with a passage, or story, that pleased me more than ordinary, I used to endeavour to imitate it, or translate it into English; and this gave rise to my Imitations published so long after." Then Spence adds the note: "He named, among other books he then read, the criticisms of Rapin and Bossu; and these might be what lead him to write his *Essay on Criticism.* He used to mention Quintilian too as an old favourite author with him."

92. Warton, *An Essay on the Genius and Writings of Pope,* 3rd ed., London, 1772, 1.78. See the doctoral study, *Quintilian's Didactic Metaphors,* by Jane Gray Carter, New York, 1910.

93. Warton, *op. cit.,* 2.230; 1.83; 2.461; 1.114.

94. Johnson, *Lives of the English Poets,* ed. by G. B. Hill, Oxford, 1905, 3.340, note 8; 2.77; 1.416.

95. No. 88 for Jan. 19, 1751. *The Works of Samuel Johnson, LL.D.,* ed. by Arthur Murphy, Dublin, 1793, 3.66.

96. Dodsley, *The Preceptor,* London, 1763 ed., p. xxiii.

97. Houston, *Doctor Johnson, A Study in Eighteenth-Century Humanism,* Cambridge, 1923, pp. 51–52.

98. Gerard, *An Essay on Taste,* London, 1759, p. 157.

99. See especially *ibid.,* p. 180.

100. *Miscellaneous Works of Edward Gibbon, Esq.,* ed. by John, Lord Sheffield, Dublin, 1796, 2.298. Also in *Gibbon's Journal,* ed. by D. M. Low, London, 1929, p. 81. For other references see *Misc. Works,* 2.417, and the *Decline and Fall of the Roman Empire,* ed. by J. B. Bury, London, 1898–1900, 5.455, note.

101. *The Letters of Philip Dormer Stanhope,* ed. by John Bradshaw, New York, 1892, 1.118.

102. Chesterfield's *Letters, op. cit.,* 1.278. The same advice is given again in *Letters of Philip Dormer, Fourth Earl of Chesterfield, to his Godson and Successor,* ed. by the Earl of Carnarvon, Oxford, 1890, p. 325.

103. Knox, *Personal Nobility,* London, 1793, pp. 68–70. See also pp. 65–66.

104. Austin, *Chironomia,* London, 1806, p. 147.

105. *Ibid.,* p. 17.

106. Edward Copleston, *A Reply to the Calumnies of the Edinburgh Review,* 2nd ed., Oxford, 1810, pp. 128–129.

107. Swinburne, *A Study of Ben Jonson,* London, 1889, pp. 167–168.

108. Ben Jonson, *Discoveries,* ed. by Castelain, pp. 83–84.

109. Swinburne, *op. cit.,* p. 124.

110. Thomas De Quincey, *Essays on Style, Rhetoric, and Language,* ed. by F. N. Scott, Boston, 1893, p. 148.

111. See the *Life and Letters of Lord Macaulay,* ed. by G. O. Trevelyan, Detroit, 1877, 1.296.

112. See the *Life, Letters, and Diaries of Sir Stafford Northcote,* ed. by Andrew Lang, Edinburgh, 1890, 2.178.

113. *Autobiography of John Stuart Mill,* Preface by J. J. Coss, New York, 1924, p. 15.

114. Saintsbury, *History of Criticism,* London, 1900–1904, 1.319.

115. Laurie, *Pre-Christian Education,* London, 1895, pp. 377–412. See also his *History of Educational Opinion from the Renaissance.*

116. In *The Quarterly Review,* 163 (1886), pp. 289–329.

117. Reprinted in Collins, *Ephemera Critica,* London, 1901, p. 67.

118. Collins, *The Study of Literature,* London, 1891, pp. 39–40.

119. *Ibid.,* p. 42.

120. *Ibid.* For other references to Quintilian see *ibid.,* pp. 78, 82, 84. See also *Ephemera Critica,* p. 278; L. C. Collins, *Life and Memoirs of John Churton Collins,* London, 1912, pp. 109, 178–180; *The Posthumous Essays of John Churton Collins,* London, 1912, p. 259; J. C. Collins, *Studies in Poetry and Criticism,* London, 1905, pp. 214, 235, 249, 287, note.

Thomas Wilson's Contributions to Rhetoric

1. Croll, M. W., *Introduction to Lyly's Euphues* (1916), p. lxiii.

2. Warton, Thomas, *The History of English Poetry* (1778) (London, 1870), p. 841.

3. Mair, G. H., *Wilson's Arte of Rhetorique* (Oxford, 1909), p. xxii.

4. *Ibid.,* p. 2. (With modern spelling.)

5. *Ibid.,* p. 116.

6. *Ibid.,* pp. 3, 4.

7. *Quarterly Journal of Speech,* XV, 140.

8. Croft, H. H. S. ed., *The Boke Named the Gouernour* (1531), by Sir Thomas Elyot (London, 1883), I, 149.

9. Baldwin, C. S., *Ancient Rhetoric and Poetic* (New York, 1924), p. 67.

10. Hallam, Henry, *Introduction to the Literature of Europe* (London, 1843), II, 209.

Bacon's Conception of Rhetoric

1. See, for example, Edwin Greenlaw, *The Province of Literary History,* Baltimore, 1931, pp. 40–45.

2. *The Advancement of Learning, Works* III, 409. Throughout this study the symbol *Works* designates *The Works of Francis Brown,* ed. by J. Spedding, R. L. Ellis, and D. D. Heath, London, 1879, 7ᵛ.

3. *Ibid.*

4. Translation of the *De Augmentis Scientiarum* VI, 3, *Works* IV, 455.

5. *Adv. of L., Works* III, 409.

6. *De Aug.* VI, 3, *Works* IV, 455.

7. *De Aug.* IV, 3, *Works* IV, 398.

8. *De Aug.* V, 1, *Works* IV, 405.

9. *De Rhetorica,* 1355b26. In *The Works of Aristotle Translated into English,* ed. by W. D. Ross, Oxford, 1924, vol. XI.

10. Letter to Sir Francis Walsingham, *Letters and Life* I, 98. In this study the symbol *Letters and Life* refers to the *Letters and Life of Francis Bacon including all his Occasional Works,* ed. by James Spedding, London, 1861–1872, 7ᵛ.

11. Letter to Mr. Secretary Cecil, *Letters and Life* III, 49.

12. *Works* VII, 100.

13. *De Aug.* VI, 3, *Works* IV, 448–454.

14. *The Works of Francis Bacon,* ed. by J. Spedding, R. L. Ellis, and D. D. Heath, 15ᵛ, Boston, 1861–1864; VI, 70–71.

15. *Adv. of L., Works* III, 342.

16. *Letters and Life* III, 49.

17. *De Aug.* VI, 3, *Works* IV, 458.

18. *Ibid.*

19. *De Aug.* VI, 3, *Works* IV, 456.

20. *Ibid.*

21. *Adv. of L., Works* III, 410.

22. *Ibid.,* 382.

23. *Adv. of L., Works* III, 329.

24. *Ibid.,* 382.

25. *Adv. of L., Works* III, 343.

26. *De Aug.* II, 1, *Works* IV, 292.

27. *De Aug.* V, 1, *Works* IV, 406.

28. *De Aug.* VI, 3, *Works* IV, 455.

29. *De Aug.* V, 4, *Works* IV, 430.

30. Spedding declares that Bacon uses the word "invent" simply as equivalent to *invenir,* to find out. *Adv. of L., Works* III, 384n.

31. *Ibid.,* 384.

32. *De Aug.* VI, 1, *Works* IV, 438–439.

33. *Ibid.,* 439–440.

34. *Ibid.,* 440.

Notes

35. *De Aug.* VI, 2, *Works* IV, 448.
36. *De Aug.* VI, 1, *Works* IV, 439.
37. *Colours of Good and Evil, Works* VII, 77.
38. *De Aug.* V, 1, *Works* IV, 406.
39. *De Aug.* VI, 3, *Works* IV, 455–456.
40. *Adv. of L., Works* III, 409.
41. *Adv. of L., Works* III, 410–411.
42. *Adv. of L., Works* III, 410.
43. *Filum Labyrinthi, Works* (Boston) VI, 425–426.
44. Dudley Fenner's *Artes of Logike and Rethoricke,* London, 1584, is typical of those books which would limit the scope of rhetoric. The second book, stating that rhetoric is the "Arte of speaking finely," divides the art into two parts: "Garnishing of speech, called Eloquution," and the "Garnishing of the maner of utterance, called Pronunciation."
45. *De Aug.* V, 4, *Works* IV, 429–430.
46. *Ibid.,* 430.
47. *Works* VII, 67–92.
48. *De Aug.* V, 4, *Works* IV, 431.
49. *De Aug.* V, 1, *Works* IV, 406.
50. *De Aug.* VII, 1, *Works* V, 3–10.
51. *Colours, Works* VII, 77.
52. *Mr. Francis Bacon to the Lord Mountjoye, Works* VII, 70.
53. *Adv. of L., Works* III, 434.
54. *De Aug.* VII, 2, *Works* V, 23.
55. See Crane, R. S., "The Relation of Bacon's Essays to His Program for the Advancement of Learning." *Schelling Anniversary Papers,* N.Y., 1923.
56. *Adv. of L., Works* III, 383.
57. *De Aug.* VI, 3, *Works* IV, 458.
58. The three quotations are from *Sylva Sylvarum, Century X, Works* II, 657.
59. *Colours, Works* VII, 77.
60. *Adv. of L., Works* III, 384.
61. For an intelligible account of the Baconian method, see that of Basil Montagu, *The Life of Francis Bacon,* London, 1833, pp. 285–290.
62. From "The Plan of the Work," part of the preface to *The Great Instauration, Works* IV, 24.
63. *Adv. of L., Works* III, 389.
64. *De Aug.* V, 3, *Works* IV, 423.

65. *Ibid.*
66. *De Aug.* III, 1, *Works* IV, 339.
67. *Adv. of L., Works* III, 411.
68. *De Aug.* V, 3, *Works* IV, 424.
69. *Ibid.*
70. *De Aug.* V, 3, *Works* IV, 423.
71. *Adv. of L., Works* III, 390.
72. *Works* VII, 78.
73. *Works* VII, 77.
74. *Ibid.*
75. *De Aug.* VI, 3, *Works* IV, 472.
76. *Ibid.,* 492.
77. *Adv. of L., Works* III, 412.
78. *De Aug.* VI, 3, *Works* IV, 492.
79. *De Aug.* II, 12, *Works* IV, 314.
80. *Ibid.*
81. *Apophthegmes, New and Old, Works* VII, 130.
82. Preface to the *Apophthegmes, Works* VII, 123.
83. *De Aug.* V, 3, *Works* IV, 421–422.
84. *De Aug.* VI, 2, *Works* IV, 453.
85. *Adv. of L., Works* III, 408.
86. *De Aug.* VI, 2, *Works* IV, 453.
87. *Adv. of L., Works* III, 408.
88. *De Aug.* VI, 2, *Works* IV, 448–454.
89. *Ibid.*
90. *Works* IV, 435–437.
91. *Works* IV, 162–163.
92. *De Aug.* V, 5, *Works* IV, 436.
93. *Ibid.*
94. *Ibid.*
95. *Ibid.,* 435.
96. *Ibid.,* 437.
97. *Of Boldness, Works* VI, 401–402.
98. *Bacon's Promus of Formularies and Elegancies,* ed. by Mrs. Henry Potts, pp. 334–336.
99. *Of the Interpretation of Nature, Works* (Boston) VI, 44.
100. *Ibid.,* 45.
101. *Ibid.,* 46.
102. *Adv. of L., Works* III, 367.
103. *De Aug.* VI, 3, *Works* IV, 454–455.
104. *De Aug.* II, *Works* IV, 288.
105. *An Advertisement touching the Controversies of the Church of England, Letters and Life* I, 91.
106. *Timber,* ed. by F. E. Schelling, Boston, 1892, p. 30.

Sources of the Elocutionary Movement in England: 1700–1748

1. See Charles A. Fritz, "From Sheridan to Rush: The Beginnings of English Elocution," *QJS*, XVI (1930), 75–88; William Phillips Sandford, *English Theories of Public Address, 1530–1828* (The Ohio State University, 1929), pp. 169–183; Warren Guthrie, "The Development of Rhetorical Theory in America 1635–1850—V, The Elocution Movement—England," *SM*, XVIII (March, 1951), 17–30; Frederick W. Haberman, "English Sources of American Elocution," *History of Speech Education in America: Background Studies*, ed. Karl R. Wallace (New York, 1954), pp. 105–126.

2. Sandford, pp. 170–175.

3. Guthrie, pp. 21, 23. For an account of Mason as one of the founders of the natural method of oral reading, see Daniel E. Vandraegen, "The Natural School of Oral Reading in England, 1748–1828," unpublished doctoral dissertation, Northwestern University, 1949.

4. W. M. Parrish, "Elocution—A Definition and a Challenge," *QJS*, XLIII (1957), 2.

5. Sandford, pp., 113, 170, 195, 209. My quotation is from p. 113. Guthrie (p. 18) speaks of Robinson's work in the same way as Sandford did, but admits that he had not seen a copy of it.

6. Robert Robinson, *The Art of Pronuntiation* (London, 1617), f.A6. Robinson's work is reproduced in *The Phonetic Writings of Robert Robinson*, ed. E. J. Dobson, Early English Text Society No. 238 (London, 1957), pp. 1–28, my quotation being taken from p. 6.

7. Dobson's edition, p. 7.

8. See E. J. Dobson, *English Pronunciation 1500–1700* (Oxford, 1957), I, 214. Robinson was presumably known to Charles Hoole, the seventeenth-century schoolmaster, and his *Art of Pronuntiation* is listed in Robert Watt's *Bibliotheca Britannica*; see Dobson, *English Pronunciation*, I, 200–201.

Otherwise Robinson does not appear to have attracted attention until recently.

9. For a full discussion of Neo-Ciceronian rhetoric of the seventeenth century, see my *Logic and Rhetoric in England, 1500–1700* (Princeton, 1956), pp. 318–341. Memory also figured as a major component of the rhetorical theory of Cicero and Quintilian, but it tended to be detached from classical theory as interpreted by several of the leading rhetoricians of the sixteenth and seventeenth centuries. Thus I am not considering it as part of my present argument.

10. *Ibid.*, pp. 276–279, 332–334, 340–341.

11. *Ibid.*, pp. 355–357, 380–381.

12. In its abridged as distinguished from its complete text published at Oxford in 1691, Henry Aldrich's *Artis Logicae Compendium* contains not only a scathing denunciation of the Port-Royalists (sig. G4ᵛ-H2ʳ) but also a reverent endorsement of the full outline of traditional logic; and this work was often reprinted in England during the eighteenth and early nineteenth centuries. But except for it, logical theory of that period did not treat the commonplaces kindly. For a typical view, see Jean Pierre de Crousaz, *A New Treatise of the Art of Thinking* [trans. John Henley] (London, 1724), II, 215–223. Incidentally, Henley's right to be called the translator of this work has been overlooked by library cataloguers, but I feel that the translation is his. See the pamphlet, *Books Written, and Publish'd, By the Reverend John Henley, M.A.* (London, 1724), p. 12.

13. For examples of the influence of this view upon English logical theory, see Isaac Watts, *Logick* (London, 1725), p. 47; also William Duncan, *The Elements of Logick*, in Robert Dodsley, *The Preceptor* (London, 1748), II, 9–11, 121.

14. See Robert Boyle, *Some Considerations Touching the Style of the H. Scriptures* (London, 1659), pp. 158–170.

15. See Thomas Sprat, *The History of the Royal-Society of London* (London, 1667), pp. 111–113.

Notes

16. For details, see Howell, pp. 146–172, 282–317.

17. Published at London in 1739 and reissued in 1755, 1789, and 1807.

18. Nicholas Burton, *Figurae Grammaticae et Rhetoricae* (London, 1702); Thomas Gibbons, *Rhetoric; or, a View of its principal Tropes and Figures* (London, 1767); Daniel Turner, *An Introduction to Rhetoric; containing all the Tropes and Figures in English Verse* (Abingdon, 1771); Anthony Blackwall, *An Introduction to the Classics . . . With an Essay, on the Nature and Use of those Emphatical and Beautiful Figures which give Strength and Ornament to Writing* (London, 1718). Blackwall's treatise on the figures went through six editions by 1748 in the form just indicated. Then it was taken over and published by Robert Dodsley in *The Preceptor*, where it had editions at London in 1748, 1754, 1758, 1763, 1769, 1775, 1783, and 1793. Titled *Rhetoric and Poetry: Extracted from the Preceptor, for the Use of the University in Cambridge*, it was given an edition at Boston in 1796.

19. See *Ecclesiastes, or, A discourse concerning the Gift of Preaching As it fals under the Rules of Art . . .* , 3rd ed. (London, 1651), pp. 5, 128-133. I have not as yet seen the first edition. A *New English Dictionary*, s.v. Elocution, gives Robert Cawdrey's *A Table Alphabeticall, containing and teaching the true writing and vnderstanding of hard vsuall English Words*, 3rd ed. (London, 1613), as the earliest English work to define elocution as delivery. The next instance listed in the *NED* is dated 1678.

20. *Ecclesiastes*, p. 128.

21. *Ibid.*, p. 132.

22. *Ibid.*, p. 133. For a full discussion of the shift of the term elocution from the context of style to that of delivery, see Frederick W. Haberman, "The Elocutionary Movement in England, 1750-1850," unpublished doctoral dissertation, Cornell University, 1947, ch. III.

23. See *Biographie Universelle*, s.v. Le Faucheur, Michel; *Nouvelle Biographie Générale*, s.v. Le Faucheur, Michel. I have not seen the first edition of his *Traitté de l'action de l'orateur;*

the title as I give it come from the *Catalogue Général des Livres Imprimés de la Bibliothèque Nationale.*

24. The title page continues: "Done out of *French. Aliud est eloquentiam callere; aliud, eloqui.* London: Printed for *Nich. Cox* at the *Golden Bible* without *Temple-Barr.*" No date is given. There is no mention in the work that Le Faucheur is author.

25. The title page continues: "*Aliud est Eloquentiam callere. Aliud est Eloqui.* London: Printed for N. Cox, in *Story's Passage, Westminster,* and sold by him and the Booksellers in *London, Oxford,* and *Cambridge.* 1727."

26. The title page continues: "London: Printed for C. Hitch, in *Paternoster-row.* MDCCL."

27. See *Dictionary of National Biography,* s.v. Henley, John, where the translation of Le Faucheur's work is treated as if it were an original work by Henley, and no first edition of it is mentioned.

28. See Donald Wing, *Short-Title Catalogue,* s.v. Le Faucher [*sic*], Michel. Wing follows the dating of the work as given in *The British Museum Catalogue of Printed Books,* and in the catalogues of other libraries.

29. *The Art of Speaking in Publick,* p. xi.

30. *An Essay Upon The Action of an Orator,* sig. A2ʳ-A5ᵛ.

31. *Ibid.*, sig. A6ᵛ-A7ʳ.

32. *The Art of Speaking in Publick,* p. xii.

33. *Dictionary of National Biography,* s.v. Wake, William.

34. *Dictionary of National Biography,* s.v. Rawlinson, Christopher (1677–1733).

35. *An Essay Upon The Action of an Orator,* p. 2.

36. *Ibid.*, p. 2.

37. For other examples, see *ibid.*, pp. 47, 78, 126.

38. *Ibid.*, p. 63.

39. *Ibid.*, pp. 92–93.

40. *Ibid.*, pp. 96, 117–118, 211.

41. In some copies of this work, the dedicatory letter to Richard Steele is signed "Charles Gildon," and this establishes Gildon's authorship. In other copies the letter is unsigned.

42. Charles Gildon, *The Life of Mr. Thomas Betterton* (London, 1710), pp. 1–4.

43. *Ibid.*, pp. 5–11.

44. *Ibid.*, pp. 11–174.

45. *Ibid.*, pp. 174–176.

46. *Ibid.*, p. 11.

47. *Ibid.*, pp. 17–18. Actually this manuscript, as Betterton's companions observe, is in "his own Hand." But we should not therefore conclude that Betterton is its author. See below, note 64. We should understand instead that Gildon is making Betterton the author as a dramatic device to emphasize the great actor's known personal modesty.

48. *Ibid.*, pp. 43–48, 89–97.

49. *Ibid.*, pp. 23–24, 38, 70–71, 81–84, 87.

50. *Ibid.*, pp. 29–30, 32–33.

51. *Ibid.*, p. 89.

52. *Ibid.*, pp. 43, 48.

53. Compare Gildon, *The Life of Mr. Thomas Betterton*, with Louis Crésol, *Vacationes Autumnales sive De Perfecta Oratoris Actione et Pronunciatione Libri III* (Paris, 1620), as follows:

For Gildon, p. 43, lines 17–23, see Crésol, p. 134, lines 3–7.

For Gildon, p. 43, lines 24–29, see Crésol, p. 109, lines 11–18.

For Gildon, p. 43, lines 30–32, see Crésol, p. 105, lines 19–22.

For Gildon, p. 44, lines 4–9, see Crésol, p. 162, lines 12–15, 17–22.

For Gildon, p. 45, lines 30–32, see Crésol, p. 367, lines 19–23.

For Gildon, p. 46, lines 1–3, see Crésol, p. 374, lines 6–10.

For Gildon, p. 46, lines 18–31, see Crésol, p. 317, lines 15–21.

For Gildon, p. 47, lines 1–2, see Crésol, p. 317, lines 15–21.

Gildon's borrowings from Crésol amount to 163 lines of text. Crésol's own discussion of the subjects from which those lines are taken amounts to some 13,000 lines of text. Thus the table just given by no means locates all of the passages Gildon used. More work is needed on this problem.

54. *The Life of Mr. Thomas Betterton*, pp. ix–x.

55. Gildon, pp. 28, 31, makes veiled references to suggest his dependence upon a translation, but they hardly suf-fice as adequate acknowledgments of his large debt to the specific translation he used.

56. Compare Gildon's text with that of *An Essay Upon The Action of an Orator*, as follows: p. 26 with p. 172; p. 26 with pp. 39–55; pp. 26–27 with pp. 39, 54–55; p. 27 with pp. 58, 175; p. 28 with pp. 115–116.

57. Compare Gildon's text with that of *An Essay Upon The Action of an Orator*, as follows: pp. 33–34 with pp. 173–177; p. 51 with pp. 171–172; p. 57 with p. 178; p. 78 with p. 202.

58. Gildon, p. 32.

59. *An Essay Upon The Action of an Orator*, p. 6.

60. Gildon, p. 72.

61. *An Essay Upon The Action of an Orator*, pp. 192–193.

62. Gildon, p. 101.

63. *An Essay Upon The Action of an Orator*, pp. 64–65.

64. The following sections of Curll's *The History of the English Stage* and of Gildon's *The Life of Mr. Thomas Betterton* may be examined for evidence that this statement is true:

Ch. I (pp. 5–12) of Curll is drawn from Gildon, pp. 2, 5–10.

Ch. II (pp. 13–31) of Curll is partly drawn from Gildon, pp. 13–17.

Ch. IV (pp. 36–54) of Curll is drawn from Gildon, pp. 23–40.

Ch. V (pp. 55–78) of Curll is partly drawn from Gildon, pp. 41–55.

Ch. VI (pp. 79–110) of Curll is partly drawn from Gildon, pp. 57–68, 71–84.

The fact that Curll's *History*, p. 36, attributes its fourth chapter to "Mr. *Betterton's* Papers" has led to the conclusion that Curll's treatment of stage gesture is taken directly from the notes of the famous actor himself. For endorsement of this conclusion see *The Cambridge Bibliography of English Literature*, II, 403. But such an opinion appears to have nothing to support it except for Curll's words as just quoted, and they, of course, are based upon Gildon's assertion in the *Life* that the manuscript read by Betterton was in his own hand. See above, note 47. Once we recognize that Curll was borrowing from Gildon, and that Gildon in turn was borrowing from the English version of Le Faucheur, the theory that the ideas are Betterton's evaporates.

Alan S. Downer, "Nature to Advantage Dressed: Eighteenth-Century Acting," PMLA, LVIII (1943), 1007, 1031–1032, was I believe the first to note that Curll's *History* borrows much of its material from Gildon's *Life.* The connection between Gildon and Le Faucheur seems not to have been pointed out until now.

65. Of the four pages assigned by Curll to voice or speaking, all are given over to reproducing Gildon's quotation and discussion of Hamlet's advice to the players. See Curll, *The History of the English Stage,* pp. 106–110.

66. See *The British Museum Catalogue of Printed Books,* s.v. Rules (col. 128).

67. *Some Rules for Speaking and Action,* 3rd ed. (London, 1716), p. 20.

68. *Ibid.,* pp. 29–31.

69. *An Essay on Elocution, or, Pronunciation. Intended chiefly for the Assistance of those who instruct others in the Art of Reading. And of those who are often called to speak in Publick* (London: Printed for M. Cooper, at the Globe in Paternoster Row, 1748), p. 27.

70. Compare *An Essay on Elocution, or, Pronunciation,* pp. 23–26, with *An Essay Upon The Action of an Orator,* pp. 97–118, 119–127.

71. Ephraim Chambers, *Cyclopaedia: or, An Universal Dictionary of Arts and Sciences,* 2nd ed. (London, 1738), s.v. Pronunciation. The italics are Chambers's.

72. See *Dictionary of National Biography,* s.v. Henley, John.

73. John Henley, *Oratory Transactions, No. I* (London, 1728), p. 5. This quotation occurs in connection with a biographical sketch of Henley included in *Oratory Transactions, No. I* and attributed to "Mr. *Welstede.*" Welstede is said in T. F. Henderson's account of Henley in *Dictionary of National Biography* to be no doubt Henley himself.

74. *Oratory Transactions, No. I,* p. 12.

75. See *Books Written, and Publish'd, By the Reverend John Henley, M.A.*

(London, 1724), pp. 5–15. See also *Oratory Transactions, No. I,* p. 12.

76. *Oratory Transactions, No. I,* p. 12.

77. See William Whiston, *Mr. Henley's Letters and Advertisements, Which concern Mr. Whiston* (London, 1727), pp. 14-16.

78. *Oratory Transactions, No. I,* p. 13.

79. For an account of the plan of The Oratory, the principles governing its conferences, the procedures followed in them, the first sermon preached there, the text of its liturgy, and so on, see John Henley, *The Appeal of the Oratory to the First Ages of Christianity* (London, 1727).

80. See John Henley, *Oratory Transactions, No. II* (London, n.d.), which contains a list of sermons, theological lectures, and academic lectures delivered at The Oratory from July 3, 1726, to August 31, 1728.

81. For the text of this sermon, see *The Appeal of the Oratory to the First Ages of Christianity,* where it is paged with the "Four Discourses," pp. 25-41. My quotation is from p. 38. In restoring the science of elocution, Henley, on July 6, 13, 20, and 27, 1726, delivered a series of lectures on the following topics: "The general Principles of Speaking"; "The general Principles of Action"; "The Antient History of Action"; "Remarks on some Rules of *Quintilian.*" On August 31, he delivered a lecture on "The Action of the Eye and Features." See *Oratory Transactions, No. II,* under "The Academical . . . Subjects of the Oratory."

82. *The Art of Speaking in Publick,* pp. x–xi. The Wood referred to here elsewhere calls himself William Wood of Christ Church, Oxford. He had offered himself in 1726 as a lecturer in The Oratory, and had been commissioned by Henley to collect for delivery at The Oratory an hour's worth of passages from Cicero on the subject of voice and gesture. But it seems that at this same time Wood was preparing to publish an attack upon Henley. When Henley discovered Wood's duplicity, he accused him of sodomy, and later threatened him with a duel. For details of

this strange business, see William Wood, *The Dueling Orator delineated* (London, 1726). It could well be that William Wood is the anonymous editor of *The Art of Speaking in Publick* and took revenge upon Henley by writing unfavorably of him in the introduction of that work.

83. *The Art of Speaking in Publick,* pp. xxiii–xxiv.

84. I have not examined the Henley manuscripts in the Guildhall Library, but I have looked at some of those in the British Museum, and have read the following ones, which, although only of minor interest, do bear upon speaking and action in oratory: "Eloquence of the Pulpit"; "The Action of the Eye, and Aspect"; "Action of the Hands"; see Additional Mss. 19,925.

85. The imprint reads: "*London:* Printed for *T. Longman,* at the *Ship* and *Black-swan* in *Pater-noster-row; J. Mac-Euen,* in the *Strand;* and sold at his shop in *Edenburgh;* and *G. Dommer,* 1725." There is a copy at the Bodleian Library.

86. My present discussion is based upon the second edition as it is given in that work.

87. *The Appeal of the Oratory to the First Ages of Christianity,* p. 15.

88. *Ibid.,* p. 15.

89. *Ibid.,* p. 19. A different note appears at this point in the first edition.

90. *Ibid.,* p. 17.

91. *Ibid.,* p. 18.

92. *Ibid.,* p. 21.

Whately and His Rhetoric

1. This is a study of the Introduction and Parts I and II of Whately's *Elements of Rhetoric,* and the statements here must be understood as applying only to those portions of the work. The two remaining, and perhaps the most original parts, are on Style and Elocution. Page references are to the seventh edition (1846).

2. See Whately, E. Jane, *Life and Correspondence of Richard Whately, D.D.,* London, 1866, I, pp. 60, 352, II, p. 80. Hereafter cited as *Life.*

3. *Life,* I, p. 19.

4. *Life of William Ewart Gladstone,* New York, 1903, I, p. 51.

5. Mozley, Rev. T., *Reminiscences, Chiefly of Oriel College and the Oxford Movement,* Boston, 1882, I., p. 18.

6. Tuckwell, W., *Reminiscences of Oxford,* London, 1907, p. 17.

7. *Life,* pp. 26–27.

8. *Memoirs,* London, 1885, p. 79.

9. *Op. cit.,* p. 20.

10. *Life,* I, p. 27.

11. CXX, Oct. 1864, p. 372.

12. "With Plato's intellectual peculiarities, on the other hand, he had little sympathy." *Life,* I, p. 19.

13. *Life,* I, pp. 24–26.

14. *Life,* I, p. 32.

15. *Life,* II, p. 47.

16. *Apologia pro Vita Sua,* London, 1921, p. 11.

17. *Op. cit.,* p. 29. See the correspondence on their break in the *Apologia,* pp. 380–387, or in Whately's *Life,* I, pp. 233–240.

18. *Life,* I, p. 28.

19. CXX, Oct. 1864, p. 389.

20. *Camb. Hist. of Lit.,* XII, p. 316.

21. *Life,* I, p. 10.

22. Though he refers twice to "Demosthenes on the Crown" (pp. 140 and 203), and once to "Cicero against Verres" (p. 197).

23. See *Life,* I, pp. 102–104.

24. See *Westminister Review,* XIII, July 1830, p. 183.

25. See Arnold's letter to Rev. Cornish, Dec. 23, 1831, in Stanley's *Life of Arnold,* I, p. 275. "Now I am sure that in point of real essential holiness, so far as man can judge of man, there does not live a truer Christian than Whately; and it does grieve me most deeply to hear people speak of him as a dangerous and latitudinarian character, because in him the intellectual part of his nature keeps pace with the spiritual."

26. Quoted in the *Life,* I, p. 454.

27. "It was in their long walks together in the woods and meadows near Oxford that they discussed and worked out such subjects as form much of the groundwork of the 'Logic'." *Life,* I, p. 14.

28. Rev. R. N. Boultbee, a former pupil, writes, "I was in the habit of walking out into the country with him

Notes

two or three times a week, and during these rambles I was made the recipient of many of his most original thoughts, preserved in his Commonplace Book. Well do I remember the shady bank in Bagley Wood, where he first read to me the draft of the 'Historic Doubts'." *Life,* I, p. 38.

29. Fitzpatrick, W. J., *Memoirs of Richard Whately,* London, 1864, I, p. 47.

30. *Life,* I, p. 14.

31. *Miscellaneous Remains from the Commonplace Book of Richard Whately, D.D.,* London, 1864, p. vi.

32. First *Reply,* p. 172.

33. See *Edinburgh Review,* CXX, p. 397.

34. Quoted from Guizot's *Mémoires* in Whately's *Life,* I, p. 454.

35. Whately said of Coleridge's dissertation, "I had thought to cut it out and burn it when I had the volume bound, but I resolve to keep it as a curious specimen of what trash a very clever man *can* write." *Life,* II, p. 316. He could not have been pleased at the publication in 1851 of Coleridge's dissertation, together with his own articles on Logic and Rhetoric under the title, "Encyclopaedia of Mental Science."

36. See Fitzpatrick's *Memoirs of Richard Whately,* I, p. 47.

37. I have been unable to find a first edition, but assume on what seems to be good evidence that the second edition, which I have examined, is a reprinting of the first. It appeared in the same year as the first. When the third edition appeared two years later it carried after the Preface the following Advertisement: "Some considerable additions having been made to the third edition, the Author has directed all of them that are of any material consequence to be printed for the accommodation of the purchasers of the former editions, separately and in such form as to be conveniently appended to the volume." The fourth edition, which is a second printing of the third, contained the same notice under the same heading, viz., "Advertisement to the Third Edition." The fifth, sixth, and seventh editions are all marked on the title page "Revised." No such notice appears in the second edition.

38. See his note, *Rhet.* I, p. 39.

39. *Rhet.* I, p. iii.

40. The *Logic* seems to have been based largely upon a work by Aldrich, then in general use at Oxford. Doubtless much of it was original with Whately and Copleston. His indebtedness to others is not as freely or as frequently acknowledged in the *Logic* as in the *Rhetoric.*

41. *Life,* I, p. 10.

Whately on Elocution

1. "From Sheridan to Rush," *Quarterly Journal of Speech,* XVI (February, 1930), 76.

2. I am keeping in Whately's excess of italics, capitals, and punctuation, for I have found that taking away these devices from a writer who has depended upon them may change the significance of a passage. Certainly without his italics the reader loses something of the tang of Whately's composition.

3. A good idea of the controversy that has raged around Whately's teaching can be gained from Corson's *Voice and Spiritual Education,* Curry's *Province of Expression,* and Parrish's *Reading Aloud.*

John Thelwall: His Life, His School, and His Theory of Elocution

1. Some biographical sources for Thelwall are the following: *DNB;* "Prefatory Memoir," an autobiographical account in *Poems,* London, 1802; *Life of John Thelwall,* by Mrs. Thelwall, London, 1837 (Vol. I only was published); obituary in *Gentleman's Magazine* (1834), II, 549; an account of his political philosophy and reforming activity in *John Thelwall, a Pioneer of Democracy and Social Reform . . . ,* Charles Cestre, London, 1906.

2. In a letter written to Joseph Cottle in 1797. Cited by John Britton, *Autobiography* (London, 1849–1850), pp. 180–181.

3. Britton, *op. cit.,* p. 185.

402

4. John Thelwall, *A Letter to Henry Cline, Esq.* (London, 1810), p. 256.

5. John Thelwall, included in *Vestibule of Eloquence* (London, 1810), pp. 17–31.

6. Henry Crabb Robinson has accounts of two visits to meetings of this society in his *Diary, Reminiscences, and Correspondence,* ed. by Thomas Sadler (London, 1869), I, pp. 492, 507–508.

7. Thomas Noon Talfourd, *Memoirs of Charles Lamb,* ed. by Percy Fitzgerald (London, 1892), p. 179.

8. London, 1761.

9. See primarily, *Elements of Elocution,* London, 1781.

10. *Prosodia Rationalis,* London, 1775.

11. Thomas Sheridan, *A General Dictionary of the English Language* (London, 1780). This work is more commonly known by its revised title, *A Complete Dictionary of the English Tongue both with Regard to Sound and Meaning.*

12. John Walker, *A Critical and Pronouncing Dictionary and Expositor of the English Language* (London, 1791).

13. *DNB.* Article on John Walker.

14. Printed in *Vestibule of Eloquence,* pp. 63–64.

15. *Vestibule of Eloquence* (London, 1810); *A Letter to Henry Cline, Esq.* (London, 1810); *Illustrations of English Rhythmus* (London, 1812); *Results of Experience* (London, 1814).

16. "Oration, on the influence of Animated Elocution," *Vestibule, op. cit.*

17. *Illustrations of English Rhythmus,* p. lv.

18. T. S. Omond, *English Metrists* (London, 1921), p. 128.

19. George Saintsbury, *A History of English Prosody* (London, 1910), III, pp. 159–160.

20. *Illustration of English Rhythmus,* p. xxi.

21. *Ibid.,* p. xxiv–xxv.

De Quincey on Rhetoric and Public Speaking

1. Appearing originally in *Blackwood's Magazine* for December, 1828, and reprinted in the Collective edition (1859) under the title "Rhetoric." I have used D. Masson's edition, *The Collected Writings of Thomas De Quincey* (London, 1897), wherein the essays on literary theory and criticism are collected in Volumes X and XI; and Professor Fred Newton Scott's edition, *De Quincey's Essays on Style, Rhetoric, and Language* (Boston, 1893).

2. "Style" appeared in *Blackwood's Magazine* in four parts, 1840–1841; the study of Greek literature in *Tait's Magazine,* December, 1838, and June, 1839. Nor should one overlook the essay, "Conversation," published in *Tait's Magazine,* October, 1847, and enlarged for the Collective edition. All are to be found in Masson, X.

3. Masson, X, 94.

4. Masson, X, 93. De Quincey goes on: "In particular, it was so taught by Aristotle: whose system we are disposed to agree with Dr. Whately in pronouncing the best as regards the primary purpose of a teacher; though otherwise, for elegance and as a practical model in the art he was expounding, neither Aristotle, nor any less austere among the Greek rhetoricians, has any pretensions to measure himself with Quintilian."

5. Masson, X, 82–85. This note contains a clear and authoritative summary of the classical concept of rhetoric and of the various permutations of that concept which have prevailed in various periods.

6. Page references in the text are to Masson, X.

7. On this point we take De Quincey *in flagrate delicto,* as witness the following passages:

"Rhetoric, in its finest and most absolute burnish, may be called an *eloquentia umbratica;* that is, it aims at an elaborate form of beauty which shrinks from the strife of business, and could neither arise nor make itself felt in a tumultuous assembly."

"My reason, however, for noticing this peculiarity [rhythm] in Isocrates is by way of fixing the attention upon the superiority, even for artificial ornaments, of downright practical business and the realities of political strife over the torpid atmosphere of a study or a school. Cicero, long after, had the same passion for *numerositas,* and the full, pompous rotundity of cadence. But in Cicero all habits and all faculties were nursed by the daily practice of life and its impassioned realities in the forum or in the senate. What is the consequence? Why this—that, whereas in the most laboured performance of Isocrates . . . few modern ears are sensible of any striking art, or any great result of harmony, in Cicero, on the other hand, the fine, sonorous modulations of his periodic style are delightful to the dullest ear of any European. Such are the advantages from real campaigns, from unsimulated strife of actual stormy life, over the torpid dreams of what the Romans called an *umbratic* experience."

The first is from "Rhetoric," written in 1828; the second from "A Brief Appraisal of the Greek Literature," written ten years later. (Masson, X, 93, 324.)

8. A. E. Phillips, in his *Effective Speaking* (Chicago, 1910), also analyzes this process helpfully, with Cumulation, Specific Instance, General Illustration, and Restatement as some of the main headings in his analysis. It is significant, in view of what is said below with reference to rhetorical invention in poetry, that most of Phillips' illustrative material is drawn from Shakespeare.

9. In *The Idea of a University.*

10. Readers familiar with the classical division of rhetoric into the steps of *inventio, dispositio, elocutio, memoria,* and *pronuntiatio,* will see that De Quincey is most full upon *inventio* and *elocutio.* The last two he virtually omits, as they have no application to written discourse. His slighting of *dispositio,* or arrangement, is a defect alike of his theory and of his practice. Another defect of his theory (attributable, perhaps, to the fact that in practice he never actually faced his audience) is his incomplete recognition of the audience as one of the determining factors in the rhetorical situation, and especially as a source of inventive topics.

11. The passage chosen appears in Masson, XI, 32.

12. The paragraph is from De Quincey's notes on Gilfillan's *Literary Portraits,* Masson, XI, 380.

13. H. M. Paull, in "De Quincey and Style" (*Fortnightly Review,* CXII

[1922], 152) argues that De Quincey does not live up to the precepts of his essay, "Style." He condemns the colloquialism of Greek writers, for instance, and yet is himself colloquial. He ridiculed the long, involved sentences of German prose, but himself writes sentences of great length and involution. The first of these points is a small one; and I think De Quincey's practice is to be preferred, in this case, to his precept. His long, involved sentences are a manifestation of that exuberant power of invention which we have discussed.

14. The phrase is Professor Brewster's, in the Introduction to his *Representative Essays on the Theory of Style,* New York, 1911.

15. Masson, X, 164–165.

16. The present writer finds himself in full accord with the judgment of J. H. Fowler, *De Quincey as a Literary Critic,* Pamphlet 52 of The English Association (July, 1922): "There is indeed one definition or distinction of his which has been widely quoted and accepted, but which, I am bound to confess, does not seem to me really profound or valuable —I mean his famous distinction between literature of knowledge and literature of power."

17. *The Aims of Literary Study,* New York, 1906, pp. 60–61. The italics are Corson's.

Some Differences between Literary Criticism and Rhetorical Criticism

1. The summary introduced in these two paragraphs and amplified below is the concluding section of a longer essay entitled, "The Literary Criticism of Oratory," originally published in *Studies in Rhetoric and Public Speaking in Honor of James Albert Winans* (New York, 1925). The entire essay was merely an attempt to spy out the land, to see what some critics have said of some orators, to discover what their mode of criticism has been. The discussion was limited in the main to Burke and a few nineteenth-century figures— Webster, Lincoln, Gladstone, Bright,

Cobden—and to the verdicts on these found in the surveys of literary history, in critical essays, in histories of oratory, and in biographies.

2. *Rhetoric*, I, 2(1355b), tr. Rhys Roberts in *The Works of Aristotle*, XI, Oxford, 1924.

3. Article "Rhetoric" in the *Encyclopaedia Britannica*, 9th and 11th editions.

4. J. L. Gerig and F. N. Scott, article "Rhetoric" in the *New International Encyclopaedia*.

5. K. H. W. Wackernagel, *Poetik, Rhetorik und Stilistik*, ed. L. Sieber, Halle, 1873, p. 11.

6. H. H. Hudson, "The Field of Rhetoric," above, pp. 3 ff. See also the same writer's "Rhetoric and Poetry," below, pp. 369 ff.

7. C. S. Baldwin, *Ancient Rhetoric and Poetic*, New York, 1924, p. 134.

8. G. E. B. Saintsbury, *History of Criticism and Literary Taste in Europe*, New York, 1900, I, 39.

9. *Ibid.*, p. 42.

10. *Ibid.*, p. 48.

11. *Ibid.*, p. 52.

12. *Op. cit.*, p. 4.

13. *Life of William Ewart Gladstone*, II, 589–590.

14. In *Cambridge History of English Literature* XI, 1–32, Cambridge, 1914.

15. For a popular but suggestive presentation of the background of rhetorical discourse, see J. A. Spender, *The Public Life*, New York, 1925.

16. New York, 1923.

Thomas Wilson's Speech against Usury

1. The speech, reported in the third person, and copied from the "Anonymous Journal Book of the House of Commons," is to be found in Sir Simonds D'Ewes' *Journals of All the Parliaments During the Reign of Queen Elizabeth* (London, 1682), pp. 172–173.

2. For a brief but excellent discussion of the subject, see *The Encyclopaedia of Religion and Ethics*, ed. James Hastings (New York, 1922), XIII,

550–558, especially the articles by John Dow and William H. Bennett; for fuller treatment see the sources listed in these articles and particularly for the problem in the sixteenth century see R. H. Tawney, *A Discourse Upon Usury by Thomas Wilson, 1572* (New York, 1925), esp. pp. 105–122. (Tawney's historical introduction in this volume owes much to the writings and assistance of George Unwin; and, in turn, has been much used in this study.)

3. Tawney, *op. cit.*, pp. 276–277. This definition is enumerated in the "Civilians or Doctours Oracion" and corresponds closely to Wilson's views expressed in the Preface and in the speech in the House of Commons.

4. *Ibid.*, p. 116.

5. *Ibid.*, p. 132.

6. D'Ewes, *op. cit.*, p. 174. Tawney, *op. cit.*, p. 159, says that only one other member supported Wilson's extreme position of opposing all interest-taking—presumably Mr. Norton who ". . . shewed, that all Usury is biting. . . ." But it is clear from their speeches, as reported in D'Ewes, that Mr. Clarke and Mr. Fleetwood were not equally opposed to interest.

7. D'Ewes, *op. cit.*, p. 175.

8. *Ibid.*, p 157.

9. *Ibid.*, p. 161.

10. J. E. Neale, *The Elizabethan House of Commons* (New Haven, 1950), p. 406. Neale states that the early Elizabethan parliaments were especially noteworthy for eloquence, listing Sir Walter Mildmay, William Fleetwood, Thomas Norton, and Peter Wentworth as the most notable orators.

11. D'Ewes, *op. cit.*, p. 167; see also pp. 163, 175.

12. Neale, *loc. cit.*

13. D'Ewes, *op. cit.*, p. 167.

14. *Ibid.*, p. 171.

15. Whether they respected him for his knowledge of business and finance is uncertain. Tawney, *op. cit.*, p. 2, says, "The most truculent of self-made capitalists could not have criticized him as a child in matters of finance. He had tried commercial cases, negotiated commercial treaties, haggled with financiers at Lisbon and Antwerp, . . ." The oblique references to Wilson and his

speech in this debate, especially in the reply by Mr. Bell, and the general tone and tenor of the speeches of Mr. Bell and of others who replied, seem definitely to indicate that they *did* choose to regard Wilson as a learned man, but one learned in book-knowledge only, and a simpleton in practical commercial and financial matters and in the knowledge of the everyday problems and behavior of men of common clay.

16. It is of interest to note that Mr. Fleetwood and Mr. Norton, two of the most eloquent and influential men in the House, also argued against the Bill and apparently agreed with and supported Wilson's position. But their speeches appear to have been well below their usual standards and seem to be much less thorough or less well reported than Wilson's.

17. G. H. Mair, ed., Wilson's *Arte of Rhetorique* (Oxford, 1909), p. 9; see also pp. 102, 104.

Milton's Rhetoric on the Tyranny of Kings

1. These introductory paragraphs are based on the first part of my "Preface" to *Milton's Rhetoric: Studies in His Defense of Liberty*, The University of Missouri Studies, Vol. XIV, Number 3, July 1, 1939, p. 5.

2. The essay that follows is a reprint of Chapter V of *Milton's Rhetoric: Studies in His Defense of Liberty*, pp. 99–110.

3. See D. Masson, *The Life of Milton*, London, 1859–1894, 7 vols., 3.611–630; 3.692–729; 4.64–77; and William T. Allison, ed., *The Tenure of Kings and Magistrates*, vi–xii.

4. "Second Defence of the People of England," *Works*, Columbia ed., 8. 135.6–137.6.

5. Professor Edward G. Ainsworth, Jr., suggests that it is interesting to conjecture what effect, if any, Milton's position in the pamphlet had in stimulating Hobbes's defense of royal authority in the *Leviathan* published two years later in 1651.

6. Allison, *op. cit.*, i–vi.

7. *Works*, Columbia ed., 5.17.23–25.
8. *Ibid.*, 18.21–23.
9. *Ibid.*, 31.15–20.
10. *Ibid.*, 40.11–13.
11. *Ibid.*, 41.7–10.
12. *Ibid.*, 55.15–22.
13. *Ibid.*, 56.12–23.
14. *Ibid.*, 45.12–24.
15. *Ibid.*, 4.14–21.
16. *Ibid.*, 39.12–40.1.
17. *Ibid.*, 40.23–41.2.
18. *Ibid.*, 55.7–15.
19. *Ibid.*, 1.8–11.
20. *Ibid.*, 42.14–27.
21. *Ibid.*, 1.1–8.
22. *Ibid.*, 2.22–3.1.
23. *Ibid.*, 3.20–26.
24. *Ibid.*, 13.18–25.
25. *Ibid.*, 12.9–10.
26. *Ibid.*, 57.28–58.20.
27. Masson, *Life*, 4.76–77.

George Whitefield: Commoner Evangelist

1. "Religion is exalted reason, refined and sifted from the grosser parts of it." Mrs. Mary Midnight, "Of Religion and the Clergy," *An Index to Mankind: or Maxims selected from the Wits of all Nations, For the Benefit of the Present Age, and of Posterity . . .* a Preface by her good Friend, the late Mr. Pope (London, 1751), p. 11.

2. John Locke, *The Reasonableness of Christianity as Delivered in the Scriptures* (London, 1695).

3. Joseph Butler, *The Analogy of Religion, Natural and Revealed, to the Constitution and Course of Nature* (London, 1736).

4. C. Harold King, "The Beginnings of Modern Science," *A History of Civilization* (New York, 1956), I, 611–617.

5. "Nature and Nature's Laws lay hid in Night: GOD said, *Let Newton be!* and all was Light." Alexander Pope, *The Poetical Works of Alexander Pope* (London, 1930), p. 461.

6. John Richard Green, *History of the English People* (London, 1880), IV, 140.

7. One contemporary reminded his readers that the knowledgeable were

aware from examples of "former times . . . what monstrous absurdities in Opinion and what vile Practices Enthusiasm will produce." *A Compleat Account of the Conduct of that eminent Enthusiast Mr. Whitefield . . .* (London, 1739), p. 11.

8. "And you gave him [Satan] advantage by reasoning with him—that is, fighting him at his own weapons; instead of simply looking up and saying, 'Thou shalt answer for me, O Lord, my God.'" John Telford, ed., *The Letters of John Wesley, A.M., Sometime Fellow of Lincoln College Oxford*, Standard Edition (London, 1931), VI, 281.

9. J. S. Simon, *The Revival of Religion in England in the Eighteenth-Century . . .* Third Thousand (London, 1907); Joseph Tracy, *The Great Awakening, a History of the Revival of Religion in the Time of Edwards and Whitefield* (Boston, 1842); Mary Hewitt Mitchell, *The Great Awakening and Other Revivals in the Religious Life of Connecticut* (New Haven, 1934); Charles Hartshorn Maxson, *The Great Awakening in the Middle Colonies* (Gloucester, 1958). Simon says that the Welch revival was a miniature of the general revivalist movement, pp. 148–149.

10. Whitefield's remains lie in the crypt of the First Presbyterian Church of Newburyport, Mass., while he may be considered to be still represented by Whitefield's Central Mission Church, Tottenham Court Road, London.

11. "Whitefield's favourite pulpit [at Hampton Common] was a long-barrow mound, just above Amberley, still known as Whitefield's Tump." Albert D. Belden, *George Whitefield—The Awakener, a Modern Study of the Evangelical Revival, . . .* (London, 1930), p. 78.

12. On the University of Pennsylvania campus.

13. The Rev. Thomas Dudley Fosbrooke, M.A. F.A.S., *An Original History of Gloucester, Supplying the Numerous Deficiencies, and Correcting the Errors, of Preceding Accounts, . . .* (London, 1819), p. 380.

14. Whitefield's publicity agent, William Seward, notes, every now and then, in his Journal such items as "Wrote letter to New York" or "Wrote letters to my dear Brethren at Savanah." William Seward, *Journal of a Voyage from Savannah to Philadelphia and from Philadelphia to England, 1740* (London, 1740), pp. 16, 2.

15. [Charles Chauncy], *A Letter from a Gentleman in Boston to Mr. George Wishart, one of the Ministers of Edinburgh, Concerning the State of Religion in New England* (Edinburgh, 1742).

16. "January 13, 1739/40. Mr. Whitefield's Name, which of late has made so much noise in *England,* could not fail drawing all sorts of People to the Church [in America]." William Stephens, Esq., *Journal of Proceedings in Georgia* (London, 1742), II, 246.

"You have no conception of the effect of Mr. Whitefield's death upon the inhabitants of the province of Georgia . . ." William Jay, *Memoirs of the Life and Character of the Rev. Cornelius Winter* (New York, 1811, First American Edition), p. 80.

Whitefield himself noticed, during a stay in Gloucester in January, 1738, "I began to grow a little popular." William Wale, ed., *Whitefield's Journals . . . To Which is Prefixed His "Short Account" and "Further Account" . . .* (London, 1905), p. 73. To be hereafter identified as *Journal.*

17. Whitefield was referred to frequently in the Diary of Rev. Solomon Reed; see entries, for example, for period Oct. 3, 1743—Jan. 9, 1745. Harriette Merrifield Forbes, ed., *New England Diaries, 1602–1800* (privately printed, Topsfield, 1923).

See also Franklin Bowditch Dexter, ed., *Extracts from the Itineraries and Other Miscellanies of Exra Stiles, 1755–1794, with a Selection from his Correspondence* (New Haven, 1916), pp. 98, 432, 594–595, 597–602.

Following Whitefield's death "the Presbyterian Church, in Arch Street [Philadelphia], was hung in black." *New York Gazette and Weekly Mercury,* Monday, October 29, 1770.

18. At Chester, judges postponed their sitting to avoid interfering with Whitefield's preaching. Tracy, *op. cit.,* p. 54.

Notes

"This year, 1741, he received the compliments of honorary Burgess Tickets from the towns of Stirling, Glasgow, Paisley . . . and Aberdeen. And in 1742, from Irvine. And in 1762, from Edinburgh." John Gillies, *Memoirs of Rev. George Whitefield, Revised and Corrected with Large Additions and Improvements, to Which is appended an extensive collection of his Sermons and Other Writings* (Middleton, 1838), p. 82n, to be hereafter referred to as *Memoirs and Sermons*.

19. The phrase "leader of the Methodists" is used in *A Letter to Mr. Foote, occasioned by his Letter to the Reverend Author of the Christian and Critical Remarks on "The Minor" . . . and a full Defense of the Principles and Practices of the Methodists* (London, 1760), p. 17.

20. Rev. Richard Green, *Anti-Methodist Publications Issued During the Eighteenth Century* (London, 1902).

21. The issue of November 26–December 3, 1739.

22. The phrase, used to describe another unconventional revivalist, applies as aptly to Whitefield. "Letter from Brother Joseph Williams to Brother Howell Harris, at Trevecka, near the Hay, Breconshire," *The Christian History* (London, 1747), p. 8.

23. James Boswell, *The Life of Samuel Johnson, LL.D.* . . . (London, 1927), I, 386–387.

24. Samuel E. Morison and Henry Steele Commager, *The Growth of the American Republic* (New York, 1950), I, 111.

25. Rev. Luke Tyerman, *The Life of the Rev. George Whitefield*, 2 vols. (London, 1876 and 1877), I, 244.

26. Arthur Stanley Turberville, *English Men and Manners in the Nineteenth Century* (Oxford, 1926), p. 308.

27. Jay, *op. cit.*, p. 21.

28. Charles Chauncy, *Seasonable Thoughts on the State of Religion in New England* (Boston, 1743), p. 80. Chauncy was representative of the more conservative who disapproved of revivals and all their works, but not actually typical of the observer who listened and watched with any degree of

scientific openmindedness. More characteristic of the testimony of the latter was the sometimes-surprised observation that Whitefield's action appeared—on the spot, at least—appropriate to the occasion.

29. *New York Gazette and Weekly Mercury*, Oct. 8, 1770.

30. Gillies, *Memoirs and Sermons*, p. 273.

31. In a period of two weeks, Whitefield preached from Kennington Common, the Moorfields, a tomb in a churchyard, a bowling green, a yard, a town hall, and a market cross. *The Gentleman's Magazine: and Historical Chronicle*, April 30, 1739 (IX, 215).

In one period from April to July, Whitefield preached 100 times to 100,-000 people. Gillies, *Memoirs and Sermons*, p. 136.

Whitefield's approach to and arrival at extempore preaching is indicated by two entries from his *Journal*. "It happened providentially that a Lecture was to be preached *that evening* at Deptford, and several importuned me to preach it; at first I was fearful. . . . But afterwards . . . I went up . . . and was enabled to preach to a large congregation without the least hesitation." *Journal*, p. 89. "This is the first time [at Islington] I have preached without notes (for when I preached at Deptford . . . , I only repeated a written sermon); but I find myself now as it were constrained to do it." *Journal*, p. 198.

His critics charged that some passages from Whitefield's sermons were "*never meditated and studied* before" because of "*that extemporaneous* Way of Preaching which we condemn." Edward Wigglesworth, *A Letter to the Reverend Mr. George Whitefield* (Boston, 1745), p. 44.

32. F. L. Chapell must be credited for noting this feature of Whitefield's role: "He is emphatically the representative man of the great revival of the eighteenth century." *The Great Awakening of 1740* (Philadelphia, 1903), p. 91.

33. Tyerman, *op. cit.*, I, 215. *The Gentleman's Magazine* refers frequently to Whitefield crowds by such terms as

"crowded audience" (XVIII, 329) or "prodigious concourse" (XXX, 245–246). Tracy, *op. cit.*, p. 58, referring to Whitefield's preaching in Philadelphia in 1740, cited an estimate of "twenty thousand hearers." The precise Franklin calculated that Whitefield could be heard by thirty thousand. See note 64 below.

34. John Wesley, *A Sermon on the Death of the Rev. Mr. George Whitefield* (London, 1770), p. 20. Wesley's idea—and language—was anticipated by "What is surprising is that numbers of all ranks, all denominations, and all characters, come constantly to hear him." *Diary of a very worthy Christian in Edinburgh*, quoted by Gillies, *Memoirs and Sermons*, p. 79n.

35. Of the "many persons" who "attended," the most numerous were "of the more illiterate sort." Henry Wilder Foote, *Annals of King's Chapel* (Boston, 1896), II, 261.

Even an unsympathetic witness conceded that Whitefield had the power "to detain five or six thousand of the vulgar from their labour." Quoted by Tyerman, *op. cit.*, I, 194.

36. On Friday, Jan. 27, 1739, "the Church was quite crowded, and many went away for want of room; some stood on the leads of the Church outside, and looked in at the top windows . . ." *Journal*, p. 109.

"It raind most of the Time, and yet they stood in the open Air." *New-York Weekly Journal*, Dec. 17, 1739.

37. His first sermon, by reports of some in the audience, drove fifteen people mad. When there were complaints of this extravagant effect, the hope was expressed that the madness would continue until the next Sunday. Gillies, *Memoirs and Sermons*, p. 20.

Whitefield frequently reports "loud amens to my sentences," "thousands of ejaculations and fervent prayers," and farewell sermons to "a weeping and affected audience." *Journal*, pp. 200, 273, 299.

During a sermon at Cambusland, at the height of his career, "You might have seen thousands bathed in tears; some at the same time wringing their hands, others swooning, and others crying out and mourning over a pierced savior." Gillies, *Memoirs and Sermons*, p. 87.

38. When one American Anglican listener said, "His doctrine is right STERLING" (*New York Gazette*, Nov. 19–26, 1739), he was both representative and exceptional. He was representative of those who, considering Whitefield's message objectively, realized that the evangelist's doctrine was not actually radical; he was exceptional in that most responded either intensely for or against Whitefield because of his unconventional *methods*.

39. George Whitefield, *The Works of the Reverend George Whitefield, M.A.*, 6 vols. (London, 1771–1772), V, 64.

40. Gillies, *Memoirs and Sermons*, p. 522.

41. George Whitefield, *The Doctrine of Election Defended and Supported, Dec. 24, 1740* (Windham, 1791), p. 10.

42. The phrase, applicable to his pamphlet position, was actually used in a letter to Howell Harris in 1738, cited by Tyerman, *op. cit.*, I, 314.

43. "The Halfway Covenant . . . seemed to many a terrific inroad upon orthodoxy." Thomas Jefferson Wertenbaker, *The First Americans, 1607–1690* (New York, 1927), pp. 110–111.

44. King, *op. cit.*, pp. 248–249; 410–416.

45. Although "right STERLING," the American Anglican listener noticed that Whitefield's doctrine "asserts the absolute Necessity of the New Birth." *New York Gazette*, Nov. 19–26, 1739.

The prominence of the conversion among eighteenth-century revivalists is also shown by Daniel Rowland's use of the phrase "new creature" to Griffith Jones. Simon, *op. cit.*, p. 137.

46. Helen C. Knight, *Lady Huntingdon and Her Friends* (New York, 1853), p. 18.

47. To understand the social power of revival movements, it is necessary to recall the convert's belief that conversion had wrought a transformation in him, as is evident, for example, in George Whitefield, *A Short Account of God's Dealings with the Reverend Mr. Whitefield* (London, 1740) and *The*

Notes

Life of Mr. J. Cennick, With an Account of the TRIALS and TEMPTATIONS which he endured till it Pleased our SAVIOUR to shew him his Love, and send him into his Vineyard, Written by Himself, for their Sakes who follow the LAMB, . . . The Second Edition (Bristol, 1745).

Not to be confused with such a retreat as the Halfway Covenant, was the quieter, more gradual process of attaining new birth as represented in the experience of Horace Bushnell; see Merle Curti, *The Growth of American Thought* (New York, 1951), pp. 630–631.

The typical eighteenth-century conversion, however, was not only a perceptibly sudden experience, but, often, could be associated with a particular hour or even minute. John Wesley, for example, always remembered his conversion as occurring "about a quarter before nine" on May 24, 1738. John Wesley, *The Journal of the Rev. John Wesley, A.M.,* in 4 volumes (London, Toronto and New York, 1906), I, 102.

The social effects of the intense revival experience were most significant. "It was more than a wave of excitement; it was a *transforming process* in the nation's life," Maxson, *op. cit.,* p. 139.

48. Fixed in the memory of one of Whitefield's contemporaries was the following: "The Lord . . . can make use of me to bring some of his elect home, when and where he pleases." Quoted by Richard Elliot, *Grace and Truth, or a Summary of Gospel Doctrine, Considered in a Funeral Discourse Preached on the Death of Rev. Mr. George Whitefield, A.M.* (London, 1770), p. 33.

49. The whole passage, from which this and other portions have been taken, becomes, "When we are once convinced of our need and helplessness, and of Jesus being a Redeemer that is mighty and willing to save, a poor soul then throws himself upon this Jesus, ventures upon this Jesus, believes the word and by venturing upon this promise, receives from Jesus the thing promised." Gillies, *Memoirs and Sermons,* p. 522.

50. *Works,* V, 249; Gillies, *Memoirs and Sermons,* p. 388; *ibid.,* pp. 505–506.

51. An incidental aspect of Whitefield's doctrine was his frequent urging of his listeners to be good, this recommendation of prudential ethics being consistent not only with eighteenth-century orthodox sermon practice but also with the routine behests of Christian ministers of all ages. Whitefield tells soldiers and wives to be obedient, and everyone to avoid swearing and drunkenness. "I took occasion, in my morning sermon, to exhort the soldiers to obey them that had rule over them. . . ." *Journal,* p. 101.

"I . . . explained the catechism to the women, and exhorted them particularly to be obedient to their husbands, which they had lately been wanting in. . . ." *Ibid.,* p. 113.

Routine indeed were such entries as "preached my sermon on Swearing," and "preached a Sermon against drunkenness." *Ibid.,* p. 133.

52. "These and others preserve the extempore style, and fully serve to discover the exactness of the preacher." Jay, *op. cit.,* p. 29.

53. *Works,* V, 174.

"He has great Mastery of Words, but studies much plainness of Speech." *New York Gazette,* Nov. 19–26, 1739.

54. Gillies, *Memoirs and Sermons,* p. 535.

55. *Ibid.,* p. 532.

56. *Ibid.,* p. 403.

57. *Ibid.,* p. 315.

58. *Ibid.,* pp. 534–535.

59. *Ibid.,* p. 405.

60. Jay, *op. cit.,* p. 20.

61. Cf. notes 60 and 63.

62. Gillies, *Memoirs and Sermons,* p. 43n.

63. Benjamin Franklin, *The Autobiography of Benjamin Franklin* (New York, 1926), p. 132.

64. The experiment consisted of Franklin's walking away from the rostrum until the speaker was no longer clearly audible, and then, using his line of march as a radius of the hypothetical circle within which a hearing audience *might* stand—even though not necessarily present on this occasion, made the calculation cited in the text. *Ibid.,* pp. 132–133.

65. Edward S. Ninde, *George White-*

field, *Prophet-Preacher* (New York and Cincinnati, 1924), p. 162.

66. Franklin, *op. cit.*, p. 133.

67. James Peterson Gledstone, *George Whitefield, M.A., Field-Preacher* (New York, 1901), p. 247.

68. *New York Gazette*, Nov. 19–26.

69. It is only fair to recognize that there have been other views of what constituted unifying or synthesizing factors. Winter speaks frequently of Whitefield's "energy" as a special quality. Jay, *op. cit.*, pp. 15, 70.

The same observer also pointed to "God in the preacher that made the word efficacious." *Ibid.*, p. 16.

A still more comprehensive attribution of Whitefield's success to divine intervention is expressed in the opinion that "the Holy Ghost, the comforter, was now moving the masses of the people, and making them anxious concerning their personal salvation; and, further, He was connecting with Whitefield's ministry a 'power from on high,' like that which distinguished the Apostle's ministry at Pentecost." Tyerman, *op. cit.*, I, 222.

70. Whitefield, at the beginning, calls the ceremonies a "Mixture of human artifice and blind Superstition," but, when the ship is about to sail, he writes, "This news, I own, was not altogether agreeable to me, because I wanted to see the Conclusion of the Lent Solemnities. . . ." George Whitefield, *A Brief Account of Some Lent and other Extraordinary Processions and Ecclesiastical Entertainments seen Last Year at Lisbon. In four letters to an English Friend* (London, 1755), Letter I, p. 6, and Letter IV, p. 22.

71. Gillies, *Memoirs and Sermons*, p. 264.

The judge role was noted by others. Winter remembered the same passage as " 'Go, ye cursed,' not without a very powerful description of the nature of the curse." Jay, *op. cit.*, p. 18.

Similarly, "When he turned himself to the *secure* Sinner, we seemed to hear the *last Thunders of the tremendous Day* he describ'd; the Pulpit seem'd almost to be a Tribunal, and the Preacher himself, if the Comparison may be pardon'd of the *Great Judge*, cloathed in Flames, and adjudging a guilty World to penal

Fire." *New York Gazette*, April 7–April 14, 1740 [Letter from Charleston about Whitefield].

72. XXX, 200, 245–246.

73. William Edward Hartpole Lecky, *A History of England in the Eighteenth Century* (New York, 1878–1890), II, 622–623.

74. The full text of the sermon from which this and following excerpts were taken can be found in Gillies, *Memoirs and Sermons*, pp. 339–350.

75. George Whitefield, *Sermons on Important Subjects, with a Memoir of the Author, by Samuel Drew, and a Dissertation on his Character, etc. by the Rev. Joseph Smith* (London, 1861), p. 65.

76. "The peculiar talents he possessed . . . can be but faintly guessed from his sermons in print," even though "the savour of them yet remains." Jay, *op. cit.*, p. 25.

77. Gledstone, *op. cit.*, p. 247.

78. *New York Gazette*, Nov. 19–26.

79. "There . . . , above all, was George Whitefield, the greatest pulpit orator of England." Lecky, *op. cit.*, II, 600.

80. Even when the fervor of the Great Awakening had lessened appreciably, Whitefield himself "never Preached one Sermon but the Meeting-House Dores and Windows was so full, that the People themselves were Astonished to see so vast an Audience." *New York Evening Post*, Sept. 2, 1745, No. 41.

Two years later, the evangelist himself reported, "Congregations are as great as ever" in New England. "Letter from the Rev. Mr. Whitefield to Mr. Howell Harris, from Boston, August 9th, 1747." Tyerman, *op. cit.*, II, 175.

81. "So prosperous was his ministry in New York, that it was found necessary immediately to enlarge the Presbyterian church in Wall-Street, by the erection of galleries; and a year or two afterwards it was again enlarged about one-third, in order to accomodate the stated worshipers." William C. Conant, *Narratives of Remarkable conversions and Revival Incidents: including a review of revivals, from the day of Pentecost to the great awakening in the last century—*

conversions of eminent persons—instances of remarkable conversions and answers to prayer—an account of the rise and progress of the Great Awakening of 1857-'8 . . . With an introduction by Henry Ward Beecher* (New York, 1858), p. 37.

82. Franklin, *op. cit.*, p. 129.

83. For the aftermath of the Great Awakening, see Eugene E. White, "Decline of the Great Awakening in New England: 1741 to 1746," *The New England Quarterly*, XXIV, March, 1951, pp. 35–52.

84. He assured a worried inquirer not to "be uneasy for my sake on account of the New Building—So that it answers any Good end for the Inhabitants of Philadelphia, I am satisfied—Persons on the spot know better than I who am at a distance. . . ." G[eorge] W[hitefield] to William Bradford; Plymouth, Feb: 24th 1749/50, a manuscript letter at American Philosophical Society Library.

85. "His maxim was, if you love me you will serve me disinterestedly; hence he settled no certain income, or a very slender one, upon his dependents, many of whom were sycophants, and while they professed to serve him, underhandedly served themselves effectually." Jay, *op. cit.*, p. 61.

86. "I leave my AFFAIRS to you, and depend on you to transact them all." "Letter from the Rev. Mr. Whitefield to Mr. H—w—l H—rr—s, New York, June 27th, 1747," Tyerman, *op. cit.*, II, 173.

87. "I hope before this Year is out to [establish a secure income] for the Orphan-House . . . (so that my poor Heart may be no more oppres'd as it has been for many Years by outward Embarrassments)." *Christian History*, p. 120.

88. At the beginning of his career, he answered the Bishop of Gloucester's suggestion to confine himself to a regular parish by writing on July 9, 1739, "I am as much convinced it is my duty to act as I do, as I am that the sun shines at noonday." *Journal*, p. 297.

Near the end of his career, he wrote, "To be a presbyter at large, is the station which, I think, divine providence hath

called me to for near these thirty years last past." G. Whitefield, A.M., *A Letter to his Excellency Governor Wright* (London, 1768), p. 9.

89. "It was truly impressive to see him ascend the pulpit. My intimate knowledge of him admits my acquitting him of the charge of affectation." Winter to Jay, Gillies, *Memoirs and Sermons,* Appendix, p. 282.

90. "The church was offered, but not being sufficient to contain a third part of the audience, . . . I preached in the fields, which put me in mind of our Lord's saying, 'Go out into the highways and hedges, and compel them to come in.' " *Journal*, p. 234.

91. "In the vast work of social organization which is one of the dominant characteristics of nineteenth-century England, it would be difficult to overestimate the part played by the Weslyan revival." Élie Halévy, *A History of the English People in 1815* (London, 1924), I, 372.

92. M. L. Greene, *The Development of Religious Liberty in Connecticut* (Boston and New York, 1905); William Thomas Whitley, *A History of British Baptists* (London, 1923); William Warren Sweet, *The Story of Religion in America* (New York, 1950); Maxson, *op. cit.*

93. Lecky, *op. cit.*, II, 691–692.

Halévy says, "We can watch between 1792 and 1815 an uninterrupted decline of the revolutionary spirit among the sects." *Op. cit.*, I, 372.

To the foregoing might be added, "It has been maintained with much force that the powerful influence of the religious revival in the British Isles strongly counteracted the spread of revolutionary ideas from France and saved the country from serious class antagonism." Turberville, *op. cit.*, p. 310.

94. "In forming the new spirit of Americanism, few events were more important than the Great Awakening. During that sudden up-surging of religious emotionalism, which for a decade rolled like a tidal wave over the colonies, provincial boundaries and the distinctions of race and creed were in some measure forgotten in a new sense of common nature and human brother-

hood." Carl Becker, *Beginnings of the American People* (Boston, New York, Chicago, 1915; reissued Ithaca, N.Y., 1960), pp. 187–188.

"With the visits of Whitefield we have the first demonstration on a large scale of one of the most important social characteristics not only of Boston but of democracy in general." Herbert Levi Osgood, *The American Colonies in the Eighteenth Century* (New York, 1924), III, 420.

The Contemporary Reception of Edmund Burke's Speaking

1. Many of Burke's critics have, perhaps, taken their cue from Sheridan, who once said to Samuel Rogers, "When posterity read the speeches of Burke, they will hardly be able to believe that during his life-time he was not considered as a first-rate speaker, not even as a second-rate one." Alexander Dyce, *Recollections of the Table-Talk of Samuel Rogers* (1887), p. 67. Rogers reports Henry Grattan also as of the opinion that Burke's speeches were much better read than heard. *Ibid.*, p. 124. These opinions might be duplicated many times over among both earlier and more recent critics.

2. "The Literary Criticism of Oratory," *Studies in Rhetoric and Public Speaking in Honor of James Albert Winans* (New York, 1925), pp. 181 ff.; also in *The Rhetorical Idiom*, ed. by Donald C. Bryant (Ithaca, N.Y., 1958), pp. 5–42 *passim*.

3. Elizabeth Carter's opinion is expressed in a letter of June 17, 1769. *Letters from Mrs. Elizabeth Carter to Mrs. Montagu, 1755–1800*, 3 vols. (London, 1817), II, 23. Goldsmith's, of course, is in *Retaliation*. The quotations, from Hazlitt, are introduced by L. E. Broughton with the remark that we may hesitate to accept Hazlitt's notion of Burke's proper place in life (*Edmund Burke—Selections* [New York, 1925], p. viii). Yet Broughton observes later, "Though eloquent, he was too good a writer to be an effective orator" (p. xlii).

4. *Selections from Edmund Burke*, edited with notes and introduction by Bliss Perry (New York, 1896), p. xi; Christopher Hobhouse, *Fox* (Boston and New York, 1935), p. 65.

5. "Edmund Burke, 1729–1797: A Portrait and an Appraisal," *History Today*, VI (1956), 729. Mahoney's principal work on Burke, *Edmund Burke and Ireland* (Harvard University Press), appeared in 1960.

6. Burke's biographer, Sir James Prior (*Life of Edmund Burke* [5th ed.; London, 1854], pp. 504–505) insists that the witticism was of late origin, invented by Fox's admirers after the split between Burke and the Foxites in 1791. Perhaps so, but Goldsmith, if he did not use the epithet "dinner-bell," came close enough to suggest a currency.

7. This aspect of Burke's effectiveness has been well investigated and well estimated by others; for example, by H. Clay Harshbarger in the introduction to his edition of "Burke's Chief American Works" (unpublished dissertation, Cornell University, 1929).

8. *Selections from Edmund Burke*, p. xi. See Prior, p. 508 fn, where the anecdote is quoted on the authority of Edward D. Clarke, the traveller, who had it from Erskine.

9. For example, Bliss Perry, *Selections*, p. xi, and Chauncey A. Goodrich, *Select British Eloquence* (New York, 1852), p. 330.

10. N. W. Wraxall, *Historical Memoirs* (2d ed.; London, 1815), II, 41; *Posthumous Memoirs* (London, 1836), I, 113, 37–38.

11. *The Correspondence of Edmund Burke*, ed. by Thomas W. Copeland, I (Cambridge and Chicago, 1958), 241. Volume II (1960) is edited by Lucy S. Sutherland, and Volume III by George H. Guttridge. Hereafter cited as *Correspondence*.

12. *Boswell's Life of Johnson*, ed. by G. B. Hill and rev. by L. F. Powell (Oxford, 1934), III, 233–234.

13. *Ibid.*, II, 151; Nathaniel W. Wraxall, *Historical and Posthumous Memoirs*, ed. by Henry B. Wheatley (London, 1884), II, 28.

14. Page 41.

15. *Memoirs of the Reign of George*

Notes

the Third, ed. by Sir Denis Le Marchant (London, 1845), II, 273.

16. "David Garrick and the Burkes," *PQ*, XVIII (1939), 369–370.

17. Loren D. Reid, "Speaking in the Eighteenth Century House of Commons," *Speech Monographs*, XVI (1949), 137–140.

18. *Correspondence*, I, 226.

19. Robert Bisset, *The Life of Edmund Burke* (2d ed.; London, 1800), I, 417.

20. *Correspondence*, I, 233.

21. XXX, 462.

22. *Correspondence*, I, 232–233.

23. Ross J. S. Hoffman, *Edmund Burke, New York Agent* (Philadelphia, 1956), p. 331.

24. *Boswell's Life of Johnson*, II, 16.

25. *Correspondence*, I, 240–241.

26. Reginald Blunt (ed.), *Mrs. Montagu, Queen of the Blues* (Boston and New York [1932?]), I, 139, 135, 168.

27. *Original Letters to Henry Flood*, p. 40, quoted in *Correspondence*, I, 243 n. 3.

28. *Hist. MSS. Comm.*, XII: x, 278.

29. *The Chatham Correspondence* (London, 1839), III, 110.

30. *Ibid.*, III, 145.

31. *Hist. MSS. Comm.*, IX: iii, 26b.

32. *The Lee Papers . . . 1754–1811* (New York, 1872–1875), I, 61.

33. *Correspondence*, I, 286.

34. *Ibid.*, I, 285.

35. *Ibid.*, I, 340.

36. O'Hara MSS. See Hoffman, p. 450 n. 12.

37. O'Hara MSS. See Hoffman, p. 472.

38. *Hist. MSS. Comm., Beaufort* (1891), p. 274.

39. *Private Papers of James Boswell . . .*, ed. by Geoffrey Scott and Frederick A. Pottle (1928–1936), VI, 83.

40. *Correspondence*, II (1960), 426.

41. *Select British Eloquence* (New York, 1872), p. 214. See James Prior, *Life of Burke* (1854), pp. 142, 144.

42. *Universal Magazine*, LVI (March 1775), 157–158.

43. *Gentleman's Magazine*, XLV (December 1775), 622.

44. *Hist. MSS. Comm.*, XIII: viii, 391. Gibbon described Burke in Parliament as "a watermill of words and images" (*Private Letters of Edward Gibbon*, ed. by Prothero [1897], I, 240); H. Walpole once asserted that "Burke could form a metaphoric vision that would satisfy no imagination but his own" (*Letters of Horace Walpole*, ed. by Toynbee, XI, 359). Flood's analysis is echoed in brief in Attorney General Kenyon's complaint to Boswell about Burke's "wildness"; said he, "I never could *cage* his opinions." *Boswell Papers*, XV, 186.

45. *Correspondence*, III, 139. That same evening Burke's brother Richard wrote to their friend Richard Champion of Bristol at greater length to the same effect. Wrote Richard, in part: "From a Torrent of Members rushing from the house when he sat down, I could hear the loudest, the most unanimous, and the highest strains of applause. That such a performance even from him was never before heard in that house." *Ibid.*

46. *Hist. MSS. Comm.*, IX: iii, 31b, 32a. See also *Letters of David Hume*, ed. by Greig (1932), II, 127.

47. *Hist. MSS. Comm.*, XIV: i, 11. Horace Walpole, who had a low opinion of Burke's wit in private conversation, admitted that in public speeches "nothing was so luminous, so striking, so abundant." *Journal of the Reign of George the Third*, ed. by Doran (1859), II, 26. And in 1782 Wraxall observed that on a certain occasion, in addition to all the arguments suggested by the nature of the subject and by the exhausted state of Great Britain, Burke "oppressed the recently appointed Minister [Mr. Ellis], under flashes of intolerable wit, supported by the keenest ridicule. Never on any occasion," continued Wraxall, "was he more happy in his allusions or more pointed in his irony. . . . Pursuing this comparison [of Ellis to a caterpillar finally come out of its comfortable 'ligaments'] with inconceivable humour, he directed the whole force of his powerful mind, in impelling his audience no longer to support a hopeless, ruinous, and unavailing conflict. On that night, the American War may indeed be said to have terminated." *Historical Memoirs* (1815), II, 140–141. Burke's ridiculing Lord North

so successfully as to make the minister himself roar with laughter is well known. Other victims did not manage to parry the assault so well, as, for example, when Burke easily turned the laugh against Martin, member for Tewkesbury, on April 26, 1786. Wraxall, *Posthumous Memoirs* (1836), II, 103.

48. Christopher Hobhouse, *Fox*, p. 25.

49. James Prior, *Life of Burke* (1854), pp. 172, 173. See also Chauncey Goodrich, *Select British Eloquence*, p. 214.

50. *Hist. MSS. Comm.*, XII: vii, 359.

51. *The Autobiographies of Edward Gibbon*, ed. by John Murray (2d ed., 1897), p. 320.

52. *Life and Letters of Gilbert Elliot, First Earl of Minto*, ed. by the Countess of Minto (1874), I, 74.

53. Nathaniel W. Wraxall, *Historical Memoirs of My Own Time* (2d ed., 1815), II, 28. See Johnson's remark that he did not envy Burke's being the first man in the H. of C. because he was the first man everywhere (*Boswell's Johnson*, ed. by Hill, V, 269, "Hebrides," September 30, 1773); and W. G. Hamilton's that "In the House of Commons I sometimes think him only the second man in England; out of it he is always the first" (Prior, *Burke* [1854], p. 484).

54. Wraxall, *Historical Memoirs*, II, 41. Italics are mine.

55. *Ibid.*, II, 108–109.

56. *Ibid.*, II, 140–141.

57. *Ibid.*, II, 449–450.

58. *Ibid.*, II, 583.

59. Wraxall, *Posthumous Memoirs* (1836), I, 258, 261–262.

60. *Ibid.*, II, 37.

61. *Ibid.*, II, 63.

62. *Ibid.*, III, 324.

63. *Boswell Papers*, XVI, 166.

64. *Hist. MSS. Comm.*, XIII: viii, 34.

65. *Life and Letters of Gilbert Elliot*, I, 124.

66. *Ibid.*, I, 194–195.

67. *Ibid.*, I, 195.

68. *Ibid.*, I, 208–209, 211, 215.

69. *Ibid.*, I, 269.

70. *Edmund Burke and His Literary Friends* (Washington University Studies; St. Louis, 1939), p. 164. See *The Diary and Letters of Madame d'Arblay*, ed. by Austin Dobson (1906), III, 448–449, 457–458, 471–472.

71. William Roberts, *Memoirs of the Life and Correspondence of Mrs. Hannah More* (2d ed., 1834), II, 108–109.

72. *Boswell Papers*, XVII, 68.

73. *Hist. MSS. Comm.*, XIII: viii, 72.

74. *Ibid.*, p. 88.

75. Hobhouse, *Fox*, p. 228.

76. *The Windham Papers*, ed. by the Earl of Rosebery (1913), I, 212.

77. *Historical Memoirs* (1815), II, 35–36.

78. "Burke's Chief American Works —An Edition" (unpublished dissertation, Cornell University, 1929), pp. cccxiii–cccxix.

79. *Hist. MSS. Comm.*, XIII: iii, 162.

80. Roberts, *Memoirs of Hannah More* (1834), III, 378.

81. In Boswell's presence on 21 April 1779, "Wilkes said Burke was eloquent, but had not the right kind of eloquence; his was wild Irish eloquence. As Appelles's painting of a fine woman had such flesh that some one said she had fed on roses, Burke's art gives us a fine woman, but fed on potatoes and whiskey; beautiful, not sublime. It does not shake you." *Boswell Papers*, XIII, 232. Cf. *Boswell's Life of Johnson*, IV, 104. Previously Wilkes had said to Boswell that "Burke was never sublime nor in good taste; there was always something low mixed." *Ibid.*, XI, 283. And the novelist, John Cleland, prodded by Boswell, said, "I don't like oratory so much drest at the toilet of Flora. I am not satisfied with flowers: I must have fruit." *Ibid.*, XIII, 220. "Burke," wrote Sir Gilbert Elliot, "has taught us that *delicacy* is the lowest of all virtues, and when it interferes with higher duties is a vice." *Life and Letters of Gilbert Elliot*, I, 310. Others could not so easily abandon "delicacy." William Maltby, a friend of Samuel Rogers, once said: "Burke always disappointed me as a speaker. I have heard him during his speeches in the House, make use of the most vulgar expressions, such as 'three nips of straw, three skips of a louse, &c.;' and on one occasion, when I was present, he introduced as an illustration, a most indelicate story about a French

Notes

king, who asked his physician why his natural children were so much finer than his legitimate." Alexander Dyce, *Recollections of the Table-Talk of Samuel Rogers* (1856), pp. 78–79. Hume said to Boswell that Burke's *Conciliation* (as printed) had a great deal of flower, a great deal of leaf, and a little fruit (*Letters of James Boswell*, ed. by Tinker [1924], I, 233); and Horace Walpole asserted that he preferred "Charles Fox's 'native wood notes' to Burke's feigned voice, though it goes to the highest pitch of the gamut of wit" (*The Letters of Horace Walpole*, ed. by Toynbee, X, 187–188).

Lord Thomas Erskine: Modern Advocate

1. J. A. Lovat-Fraser in his *Erskine* (Cambridge, 1932) gives the date as January 10, 1749, Old Style, citing the Erskine family Bible as his source (p. 1). Almost all other sources give the birth year as 1750, though a few change the day to January 21 to accommodate it to the calendar change of 1752.

2. The very brief biographical sketch here follows Lord James Campbell, *Lives of the Lord Chancellors* (New York, 1874–1881), VIII; Lloyd Paul Stryker, *For the Defense* (New York, 1947); and Lovat-Fraser, *Erskine*.

3. This hall, on Noble Street, was evidently used as a meeting place by a variety of groups. Just when Erskine participated in debates and harangues here, and on what subjects, I have not discovered. The Protestant Association, formed in 1779, met here and in this hall resolved on May 29, 1780 to accompany its President, Lord George Gordon, to the House of Commons to present the "Protestant Petition." The riots leading to Lord George's indictment for treason and Erskine's defense of him followed. See Walter Thornbury, *Old and New London: A Narrative of Its History, Its People, and Its Places* (London, 1873), I, 363.

4. *Lives of the Lord Chancellors*, VIII, 29.

5. Lovat-Fraser's view is expressed

thus: "If he had been a great advocate only, he would soon have been forgotten. He is remembered because he was also a resolute champion of liberty, a valiant defender of freedom, and a noble and far-seeing patriot" (p. xi). Most academic investigations have also focused on the treason and libel pleas. See William E. Young, "The Rhetorical Methods of Thomas Erskine," unpublished M.A. thesis (State University of Iowa, 1928); Lloyd Watkins, "Argumentation of Thomas Erskine in the Trial of Thomas Hardy," unpublished M.A. thesis (University of Wisconsin, 1951); and Merrill T. Baker, "Rhetorical Analysis of Thomas Erskine's Courtroom Defenses in Cases Involving Seditious Libel," unpublished Ph.D. thesis (State University of Iowa, 1952). Lawrence R. Rumley's "The Pleas of Thomas Erskine in Selected Trials for Criminal Conversation, 1789–1805," unpublished M.A. thesis (Cornell University, 1951), is the only exploration of Erskine's nonpolitical pleading I know of.

6. *De Oratore*, trans. J. S. Watson (London, 1881), I. viii.

7. *Lives of Eminent British Lawyers* (London, 1830), p. 381.

8. *Rhetorica ad Herennium*, trans. Harry Caplan (London, 1954), I.xvi.26. Caplan translates his author thus: "Once the Point to Adjudicate is found, the complete economy of the entire speech ought to be directed to it."

9. *Howard v Bingham*, Court of King's Bench, February 24, 1794; Lord Kenyon presiding. I have not seen the transcript of this famous trial, if one exists. Reports from *The Times*, February 25, 1794, and other sources such as C. A. Goodrich, *Select British Eloquence* (New York, 1880), pp. 708–713, are the bases for the following summary of facts.

Bernard Howard sought damages against Richard Bingham, charging criminal conversation with his wife, Elizabeth Howard. After four years of marriage to Howard and one child by him, Mrs. Howard eloped with Bingham. At the time of the trial Mrs. Howard was living with Bingham and was pregnant, admittedly by Bingham. The significant complication in the affair was that Mrs. Howard had been engaged to marry Bingham until her parents broke the engagement, determining she must make a better connection by marrying Howard, heir to the Duke of Norfolk. Under the law, Howard was clearly entitled to damages if Bingham had deprived him of "the society and comfort" of his wife. Erskine accepted Bingham's brief as an act of personal friendship.

Though Roscoe (p. 386) says there are "three or four instances" of Erskine's appearing for the defense in such cases, this is the only such plea appearing in any of the standard collections of his speeches or referred to by name in any of the standard biographical sources.

10. *Rex v Hadfield,* Court of King's Bench, June 26, 1800; Lord Kenyon presiding. The record of the trial appears in *State Trials,* comp. T. B. and Thomas J. Howell (38–40 Geo. III) (London, 1820), XXVII, 1281–1356.

As to the facts, the case was simple, but Erskine's defense made the nature of insanity and the legal responsibilities of the insane the deciding issues. James Hadfield, a wounded veteran of the war with France, discharged a pistol loaded with two slugs at George III, as the king stepped forward in his box to receive the ovation of the audience at a command performance of Colley Cibber's *She Would and She Would Not,* in Drury Lane Theatre. The king was not harmed. Hadfield was dragged from his place in the pit to a room beneath the stage, where he was interrogated before being imprisoned. Trial evidence showed he had methodically procured the pistol, made the slugs, placed himself in a strategic spot in the theatre. Evidence also showed he was subject to fits of insanity.

As traditionally interpreted and as applied by the Crown, the law stipulated that to be unaccountable for crime one must be unable "to form a judgment of that which he proposed to do, of that which he did, and of that which he had designed."

11. Lord Campbell, Goodrich, James Ridgway, Lovat-Fraser, and others report that the jury tried to bring in a verdict of damages against Howard but,

being reminded by Lord Kenyon that the adultery was admitted and Howard stood blameless before the law, granted Howard a trifling £500 where £10,000 would ordinarily be thought low. On the other hand, *The Times,* on the day after the trial, reported that the plaintiff was awarded £1,000. In either case the award was extraordinarily small.

On February 26, 1794, *The Times* editorialized: "This trial ought to serve as a very serious warning to parents, how they enforce matrimonial engagements on their children, without the parties having a mutual inclination for each other."

12. William C. J. Meredith says in his *Insanity as a Criminal Defense* (Montreal, 1931) that Erskine "upset the doctrines which until then had generally been recognized as law" by removing from Lord Kenyon's mind "the hitherto accepted doctrine of Coke and Hale" (pp. 118, 124). Twelve years after, Lord Mansfield discarded Erskine's and Kenyon's "delusion theory" in favor of the thesis that ability to distinguish right from wrong was a more precise test of sanity. Nonetheless, Erskine's argument for his principle is generally credited with having opened the way for more realistic and more merciful views of criminal insanity. See E. C. Mann, "Mental Responsibility and Diagnosis of Insanity in Criminal Cases," in *Papers Read Before the Medico-Legal Society of New York,* 3rd Ser. (New York, 1886), p. 480; John C. Bucknill, *Unsoundness of Mind in Relation to Criminal Acts* (Philadelphia, 1856), pp. 21–23.

13. Erskine's defense of Lord George Gordon offers a close parallel to the plea for Hadfield, both in the rhetorical problem to be met and in the method of meeting it.

14. The indirect suggestion that existing law was inadequate to render justice in this case may have had added force with the judges because the idea was familiar. Newspaper and magazine accounts of Hadfield's act and apprehension had represented Hadfield as a victim of mental disease.

15. When Lord Kenyon stopped the case to suggest acquittal and confine-

ment of Hadfield as an insane person, Mitford observed: "With respect to his sanity immediately preceding and subsequent to the act, I have offered the evidence I had; unquestionably, the circumstances which have now been stated, were perfectly unknown to me" (*State Trials*, XXVII, 1354). It was Garrow, assistant counsel for the Crown, who suggested that the jury be directed to "state in their verdict the grounds upon which they give it," and thus embodied Erskine's general principle in the verdict formally rendered (*ibid.*, 1356).

16. Two of Erskine's published forensic addresses are exceptions: his plea for a new trial in the case of William Shipley, Dean of St. Asaph, and his defense of Stockdale. In both, the principle of judgment is asserted very early in the address. The former is an appellate plea and this may account for the difference in method, but why the proposition that the *whole intent* of a work must be the measure of its libelous character should have been announced at the outset of the plea for Stockdale eludes me. Erskine's method here may have allowed doubts to build up in the jurors' minds, for Lord Campbell observes that "it is a curious fact . . . that the jury deliberated two hours before they found a verdict of NOT GUILTY" (*Lives of the Lord Chancellors*, VIII, 80).

17. Kenyon's almost casual promulgation of a new doctrine on criminal insanity, the jury's burst of sympathy for Elizabeth Howard and Richard Bingham, and Kenyon's frequently moralistic charges to juries in criminal conversation cases are all instances in point. Some writers imply that in the Hadfield case Kenyon was so far carried away by Erskine's supralegal persuasions that he did not even realize he was radically changing the law by his disposition of the case. His colloquy with Mitford, the prosecutor, at the end of the trial, suggests this. Henry Weihofen, in *Insanity as a Defense of Criminal Law* (New York, 1933), says "the speech of the Counsel which practically put an end to the trial" led Kenyon to render a decision which could not stand for long because it failed to define the test it endorsed (pp. 21–23). Yet Kenyon, for-

merly a specialist in the law of conveyancing, was not given to looseness in definition and detail.

18. Hugh Blair's Lecture XXVII sets out the general rule that English lawyers ought not follow too closely Ciceronian and Demosthenian arguments from topics of expediency and public welfare because at the English bar "the field of speaking is limited to precise law and statute" (*Lectures on Rhetoric and Belles Lettres*). Only in discussing introductions and statements of facts does Blair touch on the value of preparing the minds of listeners by indirect means, and in this he follows the pattern of most classical treatments of "the subtle approach." George Campbell considered neither the uses of indirect argument nor the values of alternative methods of speech organization in his *Philosophy of Rhetoric*.

19. *The Rhetoric of Aristotle*, trans. Lane Cooper (New York, 1932), I. 1. 1354b.

20. Among those with whom and against whom Erskine served as counsel were: *Lloyd Kenyon*, later Lord Chief Justice of King's Bench; *John Scott*, later 1st Earl of Eldon, Chief Justice of Common Pleas, Lord High Chancellor, and dominant member of the Cabinet for most of the period, 1801–1827; *Edward Law*, later 1st Baron Ellenborough, Chief Counsel for Warren Hastings, Chief Justice of King's Bench, member of the All-the-Talents Administration; *Sir John Mitford*, afterwards Speaker of the House of Commons, Lord Chancellor of Ireland, writer on legal subjects; *Spencer Perceval*, Attorney General, Chancellor of the Exchequer, and Prime Minister, 1809–1812. Others, who did not assume high public office, included *William Garrow, Edward Bearcroft, John Dunning, Sir Robert Dallas*, and *William Draper Best*, all greatly sought after as pleaders.

21. "Amicus Curiæ" [John Payne Collier], *Criticism on the Bar* (London, 1819), pp. 53, 59.

22. See "Proceedings in the Trial of Edward Marcus Despard, Esq., for High Treason," in *State Trials*, XXVIII, 345–528. Best was chief counsel for Despard and, in the manner of Erskine, showed

that treason should not be adjudged where *overt* acts of treason could not be proved. Having done this, he showed why some considered him a rather unsafe "leader" for he gave equal emphasis to the argument that Despard's intelligence and character were such as to make it impossible to believe he would choose to act as charged. The impossibility of demonstrating the second contention badly weakened the force of the first.

23. His plea in the trial of James O'Coigly and others for high treason, in 1798, is an excellent argument; but the style, though clear, seldom reinforces thought with feeling. See *State Trials*, XXVII, 53–90.

24. Lord Campbell, *Lives of the Lord Chancellors*, "Lord Eldon," VIII, 434.

25. Archer Polson, *Law and Lawyers* (Philadelphia, 1841), I, 188–192; "Amicus Curiæ," p. 10.

26. Attorney General Spencer Perceval neatly destroyed much of Macintosh's effect by his reply: "We are both agreed as to the illegality of printing and the illegality of publishing libels against those with whom we are at peace: the only question then for you to decide is this, whether or not these publications . . . were or were not published with the intention of vilifying the French Consul?" Lord Ellenborough [Edward Law] paraphrased Perceval in his charge, and the jury "immediately returned a verdict of—GUILTY." *State Trials*, XXVIII, 563–608, 615, 618–619.

27. From the text as published by William L. Snyder, *Great Speeches by Great Lawyers* (New York, 1882), pp. 667–676. Bartholomew Hoar (or Hoare, or Hore) was born in the County of Cork, son of Benjamin Hoar, in 1754. He received the B.A. from the University of Dublin (Trinity College) in 1775, was called to the Irish Bar in 1778, and subsequently became a King's Counsel. For at least part of his active career he resided in Dublin. (I am indebted to Professor Lewis W. Morse, Librarian, Cornell Law School, and to Mr. Arthur Cox of Dublin for this information.) Exhaustive search of records might produce additional data on Hoar, but had he been a pleader of more than ordinary powers references to him would surely be more frequent in standard sources. Had he been an inferior pleader, he would hardly have opened in a case where Curran led the plaintiff's counsel and George Ponsonby led the defense. His address, neither better nor worse than many others of the period, doubtless entered the literature of forensic oratory because Curran and Ponsonby also spoke.

28. *Ibid.*, p. 668.

29. *Ibid.*, pp. 691–707.

30. From the text as published in J. L. High, *Speeches of Lord Erskine* (Chicago, 1870), 4 vols., IV, 214–238.

31. George Ponsonby did, in fact, use this topic in behalf of the Marquis, insisting that Mrs. Massy could not have fallen so swiftly out of love with her husband unless he had, himself, been at fault (Snyder, p. 690). Curran did not reply directly.

32. Lawrence R. Rumley, p. 214. This characterization Rumley applies to "every trial which would support such treatment."

33. *Select British Eloquence*, p. 635.

34. *Lives of the Lord Chancellors*, VIII, 307.

35. One cannot assume that his legal study provided much experience in argumentation, for disputations and moots were no longer generally practiced at the Inns of Court. See W. Herbert, *Antiquities of the Inns of Court and Chancery* (London, 1804), pp. 180–181; and R. M. Jackson, *The Machinery of Justice in England*, 2nd ed. (Cambridge, 1953), pp. 209–210. His participation in debates at Coachmakers' Hall and elsewhere may, of course, have supplied enlightening experience.

36. The list of leading English works on rhetoric published between his eleventh and twenty-fifth years includes: Burgh's *Art of Speaking* (1761), Sheridan's *Lectures on Elocution* (1762), Leland's *Dissertation on the Principles of Human Eloquence* (1764), Rice's *Introduction to the Art of Reading with Energy and Propriety* (1765), Gibbons' *Rhetoric, or a View of its Principal Tropes and Figures* (1767), Enfield's *The Speaker* (1774), Steele's *Prosodia Rationalis* (1775), Cockin's

Notes

The Art of Delivering Written Language (1775).

37. Douglas Ehninger, "John Ward and His Rhetoric," *Speech Monographs,* XVIII (March 1951), 16.

38. The work was published in 1776, while Erskine was studying law.

39. *Philosophy of Rhetoric* (New York, 1841), p. 77.

40. Blair's conception of the range of forensic speaking has been cited. Campbell devotes so little attention to this form of persuasion that it seems fair to assume he had no quarrel with restrictive definitions that confined the pleader to questions of fact and legal interpretation.

41. It is worth noting that anthologists have singled out few passages from Erskine's forensic addresses as beautiful when considered apart from their context. The "Indian Chief" segment of his defense of Stockdale is such a passage, but it is the only one Goodrich was moved to call "beautiful in itself," though he published and annotated nine of Erskine's courtroom speeches.

42. Cicero, *De Oratore,* II. xxxi.

Samuel Taylor Coleridge in Lecture-Box and Pulpit

1. The following summary gives the dates, places, and leading topics of Coleridge's known lectures and sermons, together with references that include factual material, reports, and printed texts. He undoubtedly delivered many more of which records have not yet been unearthed.

1795—Three lectures in the Corn Hall, Bristol. Subjects: I, the French Revolution and the English Constitution; II, Pitt and the forces of revolution; III, censorship of the press and restrictions of free speech. A. Brandl, *Samuel Taylor Coleridge und die englische Romantik,* tr. Lady Eastlake (London, 1887), p. 106. T. M. Raysor, *Coleridge's Shakespearean Criticism* (2 vols., London, 1930), II, 3. Texts of the three lectures are given in *Essays on His*

Own Times, ed. Sara Coleridge (3 vols., London, 1850), pp. 1–98.

Two courses of six lectures each in Bristol. Subjects: first course, a comparison of the English rebellion under Charles I with the French Revolution; second course, the original condition of Christianity contrasted with its current decline. Brandl, *op. cit.,* pp. 112 ff. Joseph Cottle, *Reminiscences of Samuel Taylor Coleridge and Robert Southey* (London, 1847), pp. 17–19.

Several individual lectures in the Assembly House, on the quay, etc. Subjects: the slave trade, the hair-powder tax, the tax on corn. Brandl, *op. cit.,* p. 113.

1796—Several sermons. First two at Bath. Subjects: the corn laws and the hair-powder tax. *Ibid.,* p. 114. Another at Taunton. *Ibid.,* p. 160. Possibly a half-dozen lecture-sermons on the tour for subscriptions to the *Watchman.* Two at Birmingham and one at Nottingham are definitely mentioned by E. H. Coleridge in the fragmentary "Biographical Notes," *Coleridge: Studies by Several Hands on the Hundredth Anniversary of His Death,* ed. E. Blunden and E. L. Griggs (London, 1934), pp. 14, 16, and in the Biographical Supplement to the *Biographia Literaria,* pp. 723, 725. Another sermon at Moseley, on faith. E. K. Chambers, *Samuel Taylor Coleridge* (Oxford, 1938), p. 61. *Unpublished Letters of Samuel Taylor Coleridge,* ed. E. L. Griggs (2 vols., London, 1932), I, 57–58.

1797—Sermon at Bridgwater. Chambers, *op. cit.,* p. 76.

1798—Two or more (probably four) sermons at Shrewsbury, where he applied for the Unitarian pulpit. Subject of first: Christianity and peace. J. D. Campbell, *Samuel Taylor Coleridge* (London, 1894), p. 84; Brandl, *op. cit.,* p. 224; Chambers, *op. cit.,* pp. 88–90; *Unpublished Letters,* I, 97; R. W. Armour and R. F. Howes, *Coleridge, the Talker* (Ithaca, 1940), pp. 286–287. Sermon at Bridgwater and another at Taunton. *Unpublished Letters,* I, 91, 104. It is highly probable that Coleridge preached a number of additional sermons at Bridgwater and Taunton. See Lawrence Hanson, *The Life of S. T.*

Coleridge: the Early Years (London, 1938), p. 474. His note includes a quotation by an anonymous member of one of these congregations, who had heard "the torrent of happily expressed language."

1806–1807—Coleridge projected but probably did not deliver a series of lectures at the Royal Institution, London, on the principles of the fine arts. S. T. Coleridge, *Lectures and Notes on Shakespeare and Other English Poets*, ed. T. Ashe (London, 1908), p. 30; *Shakespearean Criticism*, II, 4.

1808—Series of lectures at the Royal Institution on the English poets. Course of 25 announced but not all given. Coleridge missed several because of illness. *Ibid.*, II, 3 ff.; Brandl, *op. cit.*, pp. 295–298.

1810—Coleridge projected but probably did not deliver a series of lectures at the Royal Institution on poetry. *Lectures and Notes on Shakespeare*, p. 32.

1811–1812—Course of 17 lectures at the Scots Corporation for the London Philosophical Society. Subject: Shakespeare and Milton illustrating the principles of poetry. *Ibid.*, pp. 33 ff.; *Shakespearean Criticism*, II, 24 ff.

1812—Course of six lectures at Willis's Rooms, London. Subject: the drama of Greece, France, England, and Spain, chiefly with reference to Shakespeare. *Ibid.*, II, 240 ff.

1812–1813—Course of 12 lectures at the Surrey Institution, London. Subject: belles lettres. *Ibid.*, II, 246 ff.

1813–1814—Series of eight lectures in the White Lion Inn, Bristol. Six of these on Shakespeare and Milton, two on education. *Ibid.*, II, 252 ff.; *Lectures and Notes on Shakespeare*, p. 455.

1814—About four lectures at Clifton, a suburb of Bristol, in the hotel. Subjects: Milton, poetry in general, literary theory. *Shakespearean Criticism*, II, 254–255.

Second course of six lectures at Bristol. Subject: Milton and Shakespeare. *Ibid.*, II, 256 ff.

Third course of four lectures at Bristol. Subject: Milton. *Ibid.*, II, 257.

Other lectures in Bristol. One on the French Revolution and probably several on Homer. *Ibid.*, II, 258.

1817—Lecture at the London Philosophical Society on principles of experimental philosophy. *Unpub. Letters*, II, 212 n.

1818—Course of 14 lectures at the Philosophical Society, London. Subjects: general literature, including Shakespeare and Milton. *Shakespearean Criticism*, II, 299 ff.; *Lectures and Notes on Shakespeare*, pp. 169 ff.; *Coleridge's Miscellaneous Criticism*, ed. T. M. Raysor (Cambridge, 1936), pp. 3 ff.

Impromptu lecture at the Philosophical Society, London. Subject: the growth of the individual mind. Gillman's *Life*, pp. 335–336. Another lecture is noted by Raysor, *Shakespearean Criticism*, II, 324 n.

1818–1819—Course of 14 lectures on philosophy and another six on Shakespeare at the Crown and Anchor Tavern, London. *Ibid.*, II, 318.

1819—Series of seven lectures at the Crown and Anchor Tavern. Subjects: Milton and other literary figures. *Ibid.*, II, 319–320.

Another series was projected, but may not have been given. *Ibid.*, II, 324–327.

2. Quite aside from the influence Coleridge exerted through the content of his lectures, he played an important role in making the delivery of lectures a fashion in London. Aaron Burr, who was there in 1812, made the following notation in his diary for Feb. 15, concerning an evening at William Godwin's: "In the evening, William, the only *son* of W. Godwin, a lad of about 9 years old, gave his weekly lecture; having heard how Coleridge and others lectured, he would also lecture; and one of his sisters (Mary, I think), writes a lecture, which he reads from the little pulpit which they have erected for him. He went through it with great gravity and decorum. The subject was, 'The Influence of Governments on the Character of the People.'" *The Private Journal of Aaron Burr* (2 vols., Rochester, N.Y., 1903), II, 326.

3. See his letter to John Britton, *Shakespearean Criticism*, II, 326. In a letter to Mudford, assistant editor of the *Courier*, printed in the *Canterbury Magazine* (Sept., 1834) and reprinted by Raysor (*Shakespearean Criticism*, II,

304), Coleridge cries, "Woe is me! that at 46 I am under the necessity of appearing as a lecturer, and obliged to regard every hour that I give to the PERMANENT, whether as poet or philosopher, an hour stolen from others' as well as my own maintenance." He echoes the belief of Dorothy Wordsworth, as expressed to Lady Beaumont in a letter probably written in 1806, that lecturing was not a satisfactory way to employ his genius. *Memorials of Coleorton*, ed. William Knight (2 vols., Edinburgh, 1887), I, 162–163.

4. See *Shakespearean Criticism*, II, 26–27, 240, 246–248, 299–304.

5. This sentence is from the letter to Britton mentioned in note 3 above.

6. This letter, which Collier says he received late in 1817, refers specifically to the proposed lectures of 1818. See *Coleridge the Talker*, p. 378.

7. *Letters*, II, 506.

8. Collier reports that Coleridge said (on Oct. 29, but in what year is a matter of dispute) that "last year he had delivered Lectures upon Poetry at the Royal Institution. For the first of the series he had prepared himself fully, and when it was over he received many high-flown, but frigid compliments, evidently, like his lecture, studied. For the second lecture he had prepared himself elaborately, and was much applauded. For the third lecture, and indeed for the remainder of the course, he made no preparation, and was liked better than ever, and vociferously and heartily cheered. The reason was obvious, for what came warm from the heart of the speaker, went warm to the heart of the hearer; and although the illustrations might not be so good, yet being extemporaneous, and often from objects immediately before the eyes, they made more impression, and seemed to have more aptitude." *Shakespearean Criticism*, II, 46–47. Cf. Coleridge's Lecture IV in the series of 1811–1812 (*ibid.*, II, 113–114).

9. *Ibid.*, II, 324–325.

10. Raysor (*ibid.*, I) has gathered 246 pages of fragments having to do with Shakespeare. Much of this material he has shown to have been used in various lectures, and the rest must also

have served as background when Coleridge spoke.

11. To Coleridge's own assertion, already quoted, that he planned to write some of his lectures, may be added the fact that a few were actually printed as written (see note 1 above) and that long passages such as that on "The Definition of Taste and the Origin of Drama" (*ibid.*, I, 176 ff.) are not infrequent among the extant manuscripts. See also James Gillman, *Life of Samuel Taylor Coleridge* (London, 1838), p. 335.

12. A note by Coleridge to the Morgans, Oct. 25, 1813, asks that they "hunt out . . . my two *square* thick memorandum books. . . . You will remember that I used to take them to the Surrey Institution." *Shakespearean Criticism*, II, 260 n.

13. Raysor describes one such lecture in these terms, "He excavated . . . a lecture on the relation of the fine arts to nature from Schelling's lecture on the same subject." *Ibid.*, II, 310.

14. Crabb Robinson wrote Mrs. Clarkson on Dec. 13, 1811, "He *will not* look into Shakespeare. The Morgans are continually laying the book in his way; but as if spell-bound, he cannot prepare himself for his lecture. The consequence is that he has recourse to his old MS. commonplace book, which I dare say you will recollect; and instead of a lecture on a definite subject, we have an immethodical rhapsody." *Ibid.*, II, 226.

Robinson reiterated the charge in a letter to his brother Thomas three days later, adding that from "his old commonplace books . . . he reads whatever chances to catch his eye, in which he certainly finds very beautiful things, which only offend me from their being thus impertinently and irrelevantly brought forward." *Ibid.*, II, 228.

15. On one occasion, according to Jerningham, he told his audience that his notes had been stolen as he entered the hall. *Ibid.*, II, 21. From Clifton Coleridge wrote the Morgans in 1813, "I have made a famous lecture to a crowded room, and all the better, because . . . I had not prepared one single word or thought till ten minutes

before the lecture commenced." *Ibid.*, II, 255.

At times this lack of preparation seems to have led him inadvertently to surprising and dramatic openings. Prince Hoare, secretary of foreign correspondence of the Royal Society, described to Farington the beginning of one lecture in the London series of 1808 as follows: "When Coleridge came into the Box there were several Books laying. He opened two or three of them silently and shut them again after a short inspection. He then paused, & leaned His head on His hand, and at last said, He had been thinking for a word to express the distinct character of Milton as a Poet, but not finding one that wd. express it, He should make one *'Ideality.'* He spoke extempore." Joseph Farington, *The Farington Diary* (8 vols., London, 1922–1928), V, 62. Diary note for May 16, 1808.

16. See her letter to Sir William Elford, Dec. 15, 1811. She says in part, "You would certainly have been enchanted, for, though his lectures are desultory in the highest degree . . . he has so much of . . . that power which fixes the attention by rousing at once the fancy and the heart—that the ear has scarcely the wish to condemn that which so strongly delights the intellect." A. G. L'Estrange, *The Life of Mary Russell Mitford* (3 vols., London, 1870) I, 162–163.

17. Katharine Byerley Thomson was thrilled even by one of the lectures of the Royal Institution course in 1808. She speaks of the fashionable audience assembled, and continues, "He came unprepared to lecture. The subject was a literary one, and the poet had either forgotten to write, or left what he had written at home. His locks were . . . trimmed, and a conscious importance gleamed in his eloquent eyes, as he turned them towards the fair and noble heads which bent down to receive his apology. Every whisper (and there were some hundreds of ladies present) was hushed, and the poet began. I remember there was a stateliness in his language, and the measured tones did not fall so pleasantly upon my ear as the half-whispered accents in which 'Mary of

Buttermere' was described to my childish understanding. 'He must acknowledge,' he said, 'his error—the lecture was *not;* but the assembly before him must recollect, that the Muses would not have been old maids, except for want of a dowry.' The witticism was received with as much applause as a refined audience could decorously manifest, and the harangue proceeded. I began to think, as Coleridge went on, that the lecture had been left at home on purpose; he was *so* eloquent—there was such a combination of wit and poetry in his similes—such fancy, such a finish in his illustrations; yet, as we walked home after the lecture, I remember that we could not call to mind any real instruction, distinct impression, or new fact imparted to us by the great theorist. It was all fancy, flourish, sentiment, that we had heard." Katharine Byerley Thomson, *Recollections of Literary Characters and Celebrated Places* (2 vols., London, 1854), II, 59–60.

18. At times his health was so poor that audiences had no assurance that he would arrive at all. This was especially true during the course of 1808. *Shakespearean Criticism*, II, 3 ff.

19. Cottle, *op. cit.*, pp. 92–97. The passage is reprinted in *Coleridge the Talker*, pp. 417–420. For a description contrasting in tone and in point of view, see William Hazlitt's "My First Acquaintance with Poets," *Works*, XII, 259 ff. The specific passage is reprinted in *Coleridge the Talker*, pp. 243–244.

20. Robinson's report for Nov. 17, 1812, is given with a revealing footnote in *Shakespearean Criticism*, II, 250.

21. *Ibid.*, II, 250.

22. *Ibid.*, II, 250. Burr has a similar comment, dated Dec. 2, 1811: *"Tous allames entendre une discours, en english. Lecture d'une philosophe nom. Coleridge, ami des* God[win]*'s. Il parlait une heure sans ordre ou suite ou connection. C'etait une tissue des tentatives tres plats pour wit."* *The Private Journal*, II, 256.

23. De Quincey, writing of the lectures of 1808, has painted a distressing picture of Coleridge at his worst: "His appearance was generally that of a person struggling with pain and overmas-

tering illness. His lips were baked with feverish heat, and often black in colour; and, in spite of the water which he continued drinking through the whole course of his lecture, he often seemed to labour under an almost paralytic inability to raise the upper jaw from the lower." *Collected Writings*, II, 189.

24. S. C. Hall, *A Book of Memories* (new ed., London, n.d.), p. 43.

25. *Shakespearean Criticism*, II, 7.

26. *Ibid.*, II, 309.

27. *Ibid.*, II, 299 ff.

28. *Ibid.*, II, 307.

29. *Ibid.*, II, 316–317. Gillman, who heard Coleridge lecture for the first time in 1818, is less critical of the series: "These lectures, from his own account, were the most profitable of any he had before given, though delivered in an unfavorable situation; but being near the Temple, many of the students were his auditors. It was the first time I had ever heard him in public. He lectured from notes, which he had carefully made; yet it was obvious, that his audience was more delighted when, putting his notes aside, he spoke extempore;—many of these notes were preserved in, and have lately been printed in the Literary Remains. In his lectures he was brilliant, fluent, and rapid; his words seemed to flow as from a person repeating with grace and energy some delightful poem. If, however, he sometimes paused, it was not for the want of words, but that he was seeking the most appropriate, or their most logical arrangement.

"The attempts to copy his lectures verbatim have failed, they are but comments. Scarcely in anything could he be said to be a mannerist, his mode of lecturing was his own. Coleridge's eloquence, when he gave utterance to his rich thoughts, flowing like some great river, which winds its way majestically at its own 'sweet will,' though occasionally slightly impeded by a dam formed from its crumbling banks, but over which the accumulated waters pass onward with increased force, so arrested his listeners, as at times to make them feel almost breathless. Such seemed the movement of Coleridge's words in lecture or in earnest discourse, and his countenance retained the same charms

of benignity, gentleness, and intelligence, though his expression varied with the thoughts he uttered, and was much modified by his sensitive nature. His quotations from the poets, of high character, were most feelingly and most luminously given, as by one inspired with the subject. In my early intimacy with this great man, I was especially struck with the store of knowledge he possessed, and on which I ever found one might safely rely." *Life*, pp. 335–336.

30. *Shakespearean Criticism*, II, 11.

31. *Ibid.*, II, 218.

32. *Ibid.*, II, 219.

33. *Ibid.*, II, 250.

34. *Ibid.*, II, 251. Coleridge makes a similar remark about another lecture in a letter to J. H. Green, Dec. 13, 1817: "The lecture went off beyond my expectations; and in several parts, where the thoughts were the same, more happily expressed extempore than in the Essay on the Science of Method for the 'Encyclopaedia Metropolitana.'" *Letters*, II, 680–681.

An enthusiastic account of still another impromptu lecture is given by Gillman. Sometime in 1818, he says, Coleridge was asked to speak in the rooms of the London Philosophical Society. The request was received in the morning, and the lecture scheduled for that evening. When Coleridge and Gillman arrived, the president of the society announced that Coleridge would speak on "The Growth of the Individual Mind." "A pretty stiff subject they have chosen," whispered the lecturer to his companion, and asked him to clasp his ankle when the time seemed right to bring the lecture to a close.

"The lecture I am about to give this evening," Coleridge began, "is purely extemporary. Should you find a nominative case looking out for a verb or a fatherless verb for a nominative case you must excuse it; it is purely extemporary, though I have thought and read much on the subject."

Gillman goes on with the story: "I could see the company beginning to smile, and this at once inspired him with confidence. He was brilliant, eloquent and logically consecutive. The time moved so quickly that on looking at my watch, I found that an hour and a half had passed. Waiting therefore for a desirable moment, I prepared myself, to use his own playful words, to punctuate his oration and I pressed his ankle, when bowing graciously and with a benevolent and smiling countenance he presently descended.

"The lecture was quite new to me, and I believe quite new to himself at least so far as the arrangement of his words were concerned. The floating thoughts were most beautifully arranged and delivered on the spur of the moment. What accident gave rise to the singular request, that he should deliver this lecture impromptu, I never learned nor did it signify, as it afforded a happy opportunity to many of witnessing in part the extent of his reading and the extraordinary strength of his powers." *Life*, p. 336.

One is tempted to infer that Coleridge always lectured more brilliantly when entirely unprepared, but the evidence of Crabb Robinson and others to the contrary is too strong. It may still be said, however, that when the subject allowed Coleridge to discuss it impromptu and at the same time with full knowledge, the conditions were conducive to his highest achievements on the platform.

35. Coleridge, in a letter to Thomas Allsop concerning a forth-coming lecture, speaks of "the pain, the restless aching, that comes instantly with the thought of giving out my soul and spirit where you cannot be present, where I could not see your beloved countenance glistening with the genial *spray* of the outpouring." Allsop, *Letters, Conversations, and Recollections of S. T. Coleridge* (New York, 1836), p. 175. If this means, as it seems to mean, that Coleridge in lecturing often spoke directly to his friends rather than to the audience as a whole, it explains in part his many failures to adapt his material to the majority of his listeners.

36. *Shakespearean Criticism*, II, 227.

37. *Ibid.*, II, 227.

38. L'Estrange, *op. cit.*, I, 162–163. Another listener who seemed quite content to accept Coleridge on his own terms was James Amphlett, who attended a lecture at Fetter Lane in 1812 and contributed an article to the *Rifleman*, a folio Sunday paper he was then editing. What follows is, he says, copied directly from that article:

"We have always been aware that a man of Mr. Coleridge's powers of mind, could never in a lecture, do himself anything like justice. So refining and multifarious are his habits of thought, that he cannot subject even his pen to any order or arrangement in his subject. In his writings we find him continually changing his course, to catch the interesting impulse of some new thought, elicited from, or crossing his subject. There is only one thing in him that is certain, and that is, though his subject should be *physics*, a *metaphysical* conclusion. It is his governing tendency, and beats him out of that which is simple into that which is complex; from individualities to generalities, in defiance of himself.

"There is another peculiarity in him which ought to be particularised, and which seems to be an illustration of the affinity that is said to exist in extremes. If he begins on any particular passion or principle, he commonly works about it, from some strange and incomprehensible impetus, till he involves himself in a mass of nebulous matter, that is as remote from the nature of his text as possible! A great portion of one of his lectures, on the passions of love (as exemplified in Juliet) consisted in a decomposition of the characteristics of garrulous age; and of contrasted powers and habits of memory, in educated and uneducated minds. He pursued wilds of thought; and Shakespeare himself disappeared in the ocean of human nature. But all these things are rather a proof of Mr. Coleridge's powers of mind than anything else. If the female part of his audience be sometimes disappointed they are sometimes as agreeably surprised. For a cross wind and current of feeling, will frequently drive the lecturer from the most rugged and masculine philosophy, into the calm and captivating confines of the circle of the affections, and influences of the heart." *The Newspaper Press . . . Recollections of James Amphlett* (London, 1860), quoted by William E. A. Axon in "James

Notes

Amphlett and Samuel Taylor Coleridge," *Library*, 3rd series, II (1911), 38–39.

39. *Op. cit.*, p. 355. The passage, which refers specifically to lectures given in Bristol in 1814, reads: "I should here mention, that Mr. Coleridge's lectures bore but a small resemblance to the polished compositions of Sir James Mackintosh. They were all of a conversational character, and were little other than the earnest harangues, with which on all possible occasions, he indulged his friends, so that there was little or no toil of preparation with him, and if the demand had been equal to the supply, he might have lectured continuously. But if there was little of formal and finished composition in Mr. C.'s lectures, there were always racy and felicitous passages, indicating deep thought, and indicative of the man of genius; so that if polish was not always attained, as one mark of excellence, the attention of his hearers never flagged, and his large dark eyes, and his countenance, in an excited state, glowing with intellect, predisposed his audience in his favor."

40. See note 29 above.

41. H. C. Robinson, *Blake, Coleridge, Wordsworth, Lamb, etc.*, ed. Edith Morley (Manchester, 1922), p. 122.

42. *Shakespearean Criticism*, II, 128–146.

43. See the reports in *Coleridge the Talker, passim*. Even Collier did not make shorthand notes of Coleridge's conversation, thinking the procedure out of place in the drawing-room. See his own statement concerning his method, *ibid.*, p. 167.

44. See note 51 below. Coleridge wrote the Rev. John P. Estlin on April 9, 1814. "My Lectures, with exception only of the general Plan of leading Thoughts, are literally and strictly extempore, the words of the moment." *Unpub. Letters*, II, 105.

45. *Shakespearean Criticism*, II, 203–205.

46. See note 38 above.

47. *Shakespearean Criticism*, II, 205.

48. *Ibid.*, II, 216.

49. See note 38 above.

50. See *Shakespearean Criticism*, I, 229, note 3, and 230, notes 1 and 2.

51. *Ibid.*, I, 229–230.

52. *Ibid.*, II, 145–146.

53. *Ibid.*, II, 146.

54. *Ibid.*, II, 146.

55. See *Coleridge the Talker*, p. 150.

56. *Shakespearean Criticism*, II, 111–128.

57. *Ibid.*, II, 215.

58. *Ibid.*, II, 215–216.

59. *Ibid.*, II, 216.

60. *Ibid.*, II, 114.

61. *Ibid.*, II, 115.

62. *Ibid.*, II, 117.

63. *Ibid.*, II, 118.

64. *Ibid.*, II, 119.

65. *Ibid.*, II, 121.

66. *Ibid.*, II, 122.

67. *Ibid.*, II, 124.

68. *Coleridge the Talker*, p. 145.

69. *Shakespearean Criticism*, II, 115–116.

70. *Ibid.*, I, 210–211.

71. *Henry Crabb Robinson on Books and Their Writers*, ed. Edith J. Morley (3 vols., London, 1938), p. 51.

72. Letter dated Jan. 16, 1798, quoted by Campbell, *op. cit.*, p. 84.

73. Here is the meat of the passage: "We that were . . . constant too often found reason to be disappointed with the quality of his lecture. His appearance was generally that of a person struggling with pain and overmastering illness. . . . In such a state, it is clear that nothing could save the lecture itself from reflecting his own feebleness and exhaustion, except the advantage of having been precomposed in some happier mood. But that never happened: most unfortunately he relied upon his extempore ability to carry him through. Now, had he been in spirits, or had he gathered animation, and kindled by his own motion, no written lecture could have been more effectual than one of his unpremeditated colloquial harangues. But either he was depressed originally below the point from which any reascent was possible, or else this re-action was intercepted by continual disgust from looking back upon his own ill-success; for assuredly he never once recovered that free and eloquent movement of thought which he could command at any time in private company." *Collected Writings*, II, 189–190.

74. Robinson mentions this habit of apologizing in a letter to Mrs. Clarkson, Nov. 29, 1811: "He has certain unfortunate habits which he *will* not (perhaps *can* not) correct. . . . I mean the vice of apologizing, anticipating, and repeating." *Shakespearean Criticism*, II, 224. In the opening of the first lecture of the series to which Robinson refers, Coleridge requested "those who hear me to allow for deficiencies. . . . What I must rely on is your sympathy; and, as I proceed, I trust that I shall interest you." Collier report, *ibid.*, II, 56. The Tomalin report of the fourth lecture ends with this sentence: "Mr. Coleridge concluded by apologizing for speaking what he conceived to be the truth, etc." *Ibid.*, II, 87. Coleridge also apologized for his extempore delivery in the fifth lecture. See the Collier report, *ibid.*, II, 114. These random samples can be matched in many other lectures.

75. Robinson comments in 1811: "The concluding lectures . . . were but indifferently attended, and scoffers were not unfrequently among the number." *Ibid.*, II, 211. In his diary note for Nov. 18 of that year, he records, "Meggison very loudly and before the lecturer had left his rostrum began to abuse him." *Ibid.*, II, 213.

76. Robinson records this remark, *Crabb Robinson on Books, etc.*, p. 55.

77. Cottle, *op. cit.*, p. 97.

Matthew Arnold: The Critic as Rhetorician

1. *Poetry and the Criticism of Life*, Harvard Press, 931, p. 80.

2. Essay on rhetoric (D. Masson ed., Edinb. 1890), Vol. XI. See also H. H. Hudson, "De Quincey on Rhetoric and Public Speaking," above.

3. A. P. Stanley, *Life and Correspondence of Thomas Arnold* (London, 1881), p. 16: "But his passion at the time I am treating of was for Aristotle and Thucydides; . . . those who knew him intimately or corresponded with him will bear me witness how deeply he was imbued with the language and ideas of the former; how in earnest conversation, or in writing, his train of thought was affected by the *Ethics* and *Rhetoric;* how he cited the maxims of the Stagyrite as oracles, and how his language was quaintly and racily pointed with phrases from him."

In a letter to Mr. Justice Coleridge, dated June 26, 1841, Thomas Arnold writes: "We have been reading some of the Rhetoric in the Sixth Form this half year, and its immense value struck me again so forcibly that I could not consent to send my son to an University where he would lose it altogether." *Ibid.*, II, 224.

4. For this distinction between rhetoric and dialectic, see E. L. Hunt, "Dialectic, A Neglected Method of Argument," *Q.J.S.E.*, VII (1921), 221–232.

5. *Culture and Anarchy* (Smith Elder and Co., London, 1889), p. 31.

6. See Max Eastman, *The Literary Mind* (1931), and J. M. Robertson, *Modern Humanists Reconsidered* (London, 1927).

7. See Plato's *Gorgias*.

8. London, 1882, p. 216.

9. *Irish Essays* (London, 1882), p. 32.

10. *Culture and Anarchy* (London, 1889), pp. 76, 78.

11. *Ibid.*, p. 165.

12. "A French Critic on Milton," *Mixed Essays* (London, 1880), p. 244. This classical passage in the criticism of rhetoric should have set beside it the vigorous defense of Macaulay as a lover of common people who made them love literature, which is called forth from Henry Sidgwick. See his attack on Arnold entitled "The Prophet of Culture," *Macmillan's Magazine*, XVI (1867), 278.

13. "The Literary Influence of Academies," *Essays in Criticism*, first series (London, 1902), p. 74.

14. *Ibid.*, p. 72.

15. "The Function of Criticism at the Present Time," *ibid.*, p. 21.

16. *Letters of Matthew Arnold* (ed. by G. W. Russell, London, 1901), I, 285.

17. *Ibid.*, I, 360.

18. *Ibid.*, I, 270.

19. *Ibid.*, I, 184.

20. *Ibid.*, I, 165.

21. *Ibid.*, II, 429.

Notes

22. See Russell Wagner, "Rhetorical Theory of Isocrates," *Q.J.S.E.*, VIII (1922), 323–337; also George Norlin's introduction to his translations of Isocrates in the Loeb Classical Library (1928).

23. *Letters*, I, 234. All the italics in the citations in this essay are Arnold's. His habit of italics has been much criticized. It seems to suggest that he heard his words.

24. *Ibid.*, I, 240.

25. *Ibid.*, I, 250.

26. *Ibid.*, I, 255.

27. "Mr. Matthew Arnold and his Countrymen," *Saturday Review*, December 3, 1864. Reprinted in Stephen's *Horae Sabbaticae* (London, 1892).

28. *Letters*, I, 282.

29. "Culture: A Dialogue," in *Choice of Books* (London, 1886).

30. The second paragraph appears in the 1865 edition; Arnold removed it in later editions.

31. Arnold seems to have remained mercifully insensible of how irritating this manner, when combined with condescension, can be. His critics pointed it out to him vigorously and frequently enough, but as he said, one never makes the slightest impression on the mind of an opponent.

32. *Letters*, I, 447.

33. *Literature and Dogma* (London, 1873), p. xvii. In the popular edition of 1886 Arnold deleted this passage.

34. The irritation at this immoderate moderation of Arnold's is most vigorously expressed in the speech of Arminius von Thunder-ten-dronck, in Harrison's "Culture; a Dialogue." "Here we are in this generation, face to face with the passions of fierce men; parties, races, sects, glare in each others' eyes before they spring; death, sin and cruelty stalk among us, filling their maws with innocence and youth; humanity passes onwards shuddering through the raging crowd of foul and hungry monsters, bearing the destiny of the race like a close-veiled babe in her arms, and over all sits Culture high aloft with pouncet box to spare her senses aught unpleasant, holding no form of creed, but contemplating all with infinite serenity, sweetly chanting snatches from graceful sages and ecstatic monks, crying out the most pretty shame upon the vulgarity, the provinciality, the impropriety of it all." This judgment is echoed in William Watson's lines,

The deep, authentic mountain thrill
  Ne'er shook his page!

35. Arnold's American tour is worth special attention as a rhetorical study. E. P. Lawrence has given an interesting account in the *Philological Quarterly*, X (1931) under the title "An Apostle's Progress, Arnold in America."

36. *Letters*, II, 264.

37. *Letters*, II, 268. This account was confirmed by the *New York Tribune* for November 8, 1883, which says that Arnold's second lecture was plainly heard because of changed elocutionary methods. Quoted by E. P. Lawrence, *op. cit.*

38. *Letters*, II, 274. A British observer wrote to the *New York Tribune* for January 16, 1884, "Mr. Arnold, piloted by Mr. D'Oyly Carte, and inaudibly lecturing to New York Society, too painfully recalls Sampson grinding corn for the Philistines." Quoted by E. P. Lawrence, *op. cit.*

39. *Unpublished Letters of Matthew Arnold* (ed. by Arnold Whitridge, Yale Press, 1923), p. 53.

40. *Letters*, II, 424.

41. We should not be too much influenced by the fact that Arnold delivered lectures as Professor of Poetry at Oxford. He was elected to this chair solely on the basis of his then little read poetry, he did not take seriously the title of Professor or feel that the duty of occasional lectures in the criticism of poetry imposed upon him the responsibilities of specialized scholarship.

42. *On Translating Homer* (London, 1896), pp. 116–117. Since this distinction between scholar and critic is so important to Arnold, I will add a passage from the Preface to the 1873 edition of *Literature and Dogma* (later greatly abbreviated by Arnold for the popular edition of 1886). "But perhaps the quality specially needed for drawing the right conclusion from the facts, when one has got them, is best called perception, delicacy of perception. And

this no man can have who is a mere specialist, who has not what we call *culture* in addition to the knowledge of his particular study; and many theologians, in Germany as well as elsewhere, are specialists. And even when we have added culture to special knowledge, a good fortune, a natural tact, a perception must go with our culture to make our criticism sure. . . . This, I say, shows how large a thing criticism is; since even of those from whom we must take what we now in theology most want, knowledge of the facts of our study, and to whom we are, therefore, and ought to be under deep obligation, even of them we must not take too much, or take anything like all they offer; but we must take much and leave much, and must have experience enough to know what to take and what to leave."

43. *Ibid.,* p. 62. Other passages on the formative power of noble poetry, especially interesting to teachers of interpretive reading, are cited in Sir Joshua Fitch's *Thomas and Matthew Arnold and their Influence on English Education* (London, 1897), pp. 175–185. See also *Thoughts on Education from Matthew Arnold* (ed. by Leonard Huxley, London, 1912). Consult index under Reading books and culture, and Recitations.

44. For an attack on Arnold as "the greatest of modern English sophists," with the *Celtic Literature* as the chief illustration, see Lane Cooper's essay "Teacher and Student," in *Two Views of Education* (New Haven, 1922). Professor Cooper treats Arnold as another professor. Professor Garrod offers this reply to the charge of sophistry: "If I conceive rightly his aim in criticism it was the exact opposite of that of the sophists. For the crime of the sophists was this, that they taught an interested love of knowledge. They taught, not a pure interest in ideas, but a love of ideas essentially related to practice, to politics, to party." *Op. cit.,* p. 74.

45. *The Study of Celtic Literature* (ed. by Alfred Nutt, London, 1910), p. 150.

46. *Ibid.,* p. v.

47. *Letters,* I, 382.

The Gladstone-Huxley Controversy on Genesis

1. *The Writings of Mrs Humphry Ward,* Boston and New York, 1909, vol. 1, pp. xxxii–xxxiii.

2. *Ibid.,* p. xxxiii.

3. Quoted from John Richard Green's recollection of the meeting, in Leonard Huxley's *Life and Letters of Thomas Henry Huxley,* New York, 1900, 2 vols., vol. 1, p. 199. For other recollections of Huxley's retort, differing in wording, but agreeing in substance, see pp. 198–202.

4. Vol. 18, pp. 685–706.

5. *Ibid.,* p. 689.

6. *Ibid.,* pp. 695–696.

7. *Ibid.,* p. 696.

8. Leonard Huxley, *op. cit.,* vol. 2, pp. 122–123.

9. Vol. 18, pp. 849–860.

10. Quoted on p. 851.

11. *Ibid.*

12. Vol. 19, pp. 1–21.

13. *Ibid.,* pp. 2–3.

14. *Ibid.,* pp. 3–4.

15. *Ibid.,* pp. 4–5.

16. *Ibid.,* p. 5.

17. *Ibid.,* pp. 10–13.

18. *Ibid.,* pp. 16–17.

19. Vol. 19, pp. 191–205.

20. *Ibid.,* p. 191.

21. *Ibid.,* p. 192.

22. *Ibid.,* pp. 192–198.

23. *Ibid.,* p. 198.

24. Vol. 18, pp. 900–922.

25. *The Nineteenth Century,* vol. 19, pp. 160–175.

26. *Ibid.,* p. 169.

27. *The Nineteenth Century,* vol. 19, pp. 206–214.

The Nazi Rhetorician

1. Konrad Heiden, *A History of National Socialism* (New York, 1935), p. 12.

2. As a matter of fact, it was Hitler who publicly announced the famous Twenty-Five Points at a meeting February 24, 1920. How little the party

Notes

propagandist actually cared for some of his colleagues' contributions to party ideology is perhaps best shown by the following: fully six years after Hitler became the supreme power in the Reich the Party Speaker System was being coached, through its official bulletin *Aufklärungs- und Rednerinformationsmaterial*, on how to answer complaints that so little had been done with some of these points. See my article, "The Nazi Party Speaker System, II," *SM*, XVII (June, 1950), 141–142.

3. Tr., Ralph Manheim (Cambridge, Mass., 1943), pp. 176–186, 469–479.

4. Following Hitler's lead, this became a standard theme among Nazi writers on propaganda. See, e.g., Eugen Hadamovsky, *Propaganda und nationale Macht* (Oldenburg i.O., 1933), pp. 42 ff., and Franz Alfred Six, *Die politische Propaganda der NSDAP im Kampf um die Macht* (diss. Heidelberg, 1936), pp. 9, 43.

5. See, e.g., Hugo Ringler, "Der Redner, der aktivste Träger der nationalsozialistischen Propaganda," *Unser Wille und Weg*, IV (Aug. 1934), 234–240; Eugen Wiesenborn, "Der Redner, Stosstruppmann der vordersten Front," *Unser Wille und Weg*, IV (Oct. 1934), 304–307; A. E. Frauenfeld, "Die Macht der Rede," *Unser Wille und Weg*, VII (Aug. 1937), 240–245, esp. 241.

6. See, e.g., Hans Riess, "Ein Wort zur Reichsrednerschule," *Unser Wille und Weg*, VI (Oct. 1936), 329–332, esp. 330.

7. See, e.g., Erich Fehlberg, "Redner der Hitlerjugend," *Unser Wille und Weg*, VII (Feb. 1937), 38–41.

8. The *Hochschule für Politik* (Berlin) is a notable example. Taken over as an official institution, i.e., *Anstalt des Reiches*, by Hitler's decree on September 30, 1937, it became a college for high ranking units of the speaker system.

9. The principal publication for this purpose was *Unser Wille und Weg* which was issued monthly from April, 1931, until wartime shortages obliged it to suspend operations in June, 1941.

10. Thus Goebbels: "It seems as if the different races are very differently endowed for public speaking, as if some

peoples have national characteristics that are too reserved and inflexible for this very social art, while others have qualities exactly predestined for it. Otherwise, one could not speak properly of Latin eloquence. The great abundance of both ordinary and exceptional talents among the Roman people give the word "rhetoric" a special significance applied to them." "Der Führer als Redner," *Unser Wille und Weg*, IX (April 1939), 76.

11. Hans Krebs, *Redner-Fibel*, 9th ed. (Berlin, 1935), p. 9.

12. Hadamovsky, *op. cit.*, p. 44.

13. *Der deutsche Erzieher* (Stuttgart, 1938).

14. *Zeitschrift für Neusprachlichen Unterricht*, XXXVIII (1939), 65–82.

15. *Mein Kampf*, pp. 476–477.

16. These sources, Schönemann, Hadamovsky, and Six suggest that the Germans were particularly impressed with the work of the "Four-Minute-Man" organization in America, a fact which may well have prompted the establishment of the Nazi Party Speaker System.

17. The persistent lack of interest in the rhetorical theories of other people may be explained in three ways: many Nazi propagandists regarded Hitler and Goebbels as sufficient fountainheads for all theory; many regarded themselves as practical men who, apart from their debt to Hitler and Goebbels, learned all they needed to know from their own practical experience as party speakers; and all were imbued with the basic Nazi doctrine that their people and their time in history required unique operation. In any case, it does not seem to have concerned them greatly that there might be certain universals in rhetoric which other cultures could teach them.

18. 1807–1808.

19. "Der Führer als Redner," p. 76.

20. "What Karl Marx worked out as his doctrine in books incomprehensible to the masses the orator, Bebel, and his fellow-travelers (*Gesinnungsgenossen*), with deadly seductiveness, translated into the German of the common man. . . . Thus, through the power of speech, an unnatural doctrine grew." Emil Dovifat, *Rede und Redner: Ihr Wesen und*

Ihre Politische Macht (Leipzig, 1937), pp. 9–12.

21. The Nazi drew at least one distinction, however, between his own and Communist technique that is important in reconstructing a Nazi theory of rhetoric. In Communist agitation he saw a form of rhetoric adapted almost entirely to appeal to lower social classes. Nazi rhetoric, on the other hand, must be suitable, even variously adapted, to all social classes, for the Nazis did not propose the abolition of class differences.

22. For sources of information on the career of Hans Krebs I am especially indebted to the Wiener Library in London.

23. *Ein Sudeten Deutscher Ergibt Sich Nicht: ein Buch um den sudetendeutschen nationalsozialistischen Führer, Hans Krebs*, ed. Hans Christoph Kaergel (Breslau, 1938), p. 46.

24. *Ibid.*, pp. 12, 36, 48–50.

25. See, e.g., *Four Fighting Years*, "published on behalf of the Czechoslovak Ministry of Foreign Affairs" (London, 1943), p. 26.

26. Kaergel, *op. cit.*, p. 52.

27. Documentation for this and other events in Krebs' career is to be found in *Der Grossdeutsche Reichstag 1938, IV Wahlperiode, nach dem 30. Januar 1933* (Berlin, 1938); see "Krebs, Hans."

28. This line of policy was achieved at a conference between German and Austro-Sudeten leaders in 1921. Krebs later said of this meeting with Hitler: "It belongs to the greatest experience of my life that my very first interview with the Führer gave me the certain conviction, not only that the fundamental principles of the NSDAP fully agreed with our own ideals, indeed conceived them much more fully and compellingly, but that I, in a personal sense, brought away from the conference the unshakable certainty of having found, in Adolf Hitler, the true spiritual leader who would lead the movement to free our nation." *Kampf in Böhmen* (Berlin, 1938), p. 82.

29. *Ein Sudeten Deutscher, etc.*, p. 65.

30. *Ibid.*, p. 104.

31. *Ibid.*, p. 78.

32. P. 5. As indicated in the text of this paper, this and all subsequent quotations are taken from the *Redner-Fibel;* the translations throughout are mine.

33. Pp. 5–6.

34. P. 21.

35. P. 17.

36. P. 21.

37. P. 29.

38. Pp. 7–8.

39. Pp. 31–32.

40. P. 49, Krebs's punctuation and italics.

41. P. 50.

42. P. 53.

43. P. 54.

44. P. 56.

45. P. 58.

46. Pp. 59–62 for all material dealing with style.

47. Pp. 10–11.

Rhetoric and Poetry

1. *Early Essays by John Stuart Mill*, edited by J. W. M. Gibbs (London, 1897), p. 209.

2. Prof. Fred Newton Scott, in his well-known article, "The Most Fundamental Differentia of Poetry and Prose" (*Publications of the Modern Language Association*, XIX, 250), goes further and practically substitutes "prose" for Mill's "eloquence," concluding that "poetry is communication in language for expression's sake; prose is expression in language for communication's sake." The present writer has drawn, as one must in discussing this subject, upon Professor Scott's article; but he believes that Mill's apothegm expresses more accurately the distinction between rhetoric and poetry than that between prose and poetry.

3. Compare Aristotle's *Rhetoric* (Welldon's translation, I, iii): "For a speech is composed of three elements, viz. the speaker, the subject of the speech, and the persons addressed; and the end or object of the speech is determined by the last, viz. by the audience."

4. *Poetry and Prose, Being Essays on Modern English Poetry* (New York, 1912), pp. 136–137.

Notes

5. XIX, 1 (Butcher's translation).

6. *Timber or Discoveries Made upon Men and Matter* (Schelling's edition), p. 78.

7. *Wordsworth's Literary Criticism,* edited by Nowell C. Smith (London, 1905), p. 23.

8. Johnson, C. F., *Forms of English Poetry* (New York, 1904), p. 18.

9. There are honorable exceptions, such as the funeral orations of Bossuet and Massillon.

10. As the reader, if I still have one, must be aware, the word "poetry" in this paper is used in a broad sense, equivalent to that of the German *Dichtung,* inclusive of all imitative or imaginative literature.

BIOGRAPHICAL SKETCHES OF THE AUTHORS AND ACKNOWLEDGMENTS TO PUBLISHERS

CARROLL C. ARNOLD has been a member of the faculty of arts and sciences at Cornell since 1946 and is now professor and chairman in the Department of Speech and Drama. He received the A.B. degree from Sioux Falls College (1933) and the M.A. (1940) and Ph.D. (1942) from the State University of Iowa. Before moving to Cornell he taught English and speech in the public schools and served as instructor in speech at the University of Akron and at Pennsylvania College for Women (now Chatham College).

Professor Arnold's writings include *Handbook of Group Discussion*, of which Russell H. Wagner was co-author, several essays on the teaching of speech and discussion, and rhetorical studies of the public addresses of Benjamin Disraeli, George William Curtis, and Thomas Erskine. He has served as an associate editor of the *Quarterly Journal of Speech* since 1951.

"Lord Thomas Erskine: Modern Advocate," is reprinted, by permission, from the *Quarterly Journal of Speech*, where it first appeared in February 1958.

DONALD C. BRYANT has been professor of speech at the State University of Iowa since 1958. He began his association with the Department of Speech and Drama at Cornell in 1924 under Everett Hunt and Herbert Wichelns. He received the A.B. degree from Cornell in 1927, the M.A. in public speaking and ancient history in 1930, and the Ph.D. in speech and English under Professor Wichelns in 1937. From 1927 to 1929 he taught history and mathematics at the Ardsley (New York) High School. From 1929 to 1937 he was instructor in English and speech at the New York State College for Teachers in Albany. In

1937 he joined the faculty of Washington University (St. Louis), where he became professor of English and speech in 1948 and served as chairman of the Department of English from 1956 to 1958.

Since 1929 he has contributed various articles, principally on Edmund Burke and rhetorical subjects, to the *Quarterly Journal of Speech*, of which he served as editor from 1957 through 1959. With Karl R. Wallace he is the author of two textbooks in public speaking, *Fundamentals of Public Speaking* (2nd ed., 1953) and *Oral Communication* (2nd ed., 1954). His *Edmund Burke and His Literary Friends* appeared in 1939. He was a member of the editorial committee and a contributor to *Studies in Speech and Drama* in honor of Alexander M. Drummond in 1944 and was editor of *The Rhetorical Idiom*, in honor of Herbert A. Wichelns, which appeared in 1958.

His contribution to this volume, "The Contemporary Reception of Edmund Burke's Speaking," is based primarily on an essay in *Studies in Honor of Frederick W. Shipley* (1942), amplified by material from "Edmund Burke: New Evidence, Broader View," *Quarterly Journal of Speech*, December 1952. Permission to reprint has been granted by the editors of "Washington University Studies" and the *Quarterly Journal of Speech*. The quotation from "Edmund Burke, 1727–1797; A Portrait and an Appraisal," by Thomas H. D. Mahoney, is reproduced by permission of the editors of *History Today*.

HARRY CAPLAN has been a member of the faculty of arts and sciences at Cornell University since April 1919, serving first, with Everett Hunt, in the Department of Public Speaking and after January 1924 in the Department of Classics. He received the A.B. degree from Cornell in 1916, the M.A. in 1917, and the Ph.D. in 1921. Since 1941 he has held the Goldwin Smith professorship in classics. He has taught also in summer sessions at the University of Wisconsin, the University of Michigan, Northwestern University, Stanford University, the University of Chicago, and Columbia University.

An outstanding scholar in classics, Professor Caplan has written books and articles on ancient and mediaeval rhetorical theory and on the theory of preaching. His edition, with translation, of the *Rhetorica ad Herennium*, published in the Loeb Classical Library in 1954, is widely used by scholars and students. He is a former president of the American Philological Association, a fellow of the Mediaeval Academy of America, an active contributor to the journals of the Speech Association of America, and a member of a number of classical and philological societies in the United States and abroad.

"Classical Rhetoric and the Mediaeval Theory of Preaching," the essay that appears here, was first published in *Classical Philology* in April 1935. It is reprinted by permission of the journal and its publisher, the University of Chicago Press. Slight revisions have been made, primarily to bring the notes up to date.

WILBUR E. GILMAN has been chairman of the Department of Speech at Queens College, Flushing, New York, since 1945. He studied under Harry Caplan and Everett Hunt at Cornell while a candidate for the A.B. degree, which he received in 1923, and under Herbert Wichelns and Lane Cooper at Cornell while a candidate for the Ph.D. degree, which he received in 1937. As an instructor he taught English and speech at the University of Missouri (1923–1925) and public speaking at Cornell (1925–1926). As assistant professor at Missouri (1927–1930) and associate professor (1930–1944) he taught courses in public speaking, interpretation, argument and debate, and rhetoric and public address. He served as the first chairman of the Department of Speech and Dramatic Art at the University of Missouri (1940–1942). In 1944 he moved to Queens College, where he has been a professor since 1955. He has taught in summer sessions at City College, Brooklyn College, and Teachers College, Columbia University, in New York, and at the University of Michigan.

He has served as president of two state speech associations—Missouri (1935–1939) and New York (1956–1957)—of two regional speech associations—Central States (1940–1941) and Eastern States (1948–1949) —and of the Speech Association of America (1951). He has contributed to the *English Journal* and the *Quarterly Journal of Speech* and to textbooks on speech. He is author with Bower Aly and Loren D. Reid of *The Fundamentals of Speaking* (1951).

His contribution to this volume, "Milton's Rhetoric on the Tyranny of Kings," is reprinted, by permission of the editor of the "University of Missouri Studies," from *Milton's Rhetoric: Studies in His Defense of Liberty* (1939). Milton's pamphlet analyzed in this essay is entitled "The Tenure of Kings and Magistrates."

FREDERICK W. HABERMAN joined the staff of the Department of Speech of the University of Wisconsin in 1947, and since 1954 he has acted as chairman of the department. He earned the B.A. degree from Allegheny College in 1930, the M.A. degree from the University of Wisconsin in 1936, and the Ph.D. in 1947 from Cornell University under Professor Wichelns.

He began his teaching career in a high school near Erie, Pennsylvania, then returned to Allegheny College as instructor. From graduate studies at Cornell he went as instructor to Princeton University. Subsequently he returned to Cornell to complete the doctorate and from there went to Wisconsin.

For nine years he was an assistant editor of the *Quarterly Journal of Speech* and for six a contributing editor to *Speech Monographs*. He instituted and edited for nine years the annual "Bibliography of Rhetoric and Public Address," has edited several symposiums for the *Quarterly Journal of Speech,* and has contributed articles to various speech journals.

The essay published in this volume, "John Thelwall: His Life, His School, and His Theory of Elocution," is reprinted, by permission, from the *Quarterly Journal of Speech,* October 1947.

HAROLD F. HARDING has been professor of speech at the Ohio State University since 1946. He is a graduate of Hamilton College, A.B. 1925, and of Cornell University, M.A. 1929, Ph.D. 1937. While a senior at Hamilton he first met the Hamilton graduates, Professors Winans of Dartmouth and Drummond of Cornell. He has taught at Iowa State University, Cornell University, and George Washington University. At Ohio State he served as director of the Rhetoric and Public Address Area and as chairman of the graduate committee of the Department of Speech. In 1956–1957 he was assistant dean of the College of Arts and Sciences and since 1957 has been executive secretary of defense studies.

From 1948 to 1951 he was editor of the *Quarterly Journal of Speech.* He is also the author of various articles in professional journals and has edited several books, including the proceedings of the *Eastern Public Speaking Conference,* 1940, and *The Age of Danger: Major Speeches on American Problems,* 1952.

His contribution to this volume, "Quintilian's Witnesses," is reprinted from Volume I, Number 1, of *Speech Monographs* (1934) by permission of the present editor and the Speech Association of America. The article was read by Everett Hunt in draft form and was accepted by the first editor of *Speech Monographs*, Hoyt Hudson.

WILBUR SAMUEL HOWELL, professor of rhetoric and oratory at Princeton University, joined the faculty of Princeton in 1934 as associate of the late Hoyt Hudson, after having taught at Iowa State College, Washington University (St. Louis), Harvard University, and Dartmouth College. He earned the A.B., M.A., and Ph.D. degrees at Cornell University, where he studied under Lane Cooper, Herbert Wichelns, Harry Caplan, Everett Hunt, Alexander Drummond, and William Strunk, Jr. He studied at the University of Paris in 1928–1929, was holder of a Guggenheim Fellowship in 1948–1949, and again in 1957–1958, and was also holder of a Huntington Library Fellowship in 1951–1952. He served from January 1953 to December 1956 as editor of the *Quarterly Journal of Speech*.

In addition to articles and reviews in scholarly journals, he has published the following books: *The Rhetoric of Alcuin and Charlemagne* (1941); *Problems and Styles of Communication* (1945); *Fénelon's Dialogues on Eloquence* (1951); and *Logic and Rhetoric in England, 1500–1700* (1956).

His article in this volume, "Sources of the Elocutionary Movement in England: 1700–1748," reprinted, by permission, from the *Quarterly Journal of Speech*, February 1959, is part of his projected history of English rhetoric and logic in the eighteenth century.

RAYMOND F. HOWES has been a staff associate of the American Council on Education since 1951. He studied under Everett Hunt while earning his A.B. degree at Cornell (1924), under Hoyt Hudson at the University of Pittsburgh (M.A. 1926), and subsequently under Herbert Wichelns in the graduate school at Cornell. He taught public speaking at the University of Pittsburgh (1924–1926), and English, speech, and journalism from 1926 to 1936 at Washington University (St. Louis). From 1936 to 1951 he held a series of administrative posts at Cornell, including director of public information and secretary of the University. Northeastern University awarded him the L.H.D. degree in 1960.

He has contributed to a number of magazines, including the *Quarterly Journal of Speech*, of which he was an associate editor, 1933–

1936. He edits two periodicals of the American Council on Education, *Higher Education and National Affairs* and *The Educational Record*. He has also edited several books, including *Debating* (1931) and *Higher Education and the Society It Serves* (1957).

His contribution to this volume, "Samuel Taylor Coleridge in Lecture-Box and Pulpit," is reprinted, by permission of Cornell University Press, from *Coleridge the Talker* by Richard W. Armour and Raymond F. Howes (1940). Dr. Armour has generously agreed that Mr. Howes may assert his sole authorship of this portion of the book.

HOYT HOPEWELL HUDSON was professor of English at Stanford University at the time of his death in 1944. Prior to that he had been professor of rhetoric and oratory and chairman of the Department of English at Princeton University, 1933–1942; professor of English at the University of Pittsburgh, 1925–1927; assistant professor of English and public speaking, Swarthmore College, 1923–1925; and instructor in public speaking, Cornell University, 1920–1923. He received the A.B. degree from Huron College, 1911; M.A., University of Denver, 1913; Ph.D., Cornell, 1923; and Litt.D., Huron College, 1938.

Among his publications are *Poetry of the English Renaissance*, with J. W. Hebel, 1929; *A First Course in Public Speaking*, with J. A. Winans, 1931; *Principles of Argument and Debate*, with J. W. Reeves, 1931; a translation of Kant's *Religion within the Limits of Reason Alone*, with T. M. Greene, 1934; *John Hoskin's Directions for Speech and Style*, 1935; a translation of Thomas Moffet's *Nobilis*, with V. R. Heltzel, 1940; and a translation and commentary, Erasmus' *The Praise of Folly*, 1941. He served as editor of the *Quarterly Journal of Speech*, 1933–1935. Posthumous publications arranged by friends include *Celebration*, a book of poems, 1945; *The Epigram in the English Renaissance*, 1947; and *Educating Liberally*, 1947.

Of Hoyt Hudson's studies reprinted in this volume, "De Quincey on Rhetoric and Public Speaking" is taken from *Studies in Rhetoric and Public Speaking in Honor of James Albert Winans*, copyright 1925 by the Century Co., by permission of Appleton-Century-Crofts, Inc.; the essays "The Field of Rhetoric" and "Rhetoric and Poetry" appeared in the *Quarterly Journal of Speech* for April 1923 and April 1924, and are reprinted by permission. All are included in this book with the approval of his widow, Mrs. Margaret Hudson. The quotation in the last essay from Dorothy Canfield Fisher's *Raw Material* is reproduced by permission of the publisher, Harcourt, Brace and Company. Several time references have been changed in "The Field of Rhetoric."

EVERETT LEE HUNT served as dean of Swarthmore College from 1939 to 1956. He was professor of English from 1932 until his retirement in 1959. He had previously served as professor of rhetoric and oratory at Swarthmore from 1926–1932. He was instructor in rhetoric and oratory at Huron College from 1913 to 1918 and was assistant professor of public speaking at Cornell from 1918 to 1926. He received the A.B. degree at Huron College in 1913, the M.A. from the University of Chicago in 1921, and the Litt.D. from Huron College in 1938.

He served as president of the Eastern Public Speaking Conference 1922–1924 and was editor of the *Quarterly Journal of Speech Education,* 1927–1930. With A. M. Drummond he edited *Persistent Questions in Public Discussion,* 1924. He has contributed essays and studies on literature and education to various periodicals.

"Plato and Aristotle on Rhetoric and Rhetoricians" is reprinted from *Studies in Rhetoric and Public Speaking in Honor of James Albert Winans,* copyright 1925 by the Century Co., by permission of Appleton-Century-Crofts, Inc. "Matthew Arnold: The Critic as Rhetorician" is reprinted, by permission, from the *Quarterly Journal of Speech,* November 1934.

C. HAROLD KING has been professor of history at the University of Miami since 1948 (associate professor, 1946–1948). He studied as an undergraduate at Cornell under Everett Hunt. After graduating from Cornell in 1920, he did graduate work in biography, literature, history, psychology, and speech at Columbia University, the University of Minnesota, the University of Virginia, New York University, and Cornell. He acquired an M.A. in literature at New York University in 1930 and a Ph.D. in history under Carl Becker at Cornell in 1935.

His academic positions have involved interrelationships among the fields of his interests at Minnesota, New York University, Colgate, and Miami, including teaching and writing in the American Civilization Program at the last institution.

He is author of Volume I of *A History of Civilization* (1956) and of articles on Whitefield in the *Quarterly Journal of Speech,* in *Proceedings of the Middle States Association of History Teachers,* and in *Studies in Speech and Drama* (1945).

Authors and Acknowledgments

His article, "George Whitefield: Commoner Evangelist," represents a complete rewriting of Whitefield material. It was composed at the University of Miami, with the assistance of talented scholarship students and the author's wife, Helen Garlinghouse King, professor of English at the University.

WAYLAND MAXFIELD PARRISH is professor of speech, emeritus, at the University of Illinois, having retired in 1955. He is a graduate of Ohio Wesleyan University (A.B. 1908) and of Cornell (M.A. 1922, Ph.D. 1929). From 1908 to 1921 he taught English and public speaking and directed debating at high schools in Michigan and Minnesota.

Influenced by the writings of Professor Winans, Mr. Parrish went to Cornell University in 1921 to study rhetoric and public speaking. In the summer of 1922 he taught at the University of Minnesota and in the fall went to Dartmouth College to fill Professor Winans' position while he was on leave. From 1923 to 1936 Professor Parrish was chairman of the Division of Public Speaking at the University of Pittsburgh. A year of this period, 1927–1928, was spent on sabbatical leave at Cornell in study for the Ph.D. degree. In 1936 he became chairman of the division of speech in the Department of English, University of Illinois. Under his direction the division was developed into the Department of Speech.

He is the author of *Reading Aloud,* first published in 1932 and reissued in 1953; *The Teacher's Speech,* 1939; and *Speaking in Public,* 1947; and the editor, with Marie Hochmuth, of *American Speeches,* 1954. He has also contributed to several books of studies in rhetoric and public speaking and has written numerous articles for the *Quarterly Journal of Speech* and other magazines.

"Whately and His Rhetoric" is reprinted, by permission, from the *Quarterly Journal of Speech* for February 1929.

ROSS SCANLAN was professor of speech at the City College of New York at the time of his death in the spring of 1961. Previously he had taught at the University of Pittsburgh, Washington University (St. Louis), Cornell University, and Dartmouth College. He held the M.A. degree from the University of Pittsburgh, the B.A. and Ph.D. from Cornell. He studied under Professors Drummond, Wichelns, Hunt, Caplan, and Hudson. He was assistant editor and then associate editor of the *Quarterly Journal of Speech* from 1951 to 1956 and resumed the post in 1960.

He contributed to *Debating*, compiled and edited by R. F. Howes (1931), and with Lester Thonssen was co-author of *Speech Preparation and Delivery* (1941). An essay, "The Challenge of Ibsen: A Study in Critical Contradictions," appeared in *Studies in Speech and Drama in Honor of Alexander M. Drummond* (1944), and more recently "Adolph Hitler and the Technique of Mass Brainwashing" was included in *The Rhetorical Idiom* (1958). He has also contributed a number of articles to the *Quarterly Journal of Speech*.

In 1949 Dr. Scanlan began a study of the Nazi organization and techniques for domestic propaganda. Two of his papers on the official Nazi Speaker Organization appeared in issues of *Speech Monographs* for 1949 and 1950. In 1952 he received a grant from the Rockefeller Foundation to continue this study. His article in this book, "The Nazi Rhetorician," is reprinted, by permission, from the *Quarterly Journal of Speech*, December 1951.

C. K. THOMAS has been professor of speech and director of the English Language Institute at the University of Florida since 1958. He received the A.B. degree in 1922, the M.A. in 1924, and the Ph.D. in 1930 from Cornell University. He studied public speaking, argumentation and debate, and classical rhetoric under Everett Hunt. He taught at Cornell from 1922 to 1958, becoming director of the Speech Clinic in 1927 and professor of speech in 1947.

His studies in American linguistic geography have been published in both technical and popular magazines, and articles about his work have been published in such diverse magazines as *Ethyl News, Parade, Aramco World,* and *Pageant.* He is the author of two books: *An Introduction to the Phonetics of American English,* 1947, and *Handbook of Speech Improvement,* 1956. He has done editorial advisory work for the Thorndike-Century, Thorndike-Barnhart, and Funk and Wagnalls dictionaries and is the author of an article on regional varieties of American pronunciation to be included in the forthcoming college edition of the Funk and Wagnalls dictionary.

"The Gladstone-Huxley Controversy on Genesis" is a paper read in December 1959 at a section of the annual meeting of the Speech Association of America honoring Everett L. Hunt.

Authors and Acknowledgments

RUSSELL HALDERMAN WAGNER was born in Greenville, Ohio. He was a graduate of Monmouth College and of Cornell (Ph.D. 1928) and during his career served appointments at Adrian College, Davidson College, and Iowa State College before going to Cornell, where from 1926 to 1947 he was successively instructor, assistant professor, and associate professor of speech. From September 1947 until his death he was professor of speech and chairman of the School of Speech and Drama at the University of Virginia. He died at Charlottesville in 1952 at the age of fifty-seven.

He served the Speech Association of America as executive councilor and as editor of *Speech Monographs,* and the Eastern Public Speaking Conference as president. He was widely known as the foremost authority on the life, works, and times of Thomas Wilson, the rhetorician.

Of his two contributions to this book, the first, "Thomas Wilson's Contributions to Rhetoric," is reprinted, by permission, from *Papers in Rhetoric,* edited by Donald C. Bryant and privately printed in St. Louis in 1940. The second, "Thomas Wilson's Speech against Usury," is reprinted, by permission, from the *Quarterly Journal of Speech,* February 1952. Both appear with the approval of his widow, Mrs. Helen Friend Wagner.

KARL R. WALLACE has been head of the Department of Speech at the University of Illinois since 1947. His A.B. degree from Cornell (1927) combined the studies of English and public speaking. Everett Hunt was his first college teacher of public speaking. From 1930 to 1933 he was an assistant in the Department of Public Speaking at Cornell while a graduate student under the guidance of Herbert A. Wichelns, Alexander M. Drummond, and Frederick G. Marcham. Cornell granted him the M.A. degree in 1931 and the Ph.D. in 1933.

He taught speech at Iowa State University (Ames) for six years, at Washington University (St. Louis) for one year. At the University of Virginia for ten years, he was head of the Department of Speech, then head of the Department of Speech and Drama. He has long been associated with the Speech Association of America. On its council for fifteen years, he has been president of the association (1954) and editor of the *Quarterly Journal of Speech* (1945–1947) and of *Background Studies in the History of Speech Education* (1954).

The *Quarterly Journal of Speech, Speech Monographs,* and the *Speech Teacher* have published a number of his articles, a large pro-

444

portion of which reflect his interest in Renaissance rhetoric. He has contributed also to *History and Criticism of American Public Address* (1943), *Humanistic Studies in Honor of James Calvin Metcalf* (1941), *The Rhetorical Idiom* (1958), and *Studies in Speech and Drama in Honor of Alexander M. Drummond* (1944). He served on the editorial committee for the last volume. His books have been *Francis Bacon on Communication and Rhetoric* (1943) and, in collaboration with Donald C. Bryant, *Fundamentals of Public Speaking* and *Oral Communication.*

His contribution to this volume, "Bacon's Conception of Rhetoric," is reprinted by permission from *Speech Monographs,* III (1936).

HERBERT AUGUSTUS WICHELNS has long been professor of speech at Cornell and served as chairman of the department from 1940 to 1948. He received the A.B. degree from Cornell in 1916 and the Ph.D. in 1922, working largely with Lane Cooper. He followed his chief, Professor Winans, to Dartmouth and also taught briefly at New York University and the University of Pittsburgh before returning to his alma mater for a distinguished career in teaching. From his graduate courses have come the heads of departments at a half-dozen institutions, outstanding professors at numerous other colleges and universities, and several editors of the *Quarterly Journal of Speech.*

Professor Wichelns was president of the Speech Association of America in 1937. His active participation in the affairs of the Eastern Public Speaking Conference led to his appointment as author-in-chief of the comprehensive history of the Speech Association of the Eastern States, which was published for its golden jubilee in 1959. His understanding study of Emerson is highly regarded by scholars.

The study printed in this volume is a portion of an essay first published in *Studies in Rhetoric and Public Speaking in Honor of James Albert Winans,* copyright 1925 by the Century Co., and is reproduced by permission of Appleton-Century-Crofts, Inc. The essay was reprinted in full in *The Rhetorical Idiom,* a volume of studies presented to Dr. Wichelns in 1958 by his former students, published by the Cornell University Press. Professor Bryant has said that this essay "has had a greater and more continuous influence upon the development of the scholarship of rhetoric and public address than any other single work published in this century."

Authors and Acknowledgments

JAMES ALBERT WINANS (1872–1956) retired in 1942 from a professorship of public speaking at Dartmouth College, after having taught public speaking and related subjects for forty-five years, at first in the Middleton (New York) High School (1897–1899), and successively thereafter at Cornell University (1899–1902), at the University of California at Berkeley (1902–1903), and again at Cornell (1903–1920). He earned the A.B. and M.A. degrees at Hamilton College, and at Cornell the LL.B. degree. He was one of the founders and an early president (1915–1916) of the organization now officially known as the Speech Association of America. After his retirement from Dartmouth College he served for a year as visiting professor of speech at the University of Missouri.

The following publications have established him as the most influential American college teacher of public speaking of his generation, quite possibly of this century: *Notes on Public Speaking* (1911); *Public Speaking* (1915); *Argumentation*, with William E. Utterback (1930); *A First Course in Public Speaking*, with Hoyt Hudson (1931); *Speech-Making* (1933, 1934, 1938); and *Daniel Webster and the Salem Murders*, with Howard A. Bradley (1956).

His article in this volume, "Whately on Elocution," appeared originally in the *Quarterly Journal of Speech*, February 1945, and is one of several essays of scholarly or pedagogical interest contributed by him to that periodical. His daughter, Mrs. E. Lloyd Boutilier, has authorized republication, as has the Speech Association of America.